THE BUDDHIST PATH TO AWAKENING

OTHER BOOKS IN THIS SERIES

Approaches to Islam in Religious Studies, edited by Richard C. Martin, ISBN 1–85168–268–6

Buddhist Texts through the Ages, translated and edited by Edward Conze, I.B. Horner, David Snellgrove and Arthur Waley, ISBN 1–85168–107–8

The Faith and Practice of Al-Gházáli, W. Montgomery Watt, ISBN 1–85168–062–4

Islam and the West, Norman Daniel, ISBN 1–85168–129–9

The Qur'án and its Exegesis, Helmut Gätje, ISBN 1–85168–118–3

What the Buddha Taught, Walpola Sri Rahula, ISBN 1–85168–142–6

RELATED TITLES PUBLISHED BY ONEWORLD

Buddhism: A Short History, Edward Conze, ISBN 1–85168–221–X

Buddhism: A Short Introduction, Klaus K. Klostermaier, ISBN 1–85168–186–8

The Buddha: A Short Biography, John S. Strong, ISBN 1–85168–256–2

A Concise Encyclopedia of Buddhism, John Powers, ISBN 1–85168–233–3

What Buddhists Believe, Elizabeth Harris, ISBN 1–85168–168–X

The Wisdom of Buddhism, compiled by Mel Thompson, ISBN 1–85168–226–0

The Wisdom of Zen, compiled by Anne Bancroft and Roger England, ISBN 1–85168–281–3

THE BUDDHIST PATH TO AWAKENING

R. M. L. GETHIN

ONEWORLD
OXFORD

THE BUDDHIST PATH TO AWAKENING

Oneworld Publications
(Sales and Editorial)
185 Banbury Road
Oxford OX2 7AR
England
www.oneworld-publications.com

Previously published by E.J. Brill 1992
Converted to digital printing 2003

A CIP record for this title is available
from the British Library.

ISBN 1–85168–285–6

Cover design by Design Deluxe
Cover image shows a Burmese statue of Sāriputta

For my mother and father

CONTENTS

PART TWO

THE SEVEN SETS COLLECTIVELY

LIST OF TABLES

PREFACE

The present work was originally submitted, in substantially the present form, as a doctoral dissertation to the Department of Comparative Religion at the University of Manchester in 1987. A constant theme of Buddhist thought is that things do not exist by virtue of their own inherent power, but rather owe their existence to numerous and diverse conditions; in fact on close examination the things in themselves vanish, and the various contributory conditions are seen to be the only true reality anything has. The particular focus of the present work is the *bodhipakkhiyā dhammā*—the conditions that contribute to awakening. While the book itself may fall somewhat short of its subject matter, at least its genesis aptly illustrates the principle of dependence upon conditions. However, it is said that it takes the mind of an all-knowing Buddha to encompass fully the complex of supporting conditions; I can indicate only rather inadequately what is owed and to whom.

The University of Manchester, where I was an undergraduate and postgraduate student, nurtured my interest in the study of Buddhism and Pali in a tradition established there by T.W. Rhys Davids, the first Professor of Comparative Religion. For that I am grateful, and I should like to express my gratitude especially to Lance Cousins, my supervisor, a true *paṇḍita*, who first opened my eyes to many things—whatever is of merit in the present study is the result of his guidance. I am also grateful to K.R. Norman (of the Faculty of Oriental Studies, Cambridge), who introduced me to some of the intricacies of Middle Indo-Aryan philology and provided advice and criticism on a number of points; to Professor John Hinnells (of the Department of Comparative Religion, Manchester), who also provided advice and criticism; to Dr Stuart McFarlane (of the Department of Religious Studies, Lancaster), who advised on the Chinese rendering of *ekâyana/eka-yāna*; to Venerable Ānanda Maitreya and Venerable Dr Rewatadhamma, who discussed a number of Abhidhamma points with me; to all those involved with the Samatha Association and Trust, who all contributed however unwittingly; to Dr Steven Collins (then of the University of Bristol, now of the University of Chicago) for his advice and criticism in the role of external examiner for the original thesis. The initial financial support for my research was provided by the Department of Education and Science; later the Pāli Text Society came to my rescue and supported me with a studentship for a further year, which allowed me to finish what I had begun.

I should also like to thank the following: Doreen Boardman, who initially typed a difficult manuscript; Gillian Binks for her generosity and tolerance in the course of providing an environment suited to writing; John Gittins for the use of his typewriter and help with photocopying; Candida Sturdy for help with proofreading; and finally my mother, father and sister, who over the years never failed to provide support and encouragement.

The book was prepared for publication after I had taken up a post as a lecturer in religious studies at the University of Bristol. I am grateful to the University for financial assistance with the preparation of camera-ready copy; to Ann French (of the Computing Service), who initiated me into the mysteries of the PC, Unix, VMS, and the Lasercomp; to the Oxford University Computing Service where the book was typeset; to the British Academy for a grant contributing towards publication costs; and to Dr F. Th. Dijkema, E.J. Brill's Oriental Editor, who waited patiently.

siddhir astu
śubham astu

Bristol 26 September 1991

PREFACE TO THE SECOND EDITION

The nine years since the first edition of *The Buddhist Path to Awakening* was published have seen the publication of many articles and books in the field of Buddhist studies. Not a few of these have some bearing on the general topic of the present study, namely the theory of early Buddhist 'meditation' and the stages of the Buddhist spiritual path. However, to my knowledge there has been no other work specifically devoted to the '*dhammas* that contribute to awakening' (*bodhi-pakkhiyā dhammā*). Nor does it seem to me that in the intervening years scholarly discussions of the relationship between the various elements of early Buddhist meditation—the *jhānas*, the formless attainments, calm and insight, concentration and wisdom, the 'immeasurables' or 'divine abidings', etc.—have reached definite or generally accepted conclusions.

One of the things I suggested in my conclusion was that before we throw away the Abhidhamma and the commentaries, we need to be very sure we have understood what it is they are saying, and how it is they are actually interpreting the earlier texts (p. 344). What prompted that suggestion then was a sense that in dealing with the theory of the Buddhist path in the Nikāyas scholars had tended to dismiss the views of the Abhidhamma and commentaries without fully understanding them. Yet my own investigation of the treatment of the *bodhi-pakkhiyā dhammā* in the Nikāyas and *abhidhamma/abhidharma* texts had led me to the conclusion that in fact, while the understanding of the later texts might not be precisely the same in all matters of detail, it was, when worked out and carefully considered, broadly consistent with that found in the Nikāyas.

So let me take this opportunity to restate what I think to be the main import of the present study for the scholarly investigation of early Buddhist meditation theory. While my study of the *bodhi-pakkhiyā dhammā* does not address directly all the specific points raised by those following in the footsteps of La Vallée Poussin and Frauwallner, it does at least, I think, place a question mark against some of the claims of 'contradiction' and 'inconsistency' in the way the texts (the Pali Nikāyas, the Abhidhamma, and the commentaries) present the theory of Buddhist meditation. What I want to suggest is that a close reading of the material concerned with the *bodhi-pakkhiyā dhammā* with attention to the subtleties and nuances of the presentation reveals a basically coherent and consistent understanding of the process whereby the 'ordinary' (*lokiya*), unawakened mind transforms itself into the 'world transcending' (*lokuttara*), awakened mind.

More specifically my suggestion is that the treatment of the *bodhi-pakkhiyā dhammā* in general and 'the factors of awakening' (*bojjhaṅga*) in particular provides something of a key to understanding the relationship between calm and insight, between concentration (*samādhi*) and wisdom (*paññā*) in early Buddhist meditation theory. The very list of the *bojjhaṅgas* is precisely intended to bring together the practice of *jhāna* with the development of wisdom (see Chapter Five). The summary statement of the path as consisting of the abandoning of the five hindrances, practice of the four establishings of mindfulness, and development of the awakening factors points towards the way in which discourses such as the *(Mahā-)Satipaṭṭhāna-sutta* and *Ānâpānasati-sutta* are intended to show how calm and insight are in practice combined (see pp. 57–9, 172, 258).

My conclusion is then that, contrary to what is sometimes suggested, there are not two radically different conceptions of the Buddhist path vying with each other: there is no great struggle going on between the advocates of the way of 'calm' (*samatha*) and 'meditation' (*jhāna*) on the one hand, and the advocates of the way of 'insight' (*vipassanā*) and understanding (*paññā*) on the other. In fact it turns out that the characteristically early Buddhist conception of the path leading to the cessation of suffering is that it consists precisely in the combining of calm and insight. It is not surprising then to find that the texts are concerned to explore the precise relationship between these. The development of the early Buddhist theory of the path does not then consist so much in the worsting of one side in a debate, as in the providing of more refined, sophisticated, and varied accounts of how understanding is related to and emerges from the stillness of mind developed in the practice of *jhāna*. Put another way, Indian Buddhist meditation theory was always precisely concerned with articulating the relationship between the process of stilling the emotions associated with 'craving' (*taṇhā*) and the process of ridding the mind of the distorted view of the world that comes from 'delusion' (*moha*) or 'ignorance' (*avijjā*). The relationship between these processes was seen as crucial because of the way in which in actual experience (as opposed to logical abstraction) craving and delusion are confused: in craving we *also* have a distorted view of the world, and in having a distorted view of the world we *also* crave. Of course, I do not wish to claim an absolute freedom from contradiction and inconsistency for the textual accounts of the Buddhist path, but I do want to suggest that the texts (from the early Nikāyas, through the early Abhidhamma to the commentaries) do provide a broadly consistent and coherent understanding of how stilling the mind is to be in some way combined with investigating the process of conditionality (*paṭiccasamuppāda*)—the rise and fall of things—as the effective way of bringing the mind to the point of awakening.

The text of this second edition is the text of the first edition with minor corrections. In addition to the reviewers (listed at the end of this preface), who drew my attention to various errors, I would like to thank Bhikkhu Bodhi and Costel Harnasz for pointing out others. I would also like to draw the reader's attention to several points in the first edition where I would make more substantial changes or additions if I were to revise this material fully.

The discussion of *satipaṭṭhāna* (pp. 30–31) should include a reference to K. R. Norman's discussion of the term in *JPTS* 10 (1985), pp 31–32 (a section of 'Pāli Lexicographical Studies III'), reprinted in *Collected Papers* III (Oxford, 1992), pp. 91–92. And the discussion of *apilāpanatā* (pp. 38–40) which refers to private communications with Norman should include a reference to his published discussion of *apilapati* in *JPTS* 12 (1988), pp 49–52 (a section of 'Pāli Lexicographical Studies V'), reprinted in *Collected Papers* III (Oxford, 1992), pp. 257–59.

I have altered my note on the commentarial interpretation of *samudaya-dhamma* and *vaya-dhamma* (p. 55, n. 111) in the light of the full discussion of the issue in

Alexander von Rospatt's *The Buddhist Doctrine of Momentariness* (Stuttgart, 1995), pp. 203–5, n. 433.

The one to one correspondence between the seven factors of awakening (*bojjhaṅga/bodhy-aṅga*) and the seven treasures of the wheel-turning king (see pp. 182–3) is not confined to the Pali texts, but is also found in the *Mahāyānasūtrâlaṃkāra* (XVIII 57–63).

I would add to the discussion of the variation *pakkhiya/pakkhika* (pp. 284-85) a reference to K. R. Norman's consideration of the issue of 'eastern' or 'anomalous' forms in his *A Philological Approach to Buddhism*, London, 1997, pp. 62–63, 66.

In Chapter Ten and in my Conclusion (pp. 340–42, 352) I draw attention to two different *abhidhamma/abhidharma* perspectives on the *bodhi-pakkhiyā dhammā/ bodhi-pākṣikā dharmāḥ*: the Theravādin perspective which emphasises how all thirty-seven *dhammas* are present in a single moment with the final attainment of the path, and the Sarvāstivādin-Yogācārin perspective which sees each of the seven sets as characterizing a successive stage of the path. I suggest, however, that these two perspectives should not be seen as mutually exclusive and that elements of each are present in both. In this context I would add two references to the *Mahāyānasūtrâlaṃkāra* which show more clearly how the idea of the thirty-seven *dharmas*' being in a single moment is also found in the northern tradition: at XIV 36 (S. Lévi, Paris, 1995, p. 95; S. Bagchi, Dharbhanga, 1970, pp. 92–3) it is stated that 'with the path of seeing, the Son of the Conquerors always gains knowledge of all the various *dharmas* contributing to awakening' (*tena darśana-mārgeṇa saha sadā mataḥ / sarveṣāṃ bodhipakṣāṇāṃ vicitrāṇāṃ jinâtmaje // tena darśana-mārgeṇa saha bodhisattvasya sarveṣāṃ bodhi-pakṣāṇāṃ dharmāṇāṃ lābho veditavyaḥ smṛty-upasthānâdīnāṃ*); while the exposition of XX–XXI 16 (Lévi, p. 178; Bagchi, p. 170) states that at the seventh stage the bodhisattva has an understanding acquired in a single moment of consciousness through developing the thirty-seven *bodhi-pakṣas* in each moment (*saptamyām eka-citta-kṣaṇa-labdha-buddhir ... pratikṣ aṇaṃ sapta-triṃśad bodhi-pakṣa-bhāvanātaḥ*).

An additional non-Pāli source for the seven sets or *bodhipakṣyas* (pp. 357–58) is Dieter Schlingloff, *Ein Buddhistisches Yogalehrbuch* (Textband), Berlin 1964, 180–81.

For additional observations and points of criticism I refer the reader to the following reviews of the first edition: Steven Collins, *JAOS* 115 (1995), 157–58; Ute Hüsken, *Orientalische Literatur* 91 (1996), 630–34; J. W. de Jong, *IIJ* 37 (1994) 384–87; John D. Ireland, *Buddhist Studies Review* 10 (1993), 247–53; Damien Keown, *JRAS* Third Series 4 (1994), 115–17; K. R. Norman, *Religion* 24 (1994), 194–95; Ulrich Pagel *BSOAS* 60 (1997), 154–56; Ernst Steinkellner, *Zeitschrift der Deutschen Morgenländischen Gesellschaft* 60 (1996), 226–27.

Finally I would like to express my gratitude to Novin Doostdar and Victoria Warner of Oneworld, the former for taking the initial interest in my book, and the latter for seeing it through to its republication.

Rupert Gethin
Bristol
26 May 2001

INTRODUCTION

1. The academic study of religion: some reflections on methodology

That I should find myself, a European, towards the end of the twentieth century of the 'Christian' era writing about matters relating to a body of ancient Indian literature should perhaps give pause for thought. For what follows is intended as a scholarly study of certain aspects of Buddhism, and was originally submitted (in substantially the present form) as a doctoral dissertation to a department of 'comparative religion' within a 'faculty of theology' at a British university. Behind these facts lies a specific story—the story of the development of a particular cultural and intellectual tradition, namely that of the West. The story concerns, in part, the evolution of the modern academic study of religion. This part of the story, although full of complex characters, exotic locations and numerous subplots, can be told clearly enough in broad outline.[1] Its ending, however, is rather inconclusive. I mean by this that the modern academic study of religion can often appear a rather messy and untidy affair where no one is exactly sure of what they are or should be doing. Varying measures of traditional theology, philosophy, the history of ideas, sociology and social anthropology, the psychology of religious experience, historical and literary criticism, textual and philological analysis are shaken together to produce an always heady and sometimes unpalatable cocktail. The reactions of those who take of this elixir are not exactly consistent.

I do not wish to enter into the methodological debate in any major way. This is simply not the place; my concerns are elsewhere. This disinclination to stray too far into the methodological maze has one immediate and fortuitous consequence: it apparently places me in some rather distinguished company. In a recent literature review R.J.Z. Werblowsky spoke of the 'almost unbearable verbiage and pretentious bombast characteristic of the floodtide of methodological literature that is sweeping over us' and suggested that this has the effect of turning many serious scholars off the subject.[2] He goes on to conclude, however, that 'it is surely right and proper that historians of religion ask themselves, from time to time, what exactly it is that they are actually doing (or that their predecessors have been doing)'.

At the risk of touching on a number of issues, each of which has an enormous literature attaching to it, I shall, then, attempt to state briefly what it is I take it I am doing in the present study. As I indicated above, the academic study of religion is a product of the intellectual history of the West; its field of enquiry, on the other hand, ranges far beyond the confines of western culture. However, the terms of the methodological debate remain those dictated by the modern western intellectual tradition—it is a debate that is largely only

---

[1] See, for example, E.J. Sharpe, *Comparative Religion: A History*, London, 1975.

[2] *Numen* 33 (1986), pp. 241-2.

intelligible in the context of that tradition.[3] This is, of course, neither a good nor bad thing in itself. It is not that one ought to demand of the modern academic study of religion that it should become free of its cultural roots—it cannot. But it is, perhaps, appropriate to ask that in the context of the methodological debate it should become more self-aware. Thus one of the more serious shortcomings of the current methodological debate is surely its failure to take on board the full significance of the fact that someone brought up in the classical intellectual tradition of, say, India would inevitably conceive of and analyze the whole matter in rather different terms.[4] To be sure, the problem is generally recognized, but the full extent of its implications has yet to be explored. Frank Whaling comments as follows in his introductory essay to *Contemporary Approaches to the Study of Religion*:

> Although this book traces in detail the contributions of scholars of different western nationalities to different approaches, the wider question that is emerging is whether the study of religion has not been too much dominated by *western* categories. What is the significance of the fact that religions outside the West have been studied in a western way ... To what extent has this pre-1945 attitude of often unconscious superiority been superseded in the contemporary situation? To what degree, in spite of the concern for *epochē* and *Einfühlung* fostered by the phenomenological approach, do western scholars feel that it is *they* who must research and interpret the religion of others for these latter? ... One suspects that we are only just beginning to reflect seriously upon such matters.[5]

It is not difficult to see why these questions remain largely unanswered. Any real understanding of them requires an insight into the nature of *both* western culture *and* non-western cultures that is not easily acquired, and the easterner may misinterpret western culture just as much as the westerner may misinterpret eastern culture. It is, perhaps, almost commonplace now to point out that there is no precise word for (and hence no concept of) 'religion' in Sanskrit and other Indian languages,[6] or that many of the difficulties associated with a term such as *nirvāṇa* simply disappear when we cease to try to force it into one neat

---

[3] Ursula King suggests (*Contemporary Approaches to the Study of Religion*, Volume I, *The Humanities*, ed. F. Whaling, Berlin, 1983, pp. 44-7) that, although the methodological debate has been dominated by the Europeans and Americans, in the last 20 years or so participants from other areas have entered the debate: 'Eastern developments in the study of religion have been influenced by earlier work done in Europe and even more the USA, but these influences have been blended with strong indigenous elements, especially in India and Japan. Unfortunately, far too little is generally known about these important eastern developments.' But this blending, perhaps, has the effect of adding further complications; cf. E. Conze's comments on the question of contemporary cultural confusion in *Indianisme et Bouddhisme: Mélanges offerts à Mgr Étienne Lamotte*, Louvain, 1980, p. 51.

[4] Those such as, for example, N. Smart (*Secular Education and the Logic of Religion*, London, 1968) and E.J. Sharpe (*Understanding Religion*, London, 1983), who respectively draw up lists of the dimensions (doctrinal, mythological, ethical, ritual, experiential, social) and modes (existential, intellectual, institutional, ethical) of religion, fail to consider in any depth the extent to which the categories of their schemata might be rooted in the western intellectual tradition. As Whaling asks (*CASR*, p. 433): 'to what extent is the western framework for the study of religion western rather than universal?'

[5] Whaling, *CASR*, pp. 11-2; see also Whaling's whole essay 'The study of religion in a global context', id., pp. 391-443.

[6] Cf. Sharpe, *Understanding Religion*, pp. 43-4.

western metaphysical pigeonhole.[7] But such examples are (to use an old cliché) only the tip of an iceberg, the submerged mass of which is always there to tear a nasty hole in the hull of any understanding we formulate in our attempts to sail from one culture to another. Thus it is not enough to identify isolated concepts and think the problem solved. The whole conceptual pattern of the relevant systems of thought is involved here, and not only this; systems of thought evolve and operate in particular cultural settings and contexts—these too need to be taken into account. To give a very general illustration, Buddhism has often tended to be presented in the West as a rather depressing and negative affair: it teaches that life is suffering and that all desire is to be given up. But even the most casual of observers must conclude that the ordinary Buddhist practice of the Sinhalese does not appear especially depressing. Of course, there may be various explanations and ways of understanding this apparent discrepancy, but it often seems that the scholarly world has, at least until recently, been readier to countenance the fact that the Sinhalese have got it wrong, than that there is something awry with their own scholarly presentation of Buddhist thought.[8] One of the reasons underlying this is, perhaps, that at precisely this point the western academic tradition tends artificially to polarize the study of other cultures: the orientalist studies texts, and the anthropologist goes into the field. In any event, it remains clear, I think, that in the general context of the modern academic study of religion there is not only room but a need for further detailed study of and reflection on the intellectual and spiritual traditions of India. In the first place, then, the present study endeavours to make some contribution to this.

My work is based primarily on the ancient Pāli literary sources. This is largely a matter of convenience and of circumstances, and not because the study of the literary sources in general or the Pāli sources in particular is taken as necessarily bringing us closer to the true essence of Buddhism (whatever that might be) than other approaches. In the context of Buddhist studies the justification for the study of the Pāli sources is simply that these texts represent an important facet of both ancient and modern Buddhist culture. Clearly any attempt at a critical study of these sources must take cognizance of historical questions, but as J.W. de Jong has suggested this alone will fail to determine what the texts actually mean or are trying to say:

> Educated in the historical tradition of the nineteenth century, scholars believed they could learn all about Buddhism by studying its history. In the first place they tried to obtain a knowledge of the facts and data in order to form a picture of the development of Buddhist ideas. This method is doomed to failure because in the spiritual life of India the historical dimension is of much less importance than it is in Western civilisation. The most important task for the student of Buddhism is the study of Buddhist mentality. That is why contact with present day Buddhism is so important, for this will guard us against seeing the texts purely as philological

[7] Cf. G. Welbon, *The Buddhist Nirvāṇa and its Western Interpreters*, Chicago, 1968, especially pp. 297-302.

[8] On this general area cf. M. Southwold, *Buddhism in Life: The anthropological study of religion and the Sinhalese practice of Buddhism*, Manchester, 1983.

> material and forgetting that for the Buddhist they are sacred texts which proclaim a message of salvation.[9]

The aspect of the literary sources that primarily interests me in this study is that which concerns what might be variously termed 'religious experience', 'the psychology of meditation experience', 'the psychology of spiritual growth' or 'mysticism'. This aspect is to the fore in the texts; in one way or another it is largely what they are about; it appears to have been of central concern to those who first compiled and used the texts. But dealing with this aspect of the texts in an academic context is not entirely straightforward. If there are already difficulties in entering into the minds of men and women culturally removed by time and space from the interpreter, then there can only be further difficulties in attempting to enter into the minds of those who understand themselves to have had experiences that transcend the ordinary. If we cannot share the world view of ordinary men and women, how can we hope to share that of mystics? How can we understand mystics without ourselves being mystics?[10]

This and related questions have been the subject of considerable reflection.[11] In practice researchers have assumed that even without direct experience of mystical states it remains possible and valid to compare and evaluate what mystics have to say about their experiences. (Just as one might compare and evaluate reports on a foreign country that one has not oneself visited.) But, as S.T. Katz has pointed out,[12] researchers often appear to have been over confident in their ability to distinguish between a mystic's own interpretation and the essential mystical experience. In their eagerness to get at this essential and pure experience, and discard what they see as the unnecessary interpretations of the mystics, they have passed over the subtle question of how a mystical experience itself may be subject to prior conditioning. Katz, who calls into question the very notion of 'raw experience', suggests that a mystic's experience is shaped and formed from the very start by the tradition within which he works. According to Katz the particular similarities that researchers identify in mystics' descriptions of their experience are abstracted only at the expense of the real differences in their accounts. In treating mystics' own descriptions in this way, researchers effectively deny that these descriptions carry any literal meaning. But:

> If none of the mystic's utterances carry any literal meaning then they cannot serve as the *data* for any position, not mine, and certainly not the view that all mystical

---

[9] J.W. de Jong, 'The Study of Buddhism: Problems and Perspectives' (*Studies in Indo-Asian Art and Culture*, vol. 4 (1974), *Acharya Raghu Vira Commemoration Volume*, pp. 13-26) reprinted in J.W. de Jong, *Buddhist Studies*, ed. G. Schopen, Berkeley, 1979, pp. 15-28 (p. 28). Cf. E. Conze, *Buddhist Thought in India*, London, 1962, pp. 17-30; *Thirty Years of Buddhist Studies*, Oxford, 1967, pp. 2-3; J.R. Carter, *Dhamma: Western Academic and Sinhalese Buddhist Interpretations: A study of a Religious Concept*, Tokyo, 1978, pp. 57, 171.

[10] Cf. W.T. Stace, *Mysticism and Philosophy*, London, 1960, pp. 19- 22.

[11] For a useful anthology and full bibliography see *Understanding Mysticism*, ed. R. Woods, London, 1981.

[12] *Mysticism and Philosophical Analysis*, ed. S.T. Katz, London, 1978, pp. 22-74.

> experiences are the same, or reducible to a small class of phenomenological categories.[13]

Frits Staal has sought to solve the problems associated with the academic study of mysticism by arguing that mysticism might be explored 'scientifically' and 'rationally' by some form of critical personal involvement.[14] He has been criticized by among others Edward Conze, who calls into question not so much his premise that mysticism cannot be understood apart from actual experience of mystical states, but the idea that mystical states might be available to researchers *qua* researchers. The Indian documents, says Conze, 'employ a terminology derived from the specific experiences of *yoga*' and 'these must remain a closed book to someone who has not had them'.[15] But that academic researchers should seek to have them, Conze regards as a nonsense:

> (a) their motives are suspect, (b) their training and essential position blind them to the values of solitaries, and (c) they are rarely strong on religious experience. How can you judge the efficacy of prayer if you cannot pray effectively?[16]

Presumably Dr Conze would have regarded himself as something of an exception that proves the rule. But what seems to lie at the heart of Conze's objection to Staal's programme is the implication that there is a 'truth' about mystical experience apart from the mystic's own truth that is somehow open to collective human understanding and that can be got at by 'scientific' and 'rational' research.[17]

Essentially the same problem that Staal and Conze address in the context of the study of mysticism has recently been stated more generally by Martin Southwold.[18] He argues that in matters of religion it is 'practice' that should be seen as having primacy over 'belief'. Thus it is only when we begin to behave and act like Buddhist villagers in Sri Lanka, that we can begin to understand village Buddhism. Here, then, the principles of the phenomenological approach to the study of religion break down. One can only have sympathy

---

[13] Id., p. 40. While the logic of Katz's critique of the universalist position is, I think, sound, the logic by which he establishes his own pluralist position is not quite so clear: may he not be over literal in his understanding of mystics' own descriptions? does a different description always and necessarilly entail a different experience? do not mystics sometimes describe what they see as the same experience in different terms? The problem for the pluralist position is where to draw the line. The Jewish experience of *devekuth* is different from the Buddhist experience of *nirvāṇa*, but to what extent are we to regard the Theravādin experience of *nibbāna* as different from the Sarvāstivādin experience of *nirvāṇa*, or from the Mādhyamika, Yogācārin or Hua Yen experience? Cf. Conze's comment: 'It is absurd to base an appraisal of the "mystics" on their utterances which are a very slight by-product of their doings.' (*Mélanges Lamotte*, p. 51.)

[14] F. Staal, *Exploring Mysticism*, Harmondsworth, 1975.

[15] *Mélanges Lamotte*, p. 51.

[16] Id., p. 52.

[17] Certainly this appears to be the underlying tone of the concluding section of Staal's book ('How to Study Mysticism'); at one point (pp. 136-7) he actually compares the investigator of mysticism to an astronaut: 'We may have to prepare an investigator of mysticism by means of an appropriate course of fasting, just as we may prepare an astronaut by an appropriate course of eating.'

[18] Op. cit.

by active participation, but does not such active participation demand something more positive than a mere suspension of judgement?[19]

I have come full circle: the way we think and what we experience is conditioned by the particular world we live in. The modern student of religion lives in a world quite removed from those of both the Buddhist villager and the Buddhist *arahant*. How can he possibly hope to enter into them and understand them? The answer must be quite simple. Unless there is some common ground he cannot. The real question is whether there is sufficient common ground, and to this there is probably no easy or final answer. The gap of understanding between two cultures may be of a different order but it is not logically different from the gap of understanding that exists between two individuals of the same culture. They too will occupy their own particular worlds, they too may sometimes have difficulties entering into and understanding the other's world. Logically, then, we are left with the question of whether anyone can ever communicate with anyone else. At this point, rather than pursue this question further into the realms of philosophical analysis, it is perhaps appropriate to appeal directly to the texts that form the subject of this study. For, as Katz has remarked, in addition to the need for refining and rethinking philosophical issues in the study of mysticism, 'there is a great deal more "technical" work to be done on the mystical material itself' by way of understanding texts and so on.[20]

In the first place, then, it is worth remembering that the Pāli literary sources themselves do not appear to regard 'the path to awakening' as something essentially culture-bound. The fact of Buddhism's spread across much of Asia in ancient times perhaps bears witness to the fact that in this they were not entirely mistaken.[21] Secondly and more importantly, one of the arguments of the present study is that the 'spiritual psychology' of the thirty-seven *dhammas* that contribute to awakening (as presented in the Nikāyas and the Abhidhamma) is concerned to show that, while the meditation experience of the 'noble person' (*ariya-puggala*) is of a different order, it nevertheless bears some kind of resemblance to certain of the experiences of the ordinary man (*puthujjana*). Indeed, the whole purpose of 'the path to awakening' is precisely to show how 'ordinary' (*lokiya*) experiences are related to 'world-transcending' (*lokuttara*) experiences, and thus how we are to get from one kind of experience to the other. This outlook of the texts means that the experiences they describe are perhaps not quite the closed book Conze suggests.

2. *Some perspectives on the early Buddhist tradition and Pāli literature*

The historical and critical study of Buddhist literature has grown up to some extent in the shadow of the historical and critical study of biblical

---

[19] Cf. P. Moore, 'Buddhism, Christianity and the Study of Religion' in *Buddhist Studies: Ancient and Modern*, ed. P. Denwood and A. Piatigorsky, London, 1983, pp. 74-87 (p. 86).

[20] Katz, op. cit., p. 2.

[21] The sceptic, of course, might see this only as illustrating the extent to which different cultures can misunderstand each other, adapting alien cultural traditions to their own norms.

literature, especially the New Testament, and in some respects should probably be regarded as something of an immature younger sister. Perhaps the most elementary lesson to be learnt here concerns our basic attitude and approach to ancient religious literatures. It is clear that neither the Gospels nor early Buddhist literature is particularly concerned to record straight history, and in attempting to use either set of literature as a means of access to historical events and persons the historian faces considerable problems. Any given event, incident, circumstance or person described in the literature is there primarily to illustrate and further the literature's own 'truth'; at the same time it may coincide with, overlap with or bear some kind of relationship to what the historian might judge to be historical truth. What he must assess is how far it is possible or appropriate to attempt to push that coincidence. This does not mean that the historian concludes: 'This and this are historical, but this and this are not.' Rather he concludes: 'Of this and this I have the means as a historian to ask the question "Is it historical or not?" but of this and this I have not.' In other words he must determine the proper limits of historical enquiry according to the nature and availability of his sources. The delicacy of the historian's task here is well illustrated by the attempt to give an account of the historical Jesus and historical Buddha.[22] In persisting rather too long with the question 'Did this happen?' and not paying proper attention to the nature of ancient literatures, one is in danger of being too literal and even rather unsophisticated in one's handling of them.[23]

The problems associated with the assessment of early Buddhist literature are further compounded by the difficulty of establishing even the most basic date in early Buddhist history—namely the date of the Buddha. Certainly we have no real reason to doubt that underlying early Buddhist literature there must indeed be a historical personality. However, in a recent and persuasive article[24] Professor Heinz Bechert has reminded the world of Indological studies that the reasons in favour of following the Ceylonese tradition that dates the Buddha's *parinibbāna* 218 years before the accession of Aśoka are certainly no more, and may be rather less, convincing than the reasons for following the traditions of north India which date the Buddha's *parinirvāṇa* just 100 years before Aśoka. Bechert himself suggests anything between 105

---

[22] Cf. R.M. Grant, *A Historical Introduction to the New Testament*, London, 1963. pp. 284-377; G. Vermes, *Jesus the Jew: A Historian's Reading of the Gospels*, London, 1973; J.W. de Jong, *BS*, pp. 23-7; D.L. Snellgrove, 'Śākyamuni's Final Nirvāṇa', *BSOAS* 36 (1973), pp. 399-411, and *Indo-Tibetan Buddhism: Indian Buddhists and Their Tibetan Successors*, Boston, 1987, pp. 5-11, 29-38.

[23] It seems to me that, in spite of their undeniable scholarship, A. Bareau's *Recherches sur la biographie du Buddha dans les Sūtrapiṭaka et les Vinayapiṭaka anciens* (3 vols, Paris, 1963, 1970, 1971) suffer precisely in this respect. Of some pertinence here is E.E. Evans-Pritchard's observation that 'myth and history are in important respects different in character, not just in the degree to which they can be substantiated by appeal to evidence or to the laws of natural science' and that 'hence a story may be true yet mythical in character, and a story may be false yet historical in character' (*Essays in Social Anthropology*, London, 1962, p. 53).

[24] 'The Date of the Buddha Reconsidered', *IT* 10 (1982), pp. 29-36; see also his 'A Remark on the Problem of the Date of Mahāvīra', *IT* 11 (1983), pp. 287-90, and 'Remarks on the Date of the Historical Buddha', *Buddhist Studies (Bukkyō Kenkyū)* 17 (1988), pp. 97-117.

and 85 years before Aśoka as reasonable. This may bring the date of the Buddha's *parinirvāṇa* forward from 486 or 483 BCE to as late as 350 BCE.

The Pāli canon that the Buddhist tradition of Ceylon and South East Asia presents us with appears to be basically the *Tipiṭaka* that the compilers of the commentaries had before them in the fifth and sixth centuries CE.[25] The Pāli tradition itself records that the texts of the canon at first existed only orally and were committed to writing at a relatively late date, some time during the first century BCE.[26] On the basis of this tradition—and scholars have generally looked upon it quite favourably—we may be justified in concluding that the Pāli canon as we have it is substantially as it was written down at that time. Presumably this canon was brought to Ceylon from India at some earlier date, possibly by Mahinda, who, according to the Pāli tradition, came to Ceylon some time during the reign of Aśoka. This tradition may have a kind of corroboration in the form of Aśoka's thirteenth rock edict.[27] Certainly the language of the canon appears to be entirely consonant with a north Indian provenance, and any evidence for significant additions to the canon after its arrival in Ceylon is at best inconclusive.[28]

The oral origin of the literature is evident enough from the style of the texts themselves. Reference to a system of 'reciters' or 'chanters' (*bhāṇaka*) is found in post-canonical Pāli literature[29] and is borne out by inscriptional evidence on the Indian mainland that may date from the middle of the second century BCE.[30] Inscriptional evidence of a similar date also bears independent witness to the classification of early Buddhist literature into 'three baskets'.[31] However, when we take into account the literary evidence of the Buddhist tradition as a whole it becomes quite clear that it is no easy matter to know what exactly went into those 'baskets'.

The oral nature of early Buddhist literature and the diffusion of Buddhism across the Indian subcontinent means that we must think in terms of different recensions of the same or similar material gradually coming to embody more or less distinct traditions. The Pāli canon is one such recension and no doubt represents the traditions of particular schools of reciters. It is the only

---

[25] This may need some qualification. While we seem to have commentaries to all texts we possess, and no commentaries for anything we do not possess, the commentaries do seem to quote as canonical a number of passages that cannot be traced in the canon as we have it (such passages are indicated by some editors of PTS editions, e.g. Ps II 11, 27, 35-6). How far these passages are untraced because they are actually not in the canon, and how far because individual editors have been unable to trace them is unclear. Cf. Mil Trsl I xv-xvi.

[26] Dīp XX 20-1; Mhv XXXIII 100-1; cf. K.R. Norman, *Pāli Literature*, Wiesbaden, 1983, pp. 10-1.

[27] This speaks of Aśoka's *dhamma-vijaya* as far as Taṃbapaṃni (see J. Bloch, *Les Inscriptions d'Aśoka*, Paris, 1955, pp. 129-30), but R. Thapar (*Aśoka and the Decline of the Mauryas*, Oxford, 1961, pp. 48-9) prefers to see any Buddhist 'missions' as distinct from Aśoka's own 'conquest by *dhamma*'.

[28] See K.R. Norman, 'Pāli and the language of the heretics', *AO* 37 (1976), pp. 117-26, and his 'The Role of Pāli in Early Sinhalese Buddhism' in *Buddhism in Ceylon and Studies on Religious Syncretism in Buddhist Countries*, ed. H. Bechert, Göttingen, 1978, pp. 28-47.

[29] On the system of *bhāṇakas* in general see Norman, *PL*, pp. 8-9.

[30] É. Lamotte, *Histoire du bouddhisme indien*, Louvain, 1958, p. 164.

[31] Id., p. 165.

recension of the early *Tripiṭaka* that survives complete in an Indic language. Exactly how many other distinct recensions and traditions there were we do not know.[32] Our knowledge of them must be built up piecemeal: on the basis of isolated texts and fragments of texts that happen to have survived in Buddhist Sanskrit and other Middle Indo-Aryan dialects; on the basis of Chinese and Tibetan translations; on the basis of quotations from Sūtra and the traditions about the contents of different recensions that can be gleaned from later exegetical works.[33] Although the evidence is incomplete when we think in terms of what might have survived, it does seem that we have enough to come to certain conclusions.

The work of detailed comparison and assessment of even this evidence is hardly complete,[34] but it is evident that among the various ancient traditions and schools of Buddhism there appears to be a general agreement concerning the nature and core contents of the *Vinaya-* and *Sūtra-piṭakas*;[35] concerning the *Abhidharma-piṭaka* considerable divergence is observable.[36] With reference to the *Sūtra-piṭaka* all schools, as far as we can tell, appear to have agreed upon the primacy of the four great *nikāyas* (collections) or *āgamas* (traditions).[37] Two of these classify texts according to their length—long (*dīgha/dīrgha*) or middling (*majjhima/madhyama*); the third according to topic (*saṃyutta/saṃyukta*), and the fourth by a system of numerical progression (*aṅguttara/ekottarika*) from one to eleven based on the number of points or items

---

32 The traditional number of schools in the texts is eighteen, but collation of all the available sources gives rather more than this (see A. Bareau, *Les sectes bouddhiques du Petit Véhicule*, Paris, 1955). It is not necessary that each one of these formed a distinct school with its own peculiar and distinctive textual tradition. The Vinaya traditions might suggest that we should think in terms of six more or less distinct canonical traditions apart from the Pāli; these are the Mahāsāṃghika, the Vātsīputrīya/Sammatīya, the Sarvāstivāda, the Kāśyapīya, the Dharmaguptaka and the Mahīśāsaka; cf. E. Frauwallner, *The Earliest Vinaya and the Beginnings of Buddhist Literature*, Rome, 1956, pp. 7-10.

33 Lamotte, *HBI*, pp. 155-210; L. Renou and J. Filliozat, *L'Inde classique: manuel des études indiennes* (2 vols, Paris, 1947, 1953) II 361-6, 393-4, 417-9, 431-2. For an up to date indication of what is available in Indian languages see Norman, *PL*, passim.

34 Apart from the general comments of some writers, notably Lamotte, more comprehensive, if undetailed, comparison is provided by M. Anesaki, 'The Four Buddhist Āgamas in Chinese (A concordance of their parts and of the corresponding counterparts in the Pāli Nikāyas)', *TASJ* 35 (1908), pp. 1-149; C. Akanuma, *The Comparative Catalogue of Chinese Āgamas and Pāli Nikāyas*, Nagoya, 1929. Among the more detailed studies limited to specific texts the most extensive is A. Bareau, *Recherches sur la biographie du Buddha*. See also E. Waldschmidt, *Das Mahāparinirvāṇa-sūtra*, Berlin, 1950; J. Brough, *The Gāndhārī Dharmapada*, London, 1962; Thich Minh Chau, *The Chinese Madhyama Āgama and the Pāli Majjhima Nikāya: A Comparative Study*, Saigon, 1964-65; J.W. de Jong, 'The *Daśottara-sūtra*' in de Jong, *BS*, pp. 252-73; C. Vogel, *The Teachings of the Six Heretics*, Wiesbaden, 1970; K. Meisig, *Das Śrāmaṇyaphala-sūtra: Synoptische Übersetzung und Glossar der chinesischen Fassungen verglichen mit dem Sanskrit und Pāli*, Wiesbaden, 1987 and *Das Sūtra von den vier Ständen: Das Aggañña-sutta im Licht seiner chinesischen Parallelen*, Wiesbaden, 1988.

35 Lamotte, *HBI*, pp. 165-97; Frauwallner, *EVBBL*; Anesaki, op. cit.; Akanuma, op. cit.

36 Lamotte, *HBI*, pp. 197-210; Norman, *PL*, pp. 95-8, 107.

37 In what follows I follow the practice of using the term *nikāya* to refer to Pāli sources, and the term *āgama* to refer to non-Pāli sources and Chinese translations in particular. This is in some respects simply a matter of practical convenience since the term *āgama* is not unknown to Pāli sources, and the term *nikāya* not unknown to non-Pāli sources; see the relevant entries in *PED*, *CPD*, *BHSD*.

discussed in a given text. As far as the contents of these four primary collections of *sūtras* are concerned, all the indications are that there was a remarkable consensus and degree of correspondence among the various recensions. The following statement made by Étienne Lamotte with reference to the comparison of the Pāli Nikāyas and the Chinese translations of the Āgamas is of some importance:

> Cependant, exception faite pour les interpolations mahāyānistes de l'*Ekottara*, interpolations aisément décelables, les variations en question n'affectent guère que le mode d'expression ou la disposition des matières. Le fonds doctrinal commun aux āgama et aux nikāya est remarquablement uniforme. Conservés et transmis par les écoles, les sūtra ne constituent pas autant des documents d'école, mais l'héritage commun à toutes les sectes ... Tout essai de reconstruction d'un bouddhisme «précanonique» s'écartant du consensus entre āgama et nikāya ne peut aboutir qu'à des hypothèses subjectives.[38]

There appears to have been both some agreement and some disagreement among the schools concerning a number of other 'lesser' (*khuddaka/kṣudraka*) texts associated with the *Sūtra-piṭaka*.[39]

All this suggests a preliminary relative chronology for our sources. We have good reasons, then, for taking as our earliest sources for the study of Buddhism the *Vinaya-piṭaka* texts and the four primary Nikāyas or Āgamas along with certain other smaller texts associated with them; the *Abhidharma-piṭaka* literature and again certain other canonical texts, such as the *Paṭisambhidāmagga* and *Niddesa* in the Pāli tradition,[40] need to be seen as somewhat later—exactly how much later is not clear.

In trying to come to a proper assessment of early Buddhist thought the Pāli material has certain advantages over other sources for two simple but inconclusive reasons. In the first place it seems to represent a relatively full recension of the appropriate material—certainly fuller than anything else we possess. This makes the use of the Pāli canon a matter of practical convenience, and means that for the most part in assessing a particular passage we do not have to speculate about what might have been said elsewhere in the canon. Secondly, it is written in a Middle Indo-Aryan language that shows only limited signs of sanskritization.[41] Certainly it appears that the earliest Buddhist tradition preferred a Middle Indo-Aryan vernacular as its medium and only gradually gave way to the progressive sanskritization that is a feature of most Buddhist texts in an Indian language that have come down to us apart from the Pāli tradition. Yet we do not appear to have any reason for regarding the Middle Indo-Aryan of the Pāli canon as a more authentic vehicle for the Buddhist tradition than any other comparable Middle Indo-Aryan dialect; the precise

---

[38] Lamotte, *HBI*, p. 171

[39] É. Lamotte, 'Problems concerning the Minor Canonical Texts' in *Buddhist Studies in Honour of Hammalava Saddhatissa*, ed. G. Dhammapala et al., Nugegoda, Sri Lanka, 1984, pp. 148-58; Lamotte, *HBI*, pp. 171-8; Norman, *PL*, p. 9.

[40] Cf. Norman, *PL*, pp. 84-9

[41] Norman, *PL*, pp. 2-7.

nature of the language the Buddha might have used remains obscure.[42] Yet the Pāli tradition's reluctance to sanskritize may be indicative of a more general conservatism. If we are right in thinking that the Pāli Nikāyas were closed rather earlier than the Chinese Āgamas, then we may be justified in regarding the Pāli tradition as among the more conservative of early Buddhist traditions. Nevertheless, the fact remains that the Pāli canon cannot simply be taken as the last authority on questions of early Buddhism; quite clearly the traditions found in other sources may be of a similar or even earlier date.

A number of attempts have been made at providing a detailed chronology of the evolution of the Pāli Nikāyas.[43] While they have certainly provided useful insights into the texts, they have not really succeeded in their aim of satisfactorily distinguishing earlier material from later with any degree of certainty.[44] Many of the criteria employed by Winternitz, Law and Pande only work if one is already prejudiced as to the nature of early Buddhism. If one feels at the outset that the Buddha, being, as it were, a reasonable sort of chap, taught a simple ethical doctrine uncluttered by myth, legend and magic, then it is a fairly straightforward matter to stratify the Nikāyas accordingly. But in fact, given what is known of Indian thought from, say, the early Upaniṣads, there is no *a priori* reason why the earliest Buddhist thought should not have contained mythical, magical or 'unscientific' elements, or—if we need to go back one stage further—why the Buddha himself should not have employed such elements in his own teaching. In fact there seems every reason to suppose that he would have. To press the point home in a slightly different way, the positivist minded nineteenth or twentieth century scholar has no historical grounds for supposing that the Buddha did not genuinely believe that he had once been the great king Mahāsudassana;[45] all he can do, if he happens to find some of the things put into the mouth of the Buddha more congenial to his way of thinking, is hope that he did not.

It is perhaps worth pursuing this a little further by way of concrete example. The *Sakkapañha-sutta*[46] depicts the Buddha in conversation with the *deva*

---

[42] For a selection of articles indicating the current state of research on this and related matters see *The Language of the Earliest Buddhist Tradition*, ed. H. Bechert, Göttingen, 1980.

[43] M. Winternitz, *History of Indian Literature*, Volume II, Calcutta, 1933; B.C. Law, *History of Pāli Literature*, 2 vols., London, 1933; G.C. Pande, *Studies in the Origins of Buddhism*, Allahabad, 1957. These works by Winternitz, Law and Pande represent more or less systematic and comprehensive attempts at chronological stratification of the Nikāya corpus largely based on criteria internal to the Pāli texts. More recently a number of scholars have attempted a systematic study of the chronological evolution of specific texts using Pāli, Sanskrit, Chinese and Tibetan parallels; see especially works by Bareau and Meisig cited in note 34 above. Recent works by J. Bronkhorst, L. Schmithausen and T. Vetter (see works by these authors cited in the bibliography below) also argue, in a more general way, that it is possible to distinguish with some degree of certainty between earlier and later stages of the development of certain doctrines expounded in the Nikāyas; I shall have occasion to refer to their work later in the main body of my study.

[44] For a general critique of the method see L.S. Cousins' comments in Dhammapala, *BSHS*, p. 67. R.F. Gombrich, 'Recovering the Buddha's Message' (*The Buddhist Forum*, Volume 1, *Seminar Papers 1987-88*, ed. T. Skorupski, London, 1990, pp. 5-20) is also critical of some of the principles employed in the chronological stratification of the Pāli texts.

[45] D II 196: *ahaṃ tena samayena rājā Mahāsudassano ahosiṃ*.

[46] D II 276-89.

Sakka—magical, mythical and 'unscientific' stuff surely. Yet in the *Saṃyutta-nikāya* the *sutta* is mentioned by name[47] which is equally surely an indication that it is early. Again, there seem to be quite good reasons for thinking that some mythological elements are indeed early. The notion of the universal monarch (*cakra-vartin*) common to Buddhist, Jaina and brahmanical sources would seem to be a case in point.[48] It seems likely that such a notion was inherited from a common source not specifically Buddhist or Jaina. This, at any rate, is what seems to have happened in the case of certain *jātaka* stories and verses.[49] In other words, it is reasonable to think of a common stock of material, some of which was undoubtedly mythological in character, that was taken over, reworked and developed by both the Buddhist and Jaina tradition. Indeed this is quite clearly what has happened in the case of Buddhist cosmology. Finally, K.R. Norman refers to verses in *ārya* metre, usually taken as a sure sign of earliness, which on the other hand exhibit features such as a developed Buddha-legend that are sometimes regarded as indicative of lateness.[50] Once more we have no real reason for thinking that the so-called sign of lateness is such at all. All this is not to deny that certain mythical features—especially those associated with 'buddhology'—become more marked in the course of the history of Buddhist literature. It is merely to point out that we in fact have no historical grounds for supposing that this process could only have begun after the death of the historical Buddha. It may in some respects even antedate him.[51]

Some of these considerations must apply to the thought world of the Nikāyas as a whole. It seems unlikely that what we call 'Buddhist' thought should be conceived of as beginning with a *tabula rasa* at the moment of the Buddha's awakening. All the indications are that Buddhism must be understood as growing out of an existing tradition.[52] By the time of the Buddha the *śramaṇa* (striver) or *parivrājaka* (wanderer) tradition may well have been several centuries old. Just how much the Buddhist tradition owes to it we cannot know. Some idea of a common yogic heritage might be formed on the basis of a detailed comparison with the Upaniṣads, Jaina sources and the *Yoga-sūtras*, but it would probably be difficult to come to definite conclusions. What is clear, however, is that we cannot assume that the earliest forms of Buddhist thought must necessarily exhibit the traits of simplicity and lack of

---

[47] S III 13.

[48] Cf. *ERE*, s.v. chakravartin; I. Armelin, *Le Roi détenteur de la roue solaire en révolution, cakravartin, selon le brahmanisme et selon le bouddhisme*, Paris, 1975.

[49] Norman, *PL*, pp. 51, 82; cf. Norman, Th Trsl xx-i.

[50] Norman, *PL*, pp. 76-7.

[51] D.L. Snellgrove makes a similar point with regard to the cult of the stūpa, *BSOAS* 36 (1973), pp. 410-11; see also his remarks on the emergence of the Mahāyāna, *Indo-Tibetan Buddhism*, pp. 26-38.

[52] Cf. J. Pryzluski and E. Lamotte, 'Bouddhisme et Upaniṣad', *BEFEO* 32 (1932), pp. 141-69; H. Nakamura, 'Common Elements in Early Jain and Buddhist Literature', *IT* 11 (1983), pp. 303-30; A.K. Warder, 'On the Relationships between Early Buddhism and Other Contemporary Systems', *BSOAS* 18 (1956), pp. 43-63. J. Bronkhorst, *The Two Traditions of Meditation in Ancient India*, Stuttgart, 1986, offers a slightly different perspective, however; cf. pp. 180-1 below.

sophistication; the earliest portions of the Nikāyas or Āgamas may already represent a quite developed synthesis of the early Indian yogic tradition.

The other great problem that needs to be addressed in any attempt to stratify the Nikāyas into early and late is the question of the oral nature of the literature. Since Pande published what is probably the most thoroughgoing attempt at a chronological stratification of the Nikāya material in 1957 a considerable amount of research has been devoted to the nature of oral literature.[53] This research has drawn attention to the way in which an oral literature is built up around and by means of stock formulaic phrases and passages. Certainly this feature is much in evidence in the Pāli canon. Once we have recognized such a characteristic it is obvious that important criteria of stratification, such as Pande's principle of interpolation, become in many instances almost impossible to use.[54] Again, those who have espoused the cause of chronological stratification have tended to regard the proliferation of lists (*mātikā*) in the texts as a criterion pointing towards the lateness of a text.[55] While it may be correct that the number and variety of lists tended to increase as time went on, we are probably once more faced with a feature that is at the same time very old. The use of lists is an integral part of the literature and directly related to its oral nature. The lists can perhaps be seen as a counterpart in a prose oral literature to the metrical formulas in a verse literature. Both provide a vehicle for the reciter and inform the literature with a structure and, in the case of the lists, what is almost a system of cross-referencing that prevents the reciter from losing his way.[56] With the benefit of hindsight, it seems that in general attempts at stratification have suffered from envisaging the problem too much in the terms of a tradition of fixed literary texts.

The difficulties associated with the assessment of the earliest phase of Buddhist literature as represented by the Vinaya, Nikāyas and Āgamas do not automatically disappear when it comes to the later phases of Buddhist literature. The second broad phase of Buddhist literature can be represented by the canonical Abhidharma literature and, in the field of Pāli literature, such texts as the *Paṭisambhidāmagga* and *Niddesa*, and also, perhaps, by such para-canonical texts as the *Peṭakopadesa*, *Nettippakaraṇa* and *Milindapañha*.[57] It may be quite clear that the Nikāyas and Āgamas represent the common heritage of early Buddhism; it is equally clear that while these later works contain much that is apparently new and distinctive to a particular tradition, they also contain a certain amount that appears new yet at the same time is manifestly

[53] The classic work is A.B. Lord, *The Singer of Tales*, Harvard, 1960. With regard to Pāli literature see L.S. Cousins, 'Pāli Oral Literature' in Denwood and Piatigorsky, *BSAM*, pp. 1-11.

[54] According to Pande (op. cit., pp. 33-5) many *suttas* reveal 'patchwork'; but surely all we are doing here is identifying the basic formulaic units of the tradition and then seeing them being fitted together.

[55] Cf. G.C. Pande, op. cit., pp. 88, 136-7, 143.

[56] Cf. S. Collins, *Selfless Persons: Imagery and Thought in Theravāda Buddhism*, Cambridge, 1982, pp. 109-10.

[57] Chinese versions of Mil suggest that books I-III are part of the common Buddhist heritage; books IV-VII were proably added in Ceylon (Lamotte, *HBI*, p. 465).

still part of the common heritage. To anticipate the future course of this study, a simple example is provided by the expression 'thirty-seven *bodhi-pakkhiyā dhammā*'. This complete expression is not met with in the Pāli canon at all; we have either the numerically non-committal plural *bodhi-pakkhiyā dhammā* or the expression 'seven *bodhi-pakkhiyā dhammā*'.[58] Even the commentary embedded in the text of the *Vibhaṅga*, the second book of the *Abhidhamma-piṭaka*, seems not to know the number thirty-seven and prefers to understand *bodhi-pakkhiyā dhammā* as simply referring to the seven factors of awakening (*bojjhaṅga*). Yet the expression 'thirty-seven *bodhi-pakkhiyā dhammā/bodhi-pākṣikā dharmāḥ*', seems common to all traditions of Buddhism. We find it in the *Peṭakopadesa*, the *Milindapañha* and Pāli commentaries; in the *prajñā-pāramitā* literature, Mahāyāna *sūtras* and the Abhidharma traditions of the Sarvāstivādins.[59] The point is that we cannot simply regard the transition from Nikāya or Āgama to Abhidharma as a convenient cut-off point in the history of Buddhist literature; we cannot simply say that what precedes the Abhidharma literature is common heritage and early, and that everything else is the peculiar development of a particular tradition and later.

Even when we come to the later commentarial and exegetical literature of the different schools, the position is by no means cut and dried. The Pāli tradition, for example, understands its commentaries not as the original compositions of the authors whose names appear in the colophons but rather as preserving a traditional exegesis of the canon that goes back hundreds of years and which ultimately has a north Indian provenance. There are good reasons for thinking that this tradition has some basis in fact.[60] Some of the material preserved in the commentaries may well be very old and may represent traditions of exegesis that are again the common heritage of the Buddhist tradition as a whole rather than the peculiar traditions of a school.[61]

Two rather general points seems to follow from this: first, that certain elements in apparently later literature may in some cases represent very early traditions—traditions that antedate the divisions in the Saṃgha; secondly, that while it is apparent that there were divisions in the Saṃgha, it seems that the various distinct traditions must have remained in communion with each other,

---

[58] For full discussion see Chapter 9.2.

[59] Another example of a common innovation is the Abhidhamma system of five *jhānas* as opposed to the Suttanta system of four. The additional *jhāna* is achieved by distinguishing between *jhāna* that has both *vicāra* and *vitakka*, and *jhāna* that has only *vicāra*; this latter kind of *jhāna* corresponds to what is called the *dhyānântara* in Sarvāstivādin Abhidharma literature, though *avitakko vicāra-matto samādhi* is distinguished at S IV 363.

[60] Cf. E.W. Adikaram, *Early History of Buddhism in Ceylon*, Migoda, Ceylon, 1946; Sodo Mori, *A Study of the Pāli Commentaries*, Tokyo, 1984 (English summary); F. Lottermoser, 'Quoted Verse Passages in the Works of Buddhaghosa: Contributions towards the study of the lost sīhalaṭṭhakathā literature', doctoral dissertation, Göttingen, 1982.

[61] Cf. K.R. Norman, 'The Dialects in Which the Buddha Preached' in Bechert, *LEBT*, pp. 61-77 (p. 73). As examples of common commentarial traditions compare the accounts of *satipaṭṭhāna/smṛty-upasthāna* preserved in the Pāli commentaries and Abhidh-k-bh (see below, pp. 33-36), also of *ānâpāna-sati/ānâpāna-smṛti* at Vism VIII 145-244 and Abhidh-k 339-40; see also J. Brough, 'Thus Have I Heard...', *BSOAS* 13 (1950), pp. 416-26 (p. 421); the notion of access (*upacāra*) or neighbouring (*samantaka*) concentration also seems to be an 'innovation' common to the later literature of different schools, see L.S. Cousins, *Religion* 3 (1973), p. 118.

and that geographical dispersal as much as doctrinal divergence tended towards the formation of particular traditions. Our difficulties here are compounded by the fact that the various traditions concerning the first Buddhist councils and splits in the Saṃgha are full of problems. These have hardly been finally resolved, despite the undoubted scholarship that has been devoted to them.[62] The lack of any hard dates for the Buddha, for the texts and for the splits in the Saṃgha means that we are left with only the vaguest of ideas concerning the timescale for the evolution and development of early Buddhist thought and literature.

In this sea of uncertainty the one island of relatively hard facts is formed by Aśoka's edicts. Their references to various rulers in the wider Hellenic world beyond the Indian subcontinent allow Aśoka's accession to be dated with some accuracy to around 265 BCE,[63] give or take, say, five years. They would also seem to indicate that by this time Buddhism represented a movement of some significance, that the Saṃgha was becoming widely dispersed across the subcontinent, and that division within the Saṃgha was by this time a real issue—a matter of public concern and not just of interest to the Saṃgha itself.[64] The Buddhist discourses (*dhamma-pāliyayāni*) referred to in the Bhābrā edict[65] seem to correspond to particular texts in the Pāli canon,[66] and it seems reasonable to assume that by the time of Aśoka at least the Vinaya and Nikāyas or Āgamas must have existed in a form that would be readily recognizable to us. If we do not make this assumption it is difficult to understand how they come to make no allusion to Aśoka, and to represent the common heritage of the Buddhist tradition in quite the way they do.

What conclusions should one draw from this brief survey of what we know of the early history of Buddhist literature? If the task one has set oneself is broadly speaking the exposition of Buddhist thought according to the traditional literary sources, then clearly one needs to maintain some kind of awareness of the historical dimension of that literature. In practical terms this entails some kind of chronological stratification. Even if this were a more straightforward matter than it is, one would still need to ensure that any exposition of Buddhist thought was based on a representative and meaningful selection from the literary tradition. In other words, even if we think we know that certain passages and certain *suttas* are definitely older than certain others, it would be unsound simply to isolate these. Why? Because we do not know whether the Buddhist tradition ever regarded precisely these texts as embodying a proper or meaningful expression of 'Buddhism'. In general, if the contemporary scholar seeks to make sense of the earliest Buddhist thought

[62] For a discussion of the principal research see Lamotte, *HBI*, pp. 136-54; C.S. Prebish, 'A Review of Scholarship on the Buddhist Councils', *JAS* 33 (1974), pp. 239-54; J.J. Nattier and C.S. Prebish, 'Mahāsāṃghika Origins : The Beginnings of Buddhist Sectarianism', *HR* 16 (1976-7), pp. 237-72.

[63] The thirteenth rock edict; see Bloch, op. cit., pp. 129-30.

[64] The so-called 'schism' edict, see Bloch, op. cit., pp. 152-3.

[65] See Bloch, op. cit., pp. 154-5.

[66] Lamotte, *HBI*, pp. 256-8. Titles of *suttas* seem to have been very secondary and not always fixed; see D I 46; Mil Trsl xvi; M Trsl I xvi; Anesaki, op. cit., passim.

embodied in the Nikāyas, he would be wise to take heed of the sense the subsequent tradition has already made of the earliest tradition.

Thus in my approach to the Nikāya material I have endeavoured to take seriously what might be called an Abhidhamma point of view. This does not mean, I hope, that the viewpoint of the *Abhidhamma-piṭaka* is crudely pushed back and imposed unhistorically on the thought-world of the Nikāyas. It means rather that the concerns of the Abhidhamma are taken as real concerns that arise directly out of the concerns of the Nikāyas. Clearly there is a danger of introducing anachronisms into the thought-world of the Nikāyas, but I think this can be to some extent guarded against by having an eye for the consensus of the wider Buddhist tradition. Obviously if someone wished to press the charge of unhistorically interpreting the Nikāyas in the light of the later tradition it would not always be easy to prove innocence. But I would point out in my defence that we are not simply interested in history here; we are concerned also to come to grips with what actually interested the minds of those who compiled the literature. In such circumstances and in the light of what is really known with any certainty about the history of early Buddhist literature, I suggest that the burden of proof lies with those who might wish to say that the subsequent tradition has got it fundamentally wrong. However, in order to do so they would first have to demonstrate that they had properly appreciated what the subsequent tradition—the *ābhidhammikas* and commentators—has to say, and this, the world of Buddhist scholarship is not yet, I think, in a position to do.[67]

3. What does the Buddhism of the Nikāyas teach?

The processes involved in understanding an ancient literary text[68] can be considered by way of three logically distinct stages. First we need to engage in textual criticism in order to get as close as possible to the original text of the author or authors. Next we need to engage in philological analysis; we need to be sure that we have as complete a knowledge as possible of the language in which the text is written. Finally we can attempt to consider what might have been in the mind of the author or authors and ask whether we have properly understood and appreciated what the author or authors wanted to communicate. From what I have already said in the previous section it is apparent that the carrying out of these three tasks in the case of Pāli literature is no straightforward matter. Apart from difficulties connected with the Pāli manu-

---

[67] Cf. Professor Gombrich's comments (*The Buddhist Forum*, Volume I, *Seminar Papers 1987-88*, ed. T. Skorupski, London, 1990, p. 11): '[S]ome of my colleagues are finding inconsistencies in the canonical texts which they assert to be such without telling us how the Buddhist tradition itself regards the texts as consistent—as if that were not important. My own view is not, I repeat, that we have to accept the Buddhist tradition uncritically, but that if it interprets texts as coherent, that interpretation deserves the most serious consideration.'

[68] For a discussion of these processes in the New Testament context see R.M. Grant, op. cit., pp. 41-101. Cf. also K.R. Norman, 'On translating from Pāli', *One Vehicle*, Singapore, 1984, pp. 77-87 and 'Pāli Philology and the Study of Buddhism' in Skorupski, *The Buddhist Forum* I 31-39.

script tradition,[69] when we are dealing with a literature that has been composed orally and evolved orally what exactly do we mean by the original text of the author or authors? If, in the case of the Nikāyas, we take as our original text the text as it was written down possibly in the first century BCE, then we must acknowledge that this is hardly the text of the authors. On the other hand, what Ānanda might have recited at the first Buddhist council is rather too far back in the realms of conjecture and hypothesis for us to realistically conceive of it as our original. The processes by which the 'text' of the Nikāyas evolved also complicate the philological analysis. When we come to the point of appreciating what the author or authors of the texts actually wanted to say, we are confronted with the full force of the question of authorship.

The considerations I outlined in the previous section suggest that in addressing the question of what the Nikāyas teach, we should not primarily conceive of ourselves as trying to answer the question of what the historical Buddha was trying to say. It is within the realms of possibility, of course, that the Nikāyas, either as a whole or in part, represent quite accurately what the historical Buddha actually said, but we really have no means of knowing with any certainty whether this is so or which parts are the more authentic and which the less. In such circumstances it seems more realistic and safer to think of the Nikāyas as having a collective authorship. This is to some extent reflected in what the texts themselves tell us. Some *suttas* are represented as the work of individual disciples, while the whole, the tradition tells us, is the product of what might be seen as the editorial work of Ānanda and the subsequent schools of *bhāṇakas* who no doubt improvised, added and embellished as they saw fit. What we must ask, then, is what the Nikāya texts meant to those who compiled and used them probably sometime between the beginning of the fourth century BCE and the middle of the third century BCE.

Even if the problems of authorship, and of textual and philological analysis were less complicated than they are, the task facing the modern exegete would be no easy one. To anyone who has read more than a few pages of the Nikāyas it must be apparent that the Nikāyas are not immediately self-explanatory. Much is taken for granted and left unexplained. The repeated use of stock phrases and descriptions results in a rather stylized literary form that can be laconic and cryptic. The rationality and modernity of some of the sentiments that seem to find expression in the Nikāyas have often been emphasized at the expense of the apparent strangeness—to the modern mind—of much of the Nikāya thought-world. And so, as I have already pointed out, in seeking to come to know what sparked the imagination of those who compiled the Nikāyas we cannot afford to ignore the clues afforded by the wider Buddhist tradition. More particularly, in practice one cannot entirely separate the question of what the Nikāyas taught from the question of what the Abhidhamma and commentaries taught.

---

[69] See O. von Hinüber, 'On the Tradition of Pāli Texts in India, Ceylon and Burma' in *Buddhism in Ceylon and Studies on Religious Syncretism in Buddhist Countries*, ed. H. Bechert, Göttingen, 1978, pp. 48-57.

But how does one begin to answer the question: 'What does the Buddhism of the Nikāyas teach?' One way is to ask why the Nikāyas were written at all. Why do they regard what they have to say as significant? What is their *raison d'être*? The answer is surely not hard to find. The Nikāyas understand themselves as pointing towards the solution of a problem. This problem is stated in the texts in a variety of ways. Suffering, the ultimately unsatisfactory nature of life; *dukkha* (the first of the noble truths) is perhaps the most familiar. A rather more informal statement of the matter can perhaps better bring out what *dukkha* is to the Nikāyas: the problem is that many people find in life a problem. But the significance of even this basic premise of the Nikāya thought-world is, I think, sometimes misconstrued or not adequately set forth. For the Nikāyas are not seeking to persuade a world of otherwise perfectly content beings that life is in fact unpleasant; rather they address something that is, as the Nikāyas see it, universally found to exist and will sooner or later confront us all. In other words, understanding the first noble truth involves not so much the revelation that *dukkha* exists, as the realization of what *dukkha* is, or the knowledge of the true nature of *dukkha*. In their own terms, the Nikāyas teach but two things: *dukkha* and the cessation of *dukkha*. In other words, they postulate a situation where there is a problem and a situation where there is no longer a problem, and are concerned with the processes and means involved in passing from the former to the latter. If this is the Nikāyas' ultimate concern, then everything in them might be viewed as at least *intended* to be subordinate to that aim.

In the Nikāyas the processes and means that bring about the cessation of *dukkha* are conceived of primarily in terms of spiritual practice and development. What in particular seems to interest the compilers of the Nikāyas is the nature of spiritual practice and development,[70] how spiritual practice effects and affects spiritual development, how what one does, says and thinks might be related to progress towards the cessation of *dukkha*. In other words, we might say that Buddhist thought is about the Buddhist path—a path that is seen as leading gradually away from *dukkha* towards its cessation, and as culminating in the awakening from a restless and troubled sleep.

Although the notion of the path is central to Buddhist thought, it seems to be a fact that the scholarly world has been rather slow in coming forth with attempts at straightforward exposition of the notion of the spiritual path and practice especially as presented in the Pāli Nikāyas and Abhidhamma. Indeed a plain and descriptive scholarly account of just what the Nikāyas and Abhidhamma have to say on so many of the fundamental topics of ancient Buddhism is simply not to be found. In part there are no doubt good reasons for this. Buddhist studies represents a new field with relatively few workers. Those who devoted their energies to the exposition of the Pāli sources initially felt that in them they had the means of rediscovering an original unadulterated

[70] Terms such as *bhāvanā* (bringing into being), *brahma-cariya* (the holy life), *magga* (path), *paṭipadā* (way) and *yoga* (striving) are all terms which seem to entail a notion that is loosely covered by the English 'spiritual practice'.

Buddhism. Inspired by the fashions and concerns of New Testament scholarship they tended to paint a picture of Nikāya Buddhism as beginning with a simple ethical doctrine that was gradually distorted by the Buddhist 'church' and complicated by the pedantry of the *ābhidhammika* 'scholastics'.[71] This heritage has not been entirely shaken off and still can colour our attitude to the Nikāyas and Abhidhamma,[72] despite the fact that it is based on a quite arbitrary selection and reading of the sources.

Certainly the last twenty-five years have seen the publication of an increasing number of monographs concerned with Buddhist thought primarily as revealed in the Pāli sources. These represent valuable and useful contributions to our appreciation of the Nikāyas, and in the main approach their subject with sensitivity and open mindedness. However, by far the majority gravitate towards those aspects of the Nikāya thought-world that immediately capture the imagination of the mind nurtured in the traditions of modern western philosophy: conditioned arising (*paṭicca-samuppāda*), the absence of a substantial self (*anattā*), and *nibbāna*. In these scholars have seen reflections of some of the classic preoccupations of western philosophy such as causality, the logical contradictions of difference and identity involved in the notion of change, the concept of the person and personal identity, and the metaphysics of the absolute. I do not wish to suggest that one is mistaken in seeing such reflections, but only that reflections can be misleading. The point is that in Buddhist thought discussion of *paṭicca-samuppāda*, *anattā* and *nibbāna* is not pursued as an end in itself but subordinated to the notion of the spiritual path, which is hardly true of the discussion of causality, change and metaphysics in western thought. The danger is that we rather too hastily translate the Nikāyas into terms that are more congenial to us without having first understood the original language.

Those looking for a scholarly account of the Buddhist path as understood in the Nikāyas and Abhidhamma are still almost entirely dependent on the summary accounts contained in general works on Buddhism and Buddhist meditation. Apart from their introductory character many of the former are rather dated, while the latter tend to rely heavily on the classic systematization of the *Visuddhimagga*, and give little indication of what is actually contained in the canonical sources. A proper examination of the notion of the Buddhist path and spiritual practice as contained in the Nikāyas and canonical Abhidhamma texts is thus overdue. It is in the hope of contributing to this examination that the present study is undertaken.

---

71 E.g. C.A.F. Rhys Davids' article in *ERE*, s.v. *abhidhamma*; and B.C. Law, A *History of Pāli Literature*, I 235-40.

72 Even as well considered a work as Collins' *Selfless Persons* shows traces of it. Chapter 8, which considers the Abhidhamma theory of momentariness, opens with a quotation from the *Oxford English Dictionary*: 'Scholasticism. 2. Servile adherence to the methods and teaching of the schools; narrow or unenlightened insistence on traditional doctrines and forms of exposition.' P. Masefield's *Divine Revelation in Pāli Buddhism* (Colombo, 1986) is a recent attempt to show how the Abhidhamma and commentaries basically misrepresent the Nikāyas: 'the scholastic analysis of the Abhidhamma' is the province of the 'puthujjana monk' (as opposed to the 'sāvaka monk') who has 'lost contact with the Dhamma as the Deathless' (op. cit., p. 162).

But how and where should one begin? I have suggested that in a sense all Buddhist thought is about the Buddhist path, but plainly we do not have in the Nikāyas and canonical Abhidhamma a single systematic account in the manner of later manuals such as the *Visuddhimagga*. We are faced not so much with a single finished canvas as with a bewildering array of sketches and detailed studies which it is impossible to take in at once. Their subject is seen from different angles and in various aspects; it is viewed from near and afar. Our problem is how to arrange the different pictures in order to begin to see how they might relate to each other. In other words, we need a method of sorting and arranging our sources that does not rely simply on what catches our eye, or dissolve into a rather arbitrary scheme of chronological stratification. One option is to follow the lead given in the literature itself.

I have already drawn attention to a characteristic feature of canonical Buddhist literature, namely the way it likes to formulate teachings by way of lists. Two such lists that immediately spring to mind are the four noble truths (*ariya-sacca*) and the noble eight-factored path (*ariyo aṭṭhaṅgiko maggo*). But these are only two amongst literally hundreds[73] of similar lists covering the whole range of the theory and practice of ancient Buddhism. It may be initially tempting to discuss these lists as a quaint but tedious vestige of an oral culture which forms something of an obstacle to our understanding of the real essentials of Buddhist thought. Yet they are so fundamental to the literature that it seems we must resist the temptation. Indeed, it is obvious that many Nikāya discourses can be readily resolved into an elaboration of one or more of these lists. In fact this is precisely the source of our familiarity with the noble eight-factored path and the four noble truths—these two lists happen to form the basis of what the tradition tells us was the Buddha's first discourse. Examples of less familiar combinations of lists that are no less the bases for complete descriptions of the path are not hard to find.[74]

Clearly the collation of these lists in order to provide more complete yet succinct compendia of the full range of Buddhist teaching was a practice undertaken quite early on in the history of Buddhist literature. Two important and relatively early examples of such collations are the *Saṃgīti-* and *Dasuttara-suttas*. Furthermore, two of the great Nikāyas, the *Saṃyutta-* and *Aṅguttara-nikāyas*, are really in essence only more ambitious extended improvisations on the fundamental Nikāya lists. The former takes a particular list and attempts to assemble all the significant treatments and discussions of it from the available stock of material, while the latter, by means of a system of numerical progression from one to eleven, arranges its material according to the number of items or divisions involved. As soon as one begins to peruse the *Saṃyutta-* and *Aṅguttara-nikāyas* it is quite obvious that they do not provide a uniform and even treatment of their material, but instead handle it in a fashion that enhances particular themes and emphases. These two collections thus seem to

[73] How many lists there are in the Nikāyas would be difficult to say; I counted 229 in the *Saṃgīti-sutta*.

[74] E.g. the *Cetokhila-sutta* (M I 101-4) resolves into the five *ceto-khilas*, five *vinibandhas*, and four *iddhi-pādas*.

provide a convenient basis on which to begin to gauge what most interested their compilers at what is a relatively early point in the history of Buddhist thought. What then does an initial review of the contents of the *Saṃyutta-nikāya* reveal?

The first major division (*vagga*) is entitled 'accompanied by verses' (*sagāthā*) which seems to mean precisely what it says. It is a miscellaneous collection of verses each of which is usually associated with a prose piece in the normal Sutta format. The next *vagga* is entitled 'connections' (*nidāna*) and consists of ten groups (*saṃyutta*) of *suttas*.[75] Each of these groups is devoted to a particular theme. However, about one half of the whole is taken up by just one *saṃyutta*, namely the *nidāna-saṃyutta*. This is a collection devoted to the exposition of the twelve—in all—'connections' or 'links' that constitute the theory of causation or, more properly, conditioned arising (*paṭicca-samuppāda*). The third *vagga* is entitled 'aggregates' (*khandha*). There are thirteen *saṃyuttas* in all, but as with the *nidāna-vagga* one dominates the rest. This time over half the *vagga* is devoted to an exposition of the five aggregates or groups into which the sum total of conditioned existence can be resolved. The fourth *vagga*, entitled 'six spheres' (*saḷāyatana*), contains ten *saṃyuttas*. The *saṃyutta* of the title is concerned with an analysis of the way in which the whole of experience is potentially encompassed by the six spheres of sense (the eye, ear, nose, tongue, body and mind); once more it takes up around half the *vagga*.

The arrangement of the fifth and final *vagga* is slightly different. It is entitled simply the 'great division' (*mahā-vagga*) and consists of twelve *saṃyuttas*. The *mahā-vagga* is probably the largest of the five, and the treatment of the component *saṃyuttas* is rather more even than in the other *vaggas*. This becomes especially clear when the extensive abridgements (*peyyāla*) of the *mahā-vagga* are taken into account. The names of the twelve *saṃyuttas* are as follows: 'path' (*magga*), 'factors of awakening' (*bojjhaṅga*), 'establishments of mindfulness' (*satipaṭṭhāna*), 'faculties' (*indriya*), 'right endeavours' (*sammā-ppadhāna*), 'powers' (*bala*), 'bases of success' (*iddhi-pāda*), 'Anuruddha', 'meditation' (*jhāna*), 'in-breathing and out-breathing' (*ānâpāna*), 'stream attainment' (*sotâpatti*) and 'truths' (*sacca*). An immediate point of interest is that the first seven *saṃyuttas* reflect a grouping that is found in a number of Nikāya passages in the following sequence: four *satipaṭṭhānas*, four *sammā-ppadhānas*, four *iddhi-pādas*, five *indriyas*, five *balas*, seven *bojjhaṅgas*, the noble eight-factored *magga* (these are hereafter referred to collectively as 'the seven sets'). Furthermore, in post-canonical Pāli literature this composite list is given the collective designation 'thirty-seven *dhammas* that contribute to awakening (*bodhi-pakkhiyā dhammā*)'. I referred to this expression above and noted that precisely the same designation (thirty-seven *bodhi-pākṣikā dharmāḥ*) is found in a variety of Buddhist Sanskrit sources.

In general and as far as can be known, other recensions of the *saṃyukta* type seem to have followed a similar pattern to the one followed by the Pāli,

[75] But cf. L.Feer at S II vii-xi on the difficulties in determining the precise extent of some *saṃyuttas*.

giving weight to the same themes: conditioned arising, the aggregates, the sense spheres and the seven sets.[76] These same themes continue to feature prominently in the later literature, both Pāli and non-Pāli. Certainly we have here the basic framework of contents for a number of important canonical Abhidharma works such as the *Vibhaṅga*, *Dhātukathā* (of the Theravāda) and the *Dharmaskandha* (of the Sarvāstivāda),[77] while later works and manuals witness in a variety of ways to the continuing influence of what might be called the basic *saṃyukta* table of contents.

Turning now to the *Aṅguttara-nikāya*, when we look under the appropriate numerical headings for those lists that are so clearly singled out in the *Saṃyutta-nikāya* we find that they hardly feature at all and in some cases are simply not there. The obvious reason for this is because they are treated so fully in the *Saṃyutta-nikāya*; the *Aṅguttara-nikāya's* method and purpose is rather different. On closer inspection all the principal *saṃyutta* headings are in fact to be found in the *Aṅguttara-nikāya*, but they feature, as it were, secondarily. While they are generally not found as primary lists under the appropriate numerical headings, they do occur in the course of the exposition of other material.[78]

Thus it seems that the *saṃyutta* and *aṅguttara* systems are essentially complementary; although there is some overlap, there is not extensive repetition. It seems reasonable to understand the *saṃyutta* method as intended to bring to the fore what were felt to be the more fundamental themes of ancient Buddhist thought. In that case it represents what might be viewed as a fairly coarse net being drawn through the pool of available material. The *aṅguttara* method in contrast represents a somewhat finer net. With its system of eleven numerical sections it is able to catch what has slipped through the *saṃyutta* net, and incidentally anything that has overflowed from it when it was drawn from the pool. So we have in the *Saṃyutta-nikāya* especially a simple means of access to the themes and concerns of Buddhist thought at a relatively early date in its history. The lists that dominate the *Saṃyutta-nikāya* are of course scattered throughout the other Nikāyas, but the *saṃyutta* arrangement delineates something that the *dīgha*, *majjhima* and *aṅguttara* arrangements leave rather less well defined. In so far as what is delineated by the *saṃyutta* arrangement also serves as a framework for parts of the Abhidhamma literature, we can perhaps use it as a bridge to cross from the *suttas* to the Abhidhamma.

4. The thirty-seven dhammas that contribute to awakening: preliminary remarks

I stated above that my concern in this study is to contribute to our understanding of the notion of spiritual practice and the path to awakening in

---

[76] Cf. Anesaki, op. cit., pp. 68-76; J. Bronkhorst, 'Dharma and Abhidharma', *BSOAS* 48 (1985), pp. 316-7.

[77] Cf. Chapter 8.2.

[78] Cf. C.A.F. Rhys Davids' comments at A VI (*Indexes*) vii-viii; 'Curious Omissions in Pāli Canonical Lists', *JRAS* (1935), pp. 721-4; Pande, op. cit., pp. 232-3.

the Nikāyas and Abhidhamma. If I am to follow the lead suggested by the arrangement of the *Saṃyutta-nikāya*, then it is the *mahā-vagga* or 'great division' that seems to offer the obvious point of departure. The reasons for this are six. (i) The *mahā-vagga* seems to be intended as something of a culmination in the *saṃyutta* scheme; this is suggested both by its title and by the position it occupies in the scheme. (ii) Some non-Pāli recensions of the material corresponding to what is contained in the *mahā-vagga* seem to have given it the title 'path' (*mārga*) or 'noble path' (*ārya-mārga*).[79] (iii) The *mahā-vagga* opens with the collection of *suttas* on the eight-factored path (*magga-saṃyutta*). (iv) The greater part of the *mahā-vagga* concerns a group of seven sets that is found elsewhere in the Nikāyas in a sequence culminating in the noble eight-factored path. (v) The same stock sequence is taken up in a variety of later sources, both Pāli and non-Pāli, and given the name 'thirty-seven *dharmas* that contribute to awakening'. (vi) The Abhidharma traditions of both the Sarvāstivādins and Theravādins understand these same thirty-seven *dharmas* as in some sense equivalent to the 'path' (*mārga*).

This last point requires a little elaboration. For the moment I am content to follow what Buddhaghosa says in the *Visuddhimagga* for the Theravādins, and for the Sarvāstivādins what Vasubandhu says in the *Abhidharmakośa*. According to Buddhaghosa, then, all thirty-seven *bodhi-pakkhiyā dhammā* are found in a single moment of consciousness (*eka-citta*) at the time of the arising of the four knowledges concerned with the paths to stream-attainment, once-return, non-return and *arahant*-ship respectively.[80] According to Vasubandhu the path (*mārga*) can be termed 'that which contributes to awakening' (*bodhi-pākṣika*); this consists of the thirty-seven *dharmas*.[81] He then goes on to indicate how the classic sequence of the seven sets describes the successive stages of the complete path. We thus have two basic emphases. The first sees the thirty-seven *dhammas* collectively as a description of the final culmination of the path to awakening; the second sees the thirty-seven collectively as a description of the successive stages of the path. For the time being this will suffice, but I shall need to return to this difference in approach in chapter ten below.

I am now in a position to indicate rather more definitely the course I wish this investigation to follow. Its specific starting point consists in three basic facts. First, details of the seven sets *individually* are scattered throughout the Nikāyas, but without any firm indication that the seven are associated. Secondly, in a number of Nikāya and Abhidhamma contexts the seven sets are found brought together in a bare sequence, yet without any definite statement as to why. Finally, in the post-canonical literature the seven sets receive the collective appellation 'thirty-seven *dhammas* that contribute to awakening' and

---

79 See Anesaki, op. cit., p. 68; Bronkhorst, *BSOAS* 48 (1985), p. 317.

80 Vism XXII 2, 31: *sotâpatti-maggo sakad-āgāmi-maggo anāgāmi-maggo arahatta-maggo ti imesu pana catusu maggesu ñāṇaṃ ñāṇa-dassana-visuddhi nāma.* Vism XXII 39: *ime satta-tiṃsa bodhi-pakkhiyā dhammā ... imesaṃ pana catunnaṃ ñāṇānaṃ uppatti-kāle eka-citte labbhanti.*

81 Abhidh-k-bh 382: *punar apy eṣa mārgo bodhi-pakṣyâkhyāṃ labhate. saptatriṃśad-bodhi-pakṣyā dharmāḥ catvāri smṛty-upasthānāni catvāri samyak-prahāṇāni catvāra ṛddhi-pādāḥ pañcend-riyāṇi pañca balāni sapta bodhy-aṅgāni āryâṣṭâṅgo mārga iti.* Cf. Abhidh-dī 356-7.

are in some sense explicitly identified with the path. What I want to do is trace the logic behind this state of affairs. What, if any, is the relationship between the treatment of the seven sets individually in the Nikāyas and their final collective designation as 'thirty-seven *bodhi-pakkhiyā dhammā*' equivalent to the path to awakening? What I hope will emerge from this exercise is a clearer understanding not only of how early Buddhist thought actually conceived of the spiritual path, but also of the forces and concerns that governed the development of Buddhist thought.

My study of these questions falls into two main parts. In Part One I have tried to give a detailed account of how the seven sets are individually treated and defined. This account concentrates in the first place on the Nikāya material but is complemented by reference to both canonical Abhidhamma and post-canonical texts. The treatment of the seven sets individually in the Nikāyas must be regarded as constituting what is assumed in those contexts in the Nikāyas and Abhidhamma literature where the seven sets are brought together. Thus Part One provides the necessary background to Part Two of the study in which I turn my attention to the seven sets collectively and as the thirty-seven *bodhi-pakkhiyā dhammā*.

My study is intended primarily as an enquiry into the Pāli sources. Accordingly I have endeavoured to take into account every passage in the Pāli canon (and also in the para-canonical *Peṭakopadesa*, *Nettippakaraṇa* and *Milindapañha*) where the seven sets are discussed either individually or collectively.[82] It has proved impractical to discuss explicitly all canonical passages dealing with the individual sets. What I have tried to do is to identify and draw attention to what is distinctive and characteristic in the treatment of each of the seven sets, while at the same time noting anything that seems peculiar or worthy of mention in its own right. In the case of passages concerning the seven sets collectively and the expression *bodhi-pakkhiyā dhammā* I have been able to be more comprehensive.

It is perhaps useful at this stage to indicate very generally the sections of the Pāli canon most relevant to my study. Not surprisingly the *Vinaya-piṭaka*, apart from one or two (still important) passages, is largely irrevelant. All four of the primary Nikāyas, on the other hand, provide a variety of texts dealing with the seven sets both individually and collectively. These are supplemented by various passages in certain *Khuddaka-nikāya* texts: the *Khuddakapāṭha*, the *Dhammapada*, the *Udāna*, the *Itivuttaka*, the *Theragāthā* the *Therīgāthā* and *Apadāna*. This material can be considered as more or less of a piece with the four primary Nikāyas. The remaining *Khuddaka* texts are largely irrelevant,[83] the *Niddesa* and *Paṭisambhidāmagga* being two important exceptions. Both these texts refer regularly to the seven sets, but their material is best considered

---

[82] See below, Appendix (Summary of Textual References).

[83] One should note here that the seven sets are absent from the *Suttanipāta*. This cannot be explained entirely by reference to the fact that Sn is largely in verse and therefore likely not always to conform to the set patterns of Sutta prose; after all references to the seven sets are found in Dhp, Th, Thī and Ap. However, as I shall point out, the basic terminology relevant to the seven sets is to be found in Sn.

alongside the canonical Abhidhamma material. Of the seven works of the *Abhidhamma-piṭaka*, the *Dhammasaṅgaṇi* and *Vibhaṅga* are the basic texts as far as the seven sets are concerned. While the *Dhātukathā's* method encompasses the seven sets, it does so in a way that is largely self-contained and thus only incidentally impinges on the themes of the present study. The seven sets are absent from the *Puggalapaññatti*. The *Kathāvatthu* contains a number of discussions that have some bearing on the seven sets, while the *Yamaka* deals directly only with the twenty-two *indriyas*. Finally, the *Paṭṭhāna's* method, like the *Dhātukathā's*, is largely self contained; while the seven sets do not feature explicitly, it would be misleading to regard them as entirely irrelevant, but I have been content to indicate in rather general terms how this is so. In the *Peṭakopadesa*, *Nettippakaraṇa* and *Milindapañha* the seven sets and thirty-seven *bodhi-pakkhiyā dhammā* feature sporadically.

My approach to the later literature has as a matter of practical necessity been rather less systematic. For the most part I have been content to concentrate on those *aṭṭhakathā* passages that bear directly on the relevant parts of the canonical literature. I have in addition made use of the *Visuddhimagga* and *Vimuttimagga*. Throughout this study I have also made selective use of non-Pāli sources. These sources assist in two ways: either they confirm and underline something that is already apparent in the Pāli sources themselves, or by suggesting a different perspective they throw the Pāli sources into relief. As a result of this there emerges a rather clearer picture of just what is distinctive and peculiar in the Pāli tradition and of what constitutes the consensus of ancient Buddhist thought.

The importance of the thirty-seven *bodhi-pakkhiyā dhammā* has not, of course, escaped the notice of modern scholars. They frequently mention it in passing, and A.K. Warder, for example, has taken the seven sets as a basis for an account of the Buddha's own teaching.[84] The fullest treatments of the subject appear to be a chapter in Har Dayal's *The Bodhisattva Doctrine in Buddhist Sanskrit Literature*[85] and an essay incorporated in Étienne Lamotte's *Le Traité de la Grande Vertu de Sagesse de Nāgārjuna*.[86] The former, although dated and seriously misleading in a number of respects, is still cited. The latter certainly provides a clear indication of the extent to which the seven sets and thirty-seven *dhammas* feature in Buddhist literature, but hardly amounts to a systematic study. In certain respects, though, I have taken Lamotte's essay as something of a starting point.

---

[84] A.K. Warder, *Indian Buddhism*, 2nd ed., Delhi, 1980, pp. 81-105.

[85] London, 1932, pp. 80-164.

[86] Lamotte, *Traité*, III 1119-37. See also *Encyclopaedia of Buddhism*, ed. G.P. Malalasekera, Colombo, s.v. *bodhipakkhiyā dhammā*; Ledi Sayadaw, 'The Requisites of Enlightenment (Bodhipakkhiya-Dīpanī)', *The Wheel*, 71/174, Kandy, 1971.

PART ONE

THE SEVEN SETS INDIVIDUALLY

CHAPTER ONE

THE ESTABLISHING OF MINDFULNESS

1. What are the satipaṭṭhānas?

The Nikāyas answer the question 'what are the *satipaṭṭhānas*?' with the following basic formula:

> *cattāro satipaṭṭhānā. katame cattāro. idha bhikkhave bhikkhu [i] kāye kāyânupassī viharati ātāpī sampajāno satimā vineyya loke abhijjhā-domanassaṃ. [ii] vedanāsu vedanânupassī viharati ātāpī sampajāno satimā vineyya loke abhijjhā-domanassaṃ. [iii] citte cittânupassī viharati ātāpī sampajāno satimā vineyya loke abhijjhā-domanassaṃ. [iv] dhammesu dhammânupassī viharati ātāpī sampajāno satimā vineyya loke abhijjhā-domanassaṃ.*[1]

> The four establishings of mindfulness. What four? Here, *bhikkhus*, a *bhikkhu* [i] with regard to the body dwells watching body; he is ardent, he comprehends clearly, is possessed of mindfulness and overcomes both desire for and discontent with the world. [ii] With regard to feelings he dwells watching feeling ... [iii] With regard to the mind he dwells watching mind ... [iv] With regard to *dhammas* he dwells watching *dhamma*; he is ardent, he comprehends clearly, is possessed of mindfulness and overcomes both desire for and discontent with the world.

Buddhist Sanskrit sources also speak of four *smṛty-upasthānas*, but I have been unable to find a Sanskrit version of precisely this bare formula in any source available to me. However, a fuller expanded version of the formula—to which a Pāli parallel also exists—appears to be fairly common in Buddhist Sanskrit sources.[2] I shall return to this expanded version of the *satipaṭṭhāna* formula in section five of this chapter. A basic statement of the matter found in the Chinese Āgamas would seem to correspond to a Sanskrit form that enumerates the four *smṛty-upasthānas* as the *smṛty-upasthāna* of watching the body (*kāyânupaśyanā-smṛty-upasthāna*), the *smṛty-upasthāna* of watching feeling (*vedanânupaśyanā-smṛty-upasthāna*), the *smṛty-upasthāna* of watching mind (*cittânupaśyanā-smṛty-upasthāna*), and the *smṛty-upasthāna* of watching *dharma(s)* (*dharmânupaśyanā-smṛty-upasthāna*).[3]

---

[1] D II 290 = M I 55 (*Mahāsatipaṭṭhāna-* and *Satipaṭṭhāna-suttas*); see also D III 58, 141, 221, 276; M I 339-40; S V 141-92 passim, 294-306 passim, A IV 457-8. For the basic formula with no explicit allusion to *satipaṭṭhāna* see D II 94-5, 100; M III 136, 251; S IV 211; A II 256; IV 300-1. Outside the four primary Nikāyas see Nidd I 9, 19, 244, 347, 399, 475; Paṭis I 41; II 15, 18; Vibh 105, 236.

[2] For the record, I give the text as found in the Mūlasarvāstivādin *Mahāparinirvāṇa-sūtra* (Waldschmidt, *MPS* 200; parallel to D II 100): *iha bhikṣur adhyātmaṃ kāye kāyânupaśyī viharaty ātāpī samprajānaḥ smṛtimān vinīyâbhidhyā loke daurmanasyaṃ bahirdhā kāye'dhyātma-bahirdhā kāye'dhyātmaṃ vedanāsu bahirdhā vedanāsv adhyātma-bahirdhā vedanāsv adhyātmaṃ citte bahirdhā citte'dhyātma-bahirdhā citte'dhyātmaṃ dharmeṣu bahirdhā dharmeṣv adhyātma-bahirdhā dharmeṣu dharmânupaśyī viharaty ātāpī samprajānaḥ smṛtimān vinīyâbhidhyā loke daurmanasyam.* Cf. Lamotte, *Traité*, III 1121-2.

[3] See L. Hurvitz, 'Fa-sheng's Observations on the Four Stations of Mindfulness' in *Mahāyāna Buddhist Meditation: Theory and Practice*, ed. by Minoru Kyota, Honolulu, 1978, pp. 207-48 (p.

The *Mahāsatipaṭṭhāna-* and *Satipaṭṭhāna-suttas* of the *Dīgha-* and *Majjhima-nikāyas* respectively consist of a detailed and full exposition of what I have dubbed the basic *satipaṭṭhāna* formula. Before turning my attention to this, I wish to give some initial consideration to the elementary questions of what exactly a *satipaṭṭhāna* is, and what exactly *sati* is. I have translated *satipaṭṭhāna* above as 'establishing of mindfulness'. This seems to me to be a convenient and acceptable translation that conveys generally the import of the term *satipaṭṭhāna* in Pāli literature as a whole. However, 'establishing of mindfulness' is not an immediately intelligible English expression and requires further explanation. The term *satipaṭṭhāna* has been variously commented upon by scholars,[4] yet their comments add up to a slightly confused presentation of the basic facts, and of the traditional exegesis of the Pāli commentaries. Basically there are two areas of confusion. First, should Buddhist Sanskrit *smṛty-upasthāna* be taken as a correct or incorrect back-formation of Middle Indo-Aryan *satipaṭṭhāna*? Secondly, does the term *satipaṭṭhāna* refer primarily to the body, feelings, mind and *dhammas* as the objects of observation and mindfulness (i.e it is the body, etc. that are *satipaṭṭhānas*), or does it rather refer to the actual activity of observing the body, feelings, mind and *dhammas* (i.e. it is the act of watching that is a *satipaṭṭhāna*)?

To begin with the second point, it seems to me that the basic formula and the succinct statement of the *smṛty-upasthānas* as found in the Chinese Āgamas make it quite clear that in the first place the four *satipaṭṭhānas* are taken to consist in four varieties of *anupassanā*. In other words, the term *satipaṭṭhāna* refers primarily to the activity of observing or watching the body, feelings, mind and *dhammas*. The question is what is meant by terming these four varieties of *anupassanā* 'four *satipaṭṭhānas*'. What exactly does *satipaṭṭhāna* mean?

Prima facie the term *satipaṭṭhāna* might represent a combination of *sati* (= Skt *smṛti*) and *paṭṭhāna* (= Skt *prasthāna*). But this resolution of the compound is not without difficulties. In the first place, if we except *satipaṭṭhāna*, the term *paṭṭhāna* appears to be unknown to the Nikāyas;[5] it becomes current only rather later in the canonical Abhidhamma literature; even here the term is rare and of slightly obscure significance. The Theravādin and Sarvāstivādin canons both contain Abhidharma works that employ the term in their titles, namely the *Paṭṭhāna* and *Jñānaprasthāna*. In classical Sanskrit literature *prasthā* means basically 'to stand forth' and hence 'to set out', 'to depart'; a

---

211). Cf. Vibh-a 215: *kāyânupassanā-satipaṭṭhānaṃ … vedanânupassanā-satipaṭṭhānaṃ … cittânupassanā-satipaṭṭhānaṃ … dhammânupassanā-satipaṭṭhānaṃ*

[4] Cf. T.W. and C.A.F. Rhys Davids at D Trsl II 324; C.A.F. Rhys Davids at S Trsl V xiv-v; H. Dayal, *The Bodhisattva Doctrine in Buddhist Sanskrit Literature*, London, 1932, p. 85; A.K. Warder, *Indian Buddhism*, p. 83; Childers, *PED*, s.vv. *upaṭṭhāna, paṭṭhāna, satipaṭṭhāna*; *BHSD*, s.vv. *upasthāna, prasthāna, smṛtyupasthāna*; *CPD*, s.v. *upaṭṭhāna*.

[5] *PTC*, s.v. *paṭṭhāna*, gives only *paṭṭhānaṃ bhāvento sato* (Nidd I 19) and *ekatta-paṭṭhāna* (Paṭis I 15); the former is a misreading of *satipaṭṭhānaṃ bhāvento sato*, and the latter, although of interest, does not bear on *sati* (the full phrase is *ekatta-paṭṭhāna-vasena cittassa ṭhitaṭṭho abhiññeyyo*).

prasthāna is thus a 'setting forth', a 'departure' or a 'course'.[6] In the context of the title of the seventh book of the *Abhidhamma-piṭaka*, *paṭṭhāna* appears to mean something like 'point of departure' and hence 'basis', 'origin' or 'cause', or possibly it might be taken as signifying a 'course' or 'sequence (of conditions)'.[7] A *paṭṭhāna* of *sati* ought to mean, then, 'the setting out of mindfulness', 'the departure of mindfulness' in the sense of 'the beginning of mindfulness'. Clearly, one might begin to make sense of the term on this basis, but there are other factors that would seem to suggest that this might not be the most straightforward course to follow.

As C.A.F. Rhys Davids has pointed out,[8] it is nearly always derivatives from *upa-sthā* that are found associated with *sati* in the Nikāyas, and never derivatives from *pra-sthā*.[9] This fact alone would seem to weigh rather heavily against taking *satipaṭṭhāna* to represent the combination of *sati* and *paṭṭhāna*, and suggests that what we ought to have is *sati* combined with *upaṭṭhāna*. The form we might most readily expect from the combination of *sati* and *upaṭṭhāna* is **saccupaṭṭhāna*. But the possibility of confusion with *sacca* (= Skt *satya*) inherent in such a form might well have counted against its adoption in a context where *sati* is all important.[10] If *satipaṭṭhāna* is not what we might normally expect from the combination of *sati* and *upaṭṭhāna*, then strictly neither is it what we might expect from the combination of *sati* and *(p)paṭṭhāna*; the form we would expect to find at least somewhere is **sati-ppaṭṭhāna* rather than *sati-paṭṭhāna*. So *PED* and C.A.F. Rhys Davids seem to be slightly hesitant and even confused about whether we have *sati* and *paṭṭhāna*, or *sati* and *upaṭṭhāna*,[11] and others such as Har Dayal state unequivocally that Buddhist Sanskrit *smṛty-upasthāna* is a wrong backformation.[12] Both Childers and Geiger, however, suggest that Middle Indo-Aryan *satipaṭṭhāna* does indeed represent a sandhi of *sati* and *upaṭṭhāna*;[13] Childers even provides an example of a similar sandhi, namely *bhikkhunipassaya* from *bhikkhunī* and *upassaya*.[14]

---

[6] MW, s.v. *pra-sthā*.

[7] Cf. Ledi Sayadaw, *JPTS* (1915-16), pp. 22-3.

[8] S Trsl V xiv-v.

[9] Cf. *sati na upaṭṭhāti* (M I 104); *sati upaṭṭhapetabbā* (D II 141); *upaṭṭhitā sati* (Vin III 4; M I 117, 86; S IV 18, 28; V 337-9; A I 148; Thī 388); *satiṃ upaṭṭhapetvā* (Vin I 24; D I 71; M II 139; S I 179; A II 210; Th 946; Thī 182; etc.). *Sati* is associated with derivatives from verbs other than *upa-sthā*, e.g. *sati paccupaṭṭhitā* (D II 292; M I 59); *sati saṇṭhāti* (S V 222); *satiñ ca suppatiṭṭhitaṃ* (Sn 444). However, I have been unable to find any clear example of *sati* associated with *pra-sthā*. At M I 339 there is the expression *catusu satipaṭṭhānesu supaṭṭhita-cittā viharanti* but with *supatiṭṭhita* and *sûpaṭṭhita* as variants; cf. A III 155; V 195.

[10] The expression *muṭṭha-sacca* (< *-*smārtya*) is, however, found at D III 213; A V 149; Dhs 232.

[11] Cf. *PED*, s.vv. *paṭṭhāna* and *satipaṭṭhāna*; D Trsl II 324; S Trsl V xiv-v.

[12] Dayal, op.cit., p. 85.

[13] Childers, s.v. *satipaṭṭhāna*; W. Geiger, *Pāli Literature and Language*, Calcutta, 1956, p. 109. Cf. also *BHSD*, s.v. *smṛty-upasthāna*; Nyanaponika Thera, *The Heart of Buddhist Meditation*, London, 1962, p. 10.

[14] Childers, s.v. *satipaṭṭhāna*; Childers seems to be referring to *bhikkhunipassaya* in the *Mahāvaṃsa* (cf. Childers, s.v. *passaya*); the PTS edition in fact reads *bhikkhunupassaya* (see Mhv XVIII 11, XIX 68, XXXIV 36) with *bhikkhunipassaya* as variant. Elsewhere I have found *bhikkhunûpassaya* (Vin II 259; IV 56, 166, 176, 211, 224, 265, 266, 314); *bhikkhunīupassaya* (Vin IV

If we take *satipaṭṭhāna* to represent *sati* and *upaṭṭhāna*, what would it mean? The verb *upatiṣṭhati* means primarily 'to stand near' and hence 'to be present', 'to manifest' and 'to serve'.[15] The regular Nikāya expression *satiṃ upaṭṭhapetvā* means, then, 'causing mindfulness to stand near', 'causing mindfulness to be present' or even 'causing mindfulness to come into service'. According to the *Paṭisambhidāmagga* the sense of *satipaṭṭhāna*, of the faculty of mindfulness, of the mindfulness awakening-factor and of right mindfulness is to be directly known as 'standing near' or 'serving' (*upaṭṭhāna*).[16] What is meant, I think, is that *sati* is understood as a quality of mind that 'stands near' or 'serves' the mind; it watches over the mind. One might say that it is a form of 'presence of mind'. In general this would seem to tie in with the emphasis in Buddhist literature on *sati* as a quality that the *bhikkhu* needs to develop at all times, and with the notion that *sati* manifests as 'guarding'.[17] The four *satipaṭṭhānas* are, then, four *anupassanās*, four activities the purpose of which is to bring *sati* into 'service'. That is, in the process of watching the body, feelings, mind and *dhammas*, *sati* stands near, manifests and is established.

To sum up, derivatives from *upa-sthā* are regularly associated with *sati* in the Nikāyas; there appears to be no real reason why the form *satipaṭṭhāna* should not be taken as the product of the combination of *sati* and *upaṭṭhāna*; the notion of the *upaṭṭhāna* of *sati* seems to be quite intelligible. I take it, then, that *satipaṭṭhāna* is primarily a term that is used to qualify four varieties of *anupassanā* as four practices of watching or contemplation that are 'causes for the standing near of mindfulness'; the texts thus go on to speak of (translating rather literally and clumsily) 'four mindfulness-manifestings'.

This may be the *primary* significance of the term *satipaṭṭhāna*, but already in the Nikāya period the term is obviously well established enough to be the subject of a certain amount of play. In the *satipaṭṭhāna-saṃyutta* we find the following:

> I shall teach you, *bhikkhus*, the arising and disappearance of the four *satipaṭṭhānas*, listen. And what, *bhikkhus*, is the arising of the body? Due to the arising of food, there is the arising of the body; due to the disappearance of food, there is the disappearance of the body. Due to the arising of contact, there is the arising of feelings; due to the disappearance of contact there is the disappearance of feelings. Due to the arising of name and form, there is the arising of mind; due to the disappearance of name and form, there is the disappearance of mind. Due to the arising of bringing to mind, there is the arising of *dhammas*; due to the disappearance of bringing to mind, there is the disappearance of *dhammas*.[18]

101, Spk I 191); *bhikkhunupassaya* (v.l. *bhikkhunipassaya*) (Mil 124); *bhikkhunupassaya* (S II 215); *bhikkhuniupassaya* (J I 147, 428); *bhikkhunīpassaya* (v.l. *bhikkhunupassaya*) (A II 144, 145). Cf. K.R. Norman, *JPTS* 10 (1985), pp. 31-2.

[15] MW, s.v. *upa-sthā*.

[16] Paṭis I 16-17: *satipaṭṭhānaṃ upaṭṭhānaṭṭho abhiññeyyo ... satindriyassa ... sati-sambojjhaṅgassa ... sammā-satiyā upaṭṭhānaṭṭho abhiññeyyo*. Cf. Paṭis I 20-2. This seems to me a fairly clear indication that Paṭis at least took *satipaṭṭhāna* as *sati* and *upaṭṭhāna*; cf. *kāyo upaṭṭhānaṃ no sati, sati upaṭṭhānañ ceva sati ca* (Paṭis I 177, 183; II 232-3) (see below, p. 33).

[17] See below, p. 40.

[18] S V 184: *catunnaṃ bhikkhave satipaṭṭhānānaṃ samudayañ ca atthagamañ ca desissāmi. taṃ suṇātha. ko ca bhikkhave kāyassa samudayo. āhāra-samudayā kāyassa samudayo. āhāra-nirodhā kāyassa atthagamo. phassa-samudayā vedanānaṃ samudayo. phassa-nirodhā vedanānaṃ atthagamo.*

This passage quite clearly only makes sense if *satipaṭṭhāna* is taken as directly describing the body and so forth. In other words, it must be assumed that *satipaṭṭhāna* means 'the basis of *sati*', 'the foundation of *sati*', 'that which is the support of *sati*'. The term here refers to the body, feelings, mind and *dhammas* as four objective fields of *sati*. This kind of meaning can probably be reached on the basis of a derivation from either *upa-sthā* or *pra-sthā*, though as far as classical Sanskrit is concerned it would seem to fit better with *prati-ṣṭhā*, 'to stand upon'. Certainly in the explanations of the Pāli commentaries, to which I shall now turn, there seems to be a tendency to assimilate *pra-sthā* and *prati-ṣṭhā*. The play on the term *satipaṭṭhāna*, which becomes more evident in the exegetical writings, should probably be regarded as arising directly out of an ambiguity inherent in Middle Indo-Aryan *satipaṭṭhāna*.

I take the interpretation of *satipaṭṭhāna* as referring to the body and so on as the 'supports of *sati*' as secondary, but it is not to be viewed as particularly late or even peculiar to the Pāli sources. Both Buddhaghosa and Vasubandhu in fact refer to a canonical source equivalent to the one quoted above. Taking the Pāli sources first, Buddhaghosa states that there are three basic uses of the term *satipaṭṭhāna*:[19] there is *satipaṭṭhāna* that is the field or pasture of mindfulness (*sati-gocara*); there is *satipaṭṭhāna* that consists in the teacher's having gone beyond dislike and favouritism (*paṭighânunaya-vītivattatā*) concerning his disciples' achievements; and there is *satipaṭṭhāna* that is simply *sati*. Buddhaghosa then proceeds to illustrate these different uses by quotation from Sutta. He begins with the *satipaṭṭhāna-saṃyutta* passage I have already quoted:

> For with regard to 'I shall teach you, *bhikkhus*, the arising and the disappearance of the four *satipaṭṭhānas*. Listen, pay careful attention ... And what, *bhikkhus*, is the arising of body? Due to the arising of food there is the arising of body ... ' and so on, it is the pasture of mindfulness that is spoken of as *satipaṭṭhāna*. Likewise with regard to 'Body is a support, it is not mindfulness; mindfulness is both a support and it is mindfulness ... ' and so on [= Paṭis I 177, 183; II 232-3]. The meaning of this is that it is a resting place (*paṭṭhāna*) because [something] rests (*patiṭṭhāti*) there.[20] What rests? Mindfulness. A *satipaṭṭhāna* is a resting-place of mindfulness. Alternatively *paṭṭhāna* is 'a special place';[21] a *satipaṭṭhāna* is a special-place for mindfulness like a place for elephants or a place for horses, etc.[22]

---

nāma-rūpa-samudayā cittassa samudayo. nāma-rūpa-nirodhā cittassa atthagamo. manasikāra-samudayā dhammānaṃ samudayo. manasikāra-nirodhā dhammānaṃ atthagamo ti.

19 Sv III 752 = Ps I 237-8 = Vibh-a 214.

20 Strictly *patiṭṭhāti* should be derived from *prati-ṣṭhā* and is analogous to the form *upaṭṭhāti*; from *pra-sthā* we would expect *paṭṭhāti*, *patiṭṭhati*, or *paṭṭhahati* (see Geiger, op.cit., pp. 168- 9). As I suggested above, the Pāli commentaries seem to be playing on a certain ambiguity in the Pāli form.

21 The commentary here is suggesting that the force of *(p)pa-* in *(p)paṭṭhāna* is equivalent to *padhāna* in the sense of 'chief' or 'principal' (see MW, s.v. *pradhāna*; this meaning is not recorded for *padhāna* in *PED*); cf. Sadd 881 and Ledi Sayadaw, 'On the Philosophy of Relations', *JPTS* (1915-16), p. 26.

22 Sv III 752-3 = Ps I 238 = Vibh-a 214: *catunnaṃ bhikkhave satipaṭṭhānānaṃ samudayañ ca atthagamañ ca desissāmi. taṃ suṇātha sādhukaṃ manasikarotha ... pe ... ko ca bhikkhave kāyassa samudayo. āhāra-samudayā kāyassa samudayo ti ādīsu hi sati-gocaro satipaṭṭhānan ti vuccati. tathā kāyo upaṭṭhānaṃ no sati, sati upaṭṭhānañ ceva sati cā ti ādīsu. tass'attho patiṭṭhāti asmin ti paṭṭhānaṃ. kā patiṭṭhāti. sati. satiyā paṭṭhānaṃ satipaṭṭhānaṃ padhanaṃ ṭhānan ti vā paṭṭhānaṃ. satiyā paṭṭhānaṃ satipaṭṭhānaṃ hatthi-ṭṭhāna-assa-ṭṭhānâdīni viya.*

Buddhaghosa next refers to a passage detailing three *satipaṭṭhānas* that are the peculiar domain of the teacher. These three *satipaṭṭhānas* concern the teacher's ability to maintain mindfulness regardless of whether his disciples fail to understand the teaching, whether some understand and some do not, whether they all understand:[23]

> 'There are three *satipaṭṭhānas* which the noble one practises and when he practises these he is a teacher worthy to instruct the multitude'—here the teacher's threefold state of having passed beyond dislike and favouritism with regard to disciples who have entered upon the way is spoken of as *satipaṭṭhāna*. The meaning of this is that it is a *paṭṭhāna* from the point of view of what is to be established (*paṭṭhāpetabbato*); 'from the point of view of what is to be made to occur' is the meaning. From the point of view of what is to be established by what? By mindfulness. A *satipaṭṭhāna* is an establishing by mindfulness.[24]

Finally Buddhaghosa turns to the more usual and general use of *satipaṭṭhāna* in the Nikāyas:

> But with regard to 'The four *satipaṭṭhānas* when developed and made great bring to fulfilment the seven factors of awakening' and so on, it is just mindfulness that is spoken of as *satipaṭṭhāna*. The meaning is that it is 'a standing forth' (*paṭṭhāna*) because [something] stands forth (*patiṭṭhāti*); it stands near (*upaṭṭhāti*); 'coming forth and leaping forward it proceeds' is the meaning. A *satipaṭṭhāna* is just mindfulness in the sense of standing forth (*paṭṭhāna*). Alternatively *sati* is in the sense of remembering and *paṭṭhāna* is in the sense of standing near (*upaṭṭhāna*). So *satipaṭṭhāna* means simply 'mindfulness and the standing forth which that [i.e. mindfulness] is'. This is what is intended here.[25]

The 'here' in 'This is what is intended here' refers to the basic *satipaṭṭhāna* formula which I quoted at the beginning of this chapter, and which opens the *(Mahā-)Satipaṭṭhāna-sutta*. This formula is the basis of nearly the whole of the Nikāya treatment of the *satipaṭṭhānas* and it seems to be quite clear that Buddhaghosa sees his third explanation as the normative one. It is, then, hardly correct to say, as C.A.F. Rhys Davids does,[26] that Buddhaghosa rejects the interpretation of *satipaṭṭhāna* as *sati-upaṭṭhāna*; whether we have *paṭṭhāna* or *upaṭṭhāna* is in fact of little consequence to his exegesis, and he allows both.

This final explanation takes *satipaṭṭhāna* not as a *tatpuruṣa* compound ('the standing forth of mindfulness') but as a *karmadhāraya*: 'the standing forth that is mindfulness'. Yet it seems to correspond in practice to what I have suggested is the primary import of the term *satipaṭṭhāna*. Essentially a *satipaṭṭhāna* is nothing but *sati* itself; it is simply the 'standing near' of mindfulness. But as I

---

[23] M III 216, 221.

[24] Sv III 753 = Ps I 238 = Vibh-a 214: *tayo satipaṭṭhānā yad ariyo sevati, tad ariyo sevamāno satthā gaṇam anusāsituṃ arahatī ti ettha tidhā paṭipannesu sāvakesu satthuno paṭighânunaya-vīti-vattatā satipaṭṭhạnan ti vuttā. tass'attho paṭṭhāpetabbato paṭṭhānaṃ; pavattayitabbato ti attho. kena paṭṭhāpetabbato ti. satiyā. satiyā paṭṭhānaṃ satipaṭṭhānaṃ.*

[25] Sv III 753 = Ps I 238 = Vibh-a 214-5: *cattāro satipaṭṭhānā bhāvitā bahulīkatā satta bojjhaṅge paripūrentī ti ādīsu pana sati yeva satipaṭṭhānan ti vuccati. tass'attho patiṭṭhātī ti paṭṭhānaṃ; upaṭṭhāti; okkantitvā pakkhanditvā pavattatī ti attho. sati yeva paṭṭhānaṭṭhena satipaṭṭhānaṃ. atha vā saraṇaṭṭhena sati upaṭṭhānaṭṭhena paṭṭhānaṃ. iti sati ca sā paṭṭhānañ cā ti pi satipaṭṭhānaṃ. idaṃ idha adhippetaṃ.*

[26] S Trsl V xv.

have already suggested underlying both the canonical and commentarial understanding is a certain play on the term *satipaṭṭhāna*.[27] This is, I think, rather evident in the passage Buddhaghosa quotes from the *Paṭisambhidāmagga*. The notion is that watching the body, etc. is what supports mindfulness, is what causes mindfulness 'to stand near', but at the same time the very nature of mindfulness is 'to stand near' or 'to support'. Mindfulness is that which stands near, supports and guards the mind. Vasubandhu's comments on *smṛty-upasthāna* in the *Abhidharmakośa-bhāṣya* provide an interesting parallel to the Pāli commentarial material:

> Why is it that, from the point of view of essential nature, *smṛty-upasthāna* is wisdom? Because it is said [in the Sūtra] that *smṛty-upasthāna* is watching the body with regard to the body. Now what is 'watching'? It is wisdom ... Why is wisdom spoken of by the Blessed One as *smṛty-upasthāna*? The Vaibhāṣikas say that it is because of the predominance of mindfulness, which means 'because of the occurrence of forceful application of mindfulness'; it is like the support of a wedge when splitting wood. It works as follows. On account of it [i.e. wisdom] mindfulness stands near (*upatiṣṭhate*), therefore wisdom is the standing near of mindfulness (*smṛty-upasthāna*)—because of designating (*abhilapana*) what has been seen [by wisdom]. Accordingly it was said by the venerable Aniruddha, 'For one who dwells watching body with regard to the body, recollection which has the body as object stands near, is established ... ' and so on. Also it was said by the Blessed One, 'For one who dwells watching body with regard to the body, mindfulness that is unmuddled stands near.' But then this is said, 'How, *bhikṣus*, is there the arising and disappearance of the four *smṛty-upasthānas*? Due to the arising of food, there is the arising of the body; due to the ceasing of food, there is the ceasing of body.' Here *smṛty-upasthāna* is spoken of just as the object. Stating that mindfulness stands near there, they are named according to the object.[28]

Vasubandhu here gives two basic explanations of *smṛty-upasthāna* which parallel quite closely what is said of *satipaṭṭhāna* in the Pāli commentaries. His first explanation focuses on the actual activity of watching which consitutes *smṛty-upasthāna*, the second focuses on the actual support, objective field or basis of that activity. There are two points of particular interest in Vasubandhu's account. The first is the direct identification of *smṛty-upasthāna* with

---

[27] Essentially the discussion of the view that all *dhammas* are establishings of mindfulness (*sabbe dhammā satipaṭṭhānā*) at Kv 155-9 relies on the ambiguity of the term *satipaṭṭhāna*. According to Kv-a 52-3 the Andhakas arrived at their conclusion on the basis of the Sutta passage dealing with the *samudaya* and *atthagama* of the *satipaṭṭhānas*: if the *satipaṭṭhānas* are simply the four classes of object (body, feelings, mind and *dhammas*) for mindfulness then, since all *dhammas* (a term which in its widest sense embraces body, feelings and mind) can be objects of mindfulness, all *dhammas* are *satipaṭṭhānas*; but such a conclusion is not allowed by Kv because (taking *satipaṭṭhāna* as a term for mindfulness rather than its objects) not all *dhammas* are mindfulness.

[28] Abhidh-k 342: *svabhāva-smṛty-upasthānaṃ prajñeti kuta eva tat. kāye kāyânupaśyanā smṛty-upasthānam iti vacanāt. kā punar anupaśyanā. prajñā ... kasmāt prajñā smṛty-upasthānam ity uktā bhagavatā. smṛty-udrekatvād iti vaibhāṣikāḥ. smṛti-balâdhāna-vṛttitvād iti yo'arthaḥ. daru-pāṭana-kīla-saṃdhāraṇavat. evaṃ tu yujyate. smṛtir anayopatiṣṭhata iti smṛty-upasthānaṃ prajñā. yathā-dṛṣṭasyâbhilapanāt. tad yathā hy uktam āyuṣmatā Aniruddhena tasya kāye kāyânupaśyino viharataḥ kāyâlambanânusmṛtis tiṣṭhati saṃtiṣṭhata iti vistaraḥ. bhagavatâpi coktaṃ tasya kāye kāyânupaśyino viharata upasthitā smṛtir bhavaty asaṃmūḍheti. yatra tûktaṃ kathaṃ bhikṣavaś caturṇāṃ smṛty-upasthānānāṃ samudayaś ca bhavaty astaṃgamaś ca. āhāra-samudayāt kāyasya samudayo bhavaty āhāra-nirodhāt kāyasyâstaṃgama ity atrâlambanam eva smṛty-upasthānam uktaṃ smṛtir atropatiṣṭhata iti kṛtvā yathâlambanaṃ caiṣāṃ nāma.*

prajñā or 'wisdom'. This, of course, follows from the understanding of *smṛty-upasthāna* as essentially *anupaśyanā* or 'watching'. While this might appear to stand in direct contrast to the tradition of the Pāli texts that states that *satipaṭṭhāna* is just *sati*, closer consideration indicates that the difference between the two conceptions here is rather subtle. Certainly in the Pāli texts the close association of *sati* and *paññā* is brought out in a number of places, and the *Vibhaṅga* also makes an explicit identification of *anupassanā* with *paññā*.[29] The second point of some interest is the use of the term *abhilapana* (designating, elucidation, full expression)[30] in connection with *smṛty-upasthāna*. I shall return to these matters below.

2. *What is sati?*

What exactly is *sati*? So far I have been content to translate it as 'mindfulness', and something of its particular quality is perhaps already apparent from the preceding discussion of the term *satipaṭṭhāna*. The Sanskrit root *smṛ* seems to connote two basic ideas, namely 'to remember' and more simply, perhaps, 'to have in mind'. Both these uses seem to be witnessed from the *Ṛgveda* onwards.[31] Sanskrit *smṛti* can be both an act of 'remembering' or 'bearing in mind', and also what is remembered—hence the brahmanical use of *smṛti* to characterize the body of received tradition as what has been remembered, as opposed to what has been directly heard (*śruti*) from the vedic seers.[32] In Buddhist literature, however, it is the bare aspect of 'remembering' or 'having in mind' that is focused upon to the exclusion of other meanings: memory as the act of remembering, not what is remembered, or, as the commentaries put it, 'memory' in the sence of remembering (*saraṇaṭṭhena sati*).[33] The Nikāyas put it as follows:

> And what, *bhikkhus*, is the faculty of *sati*? Here, *bhikkhus*, the noble disciple has *sati*, he is endowed with perfect *sati* and intellect, he is one who remembers, who recollects what was done and said long before.[34]

But it is clear from the notion of *satipaṭṭhāna* that what the Nikāyas mean by 'remembering' is rather more than simply the ability to recall information from the distant past. Yet in terms of plain definition of *sati*, the four primary Nikāyas add very little to the definition I have just quoted. On the whole the Nikāyas prefer to proceed by way of description of the actual practice of *satipaṭṭhāna*, which is seen as the method by which *sati* naturally comes into its own. But rather than turning to the canonical account of *satipaṭṭhāna* cold, as it were, it is perhaps worth considering briefly how the later Buddhist tradition saw fit to describe what *sati* is. The early Abhidhamma literature provides a

---

29 Vibh 194.
30 *BHSD*, s.v. *abhilapana*.
31 MW, s.v. *smṛ*.
32 See J. Gonda, *Vedic Literature*, Wiesbaden, 1975, pp. 33-4.
33 Sv III 753 = Ps I 238.
34 S V 197-8: *katamañ ca bhikkhave satindriyaṃ. idha bhikkhave ariya-sāvako satimā hoti paramena sati-nepakkena samannāgato cira-kataṃ cira-bhāsitaṃ pi saritā anussaritā.*

number of terms that are intended to illustrate the nature of *sati*, and which are of some interest. As I have already pointed out, the *Paṭisambhidāmagga* makes a certain amount out of the actual term *upaṭṭhāna* or 'standing near', and seems to see this as characterizing the actual nature of *sati*.[35] The *Dhammasaṅgaṇi* gives the following register of terms for *sati*: *sati anussati paṭissati sati saraṇatā dhāraṇatā apilāpanatā asammussanatā sati satindriyaṃ sati-balaṃ sammā-sati*.[36] A number of these terms would appear to key into the various aspects under which *sati* is considered in the *suttas*: as a faculty (*satindriya*), as a power (*sati-bala*), as a factor of the path (*sammā-sati*);[37] the derivatives from the root *smṛ* echo different Nikāya contexts,[38] and reiterate the general notion of *sati* as 'remembering'. The three remaining terms are 'bearing [in mind]' (*dhāraṇatā*), 'the state of not forgetting' or 'the state of not being distracted' (*asammussanatā*),[39] and finally *apilāpanatā*. The last of these is perhaps the most interesting, and I shall comment on it presently. First I should like to turn to the *Milindapañha*. The *Milindapañha* contains what is perhaps the earliest attempt in Buddhist literature to state fully just what *sati* is. Questioned by king Milinda as to the characteristic (*lakkhaṇa*) of *sati*, the monk Nāgasena replies that it has both the characteristic of calling to mind (*apilāpana*) and the characteristic of taking hold (*upagaṇhana*). Nāgasena proceeds to explain:

> Just as, Your Majesty, the treasurer of a king who is a *cakka-vattin* causes the *cakka-vattin* king to remember his glory evening and morning [saying], 'So many, lord, are your elephants, so many your horses, so many your chariots, so many your foot soldiers, so much your gold, so much your wealth, so much your property; may my lord remember.' Thus he calls to mind the king's property. Even so, your Majesty, *sati*, when it arises, calls to mind *dhammas* that are skilful and unskilful, with faults and faultless, inferior and refined, dark and pure, together with their counterparts: these are the four establishings of mindfulness, these are the four right endeavours, these are the four bases of success, these are the five faculties, these are the five powers, these are the seven awakening-factors, this is the noble eight-factored path, this is calm, this is insight, this is knowledge, this is freedom. Thus the one who practises yoga resorts to *dhammas* that should be resorted to and does not resort to *dhammas* that should not be resorted to; he embraces *dhammas* that should be embraced and does not embrace *dhammas* that should not be embraced. Just so, Your Majesty, does *sati* have the characteristic of calling to mind ...
>
> Just as, Your Majesty, the adviser-treasure of the king who is a *cakka-vattin*

---

35 It is important to note here that *upaṭṭhāna* stands in the same relationship to *sati* as does *adhimokkha* to *saddhā*, *paggaha* to *viriya*, *avikkhepa* to *samādhi*, *dassana* to *paññā*, etc. Cf. below, Table 10, p. 309.

36 Dhs 16; cf. Nidd I 10-11.

37 Cf. the *lokuttara* register, e.g. Dhs 62, which adds *sati-sambojjhaṅga*.

38 Such as the practice of 'recollection' (*anussati*) of Buddha, Dhamma, Saṃgha, morality (*sīla*), generosity (*cāga*) and *devatās* (e.g. D III 250, 280); the association is explicit at Nidd I 10-11.

39 Pāli *asammussanatā* probably shows semantic confusion of Skt *muṣ* ('to steal') and *mṛṣ* ('not to heed'). However, the Nikāya expression *muṭṭha-ssati* (e.g. D III 252, 287; M I 20; III 6,84; S V 269, 324; A IV 229, 232), despite *PED* (s.v. *muṭṭha*), probably represents Skt *muṣṭa-* (= *muṣita*) and not *mṛṣita*, and should be rendered 'lost mindfulness' or 'with mindfulness lost'; cf. Skt *muṣita-cetas* (q.v. MW). Cf. *CPD*, s.vv. *asammuṭṭha*, *asammussanatā*, *asaṃmosa*, *asammosana-rasa*; *BHSD*, s.vv. *asaṃmosa*, *asaṃmosanatā*, *muṣita-smṛti*.

> knows those things that are beneficial and unbeneficial to the king [and thinks], 'These things are beneficial, these unbeneficial; these things are helpful, these unhelpful.' He thus removes the unbeneficial things and takes hold of the beneficial. Even so, Your Majesty, *sati*, when it arises, follows the courses of beneficial and unbeneficial *dhammas*: these *dhammas* are beneficial, these unbeneficial; these *dhammas* are helpful, these unhelpful. Thus the one who practises yoga removes unbeneficial *dhammas* and takes hold of beneficial *dhammas*; he removes unhelpful *dhammas* and takes hold of helpful *dhammas*. Just so, Your Majesty, does *sati* have the characteristic of taking hold.[40]

This account is clearly of some importance and is quoted, though not in full, by Buddhaghosa in the *Atthasālinī*.[41] Curiously one of the key terms here, namely *apilāpana*, seems to have been misunderstood—or at least reinterpreted—by the Pāli Abhidhamma tradition. It is not clear what the original source is for the association of the term *apilāpana(tā)* with *sati*.[42] Presumably the use in the *Milindapañha* post-dates the use in the *Dhammasaṅgaṇi*, yet it seems to me that it is the *Milindapañha* account that preserves the original significance of the term.

The *Dhammasaṅgaṇi* creates a pair of opposites, *apilāpanatā* and *pilāpanatā*, which are used to explain *sati* and *muṭṭha-sati* ('lost mindfulness') respectively.[43] Now *apilāpanatā* would seem to mean 'not floating [on the object of the mind]' and *pilāpanatā* 'floating [on the object of the mind]'.[44] This, at least, is evidently how the commentarial Abhidhamma tradition took the terms.[45] Accordingly, *apilāpeti* in the *Milindapañha* passage is taken by the *ṭīkā* to mean 'it does not allow any floating', or 'it plunges into'.[46] While it is not impossible

---

[40] Mil 37-8: *yathā mahā-rāja rañño cakka-vattissa bhaṇḍâgāriko rājānaṃ cakka-vattiṃ sāya-pātaṃ yasaṃ sarāpeti ettakā deva te hatthī ettakā assā ettakā rathā ettakā pattī ettakaṃ hiraññaṃ ettakaṃ suvaṇṇaṃ ettakaṃ sāpateyyaṃ taṃ devo saratū ti rañño sāpateyyaṃ apilāpeti. evam eva kho mahā-rāja sati uppajjamānā kusalâkusala-sâvajjânavajja-hīna-ppaṇīta-kaṇha-sukka-sappaṭibhāga-dhamme apilāpeti ime cattāro satipaṭṭhānā ime cattāro sammā-ppadhānā ime cattāro iddhi-pādā imāni pañc'indriyāni imāni pañca balāni ime satta bojjhaṅgā ayaṃ ariyo aṭṭhaṅgiko maggo ayaṃ samatho ayaṃ vipassanā ayaṃ vijjā ayaṃ vimuttī ti. tato yogâvacaro sevitabbe dhamme sevati asevitabbe dhamme na sevati bhajitabbe dhamme bhajati abhajitabbe dhamme na bhajati. evaṃ kho mahā-rāja apilāpana-lakkhaṇā satī ti ... yathā mahā-rāja rañño cakka-vattissa pariṇāyaka-ratanaṃ rañño hitâhite jānāti ime rañño hitā ime ahitā ime upakārā ime anupakārā ti. tato ahite apanudeti hite upagaṇhāti anupakāre apanudeti upakāre upagaṇhāti. evam eva kho mahā-rāja sati uppajjamānā hitâhitānaṃ dhammānaṃ gatiyo samannesati ime dhammā hitā ime dhammā ahitā ime dhammā upakārā ime dhammā anupakārā ti. tato yogâvacaro ahite dhamme apanudeti hite dhamme upagaṇh-āti anupakāre dhamme apanudeti upakāre dhamme upagaṇhāti. evaṃ kho mahā-rāja upagaṇhana-lakkhaṇā sati.*

[41] As 121-2; the version of Mil that Buddhaghosa had before him probably differed from ours; see Norman, *PL*, pp.110-1.

[42] The term *apilāpanatā* is also used in association with *sati* at Nidd I 10 347; II 262; Dhs 11-2, 16, 62, 64; Vibh 124, 250, Pugg 25; Nett 15, 28, 54. But cf. p. 78 n.1, below on A II 185.

[43] Dhs 11, 232; at Dhs 232 *apilāpanatā* is to be corrected to *pilāpanatā*; cf. As 405; Vibh 360.

[44] Cf. Skt *plavana* (*plu*).

[45] As 147: '*Apilāpanatā* is the state of not floating in the sense of plunging into, a term for entering into.' (*anupavisana-saṃkhātena ogāhanaṭṭhena apilāpana-bhāvo apilāpanatā.*) As 405: '*Pilāpanatā* means it floats on the object [of the mind] like a gourd-bowl in water.' (*udake alābu-kaṭāhaṃ viya ārammaṇe pilavatī ti pilāpanatā.*)

[46] Mil-ṭ 10: *apilāpetī ti anupavisanaṭṭhena ogāḷhayati.* The *Mūlaṭīkā* (Be 1960, p. 89) to As 121 explains *apilāpeti* as 'it makes for non-floating' (*apilāpe karoti*). *CPD* (s.vv. *apilāpa*, *apilāpeti*) and I.B. Horner (Mil Trsl I 50-1) follow this interpretation.

that *a-* is a negative prefix here,[47] it is, perhaps, rather unlikely. The sense of 'not floating' could possibly be preserved by taking *apilāpeti* as equivalent to Sanskrit *āplāvayati*, which might be rendered 'it immerses itself in'.[48] Yet such a meaning seems not to fit the context particularly well. It seems more reasonable to follow PED[49] and assume that we have *apilapati* (= *abhilapati*), 'to recite'; the causative *apilāpeti* then means 'to cause to be recited, to enumerate', and then 'to remind someone of something by enumerating it to them'.[50] This in fact seems to fit the *Milindapañha* use rather well.

What the *Milindapañha* account is suggesting, I think, is that *sati* should be understood as what allows awareness of the full range and extent of *dhammas*; *sati* is an awareness of things in relation to things, and hence an awareness of their relative value. Applied to the *satipaṭṭhānas* presumably what this means is that *sati* is what causes the practitioner of yoga to 'remember' that any feeling he may experience exists in relation to a whole variety or world of feelings that may be skilful or unskilful, with faults or faultless, relatively inferior or refined, dark or pure. The idea is probably clearest with regard to feeling (*vedanā*) but, of course, should be extended to cover body (*kāya*), mind (*citta*) and *dhammas*. To talk of 'remembering' one 'body' in relation to a world of different 'bodies' sounds rather strange in English, but such language is perhaps not so alien to the Nikāya thought-world: 'Among bodies, *bhikkhus*, I declare this, namely breathing in and out, to be a particular body.'[51] Thus it is only by in some sense 'remembering' the full range and extent of *dhammas* that the practitioner of yoga can come to know: 'These are the four establishings of mindfulness, these the four right endeavours, these the four bases of success, these the five faculties, these the five powers, these the seven awakening-factors, this the noble eight-factored path.'

Interestingly, in Buddhist Sanskrit sources there does not appear to be any talk of *plavana* or *aplavana* in connection with *smṛti*, there is, however, talk of *abhilapana*. As I have already noted, Vasubandhu states that the *smṛty-upasthānas* are wisdom 'because of designating what has been seen [by wisdom]' (*yathā-dṛṣṭasyâbhilapanāt*).[52] Similarly the author of the *Abhidharmadīpa* says:

> The faculty of *smṛti* is a name for that which is appropriate designation (*aviparītâbhi-*

---

[47] Cf. *CPD*, s.v. *a-* (3) for examples of *a-* being added to personal forms of verbs (although sometimes with *na* as v.l.).

[48] MW, s.v. *ā-plu*. *CPD*, however, lists a verb *apilapati* from the Sanskrit root *ā-plu* in the sense of 'it floats [before the mind]'. It cites only two tentative occurrences. One of these is at Mp III 170 where Buddhaghosa states that *sukhino dhamma-padāpilapanti* (A II 185: *dhamma-padāni pi lapanti*) means, 'they (= *dhamma-padas*) float before the happy one like an image in a clear mirror; they stand near and, having become manifest, they are known' (*sukhino ... te sabbe pasanne ādāse chāyā viya apilapanti* (v.l. *pilavanti, plavanti*) *upaṭṭhahanti pākaṭā hutvā paññāyanti*). K.R. Norman suggests (private communication) that the commentary here does not recognize the verb *api-lapati* (= *abhi-lapati*), and that we should translate at A II 185, 'the happy ones recite the words of *dhamma*'; the context here does concern *sati*, so this is a possible source of the association of *apilāpana*/*apilāpeti* and *sati*.

[49] S.v. *apilāpeti*. *CPD* does not recognize this verb.

[50] K.R. Norman, private communication.

[51] M III 83: *kāyesu kāyaññatarâhaṃ bhikkhave etaṃ vadāmi yadidaṃ assāsa-passāsaṃ*. See also Paṭis II 232.

[52] Abhidh-k 342.

> *lapanā*) with regard to the body and so on as observed by wisdom; it is recognition. In the mind that has made itself familiar with it there is no loss of the object; this absence of loss is the faculty of *smṛti*.[53]

The term *abhilapana* apart, Vasubandhu defines *smṛti* succinctly as 'not losing the object [of the mind]' (*smṛtir ālambanâsaṃpramoṣaḥ*).[54] Returning to the Abhidhamma treatment of *sati*, its formal definition by way of characteristic (*lakkhaṇa*), property (*rasa*), manifestation (*paccupaṭṭhāna*) and basis (*padaṭṭhāna*) is as follows:

> By means of it they [= other *dhammas*] remember, or it itself remembers, or it is simply just remembering, thus it is *sati*. Its characteristic is not floating; its property is not losing; its manifestation is guarding or the state of being face to face with an object; its basis is strong noting or the *satipaṭṭhānas* of the body and so on. It should be seen as like a post due to its state of being firmly set in the object, and as like a gatekeeper because it guards the gate of the eye and so on.[55]

As I have already suggested, the characteristic of *apilāpana* must, I think, be explained here with reference to the pair of opposities *apilāpanatā* and *pilāpanatā*. It seems that because the commentaries fail to recognize *api-lapati* (= *abhi-lapati*) they therefore make use of a rather different image: *sati* is the mental quality that submerges itself in the objects of the mind; when there is no *sati* the mind floats or drifts on the objects of the mind. An echo of the same kind of thinking is, I think, apparent in the statement that *sati's* manifestation is the state of being face to face with an object, and that it is like a post because it is set firmly in the object.

At this point the consideration of *sati* can perhaps be taken a little further by addressing the question of the relative understanding of *sati/smṛti* in the traditions of the Theravādins and Sarvāstivādins respectively. According to the system of Abhidhamma embodied in the Pāli *Abhidhamma-piṭaka* and commentaries, *sati* is only ever present as a mental factor (*cetasika*) in skilful states of mind (*kusala-citta*): if there is *sati*, there is skilful consciousness; and since *sati* is in fact always present in skilful states of mind, if there is skilful consciousness, there is *sati*. However, according to the Sarvāstivādin system of Abhidharma *smṛti* is a mental factor (*caitta*) that is universal to all states of mind (*citta-mahā-bhūmika*) skilful or unskilful.[56]

Nyanaponika has taken this matter up in a section of his *Abhidhamma Studies*.[57] Briefly, he pursues a question raised in the *Atthasālinī* concerning the absence of *sati* in unskilful states of mind: 'Do those of wrong views not

---

[53] Abhidh-dī 360: *smṛtîndriyaṃ nāma kāyâdīṣu prajñayopalakṣiteṣu yā khalv aviparītâbhilapanā pratyabhijñānaṃ yenâvadhārite viṣaya-saṃmoṣaś cetasi na bhavati sa khalv asaṃmoṣaḥ smṛtîndriyam*. Cf. Abhidh-dī 69 where *smṛti* is explained as 'designation of the object of the mind' (*cittasyârthâbhilapanā*).

[54] Abhidh-k 34.

[55] Vism XIV 141: *saranti tāya sayaṃ vā sarati saraṇa-mattaṃ eva vā esā ti sati. apilāpana-lakkhaṇā sati asammosa-rasā ārakkha-paccupaṭṭhānā visayâbhimukha-bhāva-paccupaṭṭhānā vā thira-saññā-pada-ṭṭhānā kāyâdi-satipaṭṭhānā pada-ṭṭhānā vā. ārammaṇe daḷhaṃ patiṭṭhitattā pana esikā viya cakkhu-dvārâdi-rakkhaṇato dovāriko viya ca daṭṭhabbā*. (Cf. As 121-2; Abhidh-av 18.)

[56] Abhidh-k 54.

[57] Nyanaponika Thera, *Abhidhamma Studies*, 3rd edition, Kandy, 1976, pp. 68-72.

remember actions done by them? They do. But that is not called *sati*, it is merely the occurrence of unskilful consciousness in that aspect.'[58] As Nyanaponika points out, as an explanation this is not entirely helpful. However, the *Mūlaṭīkā* makes a reference at this point to the association of such unskilful states with 'clear noting' (*patu-saññā*). Following this up, Nyanaponika concludes that it is in fact *saññā* that should be regarded as playing the crucial role in the psychology of remembering as far as the Theravādin Abhidhamma is concerned. The Sarvāstivādins, he suggests, failed to appreciate this and in their system 'corrected' the omission of *smṛti* from unskilful consciousness.[59] This assumes without justification that the traditions embodied in the *Dhammasaṅgaṇi* are necessarily more ancient than those preserved in the Sarvāstivādin Abhidharma system, and also that the Sarvāstivādin account of *saṃjñā* is rather different from that of the Theravādins. This apart, however, Nyanaponika's comments are of some interest. The formal Abhidhamma definition of *saññā* is as follows:

> All [*saññā*] has the characteristic of noting (*sañjānana*); its property is the making of a sign that is a condition for noting again, 'this is the very same thing'—as carpenters and so on do with wood, etc.; its manifestation is the producing of conviction by virtue of a sign that has been accordingly learnt—like the blind perceiving the elephant [Ud 68-9]; its basis is whatever object that has come near—like the idea (*saññā*) 'people' that arises for young animals in respect of scarecrows.[60]

Now it is clear from this account that in its capacity of labelling or marking (which seems to be what is intended here) *saññā* must be understood as playing a major role in the psychology of memory, at least as far as this is conceived of as a simple matter of recognition and recall. But there is little reason to think that the Sarvāstivādins would have wished to quarrel with this understanding of *saññā*/*saṃjñā*: '*saṃjñā* is noting, the taking up of the sign of the object' (*saṃjñā saṃjānaṃ viṣaya-nimittodgrah*).[61] So far, then, it is clear that both systems refer to *sati*/*smṛti* as 'not-losing', 'unforgetfulness' or 'non-confusion' (*asammosa*/*asaṃmoṣa*); both systems have more or less the same conception of *saññā*/*saṃjñā*. The Abhidhamma definition of *saññā* also suggests that it has a significantly close relationship to *sati*—strong *saññā* is in fact the basis of *sati*.

Clearly when we talk of 'memory' and 'remembering' in the context of Buddhist psychology we are dealing with quite subtle questions. From the point of view of Abhidhamma analysis it is apparent that many of one's so called 'memories' are simply conceptions or ideas based on a particular

---

58 As 250: *kiṃ diṭṭhi-gatikā attanā kata-kammaṃ na sarantī ti. saranti. sā pana sati nāma na hoti kevalaṃ tenâkārena akusala-citta-ppavatti.* Quoted Nyanaponika, *AS*, p. 68.

59 Nyanaponika, *AS*, p. 72.

60 Vism XIV 130: *sabbā va sañjānana-lakkhaṇā; tad ev'etan ti puna sañjānana-paccaya-nimitta-karaṇa-rasā dāru-ādīsu tacchakâdayo viya; yathā-gahita-nimitta-vasena abhinivesakaraṇa-paccupaṭṭhānā, hatthi-dassaka-andhā viya; yathā-upaṭṭhita-visaya-pada-ṭṭhānā, tiṇa-purisakesu miga-potakānaṃ purisā ti uppanna-saññā viyā ti.* (Cf. As 110; Abhidh-av 18.)

61 Abhidh-k 54. See also A. Wayman, 'Regarding the translation of the Buddhist technical terms saññā/saṃjñā, viññāṇa/vijñāna' in *Malalasekera Commemoration Volume*, ed. O.H. de A. Wijesekera, Colombo, 1976, pp. 325-35.

perspective of what occurred in the past. In short, they are misconceptions, the product of *saññā* associated with unskilful consciousness. The point is that as far as Abhidhamma is concerned our 'remembering' fails to reflect properly the way things truly are. This point is not particularly hard to appreciate, even conventional wisdom tells me that if I am brooding on some wrong done to me, my view of the world is likely to be coloured as a result.

What is important about *sati/smṛti* in Buddhist thought is that it is seen as a particular kind of 'remembering'—when developed it 'remembers', as it were, properly. The *Abhidharmadīpa's* explanation of the faculty of *smṛti* as *aviparīt-âbhilapanā* or 'unperverted designating' would seem to be an allusion to the four *viparyāsas* or 'perversions'.[62] Rather interestingly the *Nettippakaraṇa* states:

> One who dwells watching body with regard to body abandons the perversion [that sees] the beautiful in the ugly ... One who dwells watching feeling with regard to feelings abandons the perversion [that sees] happiness in suffering ... One who dwells watching mind with regard to mind abandons the perversion [that sees] the permanent in the impermanent ... One who dwells watching *dhamma* with regard to *dhammas* abandons the perversion [that sees] the self in what is not-self.[63]

The point is clear, I think, in the *Milindapañha* account. Because *sati* 'remembers', it knows the full variety of *dhammas*, skilful and unskilful, and so on; because *sati* 'remembers' it knows how things stand in relation to one another; it, as it were, opens up one's view. In this way it tends towards a seeing of things that reflects what the Abhidhamma considers to be the way things truly are. This is the reason why *sati/smṛti* is so intimately bound up with wisdom in the texts. Thus in the basic *satipaṭṭhāna* formula, Nikāya usage alone would suggest that such terms as *anupassin* and *sampajāna* technically connote insight and wisdom. This becomes quite explicit in the *Vibhaṅga* exposition, while those following the traditions of the Sarvāstivādins straightforwardly state that the essential nature of *smṛty-upasthāna* is wisdom.

At the beginning of this section I quoted an explanation of the faculty of *sati* that states that the noble disciple is endowed with perfect *sati* and intellect (*paramena sati-nepakkena samannāgato*) and is one who remembers and recollects what was done and said long before. With regard to this explanation the commentaries state that *nepakka* is a term for wisdom (*paññā*).[64] But why, they ask, is wisdom included in the section on *sati*? The answer is:

> In order to indicate a strong state of *sati*. For *sati* arises both with and without wisdom. When it arises with wisdom it is strong, when it arises without it is weak ... Similarly two ministers of the king may serve in two [different] districts; one of

[62] It is important to note that this explanation is given of *smṛtîndriya* in the context of the account of the development of those *dharmas* that contribute directly to progress along the path. Presumably then only *smṛti* associated with skilful consciousness is referred to here.

[63] Nett 83-4 : *kāye kāyânupassī viharanto asubhe subhan ti vipallāsaṃ pajahati ... vedanāsu vedanânupassī viharanto dukkhe sukhan ti vipallāsaṃ pajahati ... citte cittânupassī viharanto anicce niccan ti vipallāsaṃ pajahati ... dhammesu dhammânupassī anattani attā ti vipallāsaṃ pajahati.* Cf. Peṭ 103; Vism XXII 34. Abhidh-k 342 gives the four *smṛty-upasthānas* as the opposite (*vipakṣa*) of the *viparyāsas*; cf. Wayman, Śrāvakabhūmi MS, p. 98.

[64] Spk III 234; Vibh-a 311.

> them may serve along with a prince, the other just by himself by means of his own ability; the one serving along with a prince has authority both because of his own authority and also because of the prince's authority; the one serving by means of his own ability cannot match this authority. Thus the minister serving along with a prince is like *sati* that has arisen with wisdom; the one serving by means of his own ability is like *sati* that has arisen without wisdom.[65]

What all this perhaps suggests is that as far as Abhidhamma is concerned, the extent to which even unwholesome actions and states of mind are 'remembered', corresponds in some measure to a degree of *sati* and skilful consciousness. This need not count against the Abhidhamma view that *sati* is exclusive to skilful consciousness; the Theravādin conception of thought processes is such that it is quite possible to conceive of the mixing of skilful and unskilful consciousness in quick succession. In effect this conception of *sati* suggests that the stronger the quality of mind called *sati* becomes, the weaker unwholesome states of mind become, and the harder it is for these to take over and dominate thought, word and deed. The more nearly what in Abhidhamma is defined as an unwholesome course of action is properly 'remembered', the less likely it is that that course of action will be followed through.

Looked at in this way the difference between the Theravādin and Sarvāstivādin conception of *sati/smṛti* becomes rather finely balanced. For the Sarvāstivādins a lack of proper remembering of the object of the mind is not conceived of as an absolute absence of *smṛti*, but rather as *smṛti* in a weak and attenuated form such that it cannot operate as it should, and is even perhaps 'perverted' in some way. In this they preserve a straightforward understanding of the ancient canonical notion of 'wrong mindfulness' (*micchā-sati/mithyā-smṛti*), which the Theravādin Abhidhamma chose to understand as the result of the absence of *sati*.[66]

Finally in this discussion of the notion of *sati/smṛti* in ancient Abhidharma literature, mention should be made of the important term *appamāda/apramāda* or 'heedfulness'. The Sarvāstivādins include this in their list of mental factors (*caittas*) exclusive to skilful consciousness (*kuśala-mahābhūmika*).[67] Significantly where the term *appamāda* is found in the Nikāyas the commentaries take it as a term for *sati*.[68] Vasubandhu in the *Abhidharmakośa* defines *apramāda* as follows:

> *Apramāda* is the development of skilful *dharmas*. But what kind of development is

---

[65] Vibh-a 312: *satiyā balava-bhāva-dīpanattham. sati hi paññāya saddhiṃ pi uppajjati vinā pi. paññāya saddhiṃ uppajjamānā balavatī hoti, vinā uppajjamānā dubbalā ... yathā hi dvīsu disāsu dve rāja-mahāmattā tiṭṭheyyuṃ; tesu eko rāja-puttaṃ gahetvā, eko attano dhammatāya ekako va; tesu rāja-puttaṃ gahetvā ṭhito attano pi tejena rāja-puttassa pi tejena tejavā hoti; attano dhammatāya ṭhito na tena sama-tejo hoti. evam eva rāja-puttaṃ gahetvā ṭhito mahāmatto viya paññāya saddhiṃ uppannā sati; attano dhammatāya ṭhito viya vinā paññāya saddhiṃ uppannā.*

[66] As 250.

[67] Abhidh-k 55.

[68] Cf. Sv I 104 which glosses *appamāda* as 'non-absence' (*avippavāsa*) of *sati*; It-a I 80 gives the same explanation but adds: 'It is a name for permanence of established *sati*; but some say that when they occur by means of the application of *sati* and *sampajañña*, the four immaterial aggregates are *appamāda*.' (*niccaṃ upaṭṭhitāya satiyā eva c'etaṃ nāmaṃ. apare pana sati-sampajañña-yogena pavattā cattāro arūpino khandhā appamādo ti vadanti.*)

something different from these [skilful *dharmas*]? That which is attention to them. The followers of other schools take Sūtra as saying that [*apramāda*] is guarding in respect of the mind.[69]

It is not hard to see in this definition a certain overlap with the full definition of *sati* found in the *Milindapañha* and Pāli commentaries. The *Milindapañha's* notion of *sati* as 'taking hold' (*upagaṇhana*) of what is helpful and beneficial seems quite close here, while the alternative notion of *apramāda* as 'guarding' corresponds exactly to an idea expressed in the formal Abhidhamma definition of *sati*.

It is no doubt out of place to try to resolve all the various points raised in this. The tensions and dynamics of each system are balanced slightly differently, and each, it might be argued, has its own merits. There is not a radical difference in the conception of *sati/smṛti* in the Theravādin and Sarvāstivādin systems, and much the same themes recur. To sum up, it seems to me that there are basically four elements to the notion of *sati* in the literature: (i) *sati* remembers or does not lose what is before the mind; (ii) *sati* is, as it were, a natural 'presence of mind'; it stands near and hence serves and guards the mind; (iii) *sati* 'calls to mind', that is, it remembers things in relationship to things and thus tends to know their value and widen the view; (iv) *sati* is thus closely related to wisdom; it naturally tends to seeing things as they truly are.

3. The Mahāsatipaṭṭhāna- and Satipaṭṭhāna-suttas[70]

What distinguishes the *Mahāsatipaṭṭhāna-sutta* from the *Satipaṭṭhāna-sutta* is the addition in the former of a detailed exposition of the four noble truths.[71] In other respects the two *suttas* appear identical. Both are said to have been delivered by the Buddha while dwelling among the Kurus, and *prima facie* there appears to be no reason not to take the two *suttas* as two versions of one and the same discourse; the commentaries seem to make no attempt to distinguish the occasion of their delivery. In view of the *sutta's*—or *suttas'*—importance it is worth here giving a brief account of the basic structure and contents,[72] before moving on to discuss the various elements.

After the initial setting of the scene the discourse opens with what I call 'the *ekâyana* formula':

> *Ekâyana, bhikkhus*, is this path for the purification of beings, for passing beyond sorrow and grief, for the disappearance of pain and discontent, for the attainment of the right way, for the realization of *nibbāna*—that is the four *satipaṭṭhānas*.

---

[69] Abhidh-k 55: *apramādaḥ kuśalānāṃ dharmāṇāṃ bhāvanā. kā punas tebhyo'nyā bhāvanā. yā teṣv avahitatā. cetasa ārakṣeti nikāyântaritāḥ sūtre paṭhanti.*

[70] D II 290-314; M I 55-63.

[71] A.K. Warder (*Indian Buddhism*, p. 87, n. i.) mistakenly states that the four *saccas* are not given in the M version; they are (M I 62). What is missing is the extended analysis of the *saccas* (D II 305-13).

[72] For a discussion of some of the differences that exist between the Pāli version and versions that survive in Chinese, see Lin Li-Kouang, *L'Aide Mémoire de la Vraie Loi (Saddharma-smṛty-upasthāna-sūtra)*, Paris, 1949, pp. 118-27; L. Schmithausen, 'Die vier Konzentrationen der Aufmerksamkeit', *Zeitschrift für Missionwissenschaft und Religionwissenschaft*, 60 (1976), pp. 241-66; J. Bronkhorst, *BSOAS* 48 (1985), pp. 309-12. Cf. my comments below, pp. 58-9.

This is immediately followed by the basic *satipaṭṭhāna* formula as stated at the opening of this chapter. The remainder of the *sutta* consists basically of a detailed description of the practice of *kāyânupassanā*, *vedanânupassanā*, *cittânupassanā* and *dhammânupassanā*; in other words each of the four parts of the basic formula is explained by way of example and subsequently expanded.

In the account of *kāyânupassanā* there are fourteen basic sections. Each of these sections opens with a description of an activity that illustrates the practice of *kāyânupassanā*: the *bhikkhu* (i) is mindful when breathing in and out (*so sato va assasati sato passasati*); (ii) he knows (*pajānāti*) when he is walking, standing, sitting or lying down; (iii) he acts with clear comprehension (*sampajāna-kārin*) when walking up and down, looking at and around, in bending and stretching his limbs, in handling his robes and bowl, in eating, drinking, chewing and tasting, in walking, standing, sitting, lying down, sleeping, waking, speaking and remaining silent; (iv) he reflects on the body as full of different kinds of impurity (*kāyaṃ ... pūraṃ nāna-ppakārassa asucino paccavekkhati*) (thirty-one parts of the body are listed); (v) he reflects on the body by way of the elements of earth (*paṭhavī*), water (*āpo*), fire (*tejo*) and wind (*vāyo*); (vi-xiv) he compares his body to a corpse in nine different states of putrefaction, thinking, 'This body too is of such a nature, it will be such, it has not passed beyond this.' These fourteen practices that can form the basis of *kāyânupassanā* draw on themes and stock passages that are found scattered throughout the Nikāyas. In effect, then, the various Nikāya elements that might constitute *kāyânupassanā* are brought together to give something of a summary account. Appended to the description of each of these fourteen practices is what might be called the expanded *satipaṭṭhāna* formula for *kāyânupassanā*. This falls into four parts:

> [i] Thus with regard to the body he dwells watching body within; or he dwells watching body without; or he dwells watching body within and without. [ii] Or with regard to the body he dwells watching the nature of arising; or he dwells watching the nature of fall; or he dwells watching the nature of arising and fall. [iii] Or again, his mindfulness that there is body is established just for the sake of a degree of knowledge and a degree of recollection. [iv] And he dwells independent; he does not grasp anything in the world.[73]

This expanded formula is thus repeated a total of fourteen times in the course of the explanation of *kāyânupassanā* (though it is lost in the abbreviations of the text in sections vii-xiii above). This completes the description of *kāyânupassanā*.

The practice of *vedanânupassanā* is dealt with in just one section. Whatever kind of feeling the *bhikkhu* feels or experiences, he knows that he feels it (*vedanaṃ vediyamāno ... vedanaṃ vediyāmī ti pajānāti*). Examples of nine types of feeling are given. These are the basic three pleasant (*sukha*), unpleasant

---

[73] *[i] iti ajjhattaṃ vā kāye kāyânupassī viharati bahiddhā vā kāye kāyânupassī viharati ajjhatta-bahiddhā vā kāye kāyânupassī viharati. [ii] samudaya-dhammânupassī vā kāyasmiṃ viharati vaya-dhammânupassī vā kāyasmiṃ viharati samudaya-vaya-dhammânupassī vā kāyasmiṃ viharati. [iii] atthi kāyo ti vā pan'assa sati paccupaṭṭhitā hoti yāvad eva ñāṇa-mattāya paṭissati-mattāya. [iv] anissito ca viharati na ca kiñci loke upādiyati.*

(*dukkha*) and neither unpleasant nor pleasant (*adukkha-m-asukha*), along with the same three considered by way of association with sensuality (*sāmisa*) and dissociation from sensuality (*nirāmisa*). There then follow the four parts of the expanded *satipaṭṭhāna* formula for *vedanânupassanā*; that is, where before there was mention of 'body', there is now mention of 'feeling'.

Like *vedanânupassanā*, *cittânupassanā* is dealt with in one section; it consists in the *bhikkhu* knowing (*pajānāti*) various kinds of mind (*citta*). Sixteen kinds in eight pairs are distinguished by way of example: the mind with passion (*sarāga*) and the mind without it (*vīta-rāga*); the mind with hatred (*sadosa*) and the mind without it (*vīta-dosa*); the mind with delusion (*samoha*) and the mind without it (*vīta-moha*); the mind that is composed (*saṃkhitta*) and the mind that is scattered (*vikkhitta*); the mind that has become great (*mahaggata*) and the mind that has not (*amahaggata*); the mind that is surpassable (*sa-uttara*) and the mind that is not (*anuttara*); the mind that is concentrated (*samāhita*) and the mind that is not (*asamāhita*); the mind that is freed (*vimutta*) and the mind that is not (*avimutta*). The four parts of the expanded *satipaṭṭhāna* formula for *cittânupassanā* follow.

Lastly *dhammânupassanā* is dealt with in five sections. The *bhikkhu* dwells watching *dhamma(s)* with regard to the five hindrances (*nīvaraṇa*), the five aggregates of grasping (*upādāna-kkhandha*), the six internal (*ajjhatika*) and external (*bahira*) spheres of sense (*āyatana*), the seven factors of awakening (*bojjhaṅga*), and the four noble truths (*ariya-sacca*). Each of these five categories of items is enumerated in full in the text, and to conclude each section the four parts of the expanded *satipaṭṭhāna* formula for *dhammânupassanā* are given in full.

The expanded *satipaṭṭhāna* formula thus occurs a total of twenty-one times: fourteen times for *kāyânupassanā*, once each for *vedanânupassanā* and *cittânupassanā*, and five times for *dhammânupassanā*. The *(Mahā-)Satipaṭṭhāna-sutta* then concludes with the following statement:

> Now if anyone, *bhikkhus*, should develop these four establishings of mindfulness in this way for seven years, one of two fruits is to be expected for him: knowledge in the here and now, or, if there be a remainder of grasping, the state of non-return. Let alone seven years, *bhikkhus*, if anyone should develop these four establishings of mindfulness in this way for six years ... five years ... four years ... three years ... two years ... one year ... seven months ... six months ... five months ... four months ... three months ... two months ... one month ... half a month ... seven days, one of two fruits is to be expected for him: knowledge in the here and now, or, if there be a remainder of grasping, the state of non-return.[74]

The *sutta* closes with a repetition of the opening *ekâyana* formula.

---

[74] *yo hi koci bhikkhave ime cattāro satipaṭṭhāne evaṃ bhāveyya satta vassāni tassa dvinnaṃ phalānaṃ aññataraṃ phalaṃ pāṭikaṅkhaṃ: diṭṭhe va dhamme aññā sati vā upādisese anāgāmitā. tiṭṭhantu bhikhave satta vassāni yo hi koci bhikkhave ime cattāro satipaṭṭhāne evaṃ bhāveyya cha vassāni ... pañca vassāni ... cattāri vassāni ... tīṇi vassāni ... dve vassāni ... ekaṃ vassaṃ ... satta māsāni ... cha māsāni ... pañca māsāni ... cattāri māsāni ... tīṇi māsāni ... dve māsāni ... ekaṃ māsaṃ ... aḍḍha-māsaṃ ... sattâhaṃ tassa dvinnaṃ phalānaṃ aññataraṃ phalaṃ pāṭikaṅkhaṃ: diṭṭhe va dhamme aññā sati vā upādisese anāgāmitā.*

4. *The exegesis of the basic satipaṭṭhāna formula*

The basic formula, then, describes a *bhikkhu* as dwelling watching (*anupassin*) body, feeling, mind and *dhammas*; in each case he is said to be ardent (*ātāpin*), to comprehend clearly (*sampajāna*) and to possess mindfulness (*satimant*), having overcome desire and discontent for the world (*vineyya loke abhijjhā-domanassaṃ*). What does this mean? It seems reasonable to see the progression from watching body to watching *dhamma(s)* as intended to indicate a movement from clear awareness of the more immediately accessible realms of experience to an awareness of what the Nikāyas see as subtler and deeper realms. Such a hierarchial conception of the universe and consciousness alike is, of course, a consistent theme of the Upaniṣads and Buddhist literature,[75] and it seems that in the four *satipaṭṭhānas* we have another expression of it. Certainly they appear to be understood in this kind of way in later writings.[76] With regard to the notion of the four *satipaṭṭhānas* representing a progressive refining of mindfulness, it should be noted that the Nikāyas also devote a certain amount of space to the discussion of mindfulness concerned with the body (*kāya-gatā sati*) quite apart from the explicit discussion of the first establishing of mindfulness. Thus the *Kāyagatāsati-sutta* consists basically of an alternative treatment of precisely the same set of fourteen activities that are given in the *(Mahā-)Satipaṭṭhāna-sutta* under the heading *kāyânupassanā*.[77] The reason why *kāya-gatā sati* is singled out for extra treatment would seem to be that it is considered the common basis for the subsequent development of all mindfulness.

The basic *satipaṭṭhāna* formula attributed four qualities to the *bhikkhu* engaged in the practice of *satipaṭṭhāna*: he is one who watches (*anupassin*); he is ardent (*ātāpin*); he is one who comprehends clearly (*sampajāna*); he possesses mindfulness (*satimant*). The *Vibhaṅga's* 'analysis according to the principles of Sutta' (*suttanta-bhājaniya*) of the *satipaṭṭhāna* formula spells out the more or less technical association these terms had acquired by the time of the emergent Abhidhamma. The terms *anupassin* and *sampajāna* connote 'wisdom', thus in explanation of each the *Vibhaṅga* gives the appropriate *Dhammasaṅgaṇi* register of associated terms in full.[78] The implications of *satimant* are obvious enough; the *Vibhaṅga* gives the standard register of terms for *sati* in full.[79] The term *ātāpin* is taken by the *Vibhaṅga* to connote 'strength' or 'vigour' (*viriya*); once again it gives the appropriate *Dhammasaṅgaṇi* register of associated terms.[80]

---

[75] Cf. Przyluski and Lamotte, op. cit. pp. 148-54 where the Upaniṣad conception of a universe of three levels corresponding to the waking state, sleep accompanied by dreams and deep sleep is compared to the Buddhist notion of three realms or *dhātus*. On the waking state (*jāgarita-sthāna*), dream state (*svapna-sthāna*) and deep sleep (*suṣupti*) in Vedānta see K. Werner, *Yoga and Indian Philosophy*, Delhi, 1977, pp. 68-70.

[76] E.g. Abhidh-k 342 states that the order of their arising results from seeing what is gross (*audārika*) first.

[77] M III 88-99.

[78] Vibh 194-5; cf. Dhs 9-17.

[79] Ibid.

[80] Ibid.

The early para-canonical exegetical work, the *Nettippakaraṇa*, carries out a similar exercise in the analysis of the *satipaṭṭhāna* formula—but rather more succinctly:

> *Tasmāt iha taṃ bhikkhu kāye kāyânupassī viharati ātāpī sampajāno satimā vineyya loke abhijjhā-domanassaṃ*: *ātāpī*, that is to say, the faculty of strength; *sampajāno*, that is to say, the faculty of wisdom; *satimā*, that is to say, the faculty of mindfulness ... [81]

In their analysis of these terms in the *satipaṭṭhāna* formula the later *aṭṭha-kathās* follow the lead of the *Vibhaṅga* and *Nettippakaraṇa*. Clearly what the *Vibhaṅga*, *Nettippakaraṇa* and commentaries wish to do here is make connections; they wish to link the *satipaṭṭhāna* formula to the broader scheme of the Nikāya outlook. It would not, I think, be strictly correct to describe their method here as 'innovation', rather they formalize something that is looser but already present in the Nikāyas. It would be hard, for example, not to recognize in the four primary Nikāyas the special association of probably all terms derived from the roots *jñā*, 'to know', and *dṛś* and *paś*, 'to see'. From the point of view of the present study it is worth bearing in mind that the *Vibhaṅga* analysis of *anupassin*, *ātāpin*, *sampajāna* and *satimant* associates these terms directly with the faculties and powers of wisdom, strength and mindfulness; with right view, right strength and right mindfulness. As I hope will emerge in the course of this study, the kind of interweaving of the elements of the seven sets involved here lies at the very heart of the treatment of the seven sets in the Nikāyas.

The concluding phrase of the basic *satipaṭṭhāna* formula, *vineyya loke abhijjhā-domanassaṃ*, is of some interest. The *Vibhaṅga* states that the 'world' referred to here is either simply the body or the five aggregates of grasping (*upādāna-kkhandha*),[82] presumably on the grounds that, apart from the unconditioned, there is no world other than the five aggregates.[83] As for *abhijjhā* and *domanassa*, the *Vibhaṅga* explains these these by reference to registers of associated terms for desire (*rāga*) and unpleasant feeling (*dukkha*) respectively.[84] According to the *Vibhaṅga*, then, the whole phrase means that this desire for and discontent with the world are repeatedly dispelled (*vinīta, paṭivinīta*), stilled (*santa, samita, vūpasanta*), ended (*appita, vyappita*), dried up (*sosita, visosita*); an end is put to them (*vyantīkata*).[85] The *Nettippakaraṇa's* brief

---

[81] Nett 82-3.

[82] Vibh 195.

[83] Cf. R. Gethin, 'The five khandhas: their treatment in the nikāyas and early abhidhamma', *JIP* 14 (1986), pp. 35-53.

[84] Vibh 195. The register for *abhijjhā* here is *rāgo sārāgo anunayo anurodho nandī nandi-rāgo cittassa sārāgo* (see Vibh 145 where the same set of terms explains *taṇhā*); this is not the same as the register used for *abhijjhā* at Dhs 79, though it does form the opening of the explanation of *lobha* as *akusala-hetu* at Dhs 189. The register for *dukkha* at Vibh 195 is *cetasikaṃ asātaṃ cetasikaṃ dukkhaṃ cetosamphassajaṃ asātaṃ dukkhaṃ vedayitaṃ ceto-samphassajā asātā dukkhā vedanā*; cf. Dhs 84.

[85] Vibh 195.

comment here is perhaps rather more suggestive: '*Vineyya loke abhijjhā-domanassaṃ*, that is to say, the faculty of concentration (*samādhindriya*).'[86]

What the *aṭṭha-kathās* have to say on this phrase makes clear the import of the *Nettippakaraṇa's* comment. According to Buddhaghosa the term *vineyya* refers either to *tad-aṅga-vinaya* or *vikkhambhana-vinaya*,[87] which are presumably the same as *tad-aṅga-ppahāna* or 'abandoning by substitution of opposites' and *vikkhambhana-ppahāna* or 'abandoning by supression'. According to the *Paṭisambhidāmagga*, 'for one who develops the first *jhāna* there is abandoning of the hindrances by suppression', while 'for one developing concentration that partakes of penetration there is abandoning of views by substitution of opposites'.[88] The *Visuddhimagga* gives two similar but rather more general definitions: *vikkhambhana-ppahāna* is 'the suppressing of adverse *dhammas* such as the hindrances by any kind of ordinary concentration';[89] *tad-aṅga-ppahāna* is 'the abandoning of any *dhamma* that is to be abandoned by means of whatever factor of knowledge and of insight that is its opposite'.[90]

These two types of abandoning are principally contrasted with *samuccheda-ppahāna* or 'abandoning by cutting off'.[91] This operates 'for one who develops the transcendent path that leads to the destruction of the *āsavas*' [92] and consists in 'the abandoning of *dhammas* that are fetters etc. by means of the knowledge of the noble path, such that they do not occur again'.[93] Thus the basic point of contrast is that this last form of abandoning abandons defilements finally and absolutely, for once and for all, while the two preceding kinds of abandoning abandon defilements only temporarily—principally in meditation, be it calm (*samatha*) or insight (*vipassanā*).

Returning to the terms *abhijjhā* and *domanassa*, Buddhaghosa says that since these terms imply the two principal hindrances, namely sensual desire (*kāma-cchanda*) and aversion (*vyāpāda*), they in fact stand in for tiredness and lethargy (*thīna-middha*), excitement and depression (*uddhacca-kukkucca*) and doubt (*vicikicchā*) as well, so that all five hindrances are included:

> But here since taking *abhijjhā* includes *kāma-cchanda*, and taking *domanassa* includes *vyāpāda*, therefore it should be understood that the abandoning of the hindrances is spoken of by indicating the pair that is strong among those items that make up the hindrances.[94]

---

[86] Nett 83.

[87] Sv III 758 = Ps I 243 = Vibh-a 220: *tattha vineyyā ti tad-aṅga-vinayena vā vikkhambhana-vinayena vā vinayitvā.*

[88] Paṭis I 27: *vikkhambhana-ppahānañ ca nīvaraṇānaṃ paṭhama-jjhānaṃ bhāvayato, tad-aṅga-ppahānañ ca diṭṭhi-gatānaṃ nibbedha-bhāgiyaṃ samādhiṃ bhāvayato.*

[89] Vism XXII 111: *tena tena lokiya-samādhinā nīvaraṇâdīnaṃ paccanīka-dhammānaṃ vikkhambhanaṃ.*

[90] Vism XXII 112: *tena tena vipassanāya avayava-bhūtena ñāṇaṅgena paṭipakkha-vasen'eva tassa tassa pahātabba-dhammassa pahānaṃ.*

[91] Vism XXII 110.

[92] Paṭis I 27: *samuccheda-ppahānañ ca lokuttara-khaya-gāmi-maggaṃ bhāvayato.*

[93] Vism XXII 122: *ariya-magga-ñāṇena saṃyojanâdīnaṃ dhammānaṃ yathā na puna pavattanti.* Paṭis I 27 also mentions a variety of subsidiary types of abandoning.

[94] Sv III 759 = Ps I 244 = Vibh-a 220: *yasmā pan'ettha abhijjhā-ggahaṇena kāma-cchando domanassa-ggahaṇena vyāpādo saṃgahaṃ gacchati tasmā nīvaraṇa-pariyāpanna-balava-dhamma-*

At first sight the commentarial explanation of *vineyya loke abhijjhā-domanassaṃ* might seem rather complicated and involved, yet with its technical edge dulled the commentarial viewpoint is in effect simply that the *satipaṭṭhānas* are only properly practised when the mind is at least temporarily free from the five hindrances; that is to say, it is only when the mind has been made still, calm, happy and lucid that the body, feelings, the mind itself and *dhamma(s)* can be truly 'watched'. It seems to me that as much is already quite explicit in a number of Nikāya treatments of the basic *satipaṭṭhāna* formula; at the very least these treatments make it clear why the commentaries give the explanations they do.

The following *Majjhima-nikāya* passage quite plainly sees the abandoning of the five hindrances as the prelude to the practice of the four *satipaṭṭhānas*:

> He sits down, bending his legs into a crosslegged position; holding his body straight he causes mindfulness to stand near around the face. Abandoning desire for the world he dwells with a mind from which desire has been removed; he purifies his mind from desire. Abandoning the stain of aversion he dwells with a mind without aversion, compassionate and friendly towards all creatures and beings; he purifies his mind from the stain of aversion and hatred. Abandoning tiredness and lethargy he dwells with tiredness and lethargy removed, observing brightness, mindful and comprehending clearly; he purifies his mind from tiredness and lethargy. Abandoning agitation and depression he dwells unagitated with his mind stilled within; he purifies his mind from agitation and depression. Abandoning doubt he dwells as one who has crossed over doubt, not wondering about skilful *dhammas*; he purifies his mind from doubt. Abandoning these five hindrances which are defilements of the mind and weaken wisdom, with regard to the body he dwells watching body, ardent, comprehending clearly, with mindfulness, having overcome desire for and discontent with the world; with regard to feelings ... with regard to the mind ... with regard to *dhammas* he dwells watching *dhamma*, ardent, comprehending clearly, with mindfulness, having overcome desire for and discontent with the world.
>
> Just as, Aggivessana, an elephant tamer plants a great stake in the the earth and tethers a wild elephant to it by the neck in order to subdue [in him] the ways and thoughts of the wild, the distress, strain and discomforts of the wild; in order to make him pleasing to villagers; in order that he should adopt ways that are agreeable to men. Just so, Aggivessana, these four *satipaṭṭhānas* are tethers for the mind for the abandoning of the ways and thoughts of the world, for the abandoning of the distress, strain and discomforts of the world, for the obtaining of the right way, for the realization of *nibbāna*.[95]

---

dvaya-dassanena nīvaraṇa-ppahānaṃ vuttaṃ hotī ti veditabbaṃ. (The taking of *domanassa* includes *vyāpāda* because all *citta* rooted in aversion is accompanied by unpleasant mental feeling.)

[95] M III 135-6: *so abhijjhaṃ loke pahāya vigatâbhijjhena cetasā viharati abhijjhāya cittaṃ parisodheti. byāpāda-padosaṃ pahāya abyāpanna-citto viharati sabba-pāṇa-bhūta-hitânukampī byāpāda-padosā cittaṃ parisodheti. thīna-middhaṃ pahāya vigata-thīna-middho viharati āloka-saññī sato sampajāno thīna-middhā cittaṃ parisodheti. uddhacca-kukkuccaṃ pahāya anuddhato viharati ajjhattaṃ vūpasanta-citto uddhacca-kukkuccā cittaṃ parisodheti. vicikicchaṃ pahāya tiṇṇa-vicikiccho viharati akathaṃ-kathī kusalesu dhammesu vicikicchāya cittaṃ parisodheti. so ime pañca nīvaraṇe pahāya cetaso upakkilese paññāya dubbalīkaraṇe kāye kāyânupassī viharati ātāpī sampajāno satimā vineyya loke abhijjhā-domanassaṃ. vedanāsu ... citte ... dhammesu ... seyyathâpi Aggivessana hatthi-damako mahantaṃ thambhaṃ paṭhaviyaṃ nikhaṇitvā āraññakassa nāgassa gīvāya upanibandhati āraññakānañ c'eva sīlānaṃ abhinimmadanāya āraññakānañ c'eva saṃkappānaṃ abhinimmadanāya āraññakānañ c'eva daratha-kilamatha-pariḷāhānaṃ abhinimmadanāya gāmante abhiramāpanāya manussa-kantesu sīlesu samādapanāya. evam eva kho Aggivessana ariya-sāvakassa*

It is clear that as far as this passage is concerned the activity of *kāyânupassanā*, *vedanânupassanā*, *cittânupassanā* and *dhammânupassanā* is seen as associated initially with the first *jhāna*. The account continues with the instruction to the *bhikkhu* that as he dwells watching body, feeling, mind and *dhamma* he should not 'think thoughts' that are connected with body, and the rest (*mā ca kāyūpasaṃhitaṃ ... vedanūpasaṃhitaṃ ... cittūpasaṃhitaṃ ... dhammūpasaṃhitaṃ vitakkaṃ vitakkesi*). So 'as a result of the stilling of initial and sustained thought he dwells having attained the second *jhāna* [which is] inward composure, a state of unification of mind, without initial and sustained thought, born of concentration, having joy and happiness' (*so vitakka-vicārānaṃ vūpasamā ajjhattaṃ sampasādanaṃ cetaso ekodi-bhāvaṃ avitakkaṃ avicāraṃ samādhijaṃ pīti-sukhaṃ dutiya-jjhānaṃ ... upasampajja viharati*). The *bhikkhu* thus proceeds to the third and fourth *jhānas* and finally knows *dukkha*, its arising, its cessation and the way leading to its cessation; he knows that his mind is finally free of the *āsavas*.

The following *Saṃyutta-nikāya* passage again deals with the calming of the mind by the practice of the *satipaṭṭhānas* and the subsequent stilling of *vitakka* and *vicāra* or 'initial and sustained thought':

> Here, Ānanda, with regard to the body a *bhikkhu* dwells watching body, ardent, comprehending clearly, with mindfulness, having overcome desire for and discontent with the world. As he dwells watching body with regard to the body, discomfort arises in the body taking the body as its object, or the mind is depressed, or the mind is scattered without. Then, Ānanda, the *bhikkhu* should apply his mind to some sign that brings about composure. As he applies his mind to a sign that brings about composure, gladness is born; for one who is gladdened joy is born; the body of one whose mind is joyful becomes tranquil; one whose body is tranquil feels happiness; the mind of one who is happy becomes concentrated. Thus he reflects: 'The purpose for which I applied my mind is accomplished in me; now let me withhold [my mind].' He withholds and has neither initial nor sustained thought. He knows: 'I am without initial and sustained thought; mindful within, I am at ease.'[96]

Once again, then, the terminology used is elsewhere in the Nikāyas associated with the description of the attainment *jhāna*. As I shall have occasion to remark again, the sequence 'gladness is born ... the mind of one who is happy becomes concentrated' is of considerable importance in Nikāya spiritual psychology, and is classically used in the *sīlakkhandha-vagga* of the *Dīgha-nikāya* to introduce the attainment of the first *jhāna*.[97]

---

ime cattāro satipaṭṭhānā cetaso upanibandhanā honti gehasitānañ c'eva sīlānaṃ abhinimmadanāya gehasitānañ c'eva saṃkappānaṃ abhinimmadanāya gehasitānañ c'eva daratha-kilamatha-pariḷāhānaṃ abhinimaddanāya ñāyassa adhigamāya nibbānassa sacchikiriyāya.

[96] S V 155-6: *idhânanda bhikkhu kāye kāyânupassī viharati ... tassa kāye kāyânupassino viharato kāyârammaṇo vā uppajjati kāyasmiṃ pariḷāho cetaso vā līnattaṃ bahiddhā vā cittaṃ vikkhipati. tenânanda bhikkhunā kismiñcid eva pasādaniye nimitte cittaṃ paṇidahitabbaṃ. tassa kismiñcid eva pasādaniye nimitte cittaṃ paṇidahato pāmujjaṃ jayati. pamuditassa pīti jayati. pīti-manassa kāyo passambhati. passaddha-kāyo sukhaṃ vedayati. sukhino cittaṃ samādhiyati. so iti paṭisaṃcikkhati. yassa khvāhaṃ atthāya cittaṃ pañidahiṃ so me attho abhinipphanno. handa dāni paṭisaṃharāmī ti. so paṭisaṃharati c'eva na ca vitakketi na ca vicāreti. avitakkomhi avicāro ajjhattaṃ satimā sukhaṃ asmī ti pajānāti.*

[97] See below, pp. 169-70.

An extended simile in the *satipaṭṭhāna-saṃyutta* states in more general terms the principle that the successful practice of the four *satipaṭṭhānas* depends more or less on calming and concentrating the mind:

> Suppose, *bhikkhus*, that an immature, unaccomplished and unskilful cook were to serve a king or king's minister with various kinds of sauce—sour, bitter, spicy, sweet, hot and salty. Now the immature, unaccomplished and unskilful cook does not take note of his master's signals: 'Today this sauce pleases my master, or he reaches out for this one, or he takes a lot of this one, or he speaks in praise of this one ... ' The immature, unaccomplished and unskilful cook gains no clothing, no payment, no gratuities. What is the reason? Because, *bhikkhus*, the immature, unaccomplished and unskilful cook does not take note of his master's signals.
>
> Just so, *bhikkhus*, some immature, unaccomplished and unskilful *bhikkhu* with regard to the body dwells watching body, ardent, comprehending clearly, with mindfulness, having overcome desire for and discontent with the world. While he dwells watching body with regard to the body, his mind does not become concentrated, the defilements are not abandoned, he does not take up the sign ... With regard to feelings ... With regard to mind ... With regard to *dhammas* ... The immature, unaccomplished and unskilful *bhikkhu* gains no happy-dwelling in the here and now, no mindfulness and clear comprehension. What is the reason? Because, *bhikkhus*, he does not take up the sign of his own mind.[98]

The passage continues by describing the case of the masterful, accomplished and skilful (*paṇḍito vyatto kusalo*) cook and the masterful, accomplished and skilful *bhikkhu*. Such a cook does take note of his master's signals, and as a result does receive clothing, wages and gratuities. Similarly such a *bhikkhu's* mind does become concentrated, the defilements are abandoned, and he does take up the sign of his own mind. As a result he does gain 'happy dwelling' in the here and now, he does gain mindfulness and clear comprehension.

Other passages might be cited that underline the general point.[99] The *Kāyagatāsati-sutta*, for example, has the following refrain in the fourteen places where the *(Mahā-)Satipaṭṭhāna-sutta* gives the expanded *satipaṭṭhāna* formula for *kāyânupassanā*:

> For one who dwells thus heedful, ardent, with application, worldly memories and thoughts are abandoned; as a result of their abandoning the mind becomes stilled

---

[98] S V 149-50: *seyyathâpi bhikkhave bālo avyatto akusalo sūdo rājānaṃ vā rāja-mahāmattānaṃ vā nānaccayehi sūpehi paccupaṭṭhito assa ambilaggehi pi tittakaggehi pi kaṭukaggehi pi madhuragg-ehi pi khārikehi pi akhārikehi pi loṇikehi pi aloṇikehi pi. sa kho bhikkhave bālo avyatto akusalo sūdo sakassa bhattussa nimittaṃ na uggaṇhāti: idaṃ vā me ajja bhattu sūpeyyaṃ ruccati, imassa vā abhiharati, imassa vā bahuṃ gaṇhāti, imassa vā vaṇṇaṃ bhāsati ... ti. sa kho bhikkhave bālo avyatto akusalo sūdo na c'eva lābhī hoti acchādanassa na lābhī vetanassa na lābhī abhihārānaṃ. taṃ kissa hetu. tathā hi so bhikkhave bālo avyatto akusalo sūdo sakassa bhattussa nimittaṃ na uggaṇhāti. evam eva kho bhikkhave idh'ekacco bālo avyatto akusalo bhikkhu kāye kāyânupassī viharati ... tassa kāye kāyânupassino viharato cittaṃ na samādhiyati upakkilesā na pahīyanti. so taṃ nimittaṃ na uggaṇh-āti ... sa kho bālo avyatto akusalo bhikkhu na ceva lābhī diṭṭhe va dhamme sukha-vihārānaṃ, na lābhī sati-sampajaññassa. taṃ kissa hetu. tathā hi sa kho bālo avyatto akusalo bhikkhu sakassa cittassa nimittaṃ na uggaṇhāti.* (Quoted in part at Vism IV 122.)

[99] Cf. S V 145-6 which contrasts the five *nīvaraṇas* as an accumulation of non-skill (*akusala-rāsi*) with the four *satipaṭṭhānas* as an accumulation of skill (*kusala-rāsi*). At M I 301 (*Cūḷavedalla-sutta*) the four *satipaṭṭhānas* are termed 'sign of concentration' (*samādhi-nimitta*). See also S V 144-5.

within, composed, unified and concentrated. In this way, *bhikkhus*, a *bhikkhu* develops mindfulness concerned with the body.[100]

The Nikāyas and later tradition appear to be agreed, then, that the successful practice of the four establishings of mindfulness is dependent on the stilling of the mind by the abandoning of the five hindrances. Of course, for the commentaries the mind that is without the five hindrances is of two basic types—it is either stilled in 'access' concentration (*upacāra-samādhi*) or in full 'absorption' (*appanā*) equivalent to full *jhāna*; any such distinction would seem to be lacking in the Nikāyas.[101] With this proviso, it seems to me that the substance of the commentarial understanding of the basic *satipaṭṭhāna* formula is already contained in the above Nikāya passages.

To sum up, the point I wish to make is no doubt simple enough, but it can be overlooked. For the Nikāyas and later tradition the effective practice of the establishings of mindfulness is seen as presupposing a certain degree of concentration (*samādhi*) or calm (*samatha*). Of course, what is clear is that this concentration or calm is itself the outcome of the preparatory practice of the establishings of mindfulness—especially of the various exercises associated with watching the body. It might be said, then, that in order to practice the *satipaṭṭhānas* the *bhikkhu* requires concentration; in order to acquire concentration he practises the *satipaṭṭhānas*. Stated without paradox, this means that the texts distinguish between the initial stages of the establishing of mindfulness, which are preparatory in nature, and the establishing of mindfulness proper.

5. *The expanded satipaṭṭhāna formula*

The first part of the expanded *satipaṭṭhāna* formula describes a *bhikkhu* as watching body, feelings, mind and *dhammas* initially 'within' (*ajjhattaṃ*) then 'without' (*bahiddhā*) and finally 'within and without' (*ajjhatta-bahiddhā*).[102] The significance of the terms *ajjhattaṃ* and *bahiddhā* is clear enough from the Abhidhamma texts onwards: that which refers to oneself is 'within' and that which refers to other beings and persons (*para-satta*, *para-puggala*) is 'without'.[103] There seems to be little reason to suppose that their significance is any different in the Nikāyas. The *bhikkhu*, then, first watches his own body, feelings, mind and *dhammas*, next those of others, and finally his own and those of others together. This is of some interest.

The idea of watching another's body is no doubt clear enough if we are talking of the parts of a body or a corpse, but when we are talking of the breath the idea is perhaps a little harder to grasp. The subcommentary here

---

[100] M III 89-94 (passim): *tassa evaṃ appamattassa ātāpino pahitattassa viharato ye te gehasitā sara-saṃkappā te pahīyanti, tesaṃ pahānā ajjhattaṃ eva cittaṃ santiṭṭhati sannisīdati ekodihoti samādhiyati. evaṃ pi bhikkhave bhikkhu kāya-gataṃ satiṃ bhāveti.*

[101] See L.S. Cousins, 'Buddhist *Jhāna*', *Religion* 3 (1973) p. 118; Vism IV 32-3.

[102] Occasionally the triad *ajjhattaṃ/bahiddhā/ajjhatta-bahiddhā* is added straight to the basic *satipaṭṭhāna* formula (e.g. Vibh 193); the addition of *adhyātmam/bahirdhā* is standard in Buddhist Sanskrit sources, see above, p. 29, n. 2.

[103] E.g. Dhs 187-8.

makes the point that watching another's breath concerns the development of insight and not the development of full *jhāna* or absorption (*appanā*).[104] The idea of watching another's feelings, mind and *dhammas* is perhaps even more curious. The commentary is of little help here except to confirm that this is indeed the meaning intended.[105] Interestingly, though, some ancient authors give alternative explanations. Although it appears that he too had before him the terms *adhyātmam/bahirdhā*, the author of the **Mahāprajñāpāramitā-śāstra* gives an explanation in terms of feeling that is *ādhyātmika* or *bāhya*:[106] feeling that is directly associated with the five [sense-] consciousnesses (*pañca-vijñāna-samprayukta-vedanā*) is *bāhya*; feeling directly associated with bare mind-consciousness (*mano-vijñāna-samprayukta-vedanā*) is *ādhyātmika*.[107] However, this is not the only explanation given by the author of the **Mahāprajñāpāramitā-śāstra*; the rest of his discussion of this point with regard to *vedanā-*, *citta-* and *dharma-smṛty-upasthāna* suggests that he too envisaged that the yogin progressed by watching the feelings, mind and *dharmas* of others.[108]

It might be suggested that the way the *sutta* formulation includes the progression *ajjhattaṃ/bahiddhā/ajjhatta-bahiddhā* for all four *satipaṭṭhānas* is simply mechanical, and that the later exegetical works are thus left with the job of making sense of an accident. But this is much too convenient. Elsewhere the Nikāyas can be quite definite in leaving out of consideration what should be left out of consideration.[109] If this whole matter is to be given an explanation on the theoretical level, then it must be understood, I think, as to do with the blurring of distinctions between self and other—something which is, of course, entirely consistent with the notion of not-self in Buddhist thought. Thus as the *bhikkhu* watches body, feelings, mind and *dhammas* within, without, within and without, rather than seeing a world made up of distinct 'persons' or 'selves', he becomes progressively aware of a world of *dhamma* made up entirely of *dhammas* all of which are 'not-self'. Of some interest in this connection is a passage from the *Dīgha-nikāya* which tends to confirm that something of this nature is envisaged:

> Here a *bhikkhu* with regard to the body dwells watching body within, ardent, comprehending clearly, with mindfulness, having overcome desire for and discontent with the world. As he dwells watching body within with regard to the body, he

---

[104] DAṬ II 381: 'There is no arising of the sign of absorption in respect of the in-and-out-breathing-body [of another] by way of calm.' (*samatha-vasena pana assāsa-passāsa-kāye appanā-nimittuppatti eva natthi.*) Cf. Soma Thera, *The Way of Mindfulness*, 5th ed., Kandy, 1981, p. 51.

[105] E.g. Vibh-a 268; Sv III 775, 777, 782; Ps I 279, 280, 286, 287, 289, 300, 301.

[106] Cf. Pāli *ajjhattika* and *bāhira*, usually applied to the six internal *āyatanas* (*cakkhu, sota, ghāna, jivhā, kāya, mano*) and six external *āyatanas* (*rūpa, sadda, gandha, rasa, phoṭṭhabba, dhamma*) respectively (see Dhs 211, 255). See also Vibh 67: *viññāṇa-kkhandha* is *ajjhattika*; *vedanā-*, *saññā-* and *saṃkhāra-kkhandhas* are *bāhira*; *rūpa-kkhandha* may be either.

[107] *Traité*, III 1173-4.

[108] Id., 1174-5.

[109] Cf. S III 167: The *bhikkhu* in the four *jhānas* sees *rūpa*, *vedanā*, *saññā*, *saṃkhāras* and *viññāṇa* as not self, etc.; in the first three *arūpa* attainments *rūpa* is left out because there is no *rūpa* there to be seen as not self, etc.; the fourth *arūpa* attainment is left out of consideration altogether not because here *vedanā*, etc. are self, but presumably because in the sphere of 'neither *saññā* nor not *saññā*' *vedanā*, etc. are so subtle as to make it impossible to achieve *consciously* the vision of not-self, etc.

> becomes rightly concentrated thereon, rightly settled. Being rightly concentrated thereon, rightly settled, he brings about knowledge and vision with regard to the body of another without...With regard to feelings ...With regard to mind ... With regard to *dhammas* ... Being rightly concentrated thereon, rightly settled, he brings about knowledge and vision with regard to *dhammas* of another without.[110]

The second and fourth parts of the expanded *satipaṭṭhāna* formula are best dealt with together. I do not wish to comment further on the third part; suffice to say that it underlines what has already been said about the relationship between mindfulness and wisdom.

So in the course of watching body, feelings, mind and *dhamma* the *bhikkhu* goes on to watch the nature of arising (*samudaya-dhamma*), the nature of fall (*vaya-dhamma*), and the nature of arising and fall (*samudaya-vaya-dhamma*).[111] Finally he dwells 'independent' or 'unattached' (*anissita*) and does not grasp anything in the world (*na ca kiñci loke upādiyati*). Possibly this last remark should be taken as merely a variation on 'having overcome desire for and discontent with the world', but the commentary appears to read rather more into it than this. The expanded *satipaṭṭhāna* formula describes 'the way of release as far as *arahant*-ship' (*yāva arahattā niyyāna-mukhaṃ*),[112] and referring to that twenty-one occurrences of the expanded formula in the *sutta*, the *(Mahā-)Satipaṭṭhāna-sutta* is described as 'the teaching that is taught culminating in arahantship in twenty-one places' (*eka-vīsatiyā ṭhānesu arahatta-nikūṭena desitā desanā*).[113] Why are these things said in the commentaries?

The language of the second and fourth parts of the expanded *satipaṭṭhāna* formula seems to echo other Nikāya passages with particular connotations:

> And then, *bhikkhus*, after some time the *bodhisatta* Vipassin dwelt watching rise and fall with regard to the five aggregates of grasping: thus is form, thus is the arising of form, thus is the disappearance of form; thus is feeling ... perception ... formations ... consciousness, thus is the arising of consciousness, thus is the disappearance of consciousness. And as he dwelt watching rise and fall with regard to the five aggregates of grasping his mind was soon freed from the *āsavas* through not grasping.[114]

---

110 D II 216: *idha kho bhikkhu ajjhattaṃ kāye kāyânupassī viharati ātāpī sampajāno satimā vineyya loke abhijjhā-domanassaṃ. ajjhattaṃ kāye kāyânupassī viharanto tattha sammā samādhiyati sammā vippasīdati. so tattha sammā samāhito sammā vippasanno bahiddhā para-kāye ñāṇa-dassanaṃ abhinibbatteti ... ajjhattaṃ dhammesu dhammânupassī viharati ātāpī sampajāno satimā vineyya loke abhijjhā-domanassaṃ. ajjhattaṃ dhammesu dhammânupassī viharanto tattha sammā samādhiyati sammā vippasīdati. so tattha sammā samāhito sammā vippasanno bahiddhā para-dhammesu ñāṇa-dassanaṃ abhinibbatteti.*

111 As is usual in the translation of this passage, I have taken *samudaya-dhamma* and *vaya-dhamma* as meaning '(having) the nature of rise/fall'; cf. A.K. Warder, *JIP* 1 (1971), pp. 282–3 on this usage of *-dhamma* in the Nikāyas. The commentaries (*aṭṭhakathā*), however, take *dhamma* as indicating the conditions for the arising and the fall of body, etc. (see Sv III 765, 768, 769; Ps I 249–50), although the subcommentaries also allow that *dhamma* can have the sense of 'nature' here (DAṬ II 381; Ps-pṭ (Be) I 350: *pakati-vācī vā dhamma-saddo*). In the end the point would seem to make little difference to the general purport of the expression: the *bhikkhu* sees how body, etc., arise and fall away.

112 Sv III 766; Ps I 250, 270, 274, 280.

113 Sv III 806; Ps I 302.

114 D II 35: *atha kho bhikkhave Vipassī bodhisatto aparena samayena pancas' upādāna-kkhandesu udaya-vyayânupassī vihāsi: iti rūpaṃ iti rūpassa samudayo iti rūpassa atthagamo. iti vedanā ... iti*

As I have commented elsewhere,[115] the practice of watching rise and fall with regard to the five aggregates of grasping seems to be particularly associated with the gaining of the insight that leads directly to the destruction of the *āsavas*, directly to awakening. That the Nikāyas also take it that *kāyânupassanā*, *vedanânupassanā*, *cittânupassanā* and *dhammânupassanā* each lead directly to the destruction of the *āsavas* seems to be stated in the following:

> Here, Sāriputta, a *bhikkhu* with regard to the body dwells watching body, ardent, clearly comprehending, with mindfulness, having overcome desire for and discontent with the world. As he dwells watching body with regard to the body his mind becomes free from passion, is freed from the *āsavas* through not grasping ... With regard to feelings ... With regard to mind ... With regard to *dhammas* ... [116]

> Here, *bhikkhus*, a *bhikkhu* with regard to the body dwells watching body ... As he dwells watching body with regard to the body, the body is fully known; due to full knowledge of the body the deathless is realized ... With regard to feelings ... With regard to the mind ... With regard to *dhammas* ... [117]

In a rather similar way, for the *bhikkhu* who develops mindfulness concerned with the body ten benefits (*ānisaṃsā*) are to be expected; the last of these is the destruction of the *āsavas*.[118]

The implications of all this are rather interesting when considered in relationship to the notion of the thirty-seven *bodhi-pakkhiya-dhammas*. Certainly as far as the commentaries are concerned it is clear that although there may be thirty-seven *dhammas* that contribute to awakening, the very first of these, namely the first *satipaṭṭhāna*, is capable of taking the *bhikkhu* all the way to final awakening, to *arahant*-ship. What of the other thirty-six? For the moment I raise the question without attempting to offer a full answer. It is something to be borne in mind as this study proceeds.

A slightly different but perhaps complementary perspective is to be gained from the full Nikāya treatment of mindfulness of breathing in and out (*ānâpāna-sati*). Consider the following:

> [i] When a *bhikkhu* breathing in long, knows: 'I breathe in long'; breathing out long ... breathing in short ... breathing out short ... When he trains himself: 'I shall breathe in experiencing the whole body ... I shall breathe out ... I shall breathe in tranquillizing the forces of the body ... I shall breathe out ... '—at that time with regard to the body he dwells watching the body ...
>
> [ii] When a *bhikkhu* trains himself: 'I shall breathe in experiencing joy ... I shall breathe out ... I shall breathe in experiencing happiness ... I shall breathe out ... I shall breathe in experiencing the forces of the mind ... I shall breathe out ... I shall

---

saññā ... iti saṃkhārā ... iti viññāṇaṃ iti viññāṇassa samudayo iti viññāṇassa atthagamo ti. tassa pañcas'upādāna-kkhandhesu udaya-vyayânupassino viharato na cirass'eva anupādāya āsavehi cittaṃ vimucci.

[115] *JIP* 14 (1986), p. 43.

[116] S V 158: *idha Sāriputta bhikkhu kāye kāyânupassī viharati ... tassa kāye kāyânupassino viharato cittaṃ virajjati vimuccati anupādāya āsavehi ... vedanāsu ... citte ... dhammesu ...*

[117] S V 182: *idha bhikkhave bhikkhu kāye kāyânupassī viharati ... tassa kāye kāyânupassino viharato kāyo pariññāto hoti. kāyassa pariññātattā amataṃ sacchikataṃ hoti ... vedanāsu ... citte ... dhammesu ...* (Cf. S V 181.)

[118] M III 99.

breathe in tranquillizing the forces of the mind ... I shall breathe out ... '—at that time with regard to feelings he dwells watching feeling ...

[iii] When a *bhikkhu* trains himself: 'I shall breathe in experiencing the mind ... I shall breathe out ... I shall breathe in gladdening the mind ... I shall breathe out ... I shall breathe in concentrating the mind ... I shall breathe out ... I shall breathe in freeing the mind ... I shall breathe out ... '—at that time with regard to mind he dwells watching mind ...

[iv] When a *bhikkhu* trains himself: 'I shall breathe in watching impermanence ... I shall breathe out ... I shall breathe in watching dispassion ... I shall breathe out ... I shall breathe in watching cessation ... I shall breathe out ... I shall breathe in watching letting-go ... I shall breathe out ... '—at that time with regard to *dhammas* he dwells watching *dhamma* ...

Developed in this way, made great in this way, mindfulness of breathing in and out brings the four establishings of mindfulness to fulfilment.[119]

From this it seems that the first *satipaṭṭhāna* or *kāyânupassanā* is *in itself* strictly insufficient to bring the *bhikkhu* to the conclusion of the path to awakening. The treatment of mindfulness of breathing in and out in the *(Mahā-)Satipaṭṭhāna-sutta* rather pointedly breaks off after the first 'tetrad'[120]—the tetrad that in the full *ānâpāna-sati* treatment is explicitly identified with the first *satipaṭṭhāna*. This leaves three more tetrads which in the full treatment are associated with the second, third and fourth *satipaṭṭhānas* respectively. What is interesting in the full treatment is the way in which *ānâpāna-sati* begins as the vehicle for the first *satipaṭṭhāna* and finishes up as a vehicle for all four. Thus by starting with the watching of the breath as 'body' the *bhikkhu* naturally progresses to the watching of feeling, mind and *dhammas* through the medium of the breath. Finally this brings to fulfilment not only the four *satipaṭṭhānas*, but also the seven factors of awakening, and knowledge and freedom (*vijjā-vimutti*).[121]

The essential unity of the four *satipaṭṭhānas* is perhaps suggested by the following:

Suppose, Ānanda, there were a great pile of dirt at [the junction of] four highways.

---

[119] M III 83-5 = S V 329-31 = 336-7: *[i] yasmiṃ samaye bhikkhu dīghaṃ vā assasanto dīghaṃ assasāmī ti pajānāti; dīghaṃ vā passasanto ... rassaṃ vā assasanto ... rassaṃ vā passasanto ... sabba-kāya-paṭisaṃvedī assasissāmī ti sikkhati ... passasissāmi ... passambhayaṃ kāya-saṃkhāraṃ assasissāmi ... passasissāmi ... kāye kāyânupassī bhikkhave tasmiṃ samaye viharati ... [ii] yasmiṃ samaye bhikkhave bhikkhu pīti-paṭisaṃvedī assasissāmī ti sikkhati ... passasissāmi ... sukha-paṭisaṃvedī assasissāmi ... passasissāmi ... citta-saṃkhāra-paṭisaṃvedī assasissāmi ... passasissāmi ... passambhayaṃ citta-saṃkhāraṃ assasissāmi ... passasissāmi ... vedanāsu vedanânupassī bhikkhave tasmiṃ samaye viharati ... [iii] yasmiṃ samaye bhikkhave bhikkhu citta-paṭisaṃvedī assasissāmī ti sikkhati ... passasissāmi ... abhippamodayaṃ cittaṃ assasissāmi ... passasissāmi ... samādahaṃ cittaṃ assasissāmi ... passasissāmi ... vimocayaṃ cittaṃ assasissāmi ... passasissāmi ... citte cittânupassī bhikkhave tasmiṃ samaye bhikkhu viharati ... [iv] yasmiṃ samaye bhikkhave bhikkhu aniccânupassī assasissāmī ti sikkhati ... passasissāmi ... virāgânupassī assasissāmi ... passasissāmi ... nirodhânupassī assasissāmi ... passasissāmi ... paṭinissaggânupassī assasissāmi ... passasissāmi ... dhammesu dhammânupassī bhikkhave tasmiṃ samaye bhikkhu viharati ... evaṃ bhāvitā kho bhikkhave ānâpana-sati evaṃ bahulīkatā cattāro satipaṭṭhāne paripūreti.*

[120] *Catukka*, the term used in the commentary. Each *catukka* gives four ways in which the *bhikkhu* experiences the breath.

[121] M III 82 (see also S V 329-40, passim): *ānâpāna-sati bhikkhave bhāvitā bahulīkatā cattāro satipaṭṭhāne paripūreti. cattāro satipaṭṭhānā bhāvitā ... satta bojjhaṅge paripūrenti. satta bojjhaṅgā bhāvitā ... vijjā-vimuttiṃ paripūrenti.*

> A cart or chariot coming from the eastern direction would destroy that pile of dirt; a cart or chariot coming from the western direction ... the northern direction ... the southern direction would destroy that pile of dirt. Just so, Ānanda, when a *bhikkhu* with regard to the body dwells watching body he too destroys bad unskilful *dhammas* ... with regard to feelings ... the mind ... *dhammas* ... [122]

In all this we appear to have two perspectives on the same thing. On the one hand, the whole of the path to awakening is subsumed within the first establishing of mindfulness without reference to the other three. On the other hand, the first establishing of mindfulness taken to its own conclusion actually subsumes the other three establishings of mindfulness.

Finally, returning briefly to the question of the relationship of the four *satipaṭṭhānas* to the seven *bojjhaṅgas*, the notion that the development of the four *satipaṭṭhānas* leads directly to the fulfilment of the seven *bojjhaṅgas* and knowledge and freedom reflects the overall structure of the *(Mahā-)Satipaṭṭhāna-sutta* itself, which culminates in the watching of the seven *bojjhaṅgas* and the four noble truths.[123] Perhaps not surprisingly, then, a statement to the effect that the Buddhist path consists essentially in the abandoning of the five hindrances, the development of the establishings of mindfulness and subsequent development of the awakening-factors is found several times in the Nikāyas:

> All those who escaped from the world [in the past], or escape [now], or will escape [in the future], did so, do so and will [continue] to do so by abandoning the five hindrances which are defilements of the mind that weaken wisdom, and, with minds well established in the four establishings of mindfulness, by developing the seven awakening-factors thus present.[124]

This summary of the Buddhist path in terms of abandoning the five *nīvaraṇas*, establishing the four *satipaṭṭhānas* and developing the seven *bojjhaṅgas* is of some interest. First, in opposing the four *satipaṭṭhānas* to the five *nīvaraṇas*, it once more associates the practice of the *satipaṭṭhānas* with the practice of *jhāna*. Further, it seems to have some bearing on the way the practices that constitute the first and fourth *satipaṭṭhānas/smṛty-upasthānas* are specified in ancient Buddhist literature. For example, while the *Satipaṭṭhāna-sutta* gives six basic methods for *kāyânupassanā* (taking the nine corpse-contemplations as one) and five methods of *dhammânupassanā*, the *Vibhaṅga* refers only to watching the different parts of the body under *kāyânupassanā*,

---

[122] S V 325: *seyyathâpi Ānanda catu-mahā-pathe mahā-paṃsu-puñjo puratthimāya ce pi disāya āgaccheyya sakaṭaṃ vā ratho vā upahanat'eva taṃ paṃsu-puñjaṃ. pacchimāya ce pi disāya ... uttarāya ... dakkhiṇāya ce pi disāya ... evaṃ eva kho Ānanda bhikkhu kāye kāyânupassī viharanto pi upahanat'eva pāpake akusale dhamme. vedanāsu ... citte ... dhammesu ...*

[123] It is worth noting in this connection that the Chinese version apparently omits the *upādāna-skandhas* and *āyatanas* under *dharmânupaśyanā*, giving only the *nīvaraṇas* and *bodhyaṅgas* (see Warder, *IB*, pp. 86-7).

[124] A V 194-5 (cf. D II 83 = III 101 = S V 161; A III 387; Nett 94) : *ye kho keci lokamhā niyyiṃsu vā niyyanti vā niyyissanti vā sabbe te pañca nīvaraṇe pahāya cetaso upakkilese paññāya dubbalīkaraṇe catusu satipaṭṭhānesu supatiṭṭhita-cittā satta bojjhaṅge yathā-bhūtaṃ bhāvetvā evaṃ ete lokamhā niyyiṃsu vā niyyanti vā niyyissanti vā.* (In this context *yathā-bhūtaṃ* surely does not mean 'as they really are' in some kind of absolute sense, but more simply 'as they are, as existing' *consequent* on the mind's being established in the four *satipaṭṭhānas*.) (Cf. below, p. 258)

and only to watching the *nīvaraṇas* and *bojjhaṅgas* under *dhammânupassanā*.[125] In non-Pāli sources other variations are found. This has led scholars such as Schmithausen and Bronkhorst to speculate on the nature of the 'original' specification of the first and fourth *satipaṭṭhānas/smṛty-upasthānas*:[126] the former suggests that watching the body originally consisted only of watching the different postures of the body, and the latter (following the *Vibhaṅga*) suggests that it consisted only of watching the different parts of the body. Much of their discussion is at best highly speculative, and at worst misconceived.

Schmithausen, for example, suggests that the redactors of the Pāli canon have put the watching of breath first because in some canonical texts, such as the *Ānâpānasati-sutta*, it is presented as the preliminary stage (Vorstufe) of the four *satipaṭṭhānas*.[127] This is a misunderstanding. As we have seen, in the *Ānâpānasati-sutta* watching the breathing is not a preliminary of the *satipaṭṭhānas*, it actually is the *satipaṭṭhānas*. One must ask why *ānâpāna-sati* is singled out for treatment in this way. One reason might be because it is taken as the normative (not 'original' or 'only') basis on which to abandon the five *nīvaraṇas*, establish the *satipaṭṭhānas* and develop the *bojjhaṅgas*. In many ways, then, the *Ānâpānasati-sutta* is simply an expanded and full illustration of just how the Buddhist path consists in the abandoning of the *nīvaraṇas*, establishing the *satipaṭṭhānas*, and developing the *bojjhaṅgas*.

6. *The ekâyana formula*

The *(Mahā-)Satipaṭṭhāna-sutta* introduces the four *satipaṭṭhānas* with the following formula:

> *Ekâyana, bhikkhus*, is this path for the purification of beings, for passing beyond sorrow and grief, for the disappearance of pain and discontent, for the attainment of the right way, for the realization of *nibbāna*—that is the four *satipaṭṭhānas*.[128]

Two ideas are, then, coupled here. First, the path for the purification of beings, and so on, is termed *ekâyana*; secondly, the path so termed is said to consist of the four *satipaṭṭhānas*. The latter point is of some interest since it appears that in the four primary Nikāyas this formula is only applied to the *satipaṭṭhānas*. This must be of some significance, since with many of the formulas used in the *mahā-vagga* of the *Saṃyutta-nikāya*, for example, the seven sets are interchangeable. Not so with the *ekâyana* formula. Interestingly though, the late canonical *Niddesa* does extend the application of the term *ekâyana-magga* to all seven sets. The *Niddesa* comments that the Blessed One is

---

125 Vibh 193, 199-202.

126 See works cited above, p. 44, n. 72.

127 Schmithausen, *KA*, p. 250.

128 D II 290 = M I 55: *ekâyano ayaṃ bhikkhave maggo sattānaṃ visuddhiyā soka-pariddavānaṃ samatikkamāya dukkha-domanassānaṃ atthāgamāya ñāyassa adhigamāya nibbānassa sacchikiriyāya yadidaṃ cattāro satipaṭṭhānā*. The formula also occurs at S V 141, 167-8, 185; Kv 158. It does not seem to occur in full in any extant Sanskrit sources (cf. Lamotte, *Traité*, III 1121) but is found in the Chinese translations of the Āgamas (see below, p. 64, n. 154); cf. Abhidh-k-vy 529: *ekâyano'yaṃ bhikṣavo mārgo yad uta catvāri smṛty-upasthānāni*.

eka because he has travelled the *ekâyana*-path (*bhagavā ekâyana-maggaṃ gato ti eko*) and then goes on to explain the *ekâyana*-path as 'the four establishings of mindfulness, the four right endeavours, the four bases of success, the five faculties, the five powers, the seven awakening-factors, the noble eightfold path'.[129] The *Niddesa* then quotes the following verse:

> Seeing the end and destruction of birth, he knows the *ekâyana*-path in friendliness and compassion; by this path they crossed the flood in the past, they will cross [it in the future] and they cross [it now].[130]

So it is, says the *Niddesa*, that the Blessed One is *eka* because he has travelled the *ekâyana*-path (*evaṃ bhagavā ekâyana-maggaṃ gato ti eko*). At the same time as extending the term *ekâyana-magga* to all seven sets, the *Niddesa* also preserves a tradition of the term's special association with *sati* or 'mindfulness': 'that which is mindfulness, recollection ... the awakening-factor of mindfulness, the *ekâyana*-path—this is called mindfulness.'[131]

The problem is simple: what does *ekâyano maggo* actually mean, and what is the significance of the expression's special association with the *satipaṭṭhānas* in the four primary Nikāyas? Translators of the *ekâyana* formula seem largely to have passed over the difficulties involved here and assumed that we can straightforwardly render *ekâyana* along the lines of 'the one (i.e. only) way'.[132]

The Pāli commentaries, in contrast, provide five basic ways of taking *ekâyana* in the present context:[133]

(i) *Ayana* is simply one of the many words for *magga*; *ekâyano ayaṃ maggo* means, then, that this path (the path for the purification of beings) is a single path, and not a forked path (*eka-maggo ayaṃ bhikkhave maggo na dvedhā-patha-bhūto ti evaṃ attho daṭṭhabbo*).

(ii) A path that is *ekâyana* is one that is to be travelled alone (*ekena ayitabbo*); one who is 'alone' is one who has left behind the crowd and withdrawn with a mind secluded from the objects of the senses (*ekenā ti gaṇa-saṃgaṇikaṃ pahāya vūpakaṭṭhena pavivitta-cittena*).

---

[129] Nidd I 455-6: *kathaṃ bhagavā ekâyana-maggaṃ gato ti eko. ekâyana-maggo vuccati cattāro satipaṭṭhānā cattāro samma-ppadhānā cattāro iddhi-padā panc'indriyāni pañca balāni satta bojjhaṅgā ariyo aṭṭhaṅgiko maggo.* (Cf. Nidd I 457; Nidd II 112-4, 262; Paṭis I 174.)

[130] This verse is also found at S V 168, 186, and is quoted at Sv III 745, Ps I 230.

[131] Nidd I 10, 347, 506: *yā sati anussati ... sati-sambojjhaṅgo ekâyana-maggo ayaṃ vuccati sati.* (Cf. Dhs register of terms for *sati*, e.g. Dhs 11.)

[132] See Rhys Davids, D Trsl II 327 ('The one and only path, Bhikkhus, leading to the purification of beings ... is that of the Fourfold Setting up of Mindfulness.'); Horner, M Trsl I 71 ('There is this one way, monks, for the purification of beings ... that is to say the four applications of mindfulness.'); Lamotte, *Traité*, III 1122 ('Il n'y a qu'une voie pour la purification des êtres ... ce sont les quatre fixations-de-l'attention.').

[133] See Sv III 743-4; Ps I 229-30; there are a number of different readings. For the first four explanations cf. Aggavaṃsa's summary (Sadd 918): *atthi padaṃ catur-ādhippayikaṃ ... yathā: eko ayano ekâyano ekena ayitabbo ekâyano ekassa ayano ekâyano ekasmiṃ ayano ekâyano iccevam-ādi atrâyaṃ pāḷī: ekâyano ayaṃ bhikkhave maggo ... yadidaṃ cattāro satipaṭṭhānā ti.* A sixth explanation, taking *ekâyana* to signify that one goes to *nibbāna* only once (*yasmā eka-vāraṃ nibbānaṃ gacchati tasmā ekâyano*), is not allowed by Buddhaghosa.

(iii) The *ekâyana* path is the path of 'the one' in the sense of 'the best', which means 'the best of all beings', namely the Buddha (*ekassa ayano ekâyano; ekassā ti seṭṭhassa; sabba-satta-seṭṭho va bhagavā*).

(iv) An *ekâyano* path is a path that occurs or is found in just one place (*ayatī ti va ayano; gacchati pavattatī ti attho; ekasmiṃ ayano ti ekâyano*); in the present context that is in the *dhamma-vinaya* of the Buddha (*imasmiṃ yeva dhamma-vinaye pavattati na aññathā ti vuttaṃ hoti*).

(v) Finally, a path that is *ekâyana* is one that goes to one place only (*ekaṃ ayatī ti ekâyano*), namely *nibbāna* (*ekaṃ nibbānam eva gacchatī ti vuttaṃ hoti*).

Here, then, are five different grammatical resolutions of the compound *ekâyana*. Leaving this aside for the moment, what of the term *ekâyana* in other contexts both outside Buddhist literature and elsewhere in the Nikāyas? Böhtlingk and Roth distinguish what are really two basic ideas in the usage of *ekâyana* in the Upaniṣads and Epic.[134] In principle they correspond to the second and fifth explanations respectively of those offered in the Pāli commentaries. As a noun, *ekâyana* is first of all a lonely place—a place where only one person goes.[135] A second group of usages stems from the notion of 'going to one'. An *ekâyana* is a meeting place, a place where people or things become one;[136] an assembly, or gathering together as one.[137] Finally the word is understood to indicate some kind of spiritual unification—'going to the one'—or the practice that brings this about.[138] It is perhaps worth quoting some examples of this second group of usages:

> As the ocean is the meeting place (*ekâyana*) of all waters, as the skin is the meeting place of all kinds of touch, as the nose is the meeting place of all smells ... as speech is the meeting place of all *Vedas*.[139]
>
> Now all these have *citta* as their meeting place, *citta* as their *ātman*, they are based in *citta* ... so indeed is *citta* the meeting place of all these, *citta* the *ātman*, *citta* the basis.[140]
>
> Thus do men who know the *Vedas* declare the *dharma* of going to the one (*ekâyanaṃ dharmam*); all those who attain to the appropriate knowledge pass to the way beyond.[141]
>
> He who would be devoted to going to the one (*ekâyane līnaḥ*), in silence, not

[134] BR, s.v. *ekâyana*.

[135] Ein einsamer, abseits gelegener Ort; e.g.: *tad ekâyanam āsādya viṣamaṃ bhīma-darśanam/ bahu-tālocchrayaṃ śṛṅgam āruroha mahā-balaḥ//* (MBh 3.157.33)—'And he reached a rugged, terrible looking desolate place, [and] the peak, many palms in height, the mighty man climbed.'

[136] Vereinigungspunkt.

[137] Sammelpunkt aller Gedanken, Gedankenheit; BR cite only the lexicographers.

[138] Das Aufgehen in Einem, Einheitslehre, Monotheismus.

[139] Bṛh-Up 2.4.11; 4.5.12: *sa yathā sarvāsām apāṃ samudra ekâyanam evaṃ sarveṣāṃ sparśānāṃ tyag ekâyanam evaṃ sarveṣāṃ gandhānāṃ nāsike ekâyanam ... evaṃ sarveṣāṃ vedānāṃ vāg ekâyanam*.

[140] Ch-Up 7.5.2: *tāni ha vā etāni cittaikāyanāni cittâtmāni citte pratiṣṭhitāni ... cittaṃ hy evaiṣām ekâyanaṃ cittam ātmā cittaṃ pratiṣṭhā*. Cf. Ch-Up 7.4.2.

[141] MBh 12.210.28': *evam ekâyanaṃ dharmam āhur veda-vido janāḥ/ yathā jñānam upāsantaḥ sarve yānti parāṃ gatim//*

> thinking on anything, having previously practised renunciation would be one who has crossed over and is free from obstacles.[142]

Böhtlingk and Roth also list *ekâyana* as an adjective and cite by way of example *ekâyano mārgaḥ* in the sense of a footpath that is only wide enough for one. *Prima facie* this would seem to correspond most readily with the Pāli usage in connection with the *satipaṭṭhānas*—but obviously to be understood metaphorically.

Apart from the *ekâyana* formula *PTC* lists only one other occurrence of the expression *ekâyana maggo* in the four primary Nikāyas. This is the *Mahāsīhanāda-sutta*, which uses a series of similes to depict the way in which someone comes to each of the five destinies (*gati*).[143] The passage dealing with the first of these, *niraya*, runs as follows:

> Now I, Sāriputta, perceiving with my mind the mind of some person understand as follows: 'This person has set out thus (*tathā*), he goes along thus, and he has entered upon that path (*tañ ca maggaṃ*). Accordingly (*yathā*) at the breaking up of the body, after death he will arise in a descent, an unhappy destiny, a place of ruin, *niraya*.' After some time I see him, by means of the divine eye that is purified and superhuman, at the breaking up of the body ... arisen in *niraya*, experiencing feelings that are constantly painful, burning, acute. It is as if, Sāriputta, there were a pit of coals more than the height of a man in depth—full of coals without flames and without smoke. And a man might come along scorched by the hot weather, overcome by the hot weather, exhausted, parched, thirsty, heading for that pit of coals by a path that leads to that one place (*ekâyanena maggena tam eva aṅgāra-kāsuṃ paṇidhāya*). A man with sight seeing him would say as follows: 'That good man has set out thus, he goes along thus and has entered upon that path; accordingly he will come right to this pit of coals.' After a time he would see him fallen into that pit of coals experiencing feelings that were constantly painful, burning, acute.[144]

Now one might translate *ekâyanena maggena* in the above passage as 'by a narrow path', yet this would seem to me to lose the force of the image. Miss Horner translates the complete phrase: 'heading direct for that pit of charcoal

---

[142] MBh 14.19.1: *yaḥ syād ekâyane līnas tūṣṇīṃ kiṃcid acintayan/ pūrvaṃ pūrvaṃ parityajya sa tīrṇo nirārambhako bhāvet//* (v.l. *nirālambano*; *tīrṇo bandhanād* = (?) *tīrṇo'bandhanād*). Ch-Up 7.1.2 is also cited by BR in this connection. Translators have usually rendered this on the basis of Śaṃkara's explanation as 'ethics' or 'politics' (*nīti-śāstra*); cf. B. Faddegon, 'The Catalogue of Sciences in the *Chāndogya Upaniṣad*', AO 4 (1926) pp. 42-54. Faddegon considers all the meanings suggested by BR as inappropriate here: 'So the word in our passage stands isolated in its meaning. If I may guess, I should take the word in antithesis with *vākovākya* and explain: "the going by oneself, monologue, uninterrupted recital or exposition".' (Id., p.52.)

[143] M I 73: *nirayo tiracchanayoni pittivisayo manussā devā.*

[144] M I 74: *idhâhaṃ Sāriputta ekaccaṃ puggalaṃ evaṃ cetasā ceto paricca pajānāmi: tathâyaṃ puggalo paṭipanno tathā ca iriyati tañ ca maggaṃ samārūḷho yathā kāyassa bhedā param maraṇā apāyaṃ duggatiṃ vinipātaṃ nirayaṃ upapajjissatī ti. tam enaṃ passāmi aparena samayena dibbena cakkhunā visuddhena atikkanta-mānusakena kāyassa bhedā ... nirayaṃ upapannaṃ ekanta-dukkhā tippā kaṭukā vedanā vediyamānaṃ. seyyathâpi Sāriputta aṅgāra-kāsu sādhika-porisā pūr'aṅgārānaṃ vītaccikānaṃ vīta-dhūmānaṃ, atha puriso āgaccheyya ghammâbhitatto ghamma-pareto kilanto tasito pipāsito ekâyanena maggena tam eva aṅgāra-kāsuṃ paṇidhāya. tam enaṃ cakkhumā puriso disvā evaṃ vadeyya: tathâyaṃ bhavaṃ puriso paṭipanno tathā ca iriyati tañ ca maggaṃ samārūḷho yathā imaṃ yeva aṅgāra-kāsuṃ āgamissatī ti. tam enam passeyya aparena samayena tassā aṅgāra-kāsuyā patitaṃ ekanta-dukkhạ tippā kaṭukā vedanā vediyamānaṃ.*

itself by the one sole way'.[145] This interpretation of *ekâyanena maggena* seems again to be inappropriate in the present context. The point of the image seems to be that someone is seen to be following a particular path that leads to a particular place—and that place only. If one sets out along a particular road, one will inevitably arrive at the place at the end of that road.

Three occurrences of the term *ekâyana* in *Jātaka* verses are of some interest here:

> *sūkarehi samaggehi vyaggho ekâyane hato ti*[146]

The meaning 'going to one' clearly does not fit here, and the commentarial exegesis (*tattha ekâyane hato ti eka-gamasmiṃ yeva hato*) is surely correct: 'The tiger was killed at one charge by the pigs en masse.'

> *ekâyane taṃ pathe addasāsiṃ balena vaṇṇena upeta-rūpaṃ*[147]

Here the meaning of 'narrow' or possibly 'lonely' seems to fit most naturally: 'I saw stretched on that narrow path a form of strength and beauty.'

> *ekâyano eka-patho sarā sobbhā ca passato/*
> *aññaṃ maggaṃ na passāmi yena gaccheyya assamaṃ//*[148]

Here one might take *ekâyana* in the sense of 'only path', reiterated by *eka-patho* and bringing out the force of 'I see no other path'.[149] On the other hand the fact of the lake and pit on either side of the path means that 'narrow' is no less appropriate and this interpretation is suggested by the commentary:[150] 'There is a single narrow path with the lake on one side and the pit on the other; I see no other path by which I might reach the hermitage.'

It seems to me on the basis of this brief survey of the usage of *ekâyana* in Sanskrit and Pāli literature, that the term most commonly expresses two basic ideas. First, a place where only one goes, giving the senses of 'lonely' or 'narrow';[151] secondly the 'going to one'. Given that nowhere is the sense 'one and one only' clearly and definitely the proper sense, and in most cases definitely not, it seems rather perverse to adopt this sense in the *satipaṭṭhāna* context.[152]

At this point it is worth returning to the commentarial exegesis of the *ekâyana* formula, and one should note that even the commentarial explanation of *ekâyana* as a single path as opposed to a forked path (*eka-maggo ... na dvedhā-patha-bhūto*) is not to be interpreted as meaning the 'sole, exclusive' path. The image of the forked path is clearly and unambiguously associated in

---

145 M Trsl I 99.
146 Ja IV 349.
147 Ja V 172-3.
148 Ja VI 557.
149 Cf. M. Cone and R. Gombrich, *The Perfect Generosity of Prince Vessantara*, Oxford, 1977, p. 67.
150 Ja VI 558.
151 This is the sense Edgerton regards as primary (*BHSD*, s.v. *ekâyana*).
152 Conze (*BTI*, pp. 51-2) rejects the 'exclusive' sense, but fails to acknowledge that it is also given in the commentaries.

the texts with doubt (*vicikicchā*).[153] What is being said here is, I think, that the path is unified, clear, well defined and single—not confusing and difficult to follow as the result of forks, and side roads. The notion of exclusivity is in fact associated with what is the rather more contrived explanation of *ekâyana* as that which occurs in just one place; an explanation which, I think, need not be taken seriously for the earlier texts.[154]

In the examples I have given of the usage of *ekâyana* there is evident both an ordinary literal application, and also a quite specific spiritual and mystical application. Accordingly the commentaries feel it appropriate to delve deep into it for hidden meaning. And this is really where our problems start. Once we have identified *ekâyana* as a spiritual and mystical term, it seems to me that it is perhaps inappropriate to look for a single straightforward meaning; the ambiguity of the term may well be relevant already in the Nikāyas. Thus *ekâyana* might be placed alongside such terms as *kevalin*, *tathāgata* and *nibbāna*; that is, it should be included among those terms which embrace a certain range of ideas, and convey certain nuances that would have evoked something of an emotional response in those listening. In short, the term *ekâyana* is untranslatable.

This, of course, is not entirely helpful. However, one of the terms I have just mentioned, namely *kevalin*, is perhaps rather helpful here. In Buddhist and Jaina texts *kevalin* is used of one who has reached the end of spiritual endeavour, and seems to convey some kind of paradoxical notion or 'isolation' or 'separateness' on the one hand, and 'wholeness' or 'unity' on the other.[155] This is rather similar to *ekâyana* as the 'going alone' and the 'going to one'. These, I take it, are the principal notions expressed by *ekâyana* in the *satipaṭṭhāna* context, though the nuance of the path as single and not forked should perhaps also be considered as inherent. One might thus translate the *ekâyana* formula: 'Going straight to the one is this path for the purification of beings ... namely the four establishings of mindfulness.' It might be objected that 'the one' has rather inappropriate overtones of the Upaniṣads, but it is not necessary to attach any absolute metaphysical or ontological significance to such a term in a Nikāya context. What is basically being said is that the four

---

[153] S III 108-9: *dvidhā-patho Tissa vicikicchāya etaṃ adhivacanaṃ*. Dhs 85: *yā tasmiṃ samaye kaṅkhā ... dvedhā-patho ... ayaṃ tasmiṃ samaye vicikicchā hoti*. As 259: *paṭipatti-nīvaraṇena dvedhā-patho viyā ti dvedhā-patho*—'It is a forked path because it prevents arriving [at one's goal], as a forked path does.'

[154] Guṇabhadra's Chinese rendering of the *ekâyana* formula in his translation of the *Saṃyuktāgama* (see *Taisho Shinshu Daizokyo* II 171) suggests confusion or a deliberate equating of *ekâyana* and *eka-yāna* (*yi ch'eng*) and thus introduces a further range of associations from later Buddhist literature (I am grateful to Dr Stuart MacFarlane for this information); cf. L. Hurvitz, 'Fa-Sheng's Observations on the Four Stations of Mindfulness' in *Mahāyāna Buddhist Meditation: Theory and Practice*, ed. Minoru Kiyota, Honolulu, 1978. p. 212. D. Seyfort Ruegg has raised the question of a relationship between *ekâyana* and *eka-yāna*: 'Si la doctrine de l'*ekayāna* proprement dit est surtout mahāyāniste, la notion de l'unicité de la voie n'est pas entièrement inconnue aux Nikāya/Āgama. Quelques-unes de ces sources scripturaires emploient le terme d'*ekâyana* pour désigner la seule voie menant directement et sûrement au but unique autrement dit au *nirvāṇa*; c'est ainsi que les quatre *satipaṭṭhāna* constituent la voie unique de la purification des êtres animés.' (*La Théorie du Tathāgatagarbha et du Gotra*, Paris, 1969, p. 178, n. 1).

[155] See MW, *PED*, s.vv. *kevala*, *kevalin*.

satipaṭṭhānas represent a path that leads straight and directly all the way to the final goal. As the opening formula of the *(Mahā-)Satipaṭṭhāna-sutta*, this balances rather nicely with the concluding formula that states that what issues from the practice of the *satipaṭṭhānas* is one of two fruits, knowledge or the state of non-return.

Why is it, then, that in the four primary Nikāyas the four *satipaṭṭhānas*, alone of the seven sets, are given the epithet *ekâyano maggo*? Possibly it should be viewed as an accident that is put right in the *Niddesa*. But given that so much of the Nikāya treatment of the seven sets is held in common, the restriction of the epithet to the *satipaṭṭhānas* seems rather too pointed. So what is the peculiar and special quality of the *satipaṭṭhānas*?

According to the commentary, the *(Mahā-)Satipaṭṭhāna-sutta's* account concerns the repeated practice of the *satipaṭṭhānas* during the stages of ordinary (*lokiya*) calm and insight meditation prior to the arising of the transcendent path (*lokuttara-magga*), which endures for only one moment before giving way to the transcendent 'fruit' consciousness (*phala-citta*).[156] In this connection the commentary recalls a discussion that arose between two elders, a certain Tipiṭaka-Cūḷanāga and his teacher, Tipiṭaka-Cūḷasumma.[157] According to the former in the *(Mahā-)Satipaṭṭhāna-sutta* only 'the path of prior-stage *satipaṭṭhāna*' (*pubba-bhāga-satipaṭṭhāna-magga*, i.e. the ordinary path *prior* to the arising of the transcendent path)[158] is indicated; according to the latter 'the mixed path' (*missaka-magga*, i.e. both ordinary and transcendent) is indicated. Cūḷasumma apparently then recited the *sutta* from the beginning. When he reached the part which states 'whoever, *bhikkhus*, develops these four *satipaṭṭhānas* in this way for seven years ... ' he realized, the story goes, that it could only be the path of the prior-stage (*pubba-bhāga-magga*) that was intended, since 'the transcendent path having arisen certainly does not last for seven years' (*lokuttara-maggo uppajjitvā satta vassāni tiṭṭhamāno nāma natthi*). Although I am unsure how this is to be reconciled with characterization of the *sutta* as the teaching that culminates in *arahant*-ship in twenty-one places, it is of some interest in the present context. I noted above the way in which the commentary sees *ekâyana* as indicating the clear decisiveness and directness of the 'single way' as opposed to the doubt and wavering of the 'forked path'. Appropriately enough, it would seem that the stages prior to the arising of the transcendent path are precisely the domain of doubt, this is where there is a question of doubt.[159] So for the commentaries at least, the *satipaṭṭhānas* are what especially make for the crossing over of doubt, and proceeding directly to the conclusion of the path.

As for the Nikāyas, there is a sense in which, of the seven sets, the four

---

156 See Vism XXII 15.

157 Sv III 744-5; Ps I 230-1.

158 On the *pubba-bhāga-magga* see below, pp. 331-4.

159 Cf. Ps IV 39 which comments on a statement concerning the possibility of dispute about the path and way that 'there is no dispute amongst those who have attained the path, but this is said in connection with the way and path of the prior stage' (*natthi adhigata-maggānaṃ vivādo, pubba-bhāga-maggaṃ pana pubba-bhāga-paṭipadañ ca sandhāy'etaṃ vuttaṃ*). Note also that one who has gained the path of stream attainment is said to abandon the fetter of doubt.

satipaṭṭhānas are the most versatile and universally applicable, a sense in which they are more completely at once an account of the path at its most basic and most advanced. The way in which this is so anticipates my discussion of the remaining sets, but if one supposes for a moment that all one knew of Buddhism was the account of the seven sets in the four primary Nikāyas, the point becomes more or less clear. It is really only with the material associated with the full description of the *satipaṭṭhānas* that any concrete idea of the basic practice of the *bhikkhu* might be obtained; it is really only from this material that one might form an idea of how the *bhikkhu* might be expected to set about beginning his progress along the path. In other words, with the four *satipaṭṭhānas* we have the nearest thing in the four Nikāyas to basic general instruction in Buddhist '[meditation] practice' or *yoga*. As I hope will become clear, the remaining sets concern rather more exclusively what actually issues from that meditation practice and how it progresses—not that these elements are absent from the account of the four *satipaṭṭhānas*.

The reason for this peculiarity of the four *satipaṭṭhānas* would seem to be concerned with the way in which *sati* or 'mindfulness' itself is fundamental and central to the Nikāyas approach to 'yoga'. Edward Conze commented on mindfulness as follows:

> Although traces of it are not altogether absent in other religious and philosophical disciplines, in Buddhism alone mindfulness occupies a central position. If one were asked what distinguishes Buddhism from all other systems of thought, one would have to answer that it is the Dharma-theory and the stress laid on mindfulness ... On occasions it is almost identified with Buddhism itself.[160]

Whether or not one agrees that 'mindfulness' is the peculiar domain of Buddhism in quite the way suggested by Conze, its position of central importance in the Nikāyas can hardly be disputed: 'And mindfulness, *bhikkhus*, I declare to be beneficial always.'[161]

From one perspective the culmination of the Buddhist path is 'awakening' (*bodhi*) which consists in full wisdom or knowledge. Yet the key to unlock this liberating knowledge is, according to the Nikāyas, something rather simple: 'mindfulness' or a certain quality of 'presence of mind' with regard to body, feelings, mind and *dhammas*. For this reason, then, the four *satipaṭṭhānas* embrace a conception of the essentials of Buddhist practice that is clear and direct. In this sense, more than any of the remaining sets, the four *satipaṭṭhānas* provide a description of the path right from basics direct to the final goal and are, it seems, deserving of the epithet *ekâyano maggo*.

7. Conclusion

Finally I should draw attention to a number of miscellaneous treatments of the four *satipaṭṭhānas*. What underlies the first of these is the notion that the *satipaṭṭhānas* always constitute the *bhikkhu's* refuge—they guard and protect

[160] Conze, *BTI*, p. 51.
[161] S V 115: *satiñ ca khvāhaṃ bhikkhave sabbatthikaṃ vadāmi.*

him. This is a theme already noted. Thus the basic *satipaṭṭhāna* formula is several times found in explanation of the following:

> Therefore, Ānanda, you should dwell with yourselves as lamp, with yourselves as refuge, not with some other refuge; with *dhamma* as lamp, with *dhamma* as refuge, not with some other refuge. And how, Ānanda, does a *bhikkhu* dwell with himself as lamp..? In this connection a *bhikkhu* with regard to the body dwells watching body ...[162]

If this should seem to stand in contrast with what was said above concerning the blurring of self and other in connection with the expanded *satipaṭṭhāna* formula, it is perhaps worth citing the following:

> [Thinking,] 'I shall protect myself,' establishing of mindfulness is to be practised; [thinking,] 'I shall protect others,' establishing of mindfulness is to be practised. Protecting oneself, *bhikkhus*, one protects others; protecting others, one protects oneself. How, *bhikkhus*, does one protect others by protecting oneself? By continued practice, by development, by making great ... How, *bhikkhus*, does one protect oneself by protecting others? By patience, by absence of cruelty, by friendliness, by kindness.[163]

Two similes continue the theme of the four *satipaṭṭhānas* as the protection and refuge of the *bhikkhu*. These similes oppose the *satipaṭṭhānas* as the proper 'pasture and own home ground' (*gocaro sako pettiko visayo*) of the *bhikkhu*, to the five classes of sense-desire-object (*kāma-guṇa*) as not the *bhikkhu's* pasture and the ground of others (*agocaro para-visayo*). Thus the fowl that wanders away from the refuge of the clods of earth in a ploughed field is prey to the hawk, just as the *bhikkhu* who wanders from the refuge of the *satipaṭṭhānas* into the domain of the objects of sense-desire is prey to Māra,[164] or as the monkey who is held by the monkey trap by his four limbs and head is at the mercy of the hunter, so the *bhikkhu* capitivated by the objects of sense desire is at the mercy of Māra.[165] It is this way of looking at the *satipaṭṭhānas* that underlies Buddhaghosa's explanation of *satipaṭṭhāna* as the field or pasture of mindfulness (*sati-gocara*). In conclusion two short statements concerning the *satipaṭṭhānas* are worth quoting:

> As a result of the development and making great of the four *satipaṭṭhānas*, when the Tathāgata attains *parinibbāna*, the good *dhamma* is long lasting.[166]

> Those for whom you have compassion, *bhikkhus*, those who judge that there is something to be heard—whether friends, companions, relatives or kinsmen—they

---

[162] D II 100 = S V 154; D III 58, 77; S V 163, 164: *tasmāt ih'Ānanda atta-dīpā viharatha atta-saraṇā anañña-saraṇā dhamma-dīpā dhamma-saraṇā anañña-saraṇā ... kathañ c'Ānanda bhikkhu atta-dīpo viharati ... idh'Ānanda bhikkhu kāye kāyânupassī viharati ...*

[163] S V 169: *attānaṃ bhikkhave rakkhissāmī ti satipaṭṭhānaṃ sevitabbaṃ, paraṃ rakkhissamī ti satipaṭṭhānaṃ sevitabbaṃ. attānaṃ bhikkhave rakkhanto paraṃ rakkhati, paraṃ rakkhanto attānaṃ rakkhati. kathañ ca ... āsevanāya bhāvanāya bahulīkammena ... kathañ ca ... khantiyā avihiṃsāya mettatāya anuddayatāya ...*

[164] S V 146-8.

[165] S V 148-7.

[166] S V 172-3, 174: *catunnaṃ ca kho āvuso satipaṭṭhānānaṃ bhāvitattā bahulīkatattā tathāgate parinibbute sad-dhammo cira-ṭṭhitiko hoti.*

> should be caused to undertake, directed towards, established in the development of the four *satipaṭṭhānas*.[167]

The first echoes something that is in fact said of the seven sets collectively in another context,[168] while the second appears to be peculiar to the *satipaṭṭhānas*. Together they seem to underline the point that if any one of the seven sets can be characterized as setting down the basic prescription for practice of the Buddhist path, it is the four *satipaṭṭhānas*.

---

[167] S V 189: *ye bhikkhave anukampeyyātha ye ca sotabbaṃ maññeyyuṃ mittā vā amaccā vā ñātī vā sālohitā vā te vo bhikkhave imesaṃ catunnaṃ satipaṭṭhānānaṃ bhāvanāya samādapetabbā nivesetabbā patiṭṭhāpetabbā.*

[168] See Chapter 7.2.

CHAPTER TWO

THE RIGHT ENDEAVOURS

1. The basic formula: samma-ppadhāna and samyak-prahāṇa

In a number of places in the Nikāyas and canonical Abhidhamma the four *samma-ppadhānas* are explained by the following formula:

> *idha bhikkhu [i] anuppannānaṃ pāpakānaṃ akusalānaṃ dhammānaṃ anuppādāya chandaṃ janeti vāyamati viriyaṃ ārabhati cittaṃ paggaṇhāti padahati; [ii] uppannānaṃ pāpakānaṃ akusalānaṃ dhammānaṃ pahānāya chandaṃ janeti vāyamati viriyaṃ ārabhati cittaṃ paggaṇhāti padahati; [iii] anuppannānaṃ kusalānaṃ dhammānaṃ uppādāya chandaṁ janeti vāyamati viriyaṃ ārabhati cittaṃ paggaṇhāti padahati; [iv] uppannānaṃ kusalānaṃ dhammānaṃ ṭhitiyā asammosāya bhiyyobhāvāya vepullāya bhāvanāya pāripūriyā chandaṃ janeti vāyamati viriyaṃ ārabhati cittaṃ paggaṇhāti padahati.*[1]

> In this connection a *bhikkhu* [i] generates purpose, strives, initiates strength, takes hold of his mind, endeavours for the sake of the non-arising of bad, unskilful *dhammas* that have not arisen; [ii] he generates the purpose, strives, initiates strength, takes hold of his mind, endeavours for the sake of abandoning bad unskilful *dhammas* that have arisen; [iii] he generates purpose, strives, initiates strength, takes hold of his mind, endeavours for the sake of the arising of skilful *dhammas* that have not (yet) arisen; [iv] he generates purpose, strives, initiates strength takes hold of his mind, endeavours for the sake of establishing, of not losing, of increase, of abundance, of development, of fulfilment of skilful *dhammas* that have arisen.

Buddhist Sanskrit sources evidence an almost exactly parallel formula explaining four *samyak-prahāṇas*:

> *[i] anutpannānāṃ pāpakānām akuśalānāṃ dharmāṇām anutpādāya chandaṃ janayati [ii] utpannānāṃ pāpakānām akuśalānāṃ dharmāṇāṃ prahāṇāya chandaṃ janayati [iii] anutpannānāṃ kuśalānāṃ dharmāṇām utpādāya chandaṃ janayati [iv] utpannānāṃ kuśalānāṃ dharmāṇāṃ sthitāya'bhūyobhāvāya asampramoṣāya paripūraṇāya chandaṃ janayati vyayacchate vīryam ārabhati cittaṃ pragṛhnāti samyak pradadhāti.*[2]

As in the case of *satipaṭṭhāna* and *smṛty-upasthāna*, Pāli and Sanskrit

[1] D III 221; M II 11; S V 244; A II 15; IV 462; Vibh 208.

[2] E.g. *Mahāvyutpatti* 16; Lamotte (*Traité*, III 1123) quotes a version from the *Pañcaviṃśati* that parallels the Pāli more closely; the form of the final verb is sometimes given as *praṇidadhāti* (cf. my comments below). The order of the four parts of this formula is not always the same in Buddhist Sanskrit literature (a fact not noted by Lamotte); parts [i] and [ii] are sometimes inverted (e.g. Artha 29); this also seems to be the order followed by Abhidh-dī 358 and assumed by Abhidh-k 328, which comments: 'For certain things, like the *smṛty-upasthānas*, the *dhyānas*, etc., the [order of] teaching conforms with arising; for certain things, like the *samyak-prahāṇas*, it conforms with explanation, for it is not a fixed rule that one first generates desire for the abandoning of arisen things and afterwards for the non-arising of unarisen things.' (*keṣāṃcid utpatty-anukūlā deśanā. yathā smṛty-upasthāna-dhyānâdīnām. keṣāṃcit prarūpaṇânukūlā deśanā yathā samyak-prahāṇānāṃ, na hy eṣa niyamo yat pūrvam utpannānāṃ prahāṇāya cchandaṃ janayati, paścād anutpannānām anutpādāyeti.*)

sources reveal a discrepancy in the form of a term designating a parallel formula. The Pāli form is, then, *samma-ppadhāna* or 'right endeavour', while the Sanskrit equivalent appears to be *samyak-prahāṇa* or 'right abandoning'. Certainly 'four right endeavours' would appear to fit better as a general description of the formula than 'four right abandonings', since all four parts of the formula speak of one who endeavours (*padahati/pradadhāti*) while only the second part explicitly mentions abandoning (*pahānāya/prahāṇāya*). The Sanskrit version even says 'rightly endeavours' (*samyak pradadhāti/praṇidadhāti*).

A further factor that seems to count against *samyak-prahāṇa* as being a correct interpretation of an underlying original term, is that Sanskrit sources do in fact in one or two instances cite four *samyak-pradhānas*. Thus, for example, the *Mahāvastu* has the phrase, 'the four *samyak-pradhānas* are my horses'.[3] Yaśomitra's *Kośa-vyākhyā* also glosses *samyak-prahāṇa* by *samyak-pradhāna*,[4] while Vasubandhu seems to offer an explanation of *samyak-prahāṇa* (or *-pradhāna*)[5] in terms of *pra-dhā* and not *pra-hā* when he says that *vīrya* is called *samyak-prahāṇa* (or *-pradhāna*) because 'by means of it body, speech and mind are properly applied' (*tena hi samyak kāya-vāg-manāṃsi pradhīyante*).[6] Chinese translations of Buddhist texts witness both 'endeavour' and 'abandoning'.[7] Furthermore the Buddhist Sanskrit exegetical tradition is apparently unanimous in identifying four *samyak-prahāṇas/-pradhānas* with 'strength' (*vīrya*), in exactly the same way as the Pāli tradition does *samma-ppadhāna*.[8]

In the light of all this, the most straightforward explanation of the discrepancy between the Pāli and Sanskrit forms seems to be to consider *samyak-prahāṇa* as an incorrect back-formation based on a Middle Indo-Aryan form such as *samma-ppahāna* which might equally correspond to Sanskrit *samyak-prahāṇa* or *samyak-pradhāna*.[9]

Although this largely explains how the discrepancy might have arisen, it leaves the question of why it arose unanswered. After all, the notion of endeavour and application is given considerable prominence in the formula, not just with the verb *padahati/pradadhāti,* but also with the whole recurring

---

[3] *Mahāvastu* III 165: *samyak-pradhānā caturo me aśvā*. The Skt fragments of the *Dharmaskandha* also witness *samyak-pradhāna* (*Fragmente des Dharmaskandha*, ed. S. Dietz, Göttingen, 1984, p. 52).

[4] See Lamotte, *Traité* III 1123.

[5] Abhidh-k 384. Pradhan's text in fact reads *-pradhāna*, but is emended by the compilers of the index to *-prahāṇa* (Abhidh-k Index 435); the general authority for their corrigenda are the Tibetan and Chinese versions and Yaśomitra (id., p. 427); cf. Abhidh-k Trsl IV 281, n. 2.

[6] Cf. Arthan-n 214, which gives *-prahāṇa* and then comments on *-pradhāna* in very similar terms to the *Kośa*: *katamāni catvāri samyak-prahāṇāni. samyak kāya-vāg-manāṃsi dhārayantīti pradhānāni.* Abhidh-dī 358 also gives both *-prahāṇa* and *-pradhāna*.

[7] Lamotte, *Traité*, III 1123: 'Dans les sources pāli, *sammappadhāna*, "efforts corrects"; dans les sources sanskrites, *samyakprahāṇa*, "destructions correctes", traduit en tibétain par *yan dag par sponba* [= abandoning] ... Les traductions chinoises donnent le choix entre *tcheng cheng* ou *tcheng k'in* [= endeavour] d'une part, et *tcheng touan* [= abandoning] d'autre part.'

[8] E.g. Abhidh-h Trsl 194; Abhidh-k 384; Abhidh-sam Trsl 120; Abhidh-dī 358. On identification in Pāli literature, see below.

[9] Cf. Dayal, op. cit., pp. 82-3. Turner (s.v. *pradhānaka*) notes Prakrit *pahāṇa* (chief) corresponding to Pāli *padhāna*, and (s.v. *prahāṇa*) Prakrit *pahāṇa* (abandoning) corresponding to Pāli *pahāna*.

refrain: *chandaṃ janeti vāyamati viriyaṃ ārabhati cittaṃ paggaṇhāti padahati/ chandaṃ janayati vyayacchate vīryam ārabhate cittaṃ pragṛhnāti samyak pradadhāti.* Why, in a context that seems so obviously to point towards the notion of four 'endeavours', should a Middle Indo-Aryan form, albeit ambiguous out of context, have been construed in such a way as to give *samyak-prahāṇa* or 'right abandoning'? Is it simply a question of misunderstanding on the part of a rather obtuse ancient monk or group of monks? Such an explanation would appear to be historically inadequate.

As I have already indicated, an understanding in terms of right endeavour was not entirely lost to the northern Buddhist tradition. Curiously, embedded in the exegesis of the term *samma-ppadhāna* found in the Pāli commentaries is an explanation that reflects the notion of abandoning. I shall consider this commentarial treatment fully below; for the moment it will suffice to note that one explanation that Buddhaghosa offers for *samma* in *samma-ppadhāna* is that it indicates that it is 'something beautiful by virtue of its *forsaking* the ugliness of the defilements'.[10] This explanation occurs within the context of a discussion of the four *samma-ppadhānas* as constituents of the transcendent mind (*lokuttara-citta*). The point seems to be that in this context *samma-ppadhāna* is to be understood as in some sense the strength or application of the mind that forms the basis which actually enables the mind to give up the *kilesas*.

The treatises of the northern tradition generally understand the *samyak-prahāṇas* as characterizing a stage on the path somewhat prior to the arising of the transcendent path, namely the stage of *uṣma-gata*, or 'sparks'.[11] Asaṅga states that the fruit of the development (*bhāvanā-phala*) of the *samyak-prahāṇas/-pradhānas* is the complete abandoning of *dharmas* opposed (*vipakṣa*) to skilful *dharmas*, and the obtaining and growth of *dharmas* that counteract (*pratipakṣa*) unskilful *dharmas*.[12] The stage of *uṣma-gata* is the first of the four states partaking of penetration (*nirvedha-bhāgiya*) and signals the entrance into the path of application (*prayoga-mārga*). Clearly it is seen as marking a significant shift in level for the practitioner. The characterization of this stage as abandoning—though not in the absolute sense of the transcendent path—the grosser obstacles and impediments to the development of full wisdom is not entirely inappropriate.

Another reason for the form *samyak-prahāṇa* might be that the usual Sanskrit usage of *pradadhāti* and *pradhāna* hardly agrees with that of *padahati* and *padhāna* in the Nikāyas. Thus *samyak-pradhāna* according to normal Sanskrit usage does not appear to signify right endeavour or application at all, but rather something along the lines of right or proper chief or principal (thing or person). It is in fact, out of context, a not very clear or sensible Sanskrit word.[13] The uncertainty in the Sanskrit version of the formula concerning the

---

[10] Vism XXII 35: *sobhanaṃ vā taṃ kilesa-virūpatta-vijahanato.*

[11] See below, p. 338.

[12] Abhidh-sam Trsl 120

[13] However, Buddhaghosa does make an effective play on this alternative sense of *padhāna*; see below, p. 79.

form of the closing verb—*pradadhāti* or *praṇidadhāti* —underlines this point; *pra-ṇi-dhā* is found regularly in Sanskrit literature, both Buddhist and non-Buddhist, in senses similar to *padahati* and *padhāna* in the Nikāyas.[14]

In the light of all this, it seems to me that the characterization of this fourfold formula as *samyak-prahāṇa* or 'right abandoning' becomes somewhat more intelligible. The point is that one cannot exclude the possibility that the Buddhist tradition *deliberately* capitalized on the ambiguity of a Middle Indo-Aryan form from an early date—prior to any schism between the Sarvāstivāda and the Theravāda. After all, the Pāli commentaries provide other examples of word-play that works in Pāli but not in Sanskrit.[15] One cannot, then, simply characterize *samyak-prahāṇa* as an 'incorrect' backformation. Although *samma-ppadhāna* must, I think, take precedence over *samyak-prahāṇa* as reflecting the correct primary exegesis, it does seem that the Buddhist tradition as a whole preserves an explanation of the term which focuses on the notion of abandoning. In terms of Buddhist spiritual psychology, one of the significant aspects of *samma-ppadhāna* or *samyak-prahāṇa* was that it was understood as directly facilitating the abandoning of unskilful states either at the moment of attaining the transcendent path or during the prior stages.

2. The samma-ppadhāna formula in the Nikāyas

The *samma-ppadhāna* formula is given as a straightforward explanation of the 'four *samma-ppadhānas*' on some eight occasions in the four primary Nikāyas.[16] The formula is in fact found as frequently in some other context.[17] On several occasions the formula is given in explanation of *sammā-vāyāma* or 'right striving', the sixth factor of the noble eight-factored path.[18] Similarly the formula is also used to explain the faculty of strength (*viriyindriya*).[19] It is perhaps significant that this formula appears to be the standard way of explaining right striving as a factor of the noble eight-factored path—in fact there seems to be no instance where this sixth factor is explained differently. On the other hand, the faculty of strength (*viriyindriya*) and the power of strength (*viriya-bala*) are explained in a variety of ways.[20]

At any rate, one can see in this usage of the formula the beginnings of the procedure whereby the later Abhidhamma works draw up more formal correspondences between the various members of the seven sets. Thus the

---

[14] Cf. BR and MW, s.vv. *pra-dhā* and *pra-ṇi-dhā*.

[15] Cf. the play on *satthar/sattha* as 'teacher'/'caravan (leader)' at Vism VII 49; such a play is hardly appropriate to Sanskrit *śāstṛ/sārtha*. At As 49 there is a play on *citta* as 'mind' (= Skt *citta*) and *citta* as 'varigated' (= Skt *citra*); of course, Pāli also records the sanskritized form *citra*; (*PED*, s.v. *citta* (1)). An example of such a play in the Nikāyas themselves is *satta* as a 'being' (= Skt *sattva*) and *satta* as 'attached' (= Skt *sakta*) at S III 190.

[16] D III 221; M I 11; S V 244; A II 15; IV 462; at S IV 364; A I 39, 295-7, where the seven sets are treated in turn, 'four *samma-ppadhānas*' is implicit in the text; cf. Vibh 208.

[17] D II 312; M II 26-8; III 251; S V 9, 198, 268-9; A II 74, 256.

[18] D II 312; M III 251; S V 9; cf. Vibh 105, 235.

[19] S V 198.

[20] See below, pp. 116-7; 140.

samma-ppadhānas, *sammā-vāyāma*, *viryindriya*, *viriya-bala*, *viriya-sambojjhaṅga* are essentially one, namely *viriya* or 'strength'. Of course the seeds of this are also to be seen in the very wording of the *samma-ppadhāna* formula, where the various recurring phrases characterize endeavour: *vāyamati* corresponds to *sammā-vāyāma; viriyaṃ ārabhati* to *viriya* as an *indriya*, *bala* and *bojjhaṅga*; *padahati* to *samma-ppadhāna* itself. Accordingly, in the *sammappadhāna-vibhaṅga* definitions for all these recurring phrases of the *samma-ppadhāna* formula are found; *vāyamati*, *viriya* and *padahati* are all defined in identical terms, corresponding to the *Dhammasaṅgaṇi* register for *viriya.*[21] For *chanda* there is a distinct definition: *kattukamyatā* or 'desire to act'. This constitutes the first Abhidhamma definition of *chanda,* since there is no register for *chanda* in the *Dhammasaṅgaṇi.*[22] I shall return to this general theme with reference to all seven sets later.

In one *Aṅguttara-nikāya* passage, the four parts of the formula act as explanations of four endeavours (*padhānas*) without the qualification *sammā*. The four parts here represent the endeavour of restraint (*saṃvara-ppadhāna*), the endeavour of abandoning (*pahāna-ppadhāna*), the endeavour of development (*bhāvana-ppadhāna*), and the endeavour of protecting (*anurakkhaṇa-ppadhāna*) respectively.[23] These same four *padhānas* of *saṃvara*, *pahāna*, *bhāvanā* and *anurakkhaṇa* are elsewhere explained rather differently:

> [i] And what is the restraint of endeavour? In this connection a *bhikkhu*, when he sees a visible form with the eye, is not one who seizes upon the particular characteristic, is not one who seizes upon the details, since dwelling with the eye-faculty unrestrained might cause longing and dejection, bad unskilful *dhammas*, to overwhelm him; he therefore engages in restraint, he protects the eye- faculty, he achieves restraint of the eye-faculty. When he hears a sound with the ear ... smells a smell with the nose ... tastes a taste with the tongue ... feels a physical sensation with the body ... experiences a *dhamma* with the mind ... he achieves restraint of the mind-faculty.
>
> [ii] And what is the endeavour of abandoning? In this connection a *bhikkhu* does not harbour thoughts of sensual desire when they have arisen, he abandons them, dispels them, makes an end of them, brings them to a state of destruction. He does not harbour thoughts of hatred ... thoughts of cruelty ... bad unskilful *dhammas* ... he brings them to a state of destruction.
>
> [iii] And what is the endeavour of development? In this connection a *bhikkhu* develops the awakening-factor of mindfulness based on seclusion, based on dispassion, based on cessation, ripening in release. He develops the awakening-factor of *dhamma*-discrimination ... of strength ... of joy ... of tranquillization ... of concentration ... of equipoise.
>
> [iv] And what is the endeavour of protecting? In this connection a *bhikkhu* protects the auspicious sign of concentration when it has arisen—the image of the skeleton, the image of the worm-infested [corpse], the image of the discoloured

---

[21] *viriyârambho nikkamo parakkamo uyyāmo vāyāmo ussāho ussoḷhi thāmo dhiti asithila-parakkamatā anikkhitta-chandatā anikkhitta-dhuratā dhura-sampaggāho viriyaṃ viriyindriyaṃ viriyabalaṃ sammā-vāyāmo.* (See Vibh 208-9, and, e.g. Dhs 22.)

[22] Vibh 208. *Chanda* is one of what the commentaries, referring to Dhs 9, call *yevāpanakadhammas*; see As 132; Vism XIV 133. I shall discuss *chanda* in connection with the *iddhi-pādas*.

[23] A II 74.

[corpse], the image of the rotting [corpse], the image of the decayed [corpse], the image of the bloated [corpse].[24]

Essentially this schema of the four *padhānas* provides each part of the *samma-ppadhāna* formula with a specific and positive content; the difference is of the kind between a general statement of a matter and a specific and particularized statement. Thus, in order to illustrate the practice of the four aspects of *samma-ppadhāna* various themes that feature repeatedly in the Nikāyas are brought together. The endeavour of restraint is characterized by the set formula concerning the guarding of the sense-doors;[25] the endeavour of abandoning focuses on the abandoning of thoughts to do with sensual desire, hatred and cruelty—again a standard theme of the Nikāyas;[26] the endeavour of development is characterized by the development of the factors of awakening (of which more presently); finally the endeavour of protecting is illustrated by the practice of concentration based on the contemplation of ugliness (*asubha*), another sporadic theme of the Nikāyas.[27] The result is that in effect the whole of the Buddhist path is shown as being embraced by the four aspects of *(samma-)ppadhāna*; that is, the four *padhānas* provide an example of a course of practice complete in itself.

A passage from the *Nettippakaraṇa*, on the other hand, gives a different specific content to the *samma-ppadhāna* formula[28]—a specific content that appears to be more particular in its application. Unarisen bad unskilful *dhammas* are thoughts (*vitakka*) concerned with sensual desire (*kāma*), hatred (*vyāpāda*) and cruelty (*vihiṃsā*); arisen bad unskilful *dhammas* are the tendencies (*anusaya*) that constitute the roots of unskilfulness (*akusala-mūla*); unarisen skilful *dhammas* are the spiritual faculties (*indriya*) of the stream-attainer;

---

[24] A II 16-7 (= D III 225): *[i] katamañ ca bhikkhave saṃvara-ppadhānaṃ. idha bhikkhave bhikkhu cakkhunā rūpaṃ disvā na nimitta-ggāhī hoti nânuvyañjana-ggāhī hoti yatvâdhikaraṇaṃ enaṃ cakkhundriyaṃ asaṃvutaṃ viharantaṃ abhijjhā-domanassā pāpakā akusalā dhammā anvassaveyyuṃ; tassa saṃvarāya paṭipajjati rakkhati cakkhundriyaṃ cakkhundriye saṃvaraṃ āpajjati. sotena saddaṃ sutvā ... ghānena gandhaṃ ghāyitvā ... jivhāya rasaṃ sayitvā ... kāyena phoṭṭhabbaṃ phusitvā ... manasā dhammaṃ viññāya ... manindriyaṃ manindriye saṃvaraṃ āpajjati ... [ii] katamañ ca bhikkhave pahāna-ppadhānaṃ. idha bhikkhave bhikkhu uppannaṃ kāma-vitakkaṃ nâdhivaseti pajahati vinodeti vyantikaroti anabhāvaṃ gameti. uppannam vyāpāda-vitakkaṃ ... uppannaṃ vihiṃsā-vitakkaṃ ... uppannuppanne pāpake akusale dhamme ... [iii] katamañ ca bhikkhave bhāvana-ppadhānaṃ. idha bhikkhave bhikkhu sati-sambojjhaṅgaṃ bhāveti viveka-nissitaṃ virāga-nissitaṃ nirodha-nissitaṃ vossagga-pariṇāmiṃ. dhamma-vicaya-sambojjhaṅgaṃ ... viriya-sambojjhaṅgaṃ ... pīti-sambojjhaṅgaṃ ... passaddhi-sambojjhaṅgaṃ ... samādhi-sambojjhaṅgaṃ ... upekkhā-sambojjhaṅgaṃ ... [iv] katamañ ca bhikkhave anurakkhaṇa-ppadhānaṃ. idha bhikkhave bhikkhu uppannaṃ bhaddakaṃ samādhi-nimittaṃ anurakkhati aṭṭhika-saññaṃ puḷavaka-saññaṃ vinīlaka-saññaṃ vipubbaka-saññaṃ vicchiddaka-saññaṃ uddhumātaka-saññaṃ ...*

[25] E.g. D I 70.

[26] For a more elaborate treatment of this theme see the *Dvedhāvitakka-sutta* (M I 114-8) which employs almost identical terminology, e.g.: *so kho ahaṃ bhikkhave uppannuppannaṃ kāma-vitakkaṃ pajahām'eva vinodem'eva byant'eva naṃ akāsiṃ*. (Cf. discussion of *sammā-saṃkappa* below, pp. 191-4.)

[27] E.g. M I 58-9.

[28] Nett 18-9.

finally arisen skilful *dhammas* are the spiritual faculities of the person who is standing on the path (*aṭṭhamaka*).[29]

Another variation on the theme of the four aspects of the *samma-ppadhāna* formula is found in a *Saṃyutta-nikāya* passage:

> In this connection, thinking that the arising in him of unarisen bad unskilful *dhammas* might lead to what is disadvantageous, a *bhikkhu* makes an effort; thinking that his non-abandoning of arisen bad unskilful *dhammas* might lead to what is disadvantageous, he makes an effort; thinking that the non-arising in him of unarisen skilful *dhammas* might lead to what is disadvantageous, he makes an effort; thinking that the ceasing in him of arisen skilful *dhammas* might lead to what is disadvantageous, he makes an effort.[30]

Here, what is essentially the same structure as the *samma-ppadhāna* formula is couched in the most general of terms. An extended commentarial account of *samma-ppadhāna*, found in several places in the *aṭṭhakathās*,[31] quotes this passage, stating that it concerns only the ordinary non-transcendent *lokiya* path in the stages prior to the arising of the transcendent path (*lokuttara-magga*).[32] This is, in effect, a way of saying that this treatment is generally applicable to the processes of spiritual attainment, but cannot be applied to the specific attainment of the transcendent path.

Accordingly unarisen skilful *dhammas* here include not just the transcendent path but also ordinary calm and insight (*samatha-vipassanā*), while 'arisen skilful *dhammas*' here refers only to ordinary calm and insight.[33] Why only to ordinary calm and insight and not also to the transcendent path? Simply because the statement 'the ceasing in him of arisen skilful *dhammas* might lead to what is disadvantageous' cannot apply in the case of transcendent skilful *dhammas*. For ceasing—the non-arising or non-occurrence (*anuppatti*)—of ordinary skilful *dhammas*, such as calm and insight, once arisen may well result in the decline and loss (*parihāni*) of calm and insight. On the other hand, the

[29] The term *aṭṭhamaka* is problematic. *PED* and *CPD* understand as its meaning 'eighth' referring to the person who is *sotâpatti-phala-sacchikiriyāya paṭipanno*, i.e. the 'eighth' of the eight *ariya-puggalas* (cf. Pugg 73). Nowhere, it seems, do we find any mention of the seventh, etc. persons, and as Ñāṇamoli says (Nett Trsl 32, n.) there 'seems no precedent for counting the "eight persons" back'. Further at Nett 49-50 *aṭṭhamaka* describes the *anāgāmin*. Ñāṇamoli suggests (ibid.) *ā-sthā* as the correct etymology but does not demonstrate the evolution of the form *aṭṭhamaka* on this basis. Whatever the difficulties of this, his understanding of the term as equivalent to *paṭipannaka* (one who has entered on the path) must be essentially correct. It seems clear that in practice *aṭṭhamaka* signifies one standing upon the transcendent path, cf. Nett-a (Ce 1921) 95-6 (*aṭṭhamakassā ti sotâpatti-phala-sacchikiriyāya paṭipannassa … aṭṭhamakassā ti anāgāmi-maggaṭṭhassa*) ; Pugg-a 186 (which uses the term *maggaṭṭhaka*); Kv 247-51; Kv-a 68 (which glosses *aṭṭhamaka* by *sotâpatti-maggaṭṭha-puggala*). Buddhist Skt literature records *aṣṭamaka* in the same sense (*BHSD*, s.v. *aṣṭamaka*).

[30] S II 195-7: *idha bhikkhu anuppannā me pāpakā akusalā dhammā uppajjamānā anatthāya saṃvatteyyun ti ātappaṃ karoti. uppannā me pāpakā akusalā dhammā appahīyamānā anatthāya saṃvatteyyun ti ātappaṃ karoti. anuppannā me kusalā dhammā anuppajjamānā anatthāya saṃvatteyyun ti ātappaṃ karoti. uppannā me kusalā dhammā nirujjhamānā anatthāya saṃvatteyyun ti ātappaṃ karoti.* (This appears to be the only occurrence in the four Nikāyas.)

[31] Ps III 243-54; Mp II 43-9; Vibh-a 289-301.

[32] Vibh-a 291: *sā* (sc. *lokiyā sammappadhāna-kathā*) *Kassapa-saṃyutta-pariyāyena lokiya-magga-kkhaṇe veditabbā*. Cf. Ps III 243; Mp II 44.

[33] Vibh-a 291-2: *ettha ca anuppannā kusalā dhammā ti samatha-vipassanā ceva maggo ca uppannā kusalā nāma samatha-vipassanā va*. (Cf. Ps III 244; Mp II 44-5.)

ceasing of the transcendent path once arisen does not entail loss of calm and insight, on the contrary in making way for the fruit it establishes calm and insight; there is no falling away from the calm and insight established by transcendent *dhamma*.[34] The commentarial account then proceeds to recount a number of stories illustrating how ordinary calm and insight is lost and how this leads to disadvantage. In general, the commentarial interpretation of all this is really rather convincing.

So far, then, what stands out particularly clearly here, is the way in which the Nikāya use of the *samma-ppadhāna* formula can—and, I think, must—be seen as reflecting both different scales and different levels of the spiritual path. This is a feature I have already drawn attention to with regard to the *satipaṭṭhānas*, and, as I shall repeatedly try to demonstrate, is of central importance in understanding the Nikāyas' and later Buddhist literature's conception of the seven sets both collectively and individually.

3. *The Samaṇamaṇḍikā-sutta*

Perhaps the most striking of the Nikāya treatments of the *samma-ppadhāna* formula is that found in the *Samaṇamaṇḍikā-sutta*.[35] This treatment quite explicitly uses the *samma-ppadhāna* formula at four successive spiritual levels. The *sutta* opens with the Buddha stating that a person endowed with ten *dhammas* is one who has 'accomplished what is skilful, who has perfect skilfulness, an unconquerable *samaṇa*, attained to the utmost attainment' (*purisa-puggalaṃ sampanna-kusalaṃ parama-kusalaṃ uttama-patti-pattaṃ samaṇaṃ ayojjhaṃ*). The Buddha then begins his exposition of this statement by listing sixteen items in four groups of four that he declares need to be understood (*veditabba*). One needs to understand unskilful moral habits (*akusala-sīla*), from what they originate (*ito-samuṭṭhāna*), where they completely cease (*aparisesā nirujjhanti*), and how one practises in order to be practising for their cessation (*nirodhāya paṭipanno*). In the same way, one should understand skilful moral habits (*kusala-sīla*), unskilful thoughts (*akusala-saṃkappa*), and skilful thoughts (*kusala-saṃkappa*). The details of the exposition of these matters are set out in the adjoining table (p. 77). What is interesting from the present point of view is the overall pattern and the part the *samma-ppadhāna* formula plays in this. In fact the pattern of each of the four groups parallels exactly the structure of the four noble truths: an item is given, next its

---

[34] Spk II 165: '*Nirujjhamānā anatthāya saṃvatteyyuṃ:* they should be understood as *dhammas* such as *sīla*, etc. which because of non-arising by virtue of decline cease and might lead to disadvantage. And herein *lokiya [dhammas]* can decline; there is certainly no decline of *lokuttara [dhammas]*.' (*te sīlâdi-dhammā parihāni-vasena puna anuppattiyā nirujjhamānā anatthāya saṃvatteyyun ti veditabbā. ettha ca lokiyā parihāyanti, lokuttarānaṃ parihāni natthī ti.*) Vibh-a 292: 'Now the [transcendent] path having arisen just once ceases, certainly not as something leading to disadvantage; for it ceases only having provided the condition for the [transcendent] fruit.' (*maggo pana sakiṃ uppajjitvā nirujjhamāno anatthāya saṃvattanako nāma natthi. so hi phalassa paccayaṃ datvā va nirujjhati.*) Cf. Ps III 244; Mp II 45.

[35] M II 22-9.

TABLE 1. THE SCHEMA OF THE SAMAṆAMAṆḌIKĀ-SUTTA

A	1.	*ime akusala-sīlā*	*akusala-kāya-, vāci-, mano-kamma; pāpaka-ājīva*
	2.	*ito-samuṭṭhāna*	*citta: sarāga, samoha, sadosa*
	3.	*idha aparisesā nirujjhanti*	*kāya-duccaritaṃ...pahāya, kāya-sucaritaṃ...bhāveti*
	4.	*evaṃ paṭipanno akusalānaṃ sīlānaṃ nirodhāya paṭipanno*	***samma-ppadhāna*** formula
B	1.	*ime kusala-sīlā*	*kusala-kāya-, vāci-, mano-kamma; ājīva-parisuddhi*
	2.	*ito-samuṭṭhāna*	*citta: vīta-rāga, vīta-moho, vīta-dosa*
	3.	*idha aparisesā nirujjhanti*	*sīlavā hoti...tañ ca ceto-vimuttiṃ...pajānāti*
	4.	*evaṃ paṭipanno kusalānaṃ sīlānaṃ nirodhāya paṭipanno*	***samma-ppadhāna*** formula
C	1.	*ime akusala-saṃkappā*	*kāma-, vyāpāda-, vihiṃsā-saṃkappa*
	2.	*ito-samuṭṭhāna*	*kāma-, vyāpāda-, vihiṃsā-saññā*
	3.	*idha aparisesā nirujjhanti*	first *jhāna*
	4.	*evaṃ paṭipanno akusalānaṃ saṃkappānaṃ nirodhāya paṭipanno*	***samma-ppadhāna*** formula
D	1.	*ime kusala-saṃkappā*	*nekkhamma-, avyāpāda-, avihiṃsā-saṃkappa*
	2.	*ito-samuṭṭhāna*	*nekkhamma-, avyāpāda-, avihiṃsā-saññā*
	3.	*idha aparisesā nirujjhanti*	second *jhāna*
	4.	*evaṃ paṭipanno kusalānaṃ saṃkappānaṃ nirodhāya paṭipanno*	***samma-ppadhāna*** formula

origination is considered, followed by the question of its ceasing, and the practice that brings this about.[36]

So what is the significance of the repetition of the *samma-ppadhāna* formula as the exposition of the fourth part (the part, if one is to think in terms of the four noble truths, that is usually explained by reference to the noble eight-factored path)? As will be seen later, in the light of the treatment of the seven sets in the *Saṃyutta-nikāya* it is tempting to think that an exposition of any one of the seven sets might have been appropriate here, and that the substitution of another of the sets for the *samma-ppadhāna* formula would not do serious damage to the main purpose of this *sutta*. However, the repeated use of the *samma-ppadhāna* formula in this context is not, it seems to me, without a particular character and quality of its own. If one considers the details of each of the four sections a little more closely, one sees that coming to understand the origination of a particular set of items is said to lead on to a particular achievement—an achievement which constitutes the cessation of the set of items in question. In the first section the *bhikkhu* succeeds in abandoning bad conduct and developing good conduct; in the second he becomes endowed with good moral habit (*sīlavant*) and knows the subsequent freedom of mind (*ceto-vimutti*); in the third he attains the first *jhāna*; finally, in the fourth, he attains the second *jhāna*. In each instance what brings about and supports the ceasing of the given set of items, what facilitates the particular achievement, is the practice of the four aspects of *samma-ppadhāna* (not, however, referred to by name). This use of the formula, then, seems to fit in well with a general picture of the *samma-ppadhānas*— and indeed *viriya* itself—as essentially that which supports and sustains any particular achievement. This notion of *viriya* as that which supports is vividly taken up in the *Milindapañha*:

> Just as, Your Majesty, a man might shore up a house that was falling down with an extra piece of wood, and being thus shored up that house would not fall down. Even so, your majesty, *viriya* has the characteristic of shoring up; shored up by *viriya* no skilful *dhammas* are lost.[37]

4. *Commentarial definitions of* viriya *and* samma-ppadhāna

The above exposition of the *samma-ppadhāna* formula in the Nikāyas is consistent with the explanations of *samma-ppadhāna* and *viriya* offered by the commentaries. These explanations are best viewed as drawing out and further developing the implications of the Nikāya treatment. The standard definition of *viriya* in the *Visuddhimagga* reads as follows:

> *Viriya* is the state of a hero. Its characteristic is exertion, its function is the supporting of conascent [*dhammas*], its manifestation is a state of non-collapse. Since it is said [by the Blessed One] that one who is stirred endeavours properly, its proximate cause is what stirs; alternatively its proximate cause is any ground for

[36] Cf. the verbal parallels between the truths and the *Samaṇamaṇḍikā-sutta* treatment: *samudaya/samuṭṭhāna; nirodha/nirujjhanti; nirodha-gāminī-paṭipadā/nirodhāya paṭipanno.*

[37] Mil 36: *yathā mahā-rāja puriso gehe patante aññena dārunā upatthambheyya upatthambhitaṃ santaṃ evaṃ taṃ gehaṃ na pateyya, evaṃ eva kho mahā-rāja upatthambhana-lakkhaṇaṃ viriyaṃ viriyupatthambhitā sabbe kusalā dhammā na parihāyantī ti.*

> the instigation of *viriya*. Rightly instigated it should be seen as the root of all attainments.[38]

Here, then, *viriya* is seen as the strength and mental resolve that supports and maintains various kinds of spiritual achievement—at least in its skilful manifestations.

Buddhaghosa also provides the following exegesis of the term *samma-ppadhāna*:

> It is *padhāna* in that by means of it they endeavour (*padahanti*); *samma-ppadhāna* is beautiful *padhāna*; either it is *samma-ppadhāna* in that by means of it they endeavour rightly, or it is *samma-ppadhāna* in that it is beautiful because of forsaking the ugliness of the defilements, and *padhāna* because of producing (*nipphadakatta*) welfare and happiness due to bringing about the state of being best and causing the state of being chief (*padhāna*). It is a term for strength. It is fourfold in that it accomplishes the functions of abandoning and non-arising for arisen and unarisen unskilful [*dhammas*] [respectively], and the functions of arising and maintenance of unarisen and arisen skilful [*dhammas*] [respectively]. Therefore 'four *sammappadhānas*' are spoken of.[39]

The explanation here plays upon the diverse meanings of *padhāna*. To begin with, *padhāna* can be understood simply as indicating endeavour; this is its usual and normal meaning in Pāli literature. However, as has already been noted, *padhāna* corresponding to Sanskrit *pradhāna* can have another range of meanings—the normal meanings in Sanskrit literature. A *pradhāna* is, then, the chief or principal thing or person; as an adjective it signifies chief or most important. Furthermore, in Sāṃkhya theory *pradhāna* is used as a term for *prakṛti* or the primary ground from which the world of experience originates.[40] Buddhaghosa's explanation seems to reflect these kinds of usage: *samma-ppadhāna* is beautiful; it is the originator of welfare and happiness, and it brings about the state of a chief. In this Buddhaghosa echoes the understanding of *viriya* as the state of a hero and as the root of all attainments: *samma-ppadhāna* forms the basis for the abandoning of the defilements which are detrimental to welfare and happiness, and as a result one achieves the best state, one is a chief. Dhammapāla gives essentially the same explanation, although worded slightly differently:

> It is *samma-ppadhāna* in that they endeavour rightly by means of it, or it itself endeavours rightly; it is commendably or beautifully endeavouring. Alternatively,

---

[38] Vism XIV 137: *vīra-bhāvo viriyaṃ taṃ ussāhana-lakkhaṇaṃ, sahajātānaṃ upatthambhana-rasaṃ, asaṃsīdana-bhāva-paccupaṭṭhānaṃ, saṃviggo yoniso padahatī ti* [A II 115] *vacanato saṃvega-pada-ṭṭhānaṃ viriyârambha-vatthu-pada-ṭṭhānaṃ vā. sammā āraddhaṃ sabba-sampattīnaṃ mūlaṃ hotī ti daṭṭhabbaṃ*. (Cf. As 120-1, which also quotes similes found at Mil 36-7.)

[39] Vism XXII 35: *padahanti etenā ti padhānaṃ; sobhanaṃ padhānaṃ samma-ppadhānaṃ: sammā vā padahanti etenā ti samma-ppadhānaṃ; sobhanaṃ vā taṃ kilesa-virūpatta-vijahanato padhānañ ca hita-sukha-nipphadakattena seṭṭha-bhāvâvahanato padhāna-bhāva-karaṇato cā ti samma-ppadhānaṃ. viriyass'etaṃ adhivacanaṃ. tayidaṃ uppannânuppannānaṃ akusalānaṃ pahānânu-ppatti-kiccaṃ anuppannuppannānañ ca kusalānaṃ uppatti-ṭhiti-kiccaṃ sādhayatī ti catubbidhaṃ hoti, tasmā cattāro samma-ppadhānā ti vuccati*. (The correct reading of this passage is difficult to determine, it occurs with variations at Paṭis-a I 97; III 618; Nidd-a I 66.)

[40] BR and MW, s.v. *pra-dhāna*.

it is *samma-ppadhāna* because it correctly causes a state of being chief for a person. It is a term for *viriya*.[41]

The material dealt with in this chapter more or less exhausts the Nikāya treatment of the four *samma-ppadhānas* and the *samma-ppadhāna* formula outside the context of the seven sets; *samma-ppadhāna* in the context of the seven sets will be dealt with later. For the sake of completeness at this point one should also note the following. Along with the four *satipaṭṭhānas* and four *iddhi-pādas*, the four *samma-ppadhānas*, or rather the four parts of the formula, are said to constitute four *dhammas* to be developed (*bhāvetabba*) in an *Aṅguttara-nikāya* passage of the *catun-nipāta*.[42] The formula is also employed in a Nikāya passage explaining the *iddhi-pāda* formula; this will be considered in the next chapter.[43]

---

[41] Ud-a 304: *sammā padahanti etena sayaṃ vā sammā padahati; pasatthā sundarā vā padahanan ti samma-ppadhānaṃ. puggalassa vā samma-d-eva padhāna-bhāva-karaṇato samma-ppadhānaṃ. viriyass'etaṃ adhivacanaṃ.*

[42] A II 256.

[43] The following summarizes the uses of the *samma-ppadhāna* formula in the four primary Nikāyas: four *samma-ppadhānas* (D III 221; M II 11; S V 244; IV 364; A I 39, II 15, IV 462); *sammā-vāyāma* (= *maggaṅga*) (D II 312; M III 251; S V 9); *viriyindriya* (S V 198); others (M II 26-8; S V 268-9; A II 256, 74); variations (D III 221; S II 195-7; A II 16-7).

CHAPTER THREE

THE BASES OF SUCCESS

1. The basic formula

In the Pāli canon four *iddhi-pādas* are frequently cited by means of the following stock formula:

> *cattāro iddhi-pādā. katame cattāro. idha bhikkhave bhikkhu [i] chanda-samādhi-padhāna-saṃkhāra-samannāgataṃ iddhi-pādaṃ bhāveti. [ii] viriya-samādhi-padhāna-saṃkhāra-samannāgataṃ iddhi-pādaṃ bhāveti. [iii] citta-samādhi-padhāna-saṃkhāra-samannāgataṃ iddhi-pādaṃ bhāveti. [iv] vīmaṃsā-samādhi-padhāna-saṃkhāra-samannāgataṃ iddhi-pādaṃ bhāveti.*[1]

This formula is not immediately intelligible or self-explanatory, but fortunately the Nikāyas preserve an analysis of it in the *iddhi-pāda-saṃyutta.*[2] The passage in question begins by defining *chanda-samādhi*:

> If a *bhikkhu* gains concentration, gains one-pointedness of mind depending on desire [to act], this is called *chanda-samādhi.*[3]

The analysis continues by citing the four parts of the *samma-ppadhāna* formula in full, with the concluding comment that 'these are called forces of endeavour' (*ime vuccanti padhāna-saṃkhārā*). Finally the nature of the first *iddhi-pāda* is summed up as follows:

> There is thus this *chanda*, this *chanda-samādhi* and these *padhāna-saṃkhāras*; this, *bhikkhus*, is called the *iddhi-pāda* that is furnished with *chanda-samādhi-padhāna-saṃkhāra.*[4]

Each of the remaining three *iddhi-pādas* is analyzed in an exactly parallel fashion. This allows us to translate the basic *iddhi-pāda* formula as follows:

> Here a *bhikkhu* develops the basis of success that is furnished both with concentration gained by means of desire to act, and with forces of endeavour; he develops the basis of success that is furnished both with concentration gained by means of strength, and with forces of endeavour; he develops the basis of success that is furnished both with concentration gained by means of mind, and with forces of endeavour; he develops the basis of success that is furnished both with concentration gained by means of investigation, and with forces of endeavour.

This may remain rather obscure, but the *iddhi-pāda-saṃyutta* analysis makes it clear that a 'basis of success' or 'basis of growth' is here conceived of

---

1 D II 213-4; III 77, 221; M I 103; II 11; S IV 365; V 254-93 passim; A I 39, 297; II 256, III 81-2; IV 464; Vibh 216; Paṭis I 111, 113; II 205. (For the 'bases of success' formula in Buddhist Sanskrit sources see section six of this chapter.)

2 S V 268-9.

3 *chandaṃ ce bhikkhu nissāya labhati samādhiṃ labhati cittassa ekaggataṃ, ayaṃ vuccati chanda-samādhi.* (On *chanda* as the 'desire to act', see section five of this chapter.)

4 *iti ayaṃ ca chando ayaṃ ca chanda-samādhi ime ca padhāna-saṃkhārā. ayaṃ vuccati bhikkhave chanda-samādhi-padhāna-saṃkhāra-samannāgato iddhi-pādo.*

as consisting in an interplay of three basic things: meditative concentration, forces of endeavour (identified with the four right endeavours or, more simply, strength) and the particular means by which meditative concentration is gained, namely the desire to act, strength, mind, or investigation. An *iddhi-pāda* is not so much any one of these three things in particular as the interaction between them.

2. *The iddhi-pāda-saṃyutta*

The basic analysis of the *iddhi-pāda* formula that has just been considered provides some idea of the conception of the *iddhi-pādas* in the Nikāyas. But what precisely is the place of the *iddhi-pādas* in Buddhist spiritual practice as a whole? How are they to be understood in the context of the path to awakening? As far as the four primary Nikāyas are concerned, the treatment of the *iddhi-pādas* is certainly concentrated in the *iddhi-pāda-saṃyutta*, and this is the most convenient place to pursue such an enquiry into their nature.

Several times in the *iddhi-pāda-saṃyutta* we find a set explanation of the following: *iddhi*, *iddhi-pāda*, *iddhi-pāda-bhāvanā* and *iddhi-pāda-bhāvanā-gāminī paṭipadā*.[5] Thus *iddhi* is explained by the following stock description of eightfold *iddhi*:

> A *bhikkhu* enjoys various kinds of *iddhi*: [i] being one he becomes many, being many he becomes one; [ii] unhindered he passes into a visible state, into an invisible state, [iii] through house-walls, through city-walls and through mountains, as if through space; [iv] he goes down into the earth and comes up, as if through water; [v] he goes over firm water, as though over earth; [vi] he travels through the sky cross-legged, as if he were a bird with wings; [vii] he touches and strokes with his hand the sun and moon, [things] of such great *iddhi* and such great power; [viii] he holds mastery with his body as far as the world of Brahmā.[6]

Next, *iddhi-pāda* is explained as 'that path or way that conduces to the gaining of *iddhi*, the repeated gaining of *iddhi*' (*yo maggo yā paṭipadā iddhi-lābhāya iddhi-paṭilābhāya saṃvattati*); *iddhi-pāda-bhāvanā* or 'the development of *iddhi-pāda*' is explained by the basic *iddhi-pāda* formula; finally *iddhi-pāda-bhāvanā-gāminī paṭipadā* or 'the way leading to the development of *iddhi-pāda*' is explained as the noble eight-factored path (*ariyo aṭṭhaṅgiko maggo*).

This explanation of these four expressions is significant in two ways. First, it is clear that the notion of the *iddhi-pādas* is consistently and directly linked to the stock description of eightfold *iddhi* in the Nikāyas—in fact this stock

---

[5] S V 276, 285-8 (× 4).

[6] The passages in question abbreviate this stock formula; for the full text see, e.g., S V 264: *bhikkhu ... anekavihitaṃ iddhi-vidhaṃ paccanubhoti. eko pi hutvā bahudhā hoti, bahudhā pi hutvā eko hoti; āvībhāvaṃ tiro-bhāvaṃ tiro-kuddaṃ tiro-pākāraṃ tiro-pabbataṃ asajjamāno gacchati seyyathā pi ākāse; paṭhaviyā pi ummujja-nimmujjaṃ karoti seyyathā pi udake; udake pi abhijjamāne gacchati seyyathā pi paṭhaviyā; ākāse pi pallaṅkena kamati seyyathā pi pakkhī sakuṇo; ime pi candima-suriye evaṃ mahiddhike evaṃ mahânubhāve pāṇinā parimasati parimajjati; yāva brahma-lokā pi kāyena va saṃvatteti.* (Vism XII 69 takes *āvībhāvaṃ tiro-bhāvaṃ* as involving a distinct *iddhi* which gives a list of eight *iddhis*; the syntax of the Nikāya formula might be read as suggesting only seven distinct *iddhis*.)

description occurs on no less than fifteen occasions in the *iddhi-pāda-saṃyutta.*[7] Secondly, the linking of the development of the *iddhi-pādas* to the noble eight-factored path brings the *iddhi-pādas* right into the main stream of spiritual practice as understood in the Nikāyas. In this connection one must note that, in addition to being frequently linked to eightfold *iddhi*, the *iddhi-pādas* are also linked on some sixteen occasions to the destruction of the *āsavas*, or of *dukkha.*[8] Thus it is said that Moggallāna and the Tathāgata enjoy eightfold *iddhi* as a result of developing and making great the four *iddhi-pādas*; but at the same time it is also said that as a result of making great and developing the four *iddhi-pādas* they attain and dwell in the liberation of mind that is without *āsavas.*[9] Of course, an understanding of the *iddhi-pādas* as something fundamental to the path to awakening would appear to be already inherent in their being included in the list of the seven sets. What is of interest, then, is the relationship in the Nikāyas between the specific notion of eightfold *iddhi* and the more general notion of *iddhi* as 'success' or 'spiritual growth'.

A considerable proportion of the *iddhi-pāda-saṃyutta* appears to be concerned with the analysis of the *iddhi-pādas* as skill in meditation technique; that is to say, what is emphasized is 'the gaining of success, the repeated gaining of success' and the particular skills that are needed if this is to be accomplished. In this connection we find an extended *iddhi-pāda* formula:

> Here, *bhikkhus*, a *bhikkhu* develops the *iddhi-pāda* that is furnished both with *chanda-samādhi* and *padhāna-saṃkhāras*: 'The desire to act in me will not be too slack; it will not be dispersed without.' He dwells conscious of after and before; as before, so after; as after, so before; as below, so above; as above, so below; as by day, so by night; as by night, so by day. Thus by means of an open and untrammelled mind he develops a shining consciousness.[10]

This is then repeated three more times for the remaining *iddhi-pādas*, substituting 'strength' (*viriya*), 'mind' (*citta*) and 'investigation' (*vīmaṃsā*) in turn for 'the desire to act' (*chanda*).

One version of this extended formula adds some further explanations in a form similar to the 'word analysis' (*pada-bhājaniya*) found in the *Vinaya-piṭaka*, the *Niddesa* and *Vibhaṅga.*[11] *Chanda* that is too slack is *chanda* associated with idleness (*kosajja*); *chanda* that is too vigorous is *chanda* associated with restlessness (*uddhacca*); *chanda* that is withdrawn within is *chanda* associated with sleepiness and drowsiness (*thīna-middha*); *chanda* that is dispersed without is *chanda* dispersed after the five kinds of object of sense-desire (*pañca-kāma-guṇe ārabbha anuvikkhitto anuvisaṭo*). 'Dwelling conscious of after and before' is said to mean that one's *saññā* or 'idea' of after and before is well grasped,

---

7 S V 264, 267, 271, 274, 280, 282, 283, 284, 286 (× 2), 287 (× 2), 288, 289; cf. D II 213.

8 S V 254 (× 2), 255 (× 2), 257, 266, 268, 271, 275, 280, 282, 284, 285 (× 2), 259, 290.

9 S V 288-90.

10 S V 263-4, 264, 271, 276-7, 281: *iti me chando na ca atilīno bhavissati, na ca atipaggahīto bhavissati, na ca ajjhattaṃ saṃkhitto bhavissati, na ca bahiddhā vikkhitto bhavissati. pacchā-pure saññī ca viharati, yathā pure tathā pacchā, yathā pacchā tathā pure, yathā adho tathā uddhaṃ, yathā uddhaṃ tathā adho, yathā divā tathā rattiṃ, yathā rattiṃ tathā divā. iti vivaṭena cetasā apariyonaddhena cetasā sappabhāsaṃ cittaṃ bhāveti.*

11 S V 277-8.

brought to mind well, well remembered, well penetrated by wisdom (*pacchā-pure saññā suggahītā hoti sumanasikatā sudhāritā suppaṭividdhā paññāya*). 'Dwelling as below so above' is explained with reference to contemplation of the various parts of the body from the toes to the crown of the head (described in the same terms as the relevant aspect of *kāyânupassanā*). With regard to 'as by day, so by night' it is explained that by whatever aspects, marks and signs the *bhikkhu* develops the *iddhi-pāda* furnished with *chanda-samādhi-padhāna-saṃkhāra* during the day, he develops it by those same aspects, marks and signs during the night (*yehi ākārehi yehi liṅgehi yehi nimittehi divā chanda-samādhi-padhāna-saṃkhāra-samannāgataṃ iddhi-pādaṃ bhāveti, so tehi ākārehi tehi liṅgehi tehi nimittehi rattiṃ ... bhāveti*). Finally developing a shining consciousness is further explained: the *bhikkhu's* awareness of light is well learnt, his awareness of radiance is well established (*bhikkhuno āloka-saññā suggahītā hoti divā-saññā svādhiṭṭhitā*).[12]

The terminology involved here is in part reminiscent of the description of the preparations for meditation practice and the abandoning of the five hindrances elsewhere in the Nikāyas.[13] The general tenor of the extended formula and its detailed analysis suggest that what we are concerned with is the acquiring of skill and facility in meditation attainment. It is worth noting the particular incidents and circumstances associated with the extended formula in the *iddhi-pāda-saṃyutta*.

In the first place it is given as descriptive of the practice of the Bodhisatta himself prior to his awakening. As a result of developing the *iddhi-pādas* in this way, he develops what are elsewhere called the six *abhiññās* or 'direct knowledges': eightfold *iddhi*, the divine ear (*dibba-sota*), knowledge encompassing the mind [of others] (*ceto-pariya-ñāṇa*), knowledge of the recollection of former lives (*pubbe-nivāsânussati-ñāṇa*), knowledge of the rise and fall of beings (*acutupapatti-ñāṇa*), knowledge of the destruction of the *āsavas* (*āsavānaṃ khaya-ñāṇaṃ*).[14]

Another *sutta*[15] tells how the Buddha requests Moggallāna to stir and

---

[12] I have taken *divā* in *divā-saññā* as a feminine substantive corresponding to Skt *div*, which is usually masculine but which does occur as a feminine in the Vedas and later Skt in the sense of 'heaven' or 'sky' (see MW, s.v. 3. *div*, *dyu*); MW cites the sense of 'brightness' for the masculine in the RV. It is more usual to take *divā* as an adverb, 'by day' (cf. *PED*, s.v. *divā*, which cites further examples of the expression *divā-saññā*), but this seems to make little sense in the present context. Spk III 260 comments: 'A *bhikkhu* sitting down in an open space brings to mind the awareness of light; sometimes he closes his eyes, sometimes he opens them; when he closes them after having had them open and one direction is clear to him as though he were looking around, then the awareness of light is called "arisen". *Divā-saññā* is a name for this too. When this occurs at night it is called "well learnt".' (*yo bhikkhu aṅgane nisīditvā āloka-saññaṃ manasikaroti kālena nimmīleti kālena ummīleti, ath'assa yadā nimmīlentassâpi ummīletvā olokentassa viya eka sadisam eva upaṭṭhāti tadā āloka-saññā jātā nāma hoti. divā-saññā ti pi tass'eva nāmaṃ. sā puna rattiṃ uppajjamānā suggahītā nāma hoti.*) In the *Dīgha* description of the abandoning of the five *nīvaraṇas* prior to the arising of *jhāna*, *āloka-saññā*, along with *sati* and *sampajañña*, is opposed to *thīna-middha* (D I 71).

[13] This is discussed fully in Chapter 5.

[14] S V 263-6; cf. A III 82, which also associates the *iddhi-pādas* with the practice of the *bodhisatta*. Th 233 also links the realization of the six *abhiññās* to the development of the *iddhi-pādas*.

[15] S V 269-71.

arouse (*saṃvejeti*) a group of *bhikkhus* who are described as 'excited, complacent, unsteady, noisy, talking freely, of lost mindfulness, without clear comprehension, unconcentrated, with wandering minds and faculties uncontrolled' (*uddhatā unnaḷā capalā mukharā vikiṇṇa-vācā muṭṭha-ssatino asampajānā asamāhitā vibbhata-cittā pākatindriyā*). Moggallāna then contrives an *iddhi* (*iddhābhisaṃkhāraṃ abhisaṃkhāresi*) such that with his big toe he causes the house in which the *bhikkhus* are staying to shake and tremble. Suitably stirred, the *bhikkhus* then question the Buddha about the incident, who explains that it is through developing the *iddhi-pādas* in the manner described that Moggallāna is of such great power, and dwells in the liberation of mind that is without *āsavas*. The implication is that the development of the *iddhi-pādas* is also the remedy for the *bhikkhus*' lack of mindfulness and concentration.

3. *The suttanta-bhājaniya of the Vibhaṅga*

The *suttanta-bhājaniya* or 'analysis according to Suttanta' of the *iddhi-pāda-vibhaṅga*[16] gives an exposition of the basic *iddhi-pāda* formula that is more or less the same as that given in the *iddhi-pāda-saṃyutta*. It differs in only one or two respects, and adds a basic commentary defining some of the key terms. Where the *Saṃyutta-nikāya* defines *chanda-samādhi* as concentration gained depending on the desire to act (*chandaṃ nissāya*), the *Vibhaṅga* describes it as concentration or one-pointedness of mind gained by making the desire to act the 'overlord' or 'dominant' (*chandaṃ adhipatiṃ karitvā*). The technical notion of *chanda*, *viriya*, *citta* and *vīmaṃsā* as 'dominant' is found developed in the early Abhidhamma literature, but appears to be lacking from the four primary Nikāyas.[17] According to the *Dhammasaṅgaṇi* one of *chanda*, *viriya*, *citta* or *vīmaṃsā* may act as dominant in certain kinds of consciousness.[18] This notion is then found in the *Paṭṭhāna* as the third of the twenty-four conditions (*paccayas*), namely *adhipati-paccaya*.[19] Rather little can be gleaned from the canonical texts concerning the notion of *adhipati*; the *Visuddhimagga* makes the following general comment:

> A *dhamma* that is contributory in the sense of being most powerful is an *adhipati-paccaya* ... The four *dhammas* termed *chanda*, *viriya*, *citta*, *vīmaṃsā* should be understood as *adhipati-paccaya*, but not [all] at once, for when *citta* occurs having made *chanda* the chief, the most powerful, then just *chanda* is the *adhipati* not the others. The method is the same for the others.[20]

To return to the *iddhi-pāda-vibhaṅga*, *padhāna-saṃkhāras* are once more elucidated by reference to the *samma-ppadhāna* formula. The final statement

---

16 Vibh 216-20.

17 Such expressions as *attâdhipatteyya*, *lokâdhipateyya*, *dhammâdhipateyya* (A I 147-9) and *satâdhipateyyā sabbe dhammā* (A IV 338-9; V 106-7) are found in the Nikāyas.

18 See below, p. 320.

19 See Dukap 2.

20 Vism XVII 72: *jeṭṭhakaṭṭhena upakārako dhammo adhipati-paccayo ... chanda-viriya-citta-vīmaṃsā-saṃkhātā cattāro dhammā adhipati-paccayo ti veditabbā, no ca kho ekato, yadā hi chandaṃ dhuraṃ chandaṃ jeṭṭhakaṃ katvā cittaṃ pattati, tadā chando va adhipati, na itare. esa nayo sesesu.*

summing up the *iddhi-pāda* as a whole is slightly different from the *Saṃyutta* version, but does not seem to diverge in intent:

> There is thus this *chanda-samādhi*, these *padhāna-saṃkhāras*; collecting and grouping this together, it is termed *chanda-samādhi-padhāna-saṃkhāra*.[21]

The whole of this initial analysis is given in full for each of the four *iddhi-pādas* (substituting *viriya*, *citta* or *vīmaṃsā* as appropriate). Further definitions of key terms are then appended: of *chanda*, *viriya*, *citta* or *vīmaṃsā*; of *samādhi*, *padhāna-saṃkhāras*, *iddhi* and *iddhi-pāda*. For the most part these consist in simply applying the appropriate *Dhammasaṅgaṇi* register of terms; thus *viriya* and *padhāna-saṃkhāra* are both defined by the full register of terms for *viriya*, *vīmaṃsā* by that for *paññā*, *citta* by that for *citta*, *samādhi* by that for one-pointedness of mind (*cittass'ekaggatā*). *Chanda* is the one term not defined in the *Dhammasaṅgaṇi* and is here glossed as 'purpose, purposiveness, the desire to act, skilful wholesome purpose'.[22] The explanations of 'success' (*iddhi*) and 'basis of success' (*iddhi-pāda*) are worth quoting in full:

> 'Success' is that which of these *dhammas* is success, thorough success, succeeding, thorough succeeding, gaining, regaining, attainment, thorough attaintment, experiencing, realization, accomplishment.[23]

What is interesting about this is that *iddhi* is here taken in rather general terms. If we are to take seriously the Nikāya background to this, where the *iddhi-pādas* are at once associated with eightfold *iddhi* and the ultimate spiritual goal, then the implications of the *Vibhaṅga* definition must be, I think, that eightfold *iddhi* should be seen as nothing different from meditational success in general. That is to say, both eightfold *iddhi* and the liberation of mind that is without *āsavas* are simply two aspects of what is basically one skill or facility of mind. Precisely the same 'success' that allows the *bhikkhu* to develop eightfold *iddhi* allows him to develop the liberation of mind that is without *āsavas*. As for 'basis of success' itself, it is explained as:

> The aggregate of feeling, the aggregate of conception, the aggregate of formations, the aggregate of consciousness of one who is thus [i.e. has 'success'].[24]

In other words the totality of mental *dhammas* associated with some form of meditational success is to be regarded as the basis for that success. To sum up, we can say that a 'basis of success' consists of the aggregate of *dhammas*

---

[21] Vibh 216: *iti ayañ ca chanda-samādhi ime ca padhāna-saṃkhārā, tad ekajjhaṃ abhisaṃyūhitvā abhisaṃkhipitvā chanda-samādhi-padhāna-saṃkhāro tveva saṃkhyaṃ gacchati.*

[22] Ibid.: *chando chandikatā kattu-kamyatā kusalo dhamma-cchando.* The northern tradition also defines *chanda* as the desire to act *(kartṛ-kāmatā)*; see Abhidh-k 54; Abhidh-dī 69; Abhidh-sam Trsl 7. In expressions such as *kāma-cchanda* and *chanda-rāga* in the Nikāyas, *chanda* seems to connote 'desire' in an unskilful sense; clearly this is not so in the early Abhidhamma texts. In the later Abhidhamma *chanda* is classed as a neutral *cetasika* that may be either skilful or unskilful depending on associated *cetasikas* (e.g. Vism XIV 133-84); cf. the use of *chanda* in the *samma-ppadhāna* formula.

[23] Vibh 217: *iddhī ti yā tesaṃ dhammānaṃ iddhi samiddhi ijjhanā samijjhanā lābho paṭilābho patti sampatti phusanā sacchikiriyā upasampadā.*

[24] Ibid.: *iddhi-pādo ti tathā-bhūtassa vedanā-kkhandho saññā-kkhandho saṃkhāra-kkhandho viññāṇa-kkhandho.*

contributing to a 'success', but of particular importance in establishing and promoting that success is the interaction of concentration (gained by one of four ways) and forces of endeavour.

4. The commentarial analysis

The commentarial analysis, in the first place, reiterates the basic analysis of the *Saṃyutta-nikāya* and *suttanta-bhājaniya*: *chanda-samādhi* is concentration motivated by *chanda* (*chanda-hetuka*), or headed by *chanda* (*chandâdhika*); it is a term for *samādhi* that has been achieved by making *chanda*, which is the desire to act the *adhipati*; *padhāna-saṃkhāras* are *saṃkhāras* that constitute *padhāna*, and is an expression for *viriya* that accomplishes the four functions of right endeavour.[25] The commentaries then go on to define *iddhi* and *iddhi-pāda* in terms rather more precise than those so far encountered:

> *iddhi-pāda*, i.e. ... that which constitutes a basis in the sense of a foundation for *chanda-samādhi-padhāna-saṃkhāras* associated with skilful *citta*, such as access, *jhāna* and so on, which are [collectively] designated 'success'; the sum of remaining *citta* and *cetasika* is the meaning.[26]

In other words, 'success' is seen in terms of either access concentration (*upacāra*) or *jhāna*, and is constituted by *chanda-samādhi* (or *viriya-samādhi*, etc.) and *padhāna-saṃkhāras*; the remaining consciousness and consciousness factors are the basis for that success. This position appears to be subsequently summed up in the following:

> Here, then, the three *dhammas* termed *chanda-samādhi-padhāna-saṃkhāras* [i.e. *chanda*, *samādhi* and *viriya*] are both successes and bases of success, while the remaining associated four aggregates are just bases of success.[27]

The *Saṃyutta* commentary spells this out:

> Now, in the *iddhi-pāda-vibhaṅga* according to the method beginning [with the words] 'the aggregate of feeling of one who is thus', the remaining immaterial *dhammas* that are furnished with these [three] *dhammas* are said to be 'bases of success'. Moreover these three *dhammas* are both successes and bases of success. How? Because for one who is developing *chanda*, *chanda* is called the success, *samādhi* and *padhāna-saṃkhāras* are called the basis for the success of *chanda*; for one developing *samādhi*, *samādhi* is called the success, *chanda* and *padhāna-saṃkhāras* are called the basis for the success of *samādhi*; for one developing *padhāna-saṃkhāras*, *padhāna-saṃkhāras* are called the success, *chanda* and *samādhi* are called the basis for the success of *padhāna-saṃkhāras*. For in the case of associated *dhammas*, when one succeeds, the remaining succeed too.[28]

---

[25] Sv II 641 = Vibh-a 303.

[26] Sv II 641 = Vibh-a 303 = Vism XII 52: *iddhi-pādaṃ ti ... iddhī ti saṃkhyaṃ gatānaṃ upacāra-jjhānâdi-kusala-citta-sampayuttānaṃ chanda-samādhi-padhāna-saṃkhārānaṃ adhiṭṭhānaṭṭh-ena pāda-bhūtaṃ sesa-citta-cetasika-rāsī ti attho.*

[27] Vibh-a 306: *ettha tayo chanda-samādhi-padhāna-saṃkhāra-saṃkhātā dhammā iddhī pi honti iddhi-pādā pi. sesā pana sampayuttakā cattāro khandhā iddhi-pādā yeva.*

[28] Spk III 255-6: *iddhi-pāda-vibhaṅge pana yo tathā-bhūtassa vedanā-kkhandho ti ādinā nayena imehi dhammehi samannāgatā sesa-arūpino dhammā iddhi-pādā ti vuttā. api ca ime pi tayo dhammā iddhī pi honti iddhi-pādā pi. kathaṃ. chandaṃ hi bhāvayato chando iddhi nāma hoti, samādhi-padhāna-saṃkhārā chandiddhi-pādo nāma. samādhiṃ bhāventassa samādhi iddhi nāma hoti, chanda-padhāna-*

Both the *Saṃyutta* and *Vibhaṅga* commentaries devote some considerable space to an analysis of the details of all this for each of the four *iddhi-pādas*. From the point of view of present concerns the above suffices. What has been presented of the commentarial analysis so far considers the notion of *iddhi-pāda* by way of the internal relationships that exist between various mental factors at the time the *bhikkhu* achieves access concentration or *jhāna*. But this does not exhaust the matter, the full significance of the notion of *iddhi-pāda* has yet to be brought out:

> It should be understood that the prior stage is also called the basis of success and that [subsequent] acquisition [of *jhāna*, etc.] is called the success. The meaning of this should be explained in terms of either access or insight: the preparation for first *jhāna* is called the basis of success, first *jhāna* is the success ... the insight for the path of stream-attainment is called the basis of success, the path of stream-attainment is called the success ... It can also be explained just in terms of acquisition: the first *jhāna* is called the basis of success, the second *jhāna* the success; the second *jhāna* is called the basis of success, the third *jhāna* success ... [29]

The significance of this is that it shifts the scale. From considering the dynamic of 'success' at a given moment within a particular variety of consciousness, we move to a consideration of it from the point of view of a series of successes: how one success leads to another. This notion of *iddhi-pāda* is, then, a relative one. What is to be regarded as *iddhi* and what as *iddhi-pāda* depends on the particular perspective adopted. In particular, however, the notion of *iddhi-pāda* points to the significance of the interplay between *samādhi* and *padhāna-saṃkhāras* along with *chanda*, *viriya*, *citta* and *vīmaṃsā* in consolidating and furthering the process of meditational attainment:

> The *iddhi-pādas*: here *iddhi* [means] 'it succeeds'; 'it succeeds fully, it is accomplished' is the meaning. Alternatively *iddhi* also [means] 'by means of it beings succeed, are successful, matured, exalted'. According to the first meaning an *iddhi-pāda* is 'a *pāda* that is just *iddhi*'; an item of *iddhi* is the meaning. According to the second meaning an *iddhi-pāda* is 'a *pāda* for *iddhi*'; *pāda*, i.e. foundation; 'the means of acquiring' is the meaning. For, since by means of it they [beings/*dhammas*?] reach and obtain success in the sense of progressively higher attainments, therefore it is called a *pāda*.[30]

In summing up, the *Vibhaṅga* commentary reiterates that neither *iddhi* nor

---

saṃkhāra samādhiddhiyā pādo nāma. padhāna-saṃkhāre bhāventassa padhāna-saṃkhārā iddhi nāma hoti, chanda-samādhi padhāna-saṃkhāriddhiyā pādo nāma. sampayutta-dhammesu hi ekasmiṃ ijjhamāne sesā pi ijjhanti yeva.

[29] Vibh-a 307: *api ca pubba-bhāgo iddhi-pādo nāma paṭilābho iddhi nāmā ti veditabbo. ayaṃ attho upacārena vā vipassanāya vā dīpetabbo. paṭhama-jjhāna-parikammaṃ hi iddhi-pādo nāma, paṭhama-jjhānaṃ iddhi nāma ... sotâpatti-maggassa vipassanā iddhi-pādo nāma, sotâpatti-maggo iddhi nāma ... paṭilābhenâpi dīpetuṃ vattati yeva. paṭhama-jjhānaṃ iddhi-pādo nāma, dutiya-jjhānaṃ iddhi nāma; dutiya-jjhānaṃ iddhi-pādo nāma, tatiya-jjhānaṃ iddhi nāma ...* (Cf. Sv II 642; Spk III 256. The notion of *pubba-bhāga* and its connection with the concepts of *upacāra* and *parikamma* is taken up below, Chapter 10.5.)

[30] Vibh-a 303 (cf. Ud-a 304-5; Nidd-a I 66): *iddhi-pādā ti ettha ijjhatī ti iddhi; samijjhati nipphajjatī ti attho. ijjhanti vā etāya sattā iddhā vuddhā ukkaṃsagatā hontī ti pi iddhi. paṭhamenaṭṭhena iddhi eva pādo ti iddhi-pādo; iddhi-koṭṭhāso ti attho. dutiyenaṭṭhena iddhiyā pādo ti iddhi-pādo. pādo ti patiṭṭhā, adhigamūpāyo ti attho. tena hi yasmā uparūpari visesa-saṃkhātaṃ iddhiṃ pajjanti pāpuṇanti tasmā pādo ti vuccati.*

pāda is a term for anything other than the four aggregates in association.[31] The notion of *iddhi-pāda* simply provides one way of looking at the relationships that exist between the *dhammas* that make up the aggregates. But the commentary continues:

> But while this is said, they say that it [i.e. *iddhi-pāda*] would be an expression just for the four aggregates had not the Teacher further on given what is called the *uttara-cūḷa-bhājaniya*, because in the *uttara-cūḷa-bhājaniya* it is said that just *chanda* is *chandiddhi-pāda*, just *viriya* ... just *citta* ... just *vīmaṃsā* is *vīmaṃsiddhi-pāda*.[32]

The *uttara-cūḷa-bhājaniya* appears to refer to the final section of the *abhidhamma-bhājaniya* of the *iddhi-pāda-vibhaṅga*.[33] According to the method of the *uttara-cūḷa-bhājaniya*, at the time of *lokuttara* or 'transcendent' skilful consciousness, *chanda* alone (or *viriya, citta* or *vīmaṃsā)* is to be viewed as the 'basis of success' and remaining *dhammas* are associated with the basis of success, *chanda*.[34] In other words the four *iddhi-pādas* are simply *chanda*, *viriya*, *citta* and *vīmaṃsā* in association with *lokuttara-kusala-citta*.

This brings us to the question of the *iddhi-pādas* as *nipphanna* and *anipphanna*. The precise significance of this pair of terms is not entirely clear; their application to the list of twenty-eight varieties of materiality or 'form' (*rūpa*) is perhaps most easily intelligible. According to this classification the ten *anipphanna-rūpas* are simply terms for different modes or aspects of the eighteen *nipphanna-rūpas* in combination; *anipphanna-rūpas* are not separate realities in their own right.[35] Rather similarly, then, it might be argued that *iddhi* and *iddhi-pāda* simply describe different relations and aspects of the four mental aggregates in combination, they do not designate particular really existing *dhammas*.[36] The view that either *iddhi* or *iddhi-pāda* is *anipphanna* is rejected, however, in the *aṭṭhakathās*.[37] The *Vibhaṅga* commentary does not say why

---

[31] Vibh-a 308: *evaṃ idhâpi iddhī ti vā pado ti vā na aññassa kassaci adhivacanaṃ sampayuttakānaṃ catunnaṃ khandhānaṃ yeva adhivacanan ti.*

[32] Ibid.: *evaṃ vutte pana idam ahaṃsu catunnam khandhānaṃ eva adhivacanaṃ bhāveyya yadi satthā parato uttara-cūḷa-bhājaniyaṃ nāma na āhareyya; uttara-cūḷa-bhājaniye pana chando yeva chandiddhi-pādo, viriyaṃ eva, cittaṃ eva, vīmaṃsā va vīmaṃsiddhi-pādo ti kathitan ti.*

[33] Vibh 223.18-224.16.

[34] This is discussed more fully in Chapter 10; see pp. 326-7, 337.

[35] Cf. Y. Karunadasa, *The Buddhist Analysis of Matter*, Colombo, 1967, pp. 67-8. The distinguishing of the different classes of *rūpa* (*upāda/no upāda; nipphanna/anipphanna*) seems to concern distinctions of the relative order of things. From the point of view of the primary order there are only the four *mahā-bhūtas* (*paṭhavi, āpo, tejo, vāyo*). Dependent on these arises the body of a being: *cakkhu, sota, ghāna, jivhā, kāya, rūpa, sadda, gandha, rasa, phoṭṭhabba* (not distinguished from *paṭhavi, tejo* and *vāyo*), *itthindriya, purisindriya, jīvitindriya, hadaya-vatthu, kabaḷiṅkāra-āhāra*. All the preceding are *nipphanna* or conditioned 'realities', but there is a further order: the two *viññattis*; *lahutā, mudutā, kammaññatā*; *upacaya, santati, jaratā, aniccatā*; *ākāsa*. These last ten items are *anipphanna*, they have no separate existence.

[36] DAṬ II 268 defines *anipphanna* in the present context as 'unsubstantiated from the point of ultimate meaning; "it does not exist" is the meaning' (*paramatthato asiddho, natthī ti attho*).

[37] There is some confusion in the MSS and editions concerning the precise nature of the view to be rejected. Sv II 642 has *keci pana nipphannā iddhi anipphanno iddhi-pādo ti vadanti* (though all Sinhalese MSS apparently omit the words *nipphannā iddhi*); Spk III 256 has just *keci pana anipphanno iddhi-pādo ti vadanti* (no variants recorded); Vibh-a 308 has *keci pana iddhi nāma anipphannā iddhi-pādo nipphanno ti vadiṃsu* (no variants recorded). DAṬ II 268 attributes the view to the Abhayagirivāsins, commenting that some among them were of the view that *iddhi* is *anipphanna*, but *iddhi-pāda nipphanna*, while others that *iddhi-pāda* also is *anipphanna* (*kecī ti*

exactly,[38] but the *Dīgha* and *Saṃyutta* commentaries regard the view as refuted by the *uttara-cūḷa-bhājaniya*.[39] Presumably the point is that in the *uttara-cūḷa-bhājaniya* the terms *iddhi* and *iddhi-pāda* do refer to distinct really existing *dhammas*, namely *chanda/viriya/citta/vīmaṃsā* and *lokuttara-citta* respectively.

5. The desire to act, strength, mind and investigation

The Nikāyas and Abhidhamma talk of gaining *samādhi* or 'concentration' depending on or by making dominant the desire to act (*chanda*), strength (*viriya*), mind (*citta*) or investigation (*vīmaṃsā*). How is this understood? Nothing more is said in the canonical texts, but the commentarial tradition preserves a full and vivid simile that is of some interest:

> It is like the case of four ministers who, aspiring to a position, lived in close association with the king. One was energetic in waiting upon [the king]; knowing the king's wishes and desires, he waited upon him night and day; he pleased the king and obtained a position. The one who produces transcendent *dhamma* with *chanda* as chief should be understood as like him. Another, however, thought: 'I cannot wait upon the king daily; when a task needs to be done I shall please him by my valour.' When there was trouble on the borders he was posted by the king, and having crushed the enemy by means of his valour he obtained a position. The one who produces transcendent *dhamma* with *viriya* as chief should be understood as like him. Another thought: 'Waiting upon the king daily, taking swords and arrows on the chest is burdensome. I shall please the king by the power of my counsel.' Having pleased the king by providing counsel by means of his grasp of state craft, he obtained a position. The one who produces transcendent *dhamma* with *citta* as chief should be understood as like him. Another thought: 'What need of waiting upon [the king], and so on? Surely kings grant positions to those of [good] birth. When the king grants [a position] to such a one he will grant it to me.' So relying solely on his possession of [good] birth, he obtained a position. The one who produces transcendent *dhamma* with *vīmaṃsā* as chief, relying on thoroughly purified *vīmaṃsā* should be understood as like him.[40]

Abhayagiri-vāsino tesu ekacce iddhi nāma anipphannā iddhi-pādo nipphanno ti vadanti. ekacce iddhi-pādo pi anipphanno ti vadanti).

[38] Vibh-a 308: 'In refutation of their opinion it was agreed that both *iddhi* and *iddhi-pāda* are *nipphanna* and afflicted by the three marks.' (*tesaṃ vacanaṃ paṭikkhipitvā iddhi pi iddhi-pādo pi nipphanno ti-lakkhaṇabbhāhato ti sanniṭṭhānaṃ kataṃ.*)

[39] Sv II 64-2 = Spk III 256: 'In order to defeat their view what is called the *uttara-cūḷika-vāra* has come down in the *Abhidhamma [-piṭaka]*.' (*tesaṃ vāda-maddanatthāya abhidhamme uttara-cūḷika-vāro nāma āgato.*)

[40] Sv II 642-3 = Spk III 256-7: *tattha yathā catusu amaccesu ṭhānantaraṃ patthetvā rājānaṃ upanissāya viharantesu eko upaṭṭhāne chanda-jāto rañño ajjhāsayañ ca ruciñ ca ñatvā divā ca ratto ca upaṭṭhahanto rājānaṃ ārādhetvā ṭhānantaraṃ pāpuṇi. yathā so evaṃ chanda-dhurena lokuttara-dhamma-nibbattako veditabbo. eko pana divase divase upaṭṭhātuṃ na sakkomi, uppanne kicce parakkamena ārādhessāmī ti kupite paccante raññā pahito parakkamena sattu-maddanaṃ katvā ṭhānantaraṃ pāpuṇi. yathā so evaṃ viriya-dhurena lokuttara-dhamma-nibbattako veditabbo. eko divase divase upaṭṭhānaṃ urena satti-sara-paṭicchanaṃ pi bhāro yeva, manta-balena ārādhessāmī ti khatta-vijjāya kata-paricayatā manta-saṃvidhānena rājānaṃ ārādhetvā ṭhānantaraṃ pāpuṇi. yathā so evaṃ citta-dhurena lokuttara-dhamma-nibbattako veditabbo. aparo kiṃ imehi upaṭṭhānâdīhi rājāno nāma jāti-sampannassa ṭhānantaraṃ denti, tādisassa dento mayhaṃ dassatī ti jati-sampattiṃ eva nissāya ṭhānantaraṃ pāpuṇi. yathā so evaṃ suparisuddhaṃ vīmaṃsaṃ nissāya vīmaṃsā-dhuro lokuttara-dhamma-nibbattako veditabbo ti.*

The above version is taken from the *Dīgha* and *Saṃyutta* commentaries. Its basic import is plain enough. What we have are four different means by which one achieves one's purpose. The illustrations for *chanda* and *viriya* are in keeping with the way these two terms are explained elsewhere in the literature, but when it comes to *citta* and *vīmaṃsā* there are problems. The *Vibhaṅga* commentary's version of this simile inverts the illustrations for *citta* and *vīmaṃsā*, so we have *citta* illustrated by good birth, and *vīmaṃsā* by the power of counsel.[41] Are we to assume that one version is simply a mistake? Or does each version have its own logic? The reasoning behind the *Dīgha* and *Saṃyutta* commentaries version would seem to be that *chanda*, *viriya*, *citta* and *vīmaṃsā* represent progressively easier means of achieving one's purpose: the one who most easily achieves his purpose spiritually is the one in whom *vīmaṃsā* (identified with *paññā* or 'wisdom' in the *Vibhaṅga*) is thoroughly purified; he is therefore likened to someone easily obtaining a desired position simply on account of his good birth.

On the other hand, it would seem more natural to associate *manta* ('counsel') with *vīmaṃsā* ('investigation', 'inspection', 'reflection' and, like *manta*, a derivative from the root *man*) than with *citta* ('mind', 'consciousness'). It is easy to see why *vīmaṃsā's* nature should be illustrated as giving wise counsel, but not so easy to see why *citta's* should. Why might *citta's* nature be likened to good birth? One function of the notion of *citta* in the Abhidhamma literature is to indicate a hierarchy of 'minds' or 'consciousnesses'. *Citta* may be of many different kinds and of different levels. For example it may belong to the sphere of sense-desire (*kāmâvacara*), to the sphere of form (*rūpâvacara*), to the sphere of the formless (*arūpâvacara*) or it may transcend these (*lokuttara*). Thus the lengthy account of the term *citta* in the *Atthasālinī* lays great emphasis on the variegated nature of *citta*, and *citta* is sometimes expressly said to be of different 'births' or 'classes' (*jāti*)[42] it is mind that ultimately distinguishes beings. This conception of *citta* would seem to fit rather well with its being likened to good birth. One who achieves his purposes by *citta*, achieves it by his own nature, his own natural level of mind, like one who gets what he wants by virtue of his good birth. But this may not always be enough:

> 'Although of good birth someone might not be a counsellor; when some matter arises that must be dealt with by counsel, I shall gain a position.' Thinking this the fourth relied on counsel.[43]

On balance, it seems to me that the *Vibhaṅga* commentary's assignation of the four illustrations works rather better than the *Saṃyutta* commentary's.

---

[41] Vibh-a 305-6; cf. Moh 160. DAṬ II 269 notes the discrepancy, but offers no explanation (*sammohavinodanīyaṃ pana cittiddhi-pādassa jāti-sampatti-sadisatā vīmaṃsiddhi-pādassa manta-bala-sadisatā ca yojitā*).

[42] As 63-6; a considerable amount is made of the play on *citta/citra* meaning 'variegated' (As 63). Vism XIV 82 (cf. Abhidh-av 2): *jāti-vasena tividhaṃ kusalaṃ akusalaṃ avyākatañ ca.*

[43] Vibh-a 305-6: *catuttho jātimā pi eko amantaniyo hoti, mantena kattabba-kicce uppanne āhārapessām'etaṃ ṭhānantaran ti mantaṃ avassayi.*

6. *The northern tradition and the Nettippakaraṇa*

Buddhist Sanskrit sources preserve a slightly different version of the 'bases of success' formula; I quote from the *Arthaviniścaya-sūtra* as a representative source:

> *catvāra ṛddhi-pādāḥ. tatra bhikṣavaḥ katame catvāra ṛddhi-pādāḥ. iha bhikṣavo bhikṣuś [i] chanda-samādhi-prahāṇa-saṃskāra-samanvāgatam ṛddhi-pādaṃ bhāvayati viveka-niśritaṃ virāga-niśritaṃ nirodha-niśritaṃ vyavasarga-pariṇataṃ; ātma-chando nâtilīno bhāviṣyati nâtipragṛhītaḥ. [ii] vīrya-samādhi-prahāṇa-saṃskāra-samanvāgatam ṛddhi-pādaṃ ... nâtipragṛhītaḥ. [iii] citta-samādhi-prahāṇa-saṃskāra-samanvāgatam ṛddhi-pādaṃ ... nâtipragṛhītaḥ. [iv] mīmāṃsā-samādhi-prahāṇa-saṃskāra-samanvāgatam ṛddhi-pādaṃ ... nâtipragṛhītaḥ.*[44]

The differences between this and the Pāli version are in many ways minor, but neverthless rather interesting. An obvious difference is the addition of the *viveka-niśrita* formula ('dependent on seclusion, dependent on dispassion, dependent on cessation and ripening in release'). The *viveka-nissita* formula is certainly common in the Nikāyas, and I shall have occasion to discuss it some detail in connection with the seven *bojjhaṅgas*, but I have been unable to find any canonical source that applies it to the four *iddhi-pādas*. One passage of the paracanonical *Nettippakaraṇa*, however, does do so. I shall consider this presently. It is difficult to believe that the Chinese Āgamas do not preserve a version of the *ṛddhi-pāda* formula without the *viveka-niśrita* formula, but in extant Buddhist Sanskrit sources the inclusion of the *viveka-niśrita* formula appears to be the rule.[45] In the *Arthaviniścaya-sūtra's* version we also have the addition of the refrain '*chanda* (*vīrya, citta, mīmāṃsā*) will not be too slack in me, [it will not be] too vigorous in me'. This is not included in other Buddhist Sanskrit sources, but is of some interest since it parallels the extended *iddhi-pāda* formula of the *iddhi-pāda-saṃyutta*.

The basic way of taking the *ṛddhi-pāda* formula in Buddhist Sanskrit sources closely parallels that of the Pāli sources. Thus the four *ṛddhi-pādas* as 'bases of success' are closely associated with the general notion of meditation attainment. Where the Pāli commentaries talk of access and *jhāna*, Buddhist Sanskrit sources talk of the particular nature of the *ṛddhi-pādas* as *samādhi*.[46] The first *ṛddhi-pāda* is taken as furnished with *chanda-samādhi* and *prahāṇa-saṃskāra*;[47] *chanda-samādhi*, and so on, is *samādhi* gained by making *chanda*,

44 Artha 30-1.

45 I have been unable to find any exception to this rule apart from Konow's reconstruction of the Skt text of the *Daśasāhasrikā* (pp. 96-7) which does not have the *viveka-niśrita* formula for any of the sets. Lamotte (*Traité*, III 1124) cites *Pañcaviṃśati*, *Śatasāhasrikā*, *Daśabhūmika* and *Mahāvyutpatti* as all including *viveka-niśrita*, etc., and was also apparently unable to find an exception to the rule. The Chinese Āgama version of the *Cetokhila-sutta* appears to include the *viveka-nissita* formula where the Pāli does not (see M I 103, Thich Minh Chau, op. cit., p. 95).

46 *Bhāṣya* at Abhidh-k 385 gives two basic methods: either *pāda* is *samādhi* which is the basis for cumulative success (*ṛddhi*) i.e. the accomplishment of all excellent qualities *(sarva-guṇa-sampatti*); alternatively *ṛddhi* itself is *samādhi*, and *chanda*, etc., are the *pādas* (cf. *uttara-cūḷa-bhājaniya* method, and see below, p. 337). Cf. Abhidh-h Trsl 117-9; Abhidh-sam Trsl 121; Satya Trsl 448; Artha-n 219.

47 Artha-n 221: *chanda-samādhiś ca prahāṇa-saṃskāraś ceti chanda-samādhi-prahāṇa-saṃskārau. tābhyāṃ samanvāgataṃ sahitaṃ yuktam ṛddhi-pādaṃ bhāvayatîti.*

and so on, dominant (*adhipati*).[48] However, *prahāṇa-saṃskāras* are, of course, 'forces of abandoning' rather than 'forces of endeavour'. Much of what has already been said concerning *samyak-prahāṇa* is relevant here, though one should note that the literature does not identify *prahāṇa-saṃskāras* with *vīrya*, as it does the four *samyak-prahāṇas*. Instead the northern literature provides a list detailing just what forces of abandoning are intended: desire to act (*chanda*), striving (*vyāyāma*), confidence (*śraddhā*), tranquillity (*praśrabdhi*), mindfulness (*smṛti*), clear comprehension (*samprajanya*), volition (*cetanā*), equipoise (*upekṣā*).[49] This, then, constitutes a rather more definite difference in interpretation between the Pāli tradition and the northern tradition, than does the case of *samma-ppadhāna*/*samyak-prahāṇa*. This makes all the more interesting the following treatment of the *iddhi-pādas* preserved in the *Nettippakaraṇa*:

> Therein, one-pointedness of mind that has confidence as dominant—this is *chanda-samādhi*. When consciousness is concentrated due to suppression of the defilements either by the power of reflection or by the power of development—this is abandoning (*pahāna*). Therein, breathing in and out, initial and sustained thought, ideas and feelings, mindfulness and thought—these are forces. Thus there is the initial *chanda-samādhi*, there is abandoning due to suppression of the defilements, and there are these forces; [taking] both he develops the *iddhi-pāda* furnished with *chanda-samādhi-padhāna*[sic]-*saṃkhāra*, dependent on seclusion, dependent on dispassion, dependent on cessation, ripening in release.[50]

One-pointedness of mind that has *viriya*, *citta* and *vīmaṃsā* as dominant is then treated in precisely the same way. Both the notion of *pahāna(-saṃkhāra)* and the association of the *iddhi-pādas* with the *viveka-nissita* formula are

---

[48] Abhidh-k-vy 601-2 quotes a Sūtra source: *sūtrāt. uktaṃ hi chandaṃ câpi bhikṣur adhipatiṃ kṛtvā labhate samādhiṃ so'sya bhavati chanda-samādhiḥ. cittaṃ* [sic] *vīryaṃ mīmāṃsāṃ câpi adhipatiṃ kṛtvā labhate samādhiṃ so'sya bhavati mīmāṃsā-samādhir iti.* Cf. Abhidh-dī 359; Artha-n 220. Abhidh-sam Trsl 121 defines *chanda-*, *vīrya-*, *citta-* and *mīmāṃsā-samādhi* respectively as one-pointedness of mind attained by means of proper application of *chanda*, constant application of *vīrya*, the power of concentration previously cultivated, hearing dharma and insight respectively. The technical notion of *adhipati* does not appear to be developed in quite the same way in northern Abhidharma treatises. Adhidh-h and Abhidh-k know the concept of *adhipati-pratyaya* but it is not specifically related to *chanda*, *vīrya*, *citta* and *mīmāṃsā*; it is rather an alternative term for *kāraṇa-hetu* (productive cause) which is *hetu* in its most general aspect; see Abhidh-h Trsl 24; Abhidh-k 82-3, 98-100.

[49] Satya Trsl 42; Abhidh-sam Trsl 121; *Madhyântavibhāga-bhāṣya* IV 4 (Anacker, op. cit., pp. 247-8, 447); Abhidh-dī 359 gives the same eight items substituting *buddhi* for *samprajanya*; Amṛta Trsl 205 gives a slightly different list of five: *chanda*, *vīrya*, *smṛti*, *samprajanya*, *prīti*, *praśrabdhi*.

[50] Nett 15: *tattha yā saddhâdhipateyyā cittekaggatā ayaṃ chanda-samādhi. samāhite citte kilesānaṃ vikkhambhanatāya paṭisaṃkhāna-balena vā bhāvanā-balena vā idaṃ pahānaṃ. tattha ye assāsa-passāsa-vitakka-vicāra-saññā-vedayita-sara-saṃkappā ime saṃkhārā. iti purimako ca chanda-samādhi kilesa-vikkhambhanatāya ca pahānaṃ ime ca saṃkhārā, tad-ubhayaṃ chanda-samādhi-padhāna-saṃkhāra-samannāgataṃ iddhi-pādaṃ bhāveti viveka-nissitaṃ virāga-nissitaṃ nirodha-nissitaṃ vosagga-pariṇāmiṃ.* Nett-a (216) comments: '"This is abandoning"—concentration that achieves abandoning by suppression is "abandoning" is what is said, denoting that one abandons by means of it; *padhānaṃ* is also a reading; "the pinnacle" is the meaning.' (*idaṃ pahānan ti vikkhambhana-pahāna-sādhako samādhi pahānan ti vutto; pajahati etenā ti katvā. padhānan ti pi pāṭho; aggo ti attho*); *padhāna* (as an alternative reading) is thus taken in the sense of 'principal' and not 'endeavour'. For the association of *chanda* and *saddhā* see below, pp. 114-5.

characteristic of the northern tradition, and apart from this *Netti* passage seem to be absent from the Pāli tradition.[51]

However, the *Netti* interpretation still differs from that offered by Buddhist Sanskrit texts; *pahāna-saṃkhāra* seems to be taken as a *dvandva* ('abandoning' and 'forces') rather than a *tatpuruṣa* ('forces of abandoning'), and the list of *saṃkhāras* bears little resemblance to the one found in the northern texts. But the fact that the *Nettippakaraṇa's* treatment of the *iddhi-pādas* diverges from the usual treatment in Pāli texts constitutes further evidence that at least portions of the *Netti* 'were composed in North India at some time prior to the introduction of the text into Ceylon'.[52]

In conclusion one might suggest that *pahāna* (abandoning) perhaps makes better sense than *padhāna* (endeavour) as the original intention of the *iddhi-pāda* formula, in that it avoids the overlap with *viriya* in the second *iddhi-pāda*. It would be interesting to know whether the Chinese Āgamas preserve a parallel to the *iddhi-pāda-saṃyutta* passage that associates the *samma-ppadhāna* formula with *padhāna-saṃkhāra*.

7. *The iddhi-pādas and the prolongation of life*

The *Mahāparinibbāna-sutta* in the lead up to the Buddha's announcement of his imminent *parinibbāna* represents the Buddha as declaring that 'anyone who has developed and made great the four *iddhi-pādas* can, if he should so wish, live on for a *kappa* or what remains of a *kappa*'.[53] It is apparent from the Pāli *aṭṭhakathās* and from Buddhist Sanskrit sources that the proper interpretation of this statement was already the subject of some controversy in ancient times. Some of the views and issues involved in that controversy have been discussed by P.S. Jaini, though his treatment is by no means exhaustive, and remains rather inconclusive.[54] The problems posed by the notion of the prolongation of life by means of the *iddhi-pādas* seem to have been seen as basically two in number. First, given that the maximum potential lifespan of a given individual is understood in Buddhist thought to be determined by past *kamma* already at the time of conception, how precisely does a life-span come

---

[51] The general equivalence of the *iddhi-pādas* to 'abandoning by suppression' and hence to meditative absorption, however, is stated; e.g. Ps II 69: *imehi catuhi iddhi-pādehi vikkhambhana-ppahānaṃ*.

[52] Norman, *PL*, p. 110. Cf. Warder, *IB*, p. 342.

[53] D II 103: *yassa kassaci cattāro iddhi-pādā bhāvitā bahulīkatā yānikatā vatthu-katā anuṭṭhitā paricitā susamāraddhā, so ākaṅkhamāno kappaṃ vā tiṭṭheyya kappâvasesaṃ vā*. The Buddha then goes on to say that the Tathāgata is one who has so developed the *iddhi-pādas*. Ānanda fails to respond to the hint, whereupon the Buddha resolves to pass away in three months. When Ānanda subsequently exhorts him to live on for a *kappa*, the Buddha reprimands him and relates how on fifteen previous occasions (which are listed) he also told Ānanda how one who developed the *iddhi-pādas* might live on for a *kappa*. This whole incident is related at D II 102-9; S V 258-62; A IV 308-12; Ud 62-4; it is also found in all extant versions of the *Mahāparinirvāṇa-sūtra*, see Bareau, *RBB* II 147-94; for Bareau's discussion of the present *iddhi-pāda* formula, see id., pp. 151-6. The formula concerning the *iddhi-pādas* and the prolongation of life is also found in the *Cakkavatti-sīhanāda-sutta* at D III 77; this does not appear to count as one of the fifteen occasions referred to in the *Mahāparinibbāna-sutta*.

[54] P.S. Jaini, 'The Buddha's Prolongation of Life', *BSOAS* 21 (1958), pp. 546-52.

to be subsequently extended by the development of the *iddhi-pādas* without violating the laws of *kamma-vipāka*? Secondly, does *kappa* in this passage refer to a *mahā-kappa* (i.e. cosmic aeon) or an *āyu-kappa* (i.e. normal maximum potential lifespan of a human being, namely one hundred years)?[55] With regard to the first point, a full exposition of the various moot points of Abhidhamma raised here would, I think, need to be more extended and searching than Jaini's introductory account, which seems to me to pass over some of the subtleties.[56] I do not wish to embark on a full comparative Abhidharma study on this question here, but shall confine myself to a few comments on what I take to be the basic Theravādin Abhidhamma conception of the issue.

The *Visuddhimagga* states that there are two kinds of death, namely timely (*kāla-maraṇa*)—of which there are three varieties—and untimely (*akāla-maraṇa*).[57] The *Visuddhimagga's* discussion here suggests that there are three factors involved: the maximum potential lifespan of the human being in general; the particular potential lifespan of a given individual; any adventitious circumstances that might interfere with this and bring about untimely death. The particular potential lifespan of a given individual will vary according to the merit (*puñña*) acquired as a result of previous *janaka* or 'productive' *kamma*. What I have termed 'adventitious circumstances' are, of course, understood to work within the law of *kamma-vipāka*, and are determined in principle by what is called 'destructive' (*upaghātaka*) or 'intervening' (*upacchedaka*) *kamma*.[58] This kind of *kamma* overrides and supplants weaker *kamma*, and may be both skilful and unskilful. Presumably then, whether or not an individual's potential lifespan is fulfilled depends on any unskilful destructive *kamma*. When these principles are applied to the question of the *iddhi-pādas* and the prolongation of life, what seems to be envisaged—at least as far as the Pāli commentaries are concerned—is that anyone in whom the *iddhi-pādas* are fully developed will have complete mastery over any untimely death and live out his full potential lifespan. In other words, the development of the *iddhi-pādas* constitutes a skilful 'destructive' *kamma* of a kind that overrides any unskilful 'destructive' *kamma*.

How might this operate in the case of a Buddha? Presumably his merit would be such that his potential lifespan would be more or less equivalent to the maximum potential for a human being. Or perhaps, strictly speaking, a Buddha's merit should be properly considered as infinite. In this case his potential lifespan might in fact correspond to the duration of a great aeon. Bareau gives the following as the outlook of the Mahāsāṃghikas:

> Puisque le corps de rétribution du Buddha a été obtenu par lui pour avoir cultivé les mérites pendant beaucoup d'ères cosmiques (*kalpa*) infinies, sa vie est vraiment

---

[55] Cf. Vibh 422: *manussānaṃ kittakaṃ āyu-ppamāṇaṃ. vassa-sataṃ appaṃ vā bhiyyo vā.*

[56] Specifically on the present passage see Sv II 554-5; Mil 141-2; Kv 456-8; Kv-a 131-2; Abhidh-k 43-4.

[57] Vism VIII 2-3.

[58] Vism VIII 2-3, XIX 13-6; Cf.Ps V 11-13.

> sans fin et indestructible. C'est pour le profit des êtres vivants qu'il a cultivé la voie (*mārga*) pendant beaucoup d'ères cosmiques et a reçu une vie illimitée.[59]

Certainly it seems that the understanding of *kappa* in the *Mahāparinibbāna-sutta* to mean *mahā-kappa* is consistent with certain trends in Buddhist thought. Even if the above was not actually the view of the Mahāsāṃghikas, one might speculate that anyone or any school that interpreted *kappa* here to mean *mahā-kappa* would be basing their view on exactly this kind of thinking. This would include a certain Mahāsīva-tthera, whose views are rejected by Buddhaghosa.[60] For Buddhaghosa *kappa* here means not *mahā-kappa* but *āyu-kappa*.

So which is the correct interpretation of *kappa* in the *Mahāparinibbāna-sutta* formula—*mahā-kappa* or *āyu-kappa*? I think on balance the text of the *Mahāparinibbāna-sutta* as we have it, in its various recensions,[61] points towards *mahā-kappa* as being the correct interpretation. A significant factor here is the word *kappâvasesa*. The most likely meaning of this is surely 'the remainder of a *kappa*'.[62] For someone to say that he can live on 'for his lifespan or the remainder of his lifespan' seems not to make very good sense; 'remainder of his lifespan' in fact becomes redundant. However, if one is thinking of an incalculable aeon, and envisaging someone speaking at some point during that aeon, for him to say that he might live 'for an aeon or [at least] the remainder of the aeon' makes rather better sense. Accordingly, in order to give *kappa* the value he thinks it ought to have, Buddhaghosa must ignore the more natural way of taking *kappâvasesa*. So, he says, *kappâvasesa* does not mean 'the remainder of a *kappa*', it means 'a little bit more than a *kappa*', that is, more than a man's normal lifespan of a hundred years.[63]

Textual and philological considerations aside, Buddhaghosa's interpretation would seem—at least to the twentieth century mind—to be the more reasonable and realistic. And perhaps not only to the twentieth century mind. Since Buddhaghosa's explanation goes against the natural way of taking the text he had before him, he, or the tradition he was following, was clearly rather unhappy with the notion of a Buddha living for a whole cosmic aeon. In fact, the tradition certainly goes back as far as the *Kathāvatthu* which states that 'it should not be said that one possessing the power of *iddhi* might live on for a *kappa*'.[64] The *Milindapañha* also states that *kappa* means *āyu-kappa* in the

---

[59] Bareau, *SBPV*, p. 59. (Bareau's source is K'OUEI-KI, II pp.18b-19a = Oyama, *Yi pou tsong louen louen chou ki fa jen*, Kyoto, 1891.)

[60] Sv II 554; cf. Jaini, *BSOAS* 21 (1958), p. 549.

[61] Cf. Bareau, *RBB* II 152.

[62] See *CPD*, s.v. *avasesa*; MW, s.v. *avaśeṣa*. I fail to see that Edgerton (*BHSD*, s.v. *kalpâvaśeṣa*) has shown that *kappâvasesa* probably means 'more than a *kappa*' as Jaini suggests (*BSOAS* 21 (1958), p. 547).

[63] Sv II 555: *kappâvasesaṃ vā ti appaṃ vā bhiyyo ti vutta-vassa-satato atirekaṃ vā*. See also Spk III 251; Mp IV 149; Ud-a 322; Mp-ṭ (Be 1961) III 252. K.R. Norman has suggested to me that what Buddhaghosa may be doing is taking *kappâvasesa* as a *bahuvrīhi* in the sense of '[a period of time] having a lifespan as remainder' (cf. adjectival usage of *ardha-śeṣa* and *ardhâvaśeṣa*, q.v. MW).

[64] Kv 458: *tena hi na vattabbaṃ iddhi-balena samannāgato kappaṃ tiṭṭheyyā ti*. (The *kappa* under discussion here is a *mahā-kappa*; cf. Kv-a 131-2.)

present context.[65] Given the existence of the two ways of taking *kappa*, one would, however, expect Buddhaghosa's to be the earlier, on the grounds that the *mahā-kappa* interpretation ought to reflect the continued process of the elaboration of the notion of Buddhahood which we find evidenced in the history of Buddhist thought. But once again we seem to have an example of a line of thinking, sometimes assumed to be later, being found latent in the text of the Pāli canon. Nevertheless one might speculate that the *Kathāvatthu* and *Milindapañha* here preserve a tradition that antedates the text of the Pāli canon, and that the statement concerning the *iddhi-pādas* and the prolongation of life, as it is now preserved, rests on an earlier version which corresponded in intent to the *āyu-kappa* interpretation.

What does all this signify for the understanding of the *iddhi-pādas*? Ignoring the question of *āyu-kappa* and *mahā-kappa*, the answer is, I think, quite straightforward. One who develops fully the *iddhi-pādas* is clearly understood to have at least some power to extend his life; he has at least some control over the particular factors that determine the time of death. This, in fact, accords quite well with the treatment of the *iddhi-pādas* elsewhere in the texts. As I have tried to illustrate, the *iddhi-pādas* are primarily concerned with the development of skill and facility in *samādhi* or types of meditative attainment, and they are frequently explicitly associated with various meditative powers that are linked to the development of *jhāna*. That an aspect or by-product of this kind of mastery of the forces of the mind is seen as the ability to have some measure of control over the factors that determine the moment of death, is not a notion peculiar to the Nikāyas, but entirely consistent with the wider Indian yogic tradition.[66]

8. The notion of iddhi *in the Nikāyas*

So far I have pointed out that the *iddhi-pādas* are associated in the Nikāyas especially with the practice of eightfold *iddhi*, and at the same time frequently linked to the ultimate goal of the spiritual life, namely the destruction of the *āsavas*.[67] In addition to eightfold *iddhi*, the *iddhi-pādas* are associated with other feats of meditational power: the ability to prolong one's life, the ability to create a kingdom by *dhamma*, without slaughter, or to make Himavant a mountain of gold.[68] Alongside this we have the less specific characterization of *iddhi* as general 'success' or 'repeated success' in meditation.[69]

---

[65] Mil 141; Bareau comments (*RBB* II 152) that the relevant portion is missing from the two Chinese versions of *Milindapañha*.

[66] Cf. Jaini, *BSOAS* 21 (1958), p. 546.

[67] Outside the *iddhi-pāda-saṃyutta* the association of the *iddhi-pādas* with general spiritual attainment is evident in a number of places. They are linked to *sambodha* and the 'attainment of the unsurpassable escape from bonds' (*anuttarassa yoga-kkhemassa adhigamo*) (M I 103-4); to 'knowledge' (*aññā*), non-return (*anāgāmitā*), eightfold *iddhi*, and *anāsava-ceto-vimutti* (A III 81- 3); to the six *abhiññās* (Th 233).

[68] S I 116-7.

[69] One should note here the less technical usage of *iddhi* in Pāli literature to denote any kind of natural facility or acquired skill from the good looks of a king to the hunter's skill in trapping animals (see *PED*, *CPD*, s.v. *iddhi*). For an account of the various *iddhis* distinguished in Pāli

The *Paṭisambhidāmagga's* list of ten categories of *iddhi* embraces the full range of the notion of *iddhi* in early Buddhist literature: *iddhi* by resolve (*adhiṭṭhāna*), *iddhi* by transformation (*vikubbanā*), mind-made (*mano-mayā*) *iddhi*, *iddhi* by expansion of knowledge (*ñāṇa-vipphārā*), *iddhi* by expansion of concentration (*samādhi-vipphārā*), noble (*ariyā*) *iddhi*, *iddhi* that is the result of past actions (*kamma-vipākajā*), the *iddhi* of one who is meritorious (*puññavato*), *iddhi* that consists in crafts (*vijjā-mayā*), *iddhi* in the sense of succeeding by right application to various tasks (*samma-ppayoga-ppaccayā ijjhanaṭṭhena*).[70] Here *iddhi* includes virtually the whole of Buddhist spiritual practice: *adhiṭṭhānā iddhi* (which corresponds to eightfold *iddhi*), *vikubbanā iddhi* and *vijjā-mayā iddhi* are all aspects of what might be called 'miraculous' *iddhi*; *ñāṇa-vipphārā* and *samādhi-vipphārā iddhi* are illustrated by insight into impermanence and so on, and the practice of the *jhānas* respectively; *ariyā iddhi* is characterized by the contemplation of the unloathsome in the loathsome, etc.; *kamma-vipākajā iddhi* consists of innate skills such as the ability of a bird to fly; *puññavato iddhi* is exemplified especially by the *rājā cakka-vattī* or 'universal monarch'; the final category concerns skill in various attainments of *jhāna* and insight.

But, one might ask, is not such an integrated account of the notion of *iddhi* at odds with what is said in some parts of the Pāli canon? Surely the practice of eightfold *iddhi* and other varieties of miraculous *iddhi* is roundly condemned in certain passages? The principal passages that might convey this impression are the Vinaya ruling on the display of miraculous *iddhi* (*iddhi-pāṭihāriya*)[71] and a section of the *Kevaddha-sutta* devoted to a discussion of three kinds of 'wonder' (*pāṭihāriya*).[72] These deserve rather careful consideration.

The intellectual climate at the beginning of this century was such that it tended to demand that the 'rational' ethical and spiritual elements of religion be seen as distinct from the 'irrational' supernatural and miraculous elements. In an article entitled 'The Bodhisattva as Wonderworker', Luis O. Gomez no doubt rightly points to Edward Conze as breaking the spell of 'Buddhist rationalism' in scholarly circles.[73] Yet T.W. Rhys Davids' introduction to and translation of the *Kevaddha-sutta*, along with the *PED* entry for *iddhi*, still exercise some influence—indeed it is largely due to Rhys Davids, I think, that Gomez himself styles the opening of the *Kevaddha-sutta* as 'perhaps one of the most "rationalistic" of the *Nikāya* passages on wonder-working'.[74] But is it as 'rational' as Rhys Davids and *PED* suggest?

The *Kevaddha-sutta* begins with the householder Kevaddha requesting three times that the Buddha should invite some *bhikkhu* to undertake a display of miraculous *iddhi* (*iddhi-pāṭihāriya*) beyond the capacity of ordinary men (*uttari-manussa-dhamma*). One should note straightaway that *uttari-manussa-dhamma*

---

literature see H.W. French, 'The Concept of *iddhi* in Early Buddhist Thought', PBR II (1977), pp. 42-77. .

[70] Paṭis II 205-14. Vimutt Trsl 209-12 also considers *iddhi* fairly broadly.

[71] Vin II 112.

[72] D I 211-15.

[73] See 'The Bodhisattva as Wonder Worker' in *Prajñāpāramitā and Related Systems*, ed. L. Lancaster, Berkeley, 1977, pp. 221-61 (p. 221).

[74] Ibid.

is elsewhere taken to signify any kind of meditational attainment, and is not restricted to eightfold *iddhi*.[75] The Buddha twice repeats that it is not his custom to teach *dhamma* to *bhikkhus* by asking them to perform miraculous *iddhi* for householders. On the third occasion the Buddha explains precisely why. There are, he says, three kinds of *pāṭihāriya* or 'wondrous display': the wondrous display of *iddhi*, the wondrous display of showing [the thoughts of others] (*ādesanā*), and the wondrous display of instruction (*anusāsanī*). He then comments on each of these *pāṭihāriyas* in turn. Of *iddhi-pāṭihāriya*, he comments that a person of confidence and trust (*saddho pasanno*) might witness a *bhikkhu* enjoying eightfold *iddhi* and subsequently relate the matter to someone lacking in confidence and trust (*asaddho apasanno*). The former is inspired with trust: 'Wonderful! Marvellous! This *samaṇa* has great *iddhi*, great power.'[76] But the latter remains singularly unimpressed: 'There is a [magical] art called *gandhārī*; it is by means of this that this *bhikkhu* enjoys various kinds of *iddhi*.'[77] The Buddha then asks Kevaddha whether he agrees that a person lacking in confidence and trust might react in this way. Kevaddha replies that he does. The Rhys Davids translation of the Buddha's response is as follows:

> Well, Kevaddha! It is because I perceive danger in the practice of mystic wonders that I loathe, and abhor, and am ashamed thereof.[78]

Before stating exactly why I think this misrepresents the meaning, I wish briefly to turn to some of the comments Rhys Davids makes in his introduction to the *sutta*. With regard to the notion of 'miracles' in Buddhist literature, he remarks quite rightly; I think, that:

> They were not, however, miracles in our Western sense. There was no interference by an outside power with the laws of nature. It was supposed that certain people by reason of special (but quite natural) powers could accomplish certain special acts beyond the power of ordinary men.[79]

Yet he seems rather to forget the implications of this when he immediately says: 'These acts are eight in number.'[80] This straightaway marks off eightfold *iddhi* from other attainments 'beyond the capacity of ordinary men' (*uttari-manussa-dhamma*) in a way that is not quite faithful to the spirit of the texts. For as Rhys Davids himself points out the eight miraculous *iddhis* are quite 'natural' according to the Nikāya outlook. They are the result of meditation success in exactly the same way as, for example, the *jhānas*. True, as Rhys Davids again points out,[81] they are termed *puthujjanika-iddhi* or *iddhi* that may

---

[75] E.g. at Vin III 87 it refers to the four *jhānas*, stream-attainment, once return, non-return, *arahant*-ship and the six *abhiññās*; at Vin III 91 it is defined as *jhāna*, liberation (*vimokkha*), *samādhi*, attainment (*samāpatti*), knowledge and vision (*ñāṇa-dassana*), development of the path (*magga-bhāvanā*), realization of the fruit (*phala-sacchikiriyā*), absence of the hindrances from the mind (*vinīvaraṇatā cittassa*), delight in empty dwellings (*suññāgāre abhirati*).

[76] D I 213: *acchariyaṃ vata bho abbhutaṃ vata bho. samaṇassa mahiddhikā mahânubhavatā.*

[77] Ibid.: *atthi kho bho gandhārī nāma vijjā tāya so bhikkhu aneka-vihitaṃ iddhi-vidhaṃ paccanubhoti.*

[78] D Trsl I 278.

[79] Id., p. 272.

[80] Ibid.

[81] D Trsl I 272-3.

belong to ordinary men as opposed to the *ariyas* or 'noble ones' (stream-attainers, once-returners, non-returners and *arahants*). But then this is also true of the four *jhānas* in general and does not constitute any kind of condemnation *per se* as Rhys Davids seems to want to imply.

So why, then, is eightfold *iddhi* singled out by the Buddha in the *Kevaddha-sutta*? Is it really simply that the Buddha 'loathes the practice of them' as Rhys Davids suggests?[82] I think not. The reason is actually quite straightforward. It is not because eightfold *iddhi* is in a category of its own, fundamentally removed from other attainments; nor because the Buddha loathes its practice; nor because it is 'not the exclusive property of the enlightened' which is how Gomez views the *Kevaddha-sutta* (presumably following Rhys Davids' lead).[83]

The point, it seems to me, is this. The passage concerns the request for a *bhikkhu* to undertake a display of miraculous *iddhi* for the benefit of householders or layfollowers. Eightfold *iddhi* constitutes *iddhi-pāṭihāriya* precisely because what is at issue is the question of display.[84] Eightfold *iddhi* can constitute display in a way that the plain attainment of *jhāna* or *arahant*-ship cannot: the saint is somehow less impressive than the wonder-worker flying through the air. So what is the point that the Buddha is here depicted as wishing to make about *iddhi-pāṭihāriya*? Simply this: the display of miraculous *iddhi* as a rule achieves nothing worthwhile. The man already of confidence and trust sees it as wonderful (and is perhaps impressed for the wrong reasons), while the man without such confidence mistrusts it and sees it as a trick with no deeper significance.[85]

What of the sentence Rhys Davids' rendering of which I called into question? The Pāli reads:

> *imaṃ kho ahaṃ Kevaddha iddhi-pāṭihāriye ādīnavaṃ samanupassamāno iddhi-pāṭihāriyena aṭṭiyāmi harayāmi jigucchāmi.*

It is immediately apparent that Rhys Davids has left an emphasized and significant word untranslated: *imaṃ*. I translate as follows:

> Perceiving *this* danger, Kevaddha, in [the display of] miraculous *iddhi*, I am troubled by, ashamed of, and shun [the display of] miraculous *iddhi*.

As soon as *imaṃ* is translated the particularity rather than the generality of the condemnation of eightfold *iddhi* becomes obvious. The Buddha is condemning the display of miraculous eightfold *iddhi* to householders because he views it as unhelpful and dangerous for precisely the reasons I have just outlined. He is not making a general judgement about the practice of eightfold *iddhi* at all.

The interpretation I have just offered of the *Kevaddha-sutta* is in fact borne out by the Vinaya rulings on *iddhi-pāṭihāriya* and *uttari-manussa-dhamma*. The

---

[82] Id., p. 272.

[83] Gomez, op.cit., p. 221-2.

[84] The notion of 'display' or 'spectacle' is really inherent in the word *pāṭihāriya/prātihārya*; cf. MW, *BHSD*, s.v. causative *pratihārayati*; both record the meaning 'to have oneself announced'.

[85] The twentieth century reaction to the 'paranormal' is not very different: the faithful tend to point enthusiastically to various people and incidents, while the sceptics, maintaining that trickery or self-deceit has been involved, doggedly seek out 'rational' explanations.

principal ruling is preceded by the story of Pindola Bhāradvāja's performance of a miracle before the citizens of Rājagaha in response to a challenge.[86] This incident is said to have prompted the Buddha to make the following rule: *Bhikkhus*, a display of miraculous *iddhi* beyond the capacity of ordinary man is not to be exhibited to householders. If someone exhibits [such], there is *dukkaṭa* offence.[87] The reason for the ruling is precisely that those lacking in faith and trust will fail to be impressed,[88] and the exhibition of miraculous *iddhi* is likened to a woman exposing herself for a few coins. Once again it is clear that it is the display of miraculous *iddhi* that is condemned, and not its practice *per se*.

The Vinaya ruling on *iddhi-pāṭihāriya* can be usefully compared with the rulings concerning the fourth *pārājika* and eighth *pācittiya* offences. The fourth *pārājika* involves laying false claim to any kind of *uttari-manussa-dhamma*; this concerns any false claim, though the incident leading up to the ruling concerns a *bhikkhu* who makes a false claim in front of householders.[89] The eighth *pācittiya* involves announcing the possession of an *uttari-manussa-dhamma* that one does genuinely possess to one who has not received higher ordination (*upasampāda*); the introductory incident concerns *bhikkhus* announcing their genuine attainments to householders once more.[90] While these last two Vinaya rulings concern wider issues than just the display of miraculous *iddhi*, they serve to reiterate how it is display or boasting outside the confines of the Saṃgha that is considered detrimental to all concerned.

9. The method of developing iddhi

That *iddhi* is understood to be nothing different from skill or facility in meditative concentration is again brought out by the instructions given for the development of the various kinds of *iddhi* in the later literature. The preparation for *iddhi* is considered in the *Paṭisambhidāmagga*[91] by way of four 'levels of success' (*iddhiyā bhūmiyo*), the four *iddhi-pādas*, eight 'footings of success' (*iddhiyā padāni*), and sixteen 'roots of success' (*iddhiyā mūlāni*). The four levels are in fact the four *jhānas*. The eight footings are the *iddhi-pādas* again, each

---

[86] The account of Pindola Bhāradvāja's *iddhi-pāṭihāriya* is found in all extant *Vinayas* (with some variations); see J.S. Strong, 'The Legend of the Lion-Roarer: A study of the Buddhist Arahat Pindola Bhāradvāja', *Numen* 26 (1979), pp. 71-2, and S. Lévi and E. Chavannes, 'Les seize arhat protecteurs de la loi', *JA* 7 (1916), pp. 233-47. For the account in the Pāli sources see Vin II 110-2; in post-canonical sources the Pindola Bhāradvāja incident forms the prelude to the Buddha's performance of the 'twin miracle' (*yamaka-pāṭihāriya*); see Sv I 57; Dh-a III 204; Sn-a 570; J IV 263.

[87] Vin II 112: *na bhikkhave gihīnaṃ uttari-manussa-dhammaṃ iddhi-pāṭihāriyaṃ dassetabbaṃ. yo dasseyya āpatti dukkaṭassa.*

[88] Ibid. A stock Vinaya formula is employed (cf. Vin II 2; *PTC*, s.v. *appasīdati*): 'It is neither [conducive] to trust for those without trust, nor to growth for those with trust; indeed, *bhikkhus*, it is [conducive] to lack of trust for those without trust, and to loss [of trust] for some of those with trust.' (*n'etaṃ bhikkhave appasannānaṃ vā pasādāya pasannānaṃ vā bhiyyo-bhāvāya, atha kho taṃ bhikkhave appasannānañ c'eva appasādāya pasannānañ ca ekaccānaṃ aññathattāyā ti.*)

[89] Vin III 87-109; the ruling is qualified to exempt those who make a false claim mistakenly because of over estimation of themselves.

[90] Vin IV 23-30.

[91] Paṭis II 205-6; quoted Vism XII 49-50, 54-5.

one considered as two footings: concentration and its basis (*chanda*, *viriya*, *citta*, *vīmaṃsā*). The sixteen roots concern counteracting various obstacles to unperturbed (*aneñja*) consciousness.

According to the *Visuddhimagga* the *bhikkhu* who wishes to develop eightfold *iddhi* must have complete mastery and control of the four *jhānas* and four formless attainments. This mastery adds up to the ability to attain all eight attainments on the basis of all eight *kasiṇas* at will.[92] According to Buddhagosa such mastery of *jhāna* is very difficult and only to be accomplished by very few.[93] However, Buddhas, Paccekabuddhas and chief disciples, because of their endeavour in past lives, can achieve the various *iddhis* spontaneously as a result of attaining *arahant*-ship.[94] Others who have developed the necessary conditions in previous lives are said to need only mastery of the fourth *jhāna* in the *kasiṇas*.[95] The *Vimuttimagga*, however, states that all who attain to the fourth *jhāna* with facility develop *iddhi*.[96]

In sum, it can be said that in general the *iddhi-pādas* are seen as concerned with the development of facility and mastery in *samādhi* or 'meditative' concentration. More particularly this facility and mastery is directly linked to the development of various 'miraculous' *iddhis*. Precisely the same facility and mastery is also linked to furthering the *bhikkhu's* progress along the path to awakening.[97] There is understood to be no opposition between the development of *iddhi* and the development of *samatha* and *vipassanā* conducive to the final goal; they are of a piece.

In conclusion it is worth drawing attention to an important treatment found in the *Paṭisambhidāmagga*. The passage in question concerns how the meaning (*aṭṭha*) of *chanda*, *viriya*, *citta* and *vīmaṃsā* is to be directly known (*abhiññeyya*):

> The meaning of *chanda* is to be directly known as root; it is to be directly known as basis; it is to be directly known as endeavour; it is to be directly known as succeeding; it is to be directly known as commitment; it is to be directly known as taking hold; it is to be directly known as standing near; it is to be directly known as non-distraction; it is to be directly known as seeing.[98]

The meaning of *viriya*, *citta* and *vīmaṃsā* is to be directly known in precisely the same nine ways. The first four of these 'meanings' (root, basis, endeavour, succeeding) clearly relate to the basic *iddhi-pāda* formula. The five further 'meanings' in fact relate to the five spiritual *indriyas*: the *Paṭisambhidāmagga* throughout defines *saddhā* as 'commitment' (*adhimokkha*), *sati* as 'standing

---

[92] Vism XII 2-7.

[93] Id., XII 9.

[94] Id., XII 11.

[95] Id., XII 12.

[96] Vimutt Trsl 212.

[97] In Japanese the four *ṛddhi-pādas* are apparently understood as the four 'at-will-nesses' (*shijinsoku*) (K. Mizuno, *Primitive Buddhism*, Yamaguchi-ken, 1969, p. 178), an understanding that seems to bring out this aspect of the *ṛddhi-pādas* rather well.

[98] Paṭis I 19; II 123: *chandaṭṭho abhiññeyyo, chandassa mūlaṭṭho abhiññeyyo, chandassa pādaṭṭho abhiññeyyo, chandassa padhānaṭṭho abhiññeyyo, chandassa ijjhanaṭṭho abhiññeyyo, chandassa adhimokkhaṭṭho abhiññeyyo, chandassa paggahaṭṭho abhiññeyyo, chandassa upaṭṭhānaṭṭho abhiññeyyo, chandassa avikkhepaṭṭho abhiññeyyo, chandassa dassanaṭṭho abhiññeyyo.*

near' (*upaṭṭhāna*), *viriya* as 'taking on' (*paggaha*), *samādhi* as 'non-distraction' (*avikkhepa*) and *paññā* as 'seeing' (*dassana*). The choice of the *indriyas* here is perhaps not without significance. As I shall argue in the next chapter, the *indriyas* represent the most generally applicable category of the seven sets. So this passage neatly integrates the development of the *iddhi-pādas* and general spiritual practice.

CHAPTER FOUR

THE FACULTIES AND POWERS

1. The notion of indriya: the twenty-two indriyas

With the five *indriyas*, five *balas*, seven *bojjhaṅgas* and the *aṭṭhaṅgika-magga* the lists of the seven sets take on a slightly different character. As has been seen, the four *satipaṭṭhānas* are explained by describing four different aspects of developing what is essentially one, namely *sati* or 'mindfulness'. Similarly the four *samma-ppadhānas* are seen as four functions of *viriya* or 'strength'. While each of the *iddi-pādas* introduces a particular *dhamma—chanda, viriya, citta* or *vīmaṃsā*—as a whole, what is important in each case is the interaction of these with *samādhi* and *padhāna-saṃkhāras*; the *iddhi-pādas* seem ultimately to be understood as focusing on one particular thing, namely success in *samādhi*. In contrast the next four of the seven sets present four more or less bald lists of different *dhammas* characterized as faculties (*indriya*), powers (*bala*), factors of awakening (*bojjhaṅgas*), factors of the noble path (*ariya-magg-aṅga*) respectively. In the case of the *indriyas*, then, these five different items are confidence (*saddhā*), strength (*viriya*), mindfulness (*sati*), concentration (*samādhi*) and wisdom (*paññā*). The first point to consider is the significance of these items being collectively termed *indriyas*. What is an *indriya*?

The concept of *indriya* is one that is common to Indian thought in its generality and not something peculiar to the Buddhist tradition. The word *indriya* is, of course, derived from the name of the chief of the Vedic gods, Indra,[1] bearer of the thunderbolt (*vajra-dhara*) and counting among his mighty deeds the slaying of the dragon Vṛtra. An *indriya*, then, might be basically thought of as anything that has something of the quality of the mighty god Indra. Thus, in its application to a variety of categories in different systems of Indian thought, an *indriya* should be understood as an item or faculty that is seen as exercising some kind of power, force, influence or control over whatever is its domain; '(controlling) faculty' seems a more or less apt translation. The word *indriya* in Indian literature as a whole most commonly refers to the five sense organs of the eye, ear, nose, tongue and body, often—though not always—with the mind as the sixth. But the various schools of Indian thought, including Buddhism, also compiled elaborate lists of items considered as *indriyas* alongside these basic six which were held in common.[2]

---

[1] Mayrhofer, s.vv. *indraḥ, indriyaṃ*.

[2] Cf. the list of five *jñāna-indriyas* and five *karma-indriyas* in Sāṃkhya.

The classic complete list of *indriyas*, probably common to all ancient Buddhist schools,[3] contains twenty-two items:

1. eye-faculty (*cakkhundriya*)
2. ear-faculty (*sotindriya*)
3. nose-faculty (*ghānindriya*)
4. tongue-faculty (*jivhindriya*)
5. body-faculty (*kāyindriya*)
6. mind-faculty (*manindriya*)

7. female-faculty (*itthindriya*)
8. male-faculty (*purisindriya*)
9. life-faculty (*jīvitindriya*)

10. pleasure-faculty (*sukhindriya*)
11. pain-faculty (*dukkhindriya*)
12. happiness-faculty (*somanassindriya*)
13. unhappiness-faculty (*domanassindriya*)
14. neutral-feeling-faculty (*upekkhindriya*)

15. confidence-faculty (*saddhindriya*)
16. strength-faculty (*viriyindriya*)
17. mindfulness-faculty (*satindriya*)
18. concentration-faculty (*samādhindriya*)
19. wisdom-faculty (*paññindriya*)

20. faculty of coming to know the unknown (*anaññātaññassāmītindriya*)
21. faculty of knowing (*aññindriya*)
22. faculty of having known (*aññatāvindriya*)

From this list of twenty-two *indriyas* it can be seen that they fall into various groupings. The three groups most commonly treated in the Nikāyas are the six sense *indriyas* (1-6), the five 'spiritual' *indriyas*, with which we are principally concerned (15-19), and the five feeling *indriyas* (10-14).

The canonical literature tells us little more than that these twenty-two items can all be considered *indriyas*, so it is worth pausing for a moment to consider how the commentarial tradition views the common characteristic possessed by these twenty-two *indriyas*. Principally the commentaries reiterate what has already been said concerning the derivation of the word *indriya*. According to the *Vibhaṅga* commentary each *indriya* 'carries out the purpose of a ruler' (*indaṭṭhaṃ kāreti*) with regard to its particular realm.[4] Thus in the case of the five spiritual *indriyas*, *saddhindriya* carries out the purpose of a ruler in the manner (*lakkhaṇe*) of *adhimokkha* or 'commitment'; *viriyindriya* in the manner

---

[3] The twenty-two *indriyas* are first explicitly mentioned at Vibh 122, though all twenty-two are in fact found scattered throughout the *indriya-saṃyutta*: e.g. S V 203-7; eighteen are explicit in the *Saṃgīti-sutta* (D III 219, 239)—missing are *manindriya*, *jīvitindriya*, *itthindriya* and *purisindriya*. For the twenty-two in the literature emanating from the north of India see, e.g. *Mahāvyutpatti* 33, Abhidh-h Trsl 146-7 Abhidh-k 38-40 (*bhāṣya*); Abhidh-sam Trsl 48, Satya Trsl 41.

[4] Vibh-a 125.

of *paggaha* or 'taking on'; *satindriya* in the manner of *upaṭṭhāna* or 'standing near'; *samādhindriya* in the manner of *avikkhepa* or 'non-distraction'; *paññindriya* in the manner of *dassana* or 'seeing'. In addition all twenty-two *indriyas* are *indriyas* in the sense of lordship (*issariya*) understood as a term for overlordship or predominance (*ādhipacca*).[5] This last explanation corresponds exactly to what Vasubandhu says of the *indriyas* in the *Abhidharmakośa*:

> What is the meaning of *indriya*? [The root] *idi* [is used] with regard to supreme lordship. They are *indriyas* in that they exercise control over something. Thus the meaning of *indriya* is overlordship.[6]

Thus although we are primarily concerned with the five spiritual *indriyas* of *saddhā*, *viriya*, *sati*, *samādhi* and *paññā*, the wider perspective of all twenty-two *indriyas* is of some importance and significance, especially in the *Saṃyutta-nikāya* and Abhidhamma texts.

2. *Faith, truth and knowledge*

The word *saddhā* is most often translated as 'faith'. Even a brief perusal of the fairly extensive scholarly discussion of the notion of *saddhā* in Buddhist thought, however, serves to indicate the potential confusion inherent in such a translation.[7] Although the notion of 'faith' may possibly embrace the notion of *saddhā* at least as well as any other English word, the trouble is that it embraces so much more besides. The word 'faith' brings in its train a host of theological and philosophical connotations from the traditions of western thought inappropriate to the discussion of *saddhā*, and which can only serve to obscure the nature of its understanding in Buddhist literature. Yet scholars often seem to have been unaware of the extent to which these inappropriate associations have coloured their treatment; a case in point would seem to be Jayatilleke's account in his *Early Buddhist Theory of Knowledge*, of which more

---

[5] Vibh-a 126: *ādhipacca-saṃkhātena issariyaṭṭhenâpi etāni indriyāni*. Vibh-a 125-6 in addition states that either the Bhagavant or *kusalâkusala-kamma* may be considered the ruler or master (*inda*). Accordingly, the *indriyas* that are produced by *kamma* (*kamma-sañjanita*) are *indriyas* in the sense of bearing the mark of the ruler (*inda-liṅga*) and being the outcome of the ruler (*inda-siṭṭha*) where the ruler is *kamma*. All twenty-two have been declared (*pakāsita*) and awakened to (*abhisambuddha*) by the Bhagavant and so are *indriyas* in the sense of having been taught by the master (*inda-desita*) and seen by the master (*inda-diṭṭha*); they are also all *indriyas* in the sense of having been enjoyed by the master (*inda-juṭṭha*) since they are practised as pasture (*gocara*) or development (*bhāvanā*).

[6] Abhidh-k 38: *kaḥ punar indriyârthaḥ. idi paramaiśvarye. tasya idantîti indriyāṇi. ata ādhipatyârtha indriyârthaḥ*.(Cf. La Vallée Poussin, Abhidh-k Trsl I 103.)

[7] See La Vallée Poussin, 'Faith and Reason in Buddhism', *Transactions of the Third International Congress for the History of Religions*, (1908), II 32-43; E. Gyomroi-Ludowyk, 'The Valuation of Saddhā in Early Buddhist Texts', *UCR* V 32-49; 'Note on the Interpretation of pasidati', *UCR* I 74-82; B.M. Barua, 'Faith in Buddhism', *Buddhistic Studies*, ed. B.C. Law, Calcutta, 1932, pp. 329-49; Dayal, op. cit., pp. 145-7; N. Dutt, 'The Place of Faith in Buddhism', *IHQ* XVI 639-46; E. Conze, *Buddhist Thought in India*, London, 1962, pp. 47-50; K.N. Jayatilleke, *Early Buddhist Theory of Knowledge*, London, 1963, pp. 382-400; H. Köhler, *Śrad-dhā in der vedischen und altbuddhistischen Literatur*, Wiesbaden 1973; H.V. Guenther, *Philosophy and Psychology in the Abhidharma*, 3rd ed., Berkley, 1976, pp. 61-4; J.T. Ergardt, *Faith and Knowledge in Early Buddhism*, Leiden, 1977, pp. 140-6; J.R. Carter, *Dhamma*, pp. 99-114.

below. J.R. Carter, on the other hand, draws attention to the problem in the following:

> In an attempt to catch the force of "faith" (*saddhā*) one should avoid a pitfall presented by Western categories, especially as in the so-called faith and reason problems.[8]

To trace the vicissitudes of the notion of 'faith' in the history of western thought—religious and philosophical—would be a task of some considerable magnitude, and I shall not attempt it. One or two comments are, though, in order. Two dimensions of the notion of faith are often distinguished, namely the cognitive and affective.[9] Faith in its cognitive dimension is seen as concerning belief in propositions or statements of which one does not—or perhaps cannot—have knowledge proper (however that should be defined); cognitive faith is a mode of knowing in a different category from that knowledge. Faith in its affective dimension is a more straightforward positive response of trust or confidence towards something or somebody. Contemporary religious and philosophical discussion of faith is almost entirely concerned with faith in its cognitive aspect.[10] This preoccupation with the cognitive aspect of faith appears to be the particular legacy of post-Cartesian philosophy and Lutheran theology. The understanding of faith in Christian theology as a whole is obviously of great complexity and depth: the concerns of the Greek and Latin medieval writers were perhaps not always the same as those of their modern counterparts. Thus the question of whether or not such famous dicta as *credo ut intellegam* and *fides quaerens intellectum* operate with the same notions of faith and knowledge that the modern philosopher or religious thinker has, becomes another problem that in the present context only further compounds the difficulties of our understanding *saddhā* as 'faith'.[11]

In contrast to this, the conception of *saddhā* in Buddhist writings appears almost, if not entirely affective; the cognitive element is completely secondary; as Jan T. Ergardt says:

> To sum up: faith in these texts [*Majjhima-nikāya*] is mainly an affective and conative faculty that functions in the disciple's good decisions on the way to the goal. Its cognitive aspect is secondary and derived from the dhamma, of which the utmost knowledge is the knowledge and experience of release and nibbāna.[12]

I shall consider the affective nature of *saddhā* in Buddhist literature in more detail below. For the moment it will suffice to note that its affective nature is

---

[8] Carter, *Dhamma*, p. 104; both Conze's and Ergardt's discussion also show some appreciation of the problem.

[9] E.g. *ERE*, s.v. Faith (Christian); Jayatilleke, op. cit., p. 387.

[10] E.g. see J. Hick, *Faith and Knowledge*, New York, 1957, p. ix: 'Whether or not there be a God, great numbers of people have reported an experience which they describe as "knowing God" or "being aware of God". We are to be concerned with the mode of this putative knowledge or awareness, a mode which has long been accorded the special name of "faith". We wish to know in what it consists and how it is related to knowing and believing in general.'

[11] Cf. the following comment of Conze's, *BTI*, p. 48: 'This sceptical age dwells anyway far too much on the intellectual side of faith. *Śraddhā*, the word we render as "faith", is etymologically akin to Latin cor, "the heart", and faith is much more a matter of the heart than the intellect.'

[12] J.T. Ergardt, op. cit., p. 145.

more or less implicit in the fact that in the Nikāyas the objects of *saddhā* and the related term *pasāda* (trust) are not beliefs but, most commonly, the Buddha, Dhamma and Saṃgha. The affective nature of *saddhā* becomes explicit in the psychology of the Abhidhamma, where it is understood as having an affinity with greed or attraction to things (*rāga*).[13]

Significantly, some modern thinkers would not allow faith *qua* belief any cognitive status at all, and so effectively reduce faith to its affective dimension: to express belief in God is merely to expose a positive emotional response to the statement 'God exists'—a response, however, that may have quite definite consequences for the way one lives one's life.[14] Now this would seem to have something in common with Abhidhamma analysis, where the affirmation of mere 'beliefs' is seen as 'view' (*diṭṭhi*) that is rooted in attachment (*lobha*); but *saddhā*, although possessing a certain psychological kinship to *lobha*, is seen as a distinct and skilful positive emotional response of confidence.

What is *saddhā's* relationship to knowledge and truth? Jayatilleke finds elements of correspondence, consistency and pragmatist theories of truth in the Nikāyas, although he argues against any one theory being considered as the 'Buddhist' theory of truth.[15] It seems to me, however, that the evidence he presents clearly favours the conclusion that a pragmatist theory of truth comes *closer* to the Nikāya conception of truth than the others.[16] More recently K.H.

---

[13] Vism III 75: 'In one of greed temperament, when skilful [consciousness] occurs, *saddhā* is strong because its quality is close to that of greed, therefore one of *saddhā*-temperament has an affinity with one of greed-temperament. For, just as greed is affectionate and not mean on the unskilful side, so is *saddhā* on the skilful; just as greed seeks out the objects of sense desire, so *saddhā* seeks out the qualities of virtue, etc.; just as greed does not give up what is unhelpful, so *saddhā* does not give up what is helpful.' (*tattha yasmā rāga-caritassa kusala-ppavatti-samaye saddhā balavatī hoti rāgassa āsanna-guṇattā—yathā hi akusala-pakkhe rāgo siniddho nâtilūkho evaṃ kusala-pakkhe saddhā, yathā rāgo vatthu-kāme pariyesati evaṃ saddhā sīlâdi-guṇe, yathā rāgo ahitaṃ na pariccajati evaṃ saddhā hitaṃ na pariccajati—tasmā rāga-caritassa saddhā-carito sabhāgo.*)

[14] I.e. 'religious language' is acknowledged (following Ayer and Flew) as not meaningful descriptively, but like moral language it is to be understood as 'emotive' and 'prescriptive'. The classic essay is R.B. Braithwaite's 'An Empiricist's View of the Nature of Religious Belief' (I.T. Ramsey, ed., *Christian Ethics and Contemporary Philosophy*, London, 1966, pp. 53-73); cf. M.J. Charlesworth, *Philosophy of Religion: The Historic Approaches*, London 1972, pp. 155-9.

[15] Jayatilleke, op. cit., pp. 351-68.

[16] Jayatilleke's denial of this is rather curious. Commenting on the absence at M I 395 of a category of statements that can be 'false' (*abhūtaṃ, atacchaṃ*) and at the same time useful or beneficial (*attha-saṃhitaṃ*), he says that this might be 'either because it was considered self-contradictory to say of a statement that it was false but useful or because such statements did not in fact exist' (op. cit., p. 358) but, he continues, this is 'not because of any pragmatic theory of truth but because of the peculiarly Buddhist use of the term "useless" (*na attha-saṃhitaṃ*).' He then comments that this last term connotes 'what is useful for the attainment of the goal Nirvāṇa' and concludes that since a false statement is considered a 'moral evil' it is logically or causally impossible that it should result in what is 'morally advantageous or good (*attha-saṃhitaṃ*)' (p. 359). But surely this is to get things the wrong way round: a 'false statement' is a 'moral evil' precisely because it is not helpful for the attainment of *nibbāna*—it conduces to suffering rather than its cessation. More relevant to Jayatilleke's case is the possibility of statements that are at once 'true' and 'unhelpful'. The question then arises as to whether statements that are 'true ' but 'unhelpful' and statements that are 'true' and also 'helpful' are necessarily absolutely distinct classes, or whether it may not be simply circumstances and occasion that determines whether or not a given statement is helpful or unhelpful; the Nikāya passage under discussion notes that the Tathāgata is 'one who knows the right occasion' (*kālaññu*) for the uttering of helpful speech.

Potter has argued that *all* Indian schools of philosophy work with what is essentially a pragmatist theory of knowledge; that is, to know something as true is to be aware of its 'workability' (*prāmāṇya*), its effectiveness in accomplishing whatever is the aim or purpose (*artha*).[17] While a number of scholars have taken issue with Potter on various points,[18] what is clear from the debate is how careful we must be when we translate various Sanskrit or Pāli terms as 'knowledge', 'truth', 'belief' or 'faith'. Although such translations may be innocent enough in many contexts, when we engage in technical and philosophical discussion of the concepts behind them, we cannot silently or inadvertently assume that the terms of the discussion will be straightforwardly equivalent to those of modern western philosophical debate.

In order to illustrate the extent to which *saddhā* is of a purely affective nature in the Nikāyas, I wish now to consider a passage that treats *saddhā* and *ñāṇa* together.[19] In such a case it is all too easy to assume, as does Jayatilleke, that in fact *saddhā* must have a simple cognitive dimension. I give Jayatilleke's rendering of the passage in question:

> Nigaṇṭha Nātaputta: Do you *believe* in the statement of the recluse Gotama that there is a jhānic state (trance) in which there is no discursive or reflective thought and there is a cessation of discursive thought and reflection?
> Citta: I do not accept this as a *belief*.
> Nigaṇṭha Nātaputta: See what an honest, straightforward and upright person the householder Citta is ...
> Citta: What do you think? Which is better—*knowledge or belief*?
> Nigaṇṭha Nātaputta: Surely knowledge is better than belief.
> Citta: (I can attain up to the fourth jhāna) ... *Knowing and seeing thus, why should I accept this on the ground of faith* in any recluse or brahmin, that there is a trance in which there is no discursive or reflective thought ... [20]

This in places is more of a paraphrase than a translation. Jayatilleke takes the passage as contrasting an inferior mode of knowing, namely 'belief', with a superior one, namely 'knowledge'. The passage is, I think, doing something rather different. If one translates *saddahati* and *saddhā* by means of the notions of trust and confidence, the effect is rather different from the one Jayatilleke's translation produces:

> Do you trust the *samaṇa* Gotama [when he says] that there is a state of concentra-

---

[17] K.H. Potter, 'Does Indian Epistemology concern Justified True Belief?' *JIP* 12 (1984), pp. 307-27.

[18] See articles by J.N. Mohanty, and K.K. Chakrabarti in *JIP* 12 (1984), pp. 329-55.

[19] S IV 298-9: *saddahasi tvaṃ gahapati samaṇassa Gotamassa: atthi avitakko avicāro samādhi, atthi vitakka-vicārānaṃ nirodho ti. na khvāham ettha bhante bhagavato saddhāya gacchāmi: atthi ... ti. evaṃ vutte Nigaṇṭho Nātaputto sakaṃ parisaṃ ulloketvā etad avoca: idaṃ bhavanto passantu yāva ujuko câyaṃ Citto gahapati yāva asaṭṭho ... yāva amāyāvī câyaṃ Citto gahapati. vātaṃ vā so jalena bhadetabbaṃ maññeyya yo vitakka-vicāre nirodhetabbaṃ maññeyya, saka-muṭṭhinā vā Gaṅgāya sotaṃ āvāretabbaṃ maññeyya yo vitakka-vicāre nirodhetabbaṃ maññeyyā ti. taṃ kiṃ maññasi bhante. katamaṃ nu kho paṇītataraṃ ñāṇaṃ vā saddhā vā ti. saddhāya kho gahapati ñāṇaṃ eva paṇītataraṃ. ahaṃ kho bhante yāvad eva ākaṅkhāmi ... catutthaṃ jhānaṃ upasampajja viharāmi. so khvāhaṃ bhante evaṃ jānanto evaṃ passanto kassaññassa samaṇassa vā brāhmaṇassa vā saddhāya gamissāmi: atthi ... ti.*

[20] Jayatilleke, op. cit., p. 398; Jayatilleke's emphasis.

> tion without initial and sustained thinking, that there is cessation of initial and sustained thinking?

Note that it is *samaṇassa Gotamassa* that is the indirect object of *saddahasi*; Jayatilleke's introduction of the word 'statement' is really rather misleading. To continue:

> In this matter I do not have trust in the Blessed One [when he says] that there is a state of concentration without initial and sustained thinking ...

The ambiguity of Citta's reply is rather awkward to convey in translation. It is clear from Nigaṇṭha Nātaputta's response that he understands Citta as having said that he does not trust the Buddha, and that therefore Citta does not think that there is a state of concentration without initial and sustained thinking:

> When this had been said, Nigaṇṭha Nātaputta surveyed his own assembly and said: 'See what an honest man Citta the householder is ... Anyone who could think that initial and sustained thinking might be stopped would think the wind could be caught in a net ... or that the flow of the Gaṅgā could be obstructed with his own fist.'

Citta is then able to come back at Nigaṇṭha Nātaputta for assuming that the only grounds he might have for thinking that there is a state of concentration without initial and sustained thinking is because the Buddha had said so:

> 'What do you think, sir? Which is more refined, trust or knowledge?'
> 'Knowledge is more refined than trust, householder.'
> 'If I so desire, sir ... I dwell having attained to the fourth *jhāna*. Knowing and seeing thus, sir, who is the *samaṇa* or *brāhmaṇa* that I shall [need to] have trust in [when he says] that there is ... ?'

What this passage is doing, then, is contrasting the grounds for thinking or believing (*maññati*) something exists (*atthi*). One possible ground is the positive feeling of confidence or trust (*saddhā*) that one might have in someone who states that such and such exists, but however justified one's confidence is, a more subtle and refined reason or ground for thinking that something exists, is direct and personal knowing and seeing that something exists.[21]

Thus there seems to be no need to impart *saddhā* with the meaning 'belief', and understand it as directly cognitive in nature, an inferior kind of 'knowledge'. It seems to me that even in contexts such as the above, *saddhā* is still best understood as a positive mental attitude of trust or confidence.[22] Obviously from the point of view of translation having a positive mental attitude towards something—when, for example, that something is a proposition—can be very little different from 'believing' it. But from the point of view of the technical philosophical understanding of the Nikāyas, the point is of some importance:

---

[21] Cf. M I 294: *dve ... paccayā sammā-diṭṭhiyā uppādāya: parato ca ghoso yoniso ca manasikāro.* (See below, pp. 221-3.)

[22] The nearest one gets to *saddhā* as 'belief' and having cognitive value is perhaps M II 211: there are some *samaṇas* and *brāhmaṇas* who affirm (*paṭijānāti*) a basis for the holy life (*brahmacariya*) solely on account of *saddhā*, such as those who reason (*takkī*) and speculate (*vīmaṃsī*). Here those who place confidence or trust in their own reason as *grounds* for belief are contrasted with those whose ground is the authority of the Vedas; cf. Jayatilleke, op. cit., pp. 170-1.

saddhā is always essentially affective in nature. Terms such as *pema* ('affection') and *bhatti* ('devotion'), which are often juxtaposed and associated with *saddhā* in the Nikāyas, only serve to reiterate this essentially affective nature.[23]

Jayatilleke's assumption that one can understand *saddhā* as having a straightforward cognitive value like 'belief' leads him to some serious misunderstandings. Thus he talks in terms of the 'belief' with which the *bhikkhu* or *ariya-sāvaka* starts with, being '*replaced* by direct personal knowledge'.[24] But this is to ignore much of the treatment of the five *indriyas* in the Nikāyas.[25]

The relationship between *saddhā* and *ñāṇa* or *paññā* is in fact more in the nature of that between two different but complementary factors. *Saddhā* is seen primarily as important as initiating spiritual practice, but although it may not be as crucial in the higher stages of the Buddhist path, it is certainly misleading to talk of it as being *replaced* by *ñāṇa*. The reciprocal relationship that exists between *saddhā* and *paññā* is well illustrated by the following passage:

> The confident (*saddha*) *ariya-sāvaka* having repeatedly endeavoured so, having repeatedly been mindful so, having repeatedly practised concentration so, having repeatedly known so, thus becomes fully confident (*abhisaddahati*): 'Those *dhammas* which were previously only heard of by me—I now dwell having experienced them with my own body; having penetrated them by wisdom, I see them.'[26]

Thus *saddhā* is the instigator of a process which culminates in *paññā* which in turn reinforces *saddhā*. As J. R. Carter expresses it:

> *Saddhā* and *paññā* when taken together do not fit into "faith and reason". Rather, they express a dynamic process where *saddhā* is active in one wanting to know, coming to know in part and *paññā* becomes more pervasive in one coming to know and knowing fully, in truth.[27]

This basic conception of *saddhā* as initiating and providing a continuing support for a process that culminates in knowledge (*ñāṇa*) has been well traced and commented upon by a number of scholars,[28] and I shall not dwell on it.

In conclusion it is worth drawing attention to some of the findings of Köhler's study, *Śrad-dhā in der vedischen und altbuddhistischen Literatur*.[29] Köhler argues that in Vedic literature *śraddhā* should be understood primarily as denoting generosity (Spendefreudigkeit). As for *saddhā* in the Nikāyas, despite its title, Köhler's work proves rather disappointing. Just over four

---

23 M I 142, 444, 479: *tathāgate cassa saddhā-mattaṃ hoti pema-mattaṃ*. A III 165: *ekacco puggalo ittara-saddho hoti ittara-bhatti ittara-pemo ittara-ppasādo*.

24 Jayatilleke, op. cit., p. 399; my emphasis.

25 In fact Jayatilleke can maintain his thesis only by dismissing certain passages as later and so reflecting an entirely different conception of *saddhā*; op. cit., pp. 399-400.

26 S V 226: *saddho so bhante ariya-sāvako evaṃ padahitvā padahitvā evaṃ saritvā saritvā evaṃ samādahitvā samādahitvā evaṃ pajānitvā pajānitvā evaṃ abhisaddahati: ime kho te dhammā ye me pubbe sutavā ahesuṃ, te dānâhaṃ etarahi kāyena ca phusitvā viharāmi, paññāya ca ativijjha passāmī ti*.

27 J.R. Carter, *Dhamma*, p.104.

28 See especially J.R. Carter, *Dhamma*, pp. 103-6; cf. also J.T. Ergardt, op. cit., pp. 144-6.

29 Wiesbaden, 1973; originally submitted as a doctoral thesis, Göttingen, 1948. Cf. review by M. Hara, *IIJ* 19 (1977), pp. 105-8.

pages out of sixty-five pages are devoted to 'altbuddhistischen Literatur'.[30] Significantly, however, he does suggest here that the meaning of 'generosity' is once more relevant in certain contexts.[31] Otherwise, where *saddhā* is directed towards Buddha, Dhamma and Saṃgha, Köhler seems rather uncritically to accept that it means 'belief' (Glaube) and can be straightforwardly understood as 'das buddhistische Credo'.[32] Yet, if Köhler is right about *śraddhā* meaning 'generosity' in Vedic literature—and Minoru Hara has brought forward additional material that tends to support this conclusion[33]—then it seems to me that it also lends support to the view that the notion of *saddhā*, at least in the Nikāyas, must primarily be affective.[34] What I wish to turn to now is a consideration of the particular psychological features of *saddhā* that Buddhist literature has focused upon.

3. Saddhā, pasāda and sotâpatti

In the Nikāyas *saddhā* is most frequently explicitly directed towards the Buddha or his awakening: having heard *dhamma*, one acquires confidence (*saddhā*) in the Tathāgata;[35] the *ariya-sāvaka* is described as confident (*saddha*), he has confidence (*saddahati*) in the awakening of the Tathāgata.[36] A word closely related to *saddhā* in meaning is *pasāda. Pasāda* conveys at the same time notions of a state of mental composure, serenity, clarity or purity, and trust;[37] it is almost impossible to translate effectively. As I shall indicate below, the term *pasāda* is of particular significance in pointing towards a psychology of *saddhā* or 'confidence' which is elaborated upon in the later literature. The object of *pasāda* is once more the Buddha—along with the Dhamma and the Saṃgha. Thus a *bhikkhu* has trust in the Teacher (*satthari pasīdati*) thinking that the Blessed One is fully awakened; Dhamma is well declared by the Blessed One; the Saṃgha is well entered upon the way.[38] Similarly there are the four kinds of trust in that which is reckoned chief or highest, the four *agga-ppasādas*:

> [i] In so far as there are beings without feet, or with two feet or with four feet or with many feet, with form or formless, conscious or unconscious, or neither-conscious-nor-unconscious—of these the Tathāgata is called the highest, an *arahant*, a fully awakened one. Whoever has trust in the Buddha, has trust in what is highest, and for those who have trust in the highest, the highest is the result.
>
> [ii] In so far as there are conditioned *dhammas*, the noble eight-factored path is

[30] These are pp. 59-63.

[31] He cites S I 22, 32, 42; A III 34. Cf. also the expression *saddhā-deyyāni bhojanāni* (D I 9-12 passim): food given out of 'generosity' rather than out of 'faith'?

[32] Op. cit., pp. 60-2.

[33] M. Hara, 'Note on two Sanskrit religious terms *bhakti* and *śraddhā*', *IIJ* 7 (1964), pp. 123-45; '*Śraddhâviśeṣa*', *IT* 7 (1979), pp. 262-3.

[34] This is in contrast to Jayatilleke, who seems to see *saddhā* as 'belief' as primary and the affective, more emotional notion of *saddhā* as indicative of a later stratum of literature, op. cit., p. 400.

[35] D I 63; M I 179; etc.

[36] D III 237; M I 356; II 95; S V 197; A III 65; cf. Jayatilleke, op. cit., p. 389; Conze, *BTI*, p. 48.

[37] MW s.v. *pra-sāda*; *PED*, s.v. *pasāda*.

[38] M I 320.

called the highest of these. Whoever has trust in the noble eight-factored path … the highest is the result.

[iii] In so far as there are *dhammas* either conditioned or unconditioned, dispassion is called the highest of these *dhammas*, that is … *nibbāna*. Whoever has trust in Dhamma … the highest is the result.

[iv] In so far as there are communities or groups, the community of the disciples of the Tathāgata is called the highest of these, that is … an unsurpassed field of merit. Whoever has trust in the Saṃgha … the highest is the result.[39]

There is some reason for thinking that *pasāda* is often thought of as denoting a more refined and developed stage of *saddhā*; it is used especially in contexts where this seems appropriate. In this case *pasāda* is especially *avecca-ppasāda*, that is full-trust, trust that results from a certain degree of understanding.[40] Certainly this seems to accord with the comments made by Harivarman in the **Satyasiddhiśāstra*. Referring to a well known riddle[41] he describes the *arhant* as without confidence or trust (*aśraddha*). But he continues:

> When one perceives *dharma* for oneself, one's mind becomes clarified. This is also termed *śraddhā*. Having first heard *dharma* one perceives it face to face in one's own body; one thinks that the Dharma is absolutely true and not false. On account of this one's mind becomes pure (*prasīdati*); *śraddhā* is included in the four *avetya-prasādas*.

At this point I wish to consider further the way in which the post-Nikāya literature highlights two reciprocal aspects of *saddhā*—two aspects that are already implicit in the Nikāyas' use of the two terms *saddhā* and *pasāda*. In the first place, then, *saddhā* is the confidence at the heart of what motivates and spurs on spiritual activity; at the same time this confidence involves and is characterized by a mental clarity or purity. These two complementary aspects of *saddhā* are brought out especially clearly in a passage from the *Milindapañha*. Nāgasena explains:

> *Saddhā*, your majesty, when it arises averts the hindrances; a mind that is without

---

[39] A II 34: *yāvatā bhikkhave sattā apadā vā dipadā vā catup-padā vā bahuppadā vā rūpino vā arūpino saññino vā asaññino neva-saññi-nâsaññino vā tathāgato tesaṃ aggaṃ akkhāyati arahaṃ sammāsambuddho. ye bhikkhave buddhe pasannā agge te pasannā. agge kho pasannānaṃ aggo vipāko hoti. [ii] yāvatā bhikkhave dhammā saṃkhatā ariyo aṭṭhaṅgiko maggo tesaṃ aggaṃ akkhāyati. ye bhikkhave ariye aṭṭhaṅgike magge pasannā … aggo vipāko hoti. [iii] yāvatā bhikkhave dhammā saṃkhatā vā asaṃkhatā vā virāgo tesaṃ dhammānaṃ aggaṃ akkhāyati yadidaṃ … nibbānaṃ. ye bhikkhave dhamme pasannā … aggo vipāko hoti. [iv] yāvatā bhikkhave saṃghā vā gaṇā tathāgata-sāvaka-saṃgho tesaṃ aggaṃ akkhāyati yadidaṃ … puñña-kkhettaṃ lokassa. ye bhikkhave saṃghe pasannā … aggo vipāko hoti.* (Cf. *buddhe, dhamme, saṃghe avecca-ppasādo* at D II 217; M I 37, etc.)

[40] Cf. Jayatilleke's treatment of *avecca-ppasāda*, op. cit., p. 386.

[41] Cf. Dhp 97: *assaddho akataññu ca sandicchedo ca yo naro/ hatâvakāso vantāso sa ve uttama-poriso//* A similar play is perhaps also intended by the phrase with which Buddhas declare their intention to teach: 'May those who have ears release their faith, the gates of the deathless are open to them.' (D II 39 = M I 169 = S I 138 = Vin I 7: *apārutā tesaṃ amatassa dvārā/ ye sotavanto pamuñcantu saddhaṃ*) A number of scholars have deliberated over the verb *pamuñcantu* (does it mean 'give up' or 'put forth'?) apparently unable to countenance the idea that it might be deliberately ambiguous (see Lamotte, *Traité*, I 60-2; P. Masefield, *Divine Revelation in Pāli Buddhism*, Colombo, 1986, pp. 76-9). The association of *saddhā* and *adhimokkha* in the Pāli tradition is also surely relevant here. (Quotation adapted from Satya Trsl 182.)

> hindrances is clear, composed (*vippasanna*), undisturbed; just so, Your Majesty, *saddhā* has the characteristic of composure (*sampasādana*).[42]

In an extended simile *saddhā's* operation is likened to the throwing of a *cakkavattin's* water-clearing jewel (*udaka-ppasādakaṃ maṇi*) into water that is stirred up, disturbed, agitated and muddy (*khubhitaṃ āvilaṃ lulitaṃ kalalī-bhūtaṃ*), and which as a consequence immediately becomes clear and undisturbed (*vippasannaṃ anāvilaṃ*) and fit for drinking. Nāgasena then goes on to explain how *saddhā* also has the characteristic of leaping forward:

> When the practitioner sees that the minds of others are freed, he leaps forward after the fruit of stream-attainment, of once-return, of never-return or of *arahant*-ship. He makes an effort for the attaining of the unattained, for the obtaining of the unobtained, for the realization of the unrealized. So, your majesty, *saddhā* has the characteristic of leaping forward.[43]

This aspect of *saddhā* is likened to the way in which a crowd of people might be inspired to cross a swollen river after having first seen a strong man leap over (*pakkhandati*).

The two aspects of *saddhā* referred to in these similes are reiterated again and again not just in Pāli sources, but also in the treatises of the northern tradition.[44] The sequence of terms offered by the *Dhammasaṅgaṇi* in explanation of *saddhindriya* perhaps further suggests the particular dynamic that exists between confidence as spurring on and clarifying the mind: *saddhā saddahanā okappanā abhippasādo saddhā saddhindriyaṃ saddhā-balaṃ*.[45] The sequence might be interpreted as indicating a process beginning with straightforward trust (*saddahanā*) which leads to making ready and mental composure (*okappanā*), followed by complete clarity of mind (*abhippasāda*) which in turn is a strengthening of *saddhā*.

The way in which *saddhā* is seen as active in initiating spiritual activity is also brought out in the exegetical literature by the way *saddhā* is related to *chanda* (purpose, intention, the desire to act), *adhimokkha* (decision, commitment) and also *viriya* (strength). Thus Asaṅga in the *Abhidharmasamuccaya* states that the function of *śraddhā* is to provide a base for *chanda* which in turn serves as a base for *vīrya*.[46] I have already pointed out that the *Nettippakaraṇa*

---

[42] Mil 34-5: *saddhā kho mahārāja uppajjamānā nīvaraṇe vikkhambeti vinīvaraṇaṃ cittaṃ hoti acchaṃ vippasannaṃ anāvilaṃ. evaṃ kho mahārāja sampasādana-lakkhaṇā saddhā.*

[43] Mil 35: *yathā mahārāja yogâvacaro aññesaṃ cittaṃ vimuttaṃ passitvā sotâpatti-phale vā sakadāgāmi-phale vā anāgāmi-phale vā arhatte vā sampakkhandati. yogaṃ karoti appattassa pattiyā anadhigatassa adhigamāya asacchikatassa sacchikiriyāya. evaṃ kho mahārāja sampakkhandana-lakkhaṇā saddhā.*

[44] Cf. H.V. Guenther, *Philosophy and Psychology in the Abhidharma*, pp. 63-4. The image of the water-clearing gem is also found in Buddhist Sanskrit literature, cf. Abhidh-dī 71; *Vyākhyā* to Abhidh-k II 25. The term *prasāda* and an indication of *śraddhā's* initiating capacity are almost universal in definitions of *śraddhā*, see Abhidh-k 66; Abhidh-dī 71; Abhidh-sam Trsl 8.

[45] Dhs 10-11

[46] Abhidh-sam Trsl 7, 8. Interestingly the list of the eighteen *āveṇika-dharmas* peculiar to Buddhas in the *Mahāvastu* (I 160) and *Mahāvyutpatti* (No. 9, p. 3) has *chanda* and not *śraddhā* followed by *vīrya*, *smṛti*, *samādhi* and *prajñā*; Dayal's conclusion (op. cit. p. 141) that we can see in this an early state of affairs before *chanda* gave way to 'faith' is surely based on a misunderstanding of the nature of *śraddhā*. The *āveṇika-dhammas* are mentioned in Pāli sources but are not

defines *chanda-samādhi* in the context of the *iddhi-pādas* as one-pointedness of mind that has *saddhā* as its overlord or dominant factor.[47] The Pāli commentaries appear to focus more on *adhimokkha*: *saddhindriya* performs the purpose or aim (*aṭṭha*) of a ruler in the manner of commitment;[48] or as the *Visuddhimagga* and *Atthasālinī* put it, the manifestation of *saddhā* is commitment (*adhimutti-paccupaṭṭhāna*).[49] The Pāli commentaries also understand a direct relationship between *saddhā* and *viriya*: for one whose trust in the Buddha, etc., is strong, endeavour and strength increase.[50]

This understanding of the psychology of *saddhā* can be summed up in the following way. The arising of confidence provides the motivation to act; this involves decision and commitment. The combined effect of this is that the muddy water of the mind becomes clear and bright; free from disturbances the mind is strong and effective in applying itself. To play on the image: strength of purpose naturally crystallizes in the clear water of confidence. In conclusion I quote the standard definition of *saddhā* given in the *Visuddhimagga*:

> It is trust in that by its means they trust, or it itself trusts, or it is just trusting. Its characteristic is trusting or making ready; its function is clearing like the water-clearing gem, or leaping forward like crossing a flood; its manifestation is the absence of impurity, or commitment; its proximate cause is any ground for trust, or the factors of stream-attainment such as hearing the good *dhamma*. It should be seen as a hand, property and seed.[51]

Saddhā and sotâpatti

The passage just quoted from the *Visuddhimagga* states that *saddhā* should be understood as having its proximate cause (*pada-ṭṭhāna*) in the factors of stream-attainment (*sotâpatti-aṅga*). A passage of the *indriya-saṃyutta* similarly says that *saddhindriya* should be seen in terms of the four *sotâpattiyaṅgas*.[52] The four *sotâpattiyaṅgas* are listed in the *Saṃgīti-sutta* and *Saṃyutta-nikāya* as association with good people (*sappurisa-saṃseva*), hearing the good *dhamma* (*saddhamma-savaṇa*), proper attention (*yoniso manasikāra*) and practice in

---

actually listed (*CPD*, s.v. *āveṇi*); however, a list of eighteen qualities exactly parallel to the Buddhist Skt, with *chanda* instead of *saddhā*, is found in the *Vimuttimagga* Trsl p. 146.

47 Nett 15: *saddhâdhipateyya cittekaggatā ayaṃ chanda-samādhi.*

48 Ud-a 305 = Vibh-a 125: *adhimokkha-lakkhaṇe indaṭṭhaṃ karoti.*

49 Vism XIV 140; As 120. The emphasis on *adhimokkha* appears to be derived from the *attha* given for *saddhā* in Paṭis; see below, Chapter 10.2.

50 Sv III 1029 = Ps III 326 = Mp III 65: *yassa hi buddhâdīsu pasādo balavā tassa padhānaṃ viriyaṃ ijjhati.*

51 Vism XIV 140 (cf. As 120): *saddahanti etāya sayaṃ vā saddahati saddahana-mattaṃ eva vā esā ti saddhā. sā saddahana-lakkhaṇā okappana-lakkhaṇā vā, pasādana-rasā udaka-ppasādaka-maṇi viya pakkhandana-rasā vā oghuttaraṇaṃ viya. akālussiya-paccupaṭṭhānā adhimutti-paccupaṭṭhānā va. saddheyya-vatthu-pada-ṭṭhānā saddhamma-savaṇâdi-sotâpatti-aṅga-pada-ṭṭhānā vā. hattha-vitta-bījāni viya daṭṭhabbaṃ.* (The commentaries, e.g. Sv II 529, also give a fourfold definition of *saddhā*: confidence to be reached (*āgamanīya-saddhā*), of omniscient *bodhisattas*; confidence of attainment (*adhigama-saddhā*), of noble pesrsons; confidence of trust (*pasāda-saddhā*), which arises in response to the words 'Buddha, Dhamma, Saṃgha'; confidence of making ready (*okappana-saddhā*), which is the confidence that arises after making ready.)

52 S V 196: *catusu sotâpattiyaṅgesu ettha saddhindriyaṃ daṭṭhabbaṃ.*

accord with *dhamma* (*dhammânudhamma-paṭipatti*).[53] The *Saṃgīti-sutta* also gives a different list of four limbs of the stream-attainer (*sotâpannassa aṅgāni*).[54] Thus the stream-attainer is endowed with 'trust based in understanding' (*avecca-ppasāda*) in the Buddha, Dhamma and Saṃgha, and also has the virtues pleasing to the noble ones (*ariya-kantehi sīlehi samannāgato*). In this list the direct association of *saddhā* with stream-attainment is once more implicit in the use of the term *avecca-ppasāda*.

What then is the significance of this explicit association of *saddhā* with stream-attainer? The answer is best sought in the way stream-attainer is defined and explained in the Nikāyas and other Buddhist literature. The *sotâpanna* is said to abandon three *saṃyojanas* or 'fetters', namely the view of individuality (*sakkāya-diṭṭhi*), doubt (*vicikicchā*), and holding on to precept and vow (*sīla-bbata-parāmāsa*).[55] The *Dhammasaṅgaṇi* explains both *sakkāya-diṭṭhi* and *sīla-bbata-parāmāsa* as examples of wrong view (*micchā-diṭṭhi*) only associated with *citta* that has as a component greed or attachment (*lobha*);[56] *sakkāya-diṭṭhi* and *sīla-bbata-parāmāsa* are particular manifestations of that attachment. *Vicikicchā* is explained as doubting with regard to the Teacher, Dhamma, Saṃgha, the training, the past, the future, the past and future, and finally one is uncertain with regard to the way in which various *dhammas* have arisen according to various conditions.[57] Thus in principle *vicikicchā* is defined in exactly opposite terms to *saddhā* and *pasāda*. *Saddhā* is composed and steady clarity with regard to the Buddha, Dhamma and Saṃgha. While *vicikicchā* is wavering and uncertainty with regard to them.[58]

The thinking behind the association of *sotâpatti* and *saddhā* can perhaps be expressed in the following way. The relinquishing of attachment to individuality and precept and vow makes way for the establishing of firm confidence (regarded as having a psychological affinity with attachment); this in turn disperses doubt and uncertainty. The proper establishing of *saddhā*, the abandoning of *sakkāya-diṭṭhi*, *vicikicchā* and *sīla-bbata-parāmāsa* are, according to the logic of the dynamics of Buddhist thought, different aspects of the same process, each one involving each of the others.

4. *The remaining indriyas*

Viriyindriya

I have already discussed the nature of *viriya* in the context of the four *samma-ppadhānas*. In the present context it will suffice to remind ourselves of

---

53 D III 227; S V 347, 404.

54 D III 227; cf. S V 357, 362; A III 12; IV 405.

55 M I 9; S V 357; Dhs 182.

56 Dhs 75-80, 182-3.

57 Dhs 183: *satthari kaṅkhati vicikicchati, dhamme kaṅkhati vicikicchati, saṃghe kaṅkhati vicikicchati, sikkhāya kaṅkhati vicikicchati, pubbante kaṅkhati vicikicchati, aparante kaṅkhati vicikicchati; pubbantâparante kaṅkhati vicikicchati, idapaccayatā-paṭiccasamuppannesu dhammesu kaṅkhati vicikicchati.*

58 Cf. M I 101 where the five *cetokhilas* are defined as uncertainty with regard to the Teacher, Dhamma, Saṃgha, training and fellow *brahmacārins*.

how *viriyindriya* is explained in the two *vibhaṅga* or 'analysis' *suttas* of the *indriya-saṃyutta*. The first gives the following definition:

> And what is the faculty of strength? Here the noble disciple dwells as one who has produced strength; for the sake of abandoning unskilful *dhammas* and arousing skilful *dhammas* he is firm, of steady valour, unrelinquishing in purpose with regard to skilful *dhammas*.[59]

This definition echoes and is, in effect, an abbreviated version of the *samma-ppadhāna* formula—the four *samma-ppadhānas* are here reduced to two, just abandoning unskilful *dhammas* and arousing skilful. As if to drive this point home the second *vibhaṅga-sutta*, which immediately follows the first, gives exactly the same definition but appends the *samma-ppadhāna* formula in full, though without actually explicitly mentioning the *samma-ppadhānas*.[60] Two *suttas*, however, one immediately preceding the *vibhaṅga-suttas* and the other immediately following them, simply refer to the four *samma-ppadhānas* to explain *viriyindriya*:

> In respect of the four right endeavours—here is the faculty of strength to be seen.[61]

> That strength which he [= *ariya-sāvaka*] acquires having produced the four right endeavours, this is called the faculty of strength.[62]

Satindriya

The nature of *sati* too has already been discussed in some detail, so in the present context I shall simply confine myself to the definitions of *satindriya* in the *indriya-saṃyutta*. The first *vibhaṅga-sutta* explains *satindriya* like this:

> Here the noble disciple has mindfulness, he is possessed of the highest mindfulness and awareness; he is one who remembers and recalls what was done and said long before.[63]

The immediately following *vibhaṅga-sutta*, in a similar fashion to the procedure adopted with *viriyindriya*, then appends the basic *satipaṭṭhāna* formula to the very same definition, but without actually mentioning the *satipaṭṭhānas*. Further, the two other *suttas* mentioned in connection with *viriyindriya*, likewise simply refer to the four *satipaṭṭhānas* when explaining *satindriya*:

> In respect of the four establishings of mindfulness—here is the faculty of mindfulness to be seen.[64]

---

59 S V 197: *katamañ ca bhikkhave viriyindriyaṃ. idha bhikkhave ariya-sāvako āraddha-viriyo viharati akusalānaṃ dhammānaṃ pahānaya kusalānaṃ dhammānaṃ upasampadāya thamavā daḷha-parakkamo anikkhitta-dhuro kusalesu dhammesu.*

60 S V 198.

61 S V 196: *catusu samma-ppadhānesu, ettha viriyindriyaṃ daṭṭhabbaṃ.*

62 S V 199: *yaṃ kho bhikkhave cattāro samma-ppadhāne ārabbha viriyaṃ paṭilabhati idaṃ vuccati bhikkhave viriyindriyaṃ.*

63 S V 197: *idha bhikkhave ariya-sāvako satimā hoti paramena sati-nepakkena samannāgato cira-kataṃ cira-bhāsitaṃ pi saritā anussaritā. idaṃ vuccati bhikkhave satindriyaṃ.*

64 S V 196: *catusu satipaṭṭhānesu, ettha satindriyaṃ daṭṭhabbaṃ.*

The mindfulness which he acquires having produced the four establishings of mindfulness, this is called the faculty of mindfulness.[65]

Samādhindriya

The sources I have just referred to in defining *viriyindriya* and *satindriya* explain *samādhindriya* in the following ways. To begin with the first *vibhaṅga-sutta* once more:

> Here the noble disciple making release the object gains *samādhi*, gains one-pointedness of mind.[66]

The following *sutta* appends the formula of the four *jhānas* to this,[67] while the preceding *sutta* simply states that *samādhindriya* is to be seen in respect of the four *jhānas*.[68] So *samādhi* is understood as one-pointedness of the mind; it is the unifying of the mind, the collecting together and uniting of mental states or factors upon one object (*ārammaṇa*). As such, its characteristic is most clearly manifest in the states of *jhāna*.[69]

Once again the *Milindapañha* provides important similes illustrating the operation of *samādhi*. Its characteristic is said to be that it is 'at the head' or 'takes the lead' (*pamukha-lakkhaṇo samādhi*):

> As, Your Majesty, whatever rafters there are in a house with a ridge roof, they all lead to the ridgepole, incline towards the ridgepole, converge at the ridgepole and the ridge is termed their pinnacle—just so, Your Majesty, whatever skilful *dhammas* there are, all these are headed by concentration, incline towards concentration, lean towards concentration, tend towards concentration ...
>
> As, Your Majesty, a king might enter battle with an army of four parts, and the whole army, the elephants, horses, chariots and foot-soldiers would be headed by him, incline towards him, lean towards him, tend towads him, would follow after just him—just so ... [70]

The standard commentarial definition is as follows:

> It is concentration in that it places the mind evenly on the object, or it places rightly, or it is simply the collecting together of the mind. Its characteristic is absence of wandering or absence of dispersal; its function is the binding together of

---

[65] S V 200: *yaṃ kho bhikkhave cattāro satipaṭṭhāne ārabbha satiṃ paṭilabhati idaṃ vuccati bhikkhave satindriyaṃ.*

[66] S V 197: *idha bhikkhave ariya-sāvako vossaggârammaṇaṃ karitvā labhati samādhiṃ labhati cittassa ekaggataṃ.* (The use of the term *vossagga* perhaps should be thought to imply what, in the later terminology, would be called *lokuttara-jjhāna*; cf. below, pp. 165-6, 167).

[67] S V 200.

[68] S V 196: *catusu jhānesu, ettha samādhindriyaṃ daṭṭhabbaṃ.* (The *sutta* following the two *vibhaṅga-suttas* this time does not refer to the four *jhānas* in defining *samādhindriya*, but merely repeats the definition of the first *vibhaṅga-sutta* at S V 197.)

[69] In terms of the commentarial understanding we should perhaps understand the Nikāya use of *jhāna* as embracing both access concentration (*upacāra-samādhi*) and full absorption (*appanā*); cf. L.S. Cousins, *Religion* 3 (1973), p. 118.

[70] Mil 38: *yathā mahārāja kūṭâgārassa yā kāci gopānasiyo sabbā tā kūṭaṃ-gamā honti kūṭa-ninnā kūṭa-samosaraṇā kūṭaṃ tāsaṃ aggaṃ akkhāyati, evam eva kho mahārāja ye keci kusalā dhammā sabbe te samādhi-pamukhā honti samādhi-ninnā samādhi-poṇā samādhi-pabbhārā ... yathā mahārāja koci rājā catur-aṅganiyā senāya saddhiṃ saṃgāmaṃ otareyya, sabbā va senā hatthī ca assā ca rathā ca pattī ca tap-pamukhā bhaveyyuṃ tan-ninnā tap-poṇā tap-pabbhārā taṃ yeva anupariyāyeyyuṃ, evam eva kho ...* (A slightly different version is quoted at As 118.)

conascent [*dhammas*]—as water does for bath-powder; its manifestation is calming down; its proximate cause is especially happiness. It should be seen as steadiness of mind, like the steadiness of lamp-flames in the absence of wind.[71]

L.S. Cousins sums up the nature of *cittass'ekaggatā* as a *jhāna*-factor as follows:

> It refers specifically to a state in which the mind is absorbed in a single object. In the present context [i.e. as *jhāna*-factor] it is the ability to keep the attention, without wavering or trembling, aware only of the object of meditation.[72]

Samādhi is a state of firm concentration where the mind is completely absorbed in and content with its object. I shall consider further the nature of *jhāna* and *samādhi* in the context of my discussion of the awakening-factors in chapter five.

Paññindriya

The relevant *indriya-saṃyutta suttas* that we have been considering explain *paññindriya* as wisdom (*paññā*) concerning the rise and decay (of things) (*udayattha-gāminī*); wisdom that is 'noble, penetrating and that leads to the true destruction of suffering'.[73] This is then further characterized as knowing (*pajānāti*) the four noble truths.[74]

I do not wish to dwell on the nature of *paññā* here. Something of its nature has already come out in the discussion of *saddhā*, and I shall return to the subject when discussing *dhamma-vicaya* (chapter five) and *sammā-diṭṭhi* (chapter six). As the *indriya-saṃyutta* and other definitions indicate, *paññā* actually knows and sees the rise and decay of things; as a consequence it knows things as *anicca*, *dukkha* and *anattā*; it understands *dukkha*, its arising, its ceasing and the way leading to its ceasing; it understands how things are interdependent, conditioned by one another (*paṭiccasamuppanna*). What all this adds up to is that *paññā* knows the relationships and what governs the relationships between things; it understands how they interact. In short, it knows *dhamma* and *dhammas*. For this reason, it seems to me, Potter must be basically right, at least as far as Buddhist schools are concerned, in understanding *ñāṇa* to entail knowledge or awareness of the suitability of something for achieving the goal, which for all Buddhist schools is the ceasing of suffering for both self and others.

5. The indriya-saṃyutta: the samudaya, etc. formula

When considered in relation to the treatment of the other six sets in the *mahā-vagga*, within the *indriya-saṃyutta*[75] three formulaic treatments in par-

---

[71] Vism XIV 139: *ārammaṇe cittaṃ samaṃ ādhiyati sammā vā ādhiyati samādhāna-mattam eva vā etaṃ cittassā ti samādhi. so avisāra-lakkhaṇo avikkhepa-lakkhaṇo vā, sahajātānaṃ sampiṇḍana-raso nhāniyacuṇṇānaṃ udakaṃ viya, upasama-paccupaṭṭhāno, visesato sukha-pada-ṭṭhāno, nivāte dīpaccīnaṃ ṭhiti viya cetaso ṭhitī ti daṭṭhabbo.* (Cf. As 119.)

[72] L.S. Cousins, *Religion* 3 (1973), p. 122.

[73] S V 197: *ariyā nibbedhikā sammā-dukkha-kkhaya-gāminī.*

[74] S V 196, 199, 200.

[75] S V 193-43.

ticular stand out as being peculiar to the treatment of the (five spiritual) faculties. These consist of variations on (i) a formula concerning the arising (*samudaya*), disappearance (*atthagama*), delight (*assāda*), danger (*ādīnava*) and letting go (*nissaraṇa*) of the faculties;[76] (ii) a formula explaining that due to the relative strength of these five faculties one is an *arahant*, non-returner, once returner, stream-attainer etc;[77] (iii) a formula characterizing the five faculties as *bodhi-pakkhiya-dhammas*.[78] Variations on these three formulas collectively quite clearly constitute what is most important and distinctive in the Nikāya treatment of the faculties (within the *indriya-saṃyutta* at least). I wish now to consider especially the first two of these three treatments; the third I shall deal with in another context (chapter nine).

Immediately after the opening *sutta* of the *indriya-saṃyutta* (which merely lists the five spiritual faculties) we find the following:

> There are, *bhikkhus*, these five faculties. Which five? The faculty of confidence, the faculty of strength, the faculty of mindfulness, the faculty of concentration, the faculty of wisdom. As a result of the proper understanding of the delight, the danger and the letting go of these five faculties, one is called, *bhikkhus*, a noble disciple, a stream-attainer, not subject to ruin,[79] safe,[80] destined to full awakening.[81]

This constitutes the most succinct version of this *samudaya*, etc. formula. The principal variation, from the present point of view, is the addition to the beginning of the sequence 'delight, danger, letting go' of the two terms 'arising' (*samudaya*) and 'disappearance' (*atthagama*). A number of other slight variations occur combined with this; most of these do not affect the basic pattern of the formula.[82] Of some interest, however, is a variation which talks not of the '(arising, disappearance,) delight, danger, and letting go' of the five faculties, but instead of their arising (*samudaya*), cessation (*nirodha*) and the path leading to their cessation (*nirodha-gāminī-paṭipadā*):

> Any *samaṇas* or *brāhmaṇas*, *bhikkhus*, who understand the faculty of confidence, who understand the arising of the faculty of confidence, who understand the cessation of the faculty of confidence, who understand the way leading to the cessation of the faculty of confidence; who understand the faculty of strength ... who understand the faculty of mindfulness ... who understand the faculty of concentration ... who understand the faculty of wisdom, who understand the arising of the faculty of wisdom, who understand the cessation of the faculty of wisdom, who understand the way leading to the cessation of the faculty of

[76] S V 193-5, 195-6, 203-4.

[77] S V 200-2, 204-5.

[78] S V 227-8, 231, 237-9.

[79] *avinipāta-dhamma*, i.e. not liable to rebirth in *niraya* hell, or as an *asura*, animal or *peta*; a technical term of stream-attainment.

[80] *niyata*, literally 'restrained'; i.e. fixed, sure, assured of freedom.

[81] S V 193: *pañcimāni bhikkhave indriyāni. katamāni pañca. saddhindriyaṃ viriyindriyaṃ satindriyaṃ samādhindriyaṃ paññindriyaṃ. yato kho bhikkhave ariya-sāvako imesaṃ pañcannaṃ indriyānaṃ assādañ ca ādīnavañ ca nissaraṇañ ca yathābhūtaṃ pajānāti ayaṃ vuccati bhikkhave ariya-sāvako sotâpanno avinipāta-dhammo niyato sambodhi-parāyano ti.*

[82] E.g. the conclusion of the formula may be varied; thus instead of stream-attainment, by knowing the *samudaya*, etc. of the *indriyas* 'one is freed through absence of grasping (*anupādā vimutto*) and is called an *arahant*, one who has destroyed the *āsavas*' (S V 194). For the variations in full compare S V 193-5, 203-4.

wisdom—those *samaṇas* or *brāhmaṇas* are considered by me as *samaṇas* among *samaṇas*, as *brāhmaṇas* among *brāhmaṇas*.[83]

Here, then, the terminology of the four noble truths (*ariya-sacca*) is applied to the five spiritual faculties. In fact the *samudaya*, etc. formula is clearly closely related to the four-noble-truths formula in the Nikāyas. This is perhaps clear enough from the similarities in terminology used in the two formulas, but it is also apparent from the way in which the two are juxtaposed in some contexts, and are applied to the same categories and items, or at least to categories and items that have certain features in common. In the *khandha-saṃyutta* a whole cycle of *suttas* is found applying the formula of the four truths and the *samudaya*, etc. formula to the five aggregates of form (*rūpa*), feeling (*vedanā*), ideation (*saññā*), volitional forces (*saṃkhāras*) and consciousness (*viññāṇa*); this is what the *ariya-sāvaka* understands.[84] It seems, then, that knowing the arising, disappearance, delight, danger and letting go of something should be considered as more or less equivalent to knowing the four noble truths. Within the four primary Nikāyas the *samudaya*, etc. formula is found applied to the following items (in addition to the faculties and aggregates): feeling (*vedanā*); the seven footings of consciousness (*viññāṇa-ṭṭhiti*); two kinds of view (*diṭṭhi*)—the views of existence (*bhava*), and non-existence (*vibhava*); the objects of sensual desire (*kāma*), forms (*rūpa*), and feelings (*vedanā*); the elements (*dhātu*) of earth, water, fire and wind; gain, honour and fame (*lābha-sakkāra-siloka*); six classes of sense-object; the world (*loka*).[85] The four-noble-truths formula is also applied to many of these categories.[86]

So in the first place both formulas are characteristically applied to anything that can stand in place of *dukkha* as the first truth, or anything that might stand in for the 'world', such as the five *upādāna-kkhandhas*. Secondly the formulas are applied to that world especially as the potential object of attachment, such as the five classes of objects of sensual desire (*kāma-guṇas*), the seven footings of *viññāṇa*, feelings and so on. Precisely because all these things are potentially objects of attachment, the *bhikkhu* needs to know them as they are (*yathā-bhūtaṃ*); he needs to know their arising, their cessation and the way leading to their cessation; he needs to know their arising, their disappearance, their delight, their danger and their letting go.

Now, as will become clearer in a later chapter, the seven sets are repeatedly and most characteristically considered in the Nikāyas as items or *dhammas* that should be developed (*bhāvetabba*); the virtues of and benefits that accrue from developing them are set out and reiterated on nearly every page of the

---

83 S V 195-6: *ye hi keci bhikkhave samaṇā vā brāhmaṇā vā saddhindriyaṃ pajānanti saddhindriya-samudayaṃ pajānanti saddhindriya-nirodhaṃ pajānanti saddhindriya-nirodha-gāminī-paṭipadaṃ pajānanti viriyindriyaṃ pajānanti pe satindriyaṃ pajānanti pe samādhindriyaṃ pajānanti pe paññ-indriyaṃ pajānanti paññindriya-samudayaṃ pajānanti paññindriya-nirodhaṃ pajānanti paññindriya-nirodha-gāmini-paṭipadaṃ pajānanti, te kho pana me bhikkhave samaṇā vā brāhmaṇā vā samaṇesu ceva samaṇa-sammatā brāhmaṇesu ca brāhmaṇa-sammatā.*

84 Cf. R. Gethin, *JIP* 14 (1986), p. 43.

85 See D I 17-64 passim; II 68-70; M I 65, 85, 87-8, 504; III 18; S II 170-2; IV 43, 127-8, 192-4, 220-3, 232; A I 258-60; II 10-1; cf. *PTC*, s.vv. *assāda, ādīnava*.

86 E.g. S II 237.

respective *saṃyuttas* in the *mahā-vagga*. So for all later Buddhism these seven sets belong above all to the truth of the path (*magga-sacca*), the fourth of the noble truths. Given this fact it is slightly curious to find being applied to the five spiritual faculties a formula that is most usually applied to that which is seen as representing the conditioned world as tending to form the object of attachment—that is, what primarily constitutes the first truth, the truth of suffering (*dukkha-sacca*).

I say slightly curious, because there is, of course, no real problem here, at least when the question is considered in terms of Abhidhamma. The *dhamma-hadaya-vibhaṅga* states that the truth of suffering is to be understood (*pariññeyya*); the truth of the arising of suffering is likewise to be understood, but, in addition, its distinctive characteristic is that it is to be abandoned (*pahātabba*); similarly the truth of the cessation of suffering is to be understood, but its distinctive characteristic is that it is to be realized (*sacchikātabba*); finally the truth of the path that leads to the cessation of suffering is once more to be understood, but its distinctive characteristic is that it is to be developed (*bhāvetabba*).[87] So the five spiritual faculties, even when associated with the *lokuttara* mind at the time of the attainment of any of the four paths or four fruits, are 'to be understood' just like the truth of suffering, just like everything else. Moreover, we can also bear in mind in this connection the Abhidhamma view that the *lokuttara* mind along with its associated mental factors (*cetasika*) is of such a nature that it cannot be or subsequently become the object of any kind of unskilful *citta*, it cannot be an object of attachment. On the other hand, any other kind of skilful mind which includes among its associated mental factors *saddhā*, *viriya*, *sati*, *samādhi* and *paññā*[88] can be the object of unskilful *citta*, can be an object of attachment, either where someone subsequently becomes attached to his own skilful *citta* or is attached to the skilful *citta* of someone else.[89] What this means, then, is that there is not necessarily any conflict with the general outlook of ancient Buddhism involved in saying that a *bhikkhu* knows the arising, disappearance, delight, danger and letting go of *saddhindriya*, *viriyindriya*, *satindriya*, *samādhindriya* and *paññindriya*. There is no *a priori* reason why *saddhā*, *viriya*, *sati*, *samādhi* and *paññā* should not be seen as the world that is the potential object of attachment.

Yet the fact remains that the application of the *samudaya*, etc. formula to *saddhindriya*, etc. is rather striking. Why should the formula be applied only to the faculties and to none of the other six sets? A clue to the answer would seem

---

[87] Vibh 426-7. That the four truths are to be fully understood, abandoned, realized and developed respectively is, of course, already stated in the *Dhammacakkappavattana-sutta* (Vin I 10-12 = S V 422-3). Of course, one should understand here that is it not so much the 'truths' that are to be fully understood, abandoned, realized and developed as *dukkha*, *samudaya*, *nirodha* and *magga* themselves; cf K.R. Norman, 'The Four Noble Truths: A Problem of Pāli Syntax' in *Indological and Buddhist Studies*, ed. L.A. Hercus *et al.*, Canberra, 1982, pp. 377-91.

[88] All this is shown in the exposition of the *hetu*, *āsava*, *saṃyojana*, *gantha*, *ogha*, *yoga*, *nīvaraṇa*, *parāmāsa*, *upādāna* and *kilesa* couplets in the *Dhammasaṅgaṇi*, see Dhs 190-2, 195-209, 212-21, 242-2, 245-53, 256-9.

[89] According to the Theravādin system *saddhā*, *viriya*, *sati* and *samādhi* are always present in *kusala-citta*, *paññā* only sometimes; in the Sarvāstivādin system *śraddhā*, *vīrya*, *smṛti*, *samādhi* and *prajñā* are all present in all *kuśala-citta*.

to lie in the fact of the extended list of twenty-two faculties. For the *indriya-saṃyutta* is not confined to a consideration of just the five faculties of *saddhā*, *viriya*, *sati*, *samādhi* and *paññā*. Accordingly the *samudaya*, etc. formula is applied to the six sense faculties and to the five feeling faculties.[90]

Once the context of the extended list of faculties is taken into account, that the *samudaya*, etc. formula should be applied to the faculties of *saddhā*, *viriya*, *sati*, *samādhi* and *paññā* becomes rather more intelligible. For the list of twenty-two faculties does in fact have something of the quality of lists such as that of *rūpa*, *vedanā*, *saññā*, *saṃkhāras* and *viññāṇa* or of the six kinds of sense-object. Like them, the list of the twenty-two faculties embraces a kind of totality—a world complete in itself that might form the object of attachment. Indeed, from the point of view of the Nikāyas, the extended list of faculties can be seen as singling out what are considered to be the principal motive powers in the world of experience. Thus it is no surprise to find, when one turns to the canonical Abhidhamma texts, that the faculties (all twenty-two) are not dealt with in the contexts of the seven sets, but constitute a topic in what seems a traditional sequence: *khandhas*, *āyatanas*, *dhātus*, *saccas*, *indriyas*, *paccayâkāra* (= *paṭicca-samuppāda*).[91]

Of some interest in this connection is the *diṭṭhi-kathā* of the *Paṭisambhidā-magga*,[92] which quite clearly shows an extended list of faculties (nineteen in this case) being used in exactly the same way as *rūpa*, *vedanā*, *saññā*, *saṃkhāras* and *viññāṇa* and so on, in order to illustrate how the world becomes the object of attachment. The *diṭṭhi-kathā* begins by defining *diṭṭhi*, as *abhinivesa-parā-māsa* or 'holding on to conviction'. It then proceeds to illustrate how this takes place; it is due to having the attitude towards various items: 'this is mine, I am this, this is my self' (*etaṃ mama, eso'haṃ asmi, eso me attā*). Not surprisingly, given the nature of the characterization of the attitude, the series of items subject to it begins with *rūpa*, *vedanā*, *saññā*, *saṃkhāras* and *viññāṇa*.[93] We then have six senses (eye, ear, nose, tongue, body and mind); the six kinds of sense object (visible forms, sounds, smells, tastes, bodily sensations and *dhammas*); six classes each of consciousness (*viññāṇa*), ideation (*saññā*), volition (*sañcetanā*), craving (*taṇhā*), initial and applied thinking (*vitakka*, *vicāra*);

---

[90] S V 205-9; the formula is thus applied to sixteen of the twenty-two *indriyas*; *itthindriya*, *purisindriya*, *jīvitindriya*, along with the three special knowledge *indriyas*, are listed only briefly once in the *indriya-saṃyutta*. The first three do not feature prominently in the Nikāyas (is this their only listing?), while it would be inappropriate to apply the *samudaya*, etc. formula to the three knowledge *indriyas*, since in Abhidhamma they are quite definitely seen as exclusively characterizing the *paññā* of *lokuttara-citta*.

[91] Cf. the order of the eighteen *vibhaṅgas* and the order of topics in the *dhammahadaya-vibhaṅga* in the *Vibhaṅga* and also the *Dhātukathā* and *Yamaka*. This traditional order of topics is not, it seems, a peculiarity of Theravādin texts, but is also found in Buddhist Skt sources; e.g. *Arthaviniścaya-sūtra* (this text, having dealt with the twenty-two *indriyas*, subsequently goes on to deal with the five spiritual *indriyas* again in the context of the seven sets). See also Warder's essay 'The Mātikā' in the *Mohavicchedanī*.

[92] Paṭis I 135-61.

[93] Cf. Vin I 13 = S III 66-8 where the *khandhas* are analyzed as *anicca*, *dukkha* and *anattā* and the conclusion is reached with regard to each one in turn that it is not proper to have the view 'this is mine, I am this, this is my self'.

six elements (*dhātu*) of earth, fire, wind, water, consciousness and space;[94] thirty-two parts of the body; twelve *āyatanas*, eighteen *dhātus*, nineteen *indriyas*;[95] the sense (*kāma-*), form (*rūpa-*) and formless (*arūpa-*) realms (*dhātu*); nine kinds of existence (*bhava*); four *jhānas*; four kinds of *ceto-vimutti* (loving kindness, compassion, sympathetic joy and equipoise); four formless attainments, and finally twelve links of *paṭicca-samuppāda*.

Is there any significance in all this for the interpretation of the five spiritual faculties? The answer, I think, is yes. The very existence of the extended list of faculties, the way the *samudaya*, etc. formula is applied to it, the way it features in the Abhidhamma texts and is treated in the *diṭṭhi-kathā* of the *Paṭisambhidāmagga*—all these factors suggest that the special import of the list of the five spiritual faculties is that it characterizes *saddhā*, *viriya*, *sati*, *samādhi* and *paññā* in their most universal aspect: wherever and whenever these *dhammas* occur their characteristic is that they function in some respects as faculties. This is—to anticipate what I shall have to say about the *bojjhaṅgas* and *ariyo aṭṭhaṅgiko maggo*—in contra-distinction to the more specialized and specific functions of *viriya*, *sati*, *samādhi* and *paññā* as *bojjhaṅgas* and factors of the *ariya-magga*.[96]

That *saddhindriya*, *viriyindriya*, *satindriya*, *samādhindriya* and *paññindriya* should be understood as representing *saddhā*, etc., in their general aspect seems to be corroborated by a comparison of the treatment of the faculties (the twenty-two) and the other six sets in the *Vibhaṅga*. What is quite clear from the treatment according to the Abhidhamma method[97] is that while the *satipaṭṭhānas*, *samma-ppadhānas*, *iddhi-pādas*, *bojjhaṅgas* and *ariyo aṭṭhaṅgiko maggo* are all treated exclusively from the point of view of the *lokuttara* mind, *saddhindriya*, etc. are treated generally, as being associated with sense sphere (*kāmâvacara*), form sphere (*rūpâvacara*), formless sphere (*arūpâvacara*) or the *lokuttara* mind.[98]

One should note here that the Pāli commentaries do in fact allow that there are ordinary non-transcendent (*lokiya*) *satipaṭṭhānas*, *samma-ppadhānas*, *iddhi-pādas*, *balas*, *bojjhaṅgas* and *maggaṅgas*. This does not, I think, imply any real difference of view between the *Vibhaṅga* and commentaries. The Theravādin outlook on this point can be summed up as follows. Strictly speaking, from the point of view of Abhidhamma, we can only say that the *satipaṭṭhānas*, *samma-ppadhānas*, *iddhi-pādas*, *balas*, *bojjhaṅgas* and *maggaṅgas* function truly and fully when brought to the stage of *lokuttara-citta*; this is their natural and proper level. However, in certain kinds of ordinary skilful *citta*—just what kinds I shall consider later—the *satipaṭṭhānas* and other sets (excepting the faculties) may function in a manner that approximates to this stage or level of

---

[94] In the *Cūḷa-rāhulovāda-sutta* (M III 278-80) more or less the same series of items, to this point, is considered as *anicca, dukkha, anattā*.

[95] Missing are the three knowledge *indriyas*.

[96] I.e. *viriya* as *viriya-sambojjhaṅga* and *sammā-vāyāma*; *sati* as *sati-sambojjhaṅga* and *sammā-sati*; *samādhi* as *samādhi-sambojjhaṅga* and *sammā-samādhi*; *paññā* as *dhamma-vicaya-sambojjhaṅga* and *sammā-diṭṭhi*.

[97] I.e. in the *abhidhamma-bhājaniya* and *pañhâpucchaka* sections.

[98] See Chapter 10.

full development.[99] When it comes to the five spiritual faculties, however, these considerations and provisos are not relevant; when there is *saddhā* it functions as an *indriya*; sometimes more, sometimes less fully perhaps, but it never loses its basic quality of being an *indriya*; similarly for *viriya*, *sati*, *samādhi* and *paññā*.

This, then, is the understanding of the faculties that has emerged so far, based on a consideration of the application of the *samudaya*, etc. formula to the five spiritual faculties, and questions raised thereby. Matters, however, are not quite as straightforward as this. As soon as one turns to the other *indriya* formulas, and to the *Kathāvatthu* and the treatises of northern India, it becomes apparent that just when *saddhā*, etc. should be properly called faculties is something of a moot point.

The *indriya-kathā* of the *Kathāvatthu* addresses itself to the question of whether it is proper to distinguish 'confidence' (*saddhā*), etc. from 'the faculty of confidence' (*saddhindriya*), etc. on the grounds that the former is 'ordinary' (*lokiya*) while the latter is exclusively and strictly speaking 'transcendent' (*lokuttara*).[100] The position the *indriya-kathā* adopts is that this would not be an appropriate conclusion. On the contrary, just as it is perfectly correct to term ordinary mind (*lokiyo mano*) 'the faculty of mind' (*manindriya*) and so forth, so it is perfectly correct to call ordinary confidence (*lokiyā saddhā*) 'the faculty of confidence' (*saddhindriya*). The *Kathāvatthu* takes up its position by appealing to the extended list of faculties. The list is understood as attributing the *common* characteristic of *indriya* to twenty-two different items; all are termed faculties because they have a certain property in common irrespective of whether they are *lokiya* or *lokuttara*. If *saddhā* is called *saddhindriya* only when (i.e. by virtue of its being) *lokuttara*, then it is necessarily an *indriya* in a totally different sense from, for example, the eye-faculty (*cakkhundriya*), to which the categories of *lokiya* or *lokuttara* simply do not apply. The final appeal for the *Kathāvatthu's* viewpoint is the famous passage where the Buddha, requested to teach by Brahmā Sahampati, surveys the world with his buddha-eye and sees beings of different and varying propensities, some with weak faculties (*mudindriya*), some with sharp or acute faculties (*tikkhindriya*).[101] It is this general sense of *indriya* that the *Kathāvatthu* argues is relevant to the five spiritual faculties.

The *Kathāvatthu* commentary informs us that it was the Hetuvādins and Mahiṃsāsakas who held the view that *lokiyā saddhā* is just called *saddhā* and not *saddhindriya* and so forth for *viriya*, *sati*, *samādhi* and *paññā*.[102] According to the material collated by André Bareau a number of other schools also adopted this outlook on the five faculties. They are the Vibhajyavāda, the

[99] The details of all this, and the rather different way the matter is treated in other systems of Abhidharma are considered in Chapter 10.

[100] Kv 589-92.

[101] E.g. M I 169.

[102] Kv-a 183-4 : *idāni indriya-kathā nāma hoti. tattha lokiyā saddhā saddhā yeva nāma na saddhindriyaṃ tathā viriyaṃ ... sati ... samādhi ... paññā paññā yeva nāma na paññindriyan ti yesaṃ laddhi seyyathâpi Hetuvādānañ c'eva Mahiṃsāsakānañ ca, te sandhāya pucchā sakavādissa, paṭiññā itarassa.*

Mahāsāṃghika and the school to which the *Śāriputrâbhidharma-śāstra* belongs.[103] The *pudgalavādin* Vātsīputrīyas, on the other hand, adopted the position that the five spiritual faculties should be understood as pertaining to the stage of *laukikâgra-dharma*, that is the stage immediately prior to the arising of *lokottara* consciousness.[104] The Sarvāstivādins seem to have been in accord with the Theravādins on this issue, and viewed *śraddhendriya*, *vīryendriya*, *smṛtîndriya*, *samādhîndriya*, and *prajñendriya* as characterizing *śraddhā*, *vīrya*, *smṛti*, *samādhi* and *prajñā* in their generality.[105]

Bareau records that the reason for the Vibhajyavādin view that the five spiritual faculties should be regarded as exclusively *lokottara* is because of the *sūtra* 'd'après lequel, selon le degré de culture de ces cinq facultés, on obtient l'un ou l'autre des quatre fruits de Sainteté, alors que celui qui en est complètement dépourvu est un profane'.[106] This *sūtra* in fact corresponds to one of the variations in the cycle of *suttas* concerning the relative strength of the faculties and the consequent fruit;[107] this constitutes the second of the three principal *indriya-saṃyutta* formulas I referred to earlier, and it is this formula which I shall now consider.

6. *The indriya-saṃyutta: the 'relative strength' formula*

A total of eight *suttas*[108] in the *indriya-saṃyutta* can be said to present a variation on the following formula:

> There are these five faculties. Which five? The faculty of confidence, the faculty of strength, the faculty of mindfulness, the faculty of concentration, the faculty of wisdom. Due to the accomplishment and fulfilment of these five faculties one is an *arahant*; with faculties weaker than this one is a never-returner; with faculties weaker than this one is a once-returner; with faculties weaker than this one is a stream-attainer; with faculties weaker than this one is a follower by *dhamma*; with faculties weaker than this one is a follower by confidence.[109]

The variations on this formula are achieved in two ways. First by varying the types of different person who correspond in descending order to the relative strength of the five spiritual faculties; the relevant different lists of persons are set out in the table on page 127. Secondly by on occasion adding different closing comments; these are three in number:

> Thus difference in faculties means difference in the fruits; difference in the fruits means difference in persons.[110]

---

103 Bareau, *SBPV*, pp. 66-7, 172, 195, 197, 199.

104 Id., p. 118; this understanding seems to tie in with the notion of each one of the seven sets being associated with a particular stage in the Buddhist path, see Chapter 10.6.

105 Id., pp. 143, 145, 146.

106 Id., p. 172.

107 The *sutta* in question is to be found at S V 202 entitled *paṭipanno*.

108 For all eight, see S V 220-2, 204-5.

109 S V 200: *imesaṃ kho bhikkhave pañcannaṃ indriyānaṃ samattā paripūrattā arahaṃ hoti; tato mudutarehi anāgāmī hoti; tato mudutarehi sakadāgāmī hoti; tato mudutarehi sotâpanno hoti; tato mudutarehi dhammânusārī hoti; tato mudutarehi saddhânusārī hoti.*

110 S V 200, 201: *iti kho bhikkhave indriya-vemattatā phala-vemattatā hoti; phala*-vemattatā puggala-vemattatā hoti.* (*Reading, with Be and Ce, *phala-* for PTSe's *bala-*.)

TABLE 2. PERSONS ACCORDING TO STRENGTH OF INDRIYAS IN DESCENDING ORDER

arahant	*arahant*	*arahant*	*arahant*
arahatta-phala-sacchikiriyāya paṭipanno			
		antarā-parinibbāyin	*antarā-parinibbāyin*
		upahacca parinibbāyī	*upahacca parinibbāyī*
anāgāmin	*anāgāmin*	*asaṃkhāra-parinibbāyin*	*asaṃkhāra-parinibbāyin*
		sasaṃkhāra-parinibbāyin	*sasaṃkhāra-parinibbāyin*
		uddhaṃ-soto akaniṭṭha-gāmī	*uddhaṃ-soto akaniṭṭha-gāmī*
anāgāmi-phala-sacchikiriyāya paṭipanno			
sakadāgāmin	*sakadāgāmin*	*sakadāgāmin*	*sakadāgāmin*
sakadāgāmi-phala-sacchikiriyāya paṭipanno			
			eka-bījin
			kolaṃ-kola
sotâpanna	*sotâpanna*	*sotâpanna*	*satta-kkhatthu-parama*
	dhammânusārin	*dhammânusārin*	*dhammânusārin*
	saddhânusārin	*saddhânusārin*	*saddhânusārin*
sotâpanna-phala-sacchikiriyāya paṭipanno			
puthujjana			
S V 202	S V 200-1	S V 201-2	S V 204-5

> Thus the one who does the full amount achieves the full amount; the one who does part achieves part. I declare that these five faculties are not barren, *bhikkhus*.[111]
>
> The one who is in every way and everywhere wholly without these five faculties, him I declare an outsider, one who stands in the ranks of the ordinary man.[112]

At first sight the way in which the relative strength of the faculties corresponds to a range of attainments might well seem to support the view that the five *faculties* should be thought of as characterizing *saddhā*, etc., in their generality. But what is crucial here is how the Nikāyas understand the terms 'follower by confidence' (*saddhânusārin*), 'follower by *dhamma*' (*dhammânusārin*), and 'ordinary man' (*puthujjana*).[113] The statement to the effect that one completely without the five faculties should be considered a *puthujjana* seems to correspond exactly to the Sūtra passage upon which the Vibhajyavāda based its understanding of the faculties as exclusively *lokottara*.

Later Buddhist literature that postdates the Nikāyas or Āgamas seems agreed in understanding the term *puthujjana/pṛthagjana* as referring to anyone who has not attained one of the four paths or four fruits.[114] Similarly there appears to be general agreement that *saddhânusārin/śraddhânusārin* and *dhammânusārin/dharmânusārin* should be understood as two varieties of persons who are standing upon or who have just gained the path of stream-attainment, and who, immediately they gain the fruit, are designated 'freed by confidence' (*saddhā-vimutta/śraddhâdhimukta*) and 'one who has obtained vision' (*diṭṭhi-patta/dṛṣṭi-prāpta*) respectively.[115] To this extent these definitions should, it seems, be considered as belonging to the common heritage of ancient Buddhism. There were, no doubt, differences of detail between the Abhidharma systems on these points. For instance according to the Theravādin system the *saddhânusārin* and *dhammânusārin* will each exist for only one thought moment, while in the Sarvāstivādin system the *śraddhânusārin* and *dharmânusārin* will exist for fifteen thought moments. But in both systems the fruit moment follows immediately and inevitably upon the path; in both systems the essential difference between the *saddhânusārin/śraddhânusārin* and *dhammânusārin/dharmânusārin* relates to the difference between weak (*mudu/mṛdu*) faculties in the case of the former, and sharp (*tikkha/tīkṣṇa*) faculties in the case of the latter.[116]

These facts seem to show that certain portions of the *indriya-saṃyutta* in

---

[111] S V 201, 202: *iti kho bhikkhave paripūraṃ paripūra-kārī ārādheti. padesaṃ padesa-kārī ārādheti. avañjhānī tv evâhaṃ bhikkhave pañcindriyāni vadāmī ti.*

[112] S V 202: *yassa kho bhikkhave imāni pañcindriyāni sabbena sabbaṃ sabbathā sabbaṃ natthi, taṃ ahaṃ bāhiro puthujjana-pakkhe ṭhito ti vadāmi.*

[113] The technicalities of the exact distinctions between the five types of person beginning with the *antarā-parinibbāyin*, and between the three types of person beginning with the *eka-bījin* need not concern us here. The later literature is in broad agreement that they refer to distinctions within the general class of *anāgāmin* and *sotâpanna* respectively; see Pugg 14-7; Vism XXIII 55-7.

[114] E.g. Pugg 12; Vism XXII 5; Abhidh-h Trsl 159; Abhidh-sam Trsl 158.

[115] Vism XXI 75; Abhidh-k 353; Abhidh-h Trsl 73-5.

[116] Abhidh-h Trsl 75; Abhidh-k 353. The reference to *indriyas* as *mudu* or *tikkha* is not quite explicit in the Pāli sources, but is clearly enough indicated: see Ps III 190; Spk III 235; Pugg-a 193-4.

fact support the view that the five faculties should be understood as referring only to the *saddhā*, *viriya*, *sati*, *samādhi* and *paññā* of the *ariya-puggala*, the person who has gained one of the four paths or four fruits; the five faculties must, in other words, be exclusively *lokuttara*. Or should one conclude that the later tradition has straightforwardly imposed entirely inappropriate technical interpretations upon the terminology of the Nikāyas? Here we move into something of a problematic area. Clearly one of the reasons for the explicit interpretation and definition of the term *puthujjana* in the *Puggalapaññatti* is precisely this kind of passage that contrasts the *puthujjana* with the eight kinds of *ariya-puggala*. Similarly there are other Nikāya passages that use the term *puthujjana* which can be viewed as supporting the traditional interpretation.[117] No doubt the tighter technical definition of terminology should be seen as the end product of a gradual and continuous process, and not as what amounts to a radical reinterpretation of earlier material.

Saddhânusārin and dhammânusārin

A passage in the *khandha-vagga* of the *Saṃyutta-nikāya* appears to provide the nearest thing to a definition of *saddhânusārin* and *dhammânusārin* in the Nikāyas:

> The eye, *bhikkhus*, is impermanent, changing, becoming otherwise; the ear ... the nose ... the tongue ... the body ... the mind is impermanent, changing, becoming otherwise ... He who is confident in, decided upon these *dhammas* thus, is called a *saddhânusārin*, one who has entered into the way of perfection, has entered into the level of good men, has passed beyond the level of the *puthujjana*; he is incapable of committing that deed whose performance would cause him to rise in Niraya, or in the womb of an animal, or in the realm of the *petas*, he is incapable of dying until he has realized the fruit of stream-attainer. One whose insight these *dhammas* thus partially satisfy by means of wisdom is called a *dhammânusārin*, one who has entered into the way of perfection ... [as for the *saddhânusārin*]. He who knows and sees these *dhammas* thus, is called a stream-attainer, not subject to ruin, safe, assured of full awakening.[118]

Clearly here the *saddhânusārin* and *dhammânusārin*, although distinguished from the stream-attainer proper, are certainly very close to being stream-attainers. Like the stream-attainer they cannot suffer rebirth in any of the inferior realms; and they are distinguished from the *puthujjana*—they have passed beyond his level. Finally it is said that they cannot die without realizing the

---

[117] A clear example is S V 397: 'The one who is in everyway and everywhere completely without the four factors of stream-attainment, him I declare to be an outsider, one who stands in the ranks of the *puthujjana*.' Cf. S V 362-3, 381, 386.

[118] S III 225: *cakkhuṃ bhikkhave aniccaṃ vipariṇāmiṃ aññathābhāvi. sotaṃ ... ghānaṃ ... jivhā ... kāyo ... mano anicco vipariṇāmī aññathābhāvī. yo bhikkhave ime dhamme evaṃ saddahati adhimuccati ayaṃ vuccati saddhânusārī okkanto sammatta-niyāmaṃ sappurisa-bhūmiṃ okkanto vītivatto puthujjana-bhūmiṃ. abhabbo taṃ kammaṃ kātuṃ yaṃ kammaṃ katvā nirayaṃ vā tiracchāna-yoniṃ vā petti-visayaṃ vā uppajjeyya. abhabbo ca tāva kālaṃ kātuṃ yāva na sotâpatti-phalaṃ sacchikaroti. yassa kho ime dhammā evaṃ paññāya mattaso nijjhānaṃ khamanti ayaṃ vuccati dhammânusārī okkanto sammatta-niyāmaṃ ... yo bhikkhave ime dhamme evaṃ jānāti passati ayaṃ vuccati sotâpanno avinipāta-dhammo niyato sambodhi-parāyano ti.*

fruit of stream-attainment. It seems hardly surprising then that the later tradition views the *saddhânusārin* and *dhammânusārin* as it does.

In a number of places in the Nikāyas the terms *dhammânusārin* and *saddhânusārin* occur as the last two members of a list of seven persons: (i) one who is freed both ways (*ubhatobhāga-vimutta*); (ii) one who is freed by wisdom (*paññā-vimutta*); (iii) one who realizes with the body (*kāya-sakkhin*); (iv) one who has obtained vision (*diṭṭhi-patta*); (v) one who is freed by confidence (*saddhā-vimutta*); (vi) *dhammânusārin*; (vii) *saddhânusārin*.[119] The fullest discussion of these seven terms occurs in the *Kīṭāgiri-sutta* of the *Majjhima-nikāya*.[120] As far as the first five terms are concerned I do not wish to discuss the details of the *Majjhima* definitions but merely to consider how these relate to the definitions of the final two. The 'one who is freed both ways' and the 'one who is freed by wisdom' are both said to see by means of wisdom that the *āsavas* are destroyed (*paññāya assa disvā āsavā parikkhīṇā honti*); for both of them there is nothing left to be done by heedfulness (*na appamādena karaṇīyaṃ*). The 'one who realizes with the body', the 'one who has obtained vision' and the 'one who is freed by confidence' see by means of wisdom that some of the *āsavas* are destroyed (*paññāya assa disvā ekacce āsavā parikkhīṇā honti*), and for them there is something to be done by heedfulness (*appamādena karaṇīyaṃ*). Both the *dhammânusārin* and *saddhânusārin* see by means of wisdom that the *āsavas* are not destroyed (*paññāya assa disvā āsavā aparikkhīṇā honti*); as with the previous three, for them there is something to be done by heedfulness.

Further the *dhammânusārin* is described as one whose insight the *dhammas* made known by the Tathāgata partially satisfy by means of wisdom (*tathāgata-ppaveditā assa dhammā paññāya mattaso nijjhānaṃ khamanti*). This agrees almost exactly with the *Saṃyutta* definition quoted above. The *dhammânusārin* is in addition here said to possess the faculties of confidence, strength, mindfulness, concentration and wisdom (*api c'assa ime dhammā honti seyyath-īdaṃ saddhindriyaṃ viriyindriyaṃ satindriyaṃ samādhindriyaṃ paññindriyaṃ*). The *saddhânusārin*, however, has only a measure of confidence in and affection for the Tathāgata (*tathāgate assa saddhā-mattaṃ hoti pema-mattaṃ*), but he too possesses the faculties of *saddhā*, *viriya*, *sati*, *samādhi* and *paññā*. What is it that is left to be done by heedfulness?

> Truly, this venerable sir while resorting to a suitable dwelling, keeping the company of good friends and balancing the faculties might, in the here and now, for himself have direct knowledge of, realize, attain and dwell in that unsurpassed goal of the spiritual life for the sake of which the sons of families rightly go forth from the home into homelessness. Perceiving this to be the fruit of heedfulness for this *bhikkhu*, I declare that something is to be done by heedfulness.[121]

---

[119] M I 439-40; 477-9; A I 73-4; IV 215.

[120] M I 477-9.

[121] M I 479 : *app-eva nāma ayaṃ āyasmā anulomikāni senâsanāni paṭisevamāno kalyāṇa-mitte bhajamāno indriyāni samannānayamāno yass'atthāya kula-puttā samma-d-eva agārasmā anagāriyaṃ pabbajanti tad anuttaraṃ brahma-cariya-pariyosānaṃ diṭṭhe va dhamme sayaṃ abhiññā sacchikatvā upasampajja vihareyyā ti. imaṃ kho ahaṃ imassa bhikkhuno appamāda-phalaṃ sampassamāno appamādena karaṇīyan ti vadāmi.*

Certainly, at first sight, it does not seem very appropriate to speak of someone who exists only momentarily as 'resorting to a suitable dwelling, keeping the company of good friends and balancing the faculties'. However, since the phrase is equally applied to all five persons for whom there is something left to be done—that is those who have not destroyed all the *āsavas*—it might be thought that it concerns everything that the *saddhânusārin* and *dhammânusārin* will have to do before the *āsavas* are all destroyed, and not just what is to be done by them in the capacity of *saddhânusārin* and *dhammânusārin*. Yet a number of Nikāya passages seem to quite clearly envisage all seven of these persons as walking about and performing tasks that would seem to involve the *saddhânusārin* and *dhammânusārin* in something rather more than momentary existence. A case in point is the following *Aṅguttara-nikāya* passage:

> It is wonderful that when the Saṃgha has been invited by me [for a meal], *devatās* approach and announce, 'Householder, this *bhikkhu* is *ubhatobhāga-vimutta*, this one is *paññā-vimutta*, this one is *kāya-sakkhin*, this one is *diṭṭhi-patta*, this one is *saddhā-vimutta*, this one is *dhammânusārin*, this one is unvirtuous, of bad *dhamma*.' Yet when I am serving food to the Saṃgha I do not find that the thought arises, 'I shall give a little to this one or I shall give a lot to this one.' Rather I give with an even mind.[122]

What conclusions should one draw? It is obvious that at least in certain Nikāya passages *saddhânusārin* and *dhammânusārin* are understood to indicate persons close to or approaching stream-attainment. I have already drawn attention to the fact that the arising of clear *saddhā* is associated with stream-attainment in other contexts as well. This would appear to give added weight to the association of the *saddhânusārin* with stream-attainment. It is equally clear, I think, that the strict Abhidhamma understanding is not altogether satisfactory for the Nikāyas here. In this instance the clothes of the Abhidhamma seem to hang a little awkwardly upon the Nikāyas—though precisely where they do not fit is not so easy to determine. The Abhidhamma conception of a momentary path followed immediately by the fruit is probably the likeliest place to look. So while we must assume some kind of gap to exist

---

122 A IV 215: *anacchariyaṃ kho pana me bhante saṃghe nimantite devatā upasaṃkamitvā ārocenti asuko gahapati bhikkhu ubhatobhāga-vimutto asuko paññā-vimutto asuko diṭṭhi-patto asuko saddhā-vimutto asuko dhammânusārī asuko saddhânusārī asuko sīlavā kalyāṇa-dhammo asuko dussīlo pāpa-dhammo ti. saṃghaṃ kho panâhaṃ bhante parivisanto nâbhijānāmi evaṃ cittaṃ uppādento imassa vā thokaṃ demi imassa vā bahukan ti. atha kvāham bhante sama-citto va demi.* (Cf. M I 439-40, A I 73-4.) These passages are pointed out by Kheminda Thera, *Path, Fruit and Nibbāna*, Colombo, 1965, pp. 37-9. In one instance the commentary seems to acknowledge the discrepancy; Ps III 151-2 to M I 439-40 states: 'With regard to the words beginning 'one freed both ways', *dhammânusārin* and *saddhânusārin* are two types of person in possession of the path who exist for one thought moment. But then it is not possible for all seven *ariya-puggalas* to be so commanded by the Lord, for when the Lord has commanded it is not possible for these [two?] to act accordingly. However, assuming the impossibility of the conditions this is said in order to indicate that *ariya-puggalas* are easy to talk to and that Bhaddāli-tthera is difficult to talk to.' (*ubhatobhāga-vimutto ti ādīsu dhammânusārī saddhânusārī ti dve eka-citta-kkhaṇikā magga-samaṅgi-puggalā. ete pana satta ariya-puggale bhagavatā pi evaṃ āṇāpetuṃ na yuttaṃ, bhagavatā āṇatte tesaṃ hi evaṃ kātuṃ na yuttaṃ. aṭṭhāna-parikappa-vasena pana ariya-puggalānaṃ suvaca-bhāva-dassanatthaṃ Bhaddāli-ttherassa ca dubbaca-bhāva-dassanatthaṃ p'etaṃ vuttaṃ.*)

between the Nikāyas' and early Abhidhamma's respective usages of the terms *dhammânusārin* and *saddhânusārin* along with their conceptions of path and fruit, we have no reason to presume that the gap is such that a vast and elaborate construction is needed to bridge it. On the contrary the shift in meaning appears to be of quite a subtle nature.

One is tempted to ask here what might seem rather basic questions. Why should there be any notion of path and fruit at all? What purpose is served by the moment by moment analysis of the process that leads to the arising of the transcendent path in the Abhidhamma/Abhidharma systems? What lies behind the question of whether or not the five spiritual faculties should be regarded as exclusively *lokuttara* as distinct from *saddhā*, *viriya*, *sati*, *samādhi* and *paññā*? At the heart of all these questions is a concern with the nature of the relationship of the ordinary *lokiya* mind to the transcendent *lokuttara* mind: how does the transition from the *lokiya* to the *lokuttara* occur? We are not concerned here with abstruse points of scholastic theory, but with matters of a quite definite practical and experiential import to the ancient *bhikkhu* who understood himself as poised to make that breakthrough.

The principles at work here are similar, it seems to me, to those that later provoked the debate among Chinese Buddhists concerning gradual and sudden awakening.[123] The debate might be characterized in the following way. From a strict and absolute standpoint it must be that one is either awakened or not, either one sees it or one does not; the awakening experience is of the nature of a sudden and instantaneous breakthrough—this is from the standpoint of sudden awakening. According to the standpoint of gradual awakening this is all very well, but in practice such absolute distinctions are not always entirely appropriate; that is, it is more useful sometimes to look at it in other ways.

A feature clearly manifest in the Abhidhamma texts—but not peculiar to them—is that of finer and finer examination of mental processes and events. This quite naturally entails a consideration of those events on ever smaller time scales, until, in absolute terms, all mental events are seen as radically momentary. In view of this, analyses in terms of Abhidhamma will tend to stress the absolute and instantaneous nature of transition: either one is a stream-attainer or not; therefore, at what precise moment does one become a stream-attainer? When exactly does a person change from one who can die without realizing the fruit of stream-attainment to one who cannot? Thus the essential features of the Abhidhamma understanding of path and fruit, of *saddhânusārin* and *dhammânusārin* are a prefectly natural resolution of the treatment of these matters in the Nikāyas, and, as I have already indicated, seem to be part of the common heritage of ancient Buddhism.

My point here is not that the viewpoint of gradual awakening cannot be expressed in terms of Abhidhamma—on the contrary it is, I think, in some ways enhanced by Abhidhamma—but in so far as the Abhidhamma carried to its conclusion the method of giving a final and comprehensive expression of

---

[123] For a brief account of this debate see K.K.S. Ch'en, *Buddhism in China*, Princeton, 1972, pp. 119-20.

Buddhist teaching in absolute and universally applicable terms, it tends to focus the mind first of all on the absolute and instantaneous nature of the transition from, say, the 'ordinary' (*lokiya*) to the 'transcendent' (*lokuttara*). Yet at the same time the Abhidhamma also draws attention to a similarity or relationship that exists between the ordinary *lokiya* skilful mind and the *lokuttara* mind: in terms of bare mental states (*cetasikas*) that are present, the two kinds of mind may be nearly identical—this is clear in the *Dhammasaṅgaṇi*. In this way the Abhidhamma highlights what is involved in the sudden/gradual awakening debate.

The *suttas* of the Nikāyas are presented in the first place as the prescriptions of the Buddha applicable to particular occasions. They characteristically progress from their particular starting points via a particular course of practice or teaching toward the final goal of complete awakening. To this extent the Nikāyas can be seen as drawing attention to the gradual stage by stage nature of the process of awakening. Yet at the same time what one might call the Abhidhamma tendency to more final, absolute and universally valid expressions cannot be regarded as simply extraneous or alien to Nikāya Buddhism. Within the Nikāyas there is already a certain tension created by a tendency to shift between more figurative and particular applications on the one hand, and more absolute universal statements on the other.

7. The lesser stream-attainer

At this point it is perhaps useful to consider a distinction that is found both in the Nikāyas and in the commentaries between teaching that is *pariyāyena* and that which is *nippariyāyena*. The commentaries appear to use the two terms to characterize the mode of teaching in the Suttanta and Abhidhamma respectively.[124] Thus Rhys Davids and Stede explain the meaning of *pariyāyena* as '*ad hominem*, discursively applied method, illustrated discourse, figurative language as opposed to the abstract, general statements of Abhidhamma = *nippariyāyena*'.[125]

According to Monier Williams *paryāya*, in addition to its literal meaning of 'going round' or 'revolution', acquires a number of applied meanings. A *paryāya* is a course, succession or turn; *paryāyeṇa* can thus mean 'successively' or 'alternatively'; *paryāya*, *paryāyatā*, *paryāyatra* and *paryāya-vacana* can all

---

124 See As 154, 222, 250, 289, 308 for a convenient set of examples.

125 *PED*, s.v. *pariyāya*. Mrs Rhys Davids' comment at Dhs Trsl xxxiii n. 2 is confusing. She states that *na nippariyāyena dīghaṃ rūpâyatanaṃ* (As 317) means 'that which is long is only figuratively a visual object (is really a tactile object)'. But what this whole passage seems to be saying is that since what is long can *also* be known by touch as well as sight, which is not true of colour (*yasmā dīghâdīni phusitvā pi sakkā jānituṃ, nīlâdīni pan'eva na sakkā*), therefore the sphere of visible objects cannot of itself be considered as long, short, etc. in any final or absolute sense (*tasmā na nippariyāyena dīghaṃ rūpâyatanaṃ tathā rassâdīni*). But no more can the sphere of tangible objects (*phoṭṭhabbâyatana*) be so considered; rather length, etc. are relative notions or concepts that come into being as the result of comparing different sense objects known either through the sense of sight or through the sense of touch.

apparently mean 'a convertible term or synonym'; finally a *paryāya* is a particular 'way, manner or mode of proceeding'.[126]

A series of *suttas* in the *Aṅguttara-nikāya*[127] takes a number of terms and contrasts their usage *pariyāyena* and *nippariyāyena*. The following is taken from the first *sutta* in this series:

> These five kinds of object of sensual desire are called a restriction by the Blessed One. What five? Visible forms cognizable by the eye ... sounds cognizable by the ear ... smells cognizable by the nose ... tastes cognizable by the tongue ... tactile sensations cognizable by the body ... Here a *bhikkhu*, separated from the objects of sensual desire ... attains and dwells in the first *jhāna*. So far finding an opening in respect of restriction has been spoken of by the Blessed One *pariyāyena*. But there too restriction exists. And what is the restriction there? That *vitakka* and *vicāra* that has not ceased there, that is the restriction there.[128]

So the *bhikkhu* proceeds to the second *jhāna*; this is once more described as finding an opening *pariyāyena*, for here too restriction or crowding exists in the form of *pīti* or joy. The *bhikkhu* thus progresses through the remaining two *jhānas* and the four formless attainments; each one is described as finding an opening *pariyāyena* in relationship to the previous one. But even in the sphere of neither consciousness nor unconsciousness (*neva-saññā-nāsaññâyatana*) there is restriction:

> That consciousness of the sphere of neither consciousness nor unconsciousness that has not ceased here, that is the restriction there. So again the *bhikkhu* by passing completely beyond the sphere of neither consciousness nor unconcsciousness attains and dwells in the cessation of consciousness and feeling, and sees by his wisdom that the *āsavas* are destroyed. To this extent finding an opening in respect of restriction has been spoken of by the Blessed One *nippariyāyena*.[129]

Buddhaghosa in the *Manorathapūraṇī* glosses *pariyāyena* and *nippariyāyena* in this context by *ekena kāraṇena* and *na ekena kāraṇena* respectively:

> ***Pariyāyena*** i.e. for one particular reason; the first *jhāna* is called finding-an-opening only in as much as the restriction of the objects of sensual desire is absent, it is not [one] in every respect ...
>
> ***Nippariyāyena*** i.e. not for a particular reason; now the destruction of the *āsavas* is indeed called the one and only finding-an-opening in every respect due to abandoning all restrictions.[130]

---

126 MW, s.v. *paryāya*. The notion of *paryāya*, *paryāyatra*, *paryāya-sûkta* as 'a regular recurring series or formula' is perhaps also of some interest in relationship to Suttanta literature's use of recurring themes and formulas.

127 A IV 449-56.

128 A IV 449: *pañcime āvuso kāma-guṇā sambādho vutto bhagavatā. katame pañca. cakkhu-viññeyyā rūpā ... sota-viññeyyā saddā ... ghāna-viññeyyā gandhā ... jivhā-viññeyyā rasā ... kāya-viññeyyā phoṭṭhabbā ... idhâvuso bhikkhu vivicc'eva kāmehi pe paṭhamaṃ jhānaṃ upasampajja viharati ettāvatā pi kho āvuso sambādhe okāsâdhigamo vutto bhagavatā pariyāyena.*

129 A IV 451: *yad eva tattha neva-saññā-nâsaññâyatana-saññā aniruddhā hoti ayaṃ ettha sambādho. puna ca paraṃ āvuso bhikkhu sabbaso neva-saññā-nâsaññâyatanaṃ samatikamma saññā-vedayita-nirodhaṃ upasampajja viharati paññāya cassa disvā āsavā parikkhīṇā honti. ettāvatā pi kho āvuso sambādhe okāsâdhigamo vutto bhagavatā nippariyāyenā ti.*

130 Mp IV 205: *pariyāyenā ti ekena kāraṇena; kāma-sambādhassa hi abhāva-matten'eva paṭhama-jjhānaṃ, okāsâdhigamo nāma, na sabbathā sabbaṃ ... nippariyāyenā ti na ekena kāraṇena; atha kho āsava-kkhayo nāma sabba-sambādhānaṃ pahīnattā sabbena sabbaṃ eko okāsâdhigamo*

On the basis of the foregoing one can perhaps sum up the distinction between teaching that is *pariyāyena* and that which is *nippariyāyena* as follows. In the former, terms are in some sense convertible, that is the meanings are not necessarily fixed or final, rather they conform to the particular circumstances or reasons (*kāraṇa*) that govern or motivate the particular teaching, the particular context in which they occur. In the latter, terms are used with fixed technical meanings, universally valid and not subject to the particular circumstances of their usage.

What is interesting is that the distinction between *pariyāya-desanā* and *nippariyāya-desanā* does not seem to correspond in any neat or simple way to what we now have as the four primary Nikāyas and the *Abhidhamma-piṭaka.*[131] If the distinction between *pariyāya-desanā* and *nippariyāya-desanā* is seen as operating in some degree within the Nikāyas, one possible way of looking at the various developed Abhidharma systems is as representing different versions of a final form of *nippariyāya desanā.* The commentaries and later treatises, then, see the Nikāyas through their version of this final *nippariyāya-desanā.* They thus translate the terms of a particular *sutta* into the particular absolute and final (*nippariyāyena*) terms that are considered appropriate to the particular occasion for the delivery of the *sutta.* There are differences of judgement and interpretation between the schools, or, and this is more significant, the Pāli commentaries sometimes record different interpretations, and the traditions of various teachers without discounting them as entirely invalid. All this is, in a sense, exactly how it should be. For once the particularity of *suttas* is recognized, if the particularity of any given *sutta* is considered somehow uncertain or variable in some degree, then it is clear that a certain freedom must exist as to how exactly it is to be interpreted in terms of *nippariyāya-desanā.* A single *sutta* can then be seen as capable of operating on different levels, of being taken in different ways that are equally valid.

Returning to the *Aṅguttara* cycle of *suttas* that contrasts the usage of a number of terms *pariyāyena* with their usage *nippariyāyena,* we find included among those terms *kāya-sakkhin, paññā-vimutta* and *ubhatobhāga-vimutta.* As I noted above these three terms are sometimes included in a list of seven persons that also includes the *saddhânusārin* and *dhammânusārin.* In the Theravādin Abhidhamma literature and in the exegetical literature of the Sarvāstivādins these seven persons are understood as *ariya-puggala/ārya-pudgala,* and each one is defined in relationship to the four paths and fruits and other traits peculiar to their particular attainments or method of attainment. The significant point is then that none of the seven is thought to be less than one who has attained the path of stream-attainment.

The present *Aṅguttara* passage, however, uses the term *kāya-sakkhin*

---

nāmā ti. At Sv I 136 Buddhaghosa states that *pariyāya* can mean turn (*vara*), teaching (*desanā*) and reason or cause (*kāraṇa*).

[131] Cf. the distinction already evidenced in the Nikāyas between that in which the meaning must be drawn out (*neyyattha*) and that in which the meaning is already drawn out (*nītattha*), e.g. A I 60. The distinction between conventional truth (*sammuti-sacca*) and absolute truth (*paramattha-sacca*) is also similar in kind (see Mil 160).

relatively, that is *pariyāyena*, to indicate anyone who attains to any of the four *jhānas* or four formless spheres and 'touches that sphere with his body'.[132] The term *paññā-vimutta* used *pariyāyena* refers to anyone attaining to any of the four *jhānas* or formless spheres and who 'knows that by wisdom';[133] the term *ubhatobhāga-vimutta* used *pariyāyena* refers to one who attains to the four *jhānas* or formless spheres and both 'touches that with his body and knows it by wisdom'.[134]

If these three terms can be used in this relative way, is it not possible that something of the same freedom applies or can apply to *saddhânusārin* and *dhammânusārin*?[135] Translating into more general terms the definitions of the two persons provided by the *Puggalapaññatti*, and ignoring the stipulation concerning the *ariya-magga*,[136] the *saddhânusārin* is then to be considered more loosely as one whose practice is in general characterized by or based on confidence (*saddhā*). He is in some respects analogous to the one who develops the *iddhi-pāda* that is endowed with *chanda-samādhi* and *padhāna-saṃkhāras*. The *dhammânusārin* is one whose practice is in general characterized by or based on wisdom *paññā*, like the one who develops the *iddhi-pada* that is endowed with *vīmaṃsā-samādhi* and *padhāna-saṃkhāras*. I do not, in fact, think that this can be regarded as the normal meaning of the two terms in question in the Nikāyas, but it does highlight something of the significance of the two terms, and provide what might be thought of as a 'lower limit' for their meaning. The 'upper limit' is provided by the definitions in the *Puggalapaññatti* and later literature which stress that the two terms signify *ariya-puggalas*. For reasons which I have already indicated, it seems to me that the usage of the terms *saddhânusārin* and *dhammânusārin* in the Nikāyas—at least in the *Saṃyutta-nikāya*—must be regarded as being fairly close to this 'upper limit'.

At this point it seems worth drawing attention to the commentarial notion of the 'lesser stream-attainer' (*cūḷa-sotâpanna, cullako sotâpanno*). This notion is mentioned both in Buddhaghosa's *Visuddhimagga* and in Buddhadatta's *Abhidhammâvatāra* at the conclusion of the exposition of 'purification by passing beyond doubt' (*kaṅkhā-vitaraṇa-visuddhi*); in the schema of the seven purifications, then, it marks the completion of the fourth:

> Now one of insight possessed of this knowledge [of the passing beyond doubt] is

---

[132] A IV 451-2: *yathā yathā ca tad āyatanaṃ tathā tathā naṃ kāyena phassitvā viharati ettāvatā pi kho kāya-sakkhī vutto bhagavatā pariyāyena.*

[133] A IV 453: *paññāya ca naṃ pajānāti.*

[134] The *nippariyāyena* usage of these three terms here does not seem to accord entirely with later usage, or even with usage in the *Kīṭāgiri-sutta* of the *Majjhima-nikāya*. In the *Aṅguttara* passage *kāya-sakkhin* used *nippariyāyena* refers to one who attains to the cessation of consciousness and feeling and sees that the *āsavas* are destroyed, in addition to touching the sphere with his body. The attainment of *saññā-vedayita-nirodha* and the destruction of the *āsavas*, of course, entail *arahant*-ship. However, in the *Kīṭagiri-sutta* the *kāya-sakkhin* is one who has only destroyed some of the *āsavas*, which in fact does accord with the later standard definition.

[135] Other terms whose *pariyāyena* and *nippariyāyena* usage is contrasted in a parallel way in this *Aṅguttara* passage include *nibbāna*, *amata*, *passaddhi* and *nirodha*.

[136] Pugg 15.

one who has found relief in the instruction of the Buddha, one who has found a footing, one whose destiny is sure—he is called a lesser stream-attainer.[137]

I have already noted how the Nikāyas generally associate the overcoming of doubt (*vicikicchā*) and establishing of firm *saddhā* with stream-attainment. Furthermore the lesser stream-attainer is also one whose destiny is assured. All this is rather reminiscent of the Nikāya definition of the *saddhânusārin*, *dhammânusārin* and *sotâpanna* I referred to earlier. Yet the fact remains that in terms of strict Abhidhamma one who has completed the fourth *visuddhi* has not finally and absolutely abandoned the three *saṃyojanas* which include doubt (*vicikicchā*).[138]

Therefore what seems to be envisaged with the notion of the *cūḷa-sotâpanna* is that the completion of the fourth purification marks a definite beginning of the process that culminates in the path of stream-attainment proper, the *lokuttara* path moment. One might then put it that, loosely speaking, the path of stream-attainment extends from the conclusion of the fourth purification (i.e. the acquisition of the knowledge that causes one to pass beyond doubt) up to the seventh purification ('by knowledge and seeing'). This perhaps can be understood as paralleled in the relationship of access concentration (*upacāra-samādhi*) to full absorption (*appanā*). Just as the distinction between access and absorption is in a sense glossed over in the Nikāya concept of and usage of the term *jhāna*,[139] so too is the distinction between the *cūḷa-sotâpanna* (= a person who is well on the way to becoming a *sotâpanna*) and the full *sotâpanna* glossed over in the Nikāya notion of the *sotâpanna*, *saddhânusārin* and *dhammânusārin*.

Beginning with the question of the proper significance of the five spiritual faculties within the Nikāyas, the foregoing discussion has touched on a number of important and far-reaching issues. To sum up, according to the traditions of the Theravādins—and also the Sarvāstivādins—*saddhindriya*, *viriyindriya*, *satindriya*, *samādhindriya* and *paññindriya* are to be normally understood as referring to *saddhā*, *viriya*, *sati*, *samādhi* and *paññā* in their generality—these five items are universally *indriyas*, it is not that they may merely act as *indriyas* at certain times, though of course they may be weaker or sharper. Within the Nikāyas this understanding seems most appropriate in the context of the extended list of *indriyas*, and also of the application of the *samudaya*, etc. formula to the five *indriyas* along with the six sense *indriyas* and five feeling *indriyas*.[140] Other ancient traditions understand that properly speaking *śraddhendriya*, *vīryendriya*, *smṛtîndriya*, *samādhîndriya* and *prajñendriya* only apply to *śraddhā*, *vīrya*, *smṛti*, *samādhi* and *prajñā* that is associated with the *lokottara* mind. This seems to be largely because of the emphasis

137 Vism XIX 27: *iminā pana ñāṇena samannāgato vipassako buddha-sāsane laddhassāso laddha-patiṭṭho niyata-gatiko cūḷa-sotâpanno nāma hoti*. (Cf. Abhidh-av 119).

138 Possibly in this context *kaṅkhā* should be understood as doubt in its grosser manifestations and *vicikicchā* as rather more subtle doubt.

139 Cf. L.S. Cousins, *Religion* 3 (1973), p. 118.

140 According to Anesaki the version of the *indriya-saṃyukta* preserved in the Chinese Āgamas contains equivalents to the Pāli *suttas* that apply the *samudaya*, etc. formula to the *indriyas*; op. cit., pp. 103-4.

placed upon certain Sūtra passages that apparently treat the five spiritual faculties as the exclusive domain of the *ārya-pudgala*. In fact the exegetical tradition of the Theravādins is agreed that in these particular passages *saddh-indriya*, etc. refer exclusively to *saddhā*, etc. as *lokuttara* but regards this as a special restricted usage that does not affect the more normal usage.[141]

The difference between the two traditions of interpretation should thus be seen as something of a moot point rather than involving a fundamental clash of views. It concerns the final technical significance and value of terms in the Abhidhamma/Abhidharma systems, and the underlying concern appears to be the nature of the relationship between the *lokiya/laukika* and *lokuttara/lokottara* mind.

8. Conclusion: the ubiquity of the indriyas in the Nikāyas

The term *indriya*, then, can be seen as indicating a significant characteristic of *saddhā*, *viriya*, *sati*, *samādhi* and *paññā*—a characteristic held in common with other basic items. Yet among these basic items their peculiar characteristic is that they 'should be developed'; they represent in general what it is the *bhikkhu* is aiming to cultivate. Edward Conze has quite appropriately called them 'the five cardinal virtues',[142] and it seems true to say that one cannot look very far into the Nikāyas without coming across them. Indeed it is hardly an exaggeration to say that every *sutta* concerns their treatment in one way or another. In view of this it is perhaps worth considering the question of the ubiquity of *saddhā*, *viriya*, *sati*, *samādhi* and *paññā* in the Nikāyas a little further.

Already in the basic treatment of the *satipaṭṭhānas* we have seen how the *Vibhaṅga* and *Nettippakaraṇa* see the phrase *viharati ātāpī sampajāno satimā vineyya loke abhijjhā-domanassaṃ* as implying four of the five items in question, namely *viriya*, *paññā*, *sati* and *samādhi*. That the later literature should make the particular correspondences and associations that it does depends in part on direct verbal parallels (as in the case of *sampajāna* and *paññā*), but also on the association of terms in particular contexts already in the Nikāyas. There is not space to pursue this at length here but the following passage illustrates the kind of process involved:

> Exertion is to be made for the non-arising of bad unskilful *dhammas* that have not yet arisen, exertion is to be made for the arising of skilful *dhammas* that have already arisen.[143]

This quite obviously echoes the *samma-ppadhāna* formula, thus giving a quite clear precedent for the association of *ātappa*, and hence *ātāpin*, with *viriya*. Thus while some of the cross-references and correspondences are

---

[141] Cf. the passage that states that the one who is completely without the *indriyas* should be understood as standing in the ranks of the *puthujjana*; Spk III 237 states that this *sutta* speaks only of the transcendent *indriyas* (*imasmiṃ sutte lokuttarān'eva indriyāni kathitāni*).

[142] Conze, *BTI*, p. 47.

[143] A I 153: *anuppannānaṃ pāpakānaṃ akusalānaṃ dhammānaṃ anuppādāya ātappaṃ karaṇīyaṃ. anuppannānaṃ kusalānaṃ dhammānaṃ uppādāya ātappaṃ karaṇīyaṃ.*

explicit in the Nikāyas (e.g. that *samma-ppadhāna* is equivalent to *viriya* which is equivalent to *samma-vāyāma*) others are implicit—(e.g. that wherever one finds *padahati* or *vāyamati* or *ātāpin*, one can understand that *viriya* is implied). Reference to another passage will serve to illustrate how the 'faculties' are often stated less implicitly but still not exactly explicitly:

> For me *viriya* was instigated and not slack; *sati* was established and not lost, the body tranquil and not agitated, the mind concentrated and one-pointed.[144]

This common set phrase is used to introduce the attainment of *jhāna* or some other kind of attainment leading directly to the development of *paññā*.

So we can say that apart from their being mentioned explicitly, talk of the five 'faculties' or 'cardinal virtues' is scattered throughout the Nikāyas—they are repeatedly referred to either by name or by associated terminology. As a further illustration of the way in which the 'faculties' pervade the Nikāyas it is worth turning to the *Suttanipāta*. The ancient canonical commentary—the *Niddesa*—establishes at least certain portions of the *Suttanipāta* as among the oldest Buddhist works we possess. It has sometimes been suggested that, being uncluttered by the various 'scholastic' lists found elsewhere in the Nikāyas, the *Suttanipāta* preserves an older and purer 'ethical' Buddhism.[145] While it is true that none of the seven sets is explicity mentioned it does not seem to follow that the Buddhism of the *Suttanipāta* has a radically different character from that of the four primary Nikāyas as a whole. The Buddhism of the *Suttanipāta* once more centres around letting go of the world of the five senses, developing *jhāna* and coming to the highest wisdom. The following are some *Suttanipāta* verses that succinctly sum up the Buddhist path in terms of the familiar 'cardinal virtues':

> Confidence is the seed, perseverence is the rain, wisdom is my yoke and plough, fear of blame is the pole, mind is the (yoke-)tie, mindfulness is my ploughshare and goad.
>
> One who is always accomplisheded in virtue, having wisdom, well-concentrated, thinking inwardly, mindful, crosses the flood which is hard to cross.
>
> By confidence one crosses the flood, by heedfulness the ocean, by strength one goes beyond suffering, by wisdom one is purified.
>
> One with the power of wisdom, accomplished in conduct and vow, concentrated, delighting in *jhāna*, mindful, freed from clinging, without barenness, without the influxes—him the wise understand as a sage.
>
> There is confidence and thus strength; wisdom too is found in me. Why do you question me about life though my heart is thus intent on endeavour?
>
> When blood dries up, bile and phlegm dry up; when flesh withers, the mind becomes more settled, mindfulness, wisdom and concentration stand more firm.
>
> Controlling his desire for these things [i.e. the objects of the senses], mindful and

---

[144] M I 21, 117, 186, 243; III 85-7; S IV 125; V 68, 76, 331-2, etc. (see *PTC*, s.v. *āraddha*): *āraddhaṃ kho pana me viriyaṃ ahosi asallīnaṃ, upaṭṭhitā sati asamuṭṭhā, passaddho kāyo asāraddho, samāhitaṃ cittaṃ ekaggaṃ.*

[145] Cf. E.M. Hare's introduction to Sn Trsl (*Woven Cadences*, Sacred Books of the Buddhists, London, 1945); B.C. Law, op. cit., I 233, 235.

well freed a *bhikkhu*, correctly investigating *dhamma* at the appropriate time, [his mind] unified [in meditation], should destroy darkness.

Know that ignorance is the head; knowledge is what splits the head when joined with confidence, mindfulness and concentration, and with purpose and strength.[146]

9. *The balas*

In the context of the seven sets the *balas* are, it turns out, exactly the same items as the five *indriyas*, namely *saddhā*, *viriya*, *sati*, *samādhi* and *paññā*, only this time considered as 'powers' (*balas*) rather than *indriyas*. The Nikāya definitions of *saddhā-bala*, etc. correspond exactly to those of *saddhindriya*, etc.[147] Like *indriya*, though, the term *bala* is applied to a whole series of items in addition to *saddhā*, *viriya*, *sati*, *samādhi* and *paññā*. However, a standard and fixed extended list of *balas*, comparable to the list of the twenty-two *indriyas*, does not seem to have evolved. The *bala-kathā* of the *Paṭisambhidāmagga*[148] states that there are a total of sixty-eight *balas*. This list consists of various groups of *balas* most of which are to be found in the four primary Nikāyas, and appears to be an attempt to bring together all important items that are or can be termed *bala*. However, this composite list of sixty-eight *balas* appears to be peculiar to the *Paṭisambhidāmagga*, and certainly cannot be thought of as standard for ancient Buddhism in the same way as the twenty-two *indriyas*, although many—if not all—of the sub-groups were quite probably common to all Buddhist schools. What seems clear is that in its wider application the term *bala* is much less technical than *indriya*. Of the seven sets, the *balas* appear to be the least frequently mentioned in the Nikāyas, and—outside the context of the seven sets—exhibit a certain looseness. A list of seven *balas* adding 'shame' (*hiri*) and 'regard for consequence' (*ottappa*) is found in a number of places,[149] while the list can also be reduced to four by the omission of *paññā*,[150] or to two, leaving just *sati-bala* and *samādhi-bala*.[151]

Other *balas* mentioned in the Nikāyas include such things as 'the power of

---

[146] Sn 77: *saddhā bījaṃ tapo vuṭṭhi paññā me yuga-naṅgalaṃ/ hirī īsā mano yottaṃ sati me phāla-pācanaṃ//* Sn 174: *sabbadā sīla-sampanno paññavā susamāhito/ ajjhatta-cintī satimā oghaṃ tarati duttaraṃ//* Sn 184: *saddhāya tarati oghaṃ appamādena aṇṇavaṃ/ viriyena dukkhaṃ acceti paññāya parisujjhati//* Sn 212: *paññā-balaṃ sīla-vatûpapannaṃ samāhitaṃ jhāna-rataṃ satimaṃ/ saṅgā pamuttaṃ akhilaṃ anāsavaṃ taṃ vâpi dhīrā muniṃ vedayanti//* Sn 432: *atthi saddhā tato viriyaṃ paññā ca mama vijjati/ evaṃ maṃ pahitattaṃ pi kiṃ jīvam anupucchasi//* Sn 434: *lohite sussamānamhi pittaṃ semhañ ca sussati/ maṃsesu khīyamānesu bhiyyo cittaṃ pasīdati/ bhiyyo sati ca paññā ca samādhi mama tiṭṭhati/* Sn 975: *etesu dhammesu vineyya chandaṃ/ bhikkhu satimā suvimutta-citto// kālena so samma dhammaṃ parivīmaṃsamāno/ ekodi-bhūto vihane tamaṃ so//* Sn 1026: *avijjā muddhā ti jānāhi vijjā muddhâdhipātinī/ saddhā-sati-samādhīhi chanda-viriyena saṃyutā//.*

[147] Cf. the definition of the respective *indriyas* at S V 196-7, with those of the *balas* at A III 10-1; IV 3-4.

[148] Paṭis 168-76.

[149] D III 253; A IV 3-4; cf. D III 282; the *Dhammasaṅgaṇi* seems to work with this list of seven *balas* as standard, see Chapter 10.3.

[150] D III 229.

[151] D III 213.

examination' (*paṭisaṃkhāna-bala*), and 'the power of development' (*bhāvanā-bala*).[152] There are also the seven, eight or ten powers of one who has destroyed the *āsavas* (*khīṇâsava-balas*),[153] and the ten *balas* of the Tathāgata.[154] Apart from such spiritual *balas* there are lists such as the five *balas* of womankind, namely the powers of beauty, wealth, relatives, sons and virtue.[155] A *bala*, then, can be any kind of power, strength or strong point.

So why in the list of seven sets are the same five items given twice, first as 'faculties' and then as 'powers'? Étienne Lamotte comments: 'En effet on a toujours reconnu qu'entre *bala* et *indriya* il n'y a qu'une différence d'intensité.'[156] However, the *indriya-saṃyutta* passage from which he gives a brief quotation is rather obscure. The passage is worth quoting more fully along with the accompanying simile:

> There is, *bhikkhus*, a method according to which the five *indriyas* are the five *balas*, and the five *balas* are the five *indriyas*. And what is that method ... ? That which is *saddhindriya* is *saddhā-bala*, that which is *saddhā-bala* is *saddhindriya* ... that which is *paññindriya* is *paññā-bala*, that which is *paññā-bala* is *paññindriya*. It is as if, *bhikkhus*, there were a river flowing, inclining and sliding eastwards, and in the middle an island. There is a method according to which the stream of that river is counted as just one. Then again there is a method according to which the stream of that river is counted as two. And what, *bhikkhus*, is the method according to which the stream of that river is counted as just one? In that there is both water to the eastern end of the island and water to the western end of the island ... And what, *bhikkhus*, is the method according to which the stream of that river is counted as two? In that there is both water to the northern side of the island, and water to the southern side of the island ... [157]

This explanation would appear to have nothing to do with degrees of intensity. The point of the image seems to be that if one stands on the island facing east, the water in front is the same as the water behind, and so from this point of view there is only one stream; on the other hand there is water flowing on either side, and so from this point of view there are two streams. In fact the Nikāyas tell us no more about the nature of the difference between *saddhā*, etc.

---

[152] D III 213, 244: A I 52, 94; II 142.

[153] The *khīṇâsava-balas* will be discussed in more detail as they concern in part the seven sets; see Chapter 7.

[154] E.g. M I 69; A V 32-3.

[155] S IV 246-8.

[156] Lamotte, *Traité*, III 1127.

[157] S V 219-20: *atthi bhikkhave pariyāyo yaṃ pariyāyaṃ āgamma yāni pañcindriyāni tāni pañca-balāni honti yāni pañca-balāni tāni pañcindriyāni honti. katamo ca bhikkhave pariyāyo ... yaṃ bhikkhave saddhindriyaṃ taṃ saddhā-balaṃ, yaṃ saddhā-balaṃ taṃ saddhindriyaṃ ... yaṃ paññindriyaṃ taṃ paññā-balaṃ yaṃ paññā-balaṃ taṃ paññindriyaṃ. seyyathâpi bhikkhave nadī pācīna-ninnā pācīna-poṇā pācīna-pabbhārā. tassā majjhe dīpo. atthi bhikkhave pariyāyo yaṃ pariyāyaṃ āgamma tassā nadiyā eko soto tveva saṃkhyaṃ gacchati. atthi pana bhikkhave pariyāyo yaṃ pariyāyaṃ āgamma tassā nadiyā dve sotāni tveva saṃkhyaṃ gacchanti. katamo ca bhikkhave pariyāyo yaṃ pariyāyaṃ āgamma tassā nadiyā eko soto tveva saṃkhyaṃ gacchati. yaṃ ca bhikkhave tassa dīpassa puratthimante udakaṃ yaṃ ca pacchimante udakaṃ ... katamo ca bhikkhave pariyāyo yaṃ pariyāyaṃ āgamma tassā nadiyā dve sotāni tveva saṃkhyaṃ gacchanti. yaṃ ca bhikkhave tassa dīpassa uttarante udakaṃ yaṃ ca dakkhiṇante udakaṃ.* (Anesaki does not record a parallel to the *sutta* in the Chinese *Saṃyuktâgama*.)

as an *indriya* and a *bala* than can be deduced from the terms *indriya* and *bala* themselves.

Before pursuing the question of the distinction between *indriya* and *bala* in the later literature it may be as well to refer to the general significance and usage of *bala* and its derivatives within the Nikāyas:

> Just as a strong man (*balavā puriso*) might stretch out his folded arm, or might fold his stretched out arm, so Brahmā Sahampati disappeared from the Brahmā World and appeared before me.[158]

> Just as a strong man grasping a weaker man (*dubbalataraṃ purisaṃ*) by the head or shoulders might hold him down, subdue him and completely overcome him, so ... that *bhikkhu*, gritting his teeth and pressing his tongue against his palate, should mentally hold down his mind, subdue it and completely overcome it.[159]

> Just as, Aggivessana, two strong men grasping a weak man by the arms might torture and torment him in a pit of burning coals, so when breathing in and out was completely stopped by way of mouth, nose and throat my body was in excessive pain.[160]

These images illustrate how something powerful (*balavant*) completely overcomes and overrides something that is weaker, so that the latter is powerless to resist. Put simply, a *bala* would seem to be anything that has this capacity. It would not seem unreasonable to view a *bala* as an *indriya* made strong.

One of the earliest statements of the distinction between *indriya* and *bala* in the Pāli sources would appear to be found in the *Paṭisambhidāmagga*:

> The meaning of *saddhindriya* is to be directly known as commitment, the meaning of *viriyindriya* as taking on, the meaning of *satindriya* as standing near, the meaning of *samādhindriya* as non-distraction, the meaning of *paññindriya* as seeing. The meaning of *saddhā-bala* is to be directly known as unshakeability with regard to lack of confidence, the meaning of *viriya-bala* as unshakeability with regard to idleness, the meaning of *sati-bala* as unshakeability with regard to heedlessness, the meaning of *samādhi-bala* as unshakeability with regard to excitement, the meaning of *paññā-bala* as unshakeability with regard to ignorance ... The meaning of the *indriyas* is to be directly known as overlordship. The meaning of the *balas* is to be directly known as unshakeability.[161]

Again, while this is not explicit it would seem reasonable to see the *balas*

---

[158] M I 168: *atha kho bhikkhave brahmā sahampati seyyathâpi nāma balavā puriso samiñjitaṃ vā bāhaṃ pasāreyya pasāritaṃ vā bāhaṃ samiñjeyya evam evaṃ brahma-loke antara-hito mama purato pāturahosi.*

[159] M I 121: *seyyathâpi bhikkhave balavā puriso dubbalataraṃ purisaṃ sīse vā gahetvā khandhe vā gahetvā abhiniggaṇheyya abhinippīḷeyya abhisantāpeyya evam eva kho ... tena bhikkhave bhikkhunā dantehi dantam ādhāya jivhāya tāluṃ āhacca cetasā cittaṃ abhiniggaṇhitabbaṃ abhinippīḷetabbaṃ abhisantāpetabbaṃ.*

[160] M I 244: *seyyathâpi Aggivessana dve balavanto purisā dubbalataraṃ purisaṃ nānā-bāhāsu gahetvā aṅgāra-kāsuyā santāpeyyuṃ samparitāpeyyuṃ evam eva kho me Aggivessana mukhato ca nasato ca kaṇṇato ca assāsa-passāsesu uparuddhesu adhimatto kāyasmiṃ ḍāho hoti.*

[161] Paṭis I 16-7: *saddhindriyassa adhimokkhaṭṭho abhiññeyyo, viriyindriyassa paggahaṭṭho ... satindriyassa upaṭṭhānaṭṭho ... samādhindriyassa avikkhepaṭṭho ... paññindriyassa dassanaṭṭho ... saddhā-balassa assaddhiye akampiyaṭṭho abhiññeyyo, viriya-balassa kosajje ... sati-balassa pamāde ... samādhi-balassa uddhacce ... paññā-balassa avijjāya ... indriyānaṃ adhipateyyaṭṭho abhiññeyyo, balānaṃ akampiyaṭṭho abhiññeyyo.* (Cf. Paṭis I 21; II 119-20.)

freedom from being shaken by the their opposite qualities as equivalent to a firm establishment or increased power of the *indriyas*.

The treatment of the *indriyas* and *balas* in the *Dhammasaṅgaṇi* is also suggestive of the distinction between them being seen as a matter of relative power.[162] We are told in the initial determination of *dhammas* present—the commentarial *niddesa-vāra*—for the first *kiriya* mind-consciousness element (*mano-viññāṇa-dhātu*)[163] that there is *samādhindriya* and *viriyindriya*, but no mention is made of *samādhi-bala* and *viriya-bala*.[164] In the subsequent explanation of each *dhamma*—the *uddesa-vāra*—*samādhi-bala* and *viriya-bala* are, however, included in the appropriate registers of terms, (i.e. for *cittass'ekaggatā*, *samādhindriya* and *viriyindriya*). The initial omission of the two *balas* would seem to mean that an item might be counted an *indriya* without its being counted a *bala*. Once again the reason would surely be because an *indriya* is weaker than a *bala*. However, the subsequent inclusion of *samādhi-bala* and *viriya-bala* is odd. It is tempting to think that the text is corrupt: either the two *balas* should be in both places or they should be omitted altogether. Yet the text as we have it existed already in ancient times. Buddhaghosa gives the following explanation:

> Now in the *niddesa-vāra*, because this [*citta*] is stronger than the remaining *cittas* without motivation, *cittekaggatā* is obtained and stated as *samādhi-bala*; *viriya* is also obtained as *viriya-bala*. But because in the *uddesa-vāra* there is no tradition [for reading] 'there is *samādhi-bala*, there is *viriya-bala*', this pair are not called 'powers' in the full sense. Since [this *citta*] is neither skilful nor unskilful it is not stated saying 'power'. And since without regard for exposition there is no 'power', in the *saṃgaha-vāra* too it is not said that there are two powers.[165]

An understanding of the *balas* as essentially the *indriyas* made strong certainly seems to underlie Buddhaghosa's comments here. The tradition he is following is perhaps that of the *Nettippakaraṇa*, which in fact explicitly states that 'these same faculties under the influence of strength become powers'.[166] Elsewhere the *aṭṭhakathās* seem to base themselves on the *Paṭisambhidāmagga* tradition. The following three passages from the Pāli commentaries all briefly deal with the distinctive characteristics first of *indriyas* then of *bala*:

> *Indriya* is in the sense of overlordship understood as overcoming as a result of overcoming distrust, laziness, heedlessness, distraction and confusion; *bala* is in the sense of unshakeability as a result of not being overcome by distrust and the rest.

---

162 For this in general, see Chapter 10.3.

163 This is the *kiriya-mano-viññāṇa-dhātu* accompanied by *somanassa* and termed 'laughter producing' (*hāsayamāna*) at As 294.

164 Dhs 121.

165 As 295: *niddesa-vāre pan'assa sesa-ahetuka-cittehi balavataratāya cittekaggatā samādhi-balaṃ pāpetvā ṭhapitā. [viriyaṃ pi viriya-balaṃ pāpetvā.] uddesa-vāre pana samādhi-balaṃ hoti viriya-balaṃ hotī ti anāgatattā paripuṇṇena balaṭṭhen'etaṃ dvayaṃ balaṃ nāma na hoti. yasmā pana neva kusalaṃ nâkusalaṃ tasmā balan ti vatvā [na] ṭhapitaṃ. yasmā ca na nippariyāyena balaṃ tasmā saṃgaha-vāre pi dve balāni hontī ti na vuttaṃ.* (This does not entirely agree with Buddhadatta's understanding; at Abhidh-av 31 he states that there are two *cittas* that have two *balas*; if one works this out he must be referring to the two *kiriya-mano-viññāṇa-dhātus*; see below, pp. 358-60)

166 Nett 100: *tāni yeva indriyāni viriya-vasena balāni bhavanti.*

> They are both fivefold by way of *saddhā*, etc. Therefore five *indriyas* and five *balas* are spoken of.[167]

> With regard to the words beginning 'he develops *saddhindriya*', *saddhindriya* means that *saddhā* itself, with *saddhā* responsible, performs the purpose of a lord. This same method applies to *viriya* and the rest ... As for *saddhā-bala*, etc., *saddhā-bala* means that just *saddhā* is a *bala* in the sense of unshakeability. This same method applies to *viriya-bala* and the rest. For here *saddhā* is not shaken by distrust, *viriya* is not shaken by laziness, *sati* is not shaken by lost mindfulness, *samādhi* is not shaken by agitation, *paññā* is not shaken by ignorance.[168]

> 'Five *indriyas*'—the five *indriyas* beginning with *saddhā*; *saddhindriya* means that having overcome distrust it performs the purpose of a lord in the manner of commitment; [*viriyindriya*] having overcome laziness performs the task of a lord in the manner of taking on; [*satindriya*] having overcome heedlessness performs the task of a lord in the manner of standing near; [*samādhindriya*] having overcome distraction performs the task of a lord in the manner of non-distraction; *paññindriya* means that having overcome ignorance it performs the task of a lord in the manner of seeing. Just these should be understood as *balas* in the sense of unshakeability as a result of not being overcome by distrust and the rest, by virtue of their strength.[169]

As in the *indriya-saṃyutta* passage, these explanations do not hinge on the difference of intensity between *indriya* and *bala*. A little reflection reveals that, in fact, this has to be the case. These commentarial explanations take as their ideal point of reference the transcendent (*lokuttara*) mind at the moment of path when all thirty-seven *bodhipakkhiya-dhammas* can be said to be present in a single arising of consciousness (*cittuppāda*). Thus it is precisely the same *saddhā* that is considered as both *indriya* and *bala*, and not two different arisings of *saddhā*, the first of which might be weak and the second strong. Accordingly the commentaries appear to see the difference between *indriya* and *bala* essentially in terms of the former being active and the latter being passive: as an active force the *indriya* acts as a lord and overcomes or displaces its opposite force; conversely as a passive power the *bala* as a result of its strength cannot be overcome by its opposite.

Turning to the explanations provided in the north Indian treatises, however, the available sources seem agreed that the distinction between *indriya* and *bala*

---

[167] Buddhaghosa at Vism XXII 37: *asaddhiya-kosajja-pamāda-vikkhepa-sammohānaṃ abhibhavanato abhibhavana-saṃkhātena adhipatiyaṭṭhena indriyaṃ. assaddhiyâdīhi ca anabhibhavanīyato akampiyaṭṭhena balaṃ. tad ubhayaṃ pi saddhâdi-vasena pañca-vidhaṃ hoti tasmā pañcindriyāni pañca balānī ti vuccanti.*

[168] Buddhaghosa at Mp II 50-1: *saddhindriyaṃ bhāvetī ti ādīsu saddhā va attano saddhā-dhurena indaṭṭhaṃ karoti saddhindriyaṃ. viriyindriyâdīsu pi es'eva nayo ... saddhā-balâdīsu saddhā yeva akampiyaṭṭhena balan ti saddhā-balaṃ. viriya-balâdīsu pi es'eva nayo. ettha hi saddhā assaddhiyena na kampati viriyaṃ kosajjena na kampati sati muṭṭha-saccena na kampati samādhi uddhaccena na kampati paññā avijjāya na kampati.*

[169] Dhammapāla at Ud-a 305: *pañcindriyānī ti saddhâdīni pañcindriyāni. tattha assaddhiyaṃ abhibhavitvā adhimokkha-lakkhaṇe indaṭṭhaṃ karotī ti saddhindriyaṃ. kosajjaṃ abhibhavitvā paggaha-lakkhaṇe pamādaṃ abhibhavitvā upaṭṭhāna-lakkhaṇe vikkhepaṃ abhibhavitvā avikkhepa-lakkhaṇe aññāṇaṃ abhibhavitvā dassana-lakkhaṇe indaṭṭhaṃ karotī ti paññindriyaṃ. tāni yeva assaddhiyâdīhi anabhibhavanīyato akampiyaṭṭhena sampayutta-dhammesu thira-bhāvena balānī ti veditabbāni.*

is one of intensity. The following extract from the commentary to the *Arthaviniścaya-sūtra* is a clear statement of the matter:

> Just the five *indriyas*, *śraddhā*, etc., when they are strong are called *balas* ... since, as a result of there being no attack in the interim by their opposites (distrust, laziness, lost mindfulness, distraction, and lack of clear comprehension), they are not overwhelmed, therefore they are called *balas*. But the *indriyas*, as a result of persistent attack by their five opposities, are overwhelmed, therefore they are called *indriyas* due to the fact that their opposites are undefeated.[170]

As in the case of the Pāli commentaries, the explanations of the distinction between *indriya* and *bala* in the north Indian texts might be seen as reflecting the particular application of the seven sets in Abhidharma. As I shall discuss in more detail below, the northern Abhidharma treatises—at least those within the broad tradition of the Sarvāstivādins—understand each of the seven sets as characteristic of successive stages of the path. So according to the *Abhidharmakośa* the *indriyas* characterize the stage of acceptance (*kṣānti*), while the *balas* characterize the next stage, that which immediately precedes the *lokottara-darśana-mārga*, namely *laukikâgra-dharma*, the highest form of ordinary non-transcendent mind.[171]

In practice the distinction between the explanation in the Pāli commentaries and north Indian sources would appear to be quite subtle. For while it is thought appropriate, according to the Theravāda, to apply the term *indriya* to *saddhā*, etc. more or less in their generality,[172] it does appear from the *Dhammasaṅgaṇi* and *Nettippakaraṇa* that the term *bala* is not so universally applicable. Both explanations emphasize that the significance of the term *bala* lies in its indicating that an item is unshakeable or unassailable by its opposites; in practice this understanding would seem to be best interpreted as indicating that the difference between an *indriya* and *bala* is one of strength or force.

---

170 Artha 226-7: *tāny eva śraddhâdīni pañcendriyāṇi balavanti balāny ucyante ... yasmāt tad-vipakṣair aśraddhā-kausīdya-muṣita-smṛti-vikṣepâsamprajanyair antarā samudācārâbhavāt tāni nâvamṛdyante, tasmād balāny ucyante. indriyāṇi punas tad-vipakṣaiḥ pañcabhir antarântarā samudācārād avamṛdyante, tasmād anirjita-vipakṣatvād indriyāṇy ucyante.* (According to Abhid-h Trsl 140 the *indriyas* when they are weak (*mṛdu*) are called *indriyas*, but when they are sharp (*tīkṣṇa*) they are called *balas*; Satya Trsl 43 states that the *indriyas* being further developed become strong and are therefore called *balas*; Abhidh-sam Trsl 122 states that the *balas* are to be understood as the *indriyas*, but they are *balas* because they destroy and remove the dangers which are opposed to them, and because of distinction; Amṛta Trsl 206 states that when the *indriyas* are weak (*mṛdu*) they are *indriyas*, when they are great (*adhimātra*) they are *balas*.)

171 See Chapter 10.6.

172 Certain exceptions to the rule are found in Dhs (see Chapter 10).

CHAPTER FIVE

THE FACTORS OF AWAKENING

1. The bare list

Like the five *indriyas* and *balas*, the *bojjhaṅgas* or 'factors of awakening' are a list of seven distinct items: the awakening-factor of mindfulness (*sati-sambojjhaṅga*), the awakening-factor of discrimination of *dhamma* (*dhamma-vicaya-sambojjhaṅga*), the awakening-factor of strength (*viriya-sambojjhaṅga*), the awakening-factor of joy (*pīti-sambojjhaṅga*), the awakening-factor of tranquillity (*passaddhi-sambojjhaṅga*), the awakening-factor of concentration (*samādhi-sambojjhaṅga*), the awakening-factor of equipoise (*upekkhā-sambojjhaṅga*).[1] In the Nikāyas this bare list occurs quite regularly with or without the appellation *satta bojjhaṅgā*[2] in a number of contexts. Some of those contexts can be regarded as of a general nature and not necessarily specific to the *bojjhaṅgas*;[3] that is, they fit the kind of treatment common to the seven sets as a whole and found especially in the *mahā-vagga* of the *Saṃyutta-Nikāya*. Possibly more distinctive is the citing of the seven *bojjhaṅgas* in connection with the conditions that prevent decline (*aparihāniyā dhammā*) and the sixteen 'unsurpassables' (*ānuttariya*) of the Buddha:

> In so far as *bhikkhus* shall continue to develop *sati-sambojjhaṅga* ... *upekkhā-sambojjhaṅga*, growth can be expected for *bhikkhus* and not decline.[4]

However, the singling out of the *bojjhaṅgas* in this context is perhaps largely a result of their being seven of them: it seems that *aparihāniyā dhammā* come in groups of seven.[5] In the *Sampasādanīya-sutta* Sāriputta lists sixteen ways in which the Buddha is unsurpassable. Seventh in the list is this:

> Moreover this is unsurpassable, namely how the Blessed One teaches *dhamma* with regard to the highest matters—these seven *bojjhaṅgas*: *sati-sambojjhaṅga* ... *upekkhā-sambojjhaṅga*. This is what is unsurpassable with regard to the highest matters, lord.[6]

---

[1] Buddhist Sanskrit sources evidence a precisely parallel list; see *BHSD*, s.v. *bodhy-aṅga*; Lamotte, *Traité* III 1128.

[2] Seven *bojjhaṅgas* are mentioned but not listed at D II 83; III 101, 284; S V 161; A III 386; V 114-8; Th 437; Thī 21, 45; Dhs 232; see also references to seven sets. *Bojjhaṅga/bojjhaṅgas* without specifying the number seven are mentioned at Vin I 294; S I 54; A I 14; Th 161-2, 352, 595, 672, 725, 1114; Thī 170-1; Ap 13, 30, 343, 509.

[3] D III 251, 282; A II 237; IV 148; V 211.

[4] D II 79 = A IV 23: *yāvakīvañ ca bhikkhave bhikkhu sati-sambojjhaṅgaṃ bhāvessanti ... upekkhā-sambojjhaṅgam bhāvessanti, vuddhi yeva bhikkhave bhikkhūnaṃ pāṭikaṅkhā no parihāni*.

[5] In the *Mahāparinibbāna-sutta* the Buddha gives in all five sets of seven *aparihāniyā dhammā* (of which the *bojjhaṅgas* are the fourth), and finally a set of six. The Mūlasarvāstivādin *Mahāparinirvāṇa-sūtra* gives six sets of seven *aparihāṇīyā dharmāḥ* (of which the *bodhy-aṅgas* are the sixth) and one set of six (see Waldschmidt, *MPS* 128). Bareau discusses the different lists of *aparihāṇīyā dharmāḥ* in the various extant versions of the *Mahāparinirvāṇa-sūtra* at RBB, II 32-9; seven of the eight versions include the *bodhy-aṅgas*.

[6] D III 105-6: *aparaṃ pana bhante etad ānuttariyaṃ yathā bhagavā dhammaṃ deseti padhānesu; satt' ime bojjhaṅgā sati-sambojjhaṅgo ... upekkhā-sambojjhaṅgo. etad ānuttariyaṃ bhante padhānesu.*

The usage of the term *padhāna* ('highest matter') is rather odd here. I have taken it in the sense of 'most important or principal item'. This is clearly a possible meaning but not one favoured by the commentary here.[7] One should also note at this point that while the seven items are individually consistently cited as *sambojjhaṅgas*, collectively they are always *bojjhaṅgas*.[8] This suggests that in general no significance should be attached to the variation *bojjhaṅga/sambojjhaṅga*.

Aside from the bare list of seven *bojjhaṅgas*, there are two formulaic treatments of the *bojjhaṅgas* of some importance. The first of these is the application of the '*viveka-nissita* formula' to the list of *bojjhaṅgas*, and the second is what I term the '*bojjhaṅga* process formula'. Before turning to these, however, I wish to consider the four terms that, among the seven sets, are peculiar to the *bojjhaṅgas*: *dhamma-vicaya, pīti, passaddhi, upekkhā*.

2. Dhamma, dhammas and dhamma-vicaya

The awakening-factor of *dhamma-vicaya* or 'discrimination of *dhammas*' is directly related to wisdom (*paññā*) in the Nikāyas:

> When a *bhikkhu*, dwelling mindful in this way, discriminates, inspects, applies investigation by means of wisdom to that *dhamma*, then the awakening-factor of *dhamma*-discrimination is instigated for that *bhikkhu*.[9]
>
> Whatever discriminates, examines, applies investigation by means of wisdom among *dhammas* that are within, this is the awakening-factor of *dhamma*-discrimination. Whatever discriminates, examines, applies investigation by means of wisdom among *dhammas* that are without, this is the awakening-factor of *dhamma*-discrimination.[10]

This correspondence of *paññā* and *dhamma-vicaya* is taken up in the early Abhidhamma literature.[11] I have already pointed out that, as an *indriya*, *paññā* is conveniently related to the seeing of the four noble truths. But the notion of *dhamma-vicaya* raises a further issue. The issue is one that I have in fact already passed over once in dealing with *dhammesu dhammânupassanā* or 'watching *dhamma* with regard to *dhammas*', which is a convenient rendering that can be paralleled with 'watching feeling with regard to feelings' (*vedanāsu vedanânupassanā*). What we are concerned with, then, is the relationship between the notions of *dhamma* and *dhammas*. In the first quotation above what 'that *dhamma*' (*taṃ dhammaṃ*) refers to is not entirely clear.[12] In the

---

7 Sv III 891: 'Here, by virtue of endeavouring, the seven *bojjhaṅgas* are spoken of as "endeavours".' (*idha padahana-vasena satta bojjhaṅgā padhānā ti vuttā.*)

8 A stock verse (S V 24 = A V 233 = 253 = Dhp 89), however, talks of those whose minds are well cultivated in the *sambodhiyaṅgas* (*yesaṃ sambodhiyaṅgesu sammā-cittaṃ subhāvitaṃ*).

9 M III 85; S V 331; cf. Vibh 227. For Pāli text see below, p. 169, n. 123.

10 S V 111: *yad api bhikkhave ajjhattaṃ dhammesu paññāya pavicinati pavicarati parivīmaṃsaṃ āpajjati tad api dhamma-vicaya-sambojjhaṅgo, yad api bahiddhā dhammesu paññāya pavicinati pavicarati parivīmaṃsaṃ āpajjati tad api dhamma-vicaya-sambojjhaṅgo.* (Cf. Vibh 228.)

11 E.g. Dhs 11.

12 Vibh-a 312 refers *taṃ dhammaṃ* back to the initial *sati-sambojjhaṅga* paragraph of the 'process' formula, the *Vibhaṅga* version of which differs slightly from the Nikāya version; cf. M III 85-6 and Vibh 227.

second quotation *dhamma-vicaya* seems to be taken unambiguously as 'discrimination of *dhammas*'. Similarly the *Peṭakopadesa* glosses *dhamma-vicaya-sambojjhaṅga* as 'discrimination of *dhammas*' (*dhammānaṃ pavicayena*).[13] Yet in what sense would the discrimination of *dhamma* be something different from the discrimination of *dhammas*?

The scholarly literature on the notion of *dhamma/dharma* in Buddhist thought is, not surprisingly, fairly extensive. Perhaps one of the best succinct yet still sufficiently comprehensive accounts is found in Edward Conze's *Buddhist Thought in India*.[14] The Buddhist usage of the word 'dharma', Conze notes, is 'ambiguous and multivalent'. He goes on to distinguish seven 'philosophically important' meanings which may be summarized as: (i) (a) transcendent reality (*nirvāṇa*), (b) 'order of law of the universe', (c) a truly real event ('things as seen when Dharma is taken as norm'), (d) mental percepts (*dharmâyatana*), (e) characteristic or property (e.g. *vaya-dharma*); (ii) moral law, right behaviour; (iii) the texts of the Buddhist tradition (i.e. the preceding as interpreted in the Buddha's teaching). In conclusion Conze comments:

> Frequently it is not at all easy to determine which one of these various meanings is intended in a given case ... This applies to such terms as 'Dharma-body', 'Dharma-eye', the 'analytical knowledge of Dharma', the 'investigation (*pravicaya*) into dharma(s)' ... And once the Mahāyāna had identified the causually interrelated dharmas with the one and only Dharma, the very distinction between 'dharma' and 'dharmas' had to be abandoned.[15]

Conze, then, identifies various nuances of the word *dharma* and also suggests that the different nuances are by no means mutually exclusive. Conze finally points out that any difference in interpretation between the schools is 'more one of emphasis than of opinion'.[16] Indeed, it seems to me that the identification of 'causally interrelated dharmas with the one and only Dharma' must be considered virtually complete already in the Nikāyas. It is this question that I wish to consider in relationship to *dhamma-vicaya-sambojjhaṅga* (and also *dhammesu dhammânupassanā*).

It is probably true to say that the relationship between *dhamma* and *dhammas* in the early literature has been insufficiently examined by modern scholarship. This is in part the result of a tendency to view *dhammas* as the exclusive domain of the later Abhidhamma literature,[17] both canonical and

---

[13] Peṭ 103.

[14] Conze, *BTI*, pp. 92-6 The early classic work on '*dhamma*' is M. and W. Geiger's *Pāli Dhamma vornehmlich in der kanonischen Literatur*, Munich, 1921. The *PED* article on *dhamma* is still of considerable interest as is, of course, Th. Stcherbatsky's *The Central Conception of Buddhism and the Meaning of the Word "dharma"*, London, 1923. See also A.K. Warder, 'Dharmas and Data', *JIP* 1 (1971), pp. 272-95; A. Hirakawa, 'The Meaning of "dharma" and "abhidharma"', *Mélanges Lamotte*, pp. 159-75; Ñāṇamoli (Vism Trsl VII n. 1, VIII n. 68) also makes some important observations. The most comprehensive account of '*dhamma*' from the point of view of the Pāli sources is J.R. Carter, *Dhamma*, Tokyo, 1978; for further bibliographical references see Carter and Conze.

[15] Conze, *BTI*, p. 94.

[16] Id., p. 95.

[17] Carter, *Dhamma*, p. 48, draws attention to the debate among modern scholars concerning

commentarial. The assumption is that the *dhammas* of the Abhidhamma constitute a scholastic elaboration somewhat removed in spirit and time from the 'original' *dhamma* of the Buddha. In fact, of course, the four primary Nikāyas themselves use the word *dhamma* in the plural quite freely. While the notion of *dhammas* in the later literature is clearly more developed than in the Nikāyas, it is important to take the Nikāya usage of *dhamma* (plural) seriously.

A.K. Warder has provided a brief survey of the Nikāya usage of *dhamma* (plural)[18] and has commented:

> The four old *Nikāyas* are not as clear about *dhamma* meaning an "element" as is the *Abhidhamma*. They seem instead to offer discussion using the word a little more freely, apparently without defining it, out of which the precise concept of the *Abhidhamma* might have been extracted.[19]

In discussing the notion of a *dhamma* in the Nikāyas, one ought, perhaps, to be quite clear about the 'precise concept' of the Abhidhamma. This is where our difficulties start, for is the Abhidhamma literature as clear about a *dhamma* as an 'element' as Warder here suggests? While Warder himself does find difficulties with 'element' as a translation and eventually prefers 'principle', he does at one point feel able to characterize the notion of *dhammas* as yielding:

> a theory of elements in the sense of irreducibles, as in chemistry, which was propounded in the *Abhidhamma* and commentarial tradition of the Sthaviravāda school eventually as a theory of a finite number, less than 100, of elements which accounted for all experience in the universe.[20]

As Warder freely acknowledges, this understanding of what a *dhamma* is, is largely based on Stcherbatsky's pioneering study of the concept of a *dharma* according to the Vaibhāṣikas and as revealed in the *Abhidharmakośa* of Vasubandhu. This conception focuses on a *dharma* as *svabhāva* and *svalakṣaṇa*, that is to say, on a *dharma* as that which has an essential nature and characteristic peculiar to itself making it an irreducible (*dravya*).[21] However, it is not self-evident that this conception is simply transferable to the Pāli canonical Abhidhamma.

The *Dhammasaṅgaṇi* cannot really be considered an enumeration of irreducible elements. In answer to its own initial question ('Which *dhammas* are skilful?') the text goes on to list fifty-six items, commenting at the close of the list: 'these *dhammas* are skilful.'[22] Yet these fifty-six items are clearly not to be taken as irreducible. On the contrary the definitions of these items that the *Dhammasaṅgaṇi* provides show that a number of them are essentially equiva-

---

whether or not the theory of *dhammas* should be regarded as part of the original teaching of the Buddha.

18 *JIP* 1 (1971), pp. 276-86.

19 Id., p. 278.

20 Id., pp. 289-90.

21 A. Hirakawa, op. cit., pp. 161, 169-70. The term *dravya* is used, for example, in the context of the thirty-seven *bodhi-pākṣikā dharmāḥ* to indicate that they are reducible to ten *dravyas* (Abhidh-k 383). A Pāli equivalent to *dravya* does not appear to be found in this connection.

22 Dhs 9: *katame dhammā kusalā ... ime dhammā kusalā.*

lents. In this way the list of fifty-six can be reduced to twenty-eight.[23] Obviously, in indicating that certain *dhammas* can be defined in terms common to others, the *Dhammasaṅgaṇi* shows that it works with some notion of an essential characteristic and nature that particular *dhammas* share. But it is not clear that this essential nature necessarily defines what a *dhamma* is. For the *Dhammasaṅgaṇi* there does seem to be a sense in which *saddhā-bala* and *saddhindriya* remain distinct *dhammas*. In the final analysis all this means, perhaps, is that, from the point of view of the commentarial tradition the *Dhammasaṅgaṇi*, although an Abhidhamma work, uses a notion of *dhamma* that is still 'by way of exposition' (*pariyāyena*) rather than 'not by way of exposition' (*nippariyāyena*).

Yet this is possibly to underestimate the subtlety of the notion of a *dhamma*. In this regard one must guard against losing sight of the fact that a *dhamma* is a mental event or happening rather than an inert substance; its essential nature is dynamic rather than static. Thus in order to define a *dhamma* one must determine not so much what it *is*, as what it *does*. In one sense, then, *dhammas* are the different capacities or capabilities of mental events. Once we begin to view *dhammas* in this way, it seems to me, that the distinction between *saddhindriya* and *saddhā-bala*, say, is at once more real and intelligible.

Even when the *Atthasālinī* does explain the *Dhammasaṅgaṇi's* notion of a *dhamma* by way of *sabhāva*, it is not clear that this is precisely the same *svabhāva* that the northern tradition uses:

> They are *dhammas* because they uphold their own self-existence. They are *dhammas* because they are upheld by conditions or they are upheld according to their own-nature.[24]

> When the first of the great skilful *cittas* of the *kāmâvacara* arises, at that time the fifty-plus *dhammas* that have arisen by way of factors of *citta* are just *dhammas* in the sense of self-existents. Thus there is no other being, existence, man or person.[25]

As I have just pointed out, the first kind of *citta* analyzed in the *Dhammasaṅgaṇi* precisely does not consist of fifty-plus *dhammas* each having its own essential nature. Thus the force of *sabhāva* here appears to focus not so much on the essential nature of particular *dhammas*, but rather on the fact that there is no being or person apart from *dhammas*; *dhammas* are what exist.[26]

It may well be that in the final analysis the tendency to understand a *dhamma* as that which has its own particular and exclusive nature is what

---

[23] Cf. Vism XIV 133.

[24] As 39: *attano pana sabhāvaṃ dhārentī ti dhammā. dhāriyanti vā paccayehi dhāriyanti vā yathā sabhāvato ti dhammā.*

[25] As 155: *yasmiṃ samaye kāmâvacaraṃ paṭhamaṃ mahā-kusala-cittaṃ uppajjati, tasmiṃ samaye cittaṅga-vasena uppannā atireka-paññāsa dhammā sabhāvaṭṭhena dhammā eva honti. na añño koci satto vā bhāvo vā poso vā puggalo vā hotī ti.*

[26] The earliest usage of *sabhāva* in Pāli sources is even more problematic. Peṭ 104 explains *hetu* as the *sabhāva* of a *dhamma* (i.e. it acts as a cause for other *dhammas*) and *paccaya* as its *parabhāva* (i.e. other *dhammas* act as conditions for its occurrence); in fact this understanding seems to underlie the first As passage quoted above. According to Paṭis 178-9 *dhammas* are 'empty by self-existence' (*sabhāvena suññā*). Cf. Warder's comments, Paṭis Trsl xvii-xviii, xxvi-xxvii; Paṭis-a III 634-5; Paṭis Trsl 362 (n.).

prevails in Buddhist thought—this is what should define a *dhamma* 'without regard for exposition'. But this important topic is rather incidental to the present study. The point I wish to make, however, is that the usage of the word *dhamma* (in the plural) remains in the Nikāyas, canonical Abhidhamma, and even to some extent in the commentarial tradition, a somewhat ambiguous and multivalent term. Its precise understanding continues to be elusive and defies rigid or fixed definition. Possibly this is no accident and the texts delight in the very fluidity of the term.

In the Nikāyas, the question of the relationship between *dhamma* and *dhammas* is perhaps most easily seen with reference to *paṭicca-samuppāda.*[27] It is stated in the Nikāyas that he who sees *paṭicca-samuppāda* sees *dhamma*, and that he who sees *dhamma* sees *paṭicca-samuppāda.*[28] This is in fact a very succinct statement of the principle involved, for what is *paṭicca-samuppāda* apart from the interrelatedness of *dhammas*? To see *dhammas* is to see their interrelatedness; to see their interrelatedness is to see *dhamma*. One might rephrase the Nikāya saying, then, as: 'He who sees *dhammas* sees *dhamma*; he who sees *dhamma* sees *dhammas*.'

A stock phrase describes the special *dhamma*-teaching of Buddhas (*buddhānaṃ sāmukkaṃsikā dhamma-desanā*) as suffering (*dukkha*), arising (*samudaya*), cessation (*nirodha*), path (*magga*).[29] This is, of course, a shorthand for the four noble truths. So *dhamma* is the four noble truths. When the four noble truths are considered in more detail in the Nikāyas, the first is often defined as 'in short the five aggregates of grasping' (*saṃkhittena pañc'upādāna-kkhandhā dukkhā*); the second is explained by reference to three kinds of craving (*taṇhā*)—for the objects of sensual desire (*kāma*), for existence (*bhava*) and for non-existence (*vibhava*); the third truth is the cessation of this craving; finally the fourth consists of the eight factors of the noble path.[30] The *Dasuttara-sutta* takes up these various categories: the five aggregates of grasping are five *dhammas* to be fully known (*pariññeyya*); the three kinds of craving are three *dhammas* to be abandoned (*pahātabba*); nine successive kinds of cessation (*nava anupubba-nirodhā*) are termed nine *dhammas* to be realized (*sacchikātabba*); the eight factors of the path are eight *dhammas* to be developed (*bhāvetabba*).[31] This illustrates, I think, something of the way in which the Nikāyas use the notion of *dhamma* and *dhammas*: to know *dhamma* is to know the four noble truths, and knowledge of the four noble truths involves knowledge of *dhammas* in various ways.

When one comes to certain of the commentarial explanations of *dhamma* and *dhammas*, there is, I think, a danger of being misled by some of the rather specialized and technical meanings identified for the word *dhamma* in particular

---

27 As recognized by Oldenberg; see Carter, *Dhamma*, pp. 49, 53.

28 M I 190-1: *yo paṭicca-samuppādaṃ passati so dhammaṃ passati, yo dhammaṃ passati so paṭicca-samuppādaṃ passati.*

29 E.g. D I 110; M I 380.

30 D II 305-13; M I 48-9; S V 420; Vin I 10.

31 See D III 278, 275, 290, 286 respectively.

contexts.[32] None of the specific applications is entirely cut loose from the primary underlying notion. That is to say, the various usages of *dhamma* are still seen by the commentarial tradition as constituting a coherent whole. This underlying and unifying notion of *dhamma* seems at times to be so much second nature to the commentarial tradition that it can appear understated in certain of its explanations. But something of it is brought out in the etymological explanation of both *dhamma* and *dhammas*: *dhamma* is that which upholds or supports (*dhāreti*) those who have attained the paths and fruits;[33] *dhammas* uphold their own self-existence.

As J.R. Carter has pointed out, the commentarial tradition places great emphasis on a threefold and ninefold explanation of *dhamma*.[34] Thus *dhamma* is understood as *pariyatti* or *āgama*, that is to say, *dhamma* as manifested in the teaching of the Buddha and recorded in the canonical literature which is to be learnt and mastered. Secondly *dhamma* is *paṭipatti*, that is to say, the teaching as practised. Finally there is *dhamma* that is *paṭivedha* or *adhigama*, that is to say, 'penetration' or 'accomplishment' consisting of the ninefold transcendent *(lokuttara-)dhamma* (the four paths and four fruits together with *nibbāna*).[35]

How does all this relate to *dhamma-vicaya*? What does the term actually mean? Strictly *vi-caya* might be derived either from the root *ci* meaning 'to gather or accumulate' or from *ci* meaning 'to note or observe'—if indeed these two roots are ultimately separable.[36] But Whitney here suggests that words with the prefixes *vi* and *nis* are best referred to the former root, with a meaning such as 'to take apart'.[37] So *dhamma-vicaya* would mean the 'taking apart of *dhamma*'. In Buddhist thought to take *dhamma* apart is, I think, to be left with *dhammas*. *Dhamma-vicaya* means, then, either the 'discrimination of *dhammas*' or the 'discernment of *dhamma*'; to discriminate *dhammas* is precisely to discern *dhamma*.[38]

The *Pārileyya-sutta*[39] is of some interest at this point. A *bhikkhu* raises the question of what kind of knowing and seeing gives rise to the immediate destruction fo the *āsavas*.[40] The Buddha responds:

---

[32] At As 38 (cf. Sv I 99) Buddhaghosa gives a four-fold explanation quoting canonical sources: *dhamma* as 'learning' (*pariyatti*) is equivalent to the canonical literature (cf. M I 133: *ekacce mogha-purisā dhammaṃ pariyāpuṇanti suttaṃ ... vedallaṃ; te taṃ dhammaṃ pariyāpuṇitvā tesaṃ dhammānaṃ paññāya atthaṃ na upaparikkhanti*); *dhamma* as cause (*hetu*) is illustrated by the phrase 'knowledge with regard to causes is *dhamma-paṭisambhidā*' (Vibh 293); *dhamma* can be equivalent to virtue (*guṇa*) when contrasted with *adhamma* (cf. Th 304); finally, in such phrases as 'at that time there are *dhammas*' (Dhs passim) and 'he dwells watching *dhamma(s)* with regard to *dhammas*', *dhamma* indicates the absence of a substantial being (*nissatta-nijjīvita*). For a full discussion of *dhamma* in the commentaries see Carter, *Dhamma*, pp. 58-67.

[33] Ps I 131 = Mp II 107; cf. Ps I 173; Khp-a 19.

[34] *Dhamma*, pp. 131-5.

[35] E.g. Mp V 33.

[36] Cf. W.D. Whitney, *The Roots, Verb-forms and Primary derivatives of the Sanskrit Language*, 1885, Leipzig, p. 47.

[37] Ibid.

[38] Edgerton (*BHSD*, s.v. *pravicaya*) rightly, I think, calls into question the translation 'investigation'.

[39] S III 94-9.

[40] S III 96: *kathaṃ nu kho jānato kathaṃ passato anantarā āsavānaṃ khayo*.

> *Dhamma* is taught by me, *bhikkhus*, by way of discrimination; the four establishings of mindfulness are taught by way of discrimination; the [four] right endeavours are taught by way of discrimination; the four bases of success are taught by way of discrimination; the five faculties are taught by way of discrimination; the five powers are taught by way of discrimination; the seven awakening-factors are taught by way of discrimination; the noble eight-factored path is taught by way of discrimination. Thus *dhamma* is taught by me by way of discrimination.[41]

The Buddha then goes on to detail the twenty modes of what is elsewhere called the 'view of inidviduality' (*sakkāya-diṭṭhi*).[42] In each case it is pointed out that the formation (*saṃkhāra*), the craving (*taṇhā*), the feeling (*vedanā*), the contact (*phassa*) and the ignorance (*avijjā*) which add up to the view of individuality are impermanent, put together, and arisen by way of conditions (*aniccā saṃkhatā paṭicca-samuppannā*). It is knowing and seeing this that gives rise to immediate destruction of the *āsavas*.

The Sanskrit fragments of the *Dharmaskandha* preserve a parallel to this *sutta* presented as a quotation from the *Pātaleya-vyākaraṇa*.[43] It presents a number of variations:

> For the sake of discrimination of the [five] aggregates, *bhikṣus*, *dharmas* are taught by me to you, that is to say the four establishings of mindfulness, the four right endeavours, the four bases of success, the five faculties, the five powers, the seven awakening-factors, the noble eight-factored path. With regard to *dharmas* taught by me to you, *bhikṣus*, for the sake of discrimination of the aggregates, some foolish persons dwell without strong purpose, without strong devotion, without strong affection, without strong delight. Slowly indeed do they contact excellence for the sake of destruction of the *āsravas*. With regard to *dharmas* taught by me to you, *bhikṣus*, for the sake of discrimination of the aggregates, some sons of families dwell with very strong purpose, with very strong devotion, with very strong affection, with very strong delight. Quickly indeed do they contact excellence for the sake of destruction of the *āsravas*.[44]

The Sanskrit version goes on to discuss the various views of individuality in terms that closely parallel those of the Pāli version (though the phrase concerning the immediate destruction of the *āsravas* is not found). Both the Pāli and Sanskrit versions focus on the *dharma* taught by the Buddha as concerned with the discernment of the subtle operation of the view of individu-

---

41 Ibid.: *vicayaso desito bhikkave mayā dhammo, vicayaso desitā cattāro satipaṭṭhānā; vicayaso desitā samma-ppadhānā; vicayaso desitā cattāro iddhi-pādā; vicayaso desitāni pañcindriyāni; vicayaso desitāni pañca balāni; vicayaso desitā satta bojjhaṅgā; vicayaso desito ariyo aṭṭhaṅgiko maggo. evaṃ vicayaso kho desito bhikkhave mayā dhammo.*

42 Taking *rūpa*, *vedanā*, *saññā*, *saṃkhāra* and *viññāṇa* in turn as self, as what the self possesses, as in the self, as what the self is in; cf. R. Gethin, *JIP* 14 (1986), pp. 44-5.

43 *Fragmente des Dharmaskandha: Ein Abhidharma-Text in Sanskrit aus Gilgit*, ed. S. Dietz, Göttingen, 1984, pp. 52-5.

44 Id., pp. 52-3: *deśitā vo bhikṣavo mayā dharmmāḥ skandhānāṃ pravicayāya, yad uta catvāri smṛty-upasthānāni catvāri samyak-pradhānāni catvāra ṛddhi-pādāḥ paṃcendriyāṇi paṃca balāni sapta bodhy-aṃgāny āryâṣṭâṃgo mārgga. evaṃ deśiteṣu vo bhikṣavo mayā dharmmeṣu skandhānāṃ pravicayāya. atha ca punar ihaikatyā moha-puruṣā na tīvra-cchandā viharaṃti na tīvra-snehā na tīvra-premāṇo na tīvra-pramādās. te dhandham evânuttaryaṃ spṛśaṃti yad utâsravānāṃ kṣayāya. evaṃ deśiteṣu vo bhikṣavo mayā dharmmeṣu skandhānāṃ pravicayāya. atha ca punar ihaikatyāḥ kula-puttrāḥ ativa-tīvra-cchandā viharaṃti ativa-tīvra-snehā ativa-tīvra-premāṇo'tiva-tīvra-pramādās. te kṣipram evânuttaryaṃ spṛśaṃti yad utâsravānāṃ kṣayāya.*

ality with regard to the five aggregates; both understand that this is achieved by way of the practice of the *dharmas* that constitute the seven sets. In other words, the Buddha's teaching is concerned with the interaction of various groupings of *dharmas* that make up *dharma*. Put simply, he teaches the discrimination of *dharmas* and the discernment of *dharma*.

3. *Pīti and passaddhi*

Pīti

In general Sanskrit literature *prīti* means 'joy', 'delight' or 'pleasure'; it then comes to mean 'friendship', 'love' or 'affection'.[45] The word thus conveys a certain emotional intensity. In the Nikāyas a distinction is made between *pīti* that is 'carnal' (*āmisā*) and *pīti* that is free of the carnal (*nirāmisā*); the former arises dependent on the five kinds of sensual desire, the latter is especially characteristic of the *pīti* that arises in association with the first and second *jhāna*.[46] More generally it seems that *nirāmisā pīti* is the kind of joy associated with spiritual practice as a whole. The term *pīti* is especially found in association with a sequence of terms (*pāmujja, pīti, passaddhi, sukha, samādhi*) that is seen as specifically related to the process of the mind's becoming progressively contented and stilled. Thus we are told that one who has trust based in understanding (*avecca-ppasāda*) in the Buddha, Dhamma and Saṃgha gains enthusiasm for the goal and *dhamma* (*labhati attha-vedaṃ labhati dhamma-vedaṃ*); he gains gladness that is connected with *dhamma* (*labhati dhammûpa-saṃhitaṃ pāmujjaṃ*); for one who is gladdened, joy is born (*pāmuditassa pīti jayati*); the body of one who is joyful becomes tranquil (*pīti-manassa kāyo passambhati*); one whose body is tranquil experiences happiness (*passaddha-kāyo sukhaṃ vedeti*); the mind of one who is happy becomes concentrated (*sukhino cittaṃ samādhiyati*).[47] The same process occurs when one sees that the five hindrances (*nīvaraṇa*) are abandoned in oneself.[48] According to a more extended sequence proper conduct (*sīla*) leads to absence of regret (*avippaṭi-sāra*), this leads to *pāmujja*, this to *pīti*, this to *sukha*, this to *samādhi*, this to knowledge and vision (*ñāṇa-dassana*), this to disenchantment (*nibbidā*) and dispassion (*virāga*), this to knowledge and vision of freedom (*vimutti-ñāṇa-dassana*).[49]

What seems to be clear is that *pīti* and these associated ideas are intended to convey a sense of the emotional fulfilment that is seen as inherent in the spiritual life. It is to be noted that this process of emotional fulfilment which culminates in the mind's becoming concentrated is consistently seen as the precursor to the more advanced stages of the spiritual path.

The notion of *pīti* in the later literature has been fully discussed by L.S. Cousins in connection with the practice of *jhāna*.[50] In this context the

45 MW, s.v. *prīti*.
46 S IV 235-6.
47 M I 37-8; cf. A III 285-8; V 329-34; D III 241-3 = A III 21-3.
48 D I 73; cf. M I 283. For further examples see D III 288; S IV 78-9, 351-8.
49 A V 1-6; cf. S II 29-32.
50 L.S. Cousins, *Religion* 3 (1973), pp. 120-2.

commentaries give a list of five kinds of *pīti* which in effect constitute five stages of increasing intensity. These are minor (*khuddakā*), momentary (*khaṇikā*), descending (*okkantikā*), transporting (*ubbegā*) and suffusing (*pharaṇā*) *pīti*, all of which are described in some detail.[51] It is the fifth and final stage of *pīti* which is the kind associated with full absorption (*appanā*) in the commentaries: 'being the root of absorption-concentration, suffusing-*pīti* comes by growth into association with *samādhi*'.[52] It is this kind of *pīti* too, it seems, that the commentaries wish to associate with *pīti-sambojjhaṅga* when they describe its characteristic as suffusing.[53]

It is perhaps worth drawing attention to a difference in the interpretation of *pīti/prīti* among the ancient schools of Buddhism. The Theravādins and the Sautrāntikas (and the author of the **Satyasiddhi-śāstra*) regard *pīti/prīti* as a distinct *dhamma/dharma* to be classified under *saṃkhāra-kkhandha/saṃskāra-skandha*. Those who follow the traditions of the Vaibhāṣikas, however, regard it as *vedanā-skandha*, and as such a manifestation of *saumanasya* or pleasant mental feeling. This causes problems with the traditional list of factors for the first *dhyāna*, namely *vitarka*, *vicāra*, *prīti*, *sukha*, *cittaikagratā*, since one item (*saumanasya*) appears to be given twice (*prīti*, *sukha*). This is resolved by understanding *sukha* to refer to *praśrabdhi*; in the higher *dhyānas*, however, *sukha* is taken to refer to *saumanasya*.[54]

Passaddhi

The term *passaddhi* ('tranquillity', 'calm') is, then, closely associated with the term *pīti*. It is perhaps of some interest that *passaddhi* is described in the ancient formula as being mediated through the body: 'the body of one whose mind is joyful becomes tranquil; one whose body is tranquil experiences happiness'. In the *Saṃyutta-nikāya* we find a distinction being made between tranquillity of the body (*kāya-passaddhi*) and tranquillity of the mind (*citta-passaddhi*).[55] This is taken up in the canonical Abhidhamma. The *Dhammasaṅgaṇi* explains *kāya-passaddhi* as tranquillity of the aggregates of feeling (*vedanā*), recognition (*saññā*) and formations (*saṃkhāra*), and *citta-passaddhi* as tranquillity of the aggregate of consciousness (*viññāṇa*).[56]

If one is to take this at face value, it seems to indicate that *vedanā*, *saññā* and *saṃkhāras* are seen as in some sense able to bridge the gap between mind and body. They are, as it were, what mediates one's state of mind to the body, and vice versa. Some form of movement from mind to body and back again is, in fact, quite clearly indicated in the ancient formula concerned with the

---

51 Vism IV 94-98; As 115-7.

52 Vism IV 99 = As 166: *appanā-samādhissa mūlaṃ hutvā vaḍḍhamānā samādhi-sampayogaṃ gatā pharaṇa-pīti*.

53 E.g Mp II 53; the *lakkhaṇa* of *pīti* is apparently more generally described as *sampīyana* or 'delighting' at Vism IV 94 and As 115.

54 See Dhs 17; Vism IV 100; Satya Trsl 181; Abhidh-k 438-9; Abhidh-h Trsl 106-8, 168; Artha-n 230. Cf. Guenther, *Philosophy and Psychology in the Abhidharma*, 3rd ed., Berkeley, 1976, p. 121.

55 S V 66, 104, 111; cf. Vibh 228.

56 Dhs 14-5, 66.

dynamics of *pīti* and *passaddhi*. To take the *Dīgha* version that introduces the four *jhānas*, the *bhikkhu* perceives that the hindrances are abandoned in him and as a result his mind becomes joyful; as a result of this his body becomes tranquil and he feels happy; a happy mind becomes concentrated.

The notion of the reciprocal nature of the relationship between mind and body is further brought out by the way in which in the *Dhammasaṅgaṇi* (followed by the later Abhidhamma) tranquillity of body and mind forms a group with five other pairs of items. These are lightness (*lahutā*) of mind and body, softness (*mudutā*) of mind and body, readiness (*kammaññatā*) of mind and body, fitness (*pāguññatā*) of mind and body, straightness (*ujukatā*) of mind and body.[57] The relationship that these factors bear to the body is underlined by the fact that precisely the same terminology in part is applied to the physical world. Among the twenty-seven varieties of *rūpa* distinguished by the *Dhammasaṅgaṇi* are lightness, softness and readiness of *rūpa*.[58] So what at one level seems to represent a quite straightforward observation of the relationship between body and mind is potentially a conception of some subtlety and precision.[59]

In view of *passaddhi's* association in the Abhidhamma with these other terms, it is perhaps worth noting one or two characteristic Nikāya contexts for their usage. In a frequently repeated stock passage that I have already had occasion to refer to, the mind that is free from hindrances (*vinīvaraṇa-citta*) is said to be healthy (*kalla*), soft (*mudu*), enlivened (*odagga*—a term that the commentaries associate with *pīti*), trustful or clear (*pasanna*)—this is the kind of mind receptive to the special *dhamma* teaching of Buddhas.[60] In the *Sāmaññaphala-sutta* and elsewhere the mind of one who has practised the four *jhānas* is described as, amongst other things, soft (*mudu-bhūta*) and ready (*kammaniya*).[61]

To sum up, *pīti* and *passaddhi* as *bojjhaṅgas* link into a range of ideas associated with the notion of the mind as happy, content and calm. Such a mind is seen as ready and suited to the gaining and developing of insight and knowledge. Together *pīti* and *passaddhi* are terms suggestive of the positive emotional content of ancient Buddhism.

4. Upekkhā

Apart from being considered one of the seven *bojjhaṅgas*, the term *upekkhā* is quite regularly found in the Nikāyas in connection with the discussion of *vedanā*, the description of the *jhānas*, and the description of the four divine-

---

[57] Dhs 9; As 249 calls the group the six pairs (*yugalaka*). They are discussed in some detail by Nyanaponika Thera, *Abhidhamma Studies*, 3rd ed., Kandy, 1976, pp. 81-90.

[58] Dhs 134, 144.

[59] For their part Buddhist Sanskrit sources often explain *praśrabdhi* directly as readiness (*karmaṇyatā*) and lightness (*lāghava*) of mind; see Abhidh-k 55; Abhidh-dī 72; Abhidh-sam Trsl 8. Cf. Satya Trsl 187: 'When at the time of the mind's working the body and mind become calm and free from ill-being, at that moment it is termed *praśrabdhi*.'

[60] E.g. M I 379-80.

[61] D I 76-83, passim; cf. M I 347-8.

dwellings (*brahma-vihāras*). As regards *vedanā*, the relevant term is *upekkhindriya* or 'the faculty of *upekkhā*'; this is identified with feeling that is not-painful-and-not-pleasant (*adukkha-m-asukha vedanā*).[62] In the ancient *jhāna* formula[63] one who has attained the third *jhāna* is described as 'with equipoise' (*upekkhaka*) and 'one who dwells happy, with equipoise and with mindfulness' (*upekkhako satimā sukha-vihārī*). The fourth *jhāna* is termed *upekkhā-sati-pārisuddhi* which the later texts interpret as 'purity of mindfulness (brought about) by means of equipoise'.[64] Finally, as one of the four divine dwellings, *upekkhā* is practised and developed together with loving kindness or friendliness (*mettā*) towards beings, compassion (*karuṇā*) with regard to the suffering of beings, and joy (*muditā*) with regard to the happiness of beings.[65] While *upekkhā*, which is last in the traditional sequence of these four items, can be regarded as completing the practice of the four *brahma-vihāras*, as H.B. Aronson has made clear in his discussions, it should not be regarded as supplanting or superseding the other three. The four always remain essentially complementary.[66]

In the later literature a formal distinction is made between *upekkhā* as not-painful-and-not-pleasant feeling (i.e. a constituent of *vedanā-kkhandha*) on the one hand, and *upekkhā* as a skilful mental factor (i.e. a constituent of *saṃkhāra-kkhandha*) on the other.[67] The distinction is common to both Pāli and Buddhist Sanskrit sources[68] and would appear to be part of the common heritage of ancient Buddhism. Although the distinction is not formally made explicit in the Nikāyas, *upekkhindriya* is quite explicitly understood as *vedanā*, while in other contexts an understanding of the term *upekkhā* as simply not-painful-and-not-pleasant feeling would seem to be inadequate.[69] The Pāli commentarial tradition preserves a rather more comprehensive analysis that

---

[62] E.g. S V 210; Vibh 123.

[63] E.g. D I 75.

[64] This interpretation of the compound already occurs at Vibh 261 (*ayaṃ sati imāya upekkhāya vivaṭā hoti parisuddhā pariyodātā tena vuccati upekkhā-sati-pārisuddhin ti*); cf. As 178; Vism IV 194. Abhidh-k 438 takes it as *upekṣa-pariśuddhi* and *smṛti-pariśuddhi*.

[65] E.g. D I 251.

[66] H.B. Aronson, 'Equanimity (*upekkhā*) in Theravāda Buddhism', *Studies in Pāli and Buddhism*, ed. A.K. Narain, Delhi, 1979, pp. 1-18; see in particular p. 8.

[67] If worked out, the *pañhâpucchaka* treatment of the twenty-two *indriyas* (Vibh 124-34) and seven *bojjhaṅgas* (Vibh 232-4) makes clear that *upekkhindriya* is treated as *vedanā* and *upekkhā-sambojjhaṅga* as *saṃkhāra*; see Table 12, p. 328. Cf. Dhātuk 16: *satta bojjhaṅgā … ekena khandhena … saṃgahitā*.

[68] E.g. Artha-n 230 comments of *upekṣā-sambodhy-aṅga* that it is *upekṣā* as a *saṃskāra* that is meant and not *upekṣā* as *vedanā*.

[69] However, the *Dhammasaṅgaṇi* makes explicit mention of *upekkhā* only as *adukkha-m-asukhā vedanā* (e.g. Dhs 28), *upekkhā* as *tatra-majjhattatā* belonging to *saṃkhāra-kkhandha* seems to be entirely absent even though what one assumes to be *tatra-majjhattatā-upekkhā* features in the quotation of the Nikāya *jhāna* formula (Dhs 32, 35); *upekkhā* or *tatra-majjhattatā* is one of the *yevāpanaka-dhammas* (cf. Dhs 9; As 132, 173). In the treatment of *lokuttara-citta* (Dhs 60-75, 99-117) this has the effect of leaving *upekkhā-bojjhaṅga* out of the reckoning, although the other six *bojjhaṅgas* are identified (Dhs 61-8). Unfortunately since *lokuttara-citta* is expanded in full for the first *jhāna* only, and given in a much abbreviated form for the remaining *jhānas* (Dhs 70), it is impossible to verify that the *Dhammasaṅgaṇi* does *not* identify *upekkhā* as a *bojjhaṅga* with *upekkhā* as *vedanā*. The *Vibhaṅga*, however, makes it clear that *upekkhā-sambojjhaṅga* should be understood as *majjhattatā* and *saṃkhāra-kkhandha* and not *vedanā* (Vibh 230, 232).

distinguishes ten different applications or meanings of *upekkhā* in the canonical literature.[70] This list can be resolved into four basic items:

(1) *upekkhā* as 'specific balance' (*tatra-majjhattatā*)—six aspects
(2) *upekkhā* as 'feeling' (*vedanā*)—one aspect
(3) *upekkhā* as 'strength' (*viriya*)—one aspect
(4) *upekkhā* as 'wisdom' (*paññā*)—two aspects

In practice the last two items, constituting three of the ten aspects, are rather less conspicuous in the canon than the first two, and I shall not comment upon them further.

It is *upekkhā* as *tatra-majjhattatā* or 'balance with regard to things' that is of immediate concern. It is worth noting the commentarial definitions of the six aspects of this. Six-limbed *upekkhā* belongs to one who has destroyed the *āsavas*; it is *upekkhā* that has the property (*ākāra-bhūtā*) of not losing (*avijahana*) the purified condition (*parisuddha-pakati-bhāva*) in the face of wished and unwished for objects at the six sense doors. As a *brahma-vihāra*, *upekkhā* has the property of balance (*majjhatta*) with regard to beings. *Upekkhā* as a *bojjhaṅga* has the property of balance with regard to conascent *dhammas*. Similarly, in its general aspect of balance with regard to things (*tatra-majjhatta*), *upekkhā* is what causes conascent (*dhammas*) to proceed evenly (*sama-vāhita-bhūtā*). *Jhānupekkhā* produces impartiality (*apakkha-pāta-jananī*) with regard to the highest kind of pleasant feeling, namely that which occurs in the third *jhāna*. *Upekkhā* that consists of purity (*pārisuddhi-upekkhā*) is the repose (*avyāpāra*) from stilling adverse conditions (*paccanīka-vūpasamana*) that exists in the fourth *jhāna*.[71] These six are said to be one by way of meaning, namely *upekkhā* as *tatra-majjhatta*, but are distinguished by virtue of the different occasions upon which they occur.[72]

Keeping in mind these six aspects of *upekkhā* as *tatra-majjhatta*, it is worth considering a little further *upekkhā* as not-painful-not-pleasant feeling. According to the *Cūḷavedalla-sutta*, inherent in pleasant feeling is a latent tendency to attraction (*rāgânusaya*), in painful feeling a latent tendency to dislike (*paṭighânusaya*) and in not-painful-and-not-pleasant feeling a latent tendency to ignorance (*avijjânusaya*).[73] What this means, then, is that while the extremes of attraction and dislike are held in check by not-painful-and-not-pleasant feeling, this may result in a state of uncertainty and indecision. Yet because not-painful-and-not-pleasant feeling is balanced between painful and pleasant feeling, there is a sense in which it can lead either way, be either positive or negative: 'not-painful-and-not-pleasant feeling is pleasant as knowing, unpleasant as not knowing' (*adukkha-m-asukhā vedanā ñāṇa-sukhā aññāṇa-dukkhā*).[74] In other words, if the danger of ignorance is avoided, because it is evenly poised not-painful-and-not-pleasant feeling is potentially a useful position

[70] As 172-3; Vism IV 156-179; Paṭis-a 187-8; cf. Aronson's discussion in Narain, *SPB*, pp. 2-6.
[71] These six are discussed more fully by Aronson.
[72] As 173; Vism IV 167; Paṭis-a 188.
[73] M I 303.
[74] Ibid.

from which to see the dangers inherent in painful and pleasant feeling. A rather similar relationship exists between the four *brahma-vihāras*. The dangers associated with *mettā*, and *muditā*—their near enemies (*āsanna-paccatthika*), are attraction (*rāga*) and worldly happiness (*geha-sitaṃ somanassaṃ*) respectively. Associated with *karuṇā* is the danger of worldly dejection (*geha-sitaṃ domanassaṃ*). The *brahma-vihāra* of *upekkhā*, while avoiding these extremes, is associated with the danger of worldly indifference consisting of not knowing (*geha-sitā aññāṇupekkhā*).[75] This is, of course, precisely not skilful *upekkhā*, but its near enemy, which the Abhidhamma would understand as some form of unskilful *citta* rooted in delusion (*moha*).[76] Yet if the *brahma-vihāra* of *upekkhā* is stable and its near enemy does not arise, then because of its balance and impartiality it can check the near enemies of *mettā*, *muditā* and *karuṇā*, which might arise if these three were developed in isolation. If *karuṇā* and *muditā* are the natural responses of the mind that has its home in *mettā*, then *upekkhā* assures that this mind remains stable and undisturbed.

The nature of *upekkhā* is further brought out with regard to the *jhānas*. *Jhānupekkhā* is said in the commentaries to manifest at the level of the third *jhāna*. This, it seems, is specifically due to the fading out of *pīti*, which is seen as enlivening the mind to such an extent that *upekkhā*, although technically present in the first and second *jhānas*, is not fully obvious. In this context *upekkhā* plays a significant part in the process of the mind's becoming stiller, less agitated and more settled, and so less prone to becoming unbalanced or obsessed. Once again this is not seen as implying indifference or insensitivity; on the contrary this is what allows the mind to become fully sensitive and effective. The process is seen as being completed in the fourth *jhāna* by the coupling of *upekkhā* and *sati*.

The explanation of *upekṣā* in Buddhist Sanskrit sources appears essentially the same and to offer no real difficulties. It is described most generally as 'evenness of mind' (*citta-samatā*), which seems to accord well with the Abhidhamma definition of *tatra-majjhattatā* as that which causes conascent *dhammas* to proceed evenly (*sama-vāhita*).[77]

The most important characteristic of *upekkhā* in all its various manifestations would seem to be the way in which it maintains the balance of skilful

---

[75] As 193-4; Vism IX 93-101; cf. Aronson in Narain, *SPB*, p. 5.

[76] Aronson argues against the tendency of some (he cites Winston King and Melford Spiro) to understand *upekkhā* as indifference or detachment that sublimates all emotional response and feeling. He suggests that any study of particular meditational practices, such as *upekkhā*, must understand these in the wider context of Buddhist practice as presented in the Nikāyas and commentaries. He concludes that their understanding of *upekkhā* does not support the view that it is mere indifference and draws attention to the fact that the underlying motivating force for the Buddha's teaching and for those who follow it is always considered to be sympathy (*anukampa*) for the world of beings, and benefit for both self and other. Cf. the following passages cited by Aronson: A I 22; Mp I 98-9, 101; A IV 134-5; D II 119. See also H.B. Aronson, 'Love, Compassion, Sympathetic Joy and Equanimity in Theravāda Buddhism' (Ph.D. dissertation, University of Wisconsin, 1975).

[77] See Abhidh-k 55; Abhidh-dī 72; Abhidh-h Trsl 15; Abhidh-sam Trsl 9; Satya Trsl 187. For further discussion of some of the terms used in Buddhist Sanskrit texts to explain *upekṣā* see G.M. Nagao, 'Tranquil Flow of Mind: An Interpretation of *upekṣā*', *Mélanges Lamotte*, pp. 245-58.

mental factors, and prevents them from subtly shifting from the skilful to the unskilful. Aronson, in his article on *upekkhā*, draws attention to the fact that *tatra-majjhattatā* is considered in the Abhidhamma to be a universal of skilful *citta*, likewise *uddhacca* or 'restlessness' is a universal of unskilful *citta*. This is also true of *upekṣā* and *auddhatya* in the Vaibhāṣika Abhidharma. This can be turned around to make the Abhidhamma/Abhidharma point somewhat clearer, I think. It is, in a sense, precisely because mental factors have become balanced and even that *citta* is skilful; when that balance is lost and mental factors become restless *citta* necessarily becomes unskilful. So *upekkhā* or *tatra-majjhattatā* is both the balance of the skilful mind and the force which maintains that balance. All this seems to be quite precisely conveyed in the following commentarial description of *upekkhā* as a *bojjhaṅga*:

> 'He is one who oversees': he is one who oversees by means of overseeing conascent [*dhammas*]. The awakening-factor of equipoise is the property of balance termed the not-drawing-back-and-not-over-running of the [other] six awakening-factors. For it is like the case of horses that are running evenly; then there is neither any urging on on the charioteer's part, thinking, 'this one is lagging behind', nor any restraining, thinking, 'this one is running ahead'; there is just the property of stability of one who sees thus. Just so the property of balance termed not-drawing-back-and-not-over-running of these six awakening-factors is called the awakening-factor of equipoise.[78]

5. The definitions of the Paṭisambhidāmagga and the commentaries

As with the *indriyas* and *balas*, the *Paṭisambhidāmagga* assigns a particular 'meaning' or 'effect' (*aṭṭha*) to each of the *bojjhaṅgas*. The meaning of *sati-sambojjhaṅga* is to be directly known as 'standing near' (*sati-sambojjhaṅgassa upaṭṭhānaṭṭho abhiññeyyo*); the meaning of *dhamma-vicaya-sambojjhaṅga* as 'discrimination' (*pavicaya*); that of *viriya-sambojjhaṅga* as 'taking on' (*paggaha*); that of *pīti-sambojjhaṅga* as 'suffusing' (*pharaṇa*); that of *passaddhi-sambojjhaṅga* as 'stilling' (*upasama*); that of *samādhi-sambojjhaṅga* as 'non-distraction' (*avikkhepa*); that of *upekkhā-sambojjhaṅga* as 'judgement' (*paṭisaṃkhāna*).[79]

These *aṭṭhas* are apparently taken up by the commentaries when defining the individual characteristic (*lakkhaṇa*) of each of the *bojjhaṅgas*, along with its particular property (*rasa*) and manifestation (*paccupaṭṭhāna*).[80] In every case the *lakkhaṇa* given corresponds to the *aṭṭha* of the *Paṭisambhidāmagga*, though in the case of *sati*, *pīti*, *samādhi* and *upekkhā* an alternative *lakkhaṇa* is given as well. The various terms employed here are for the most part also found in the context of the general commentarial definitions of the relevant *dhammas*. But

---

[78] Ps IV 143: *ajjhupekkhitā hotī ti sahajāta-ajjhupekkhanāya ajjhupekkhitā hoti ... imesaṃ channaṃ bojjhaṅgānaṃ anosakkana-anativattana-saṃkhāto majjhattâkāro upekkhā-sambojjhaṅgo. yath'eva hi sama-ppavattesu assesu sārathino ayaṃ oliyatī ti tudanaṃ vā ayaṃ atidhavatī ti ākaḍḍhanaṃ vā natthi, kevalaṃ evaṃ passamānassa ṭhitâkāro vā hoti. evaṃ eva imesaṃ channaṃ bojjhaṅgānaṃ anosakkana-anativattana-saṃkhāto majjhattâkāro upekkhā-sambojjhaṅgo nāma hoti.* (Cf. As 133; Vism XIV 153; Abhidh-av 21.)

[79] Paṭis I 16; for further details see below, Chapter 10.2.

[80] Ps I 82-4; Mp II 52-4. See Table 3, p. 161.

TABLE 3. BOJJHAṄGAS: CHARACTERISTIC, PROPERTY AND MANIFESTATION ACCORDING TO THE COMMENTARIES

sambojjhaṅga	lakkhaṇa	rasa	paccupaṭṭhāna
sati	standing near (*upaṭṭhāna*) calling up (*apilāpana*)	not-forgetting (*asammosa*)	being faced with an objective field (*gocarâbhimukha-bhāva*)
dhamma-vicaya	discrimination (*pavicaya*)	illumination (*obhāsa*)	non-delusion (*asammoha*)
viriya	taking on (*paggaha*)	supporting (*upatthambana*)	non -collapse (*anosīdana*)
pīti	suffusing (*pharaṇa*) contentment (*tuṭṭhi*)	delighting body and mind (*kāya-citta-pīnanā*)	elation (*odagga*)
passaddhi	stilling (*upasama*)	overcoming the distress of body and mind (*kāya-citta-daratha-maddana*)	absence of trembling and the state of coolness (*apariphanda - bhūta-sīti-bhāva*)
samādhi	non-distraction (*avikkhepa*) non-diffusion (*avisāra*)	collecting together (*sampiṇḍana*)	stability of mind (*citta-ṭṭhiti*)
upekkhā	judgement (*paṭisaṃkhāna*) causing to proceed evenly (*sama-vāhitar*)	preventing deficiency or excess (*ūnâdhika - nīvāraṇa*) cutting through partiality (*pakkha-pātupacchedana*)	state of balance (*majjhatta-bhāva*)

one should note that these general definitions are not fixed and exhibit a certain amount of fluidity; this is especially clear in the *Atthasālinī's* account.[81] When we compare the *bojjhaṅga* definitions with the general definitions, a number of further variations are apparent. Thus the *Atthasālinī* gives delighting (*sampīyayana*) as the *lakkhaṇa* of *pīti* and suffusing (*pharaṇa*) as an alternative *rasa*;[82] following the tradition of the *Milindapañha* illumination (*obhāsana*) is considered the *lakkhaṇa* of *paññā*.[83]

Perhaps one of the most interesting features of the *Paṭisambhidāmagga's* and commentarial definition of the *bojjhaṅgas* is the association of the term *paṭisaṃkhāna* with *upekkhā-sambojjhaṅga*. This appears to be peculiar to *upekkhā* as a *bojjhaṅga*; *paṭisaṃkhāna* does not appear to feature in general descriptions of *upekkhā* or *tatra-majjattatā*. The Nikāyas occasionally speak of a *paṭisaṃkhāna-bala*[84] which appears to be understood in terms appropriate to insight or wisdom, and this is how the term is understood in the *Dhammasaṅgaṇi*.[85] What precisely is intended by *paṭisaṃkhāna* in the context of *upekkha-sambojjhaṅga* is unclear; 'reviewing' or 'balanced judgement' might be appropriate.

6. *The bojjhaṅgas and the viveka-nissita formula*

In chapter three I drew attention to the association of the *ṛddhi-pādas/iddhi-pādas* with the *viveka-niśrita/viveka-nissita* formula. Such an association is not apparently found in the Nikāyas, but is confined to Buddhist Sanskrit sources and the *Nettippakaraṇa*. The Nikāyas do, however, regularly apply the *viveka-nissita* formula to the *bojjhaṅgas*:

> Here a *bhikkhu* develops the awakening-factor of mindfulness, dependent on seclusion, dependent on dispassion, dependent on cessation, ripening in release. He develops the awakening-factor of *dhamma*-discrimination ... the awakening-factor of strength ... the awakening-factor of joy ... the awakening-factor of tranquillity ... the awakening-factor of concentration ... the awakening-factor of equipoise, dependent on seclusion, dependent on dispassion, dependent on cessation, ripening in release.[86]

But the usage of the *viveka-nissita* formula is not restricted to the *bojjhaṅgas* in the Nikāyas; in the *mahā-vagga* of the *Saṃyutta-nikāya*, for example, the formula is systematically applied to the factors of the *ariyo aṭṭhaṅgiko maggo*,

---

[81] See As 106-136 (*dhammuddesavāra-kathā*); cf. Vism XIV 134-55.

[82] As 115.

[83] As 122; though *visayobhāsana* is also subsequently given as a *rasa*.

[84] D III 213; A I 52-3, 94; II 142.

[85] Dhs 1354; *paṭisaṃkhāna-bala* is usually paired with *bhāvanā-bala* (see also Nett 15-6; Paṭis II 69-70) which is itself suggestive of *dassana*; at Nett 38 we have three *balas*: *paṭisaṃkhāna*, *dassana*, *bhāvanā*; this suggests that perhaps *paṭisaṃkhāna* characterizes insight prior to the *ariya-magga*.

[86] E.g. D III 226: *idha bhikkhu sati-sambojjhaṅgaṃ bhāveti viveka-nissitaṃ virāga-nissitaṃ nirodha-nissitaṃ vosagga-pariṇāmiṃ dhamma-vicaya-sambojjhaṅgaṃ ... viriya-sambojjhaṅgaṃ ... pīti-sambojjhaṅgaṃ ... passaddhi-sambojjhaṅgaṃ ... samādhi-sambojjhaṅgaṃ ... upekkhā-sambojjhaṅgaṃ bhāveti viveka-nissitaṃ virāga-nissitaṃ nirodha-nissitaṃ vosagga-pariṇāmiṃ*. Buddhist Sanskrit sources give an exactly parallel formula, e.g. Artha 34; for further references see Lamotte, *Traité*, III 1128.

the *bojjhaṅgas*, *indriyas* and *balas*.[87] However, since this constitutes a special treatment of the seven sets collectively, it is worth considering the application of the *viveka-vissita* formula elsewhere in the four primary Nikāyas in order to determine if there is any pattern to be discerned.

I calculate that the *bojjhaṅgas* are itemized on thirty occasions in the four Nikāyas:[88] on eight occasions we have just the bare list;[89] on fourteen occasions we have each item together with the *viveka-nissita* formula;[90] on two occasions the *bojjhaṅgas* are itemized in connection with the fourth *satipaṭṭhāna*;[91] on five occasions each *bojjhaṅga* is considered as descriptive of a stage in a process;[92] finally there is one *Aṅguttara* treatment that falls outside these categories.[93]

The *viveka-nissita* formula is employed on eighteen occasions in all;[94] as indicated, fourteen of these involve its application to the *bojjhaṅgas*, two to the factors of the path,[95] one to the *indriyas* and one to the *balas*.[96] The context in which the *viveka-nissita* formula is applied to the *indriyas* and *balas* also involves its application to the *bojjhaṅgas* and path-factors, and is, in fact, a collective treatment of the seven sets. So apart from the context of the seven sets, the *viveka-nissita* formula is restricted to the *bojjhaṅgas* and factors of the path.

I calculate that the factors of the *ariyo aṭṭhaṅgiko maggo* are itemized on sixty-four occasions in the four Nikāyas.[97] On thirty-eight occasions the *ariyo aṭṭhaṅgiko maggo* is cited and then itemized in a bare list;[98] on four occasions the eight factors are listed without explicit reference to the *ariyo aṭṭhaṅgiko maggo*;[99] four occasions involve the contrast of the eight factors as 'right'

---

87 I refer to the sections that are common to all seven sets and the *jhānas* (cf. Chapter 7.5); the *viveka-nissita* formula is applied in these only to the items named, however; see S V 29-31, 32-4, 35-6, 38-42, 45-62, 134-40, 239-43, 249-53.

88 In this connection I find it useful to make a distinction between the number of 'occasions' on which a given list is itemized and the number of 'times'; 'occasions' takes no account of the repeated itemizing of a list within a given *sutta* or according to an extended *Saṃyutta* or *Aṅguttara* treatment; 'times' takes into account all these repetitions, even when lost in the abbreviations of the text. E.g. at S IV 367-73 a text without any abbreviations would list the *bojjhaṅgas* thirty-two times, but this can be viewed as only one occasion. Thus the *bojjhaṅgas* are itemized on thirty 'occasions' but 235 'times'. In the *Saṃyutta-* and *Aṅguttara-nikāyas* the line between 'occasions' and 'times' can be rather arbitrary.

89 D II 79 (the Mūlasarvāstivādin parallel adds the *viveka-niśrita* formula, see Waldschmidt, *MPS* 128); III 106, 251, 282; A II 237; IV 23, 148 (× 160); V 211; taking into account all repetitions this comes to 167 'times'.

90 D III 226; M I 11; II 12; III 87-8, 275; S IV 367-73 (× 32); S V 312-3, 333, 334, 335, 340; A I 53; III 390; this comes to 45 'times'.

91 D II 303-4; M I 61-2 (2 'times').

92 M III 85-7 (× 4); S V 331-3 (× 4); 334 (× 4); 335 (× 4); 337-9 (× 4) (20 'times').

93 A I 39-40; see below, p. 269.

94 142 'times'.

95 S I 88; IV 367-8 (× 32) (33 'times').

96 S IV 365-8 (× 32) (32 'times' for both *indriyas* and *balas*).

97 372 'times'; this includes one *Vinaya* context.

98 Vin I 10 (× 2); D I 157, 165; II 251, 311; III 286; M I 15-6, 48- 55 (× 15), 118, 299-307 (× 2); II 12, 82; III 231, 251, 289; S II 42-3 (× 12), 106; III 59 (× 5), 158-9 (× 3); IV 133, 175, 195, 220, 222, 233-4 (× 3), 252-62 (× 15), 330-1; V 347, 421-2 (× 2), 425, 426; A I 177, 180, 217; III 411-6 (× 6) (89 'times').

99 A I 39-40; II 89; IV 190, 348.

TABLE 4. SUMMARY OF THE USE OF THE VIVEKA-NISSITA FORMULA IN THE FOUR NIKĀYAS (EXCLUDING MAGGA-, BOJJHAṄGA-, INDRIYA- AND BALA-SAṂYUTTAS)

BOJJHAṄGAS ITEMIZED:	TIMES	OCCASIONS
As bare list	167	8
With *viveka-nissita* formula	45	14
As process	20	5
As aspect of *satipaṭṭhāna*	2	2
Others	1	1
Total	235	30

VIVEKA-NISSITA FORMULA APPLIED:		
To *bojjhaṅgas*	45	14
To path-factors	33	2
To *indriyas*	32	1
To *balas*	32	1
Total	142	18

PATH-FACTORS ITEMIZED:		
ariyo aṭṭhaṅgiko maggo seyyathīdaṃ	89	38
8 factors/factored	4	4
8 factors/factored *micchā/sammā*	5	4
10 factors/factored	176	4
10 factors/factored *micchā/sammā*	62	9
With *viveka-nissita* formula	33	2
ariyo sammā-samādhi sa-upaniso	3	3
Total	372	64

(*sammā*) and 'wrong' (*micchā*);[100] four occasions involve a bare list of ten factors;[101] nine occasions involve the contrast of the ten factors as 'right' and 'wrong';[102] only two occasions involve the *viveka-nissita* formula;[103] finally three occasions involve right-concentration along with its supporting conditions (*ariyo sammā-samādhi sa-upaniso iti pi sa-parikkhāro*).[104] The frequency of occurrence of these various usages confirms that, apart from the context of the seven sets, the application of the *viveka-nissita* formula to the factors of the path is rather restricted.[105]

Outside the four primary Nikāyas, we find that the *Paṭisambhidāmagga* includes a treatment that once more applies the formula to the *indriyas*, *balas*, *bojjhaṅgas* and factors of the path.[106] In the *Vibhaṅga* the formula is restricted to the *bojjhaṅgas* and factors of the path.[107] Thus for the Pāli sources, Lamotte singles out the *viveka-nissita* formula with reference to those two sets of items.[108] However, the conclusion of the foregoing survey of the usage of the *viveka-nissita* formula must be, I think, that in the Nikāyas the formula is in the first place to be associated with the *bojjhaṅgas* alone; it should be seen as being applied to other sets of items by a process of attraction, that is to say, by virtue of their association or affinity with the seven *bojjhaṅgas*.

What of the four terms employed in the formula, namely *viveka*, *virāga*, *nirodha* and *vossagga*? The concept of *viveka* or 'seclusion' is probably most frequently met with in connection with the stock description of the first *jhāna*:

> Secluded from the objects of sensual desire, secluded from unskilful *dhammas*, he attains and dwells in the first *jhāna*, which is accompanied by initial and sustained thinking, born of seclusion, and possesses joy and happiness.[109]

T.W. Rhys Davids sums up the basic import of *viveka* clearly: 'the stress is upon separation from the world, taking "world" in the sense of all hindrances to spiritual progress, and especially the five chief Hindrances (Nīvaraṇa)'.[110]

Taking *vossagga* or 'release/letting go' next, it appears that this term is less

---

100 S II 168-9; III 109; A 220-1 (× 2); IV 237-8 (5 'times').

101 M I 446; A II 89 (× 2); V 221-2 (× 2), 310 (× 160) (176 'times').

102 M I 42-5 (× 4); III 76-8; S II 168-9; A II 222 (× 2), 223 (× 2), 224-5 (× 2); V 211-21 (× 8); 222-36 (× 8); 240-9 (× 34) (62 'times').

103 S I 88; IV 367-8 (× 32) (33 'times').

104 D II 216-7; M III 71; A IV 40.

105 If we exclude the sections common to all seven sets in the *mahā-vagga* and just consider the usage of the *viveka-nissita* formula in the distinctive portions of the *magga-* and *bojjhaṅga-saṃyuttas*, it still appears that it is applied to the *bojjhaṅgas* with rather greater frequency than to the path-factors; for the path-factors, see S V 2-3, 29-38; for the *bojjhaṅgas*, S V 63-4, 72, 75, 76, 78- 9, 86-8, 91, 101-2, 119-120, 128-34. Of course, S V 29-38 constitutes an exhaustive usage of the formula in connection with the path factors, though it is not entirely clear that the text of the *bojjhaṅga-saṃyutta* has not been excessively abbreviated at S V 129-34; furthermore, the way the *viveka-nissita* formula is used continually throughout the *bojjhaṅga-saṃyutta* matched in the *magga-saṃyutta*.

106 Paṭis II 219-23; the *viveka-kathā*.

107 Vibh 229, 236.

108 Lamotte, *Traité*, III 1128, 1130.

109 E.g. D I 73: *so vivicc'eva kāmehi vivicca akusalehi dhammehi savitakkaṃ savicāraṃ vivekajaṃ pīti-sukhaṃ paṭhama-jjhānaṃ upasampajja viharati.*

110 D Trsl I 84.

widely used in the Nikāyas than the other three. As a result it is rather lacking in particular association. However, its basic import of 'release' or 'letting go' as a term for the final goal of *nibbāna* or liberation seems clear.[111] The term is suggestive of an active letting go or releasing (of defilements or fetters) rather than the state of having let go or being released (*vimutti*, *vimokkha*).

Dispassion (*virāga*) and cessation (*nirodha*) are together often directly associated with a number of terms that all seem to connote, more or less, the goal or culmination of the Buddhist path. Thus fairly frequently in the Nikāyas something is described as conducing (*saṃvattati*) to disenchantment (*nibbidā*), dispassion (*virāga*), cessation (*nirodha*), peace (*upasama*), direct knowledge (*abhiññā*), full awakening (*sambodha*), *nibbāna*.[112] The fact that elsewhere the pair *nibbidā* and *virāga* occur as part of a sequence of terms that is descriptive of a process,[113] suggests that the sequence *viveka*, *virāga*, *nirodha*, *vossagga* might also be understood as progressive. In other words, the *bojjhaṅgas*, and so on, are to be developed successively as dependent on seclusion, dispassion and cessation, until they finally ripen in release. The tradition itself does not seem to understand the formula in quite these terms. What it does do, however, is suggest a number of different levels for the interpretation of each of the four terms in question. The effect is not entirely different from the interpretation I have suggested.

The earliest exegesis of the *viveka-nissita* formula we have is probably that given in the *viveka-kathā* of the *Paṭisambhidāmagga*.[114] According to this there are five kinds of *viveka*, five kinds of *virāga*, five kinds of *nirodha* and five kinds of *vossagga*:

> For one developing the first *jhāna* there is seclusion from the hindrances by suppression; for one developing concentration that partakes of penetrative wisdom there is seclusion from wrong views by substitution of opposites; for one developing the transcendent path that leads to destruction [of the *āsavas*] there is seclusion by cutting off; at the moment of fruition there is seclusion by tranquillization; cessation, *nibbāna* is seclusion by relinquishing ... With regard to these five seclusions one has purpose, one's confidence is resolved, one's mind is well set.[115]

The five kinds of *virāga*, *nirodha* and *vossagga* are defined in precisely parallel terms.[116] The full development of the *bojjhaṅgas*, factors of the path, *indriyas* and *balas* dependent on seclusion, dispassion and cessation, and ripening in release, according to the *Paṭisambhidāmagga*, involves their mastery in all these different respects.

---

[111] *BHSD*, s.v. *vyavasarga*; as Edgerton suggests, *PED* (s.vv. *vossagga* and *vavassagga*) gives unwarranted emphasis to the meaning 'handing over, donation'.

[112] E.g. M I 431; sometimes *nibbidā* is replaced by *ekanta-nibbidā*, complete or final disenchantment, see S V 82, 179, 255.

[113] See above, p. 154

[114] Paṭis II 219-24.

[115] *vikkhambhana-viveko ca nīvaraṇānaṃ paṭhama-jjhānaṃ bhāvayato, tad-aṅga-viveko ca diṭṭhi-gatānaṃ nibbedha-bhāgiyaṃ samādhiṃ bhāvayato, samuccheda-viveko ca lokuttaraṃ khaya-gāmi-maggaṃ bhāvayato, paṭippassaddhi-viveko ca phala-kkhaṇe, nissaraṇa-viveko ca nirodho nibbānaṃ ... imesu pañcasu vivekesu chanda-jāto hoti saddhâdhimutto cittaṃ cassa svadhiṭṭhitaṃ.*

[116] They correspond in part to the three kinds of *pahāna* (*tad-aṅga*, *vikkhambhana*, *samuccheda*) discussed above, p. 49.

In principle the commentaries follow the *Paṭisambhidāmagga* in explaining the *viveka-nissita* formula, but it is worth noting that they appear to save their treatment of the formula for a *bojjhaṅga* context. Thus the *Vibhaṅga* commentary again explains that there are five kinds of *viveka*: *tad-aṅga-viveka* is a name for insight (*vipassanā*); *vikkhambhana-viveka* is a name for the eight attainments (i.e. the four *jhānas* and four formless attainments); *samuccheda-viveka* is a name for the [transcendent] path; *paṭippassaddhi-viveka* is a name for fruition; *nissaraṇa-viveka* is a name for *nibbāna*, which has relinquished all signs (*sabba-nimitta-nissaṭiṃ nibbānaṃ*).[117] But having distinguished these five *vivekas*, the commentaries then suggest that three in particular could be seen as especially relevant to the development of the *bojjhaṅgas*:

> For thus the yogin who is engaged in the development of *sati-sambojjhaṅga*, at the moment of insight develops *sati-sambojjhaṅga* dependent on *tad-aṅga-viveka* as to function, and dependent on *nissaraṇa-viveka* as to aspiration; but at the time of the path [he develops it] dependent on *samuccheda-viveka* as to function, and dependent on *nissaraṇa-viveka* as to object.[118]

This, then, sees the development of the *bojjhaṅgas* as confined to moments of ordinary insight meditation, and the time of attaining the transcendent path. However, the commentaries go on to refer to a view of some (who are not contradicted) that all five kinds of *viveka* are relevant to the *bojjhaṅgas*; in other words, the *bojjhaṅgas* are also developed directly in ordinary *jhāna* by 'supression'.[119] I shall return to the significance of this below.

According to the commentaries *virāga-* and *nirodha-nissita* are to be understood according to the same method as *viveka-nissita*.[120] The term *vossagga* is, however, taken rather differently. As 'giving up' (*pariccāga*) and 'leaping forward' (*pakkhandana*) it is twofold:

> Therein *pariccāga-vossagga* is the abandoning of defilements both at the moment of insight by virtue of substitution of opposites, and at the path moment by virtue of cutting off; *pakkhandana-vossagga* is the leaping forward to *nibbāna* at the moment of insight by inclination towards it, and at the path moment by making it the object.[121]

So *vossagga* is seen both as a releasing of the defilements and as a releasing into *nibbāna*.

To sum up, while the *viveka-nissita* formula is applied to other items in the Nikāyas, it seems clear that it is to be considered as primarily characteristic of the treatment of the *bojjhaṅgas*. Generally speaking the *viveka-nissita* formula

---

117 Vibh-a 316; cf. Ps I 85; Spk III 139.

118 Ibid.: *tathā hi ayaṃ sati-sambojjhaṅga-bhāvanânuyogaṃ anuyutto yogī vipassana-kkhaṇe kiccato tad-aṅga-viveka-nissitaṃ, ajjhāsayato nissaraṇa-viveka-nissitaṃ, magga-kāle pana kiccato samuccheda-viveka-nissitaṃ, ārammaṇato nissaraṇa-viveka-nissitaṃ sati-sambojjhaṅgaṃ bhāveti.*

119 This view is confined to the explanation of the *viveka-nissita* formula in the context of the *bojjhaṅgas*; in the context of the *ariyo aṭṭhaṅgiko maggo* it is omitted and not adapted to fit the *maggaṅgas* (Spk to S I 88).

120 Ibid.: *esa nayo virāga-nissitâdīsu.*

121 Ibid.: *tattha pariccāga-vossaggo ti vipassana-kkhaṇe ca tad-aṅga-vasena magga-kkhaṇe ca samuccheda-vasena kilese-ppahānaṃ. pakkhandana-vossaggo ti vipassana-kkhaṇe tan-ninna-bhāvena, magga-kkhaṇe pana ārammaṇa-kāraṇena nibbāna-pakkhandanaṃ.* (Cf. Sv III 1019.)

appears to focus on the active development of the factors in meditation, especially that kind of meditation that immediately inclines towards *bodhi* itself. In conclusion, it is worth noting Asaṅga's rather neat correlation of the four parts of the *viveka-niśrita* formula to the four truths: *viveka-niśrita* corresponds to the first truth (*duḥkha*), *virāga-niśrita* to the second truth (*samudaya*), *nirodha-niśrita* to the third truth (*nirodha*), *vyavasarga-pariṇāta* to the fourth truth (*mārga*).[122]

7. *The bojjhaṅga process formula*

In the previous section I pointed out that one of the ways in which the list of *bojjhaṅgas* is itemized in the Nikāyas is in terms of what I call the *bojjhaṅga* process formula:

> When, *bhikkhus*, mindfulness is established for a *bhikkhu*, not lost, at that time the awakening-factor of mindfulness is instigated for him, at that time he develops the awakening-factor of mindfulness, at that time the awakening-factor of mindfulness comes to full development for a *bhikkhu*. Dwelling mindful in this way, he discriminates, inspects and applies investigation to that *dhamma* by means of wisdom.
>
> When a *bhikkhu* who dwells mindful in this way discriminates, inspects and applies investigation to that *dhamma* by means of wisdom, at that time the awakening-factor of *dhamma*-discrimination is instigated for him, at that time he develops the awakening-factor of *dhamma*-discrimination, at that time the awakening-factor of *dhamma*-discrimination comes to full development for a *bhikkhu*. Discriminating, inspecting and applying investigation to that *dhamma* by means of wisdom, strength without slackness is instigated.
>
> When for a *bhikkhu*, as he discriminates, inspects and applies investigation to that *dhamma* by means of wisdom, strength without slackness is instigated, at that time the awakening-factor of strength is instigated for him, at that time he develops the awakening-factor of strength, at that time the awakening-factor of strength comes to full development for a *bhikkhu*. For one who has instigated strength non-carnal joy arises.
>
> When there arises for a *bhikkhu* who has instigated strength a non-carnal joy, at that time the awakening-factor of joy is instigated for him, at that time he develops the awakening-factor of joy, at that time the awakening-factor of joy comes to full development for that *bhikkhu*. The body and mind of one who is joyful becomes tranquil.
>
> When both the body and mind of a *bhikkhu* whose mind is joyful become tranquil, at that time the awakening-factor of tranquillity is instigated for him, at that time he develops the awakening-factor of tranquillity, at that time the awakening-factor of tranquillity comes to full development for that *bhikkhu*. The mind of one who is tranquil in body and happy becomes concentrated.
>
> When the mind of a *bhikkhu* who is tranquil in body and happy becomes concentrated, at that time the awakening-factor of concentration is instigated for him, at that time he develops the awakening-factor of concentration, at that time the awakening factor of concentration comes to full development for that *bhikkhu*. He is one who properly oversees his mind thus concentrated.
>
> When a *bhikkhu* is one who properly oversees his mind thus concentrated, at that time the awakening-factor of equipoise is instigated for him, at that time he

[122] Abhidh-sam Trsl 122-3; in dealing with the seven sets Asaṅga here relates the *viveka-niśrita* formula to the seven *bodhy-aṅgas* alone.

develops the awakening-factor of equipoise, at that time the awakening-factor of equipoise comes to full development for that *bhikkhu*.[123]

In the four primary Nikāyas this formula is usually found in the context of discussion of mindfulness of breathing in and out (*ānâpāna-sati*),[124] and is made rather a lot of. As I have already pointed out, the detailed account of *ānâpāna-sati* in the Nikāyas is given as illustrative of how, when developed and made great it fulfils the four establishings of mindfulness; when these are developed and made great, they fulfil the seven awakening-factors; when these are developed and made great they fulfil knowledge and liberation (*vijjā-vimutti*). In this context the *bojjhaṅga* process formula is given in full four times in succession, illustrating how all seven *bojjhaṅgas* come to fulfilment by way of mindfulness established by watching body, feelings, mind and *dhammas*. That the process formula should be regarded as a significant and characteristic treatment of the *bojjhaṅgas* is surely confirmed by the way the *Vibhaṅga* singles it out at the opening of the *suttanta-bhājaniya* for the *bojjhaṅgas*.[125]

The process formula quite plainly views the *bojjhaṅgas* as arising successively, one leading on to the next. Earlier, in discussing *pīti* and *passaddhi*, I drew attention to a recurring sequence of terms in the Nikāyas: *pāmujja*, *pīti*, *passaddhi*, *sukha*, *samādhi*. Among various examples, I referred to the way in

---

[123] For references see previous section: *yasmiṃ samaye bhikkhave bhikkhuno upaṭṭhitā sati hoti asammuṭṭhā, sati-sambojjhaṅgo tasmiṃ samaye bhikkhuno āraddho hoti, sati-sambojjhaṅgaṃ tasmiṃ samaye bhikkhu bhāveti, sati-sambojjhaṅgo tasmiṃ samaye bhikkhuno bhāvanā-pāripūriṃ gacchati. so tathā sato viharanto taṃ dhammaṃ paññāya pavicinati pavicarati parivīmaṃsaṃ āpajjati. yasmiṃ samaye bhikkhu tathā sato viharanto taṃ dhammaṃ paññāya pavicinati pavicarati parivīmaṃsaṃ āpajjati, dhamma-vicaya-sambojjhaṅgo tasmiṃ samaye bhikkhuno āraddho hoti ... tassa taṃ dhammaṃ paññāya pavicinato pavicarato parivīmaṃsaṃ āpajjato āraddhaṃ hoti viriyaṃ asallīnaṃ. yasmiṃ samaye bhikkhuno taṃ dhammaṃ paññāya pavicinato pavicarato parivīmaṃsaṃ āpajjato āraddhaṃ hoti viriyaṃ asallīnaṃ, viriya-sambojjhaṅgo tasmiṃ samaye bhikkhuno āraddho hoti ... āraddha-viriyassa uppajjati pīti nirāmisā. yasmiṃ samaye bhikkhuno āraddha-viriyassa uppajjati pīti nirāmisā, pīti-sambojjhaṅgo tasmiṃ samaye bhikkhuno āraddho hoti ... pīti-manassa kāyo pi passambhati cittaṃ pi passambhati. yasmiṃ samaye bhikkhuno pīti-manassa kāyo pi passambhati cittaṃ pi passambhati, passaddhi-sambojjhaṅgo tasmiṃ samaye bhikkhuno āraddho hoti ... passaddha-kāyassa sukhino cittaṃ samādhiyati. yasmiṃ samaye bhikkhuno passaddha-kāyassa sukhino cittaṃ samādhiyati, samādhi-sambojjhaṅgo tasmiṃ samaye bhikkhuno āraddho hoti ... so tathā samāhitaṃ cittaṃ sādhukaṃ ajjhupekkhitā hoti. yasmiṃ samaye bhikkhu tathā samāhitaṃ cittaṃ sādhukaṃ ajjhupekkhitā hoti, upekkhā-sambojjhaṅgo tasmiṃ samaye bhikkhuno āraddho hoti, upekkhā-sambojjhaṅgaṃ tasmiṃ samaye bhikkhu bhāveti, upekkhā-sambojjhaṅgo tasmiṃ samaye bhikkhuno bhāvanā-pāripūriṃ gacchati.* (Lamotte's quotation and translation at *Traité*, III 1128-9 contain abbreviations that are not indicated.)

[124] The one exception is S V 67-9.

[125] Vibh 227; this is a rather barer version than the one given in the Nikāyas, but still in principle the same formula. The *bodhy-aṅga* process formula apparently does not survive in Sanskrit sources (Lamotte cites no parallel to the Pāli version at *Traité*, III 1128). But as José Van Den Broeck points out, the description of the *bodhy-aṅgas* in the *Amṛtarasa* of Ghoṣaka seems to reflect this process formula: '(Le *yogin*) commémore les *dharma* conditionnés: ils naissent et prennent fin; de multiples façons, ils sont un mal. Le *nirvāṇa* est suprême. Tel est le membre "attention". Ici, il discerne et médite—c'est le membre "discernement des *dharma*". Ici, il médite et applique l'énergie—c'est le membre "énergie". Ici, en acquérant la saveur des bons *dharma*, il se réjouit—c'est le membre "joie". Ici, quand il médite, le corps et la pensée sont légers, dociles et en sécurité et ils s'adaptent à la concentration—c'est le membre "relaxation". Ici, la pensée fixée sur l'objet reste sur place et ne se disperse pas—c'est le membre "concentration". Ici, il laise aller sa pensée à sa guise, il se repose, n'excerce plus l'attention et ne pratique pas non plus le zèle—c'est le membre "equanimité".' (Amṛta Trsl 206-7; cf. Satya Trsl 44.)

which the four *jhānas* are introduced in the *sīlakkhandha-vagga* of the *Dīgha-nikāya*. At this point it is worth considering this account more fully.[126]

It begins by describing how the *bhikkhu* retires to a secluded (*vivitta*) place, sits down crosslegged and sets up mindfulness in front of him (*parimukhaṃ satiṃ upaṭṭhapetvā*). There follows an extended description of the abandoning of each of the five hindrances (*nīvaraṇa*), each illustrated by its own simile. The arising of the first *jhāna* is then introduced:

> For one who sees (*samanupassato*) these five hindrances abandoned in himself, gladness is born; for one who is gladdened, joy is born; the body of one whose mind is joyful becomes tranquil; one whose body is tranquil feels happiness; the mind of one who is happy becomes concentrated. Secluded from the objects of sensual desire, secluded from unskilful *dhammas* he attains and dwells in the first *jhāna*, accompanied by initial and sustained thinking, and joy and happiness born of seclusion.

The second *jhāna* is without initial and sustained thought but is still accompanied by joy and happiness, now said to be born of concentration (*samādhija*). In the third *jhāna* the *bhikkhu* is said to possess equipoise (*upekkhaka*), and is mindful and clearly comprehending. Finally the fourth *jhāna* is characterized as 'purity of mindfulness [brought about] by means of equipoise' (*upekkhā-sati-pārisuddhi*).

The wording of the introduction to the *jhāna* formula here parallels, in some places exactly, the wording of the *bojjhaṅga* process formula. Clearly this is no accident. The parallels between the full *sāmañña-phala* account of the practice of *jhāna* and the list of *bojjhaṅgas* can be set out in full as follows:

sati-sambojjhaṅga	*parimukhaṃ* ***satiṃ*** *upaṭṭhapetvā …*
dhamma-vicaya-sambojjhaṅga	*bhikkhu ime pañca nīvaraṇe pahīne attani* ***samanupassati****; tass'ime pañca nīvaraṇe pahīne attani* ***samanupassato***
(viriya-sambojjhaṅga)	
pīti-sambojjhaṅga	*pāmujjaṃ jayati; pamuditassa* ***pīti*** *jayati;* ***pīti****-manassa*
passaddhi-sambojjhaṅga	*kāyo* ***passambhati****; passaddha-kāyo sukhaṃ vedeti;*
samādhi-sambojjhaṅga	*sukhino cittaṃ* ***samādhiyati*** *… savitakkaṃ savicāraṃ vivekajaṃ pīti-sukhaṃ paṭhamaṃ jhānaṃ upasampajja viharati … avitakkaṃ avicāraṃ* ***samādhijaṃ*** *pīti-sukhaṃ dutiya-jjhānaṃ upasampajja viharati …*
upekkhā-sambojjhaṅga	*sukhañ ca kāyena paṭisaṃvedeti yan taṃ ariyā acikkhanti* ***upekkhako*** *satimā sukha-vihārī ti tatiya-jjhānaṃ upasampajja viharati …* ***upekkhā****-sati-pārisuddhiṃ catuttha-jjhānaṃ upasampajja viharati.*

[126] D I 71-6.

Only *viriya-sambojjhaṅga* fails to find a direct parallel here.[127] Of course, the stock phrase that here introduces the first *jhāna* does not always do so. Elsewhere the practice of *mettā, karuṇā, muditā* and *upekkhā* is introduced in a similar fashion.[128] In this context an immediate referent for *sati-sambojjhaṅga* is also lacking. On other occasions, however, the stock description of the four *jhānas* is introduced rather differently in a way that gives rather greater prominence to both *viriya* and *sati*:

> For me strength was instigated and not slack, *brāhmaṇa*; mindfulness was established and not lost; my body was tranquil and not agitated; my mind concentrated and one-pointed.[129]

While the parallels here are not so complete, the language still echoes that of the *bojjhaṅga* process formula.

As was seen in the course of the discussion of *pīti* and *passaddhi*, the process of the mind's becoming still and concentrated is seen in terms of the mind's overcoming of the immediate factors that trouble and disturb it; a mind free of these hindrances (*vinīvaraṇa-citta*) is content and settled, and provides the ground for the realization of the special teaching of Buddhas, namely the four noble truths. This is particularly clear in the stock progressive discourse (*anupubbī-kathā*),[130] but no less clear in the full *sāmañña-phala* schema. The mind that has accomplished the practice of the four *jhānas* is described here as purified (*parisuddha*), cleansed (*pariyodāta*), without blemish (*anaṅgana*), with the immediate defilements gone (*vigatupakkilesa*), soft (*mudu-bhūta*), ready (*kammaniya*), steady (*ṭhita*), having gained an unwavering state (*ānejja-ppatta*).[131] Such a mind is seen as suited to the gaining of various kinds of knowledge,[132] culminating once more in the knowledge of the destruction of the *āsavas* and knowledge of the four truths.[133]

Essentially it would seem that the list of seven *bojjhaṅgas* is a shorthand way

---

127 The parallel between *dhamma-vicaya* and *samanupassati* is less explicit than the rest, but in this kind of context surely any derivative of *passati* can be seen as connoting *paññā* (= *dhamma-vicaya*). Cf. Vibh 194-202 (passim) which identifies *anupassanā* in the context of the *satipaṭṭhāna* formula with *paññā*.

128 M I 283: *tassa sabbehi imehi pāpakehi akusalehi dhammehi visuddhaṃ attanaṃ samanupassato vimuttaṃ attanaṃ samanupassato pāmujjaṃ jayati ... sukhino cittaṃ samādhiyati. so mettā-sahagatena cetasā ekaṃ disaṃ pharitvā viharati ...* (Cf. M I 37-8 and other references given above, p. 154, n. 47.)

129 M I 21, 117: *āraddhaṃ kho pana me brāhmaṇa viriyaṃ ahosi asallīnaṃ, upaṭṭhitā sati asamuṭṭhā, passaddho kāyo asāraddho, samāhitaṃ cittaṃ ekaggaṃ*. (Cf. M I 242-7; Vin III 4; again this stock phrase does not only introduce the four *jhānas*, see M I 286, III 85-7; S IV 125; A I 148, 282; II 14.)

130 E.g. M I 379-80: 'When the Blessed One knew that Upāli the householder's mind was fit, ready, soft, free of hindrances, happy and settled, then he revealed the special *dhamma*-teaching of Buddhas : suffering, arising, cessation, path.' (*yadā bhagavā aññāsi Upāliṃ gahapatiṃ kalla-cittaṃ mudu-cittaṃ vinīvaraṇa-cittaṃ udagga-cittaṃ pasanna-cittaṃ atha yā buddhānaṃ sāmukkaṃsikā dhamma-desanā taṃ pakāsesi: dukkhaṃ samudayaṃ nirodhaṃ maggaṃ*.)

131 See D I 76-83 (passim).

132 The eight *vijjā* (Vism VII 20), the last six of which are often referred to as *abhiññā* (D III 281), and the last three as *vijjā* (M I 482).

133 D I 83-4. The term *ariya-sacca* does not occur, but *āsavānaṃ khaya-ñāṇaṃ* is described in terms of knowing (*pajānāti*) *dukkha, dukkha-samudaya, dukkha-nirodha*, and *dukkha-nirodha-gāminī paṭipadā*.

of looking at the same process: progressive development of the factors of mindfulness, *dhamma*-discrimination, strength, joy, tranquillity, concentration and equipoise is the immediate pre-requisite of awakening. What the process formula does is make explicit the way in which the sequence of seven *bojjhaṅgas* is tied more or less specifically to the immediate course the mind is understood to follow as it becomes still in concentration. In the context of the *bojjhaṅgas* this course culminates in a point of clarity and mental balance that provides the opportunity for what the texts see as a decisive spiritual breakthrough.

I referred in chapter one to a statement that occurs several times in the Nikāyas summarizing the Buddhist path as the abandoning of the five hindrances, establishing the mind in the four *satipaṭṭhānas*, development of the seven *bojjhaṅgas* and *nibbāna*.[134] As I pointed out, the full Nikāya treatment of mindfulness of breathing in and out looks remarkably like an expanded illustration of this summary (or the latter like a short statement of the former). Thus mindfulness of breathing in and out is taken (from among various possibilities) as the vehicle for abandoning the five hindrances and developing the four *satipaṭṭhānas*; the full development of the *satipaṭṭhānas* is marked by the *bojjhaṅga* process formula—the mind becomes still in that particular kind of concentration that leads directly to knowledge and liberation (*vijjā-vimutti*).[135]

All this is of some interest. It brings to life aspects of the earlier discussion of 'with regard for exposition' (*pariyāyena*) and 'not with regard for exposition' (*nippariyāyena*). It also shows how various different elements of Nikāya teaching are interwoven, and even inextricably tangled—at least from the perspective of the modern scholar trying to unravel and arrange the material from the point of view of its historical evolution.

When the Nikāyas tell us, then, that by way of a particular exposition (*pariyāyena*) the first *jhāna* is to be regarded as *nibbāna*, this is not to be dismissed as a mere trick of language. On the contrary, it points towards the fundamental orientation of the Nikāyas as regards spiritual development. For, as implied in the *bojjhaṅga* process formula, the process whereby the mind becomes still and happy in the first *jhāna*, temporarily escaping the disturbances that arise in connection with the objects of sensual desire, is directly analogous to the process whereby the mind is stilled by turning towards *nibbāna*, escaping once and for all from suffering. In the latter we do not have a radically different process, but rather the same process brought to its proper conclusion. For the Nikāyas there is an essential unity to progress along the spiritual path. The laws that govern such progress are the same at any point along the path, for the principles that underlie the workings of the mind are always the same, whether we are talking of ordinary *jhāna* or of knowledge of the destruction of the *āsavas*. That this should be so is seen simply as the nature of things; in short, it is *dhamma*.

---

[134] See above, pp. 58-9.

[135] Cf. S V 73-4, which summarizes the path as *indriya-saṃvara*, three *sucaritas*, four *satipaṭṭhānas*, seven *bojjhaṅgas*, *vijjā-vimutti*; A V 113-8 adds to the beginning of the same sequence *saddhamma-savana*, *saddha*, *yoniso manasikāra*.

8. *The bojjhaṅga-saṃyutta*

Having considered the two basic formulaic treatments of the *bojjhaṅgas* in the Nikāyas, the most convenient place to gain an impression of their general understanding in the Nikāyas is the *bojjhaṅga-saṃyutta*.[136] The single most outstanding feature of the *bojjhaṅga-saṃyutta* is the way in which the *bojjhaṅgas* are repeatedly contrasted with the five *nīvaraṇas* or 'hindrances'—around half the *saṃyutta* is devoted to this theme.[137] This contrast of the *bojjhaṅgas* with the *nīvaraṇas* is of considerable interest and includes a number of important treatments and passages not found elsewhere in the Nikāyas.

General features of the contrast

Frequently the five *nīvaraṇas* are collectively and individually termed defilements (*upakkilesa*) or, more fully, 'obstructions, hindrances, defilements of the mind that weaken wisdom' (*āvaraṇā-nīvaraṇā cetaso upakkilesā paññāya dubbalī-karaṇā*).[138] In contrast, the *bojjhaṅgas* are 'non-obstructions, non-hindrances, non-defilements of the mind' (*anāvaraṇā anīvaraṇā cetaso anupakkilesā*).[139] In other words, bringing out the force of the particular terminology a little more fully, the *nīvaraṇas* are what cover over, close up and obscure the mind; the *bojjhaṅgas*, on the other hand, uncover the mind and open it up. The general import of this contrast is brought out rather effectively by the image of great trees which grow over smaller trees causing them to rot and fall.[140] Similarly the *nīvaraṇas* grow over the mind weakening wisdom; but the *bojjhaṅgas* 'not growing over the mind, when developed and made great conduce to realization of the fruit of knowledge and freedom' (*cetaso anajjhārūhā bhāvitā bahulīkatā vijjā-vimutti-phala-sacchikiriyāya saṃvattanti*).

In another passage the *nīvaraṇas* are described as 'causing blindness, lack of sight and lack of knowledge, destroying wisdom, contributing to distress and not conducing to *nibbāna*' (*andha-karaṇā acakkhu-karaṇā aññāṇa-karaṇā paññā-nirodhikā vighata-pakkhiyā anibbāna-saṃvattanikā*). The *bojjhaṅgas*, however, cause sight and knowledge, increase wisdom, contribute to absence of distress and conduce to *nibbāna*' (*cakkhu-karaṇā ñāṇa-karaṇā paññā-vuddhiyo avighata-pakkhiyā nibbāna-saṃvattanikā*).[141] Again, it is said that the mind possessed (*pariyuṭṭhita*) and overcome (*pareta*) by any one of the five *nīvaraṇas* constitutes the cause (*hetu*) and condition (*paccaya*) for not knowing and not seeing,

---

136 S V 63-140.

137 S V 64-7, 76-7, 84-5, 92-8, 102-15, 121-8 (= 37 pp. of the 77 pp. of the *saṃyutta* in the PTS edition). In view of the abbreviated nature of much of the rest of the material that makes up the *saṃyutta* this may slightly exaggerate the proportion of space devoted to this contrast; yet it is still quite clearly the aspect of the treatment most distinctive to the *bojjhaṅgas* since much of the other material is common to or echoes themes common to all seven sets (see Chapter 7.5). The parallels given by Anesaki would seem to indicate that this same contrast is also important in the *bodhy-aṅga-saṃyukta* in the Chinese Āgamas; see Anesaki, op. cit., pp. 105-6.

138 S V 92-3, 94-7, 115.

139 S V 93, 95-7, 115.

140 S V 96-7.

141 S V 97-8.

whereas the mind that has developed the *bojjhaṅgas* constitutes the cause and condition for knowing and seeing.[142]

Two further similes should be mentioned here. These both illustrate the way in which the *nīvaraṇas* hinder the mind, and are both immediately followed by a simple statement that the *bojjhaṅgas* are what do not hinder or obstruct the mind. In the first of these similes,[143] the defilement of the mind by the five *nīvaraṇas* is likened to the defilement of unworked gold (*jāta-rūpa*) by various impurities; as a result of this the gold is not soft, not ready or workable, not bright, liable to break up, and not properly suitable for working (*upakkiliṭṭhaṃ jāta-rūpaṃ na ceva mudu hoti na ca kammaniyaṃ na ca pabhassaraṃ pabhaṅgu ca na ca sammā upeti kammāya*).[144] In the same way the *nīvaraṇas* result in the mind's not being soft, not being ready, not being bright, being liable to break up; thus it does not become properly concentrated for [the task of] destroying the *āsavas* (*na ca sammā samādhiyati āsavānaṃ khayāya*).

The other passage[145] concerns a *brāhmaṇa* who questions the Buddha about the cause and condition whereby verses that have been long learnt sometimes become unclear (*dīgha-rattaṃ sajjhāya-katā pi mantā na paṭibhanti*), and why verses that have not been long learnt sometimes become clear. The Buddha responds with an extended and detailed simile concerning the nature of each of the *nīvaraṇas*. The mind possessed and overcome by attraction for the objects of sensual desire (*kāma-rāga-pariyuṭṭhita, kāma-rāga-pareta*) is like a bowl of water mixed with lac or turmeric, or with blue or red colouring; a person with good eyesight looking down into this bowl of water for the reflection of his own face would not know and see it as it is.[146] The mind possessed and overcome by aversion (*vyāpāda*) is like a bowl of water that has been heated on a fire and is steaming and boiling (*uda-patto agginā santatto ukkaṭṭhito usmudaka-jāto*); the mind possessed and overcome by laziness and sleepiness (*thīna-middha*) is like a bowl of water covered with moss and leaves (*uaa-patto sevāla-paṇaka-pariyonaddho*); the mind possessed and overcome by excitement and depression (*uddhacca-kukkucca*) is like a bowl of water ruffled by the wind, disturbed, stirred round and rippling (*uda-patto vāterito calito bhanto ūmi-jāto*); finally the mind possessed and overcome by doubt (*vicikicchā*) is like a bowl of water that is dirty, unclear, muddy and placed in the dark (*uda-patto āvilo lulito kalalī-bhūto andha-kāre nikkhitto*). Again, anyone looking down into any of these for the reflection of his face would not know and see it as it is. In the same way, when the mind is possessed and overcome by any one

---

142 S V 126-8.

143 S V 92-3

144 F.L. Woodward misconstrues *na ca pabhassaraṃ pabhaṅgu ca* (S Trsl V 77-8: 'nor gleaming, nor easily broken up'); *na* governs only *pabhassaraṃ*. Of the mind that has the attribute of *pabhaṅgu*, the commentary states that 'its nature is to be broken up by undergoing the state of being broken into pieces with regard to the object' (Spk III 151: *ārammaṇe cuṇṇa-vicuṇṇa-bhāvupagamena bhijjana-sabhāvaṃ*).

145 S V 121-6.

146 *seyyathâpi brāhmaṇa uda-patto saṃsaṭṭho lākhāya vā haliddiyā vā nīliyā vā mañjeṭṭhāya vā. tattha cakkhumā puriso sakaṃ mukha-nimittaṃ paccavekkhamāno yathā-bhūtaṃ na jāneyya na passeyya.*

of the *nīvaraṇas* one does not know (and see) as it is its letting go, what is of benefit to oneself, what is benefit to others, what is of benefit to both; verses which have long been learnt become unclear, let alone those which have not been learnt.[147] A mind not possessed or overcome by the *nīvaraṇas*, however, is like a bowl of water unmixed with lac or turmeric, or blue or red colouring; like a bowl of water that has not been heated on a fire, is not steaming and boiling; like a bowl of water not covered with moss and leaves; like a bowl of water not ruffled by the wind, undisturbed, not stirred round, not rippling; like a bowl of water that is clear, bright, clean and placed in the light (*accho vippasanno anāvilo āloke nikkhitto*). Anyone looking down into such a bowl of water for the reflection of his face would know and see it just as it is. In the same way, when the mind is not possessed and overcome by the *nīvaraṇas*, one knows (and sees) as it is their letting go, what is of benefit to oneself, to others and to both; verses that have not been long learnt become clear, let alone those that have.

Food for the nīvaraṇas and food for the bojjhaṅgas

One of the most important aspects of the treatment of the contrast between the *nīvaraṇas* and *bojjhaṅgas* is the account of the way in which they both have their particular sets of foods (*āhāra*). The theme of the foods for the *nīvaraṇas* and *bojjhaṅgas* is one that is repeated several times in the *bojjhaṅga-saṃyutta*.[148] The general principle is stated as follows:

> Just as, *bhikkhus*, this body needs food for its subsistence, subsists conditioned by food, and without food does not subsist, just so, *bhikkhus*, the five *nīvaraṇas* need food for their subsistence, subsist conditioned by food, and without food do not subsist ... Just so, *bhikkhus*, the seven *bojjhaṅgas* need food for their subsistence, subsist conditioned by food, and without food do not subsist.[149]

How this is so is then elaborated in some detail and in the present context is most conveniently set out in tabular form.[150] The basic principles can be summed up as follows: improper or inapproriate bringing to mind (*ayoniso manasikāra*) of particular items is food for the *nīvaraṇas;* proper or appropriate bringing to mind (*yoniso manasikāra*) of particular items is food for the *bojjhaṅgas*.

This kind of treatment directly relates actual spiritual practice in the Nikāyas to what are sometimes viewed as the more purely philosophical and theoretical portions of the Nikāyas, namely the notions of causality and conditionality. What we have here are essentially instances and illustrations of the well known general statement of conditioned arising:

---

[147] *nissaraṇaṃ yathā-bhūtaṃ na pajānāti; attatthaṃ pi tasmiṃ samaye yathā-bhūtaṃ na jānāti na passati; paratthaṃ ... ubhayatthaṃ pi tasmiṃ samaye yathā-bhūtaṃ na jānāti na passati; dīgha-rattaṃ sajjhāya-katā pi mantā na paṭibhanti pageva asajjhāya-katā.*

[148] See S V 64-7; cf. 84-5, 93-4.

[149] S V 64-5: *seyyathâpi bhikkhave ayaṃ kāyo āhāra-ṭṭhitiko āhāraṃ paṭicca tiṭṭhati anāhāro no tiṭṭhati, evaṃ eva kho bhikkhave pañca nīvaraṇā āhāra-ṭṭhitikā āhāraṃ paṭicca tiṭṭhanti anāhārā no tiṭṭhanti.*

[150] See Table 5, p. 176.

TABLE 5. FOOD AND NOT-FOOD FOR THE HINDRANCES AND FACTORS OF AWAKENING

A Food for the arising of hindrances that have not arisen, and for the increase and growth of hindrances that have arisen

Making great improper bringing to mind (*ayoniso-manasikāra-bahulīkāra*) of:	Food for:
1. the sign of the beautiful (*subha-nimitta*)	– *kāma-cchanda*
2. the sign of the hateful (*paṭigha-nimitta*)	– *vyāpāda*
3. non-delight, laziness, languor, drowsiness after eating, mental depression (*arati tandi-vijambhitā bhatta-sammado cetaso ca līnattaṃ*)	– *thīna-middha*
4. mental disquiet (*cetaso avūpasamo*)	– *uddhacca-kukkucca*
5. *dhammas* that provide a basis for doubt (*vicikicchā-ṭṭhāniyā dhammā*)	– *vicikicchā*

B Food for the arising of bojjhaṅgas that have not arisen, and for the development and completion of bojjhaṅgas that have arisen

Making great proper bringing to mind (*yoniso-manasikāra-bahulīkāra*) of:	Food for:
1. *dhammas* that provide a basis for *sati-sambojjhaṅga*	– *sati-sambojjhaṅga*
2. *dhammas* that are skilful-unskilful (*kusalâkusala*), blameworthy-blameless (*sāvajjânavajja*), inferior-refined (*hīna-paṇīta*), belong to darkness or light (*kaṇha-sukka-ppaṭibhāga*)	– *dhamma-vicaya-sambojjhaṅga*
3. the bases of instigation (*ārambha-dhātu*), exertion (*nikkama*), valour (*parakkama*)	– *viriya-sambojjhaṅga*
4. *dhammas* that provide a basis for *pīti-sambojjhaṅga*	– *pīti-sambojjhaṅga*
5. tranquillity of body and mind (*kāya-, citta-passaddhi*)	– *passaddhi-sambojjhaṅga*
6. the sign of calm (*samatha*) and of non-distraction (*avyagga*)	– *samādhi-sambojjhaṅga*
7. *dhammas* that provide a basis for *upekkhā-sambojjhaṅga*	– *upekkhā-sambojjhaṅga*

C Not food for the arising of hindrances that have not arisen, nor for the increase and growth of those that have risen

Making great proper bringing to mind of:	Not food for:
1. the sign of the ugly (*asubha*)	– *kāma-cchanda*
2. the liberation of heart that is loving-kindness (*mettā-ceto-vimutti*)	– *vyāpāda*
3. the bases of instigation, exertion and valour	– *thīna-middha*
4. mental quiet	– *uddhacca-kukkucca*
5. *dhammas* that are skilful-unskilful, blameworthy-blameless, inferior-refined, belong to darkness or light	– *vicikicchā*

D Not food for the arising of bojjhaṅgas that have not arisen, nor for the development and completion of those that have arisen

Not making great bringing to mind (*amanasikāra-bahulīkāra*) of:	Not food for:
1. *dhammas* that provide a basis for *sati-sambojjhaṅga*	– *sati-sambojjhaṅga*
2. *dhammas* that are skilful-unskilful, blameworthy-blameless, inferior-refined, belong to darkness or light	– *dhamma-vicaya-sambojjhaṅga*
3. the bases of instigation, exertion and valour	– *viriya-sambojjhaṅga*
4. *dhammas* that provide a basis for *pīti-sambojjhaṅga*	– *pīti-sambojjhaṅga*
5. tranquillity of body and mind	– *passaddhi-sambojjhaṅga*
6. the sign of calm and of non-distraction	– *samādhi-sambojjhaṅga*
7. *dhammas* that provide a basis for *upekkhā-sambojjhaṅga*	– *upekkhā-sambojjhaṅga*

> When this is, that is; due to the arising of this, that arises. When this is not, that is not; due to the ceasing of this, that ceases.[151]

In the present context the discussion of the particular foods for the *nīvaraṇas* and *bojjhaṅgas* tends to dissolve any distinctions between speculative philosophy and meditation practice. For to abandon the *nīvaraṇas* and develop the *bojjhaṅgas* is to see and understand how certain things feed the *nīvaraṇas* and certain things feed the *bojjhaṅgas*. This is to know how one thing arises conditioned by another, which is, of course, to know *paṭicca-samuppāda*.

The bojjhaṅgas and wanderers of other schools

Three of the longer *suttas* in the *bojjhaṅga-saṃyutta* concerned with the *nīvaraṇa/bojjhaṅga* contrast centre on the difference between the teaching of wanderers belonging to other schools (*añña-titthiyā paribbājaka*) and the teaching of the Buddha in this respect.[152]

The first opens with an account of how a number of wanderers belonging to other schools claim in the presence of some *bhikkhus* that they also teach *dhamma* consisting of the abandoning of the five *nīvaraṇas* and development of the seven *bojjhaṅgas*. So, ask the wanderers, what is the distinction, what the difference between the *dhamma*-teaching and instruction of the *samaṇa* Gotama and their own?[153] The *bhikkhus* make no response, but put the matter before the Buddha. There is, says the Buddha, a way of exposition (*pariyāya*) according to which the five *nīvaraṇas* are ten and the seven *bojjhaṅgas* fourteen; questioned about this, the wanderers of other schools will be unable to respond, for there is no-one in the world save a Tathāgata or the pupil of a Tathāgata or one who has first heard it from a Tathāgata who might satisfy the mind with an answer to this question.

So how are the five *nīvaraṇas* ten, and the seven *bojjhaṅgas* fourteen? In the case of the *nīvaraṇas,* sensual desire (*kāma-cchanda*), aversion (*vyāpāda*) and doubt (*vicikicchā*) can each be viewed as a pair by virtue of their being either 'within' or of oneself (*ajjhattaṃ*) or 'without' or of another (*bahiddhā*).[154] Laziness and sleepiness (*thīna-middha*) and excitement and depression (*uddhacca-kukkucca*) can each be viewed as a pair by taking laziness and excitement as separate from sleepiness and depression. As for the *bojjhaṅgas*, mindfulness, *dhamma*-discrimination and equipoise are each considered pairs by virtue of their taking as their object either *dhammas* that are within or *dhammas* that are without. Joy and concentration are pairs because they may be either associated with or dissociated from initial and sustained thinking

---

151 E.g. M II 32; S II 65: *imasmiṃ sati idaṃ hoti; imass'uppāda idaṃ uppajjati. imasmiṃ asati idaṃ na hoti; imassa nirodhā idaṃ nirujjhati.*

152 See S V 108-21.

153 S V 108: *samaṇo āvuso Gotamo sāvakānaṃ evaṃ dhammaṃ deseti. etha tumhe bhikkhave pañca nīvaraṇe pahāya ... satta bojjhaṅge yathā-bhūtaṃ bhāvethā ti. mayaṃ pi bho āvuso sāvakānaṃ evaṃ dhammaṃ desema ... idha nu āvuso ko viseso ko adhippāyo kiṃ nānā-karaṇaṃ samaṇassa vā Gotamassa amhākaṃ vā yad-idaṃ dhamma-desanāya vā dhamma-desanaṃ anusāsaniyā vā anusāsanin ti.*

154 For this understanding of *ajjhattaṃ bahiddhā*, cf. Dhs 187.

(*vitakka-vicāra*). Tranquillity and strength may be either of the body or of the mind.[155]

It is important to note that this exposition involves making distinctions between items according to principles that are taken up and explored in full in the early Abhidhamma. In effect we have a particular application of a method that finds comprehensive expression in the Abhidhamma *mātikā* of the *Dhammasaṅgaṇi*. The particularity of the method's application here is evident from the fact that from the broader perspective of the *Dhammasaṅgaṇi* it could have been done differently. That is to say, there is no absolute reason why mindfulness, like joy and concentration, should not be considered as two by virtue of its association with or dissociation from initial and sustained thinking. This suggests that there is intended to be a particular point to the way in which each item is divided into a pair. It is perhaps worth briefly considering this with regard to the *bojjhaṅgas*.

The way in which joy and concentration each form a pair by virtue of association with or dissociation from initial and sustained thinking further suggests the parallels that exist between the *bojjhaṅgas* and the description of *jhāna*, for the stilling (*vūpasama*) of initial and sustained thought is precisely what marks the transition from first to second *jhāna*. Next, strength and tranquillity seem to be viewed as complementary pairs balancing each other. Finally, mindfulness, *dhamma*-discrimination and equipoise are three items that are seen as actively involved in the discernment of *dhammas* in general. If joy, concentration, strength and tranquillity are what prepare and make the mind receptive and ready for *bodhi*, mindfulness, *dhamma*-discrimination and equipoise actively promote *bodhi*.

The theme of the particular nature of the various *bojjhaṅgas* is taken further in the second treatment[156] that concerns wanderers of other schools. This treatment is introduced in precisely the same way as the first, but this time the Buddha states that the wanderers will be unable to respond when questioned about which *bojjhaṅgas* are inappropriate and which appropriate for development when the mind is depressed or slack (*līna*), and which are inappropriate and appropriate when the mind is excited or overactive (*uddhatta*). The Buddha goes on to explain that when the mind is depressed, then is not the right time (*akāla*) to develop tranquillity, concentration and equipoise; to do so would be to act like the man who throws wet grass, and so on, on to a small fire that he wants to blaze up. However, this is the right time (*kāla*) to develop *dhamma*-discrimination, strength, and joy; just as someone should throw dry grass, and so on, on to a small fire that he wants to blaze up. When the mind is excited, then is not the right time to develop *dhamma*-discrimination, strength and joy; to do so would be to act like the man who throws dry grass, and so on, on to a great fire that he wants to put out. However, it is the right time to develop tranquillity, concentration and equipoise; just as someone should

---

[155] This fourteenfold analysis of the *bojjhaṅgas* also forms one of the principal parts of their *suttanta-bhājaniya* treatment at Vibh 228.

[156] S V 112-5.

throw wet grass, and so on, on to a great fire that he wants to put out. As for mindfulness, this is always of benefit (*sabbatthika*).[157]

In the third treatment[158] the nature of the wanderers' claim is somewhat different: like the Buddha they too teach *dhamma* that consists of abandoning the five *nīvaraṇas* and dwelling suffusing the whole world with a mind that is accompanied by love (*mettā*), compassion (*karuṇā*), sympathetic joy (*muditā*) and equipoise (*upekkhā*)—a mind that is full (*vipula*), become great (*mahaggata*), immeasurable (*appamāṇa*), without hostility (*avera*) and without hatred (*avyāpajjha*).[159] When the matter is put before the Buddha, he answers that the wanderers will not be able to respond when questioned about how these four freedoms of mind (*ceto-vimutti*) are developed (*kathaṃ bhāvitā*), their outcome (*kiṃ-gatikā*), their perfection (*kiṃ-paramā*), their fruit (*kiṃ-phalā*) and their conclusion (*kiṃ-pariyosānā*). A detailed explanation of these questions is then given.

A *bhikkhu* develops the seven *bojjhaṅgas* each dependent on seclusion, dispassion and cessation and ripening in release; in addition each is accompanied by *mettā*. He then, if he wishes, dwells with the idea of the repulsive in what is not repulsive (*so sace ākaṅkhati appaṭikkūle paṭikkūla-saññī vihareyyan ti paṭikkūla-saññī tattha viharati*). He may dwell with the idea of the unrepulsive in what is repulsive; with the idea of what is unrepulsive in both what is repulsive and unrepulsive. Avoiding both the unrepulsive and the repulsive he may dwell with equipoise, mindful, clearly comprehending (*appaṭikkūlañ ca paṭikkūlañ ca tad ubhayaṃ abhinivajjetvā upekkhako vihareyyaṃ sato sampajāno ti upekkhako tattha viharati sato sampajāno*). Or:

> He attains and dwells in the liberation that is beautiful. I declare, *bhikkhus*, that the beautiful is the perfection of the freedom of mind that is *mettā*. Here a *bhikkhu* has wisdom, [although] not penetrating to a higher freedom.[160]

The exposition for *karuṇā*, *muditā* and *upekkhā* follows that for *mettā*, except that what is declared as the perfection is different in each case: the sphere of infinite space (*ākāsânañcāyatana*) is the perfection of the freedom of mind that is *karuṇā*; the sphere of infinite consciousness (*viññāṇañcāyatana*) is the perfection of the freedom of mind that is *muditā*; the sphere of nothingness (*akiñcaññāyatana*) is the perfection of the freedom of mind that is *upekkhā*.

The development of the *bojjhaṅgas* is here considered in the context of the practice of *mettā*, *karuṇā*, *muditā* and *upekkhā*. This is perhaps slightly unexpected in that the consideration of the *viveka-nissita* formula showed that for the commentaries the *bojjhaṅgas* are characteristically developed at the time of insight practice and the arising of the transcendent path and fruit. However, as

---

157 Cf. the following analysis of the *bodhy-aṅgas* given by Harivarman (Satya Trsl 448-9) and Asaṅga (Wayman, *Śrāvakabhūmi*, p. 109): *dharma-pravicaya*, *vīrya* and *prīti* constitute *vipaśyanā*; *praśrabdhi*, *samādhi* and *upekṣā* constitute *śamatha; smṛti* is either.

158 S V 115-21.

159 The stock Nikāya description of the practice of *mettā*, *karuṇā*, *muditā* and *upekkhā* is given in full here; cf. D I 250; III 223; M II 76; A II 130; IV 300; Vibh 272.

160 S V 119: *subhaṃ vā kho pana vimokkhaṃ upasampajja viharati. subha-paramâhaṃ bhikkhave mettā-ceto-vimuttiṃ vadāmi. idha paññassa bhikkhuno uttariṃ vimuttiṃ apaṭivijjhato.*

I noted above, the commentaries do suggest that this is not quite the whole story. What they have to say on this point is now worth quoting in full:

> For there are those who bring out the *bojjhaṅgas* not in respect of the moments of strong insight, path and fruit alone; they also bring them out in respect of *kasiṇa-jjhānas* that are a basis for insight, breathing-in-and-out, ugliness, and divine-abiding *jhānas*. And they are not contradicted by the teachers of the *aṭṭhakathās*.[161]

Although it is not cited as such, the above account of the practice of *mettā*, and so on, would appear to be the kind of passage the commentaries have in mind when they say that the *bojjhaṅgas* can be brought out in respect of divine-abiding *jhānas*. A few pages later in the *bojjhaṅga-saṃyutta*, the *ānâpāna-vagga*[162] is devoted to a description of how the *bojjhaṅgas* are developed in association with various meditation subjects, including the 'divine abidings': the ideas of (i) the skeleton, (ii) the worm infested corpse, (iii) the discoloured corpse, (iv) the rotting corpse, (v) the bloated corpse; (vi) *mettā*, (vii) *karuṇā*, (viii) *muditā*, (ix) *upekkhā*, (x) breathing in and out. Here, then, we have ugliness and breathing-in-and-out *jhāna*. The development of the *bojjhaṅgas* in association with these is said to be of great fruit and benefit (*mahā-phala, mahânisaṃsa*); either knowledge in the here and now (*diṭṭhe va dhamme aññā*) or, if there is a residuum of attachment, the state of non-return (*sati vā upādi-sese anāgāmitā*) is to be expected as a result.

So how is the series of *suttas* concerning the relationship of the Buddha's teaching to that of wanderers of other schools to be interpreted? It is surely striking that in none of the three cases is the Buddha represented as categorically denying the wanderers' claim to a teaching that bears some similarity to his own—a fact which the commentary seems to want to play down.[163] In other words, the Nikāyas seem to accept some form of basic common ground between the Buddha and the wanderers.[164] So while we do have what amounts to a claim of superiority on the part of the Nikāyas, there is a certain subtlety to their argument here. The wanderers of other schools may abandon the five *nīvaraṇas* and develop the seven *bojjhaṅgas*, but the full potential inherent in this practice is not understood or fulfilled by them. In short, they do not really understand what they are doing.

Johannes Bronkhorst has argued that the four *jhānas* represent a characteristically Buddhist meditation tradition—a tradition original to the Buddha and quite distinct from the 'main stream' severely 'ascetic' non-Buddhist meditation

---

161 Ps I 85 = Spk III 139 = Vibh-a 316: *te hi na kevalaṃ balava-vipassanā-magga-phala-kkhaṇesu eva bojjhaṅgaṃ uddharanti; vipassanā-padaka-kasiṇa-jjhāna-ānâpānâsubha-brahma-vihāra-jjhānesu pi uddharanti. na ca paṭisiddhā aṭṭha-kathâcariyehi.*

162 S V 129-32; cf. the *nirodha-vagga* (S V 132-4). S V 312 also relates the *bojjhaṅgas* to *ānâpāna*.

163 The wanderers do not really teach the abandoning of the *nīvaraṇas* and the development of the *bojjhaṅgas*. They merely overhear the Buddha teaching and then return to their own *ārāma* where they teach their own followers making it appear that the method has been penetrated as a result of their own knowledge (Spk III 168-9).

164 On the question of a common ground with the *paribbājaka* tradition, cf. Frauwallner, *HIP* I 135.

tradition.[165] According to Bronkhorst, this distinctively Buddhist meditation is described in the texts as 'a pleasant experience, accompanied by joy (*pīti*), and bliss (*sukha*), or bliss alone, in all but the highest stages, whereas non-Buddhist meditation is not described as pleasurable'.[166] While Bronkhorst's basic thesis concerning the existence of two meditation traditions is not without its attractions, it seems to me that we cannot dismiss the idea of a 'pre-Buddhistic' form of 'Buddhist meditation' quite so readily as he suggests. Towards the end of his study Bronkhorst writes:

> We have become acquainted with a number of descriptions of non-Buddhist religious practice in the Buddhist canon in the course of this book. None of them ascribe to outsiders what we have come to regard as authentic Buddhist meditation.[167]

Yet, if I am right concerning the nature of the *bojjhaṅga* list (namely that it links directly into a range of ideas associated with the *jhānas* and is intended to characterize a particular variety of *jhāna*) then surely in preserving the wanderers' claim that they too taught the abandoning of the *nīvaraṇas*[168] and development of the *bojjhaṅgas* the Nikāyas do preserve a tradition of 'non-Buddhists' practising 'Buddhist meditation'. That is to say, it is not unreasonable to see in the wanderers' claim a reflection of a historical situation where various groups, among them the Buddha and his followers, practised a form of meditation distinct from what Bronkhorst identifies as the main stream ascetic tradition.

If we bear in mind the way in which the *bojjhaṅgas* are related to various meditation subjects, the point in all this would seem to be not that the Buddha teaches new or original meditation subjects, but that he is unsurpassed in defining the finer points of technique and relating these to progress towards the final goal. This further brings out the way in which the *bojjhaṅga* list focuses on *bodhi* as a kind of *jhāna*. What we are concerned with is the transition from ordinary *jhāna* to the special *jhāna* that is *bodhi* itself. The various expositions that are here presented as the particular domain of the Buddha and his followers are concerned with seeing the precise nature of the items in question; this involves knowing how they stand in relationship to each other and how they interact. This once more brings us to the realm of 'causality' or 'conditionality' represented by *paṭicca-samuppāda*, or the realm of discriminating *dhammas* and discerning *dhamma*. In terms of Nikāya psychology what we are concerned with is wisdom (*paññā*)—the wisdom that discerns *dhamma* and *dhammas*, and that knows the nature of suffering, its cessation and what brings about both. Thus what is claimed as distinctive about the teaching of the Buddha is that it always perfectly relates the

---

165 See his *The Two Traditions of Meditation in Ancient India*, Stuttgart, 1986.

166 Id., p. 17.

167 Id., p. 116.

168 Note that the phrase used here to describe the abandoning of the *nīvaraṇas* (*pañca nīvaraṇe pahāya cetaso upakkilese paññāya dubbalī-karaṇe*) is regularly used to introduce the stock description of the *jhānas*; see D III 49; M I 52, 181, 270, 276, 347; III 4, 36, 136; A III 93, 100, 386-7; IV 195.

abandoning of the *nīvaraṇas* and the development of the *bojjhaṅgas* to progress towards the cessation of suffering. It is the completeness of the Buddha's teaching in this respect that is emphasized, rather than its radical departure from the wanderers' teaching. What this seems to show is how the Nikāyas present the special *dhamma* teaching of the Buddhas not as something extra simply tacked on at the end, but as something that imbues the whole teaching.

The bojjhaṅgas and the seven treasures of the cakka-vattin king

Finally, it seems worth singling out one rather brief *sutta* that does, however, give a name to a whole *vagga* of the *bojjhaṅga-saṃyutta*:[169]

> Due to the appearance of a *cakka-vattin* king there is the appearance of seven treasures. Which seven? There is the appearance of the wheel-treasure ... the elephant-treasure ... the horse-treasure ... the gem-treasure ... the woman-treasure ... the master-treasure ... the counsellor-treasure. Due to the appearance of a Tathāgata, an *arahant*, a fully awakened one there is the appearance of the seven treasures of the awakening-factors. Which seven? There is the appearance of the treasure of the awakening-factor of mindfulness ... of the awakening-factor of equipoise.[170]

In a number of places the 'wheel-turning' king is seen as some kind of counterpart to a Buddha; they are two varieties of the 'great man' (*mahā-purusa*). The interest of the present *sutta* lies in the way it is indicative of how the world of the *cakka-vattin* king (as described in the *Mahāsuddassana-* and *Cakkavattisīhanāda-suttas*, for example) might be viewed as a more complete mythological counterpart to the teaching of a Buddha. It is in this light that the commentary appears to explore the relationship between the treasures and the *bojjhaṅgas*:

> For just as the wheel-treasure of the *cakka-vattin* is the leader of all [other] treasures, so the treasure of the awakening-factor of mindfulness is the leader of all *dhammas* belonging to the four levels. Thus in the sense of leading it is like the wheel-treasure of the *cakka-vattin* king. Next among the treasures of the *cakka-vattin* is the elephant treasure, formed of a great body, towering, vast, great. So too the treasure of the awakening-factor of *dhamma*-discrimination is formed of the great body of *dhamma*, is towering, vast, great. It is thus like the elephant-treasure. The horse-treasure of the *cakka-vattin* is swift and quick running. So too the treasure of the awakening-factor of strength is swift and quick running. Thus because of its swiftness and quick running it is like the horse-treasure. The gem-treasure of the *cakka-vattin* disperses darkness and reveals light. So too the treasure of the awakening-factor of joy, because of its extreme skilfulness disperses the darkness of defilements and by virtue of conascence condition, etc. reveals the light of knowledge. Thus because of its dispersing darkness and revealing light it is like the gem-treasure. The woman-treasure of the *cakka-vattin* tranquillizes the

---

[169] The *cakkavatti-vagga*, S V 98-102.

[170] S V 99: *rañño bhikkhave cakka-vattissa pātubhāvā sattannaṃ ratanānaṃ pātubhāvo hoti. katamesaṃ sattannaṃ. cakka-ratanassa pātubhāvo hoti. hatthi-ratanassa. assa-ratanassa. maṇi-ratanassa. itthi-ratanassa. gaha-pati-ratanassa. pariṇāyaka-ratanassa pātubhāvo hoti ... tathāgatassa bhikkhave pātubhāvā arahato sammā-sambuddhassa sattannaṃ bojjhaṅga-ratanānaṃ pātubhāvo hoti. katamesaṃ sattannaṃ. sati-sambojjhaṅga-ratanassa pātubhāvo hoti. pe. upekkhā-sambojjhaṅga-ratanassa pātubhāvo hoti.*

strain of body and mind, and soothes fever. So too the treasure of the awakening-factor of tranquillity tranquillizes the strain of body and mind, and soothes fever. Thus it is like the woman-treasure. The master-treasure of the *cakka-vattin*, by providing wealth at exactly the desired moment, cuts off distraction and makes for a one-pointed mind. So too the treasure of the awakening-factor of concentration, by virtue of its being as desired, etc. accomplishes absorption and, cutting off distraction, makes for a one-pointed mind. The adviser-treasure of the *cakka-vattin*, by everywhere accomplishing what needs to be done, makes for few concerns. So too the treasure of the awakening-factor of equipoise frees the mind from sluggishness and over-activity and, establishing it in balanced application, makes for few concerns. It is thus like the adviser treasure.[171]

9. The bojjhaṅgas according to the commentaries

With regard to the seven *bojjhaṅgas* the commentaries give the following analysis in a number of places:

> Awakening-factors are 'the factors of awakening (*bodhi*) or of the one awakening (*bodhin*)'. The following is what is said. The assemblage of *dhammas* designated by mindfulness, *dhamma*-discrimination, strength, joy, tranquillity, concentration and equipoise, and which is opposed to various dangers such as slackness and excitement, resting and exertion, engagement in sensual pleasure or [self-]torment, adherence to annihilationism or eternalism, when it occurs at the moment of the transcendent path is called 'awakening' (*bodhi*) with reference to the fact that the noble disciple awakens by means of this assemblage of *dhammas*. He awakens, i.e. he emerges from the sleep of the stream of defilements: either he penetrates the four noble truths or simply he realizes *nibbāna*, is what is said. Awakening-factors are, then, 'factors of awakening' [where awakening is] a designation for an assemblage of *dhammas*—like *jhāna*-factors, path-factors and so on. However, with reference to the fact that he is one who awakens by means of this assemblage of *dhammas* in the aforesaid manner the noble disciple is called 'awakening' (*bodhin*). [So] awakening-factors are also 'factors of one awakening'—like parts of an army, parts of a chariot and so on. Accordingly the teachers of the *aṭṭhakathās* have said: 'Awakening-factors are the factors of a person who is waking up.'[172]

---

171 Spk III 154-5: *yath'eva hi cakka-vattino cakka-ratanaṃ sabba-ratanānaṃ purecaraṃ, evaṃ sati-sambojjhaṅga-ratanaṃ sabbesaṃ catu-bhūmaka-dhammānaṃ purecaran ti purecaranaṭṭhena cakka-vatti-rañño cakka-ratana-sadisaṃ hoti. cakka-vattino ca ratanesu mahā-kāyupapannaṃ accuggataṃ vipulaṃ mahantaṃ hatthi-ratanaṃ. idaṃ pi dhamma-vicaya-sambojjhaṅga-ratanaṃ mahā-dhamma-kāyupapannaṃ accuggataṃ vipulaṃ mahantan ti hatthi ratana-sadisaṃ hoti. cakka-vattino assa-ratanaṃ sīghaṃ lahu-javaṃ. idaṃ pi viriya-sambojjhaṅga-ratanaṃ sīghaṃ lahu-javan ti imāya sīgha-lahu-javatāya assa-ratana-sadisaṃ hoti. cakka-vattino maṇi-ratanaṃ andha-kāraṃ vidhamati ālokaṃ dasseti. idaṃ pi pīti-sambojjhaṅga-ratanaṃ ekanta-kusalatā kilesandha-kāraṃ vidhamati, saha-jāta-paccayâdi-vasena ñāṇâlokaṃ dassetī ti iminā andha-kāra-vidhamana-āloka-dassana-bhāvena maṇi-ratana-sadisaṃ hoti. cakka-vattino itthi-ratanaṃ kāya-citta-darathaṃ paṭippassambheti pariḷāhaṃ vūpasameti. idaṃ pi passaddhi-sambojjhaṅga-ratanaṃ kāya-citta-darathaṃ paṭippassambhetī ti pariḷāhaṃ vūpasametī ti itthi-ratana-sadisaṃ hoti. cakka-vattino gaha-pati-ratanaṃ icchiticchita-kkhaṇe dhana-dānena vikkhepaṃ pacchinditvā cittaṃ ekaggaṃ karoti. idaṃ pi samādhi-sambojjhaṅga-ratanaṃ yathicchitadi-vasena appanaṃ sampādeti vikkhepaṃ pacchinditvā cittaṃ ekaggaṃ karotī ti gaha-pati-ratana-sadisaṃ hoti. cakka-vattino ca pariṇāyaka-ratanaṃ sabbattha kicca-sampādanena appossukkataṃ karoti. idaṃ pi upekkhā-sambojjhaṅga-ratanaṃ cittuppādaṃ līnuddhaccato mocetvā payoga-majjhatte ṭhapayamānaṃ appossukkataṃ karotī ti pariṇāyaka-ratana-sadisaṃ hoti.*

172 Vibh-a 310 (and with slight variations at Ps I 85; Spk III 138; Mp II 52-3; Paṭis-a III 600; As 217; Moh 161; cf. Ud-a 305): *bodhiyā bodhissa vā aṅgā ti bojjhaṅgā. idaṃ vuttaṃ hoti. yā esā dhamma-sāmaggī yāya lokuttara-magga-kkhaṇe uppajjamānāya līnuddhacca-patiṭṭhānâyuhana-kāma-sukhatta-kilamathânuyoga-uccheda-sassatâbhinivesâdīnaṃ anekesaṃ upaddavānaṃ paṭipakkha-*

The commentaries here take the transcendent path consciousness as the basis for the normative account of the *bojjhaṅgas*, and ignore the possibiliity of 'bringing out' (*uddharati*) *bojjhaṅgas* in the ordinary *lokiya* types of *jhāna* mentioned above. The explanation involves a play both on *bodhi*- (*bodhi* or *bodhin*) and on the various meanings of *aṅga*—'limb', 'factor', 'part'.

In the first place the *bojjhaṅgas* are seen as seven 'factors' that can collectively be called 'awakening'. This same awakening is then described as penetrating the four truths or simply realizing or making visible (*sacchikaroti*) *nibbāna*, which are presumably offered as two ways of looking at the same thing. A little after the quoted passage, the *Vibhaṅga* commentary adds that seven *bojjhaṅgas* are distinguished by reason of their each performing a particular function with regard to just one object.[173] From the point of view of Abhidhamma, then, awakening is taken as what occurs when these seven *dhammas* take *nibbāna* as their object. This is to be compared, it is suggested, to the way in which *jhāna* is what occurs when the five *jhāna*-factors, having been brought to full strength, take the 'semblance sign' (*paṭibhāga-nimitta*) as their object.[174]

Secondly, 'awakening' is taken as the 'one who is awakening' (*bodhin*) or the 'person waking up' (*bujjhanako puggalo*). The seven *bojjhaṅgas* are then seen as like the limbs or parts of the body of that person. This image is then further likened to the 'parts of an army' or the 'parts of a chariot'. Presumably what is intended is that an army requires various different parts (e.g. elephants, horses, chariots, foot soldiers)[175] in order to be effective as an army. Again, a chariot requires certain essential parts to function properly. Without these parts both are ineffectual or incapacitated. Similarly, then, the person who is awakening needs mindfulness, *dhamma*-discrimination, strength, joy, tranquillity, concentration and equipoise or else he cannot properly be that person.

Immediately following the passage quoted above, the commentaries quote the explanation of the *Paṭisambhidāmagga*:

> They are awakening factors because they conduce to awakening; they are awakening-factors because they awaken; they are awakening-factors because they awaken further; they are awakening-factors because they awaken again; they are awakening-factors because they awaken fully.[176]

These are in fact only the first five of 609 answers the *Paṭisambhidāmagga* gives

---

bhūtāya sati-dhamma-vicaya-viriya-pīti-passaddhi-samādhi-upekkhā-saṃkhātāya dhamma-sāmaggiyā ariya-sāvako bujjhatī ti katvā bodhī ti vuccati. bujjhatī ti kilesa-santāna-niddāya uṭṭhahanti; cattāri vā ariya-saccāni paṭivijjhati nibbānaṃ eva vā sacchikarotī ti vuttaṃ hoti. tassa dhamma-sāmaggi-saṃkhātāya bodhiyā aṅgānī ti bojjhaṅgā jhānaṅga-maggaṅgâdayo viya. yo pan'esa yathā-vuttappakārāya etāya dhamma-sāmaggiyā bujjhatī ti katvā ariya-sāvako bodhī ti vuccati. tassa bodhissa aṅgā ti pi bojjhaṅgā senaṅga-rathaṅgâdayo viya. tenâhu aṭṭha-kathâcariyā bujjhanakassa puggalassa aṅgā ti bojjhaṅgā ti.

[173] Vibh-a 311: *idāni nesaṃ ekasmiṃ yevârammaṇe attano attano kicca-vasena nānā-karaṇaṃ dassetuṃ tattha katamo sati-sambojjhaṅgo ti ādi āraddhaṃ.*

[174] Cf. Vism IV 31-3.

[175] The classic four parts of an ancient Indian army.

[176] Paṭis II 115: *bodhāya saṃvattantī ti bojjhaṅgā; bujjhantī ti bojjhaṅgā, anubujjhantī ti bojjhaṅgā; paṭibujjhantī ti bojjhaṅgā; sambujjhantī ti bojjhaṅgā.*

to the question: 'In what sense are they awakening-factors?'[177] The *Paṭisambhidā* commentary no doubt correctly relates 'they awaken' (*bujjhanti*), 'they awaken further' (*anubujjhanti*), 'they awaken again, (*paṭibujjhanti*) and 'they awaken fully, (*sambujjhanti*) to the four stages of the transcendent path: stream-attainment, once-return, non-return and *arahant*-ship.[178] Essentially the *Paṭisambhidā* explanations again focus on the *bojjhaṅgas* as collectively achieving the event designated *bodhi*.

Just how *bodhi* is understood is worth exploring a little further. In defining *bodhi-pakkhiya* the commentaries take *bodhi* in one of two ways: either as knowledge (*ñāṇa*) with regard to the four transcendent noble paths (*ariya-magga*) or as the noble person (*ariya-puggala*).[179] The second of these corresponds to the explanation of the *bojjhaṅgas* as the *aṅgas* of the *ariya-sāvaka*. The first, however, makes explicit a different dimension: awakening is seen as essentially a species of knowledge, that is, an awakening to something. Of course, this conception of *bodhi* is virtually stated in the *bojjhaṅga* passage when *bodhi* is equated with penetrating the four truths. However, this narrow and strict way of taking *bodhi* as a particular knowledge is already quite explicit in the *Mahāniddesa*:

> Knowledge with regard to the four paths, wisdom, the faculty of wisdom, the power of wisdom, the awakening-factor of *dhamma*-discrimination, investigation, insight, right view is called awakening.[180]

'Awakening' here, then, is not the assemblage of seven *dhammas*, but just one *dhamma*, namely *dhamma-vicaya-sambojjhaṅga*.

A discussion found in the *Milindapañha* is of some interest at this point.[181] The king, Milinda, asks Nāgasena by means of how many of the seven *bojjhaṅgas* one actually awakens (*katīhi pana bhante bojjhaṅgehi bujjhati*). Nāgasena answers that it is by means of one, namely the *bojjhaṅga* of *dhamma*-discrimination (*ekena mahā-rāja bojjhaṅgena bujjhati dhamma-vicaya-sambojjhaṅgena*). So why, asks Milinda, are seven *bojjhaṅgas* mentioned (*atha kissa nu kho bhante vuccanti satta bojjhaṅgā*)? Nāgasena responds:

> Does a sword placed in its sheath and not grasped in the hand succeed in cutting what needs to be cut? In exactly the same way, Your Majesty, one cannot awaken by means of the awakening-factor of *dhamma*-discrimination without the [other] six awakening-factors.[182]

The import of this discussion is clear enough. The essential characteristic of *bodhi* is knowledge—an aspect of wisdom or *dhamma*-discrimination. Yet this

---

177 See below, Chapter 10.2.

178 Paṭis-a 100; Paṭis makes the same distinction with *bodhenti, anubodhenti, paṭibodhenti, sambodhenti; bodhana, anubodhana, paṭibodhana, sambodhana; bodhi-pakkhiya, anubodhi-pakkhiya, paṭibodhi-pakkhiya, sambodhi-pakkhiya.*

179 See below, Chapter 9.3.

180 Nidd I 456: *bodhi vuccati catusu maggesu ñāṇaṃ paññā paññindriyaṃ paññā-balaṃ dhamma-vicaya-sambojjhaṅgo vīmaṃsā vipassanā sammā-diṭṭhi.*

181 Mil 83.

182 Ibid.: *asi kosiyā pakkhitto aggahito hatthena ussahati chejjam chindituṃ. evaṃ eva kho mahā-rāja dhamma-vicaya-sambojjhaṅgena vinā chahi bojjhaṅgehi na bujjhati.*

knowledge is only gained in association with mindfulness, strength, joy, tranquillity, concentration and equipoise—these six are needed to unsheath the sword of wisdom and make it wieldy. Rather similarly, *jhāna* might be looked at as essentially concentration (*samādhi*) or one-pointedness of mind (*cittass' ekaggatā*) supported by the other four *jhāna*-factors. Much the same way of looking at things is expressed in an analysis of the *bodhy-aṅgas* that is apparently peculiar to Buddhist Sanskrit texts. I quote from the commentary to the *Arthaviniścaya-sūtra*:

> Mindfulness is the factor of awakening that is a refuge, since by the power of mindfulness there is no wavering of the object [?]. *Dharma*-discrimination is the factor of essential nature, since the essential nature of awakening is knowledge. Strength is the factor of escape, since by means of it one passes beyond the state of an ordinary man. Joy is the factor of benefit, since by means of it there is satisfaction of body and mind. Tranquillity, concentration and equipoise are factors of non-defilement, since they counteract the defilements.[183]

What of the explanation of 'awakening' in terms of the person? From the perspective of Abhidhamma a 'person' is, of course, simply *dhammas* that might be analyzed by way of the five aggregates (*khandha*), the twelve spheres (*āyatanas*), the eighteen elements (*dhātus*) and so on.[184] Thus if the seven *bojjhaṅgas* constitute an assemblage of *dhammas* equivalent to awakening, so too, apparently, does a 'person'. For at the time of the arising of the transcendent mind (*lokuttara-citta*) the 'person' who is awakening is precisely the *dhammas* that contribute to that mind. In other words all *dhammas* that arise at that time, i.e. the complete assemblage of mind and its concomitants (*citta-cetasika*), might be viewed as constituting awakening. So here we have one perspective on 'awakening' as the person who is awakening. But this can perhaps be taken a stage further. The assemblage of mind and mental concomitants that constitutes the event of awakening has certain repercussions on future assemblages of mind and mental concomitants. That is to say, awakening in certain respects determines the kinds of mind that will arise for a 'person' in the future; awakening permanently changes the character of *dhammas* arising subsequently. Thus by stream-attainment greed types of consciousness associated with wrong-view, and consciousness associated with doubt are abandoned,[185] while by the path of non-return all consciousness associated with aversion is abandoned.[186] Finally, the path of *arahant*-ship abandons all

---

[183] Artha-n 229-30: *tatra smṛtir bodher āśrayâṅgaṃ smṛti-balena tasmād ālambanād avikṣepāt* [Samtani comments that the text appears corrupt]. *dharma-pravicayaḥ svabhāvâṅgam jñāna-svabhāvatvād bodheḥ. vīrya niryāṇâṅgaṃ tena pṛthag-jana-bhūmi-samatikramāt. prītir anuśaṃsâṅgaṃ tayā kāya-cittânugrahāt. praśrabdhi-samādhy-upekṣā asaṃkleśâṅgaṃ teṣāṃ kleśa-pratipakṣatvāt.* (Cf. *bhāṣya* to *Madhyântavibhāga* IV 8(b) (Anacker, op. cit., pp. 249-50, 448); Abhidh-sam Trsl 122-3.)

[184] Cf. R. Gethin, 'The five *khandhas*', *JIP* 14 (1986), pp. 35-53.

[185] Cf. Dhs 237: 'The four arisings of consciousness associated with views, the arising of consciousness accompanied by doubt, these are the *dhammas* to be abandoned by seeing.' (*cattāro diṭṭhigata-sampayutta-cittuppādā vicikicchā-sahagato cittuppādo, ime dhammā dassanena pahātabbā.*)

[186] This follows from the fact that by this path the five lower fetters (*orambhāgiyāni saṃyojanāni*) are abandoned; these include aversion (*vyāpāda*); cf. *Mahāmāluṅkya-sutta*, M I

unskilful consciousness. In other words, awakening brings about a fundamental change in the nature or character of a 'person'; he is now a noble person.[187]

In the various ways of looking at 'awakening'[188] we get, I think, a gradually broadening perspective on one and the same thing. First of all 'awakening' is a particular knowledge. But it is a knowledge acquired in a particular way, by a particular path, so next we see 'awakening' as an assemblage of seven *dhammas* that show it to be a meditation attainment, a kind of *jhāna*. But it is a *jhāna* that has far reaching consequences, so finally we see awakening as a 'person', that is the aggregate of *dhammas* that constitutes the moment of awakening and issues from it.

At this point I should draw attention to a slightly different usage of terminology in the northern tradition. In the main *bodhi* is defined rather more narrowly than in the Pāli texts. It is not used of the knowledges of all four of the noble paths, but only of the knowledge of the path or *arhat*-ship; that is to say, *bodhi* refers strictly to the final awakening of the disciple (*śrāvaka*), *pratyeka-buddha* or *samyak-sambuddha*.[189] This awakening is defined in terms of 'knowledge with regard to non-arising' (*anutpāda-jñāna*) and 'knowledge with regard to destruction' (*kṣaya-jñāna*) of the *āsravas*.[190] The term used for knowledge of the four truths prior to this, during the first, second and third paths, is *abhisamaya*.[191] This terminological difference, although slight, coincides with one of the characteristic ways the seven sets are treated in Buddhist Sanskrit texts. According to one way of looking at the matter, the eight path-factors are brought into being at the stage of the path of seeing (*darśana*-

---

432-7. On the general question of which defilements are abandoned by each of the paths see the lengthy discussion at Vism XXII 47-91. This passage also considers the question of whether the defilements abandoned are to be viewed as past, present or future (cf. Paṭis II 217-9).

187 S. Collins comments (*SP*, p. 160) that 'there are a variety of senses in which *puggala* is used. Generally, they may be summarised as having to do with differences in character, ethical disposition, spiritual aptitude and achievement, and karmic destiny.'

188 Aggavaṃsa (Sadd 482) sums up the possible meanings of *bodhi* as five: the tree of awakening, the path, omniscience (*sabbaññuta-ñāṇa*), *nibbāna* and a person so designated (*evaṃ paṇṇattiko puggalo*); he gives *antarā ca bodhiṃ antarā ca Gayaṃ* (Vin I 8) as an example of the first; *bodhi vuccati catusu maggesu ñāṇaṃ* (Nidd I 456) of the second; *pappoti bodhiṃ vara-bhūri-medhaso* (D III 159) of the third; *patvāna bodhiṃ amataṃ asamkhataṃ* of the fourth; *ariya-sāvako bodhi vuccati* of the last. Aggavaṃsa finishes with a mnemonic verse: *rukkhe magge ca nibbāne ñāṇe sabbaññutāya ca/ tathā paṇṇattiyañ c'eva bodhi-saddo pavattati//*. (Aggavaṃsa seems in part to be following Sp I 139.)

189 For references, see below, pp. 301–2.

190 The expressions *anuppāde ñāṇaṃ* and *khaye ñāṇaṃ* are found in the Pāli canon. (e.g. D III 214, 274). Their usage seems to be derived from the stock descriptions of the attainment of *arahant*-ship (e.g. M I 23, 183, 348), indeed this is made explicit at Nett 15. While in absolute terms the expressions thus seem clearly related to the complete knowledge of the *arahant*, As 409 (to Dhs 234) takes each path to have its own *khaye ñāṇaṃ* (knowledge that particular defilements are abandoned) and each fruit to have its own *anuppāde ñāṇaṃ* (knowledge that those particular defilements will not arise). But it would seem from Dhs 234 that we should only speak of *khaye ñāṇaṃ* and *anuppāde ñāṇaṃ* of one who is endowed with all four of the paths and all four of the fruits.

191 The term *abhisamaya* is also used in the sense of knowledge of the four truths in Pāli texts; e.g. Paṭis II 82, 107, 215-9; Vism XXII 6. Cf. *CPD*, s.v. *abhisamaya* 'nearly = sotāpatti'.

mārga), that is the path of stream attainment; the seven *bodhy-aṅgas* are only developed subsequently, during the path of development (*bhāvanā-mārga*).[192]

Finally, the commentaries preserve in several places a rather full account detailing various things conducive to the arising of each *bojjhaṅga*.[193] This account is best understood as an extension of the Nikāya treatment, already discussed, concerning the foods and occasions appropriate for the development of individual *bojjhaṅgas*; indeed in certain commentaries it is explicitly presented as such. In the *Visuddhimagga*, however, it is adapted to the account of the tenfold skill in absorption (*appanā-kosalla*) which forms part of the general description of the development of *samādhi*. The tenfold skill in absorption is concerned with the practice the meditator undertakes in order to bring the achievement of access concentration (the result of initially overcoming the hindrances) to the point of full absorption (the result of making the *jhāna* factors strong).[194] All this further brings out the particular meditational or yogic aspect of the *bojjhaṅgas*. The following are the bare headings each of which is illustrated in the commentarial account:

Conducive to the arising of the awakening-factor of mindfulness

(1) mindfulness and clear comprehension (*sati-sampajañña*)
(2) avoidance of people of lost mindfulness (*muṭṭha-ssati-puggala-parivajjana-tā*)
(3) association with people of established mindfulness (*upaṭṭhita-ssati-puggala-sevanatā*)
(4) commitment to that (*tad-adhimuttatā*)

Conducive to the arising of the awakening-factor of dhamma-discrimination

(1) asking questions (*paripucchakatā*)
(2) keeping one's person and belongings clean (*vatthu-visada-kiriyā*)
(3) balancing the faculties [of *saddhā*, etc.] (*indriya-samatta-paṭipādanā*)
(4) avoidance of unwise people (*duppañña-puggala*)
(5) association of wise people (*paññavanta-puggala*)
(6) reflection on practice with deep knowledge (*gambhīra-ñāṇa-cariya-pacc-avekkhanā*)
(7) commitment to that

Conducive to the arising of the awakening-factor of strength

(1) reflection on the dangers of the descents (*apāya-bhaya*)
(2) seeing the benefits [to be gained] (*ānisaṃsa-dassāvitā*)
(3) reflection on the course of the journey (*gamana-vīthi*)
(4) honouring alms [received] (*piṇḍa-pātâpacāyanatā*)
(5) reflection on the greatness of the inheritance (*dāyajja-mahatta*)
(6) reflection on the greatness of the Teacher (*satthu-mahatta*)
(7) reflection on the greatness of one's birth (*jāti-mahatta*)
(8) reflection on the greatness of other practitioners (*sabrahma-cārī-mahatta*)
(9) avoidance of idle people (*kusīta-puggala*)
(10) association with people of firm strength (*āraddha-viriya-puggala*)
(11) commitment to that

[192] See below, Chapter 10.6.
[193] Ps I 290-300; Spk III 155-65; Mp II 54-70; Vibh-a 275-86; Vism IV 42-65.
[194] Vism IV 31-4.

Conducive to the arising of the awakening-factor of joy

(1) recollection of Buddha (*buddhânussati*)
(2) recollection of Dhamma
(3) recollection of Saṃgha
(4) recollection of virtue (*sīla*)
(5) recollection of generosity (*cāga*)
(6) recollection of *devatās*
(7) recollection of peace (*upasama*)
(8) avoidance of rough people (*lūkha-puggala*)
(9) association with affectionate people (*siniddha-puggala*)
(10) reflection on satisfying discourses (*pasādaniya-suttanta*)
(11) commitment to that

Conducive to the arising of the awakening-factor of tranquillity

(1) taking fine food (*paṇīta-bhojana-sevanatā*)
(2) living in a pleasant climate (*utu-sukha-sevanatā*)
(3) keeping a comfortable posture (*iriyā-patha-sukha-sevanatā*)
(4) maintaining balance (*majjhatta-payogatā*)
(5) avoidance of violent people (*sāraddha-kāya-puggala*)
(6) association with tranquil people (*passaddha-kāya-puggala*)
(7) commitment to that

Conducive to the arising of the awakening-factor of concentration

(1) keeping one's person and belongings clean
(2) balancing the faculties
(3) skill with regard to the sign (*nimitta-kusalatā*)
(4) appropriate application (*samaye paggahaṇatā*)
(5) appropriate easing off (*samaye niggahaṇatā*)
(6) appropriate encouragement (*samaye sampahaṃsanatā*)
(7) appropriate overseeing (*samaye ajjhupekkhanatā*)
(8) avoidance of unconcentrated people (*asamāhita-puggala*)
(9) association with concentrated people (*samāhita-puggala*)
(10) reflection on the *jhānas* and *vimokkhas*
(11) commitment to that

Conducive to the arising of the awakening-factor of equipoise

(1) balance with regard to beings (*satta-majjhattatā*)
(2) balance with regard to mental forces (*saṃkhāra-majjhattatā*)
(3) avoidance of people with bias with regard to beings and mental forces (*satta-saṃkhāra-kelāyana-puggala*)
(4) association with people with balance with regard to beings and mental forces (*satta-saṃkhāra-majjhatta-puggala*)
(5) commitment to that

CHAPTER SIX

THE NOBLE EIGHT-FACTORED PATH

1. General: the individual factors

I come now to the last of the seven sets, namely the *ariyo aṭṭhaṅgiko maggo* or 'noble eight-factored path'. In the course of my discussion of the *viveka-nissita* formula above, I have already drawn attention to the fact that most often in the Nikāyas the *ariyo aṭṭhaṅgiko maggo* is simply stated and itemized as a bare list:

> Just this is the noble eight-factored path, namely right view, right thought, right speech, right action, right livelihood, right striving, right mindfulness, right concentration.[1]

The *ariyo aṭṭhaṅgiko maggo* is stated in this way again and again in the Nikāyas—perhaps more than any other single list, and certainly more than any other of the seven sets. As a result it seems fair to say that the *ariyo aṭṭhaṅgiko maggo* appears less clearly associated with any one particular and definite formula than the other sets. It seems to stand more in its own right. But the factors of the path are also frequently listed quite apart from the expression *ariyo aṭṭhaṅgiko maggo*. In this connection the 'right' (*sammā*) factors are nearly always contrasted with the factors as 'wrong' (*micchā*); moreover two further items, right or wrong knowledge (*sammā-/micchā-ñāṇa*) and right or wrong freedom (*sammā-/micchā-vimutti*) are often added. If any one treatment is to be considered especially characteristic of the path-factors, then it should be this.

However, before embarking on a general consideration of the relevant passages, it is as well to review briefly the way in which each of the eight factors is defined in the Nikāyas. A straightforward treatment of this matter, termed 'analysis' (*vibhaṅga*), is given at several points in the Nikāyas.[2] This factor by factor analysis can be summarized as follows. Right view is knowledge concerning suffering (*dukkhe ñāṇaṃ*), its arising, its cessation and the way leading to its cessation—in other words it is knowledge concerning the four truths or realities (*sacca*) and is therefore presented as a species of wisdom. Right thought is of three kinds: thoughts of desirelessness (*nekkhamma*), thoughts of non-hatred (*avyāpāda*), thoughts of non-cruelty (*avihiṃsā*). Right

---

[1] *ayaṃ eva ariyo aṭṭhaṅgiko maggo seyyathīdaṃ sammā-diṭṭhi sammā-saṃkappo sammā-vācā sammā-kammanto sammā-ājīvo sammā-vāyāmo sammā-sati sammā-samādhi.* (For references see above, p. 163.) Once again a parallel list is also found in Buddhist Sanskrit sources: *tatra bhikṣavaḥ katama āryâṣṭâṅgo mārgaḥ. tad-yathā samyak-dṛṣṭiḥ samyak-saṃkalpaḥ samyag-vāk samyak-karmântaḥ samyag-ājīvaḥ samyag-vyāyāmaḥ samyak-smṛtiḥ samyak-samādhiḥ* (Artha Trsl 34-5). (For further references see Lamotte, *Traité*, III 1129.)

[2] D II 311; M III 251 (*Saccavibhaṅga-sutta*); S V 8-10 (*vibhaṅga*); the analysis is also found in the *Vibhaṅga* itself (Vibh 104-5, 235-6) and at Paṭis I 40-2. According to Lamotte (*Traité*, III 1130) an exact equivalent is not found in the Chinese Āgamas.

speech is refraining (*veramaṇī*) from false speech (*musā-vāda*), divisive speech (*pisuṇā vācā*), hurtful speech (*pharusā vācā*) and idle chatter (*sampha-ppalāpa*). Right action is refraining from attack on living beings (*pāṇātipāta*), taking what is not given (*adinnâdāna*) and non-celibacy (*abrahma-cariya*). Right livelihood is simply 'abandoning wrong livelihood and making a living by means of right livelihood' (*micchā-ājīvaṃ pahāya sammā-ājīvena jīvitaṃ kappeti*). Right striving is explained by the basic *samma-ppadhāna* formula, right mindfulness by the basic *satipaṭṭhāna* formula, and right concentration by the stock account of the four *jhānas*.

It is immediately obvious that the way the factors are explained and defined is intended to key into matters that are recurring themes in the Nikāyas, and that are dealt with at length in other contexts. Of course this is also true of the five faculties and powers—right view, striving, mindfulness and concentration are explained in almost precisely the same terms as are the faculties and powers of wisdom, strength, mindfulness and concentration. But it is also clear that the scope of the *ariyo aṭṭhaṅgiko maggo* is rather wider than that of the powers and faculties. Right thought, speech, action and livelihood bring in dimensions that, while omitted in the other sets, are certainly of considerable importance in the Nikāyas as a whole. The inclusion of right speech, action and livelihood, and the way these items are defined, explicitly brings in what elsewhere is summed up in the Nikāyas as 'morality', 'virtue' or 'conduct' (*sīla*). But as we shall see later, *sīla* is regularly given as the basis or foundation for the development of the seven sets individually and collectively.[3] This has the effect, then, of presenting the *ariyo aṭṭhaṅgiko maggo* as in some sense a more fully self-contained system than the other sets. The sense in which this is so will, I hope, become apparent in the course of this chapter. Since the four factors beginning with right thought are peculiar to the *ariyo aṭṭhaṅgiko maggo* it is necessary, first of all, to consider them a little further.

Right thought

The triad desirelessness (*nekkhamma*), non-hatred (*avyāpāda*) and non-cruelty (*avihiṃsā*) is found in a number of contexts in the Nikāyas, usually in opposition to the triad of sensual desire (*kāma*), hatred (*vyāpāda*) and cruelty (*vihiṃsā*).[4] In this connection these six terms are most regularly compounded with *vitakka*, but also with *saṃkappa*, *saññā* and *dhātu*. Not surprisingly the second triad is used on occasion to explain wrong thought (*micchā-saṃkappa*).[5] But what precisely are thoughts of desirelessness, non-hatred, and non-cruelty?

I have translated *nekkhamma* as 'desirelessness' largely because in the present context it stands in opposition to *kāma*. But the derivation of *nekkhamma* has been a matter of discussion.[6] *PED* (s.v. *nekkhamma*) opts for *naiṣkramya* as the derivation, which gives a meaning such as 'leaving behind' or 'renuncia-

---

3 See below, pp. 255-7.
4 D III 215; M I 114-6; II 26-8; S II 152-3; A II 137-8; III 429, 446-7.
5 M III 73; Vibh 86.
6 Cf. Masefield, op. cit., pp. 74-5.

tion'. This derivation seems to be supported by the occurrence of *naiṣkramya* (q.v., *BHSD*) in Buddhist Sanskrit texts. *PED* recognizes, however, that there is clearly semantic confusion with *niṣkāma* ('desireless'), and that *nekkhamma* may be a Middle Indo-Aryan form corresponding to an Old Indo-Aryan **naiṣkāmya*; but, it suggests, if this were the true derivation the form ought to be **nekkamma*. Presumably this is because we find Pāli *nikkāma* as the form apparently derived from *niṣkāma*. But this is surely rather inconclusive, for Pāli witnesses as derivatives from *niṣ-kram* both *nikkama* and *nikkamati* alongside *nikkhama* and *nikkhamati* (q.vv., *PED*). So there appears to be no clear reason for thinking *nekkhamma*—as well as **nekkamma*—cannot stand for **naiṣkāmya*. However, the Pāli commentaries explain *nekkhamma* as that which has 'turned away' or 'departed' (*nikkhanta*, *nissaṭa*) from greed or desire.[7] This might seem to indicate that they at least understood the term to be derived from *niṣ-kram*. But this is, I think, to misunderstand what the commentaries intend here. Now, *kāma* in the Nikāyas is used to mean both 'desire' and 'what is desirable'; this is equally true of *kāma* in Sanskrit. From the *Niddesa* onwards this distinction is expressed in terms of 'desire as defilement' (*kilesa-kāma*) and 'desire as object' (*vatthu-kāma*).[8] Strictly, then, that which is opposed to *kāma*, namely *nekkhamma*, ought to reflect this distinction. It seems to me that this is why the commentaries seize on the possibility of taking *nekkhamma* as 'turning away' or 'departing': *nekkhamma* is absence of desire because it turns away from desire, but it also turns away from what might be desired. In other words 'turning away' is offered not so much as the actual meaning of the term as an explanation of the effect of *nekkhamma*, of what it does. In sum, then, the opposition of *nekkhamma* to *kāma* is so clear in the present context that we must accept 'absence of desire' or 'desirelessness' as its primary significance.

A *Vibhaṅga* passage[9] dealing with *kāma-dhātu*, *vyāpāda-dhātu*, *vihiṃsā-dhātu*, *nekkhamma-dhātu*, *avyāpāda-dhātu* and *avihiṃsā-dhātu* brings out certain aspects of what has just been said. As the commentary makes clear,[10] what the *Vibhaṅga* does is offer two distinct ways of taking each of these six compounds. Thus *kāma-dhātu* is either a '*dhātu* connected with *kāma*' (*kāma-paṭisaṃyuttā dhātu*) or the '*dhātu* that is *kāma*' (*kāmo yeva dhātu*); the same two possibilities exist for the rest. With regard to the first method *dhātu* is to be taken as indicating 'thought' (*takka*, *vitakka*, *saṃkappa*); with regard to the second method it is to be taken as indicating '*dhammas*' or 'a *dhamma*'. In the case of *kāma-dhātu* and *nekkhamma-dhātu* there is also difference in the way in which *kāma* and *nekkhamma* are understood. According to the first method *kāma* is desire as active defilement (*kilesa-kāma*), according to the second it is the object of that desire (*vatthu-kāma*). So *kāma-dhātu* is either a 'thought connected with desire' or the totality of *dhammas* that make up the sense sphere since

[7] E.g. Ps II 79; Vibh-a 74, 117.
[8] Nidd I 1.
[9] Vibh 86-7.
[10] Vibh-a 74-6.

these are the objects of that same desire.[11] As for *nekkhamma-dhātu*, by the first method it means 'thought connected with *nekkhamma*' where *nekkhamma* can be taken either as non-greed or the first *jhāna*; by the second method it means '*dhammas* that make up *nekkhamma*', i.e. the totality of skilful *dhammas*.[12] This follows from the fact that all skilful consciousness is associated with non-greed and hence free of desire, as well as from the fact that skilful consciousness is what turns away from what is unskilful. So just as *kāma* is at once sense-desire and everything that might be the object of sense-desire, so *nekkhamma* is at once desirelessness and everything that turns away from those objects of sense-desire.

The explanation of the other four compounds is less involved, and it is only necessary to note just how the *Vibhaṅga* understands the terms *(a)vyāpāda* and *(a)vihiṃsā*. *Vyāpāda* is simply hate (*dosa*) and as such is defined by the same register of terms that is given for *dosa* in the *Dhammasaṅgaṇi*.[13] Consequently *avyāpāda* is taken as *adosa* and as 'loving-kindness' or 'friendliness' (*mettā*).[14] *Vihiṃsā* is more extreme than general hate. It is anger of such force that it causes one to inflict actual bodily harm.[15] Just as *avyāpāda* as general friendliness stands in opposition to *vyāpāda* as general unfriendliness, so *avihiṃsā*, understood as compassion (*karuṇā*), opposes the more specific *vihiṃsā*. The point is, it would seem, that confronted with others' suffering *vihiṃsā* is the state of mind that wants it to continue, and *avihiṃsā* the state of mind that wants it to cease.

But what precisely is *saṃkappa* (= Skt *saṃkalpa*)? The root *kḷp* means 'to be in order', 'to be capable', 'to be suitable'. A *saṃkalpa* is literally, then, a 'conforming', a '(suitable) arrangement or adaptation'. However, the word is regularly used of a clearly formed thought or idea; it thus conveys the sense of 'intention' or 'purpose'. One might say, then, that *saṃkappa* is the gearing of the mind to whatever is its object in a definite and particular way. By the time of the early Abhidhamma texts this is clearly identified with the technical term *vitakka*. The overriding connotation in this connection is that of the first *jhāna*-factor. Yet, as we have seen, the association of *vitakka* and *saṃkappa* is also present in the Nikāyas, though perhaps in a fashion that suggests a rather

---

11 Vibh-a 74: *kilesa-kāmaṃ sandhāya kāma-paṭisaṃyuttā dhātu kāma-dhātu; kāma-vitakkass' etaṃ nāmaṃ. vatthu-kāmaṃ sandhāya kāmo yeva dhātu kāma-dhātu; kāmâvacara-dhammānaṃ etaṃ nāmaṃ.*

12 Ibid.: *nekkhammaṃ vuccati lobhā nikkhantattā alobho. nīvaraṇehi nikkhantattā paṭhama-jjhānaṃ. sabbâkusalehi nikkhantattā sabba-kusalaṃ. nekkhamma-paṭisaṃyuttā dhātu nekkhamma-dhātu; nekkhamma-vitakkass'etaṃ nāmaṃ. nekkhammaṃ eva dhātu nekkhamma-dhātu; sabbassâpi kusalass'etaṃ nāmaṃ.* (It is clear at Vibh 86 that *nekkhamma* as *sabbe kusalā dhammā* is restricted to the second method.)

13 Vibh 86; cf. Dhs 84, 189.

14 Vibh 86; cf. Dhs 13, 189.

15 Vibh 86: 'Here someone injures beings by various means—with his hands, with a stone, a stick, a sword, or a rope. Such injuring, severe injuring, cruelty, severe cruelty, hostility, severe hostility, such onslaught is called *vihiṃsā-dhātu*.' (*idh'ekacco paṇinā vā leddunā va daṇḍena vā satthena vā rajjuyā vā aññataraññatarena satte viheṭheti. yā evarūpā heṭhanā viheṭhanā hiṃsanā vihiṃsanā rosanā virosanā parūpaghāto, ayaṃ vuccati vihiṃsā-dhātu.*)

looser connection.[16] The general idea seems to be, then, that *saṃkappa* is equivalent to the way in which the mind applies itself to or thinks of various objects. Wrong thought turns towards various objects with thoughts and ideas of desire, hatred, or cruelty; right thought turns towards various objects with thoughts and ideas that are free of desire, friendly and compassionate.

A point of interest here is that we might have expected to find *moha-saṃkappa/amoha-saṃkappa* in place of *vihiṃsā-saṃkappa/avihiṃsā-saṃkappa*—the triad of greed, hate and delusion is after all normative in Buddhist thought.[17] Why does hate feature in this double fashion? The answers seems to be because *sammā-saṃkappa* is seen as the complement to *sammā-diṭṭhi*. It would be both inappropriate and unnecessary to bring in 'thoughts of wisdom' in the context of right view:

> Endowed with four *dhammas*, *bhikkhus*, a *bhikkhu* has entered upon the way that is excellent, and the birth of the destruction of the *āsavas* is begun for him. With which four? With thoughts of desirelessness, thoughts of non-hatred, thoughts of non-cruelty, and right view.[18]

Finally, the early Abhidhamma defines *sammā-saṃkappa* as 'thinking of, continued thinking of, thought, fixing upon, continued fixing upon, absorption of the mind, right thought'.[19] It is tempting to see in this sequence a progressive intensity. Thus wrong thought ranges from thoughts and desires that only subtly tend to desire, hatred or cruelty, to thoughts and ideas that are absorbed in and obsessed with these; right thought ranges from thoughts and ideas that only subtly tend to desirelessness, non-hatred or non-cruelty, to thoughts and ideas absorbed in and fully given to these.

Right speech, action and livelihood

The seven items included under right speech and action in the analysis of the eight path-factors turn out to constitute the core of the Nikāya account of *sīla*.[20] As such they comprise four of the five basic precepts,[21] and in principle

---

[16] M II 28, however, states that *kusala-saṃkappa* (consisting of *nekkhamma-*, *avyāpāda-*, *avihiṃsā-saṃkappa*) ceases without remainder in the second *jhāna*, which, of course, precisely lacks *vitakka* (and *vicāra*).

[17] Cf. YS II 33-4 which mentions *vitarkas* preceded by greed, anger or delusion (*lobha-krodha-moha-purvaka*), and how the yogin is to develop their opposites.

[18] A II 76: *catuhi bhikkhave dhammehi samannāgato bhikkhu apaṇṇakataṃ paṭipadaṃ paṭipanno hoti yoni cassa āraddhā hoti āsavānaṃ khayāya. katamehi catuhi. nekkhamma-vitakkena avyāpāda-vitakkena avihiṃsā-vitakkena sammā-diṭṭhiyā.*

[19] Eg. Dhs 12: *takko vitakko saṃkappo appanā vyappanā cetaso abhiniropanā sammā-saṃkappo.* (For the corresponding definition of *micchā-saṃkappo* see e.g. Dhs 78).

[20] In the *sīlakkhandha-vagga* of the *Dīgha* they account for the principal part of the *cūḷa-sīla* (D I 1-4, etc.; cf. M I 179-80, 267, 345). The items are also mentioned in many other contexts (e.g. M I 286-7, 360-2, 489-90; III 23-4, 209; S IV 313-4; A I 297-8; II 254-5).

[21] See D I 146; III 195, 235; M III 170-1, 254; A II 99, 217. Of the five, *surā-meraya-majja-pamāda-ṭṭhānā veramaṇī-sikkhā-padaṃ* is not accounted for; occasionally this appears to be unincluded in the basic list (e.g. M III 47). The other four appear to be part of the common yogic heritage; cf. the definition of *yama* at YS II 29 and the *anuvratas* of Jaina tradition (see P.S. Jaini, *The Jaina Path of Purification*, Berkley, 1979, pp. 170-8).

the four *pārājika* offences involving defeat for the *bhikkhu*.[22] The notion of right livelihood appears rather less specific. A recurring refrain of the *mahā-sīla* of the *sīlakkhandha-vagga* of the *Dīgha* is as follows:

> Whereas some *samaṇas* and *brāhmaṇas*, while enjoying food given in trust, make a living by means of the wrong livelihood of animal arts such as ... he [i.e. the *samaṇa* Gotama/the noble disciple] refrains from the wrong livelihood of such animal arts.[23]

A whole series of examples of making a living by means of the wrong livelihood of animal arts is then given. What is being questioned here is not so much the 'animal arts' themselves as their appropriateness in the context of the life of one who is living on food provided by those of confidence. These examples, as far as they are intelligible, all involve providing some definite service for some other party which is accomplished by a special knowledge or art. No doubt behind this lies the historical reality of various ancient Indian 'holy men' living in precisely this way, namely receiving alms in return for offering the service of their special knowledges and arts. But, according to the present passage, this is not the job of the 'true' *samaṇa* and *brāhmaṇa*. On the contrary, he enjoys the food given by those of confidence and trust not as payment, but only in so far as it supports the fulfilling of the spiritual life.

Much the same idea is found expressed in slightly different terms elsewhere in the Nikāyas. Thus it is said that a person who enjoys alms and the other requisites provided out of confidence and trust by *khattiyas*, *brāhmaṇas* and householders, and yet is someone of bad character (*dussīlo pāpa-dhammo*), of unclean and rotten conduct, of secret deeds, not a *samaṇa* although pretending to be a *samaṇa* (*assamaṇo samaṇa-paṭiñño*), not a celibate although pretending to be a celibate (*abrahma-cārī brahma-cārī-paṭiñño*), putrid, rotten, decayed—such a person will, at the breaking up of the body, after death arise in one of the places of regress (*apāya*).[24] On the other hand if a *bhikkhu* for just a finger snap (*accharā-saṃghāta*) should develop the first *jhāna*, or any other spiritual attainment, then he can truly be called a monk; his *jhāna* is not in vain, he carries out the teacher's instruction, takes his advice; his eating of the country's alms food is not in vain.[25]

The *Majjhima* version of the stage by stage account of the path corresponding

---

22 Sexual intercourse, taking what is not given, intentional killing of a human being, falsely claiming spiritual attainments. Considerable space is devoted in the *Vinaya* to defining the precise circumstances that constitute an infringement.

23 D I 9-12 (passim), 67-9 (passim): *yathā vā pan'eke bhonto samaṇa-brāhmaṇā saddhā-deyyāni bhojanāni bhuñjitvā te evarūpāya tiracchana-vijjāya micchâjīvena jīvikaṃ kappenti ... iti vā iti evarūpāya tiracchana-vijjāya micchâjīvā paṭivirato hoti.* (There are seven paragraphs to the *mahā-sīla*, each containing this sentence; curiously at both D I 9-12 and 67-9 *micchâjīva* is absent from the final phrase in the first two paragraphs; Rhys Davids offers no comment but translates as if it was absent in all seven paragraphs (D Trsl I 16-26: 'Gotama the recluse holds aloof from such low arts'); Buddhaghosa makes no comment, Ce (1962) I 16, however, includes *micchâjīva* in these two paragraphs.)

24 See A IV 128-35.

25 See A I 38-43 (quoted more fully below, p. 268). With regard to this matter generally cf. Sn 12-5 where the Buddha refuses food that is offered as a result of recitation of verses; in terms of the *mahā-sīla* this would appear to be *kāveyya* (D I 11).

to the *sāmañña-phala* schema uses a somewhat truncated form of the *cūḷa-* and *majjhima-sīlas*. The material that comes under the *mahā-sīla* in the *Dīgha* account is omitted. Presumably this is because it is thought of as assumed in what has already been stated. Thus the completed account of *sīla* (the term does not actually occur) here explains the expression 'he is one who has accomplished the training and common mode of livelihood of *bhikkhus*' (*bhikkhūnaṃ sikkhā-sâjīva-samāpanno*).[26] For the *bhikkhu* the sum of his conduct constitutes his livelihood.

At this point the discussion of the nature of *ājīva* in the *Atthasālinī* is of some interest.[27] This points out that *ājīva* inevitably consists of acts of speech and of body. However, skilful or unskilful acts of speech and body do not always constitute livelihood. For example, for one who lives by killing (i.e. killing beings is directly or indirectly his means of subsistence) there is both wrong action (killing beings) and wrong livelihood (living by killings beings). But for one who occasionally kills for reasons of, say, sport there is only wrong action. While this works well enough in the case of the layman, if we extend these principles to the life of the *bhikkhu* it is not at all clear how, even theoretically, one might distinguish between those acts of speech and body which constitute a means of livelihood and those which do not. In other words, for one living on alms and devoted to the spiritual life all acts of speech and body tend to become livelihood, for the spiritual life itself is his 'livelihood'.

Finally, in connection with right speech, action and livelihood, a brief comment is necessary concerning their nature as conceived in the Abhidhamma literature. According to the Nikāya formulation, will or volition (*cetanā*) constitutes action (*kamma*); having willed one performs actions by body, speech and mind.[28] This ought to mean that wrong speech, action and livelihood, and right speech, action and livelihood are essentially manifestations of mental will or volition. Up to a point this seems to be accepted as so in Abhidhamma.[29] That is to say, when volition extends to a full course of action (*kamma-patha*, *kiriyā-patha*) then it is fulfilled in actions of body and speech. However, the Pāli Abhidhamma texts understand that in the case of right speech, action and livelihood there is a little more to this. Taking up the Nikāya definitions of right speech, action and livelihood in terms of refraining (*veramaṇī*) and abandoning (*pahāya*) the *Dhammasaṅgaṇi* lists three *dhammas* that are distinct from *cetanā*;[30] these are referred to in the commentaries as the three abstinences (*virati*). Thus at the time of right speech, action and livelihood there is not only the skilful volition that manifests in this way, there is also in the mind a force that actively abstains, withdraws and refrains from wrong speech, action and livelihood.[31]

---

[26] M I 179, 267, 345.

[27] As 220-1.

[28] See A III 415: *cetanâhaṃ bhikkhave kammaṃ vadāmi. cetayitvā kammaṃ karoti kāyena vācāya manasā*. (Cf. Abhidh-k 191.)

[29] On this whole question see As 89-90, 218-21.

[30] Dhs 63-4.

[31] Mp II 71 comments: 'Right speech, etc., are three kinds of abstinence and also volition, but

One of the points at issue here is the understanding that the eight path-factors occur as a unit at the time of the arising of the transcendent path consciousness. In meditation states of this kind there is no action by body or speech, only action by mind.[32] The notion of the three *viratis* allowed the Theravādin system to overcome this difficulty. The Sarvāstivādins tackled the same problem with the notion of 'non-communicative form' (*avijñapti-rūpa*).[33] According to the Sarvāstivādins meditation attainments and communicative acts of body and speech (*kāya-vijñapti*, *vāg-vijñapti*) produce a kind of form that is unmanifest or non-communicative, and which, although it shares none of the other characteristics of form, nevertheless exists dependent on the four great elements (*mahā-bhūta*). One of the functions of this kind of form in the Sarvāstivādin system appears, then, to be to explain how particular actions of body and speech (and mind) continue to exercise a precise influence—either wholesome or unwholesome—after their occurrence. Since right speech, action and livelihood are incompatible with meditation (*samādhi*) they can only operate as factors of the transcendent path (a meditation attainment) by virtue of their producing *avijñapti*.[34]

2. *The Bārāṇasī discourse and the middle way*

Outside traditional Buddhist cultures the *ariyo aṭṭhaṅgiko maggo* is probably one of the most familiar aspects of Buddhist teaching. Unfortunately the corrollary of this is probably that it is one of the most widely misunderstood. This is perhaps excusable given that the treatment of the *ariyo aṭṭhaṅgiko maggo* in the Nikāyas and early Abhidhamma is both extensive and complex. What is less excusable is that the fact of this treatment is effectively passed over in nearly all available accounts of early Buddhist thought. Our understanding thus gets little beyond a basic familiarity with the eight factors of the path, together with the notion that these can be related to the threefold scheme of virtue, concentration and wisdom (of which more below).

While it is apparent that the *ariyo aṭṭhaṅgiko maggo* features extensively in early Buddhist literature, the immediate source of our familiarity with it is that, along with the four noble truths, it is held in Buddhist tradition to have formed the substance of the Buddha's first discourse outside Bārāṇasī. The assumption in modern writings appears to have been that if one wants a short introduction to the essentials of the Buddha's teaching, then his first discourse is a suitable place to look. The kind of attitude to the Bārāṇasī discourse involved here is well illustrated by the following statement by Frauwallner:

> The sermon of Benares with its preaching of the eightfold path stands in the beginning of his teaching activity. In it he presents the simple basic thoughts which

---

at the moment of path they are just abstinences.' (*sammā-vācâdayo tayo viratiyo pi honti cetanāyo pi; magga-kkhaṇe pana viratiyo va.*) Cf. also below, pp. 214-5.

32 Though the question of whether speech might occur at such times appears to have been a point of discussion; cf. Bareau, *SBPV*; Kv 195-203.

33 See Abhidh-k. Cf. H.V. Guenther, *PPA*, pp. 162-3.

34 Abhidh-k 196: *aṣṭâṅgaś ca na syād avijñaptim antareṇa, samāpannasya samyag-vāk-karmânt-âjīvānām ayogāt.*

> had become an irrefutable certainly to him in the hour of his illumination. It is intelligible that here he gives basic directives in general words. Then followed forty long years of his wandering life as a teacher and preacher. Again and again it turned out necessary to give more exact guidance and instructions to disciples. And thus the preaching of the Deliverance-way was continually more and more improved and widened and became more finished until finally it gained the form with which we have got acquainted above [i.e the *sāmañña-phala* schema].[35]

This appears almost naively historical, and no doubt other scholars would wish to question the extent to which the Bārāṇasī discourse of tradition can be regarded as an accurate record of an historical event.[36] But it is not primarily the historical accuracy of the contents of discourse that concerns us here. Modern western scholarship's interest in the first discourse of the Buddha has no doubt been connected with the idea that to know the original form of something is to know its essence. But this is hardly the reasoning that underlies the importance of the first discourse in Buddhist tradition. To be sure, Buddhist tradition would not deny that the Bārāṇasī discourse does contain the essentials of the Buddha's teaching. But then in this respect the tradition would not see it as any different from many, if not all, other discourses. What is special for the tradition about the Bārāṇasī discourse is precisely and simply that it is the first discourse—the discourse that sets the wheel of *dhamma* rolling (*dhamma-cakka-ppavattana*). To be too concerned with the question of the discourse as a historical record is, I think, to misconstrue its 'mythological' import. In evaluating its contents what we need to do is consider carefully the particular context in which the tradition places the discourse. Once this is done it is apparent, I think, that at least as far as the tradition is concerned the Bārāṇasī discourse should not be seen, as Frauwallner suggests, as 'basic directives in general words', but precisely as 'exact guidance and instruction to disciples'.

The first discourse of the Buddha is addressed to a group of five *bhikkhus* who are described in the tradition as having spent some time living in close association with Gotama prior to his full awakening. In choosing to address just these five first, the Buddha is said to have had in mind that there are beings with weak faculties and beings with sharp faculties; the latter are ready to see, ready for awakening. These five must be regarded, then, as ready for the special teaching of Buddhas. The clue to the specific nature of the Bārāṇasī discourse seems to lie in the presentation of the *ariyo aṭṭhaṅgiko maggo* as the middle way (*majjhima paṭipadā*) between the two extremes (*anta*) of devotion to sensual pleasure (*kāmesu kāma-sukhallikânuyogo)* and devotion to self-torment (*atta-kilamathânuyoga*). For the discourse is addressed precisely to the

---

[35] Frauwallner, *HIP*, p. 148.

[36] A. Bareau has compared the different recensions of the Buddha's first discourse (see *RBB* I 172-82) and is of the opinion that the definition of the two extremes and the 'middle way' is the older part, while the section dealing with the four truths is later. He points out that the *Majjhima* version of the corresponding events (M I 172-3) gives no indication of the contents of the first discourse, and suggests that the text of the first discourse as recorded in the three *Vinaya* recensions is 'non seulement apocryphe mais assez tardif' (p. 180); there was a point at which the Buddha's followers simply did not know what the theme of the first discourse had been.

bhikkhus who, when the *bodhisatta* gave up the practice of severe austerities (*kaṭukā dukkāra-kārikā*)[37] and took proper food, became disillusioned with him: 'The *samaṇa* Gotama is a man of excess, he has given up endeavour, he has lapsed into excess.'[38] This is represented as still being their attitude to him when he approaches them in the animal park.[39] In direct response the Buddha begins his first discourse:

> There are these two extremes, *bhikkhus*, which are not to be pursued by one who has gone forth. Which two? First, that which is devotion to sensual pleasure with regard to the objects of sensual desire—this is inferior, vulgar, of the ordinary man, not noble, not concerned with what is beneficial. Secondly, that which is devotion to self-torment—this is painful, not noble, not concerned with what is beneficial. Not following these two extremes, the Tathāgata awakened to the middle way which brings sight, knowledge and conduces to peace, direct knowledge, awakening, *nibbāna*. And which is the middle way ... ? It is just the noble eight-factored path, namely right view, right thought, right speech, right action, right livelihood, right striving, right mindfulness and right concentration.[40]

The point is, then, that this is addressed to five *bhikkhus* who are presented as committed to the view that the spiritual life consists in the wholehearted rejection of pleasure and a strict adherence to severe asceticism and self-torment. If Bronkhorst's ideas concerning the two traditions of meditation in ancient India[41] are at all correct, then one of the things the Bārāṇasī discourse appears to do is to present a kind of apologetic and polemic in one. What is taught by the Buddha is truly a spiritual life (*brahma-cariya*) in that it is free of vulgar sensual indulgence, on the other hand it is distinct from what Bronkhorst characterizes as the old severely ascetic main stream meditation tradition. From the point of view of the Bārāṇasī discourse, this is now superseded by the new middle way. What is important about the first discourse is the 'middleness' of what the Buddha teaches. From this point of view, the *ariyo aṭṭhaṅgiko maggo* is laregly incidental to the discourse. True the eight-factored path here represents the 'middle way', but this is simply because, as we shall see, the *ariyo aṭṭhaṅgiko maggo* often in the Nikāyas epitomizes the totality of the spiritual life as taught by the Buddha, and not because it is the middle way *per se*.

What I have just said seems to be borne out by the fact that when we turn to the Nikāyas as a whole the theme of the *ariyo aṭṭhaṅgiko maggo* as the middle way between sensual indulgence and self-torment is not especially outstanding. Aside from the first discourse, the middle way between sensual indulgence and

---

[37] M I 246.

[38] M I 247 = II 93 = 212: *yato kho ahaṃ oḷārikaṃ āhāraṃ āhāresiṃ odana-kummāsaṃ atha me te pañca bhikkhū nibbijjâpakkamiṃsu: bāhuliko samaṇo Gotamo padhāna-vibbhanto āvatto bāhullāyā ti.*

[39] M I 171; Vin I 8-9.

[40] Vin I 10 = S V 421: *dve'me bhikkhave antā pabbajitena na sevitabbā. katame dve. yo câyaṃ kāmesu kāma-sukhallikânuyogo hīno gammo puthujjaniko anariyo anattha-saṃhito. yo câyaṃ atta-kilamathânuyogo dukkho anariyo anattha-saṃhito. ete te bhikkhave ubho ante anupakamma majjhimā paṭipadā tathāgatena abhisambuddhā cakkhu-karaṇī ñāṇa-karaṇī upasamāya abhiññāya sambodhāya nibbānāya saṃvattati. katama ca sā bhikkhave majjhimā paṭipadā ... ayaṃ eva ariyo aṭṭhaṅgiko maggo seyyathīdaṃ sammā-diṭṭhi ... sammā-samādhi.*

[41] See above, pp. 180-1.

self-torment appears to be mentioned in only four passages. Only two of these concern the *ariyo aṭṭhaṅgiko maggo* exclusively; these are the *Araṇavibhaṅga-sutta* and a *Saṃyutta-nikāya* passage both of which describe the eight-factored path as the 'middle way' in exactly the same terms as the Bārāṇasī discourse.[42]

Of particular interest from the point of view of the present study is an *Aṅguttara* passage[43] that details three 'ways' (*paṭipadā*): that of indulgence (*āgāḷhā*), that of burning away (*nijjhāmā*) and lastly the middle way. Although not described in precisely the same terms, the first two clearly correspond to the devotion to sensual pleasure and the devotion to self-torment of the Bārāṇasī discourse.[44] However, the middle way is here illustrated not in the first instance by the *ariyo aṭṭhaṅgiko maggo*, but by the short *satipaṭṭhāna* formula. The three ways are then detailed again, the first two as before, but the middle way is this time illustrated by the basic *samma-ppadhāna* formula. The text continues, rehearsing the material five more times and illustrating the middle way by the *iddhi-pādas*, *indriyas*, *balas*, *bojjhaṅgas* and *ariyo aṭṭhaṅgiko maggo* in turn. This is not, I think, because the compiler or compilers of this *sutta* were uncertain about which of the seven sets truly represented the middle way,[45] but because, just as the *ariyo aṭṭhaṅgiko maggo* represented the totality of the spiritual life as taught by the Buddha, so too, at least by the close of the Nikāya period, did the seven sets.

Towards the end of the *Dhammadāyāda-sutta* the *ariyo aṭṭhaṅgiko maggo* is again termed the 'middle way'. But this time not in relationship to the extremes of sensual indulgence and self-torment:

> Greed is bad, hatred is bad; for the abandoning of greed and for the abandoning of hate there is the middle way ... This is just the noble eight-factored path ... [46]

Elsewhere other pairs of extremes are made quite explicit. In the *nidāna-saṃyutta* the Buddha comments on the extremes of 'all exists' (*sabbaṃ atthi*) and 'nothing exists' (*sabbaṃ natthi*), and of eternalism (*sassata*) and annihilationism (*uccheda*) in terms reminiscent of the Bārāṇasī discourse: 'not following either of these extremes the Tathāgata teaches *dhamma* by the middle' (*ete te ubho ante anupagamma majjhena tathāgato dhammaṃ deseti*).[47] The 'middle' in question is the sequence of terms that constitutes conditioned arising (*paṭicca-*

---

[42] See M III 230-1; S IV 330-1.

[43] A I 295-7.

[44] The *āgāḷhā paṭipadā* is defined as *ekacco evaṃ vādī hoti evaṃ diṭṭhi natthi kāmesu doso so kāmesu pātavyataṃ āpajjati*; the *nijjhāmā paṭipadā* is illustrated by a long list of severe practices (cf. D I 166-7 where similar practices are described).

[45] Cf. C.A.F. Rhys Davids, *JRAS*, 1932, p. 124.

[46] M I 15: *tatrâvuso lobho ca pāpako doso ca pāpako, lobhassa ca pahanāya dosassa ca pahanāya atthi majjhimā paṭipadā ... ayaṃ eva ariyo aṭṭhaṅgiko maggo* ... (Ps I 104 comments: 'Greed is one extreme, hate is the other extreme and the path does not follow or approach these two extremes; it is free of these extremes therefore "middle way" is said.' (*maggo hi lobho eko anto doso eko anto ti ete dve ante na upeti na upagacchati mutto etehi antehi tasmā majjhimā paṭipadā ti vuccati.*) However, the *sutta* goes on to repeat the same formula with seven more pairs of terms that do not seem to form extremes in the way that *lobha* and *dosa* do. The commentary gives rather a full explanation of the psychology of the terms in question (see Ps I 106-7; cf. Vibh 350, 353-6, 357-8) but there is no comment specifically on this point.)

[47] S II 17, 20, 75-6, 76-7.

samuppāda). This 'middle' would seem to be rather more significant for the subsequent development of Buddhist thought than the specific notion of the *ariyo aṭṭhaṅgiko maggo* as the middle way between sensual indulgence and self-torment. Certainly in Nāgārjuna's *Mūlamadhyamakakārikās* it is conditioned arising that appears to represent the 'middle way' *par excellence*.[48] Of course, Nāgārjuna leads one to the conclusion that all dilemmas between two extremes, all 'middle ways', are in a sense the same, and this would not seem to be an improper understanding of the Nikāyas.[49] In conclusion one can say that it is the Buddha's teaching in general that is taken as a 'middle', and that the notion of the *ariyo aṭṭhaṅgiko maggo* as the middle way between sensual indulgence and self-torment is a specific application of the general principle, and there appear to be no grounds for thinking it to be the original or earliest manifestation of the principle.

3. The way leading to the cessation of suffering

After the exposition of the 'middle way' the first discourse of the Buddha continues with an exposition of the four noble truths. Again the *ariyo aṭṭhaṅgiko maggo* is mentioned. This time it explains the nature of the fourth of the noble truths or realities: the way leading to the cessation of suffering (*dukkha-nirodha-gāminī paṭipadā*).[50] This proves to be a theme that is taken up and reiterated again and again throughout the Nikāyas, and would seem to be rather more fundamental and of more general significance than the theme of the eight-factored path as the 'middle way'. In all the *ariyo aṭṭhaṅgiko maggo* explains the fourth truth explicitly some seven times in the Nikāyas.[51] While this is not in itself excessive, the extent to which the theme is played upon is certainly striking. I refer here to passages that, while not explicitly referring to the *ariya-saccas* by name nor necessarily to *dukkha*, *samudaya*, *nirodha* and *magga*, nevertheless exploit the 'pattern' of the truths by taking some item and considering its arising, its cessation and the way leading to its cessation. A good example of this is the *Sammādiṭṭhi-sutta*.[52] In construction this is basically a sixteenfold exposition of the four truths, beginning with the unskiful (cf. first truth), the root of the unskilful (cf. second truth), the skilful (cf. third truth) and the root of the skilful (cf. fourth truth)—which is said to be the *ariyo aṭṭhaṅgiko maggo*. Fifteen items follow (mostly taken from the *paṭicca-samuppāda* formula);[53] in each case the arising, cessation and the way leading to the cessation of the item is considered, and in each case the way

---

[48] As A.K. Warder points out ('Is Nāgārjuna a Mahāyānist?' in *The Problem of Two Truths in Buddhism and Vedānta*, ed. M. Sprung, pp. 79, 81) the most frequently quoted and important canonical text for Nāgārjuna appears to be the *nidāna-saṃyukta*.

[49] Cf. Ps I 104.

[50] Vin I 10 = S V 421-2.

[51] Vin I 10; D II 311; M III 251; S V 421-2, 424, 425; A I 177; cf. Vibh 104.

[52] M I 48-55.

[53] They are *āhāra*, *dukkha*, *jarā-maraṇa*, *jāti*, *bhava*, *upādāna*, *taṇhā*, *vedanā*, *phassa*, *saḷāyatana*, *nāma-rūpa*, *viññāṇa*, *saṃkhāra*, *avijjā*, *āsavas*.

leading to the cessation is given as the *ariyo aṭṭhaṅgiko maggo*. Similar variations are scattered throughout the Nikāyas.[54]

In the *magga-saṃyutta* the theme of the *ariyo-aṭṭhaṅgiko maggo* as the way to the cessation of *dukkha* is continually expressed in other ways. The eight-factored path is the way to the full understanding of suffering (*ayaṃ maggo ayaṃ paṭipadā etassa dukkhassa pariññāya*).[55] Developed and made great the eight factors are eight *dhammas* that lead to *nibbāna*, proceed to *nibbāna*, conclude in *nibbāna* (*atth'ime dhammā bhāvitā bahulīkatā nibbāna-gamā honti nibbāna-parāyanā nibbāna-pariyosānā*).[56] The conclusion (*pariyosāna*) of the eight-factored path is also expressed as the destruction (*khaya*) or restraint (*vinaya*) of passion (*rāga*), hatred (*dosa*) and delusion (*moha*);[57] its four fruits are those of stream-attainment, once-return, non-return and *arahant*-ship;[58] it is to be developed for the sake of abandoning the five kinds of sensual desire;[59] its eight factors conduce to going from this shore to the far shore (*apārā pāraṃ gamanāya saṃvattanti*).[60] In other words, the *ariyo aṭṭhaṅgiko maggo* brings one to the conclusion, the goal of the spiritual life. This general theme is also rehearsed elsewhere in the Nikāyas. A distinctive example is a *Saṃyutta* variation on the well known raft simile; here the eight-factored path itself is directly likened to the raft for crossing a river in flood.[61]

Some of these formulas and ways of looking at the *ariyo aṭṭhaṅgiko maggo* are common to all seven sets—especially in the *mahā-vagga* of the *Saṃyutta-nikāya*.[62] Yet, it is surely true that in the case of the *ariyo aṭṭhaṅgiko maggo* this kind of treatment is rather more thoroughgoing. Indeed it would seem that it is in part precisely by association with the *ariyo aṭṭhaṅgiko maggo* that the other sets are treated in a parallel fashion. Thus it is that the seven sets come collectively to be the 'path'. For the *ariyo aṭṭhaṅgiko maggo* is obviously the essential 'path' or 'way' in an explicit sense that none of the other sets can quite match.

Accordingly the *ariyo aṭṭhaṅgiko maggo* is presented in the *mahā-vagga* of the *Saṃyutta-nikāya* as the spiritual life in its entirety: it actually is *brahma-cariya*; it is *brāhmaṇa*-ship (*brāhmañña*), it is *samaṇa*-ship (*sāmañña*).[63] The point is vividly put in a passage that likens the *ariyo aṭṭhaṅgiko maggo* to the covered chariot of the *brāhmaṇa* Jānusoṇi.[64] Seeing his chariot people think it

---

[54] Cf. S II 42-3 (based on *paṭicca-samuppāda* terms again); M I 299 = S III 159 (*sakkāya-nirodha-gāminī paṭipadā*; cf. S III 86); S III 59-61 (*rūpa-*, *vedanā-*, *saññā-*, *saṃkhāra-*, *viññāṇa-nirodha-gāminī paṭipadā*); S IV 132-3 (*kamma-*), 220-3, 233 (*vedanā-*); A III 411-6 (*kāma-*, *vedanā-*, *saññā-*, *āsava-*, *kamma-*, *dukkha-nirodha-gāminī paṭipadā*).

[55] S V 6-7; cf. 21-2, 23-4.

[56] S V 11-2.

[57] S V 5-6, 8, 16-7, 25-7, 31-2, 34-5, 37-8, 40, 42, 58-62.

[58] S V 25-6; cf. D I 157 which adds the destruction of the *āsavas*.

[59] S V 22.

[60] S V 24-5; (on this phrase cf. *CPD*, s.v. *apāra*).

[61] S IV 172-5 (the more familiar passage is M I 134-5). For further examples of the general theme cf. D I 165; M I 118; S IV 251-62; A I 180, 217; IV 348; V 318.

[62] See below, Chapter 7.5.

[63] See S V 7-8, 15-7, 25-7.

[64] S V 4-6.

a most 'divine' vehicile (*brahmaṃ vata bho yānaṃ*), similarly in the *dhamma-vinaya* of the Buddha the eight-factored path is a 'divine' vehicle (*brahma-yāna*), a vehicle of *dhamma* (*dhamma-yāna*), unsurpassedly victorious in battle (*anuttaro saṃgāma-vijayo*).

The way in which the *ariyo aṭṭhaṅgiko maggo* is seen as embracing the spiritual life in its fullness is, I think, one of the most significant aspects of its treatment in the Nikāyas. Comparison with the *bojjhaṅgas*, for example, indicates quite clearly what is distinctive. Like the *bojjhaṅga-saṃyutta*, the *magga-saṃyutta* also contains a number of passages concerning the interaction of the followers of the Buddha with wanderers belonging to other schools.[65] But in the *magga-saṃyutta* the wanderers are not represented as claiming that they too teach the *ariyo aṭṭhaṅgiko maggo* and therefore wanting to know the difference between the Buddha's teaching and their own. Their question is rather more fundamental. For what purpose, they ask, is the spiritual life lived under the *samaṇa* Gotama (*kiṃ atthiyaṃ āvuso samaṇe Gotame brahma-cariyaṃ vussati*)? The answer is that it is lived for the sake of the full understanding of suffering (*dukkhassa pariññatthaṃ*).[66] When the wanderers go on to ask whether or not there is a path (*maggo*) or way (*paṭipadā*) to such full understanding, the response is that there is the *ariyo aṭṭhaṅgiko maggo*. Here, then, is the basic problem that the teaching of the Buddha is seen as addressing, namely *dukkha*; and the *ariyo aṭṭhaṅgiko maggo* is the straightforward solution, complete in itself. So the eight-factored path, as the essence of the spiritual life, acts as the thread that runs through the Nikāyas: 'Formerly and also now, *bhikkhus*, I make known just suffering and the cessation of suffering.'[67] Accordingly, one of the five 'great dreams' (*mahā-supina*) that the *bodhisatta* has is that a *tiriyā* creeper grows up from his navel reaching the sky (*tiriyā nāma tiṇa-jāti nābhiyā uggantvā nābhaṃ ahacca ṭhitā ahosi*); this dream is said to be fulfilled in the fact that the *ariyo aṭṭhaṅgiko maggo*, having been awakened to by the Tathāgata, is well proclaimed by him to *devas* and men.[68]

The *brahma-cariya* of the *ariyo aṭṭhaṅgiko maggo*, the spiritual practice that is full and complete, stands in contrast to *brahma-cariya* that is somehow incomplete:

> At that time I was the *brāhmaṇa* Mahāgovinda. I taught my pupils the path to communion with the world of Brahmā. But that *brahma-cariya*, Pañcasikha, did not conduce to disenchantment, to dispassion, to cessation, to peace, to direct knowledge, to full awakening, to *nibbāna*, but only as far as rebirth in the world of Brahmā. But now my *brahma-cariya* conduces to complete disenchantment, to dispassion, to cessation, to peace, to direct knowledge, to full awakening, to *nibbāna*. This is just the noble eight-factored path, namely right view ... right concentration.[69]

---

65 S V 6-7, 27-9.

66 S V 6; S V 27-9 gives a series of eight different but more or less equivalent responses.

67 M I 140: *pubbe câhaṃ bhikkhave etarahi ca dukkhañ c'eva paññāpemi dukkhassa ca nirodhaṃ*.

68 A III 240-2.

69 D II 251: *ahaṃ tena samayena Mahāgovindo brāhmaṇo ahosiṃ ahaṃ tesaṃ sāvakānaṃ brahma-loka-sahavyatāya maggaṃ desesiṃ. taṃ kho pana Pañcasikha brahma-cariyaṃ na nibbidāya*

Again the *ariyo aṭṭhaṅgiko maggo* is the yardstick against which all spiritual practice should be reckoned. When the wanderer Subhadda tries to draw the Buddha on the status of Pūraṇa Kassapa's and other teachers' understanding, the Buddha responds:

> Enough, Subhadda, leave aside this question of whether all who claim direct knowledge for themselves really have not had direct knowledge, or whether some have and some have not. I shall teach you *dhamma*, Subhadda. Hear it, pay careful attention, I shall speak ... Now in the *dhamma-vinaya* where the noble eight-factored path is not found, there too the *samaṇa* is not found, there too the second ... the third ... the fourth *samaṇa* is not found. But in the *dhamma-vinaya* where the noble eight-factored path is found, there too the *samaṇa* is found, there too the second ... the third ... the fourth *samaṇa* is found.[70]

The *ariyo aṭṭhaṅgiko maggo* constitutes, then, the fourth truth, the way leading to the cessation of suffering, the essential *brahma-cariya* to that end. As the path or way, the *ariyo aṭṭhaṅgiko maggo* strictly forms part of what is considered in the Nikāyas the special teaching of Buddhas: suffering, arising, cessation and path. Accordingly, in the stage by stage *sāmañña-phala* schema of the path it is only as part of the final stage—the stage of knowledge of the destruction of the *āsavas* that the *bhikkhu* comes finally to see and know the way leading to the cessation of suffering.[71]

All this makes it clear that while the *ariyo aṭṭhaṅgiko maggo* should rightly be regarded as embracing the essence of spiritual practice as conceived in the Nikāyas, it does not follow that it is seen as the Buddha's instruction to beginners. Yet—and this is something that I have already drawn attention to—the special teaching of the Buddhas, of which the *ariyo aṭṭhaṅgiko maggo* forms a part, is at the same time not presented as something entirely different or divorced from other *brahma-cariya*, from lesser paths. On the contrary it is the proper and natural conclusion of the process begun by these other paths which may lead, for example, only as far as rebirth in the world of Brahmā. As we have seen, *nibbāna* can be understood in some sense as standing in the same relationship to the conditioned world in its entirety, as the first *jhāna* stands in relationship to the world of the five senses. Accordingly the *brahma-cariya* of the *ariyo aṭṭhaṅgiko maggo* subsumes the various other *brahma-cariyas*, which are seen as incomplete. It subsumes these not as mere incidentals or as optional sideroads and diversions, but rather as lesser manifestations of the whole. The

---

na virāgāya na nirodhāya na upasamāya na abhiññāya na sambodhāya na nibbānāya saṃvattati yāvad eva brahma-lokûpapattiyā. idaṃ kho pana me Pañcasikha brahma-cariyaṃ ekanta-nibbidāya virāgāya nirodhāya upasamāya abhiññāya sambodhāya nibbānāya saṃvattati, ayaṃ eva ariyo aṭṭhaṅgiko maggo seyyathīdaṃ sammā-diṭṭhi ... sammā-samādhi. (Cf. M I 82.)

[70] D II 151: *alaṃ Subhadda. tiṭṭhat'etaṃ sabbe te sakāya paṭiññāya abbhaññaṃsu, sabbe vā na abbhaññaṃsu udāhu ekacce abbhaññaṃsu ekacce na abbhaññaṃsū ti. dhammaṃ te Subhadda desessāmi. taṃ suṇāhi sādhukaṃ manasikarohi bhāsissāmī ti ... yasmiṃ kho Subhadda dhamma-vinaye ariyo aṭṭhaṅgiko maggo na upalabbhati, samaṇo pi tattha na upalabbhati dutiyo ... tatiyo ... catuttho pi tattha samaṇo na upalabbhati. yasmiñ ca kho Subhadda dhamma-vinaye ariyo aṭṭhaṅgiko maggo upalabbhati, samaṇo pi tattha upalabbhati, dutiyo ... tatiyo ... catuttho pi tattha samaṇo upalabbhati.*

[71] E.g. D I 83-4.

ariyo aṭṭhaṅgiko maggo is a sum and reflection of all *brahma-cariya*; it is its true and ultimate conclusion.

4. The significance of the term ariya

As P. Masefield has pointed out,[72] any discussion of the *ariyo aṭṭhaṅgiko maggo* must address itself to the significance of the term *ariya*. Masefield thinks it 'no exaggeration to say that western scholarship has, almost without exception, completely overlooked the fact that the ariyan eightfold path is supramundane and thus restricted to those who are ariyan'.[73] This, it seems to me, is in fact something of an exaggeration, and at the same time passes over the rather delicate issue of the proper relationship of the Nikāya usage of terms such as *ariya* to the Abhidhamma usage. In effect scholarship, when concerned with the Theravādin and Sarvāstivādin systems of Abhidhamma/Abhidharma, has been quite well aware that the eight-factored path is termed *ariya/ārya* and of the basic import of that fact within these systems. On the other hand, when scholarship has concerned itself with the Nikāyas it has chosen largely to ignore this fact, treating it as the later and irrelevant result of scholastic systematization, and without really considering how the Nikāyas themselves use the term.

The significance of the term *ariya/ārya* in the post-Nikāya literature is clear enough. In terms of Buddhist spiritual hierarchy it is applied to anything that is directly associated with the world-transcending (*lokuttara*) knowledge of the stream-attainer, the once-returner, the non-returner and the *arahant/arhat*—the 'noble persons' (*ariya-puggala/ārya-pudgala*). By way of contrast we have the 'world' (*loka*): the sphere of the five senses (*kāmâvacara*), the *jhānas* of the form sphere (*rūpâvacara*) and the formless sphere (*arūpâvacara*); in short, the 'world' accessible to the ordinary man (*puthujjana*).

In dealing with the *indriyas* I have already drawn attention to the fact that, as far as the general principles of this contrast are concerned, the Nikāyas' technical usage of the term *ariya* must be considered in broad agreement with, although not always as clear cut as, the usage in the Abhidhamma/Abhidharma literature. That is, it is quite possible to work out on the basis of the Nikāyas alone that the *ariya-sāvaka*, so frequently contrasted with the *puthujjana*, is at least a stream-attainer and that stream-attainment is the result of seeing the four truths.[74] So already there are strong grounds for thinking that the *ariyo*

---

[72] Op. cit., p. 37.

[73] Ibid.

[74] Tracing the logic of the Nikāya usage of a term such as *ariya* can be quite involved. For example, the *puthujjana* sees *rūpa*, etc., as 'this is mine, I am this, this is my self'; the *ariya-savaka* in contrast sees *rūpa*, etc. as 'this is not mine, I am not this, this is not my self' (e.g. S III 56); elsewhere there are given twenty ways in which the *puthujjana* might see *rūpa*, etc. as 'this is mine ... ' (e.g. M III 188, 227; S III 3, 16, 96); elsewhere these same twenty ways of seeing *rūpa*, etc. as self are termed 'the view of individuality' (*sakkāya-diṭṭhi*) (M I 300; III 17, 102); elsewhere *sakkāya-diṭṭhi* is given as one of the three *saṃyojanas* abandoned as a result of proper attention to *dukkha, dukkha-samudaya, dukkha-nirodha, dukkha-nirodha-gāminī paṭipadā* (e.g. M I 9); elsewhere the *sotâpanna* is described as one who has completely destroyed three *saṃyojanas* (D I 156; II 92-3).

aṭṭhaṅgiko maggo should be particularly associated with the notion of *sotâpatti*. This seems only to be confirmed by what is said elsewhere. Thus in the case of the path-factors the *Mahācattārīsaka-sutta*[75] makes a quite explicit distinction between *sammā-diṭṭhi*, *sammā-saṃkappa*, *sammā-vācā*, *sammā-kammanta* and *sammā-ājīva* as with *āsavas*, concerned with merit (*puñña-bhāgiya*), resulting in acquisition (*upadhi-vepakka*) and as *ariya*, without *āsavas*, transcendent (*lok-uttara*), a factor of the path (*maggaṅga*). Finally a *sotâpatti-saṃyutta* passage defines the stream and stream-attainer as follows:

> 'The "stream" is spoken of, Sāriputta. What stream is this, Sāriputta?'
> 'The stream, lord, is just the noble eight-factored path, namely right view ... right concentration.'
> 'Good, good, Sāriputta ... The "stream-attainer" is spoken of, Sāriputta. What stream-attainer is this?'
> 'Now, lord, one who is endowed with this noble eight-factored path he is said to be a stream-attainer—just a venerable one of some name, of some family.'[76]

So whether or not a term like *ariya* always carries precisely its technical significance in the Nikāyas, whether or not it is possible to trace convincingly the development of the usage of such a term within the Nikāyas themselves, its basic technical import must be considered to be fully worked out by the close of the Nikāya period and not an Abhidhamma innovation grafted on to a radically different or even vastly looser usage.

The stream-attainer has, then, abandoned the three *saṃyojanas* or 'fetters' of doubt (*vicikicchā*), holding on to precept and vow (*sīla-bbata-parāmāsa*) and the view of individuality (*sakkāya-diṭṭhi*). He is endowed with the four limbs or factors of stream-attainment, that is trust based in understanding (*avecca-ppasāda*) towards the Buddha, Dhamma and Saṃgha, and the *sīla* that is dear to the *ariyas* or 'noble ones'; he cannot commit an action of the sort that would cause him to be reborn in a place of regress.[77] In short, stream-attainment is in the Nikāyas the crucial spiritual break-through. Further it is the spiritual breakthrough that endows the one who achieves it with the *ariyo aṭṭhaṅgiko maggo*.

Of some relevance at this point is the sequence of ten factors which adds right knowledge (*sammā-ñāṇa*) and right freedom (*sammā-vimutti*) to the list of eight. I have already mentioned the fact of the contrast between the eight and ten factors in detailing the extent of the Nikāya treatment of the *ariyo aṭṭhaṅgiko maggo*. The contrast is, then, one of its principal characteristics.[78]

---

[75] M III 71-8.

[76] S V 347: *soto soto ti ha Sāriputta vuccati. katamo nu kho Sāriputta soto ti. ayaṃ eva hi bhante ariyo aṭṭhaṅgiko maggo soto, seyyathīdaṃ sammā-diṭṭhi. pe. sammā-samādhī ti. sādhu sādhu Sāriputta ... sotâpanno sotâpanno ti hidaṃ Sāriputta vuccati. katamo nu kho Sāriputta sotâpanno ti. yo hi bhante iminā ariyena aṭṭhaṅgikena maggena samannāgato. ayaṃ vuccati sotâpanno yoyaṃ āyasmā evaṃ nāmo evaṃ gotto ti.* (Cf. Ud-a 306: *sotâpanno ti magga-saṃkhāta-sotaṃ āpajjitvā pāpuṇitvā ṭhito sotâpatti-phalaṭṭho ti attho.*) On the question of the 'path' as 'stream', see also below, Chapter 7.4.

[77] D II 93.

[78] See M III 76-8; S II 168-9; A II 89, 220-5. The eight/ten contrast is not explicit in the *magga-saṃyutta*; this seems to indicate that it should be taken as focusing precisely on the 'noble eight-factored path'. In fact the principles of the contrast seem to be reflected in the two

The method of contrasting the eight and ten factors is purely a feature of Suttanta exposition and does not appear to feature in the Abhidhamma. The basic principle expressed by the contrast can be stated as follows. The primary aim of spiritual practice is to cause the noble eight-factored path to arise; endowed with the eight factors a *bhikkhu* is a *sotâpanna* or 'in training' (*sekho*) and develops the eight existing factors and also the two further factors. I shall return to this below in dealing with the *Mahācattārīsaka-sutta*.

5. *The ariyo aṭṭhaṅgiko maggo and the gradual path*

It seems to me that there are two fairly distinct dimensions to what I have so far considered of the Nikāya account of the *ariyo aṭṭhaṅgiko maggo*—two dimensions that can appear slightly paradoxical. Both these dimensions arise out of the notion of the *ariyo aṭṭhaṅgiko maggo* as the spiritual life or spiritual practice in its fullness. In the first place the *ariyo aṭṭhaṅgiko maggo* subsumes all other spiritual practice; it is, as it were, the whole of the spiritual life. Secondly, as complete and perfect spiritual practice, it is the ultimate form of spiritual practice; it is what the *bhikkhu* aspires to; it is the goal, the end, the culmination of the spiritual quest. The *ariyo aṭṭhaṅgiko maggo* is the transformation of view, thought, speech, action, livelihood, striving, mindfulness and concentration into right view, right thought, right speech, right action, right livelihood, right striving, right mindfulness and right concentration. Thus the *ariyo aṭṭhaṅgiko maggo* is at once where one wishes to arrive at, and the way one must go to get there. For the destination is not exactly something different from the journey; where one arrives is only the consummation of the way one has come.

I have already referred on several occasions to the *sāmañña-phala* stage by stage account of the Buddhist path as found in the *sīlakkhandha-vagga* of the *Dīgha-nikāya*. This account follows a well defined order: the preliminary stages of the path can be categorized as *sīla*, the middle stages as *samādhi* and the final stages as *paññā*.[79] This kind of progressive description of the Buddhist path, always following essentially the same pattern of *sīla*, *samādhi* and *paññā*, occurs again and again in the Nikāyas. The *Majjhima-nikāya* uses a version

---

ekadhamma-peyyālas: the first uses the formula 'one *dhamma* is very suited to causing the *ariyo aṭṭhaṅgiko maggo* to arise' (S V 32) and the second the formula 'I see no other single *dhamma* by which the *ariyo aṭṭhaṅgiko maggo*, not having arisen, arises, or, having arisen, reaches full development' (S V 35). Interestingly the canon does contain what is in effect a 'ten-factored path *saṃyutta*' (See A V 211-49). This passage concerns exclusively the ten factors; opens with a ten-factored version of the opening of the *magga-saṃyutta*, and contains a number of other treatments that directly parallel *magga-saṃyutta* material. Cf. S V 174-5 which contrasts *sekho* and *asekho* by way of partial and full development of the *satipaṭṭhānas*.

79 In the *sīlakkhandha-vagga* the terminology in fact varies. The *Sāmaññaphala-sutta*, while giving the account in full, does not explicitly divide it into three categories. This is true also of the *Kūṭadanta-*, *Mahāli-*, *Jāliya-*, *Kevaddha-* and *Lohicca-suttas*. (The *Poṭṭhapāda-* and *Tevijja-suttas* depart from the standard pattern after the account of the fourth *jhāna*, inserting descriptions of the four formless attainments and four *brahma-vihāras* respectively.) In the *Ambaṭṭha-sutta* the categories are just two, *caraṇa* and *vijjā*; in the *Soṇadaṇḍa-sutta* just *sīla* and *paññā*; in the *Kassapasīhanāda-sutta* they are *sīla-sampadā*, *citta-sampadā* and *paññā-sampadā*; in the *Subha-sutta* they are *sīla-kkhandha*, *samādhi-kkhanda* and *paññā-kkhandha*.

that appears to be a slightly abbreviated form of the *sīlakkhandha-vagga* material.[80] Basically the same pattern is expressed in the scheme of the seven purifications (*visuddhis*) of the *Rathavinīta-sutta*,[81] and these seven form the basis for the *Visuddhimagga's* account of the path. Other works such as the *Vimuttimagga* and *Abhidharmakośa*, while not making use of the scheme of the seven *visuddhis*, also follow the principle of *sīla, samādhi, paññā* in their systematic description of the stages of the path. It seems fair, then, to regard the scheme of the stages of *sīla, samādhi* and *paññā* as expressing the essential principles of the stage by stage description of the path, both for the Nikāyas and later Indian Buddhist literature. What concerns us here is not the actual terminology, but the principles it reveals.

One of the clearest statements of the principles of this stage by stage path in the Nikāyas is the formula of 'progressive talk' (*anupubbī-kathā*) that culminates in the special teaching of Buddhas. This formula is scattered throughout the Nikāyas and I have already had occasion to refer to it. I give it now in full:

> Then the Blessed One gave a progressive talk ... namely talk on giving, talk on *sīla* and talk on heaven; he revealed the danger, elimination and impurity of sensual desires, and the benefit of desirelessness. When the Blessed One knew that the mind of ... was ready, soft, without hindrances, uplifted, settled, then he revealed the special *dhamma*-teaching of Buddhas: suffering, arising, cessation, the path.[82]

This quite explicitly begins with *sīla*. What comes next, culminating in a mind that is soft and without hindrances, quite clearly indicates *samādhi*. Finally *paññā* is indicated by the reference to the four truths. A recurring passage in the *Mahāparinibbāna-sutta* also shows how *sīla, samādhi* and *paññā* should be seen as forming some kind of successive spiritual hierarchy:

> Such is *sīla*, such *samādhi*, such *paññā*; when imbued with *sīla, samādhi* is of great fruit and benefit; when imbued with *samādhi, paññā* is of great fruit and benefit; when imbued with *paññā*, the mind is rightly freed from the *āsavas*, namely the *āsavas* of sensual desires, the *āsavas* of becoming, the *āsavas* of views, the *āsavas* of ignorance.[83]

Thus we have in *sīla, samādhi* and *paññā* the basic principles of a spiritual hierarchy. This hierarchy is not a purely ideal schema, but is seen as reflecting the actual hierarchy of the world. When it comes to spiritual development the *bhikkhu*, in order to progress, will have to attend to *sīla, samādhi* and *paññā* more or less in that order. That is, it is understood that if one tries to develop

---

[80] Cf. M I 178-84, 267-71, 344-8; III 33-6, 134-7.

[81] M I 145-51.

[82] *atha kho bhagavā ... anupubbī-katham kathesi. seyyathīdaṃ, dāna-kathaṃ sīla-kathaṃ sagga-kathaṃ kāmānaṃ ādīnavaṃ okāraṃ saṃkilesaṃ nekkhamme ānisaṃsaṃ pakāsesi. yadā bhagavā aññāsi ... kalla-cittaṃ mudu-cittaṃ vinīvaraṇa-cittaṃ udagga-cittaṃ pasanna-cittaṃ atha yā buddhānaṃ sāmukkaṃsikā dhamma-desanā taṃ pakāsesi: dukkhaṃ samudayaṃ nirodhaṃ maggaṃ.*

[83] D II 81, 84, 91, 98: *iti sīlaṃ iti samādhi iti paññā. sīla-paribhāvito samādhi mahapphalo hoti mahânisaṃso. samādhi-paribhāvitā paññā mahapphalā hoti mahânisaṃsā. paññā-paribhāvitaṃ cittaṃ samma-d-eva āsavehi vimuccati seyyathīdaṁ kāmâsavā bhavâsavā diṭṭhâsavā avijjâsavā ti.* (A similar formula is found in the Sanskrit version; see *MPS* 160, 220. For some further examples reflecting the principles of the progressive path, cf. Jayatilleke, op. cit., pp. 396-7.)

paññā, it will become apparent that some measure of *samādhi* is a prerequisite; if one tries to develop *samādhi*, it will become apparent that some measure of *sīla* is a prerequisite. What this means in practice is that it is understood that someone can have developed *sīla* but need not necessarily have developed *samādhi* and *paññā*; someone can have developed *sīla* and *samādhi*, but not necessarily have developed *paññā* to any great degree. However, the converse cannot be so. This is reflected in a corresponding hierarchy of religious goals. The development of *sīla* alone leads to happy rebirth in the *kāma-loka*; the development of *sīla* and *samādhi* to rebirth in the *brahma-loka*; by developing *sīla*, *samādhi* and *paññā* rebirth of all kinds is transcended. This is all neatly summed up in the following passage from the *Vimuttimagga*:

> After acknowledging the Path of Freedom, through virtue he transcends the way to states of regress (*apāya*); through concentration he transcends the sense plane, through wisdom he transcends all becoming. If he practises virtue to the full and practises little of concentration and wisdom, he will reach the stage of Stream-entrant and the stage of Once-returner. If he practises virtue and concentration to the full and practises little of wisdom, he will reach the stage of Non-returner. If he practises virtue, concentration and wisdom to the full, he will reach the peerless freedom of the Consummate One.[84]

While this hierarchy stands in theory, the relationship between the three elements of *sīla*, *samādhi* and *paññā* in practice is recognized in the ancient literature as being rather subtle. A number of writers have drawn attention to this fact.[85] *Sīla*, *samādhi* and *paññā* are in fact inextricably bound up together. In other words the hierarchy does not mean that when the novice at the initial stages of the path establishes *sīla*, he does not also in some way and to some degree begin to develop *samādhi* and *paññā*, or that when the adept at the advanced stages of the path develops *paññā* he does not need *sīla* or *samādhi*:

> Just as, Gotama, one might wash hand with hand or foot with foot, even so *paññā* is fully washed by *sīla*, *sīla* is fully washed by *paññā*; where there is *sīla* there is *paññā*, where there is *paññā* there is *sīla*; one who has *sīla* has *paññā*, one who has *paññā* has *sīla*; *sīla* and *paññā* together are declared the summit of the world.[86]

What this means, presumably, is that the intent to develop *sīla* is seen as bound up with *paññā* and that the development of *sīla* naturally tends to the development of *paññā* and, one can assume, *samādhi*.[87] The latter two in turn tend to the development of *sīla*.

It is precisely in this context—the context of the inter-relationships between *sīla*, *samādhi* and *paññā*—that the structure of the *ariyo aṭṭhaṅgiko maggo* is, I

---

84 Vimutt Trsl 5; cf. A IV 380-1.

85 Cf. H. Saddhatissa, *Buddhist Ethics*, London, 1970, p. 68; Gombrich, 'Notes on the Brahmanical Background to Buddhist Ethics' in Dhammapala, *BSHS*, pp. 91-102.

86 D I 124: *seyyathâpi bho Gotama hatthena vā hatthaṃ dhopeyya, padena vā padaṃ dhopeyya, evaṃ eva kho bho Gotama sīla-paridhotā paññā; paññā-paridhotaṃ sīlaṃ, yattha sīlaṃ tattha paññā, yattha paññā tattha sīlaṃ, sīlavato paññā paññāvato sīlaṃ, sīla-paññānañ ca pana lokasmiṃ aggaṃ akkhāyatī ti.*

87 The *Soṇadaṇḍa-sutta*, from which this passage is taken, considers the stages of the path by way of just two categories *sīla* and *paññā*.

think, crucial. How the eight factors are to be classified in terms of *sīla*, *samādhi* and *paññā* is detailed in the *Cūḷavedalla-sutta*:

> Right speech, right action and right livelihood—these *dhammas* are comprised by the aggregate of *sīla*; right striving, right mindfulness and right concentration—these *dhammas* are comprised by the aggregate of *samādhi*; right view and right thought—these *dhammas* are comprised by the aggregate of *paññā*.[88]

The sequence of the eight factors thus throws the normative progression into complete disorder: instead of *sīla*, *samādhi* and *paññā* we have *paññā*, *sīla*, *samādhi*.

The order of the eight factors is really quite remarkable in this respect. It is in marked contrast with the order and structure of the eight *aṅgas* of *yoga*, for example, which appear to follow the same principles as the stage by stage account of the path.[89] The order of the factors of the *ariyo aṭṭhaṅgiko maggo* is distinctive and must be regarded as being quite deliberate and intended to convey something quite specific. Yet the question of the order of the factors has been little discussed in scholarly literature. To begin with, the order of its factors seems to show that the *ariyo aṭṭhaṅgiko maggo* is understood not primarily as a description of the successive stages of the path. Indeed, this much is quite often pointed out. Saddhatissa, an oriental monk writing here primarily for a non-specialist western readership, comments:

> The path leading to the release from suffering is said to be eight-fold. These are not consecutive steps. The eight factors are interdependent and must be perfected simultaneously, the fulfilment of one factor being unlikely without at least the partial development of the others.[90]

Yet within the world of scholarship the way in which this might be so for early Buddhist literature appears neither to have been properly appreciated nor worked out and presented. More often the account of the successive stages of the path in terms of *sīla*, *samādhi* and *paññā* is simply confounded with the *ariyo aṭṭhaṅgiko maggo*. Even as careful and accomplished a scholar as Étienne Lamotte seems to follow this trend:

---

[88] M I 301: *yā câvuso Visākha sammā-vācā yo ca sammā-kammanto yo ca sammā-ājīvo, ime dhammā sīla-kkhandhe saṃgahītā; yo ca sammā-vāyāmo yā ca sammā-sati yo ca sammā-samādhi, ime dhammā samādhi-kkhande saṃgahītā; yā ca sammā-diṭṭhi yo ca sammā-saṃkappo, ime dhammā paññā-kkhandhe saṃgahītā ti.* (Certain northern sources give a different analysis: *samyag-dṛṣṭi*, *samyak-saṃkalpa* and *samyag-vyāyāma* are *prajñā-skandha*; *samyag-vāk*, *-karmânta* and *-ājīva* are *sīla-skandha*; *samyak-smṛti* and *samyak-samādhi* are *samādhi-skandha*; see Wayman, *Śrāvakabhūmi*, p. 101; Satya Trsl 43, 448-9.)

[89] The eight *aṅgas* of *yoga* are control [of conduct] (*yama*), observance (*niyama*), posture (*āsana*), breath control (*prāṇāyāma*), withdrawal (*pratyāhāra*), composure (*dhāraṇā*), absorption (*dhyāna*), concentration (*samādhi*); see YS II 29. Vyāsa comments that 'the following up of these must be performed in succession' (J.H. Woods, *The Yoga System of Patañjali*, Harvard, 1914, p. 177); the first *aṅga* clearly corresponds more or less to what is termed *sīla* in Buddhist thought, while *samādhi* in the YS probably embraces rather more than the term *samādhi* always does in Buddhist thought. The eight *aṅgas* of *yoga* seem, then, to represent a progression or succession of stages. The logic is similar to that of the gradual path in the *sāmañña-phala* schema; while elements of the later stages are not necessarily absent from the earlier stages, the basic idea of successive stages remains. There seems to be no concept of the eight *aṅgas* adding up to a *mārga* similar in conception to the *ariyo aṭṭhaṅgiko maggo*.

[90] H. Saddhatissa, *The Buddha's Way*, London, 1971, p. 46.

> La quatrième vérité sainte ... a pour objet le chemin conduisant à la destruction de la douleur (*duḥkhanirodhagāminī pratipad*). Le noble chemin à huit branches défini dans le sermon de Bénarès comporte trois éléments: la moralité, la concentration et la sagesse.[91]

Lamotte here gives no indication of any discrepancy between the *ariyo aṭṭhaṅgiko maggo* on the one hand and the scheme of *sīla*, *samādhi* and *paññā* on the other. He continues his exposition of the fourth truth, (i.e. of the *ariyo aṭṭhaṅgiko maggo*), with a full account of *sīla*, *samādhi* and *paññā*. Yet this procedure gives the impression that in the early literaure the *ariyo aṭṭhaṅgiko maggo* and the account of the successive stages of the path in terms of *sīla*, *samādhi* and *paññā* are simply equivalent when they quite manifestly are not.

The statement just quoted from Lamotte's *Histoire du bouddhisme indien* is indicative of how, while generally following the *Cūḷavedalla-sutta's* method of classifying the eight factors in terms of *sīla*, *samādhi* and *paññā*, scholars have tended to ignore the discussion in the *sutta* that immediately precedes this:[92]

> 'Is it, sister, that the three aggregates [of *sīla*, *samādhi* and *paññā*] are comprised by the *ariyo aṭṭhaṅgiko maggo*, or is it that the *ariyo aṭṭhaṅgiko maggo* is comprised by the three aggregates?'
>
> 'The three aggregates are not, Visākha, comprised by the *ariyo aṭṭhaṅgiko maggo*, but the *ariyo aṭṭhaṅgiko maggo* is, Visākha, comprised by the three aggregates.'[93]

The commentary indicates what must be intended here:

> Herein, because the *magga* is specific while the three aggregates are all inclusive, therefore, because of its specificity, it is comprised by the three all inclusive aggregates like a city by a kingdom.[94]

So why is the *ariyo aṭṭhaṅgiko maggo* comprised by the three *khandhas* but not vice versa? Technically, what this seems to mean is that one can instance *dhammas* such as *vicāra* and *pīti*, for example, which as *jhāna*-factors have a place in *samādhi-kkhandha*, yet are left out of the reckoning in the *ariyo aṭṭhaṅgiko maggo*. More generally this must mean that the *ariyo aṭṭhaṅgiko maggo* should be understood as having a more specific import than the all embracing gradual scheme of *sīla*, *samādhi* and *paññā*. At first sight this might seem to contradict some of what I have said above, namely that the *ariyo aṭṭhaṅgiko maggo* does embrace and comprise spiritual practice in its entirety,

---

[91] Lamotte, *HBI*, p. 45.

[92] The passages Lamotte refers to in this connection rather curiously refer only to *sīla*, *samādhi* and *paññā* and make no mention of their relationship to the *ariyo aṭṭhaṅgiko maggo*.

[93] M I 301: *ariyena nu kho ayye aṭṭhaṅgikena maggena tayo khandhā saṃgahītā, udāhu tīhi khandhehi ariyo aṭṭhaṅgiko maggo saṃgahīto ti. na kho āvuso Visākha ariyena aṭṭhaṅgikena maggena tayo khandhā saṃgahīta, tīhi ca kho āvuso Visākha khandhehi ariyo aṭṭhaṅgiko maggo saṃgahīto.*

[94] Ps II 361 = Vism XVI 95: *ettha yasmā maggo sappadeso tayo khandhā nippadesā, tasmā ayaṃ sappadesattā nagaraṃ viya rajjena nippadesehi tīhi khandhehi saṃgahīto.* (The technical meanings of *sappadesa* and *nippadesa* are clear at As 37; in the case of some Abhidhamma triplets and couplets, any given *dhamma* will be classifiable by one of the three or two categories; such triplets and couplets are 'inclusive' or 'comprehensive' (*nippadesa*); in the case of others certain *dhammas* will not fall into any of the three or two categories; these triplets and couplets are of 'limited scope' or 'specific' (*sappadesa*).)

that it does represent the sum of the Buddhist path as presented in the Nikāyas. However, in fact, I think this allows us to form a clearer idea of how and in what sense this is so.

The triad of *sīla*, *samādhi* and *paññā* implies a comprehensive graded description of the stages of the spiritual path. In terms of content it comprises the successive stages in full, and while reflecting the overall general nature of the actual stages of the path, it does in part represent something of an ideal scheme. The *ariyo aṭṭhaṅgiko maggo* does something rather different. While it does not by way of content fully embrace the aggregates of *sīla*, *samādhi* and *paññā*, its eight factors do collectively touch on and comprise each of these three aspects—uniquely among the seven sets. Thus the eight factors collectively represent, as it were, an actual manifestation of all three aspects, so that the *ariyo aṭṭhaṅgiko maggo* can be seen as the essential distillation of the aggregates of *sīla*, *samādhi* and *paññā*. The *ariyo aṭṭhaṅgiko maggo* comprises the whole of the spiritual life precisely in the sense that it is the consummation of the development of *sīla*, *samādhi* and *paññā*. It is the path or way of life that issues from that development. Its end is a reflection and crystallization of the way one has come. In other words, the development of *sīla*, *samādhi* and *paññā* in all its various aspects culminates in right view, right thought, right speech, right action, right livelihood, right striving, right mindfulness, right concentration—*paññā*, *sīla* and *samādhi*, the three essential aspects of spiritual practice in perfect balance. It is only in this manner that the treatment of the *ariyo aṭṭhaṅgiko maggo* in the *Cūḷavedalla-sutta* becomes properly intelligible.

The *ariyo aṭṭhaṅgiko maggo* is not, then, primarily descriptive of the successive stages of or points along a path. The eight factors constitute a 'path' or 'way' not in the sense of a linear progression from starting line to finishing post; rather they embody a complete 'way of going along' or 'mode of practice'—a *paṭipadā*. The eight factors embrace all that is essential to spiritual progress.

6. *The eight factors in the Dhammasaṅgaṇi*

At this point the treatment of the eight factors of the path in the *Dhammasaṅgaṇi* is of some interest in that it provides an indication of how the *ariyo aṭṭhaṅgiko maggo* is considered to arise; I mean by this that it suggests a relationship between the path factors in ordinary consciousness and the *ariyo aṭṭhaṅgiko maggo* as an aspect of transcendent consciousness. While, of course, the exact details of its treatment must be viewed as belonging to a later phase of Buddhist thought, the general way in which the *Dhammasaṅgaṇi* handles the path-factors seems to me to be entirely relevant to the Nikāyas. The sense of the *Mahācattārīsaka-sutta*, which I shall consider, in some detail below, does seem to become rather clearer in the light of the early Abhidhamma treatment.

As its title suggests, much of the *Dhammasaṅgaṇi* is concerned with enumerating or listing *dhammas*—but not simply listing *dhammas*, rather listing *dhammas* according to various groupings (*saṃgaṇa*). The principles behind these various groupings are diverse, overlap and operate at different levels. Thus the triplets and couplets of the *mātikā* provide an initial set of groupings. Within the first grouping of *kusala-dhammas* various other groupings are then distinguished: there are *kāmâvacara-kusala-dhammas*, *rūpâvacara-kusala-dhammas*, *arūpâvacara-kusala-dhammas* and *lokuttara-kusala-dhammas*. However, there are, of course, other *kāmâvacara-dhammas* that are not *kusala* but *akusala* or *avyākata* (undetermined). Again within the grouping of *kāmâvacara-kusala-dhammas*, there are distinguished eight further groupings, namely eight varieties of 'mind' or 'consciousness' (*citta*). Each one of these eight *cittas* represents an assemblage of *dhammas* which comes together, arises at a particular time (*samaya*) and then passes away. The items that constitute each assemblage of *dhammas* or each *citta* can simply be listed, but once again the *Dhammasaṅgaṇi* indicates that the various *dhammas* present fall into various groupings. This is most obviously brought out in the *koṭṭhāsa-vāra* or 'section on sets',[95] a section which is apparently understood as forming part of the exposition of each kind of *citta*, although it is lost in most cases in the abbreviations of the text. I quote here the opening of the *koṭṭhāsa-vāra* for the first kind of skilful *kāmâvacara-citta*:

> Now at that time there are four aggregates, two spheres, two elements, three foods, eight faculties, there is five-factored *jhāna*, a five-factored path, there are seven powers, three causes ...

What underlies the *Dhammasaṅgaṇi's* method here is the fundamental notion of what *dhammas* really are. They are not the inert contents of the mind, but rather basic forces that collectively constitute the mind; and that mind is never stable, but always on the move. Therefore it is not enough to simply list *dhammas* as if they were static pieces of the mind. To understand the mind as active (which by nature it is) one must see its forces at work, how they come together and interact. Within the *Dhammasaṅgaṇi* the *koṭṭhāsa-vāras* play a significant part in plotting the various courses of this interaction.

The opening of the *koṭṭhāsa-vāra* for the first kind of skilful *kāmâvacara-citta* mentions a 'five-factored path'. The *koṭṭhāsa-vāra* goes on to explain this as consisting of right view, right thought, right striving, right mindfulness and right concentration. Later on we are told that for the first kind of unskilful *kāmâvacara-citta* there is a 'four-factored path' consisting of wrong view, wrong thought, wrong striving and wrong concentration.[96] This seems to be understood as applying to all *kusala-* and *akusala-citta*, though probably not to *avyākata*. The eight items that potentially make up the *ariyo aṭṭhaṅgiko maggo* thus apparently form the basis of one of the groupings of *dhammas* that indicate the ways in which *dhammas* are conceived of as coming together and interacting. In other words, a path (consisting in however many of the sixteen items—eight *sammā* or 'right' and eight *micchā* or 'wrong'—happen to be present) is always present in the mind. Considered by way of the eight aspects of *diṭṭhi*, *saṃkappa*, *vācā*, *kammanta*, *ājīva*, *vāyāma*, *sati* and *samādhi*, at any

---

95 Discussed more fully below, Chapter 10.3.

96 Dhs 78-9.

given time[97] the mind reveals a 'path'; that is, the way it is orientated, the direction in which it is moving.

Why do these eight aspects do this, and not another grouping? Partly because, as I have already suggested, in touching upon *paññā*, *sīla* and *samādhi*, they indicate, as it were, a crystallization of or a momentary window on a complete way of life. Like the mind in general, one's way of life is seen as ordinarily unstable and changing. At times of skilful *citta* the 'way of life' revealed by the eight aspects is essentially the right way of life, the right path or direction; it is potentially the *ariyo aṭṭhaṅgiko maggo*. But at times of unskilful *citta* the 'way of life' is essentially wrong, the wrong path or direction.

According to the *Dhammasaṅgaṇi* and the Abhidhamma in general it is, however, only at the time of *lokuttara-citta* that all eight factors of the path come together within a single 'mind' or *citta*.[98] In the case of *lokuttara-citta* the *Dhammasaṅgaṇi* adds to the standard definitions of each factor (i.e. the definition used in the context of *kāmâvacara*, *rūpâvacara* and *arūpâvacara* consciousness) the epithets 'factor of the path' (*maggaṅga*) and 'included in the path' (*magga-pariyāpanna*).[99] This can only be to bring out the point that here we have the *ariyo aṭṭhaṅgiko maggo* itself.

The *Dhammasaṅgaṇi* in fact never explicitly considers the 'path' of ordinary *citta* as more than five-factored, and neither right nor wrong speech, action and livelihood are ever mentioned in the context of ordinary *citta*. The *Atthasālinī* explains—and there seems no reason to doubt that this is basically the correct interpretation of the *Dhammasaṅgaṇi*—that in ordinary *citta* only one of right or wrong speech, action and livelihood can ever occur at a given time.[100] The logic behind this would seem to be that it is understood that the ordinary skilful mind may well temporarily refrain from one of wrong speech, action or livelihood—which one depending on particular circumstances. However, each of the four *lokuttara-maggas* turns away from all three at once because it results in the refraining from certain kinds of wrong speech, action and livelihood for once and for all. The *magga* of stream-attainment, for example, is understood as refraining finally from the more extreme kinds of wrong speech, action and livelihood such as would result in rebirth in the places of regress (*apāya*).

With this discussion one comes up against what appears to be another ancient Abhidhamma moot point: can the *lokuttara-magga* ever be anything other than eight-factored? The debate seems to have centred around an account of the path as found in the *Mahāsaḷāyatanika-sutta*.[101] The passage considers the fulfilment of the development of the *ariyo aṭṭhaṅgiko maggo* in terms of the arising of right view, thought, striving, mindfulness and concen-

---

[97] One must understand 'any given time' slightly loosely here since, as I shall discuss, ordinarily a single arising of consciousness has only a maximum of six path-factors.

[98] Dhs 60-9.

[99] Ibid.

[100] As 154; but As 220-2 (discussed above, p. 196) would lead one to think that either *sammā-vācā* and *sammā-ājīva*, or *sammā-kammanta* and *sammā-ājīva* could occur together in ordinary *citta*.

[101] M III 289; quoted in full below, p. 241; cf. S IV 195.

tration in the context of acts of body, speech and livelihood having previously been purified.

The implication is that at the time of the fulfilment of *ariyo aṭṭhaṅgiko maggo* (that is, according to the later terminology, at the time of the *lokuttara-magga*) in certain circumstances only the five factors of the path concerned with *paññā* and *samādhi* need be relevant, and that the three factors concerned with *sīla* can be left out of the reckoning. This is basically a manifestation of the principles of the consecutive stages of the path or of the hierarchy of *sīla*, *samādhi* and *paññā*: the essential work of *sīla* is understood as being completed in the lower stages of the path and as providing the basis for the development of *samādhi* and *paññā*. Of course, this is not to be taken as implying that the *bhikkhu* at the higher stages of the path no longer keeps *sīla*, but simply that he does not have to work at it—he keeps *sīla* naturally and, as it were, spontaneously. The question is at what point exactly *sīla* can be said to have been purified. The Pāli commentaries strongly resist the notion of a transcendent five-factored path.[102] Although they largely appeal simply to the authority of the *sutta*, the logic behind their point of view would appear to be that, although to all practical intents and purposes *sīla* may well be purified at some stage prior to the arising of the *lokuttara-magga*, still the possibility of decline exists. It is of the nature of the *lokuttara magga* to cut off the possibility of decline and finally purify *sīla*. Until it has arisen, the *bhikkhu* may still lapse back into the wrong speech, wrong action and wrong livelihood from which he has turned away by means of the *lokiya-magga* or ordinary spiritual practice.

Before passing on to the *Mahācattārīsaka-sutta*, I should perhaps make it clear exactly how I view the relevance of the *Dhammasaṅgaṇi's* treatment of the eight factors. The *Dhammasaṅgaṇi* shows how the notion of the *ariyo aṭṭhaṅgiko maggo* cuts across the notion of the progressive path characterized by the sequence of *sīla*, *samādhi* and *paññā*. If this sequence can be seen as highlighting the conception of the spiritual path as a vertical hierarchy with *sīla* at the bottom, *samādhi* in the middle and *paññā* at the top, then the notion of the *magga* as eight-factored cuts a horizontal cross-section through this, indicating that elements of *sīla*, *samādhi* and *paññā*—or their unskilful counterparts—are present and interacting wherever we are in that hierarchy. At any time they move the mind inevitably either in a skilful or unskilful direction. The basic principles of this psychology of the eight-factored path are, I think,

---

102 The point is discussed at Ps V 104; As 154; Vibh-a 319-21; Kv-a 188-9. A five-factored *lokuttara-magga* is detailed at Vibh 237-41 but this is taken by the commentary to be purely a matter of exposition (see below, pp. 330-1). Kv 599-601 takes issue with the Mahiṃsāsaka (so Kv-a 188) for upholding the notion of the five-factored path. The commentaries, however, do allow a seven-factored *lokuttara-magga* corresponding to the second, third, fourth, fifth *jhānas* that lack *vitakka* (= *saṃkappa*) (see Ps V 104; As 226-228; and below, p. 330). Underlying these discussions is the question of the conception of the three factors of speech, action and livelihood. As mentioned, the Sarvāstivādins used the notion of *avijñapti-rūpa* to maintain all eight factors in the *lokottara-mārga*; the Theravādins conceived of the matter in different terms. Some cited a Sūtra equivalent to the *Mahāsaḷāyatanika* passage as contrary to the notion of *avijñapti-rūpa* (Abhidh-k 196). Those who denied *avijñapti* but did not adopt a specific notion of *virati* like the Theravādins were left only with *cetanā*, and since the transcendent path was taken as an act of 'thought', and not of speech or body, how all eight factors were encompassed was problematic.

quite evident in the *Mahācattārīsaka-sutta* and are generally valid for the Nikāyas.

The notion of the *ariyo aṭṭhaṅgiko maggo* is understood as an expression of the fact that the immediate way or approach (*paṭipadā*) to perfection consists in bringing into being the *collective* rightness (*sammatta*) of view, thought, speech, action, livelihood, striving, mindfulness and concentration.[103]

7. The Mahācattārīsaka-sutta: the law of the eight-factored path

The *Mahācattārīsaka-sutta*[104] is an exposition of noble right concentration (*ariya-sammā-samādhi*) along with its supports (*sa-upanisā*) and its equipment (*sa-parikkhāra*). These supports and equipment of noble right concentration are right view, right thought, right speech, right action, right livelihood, right striving and right mindfulness; in other words, the seven remaining items that make up the *ariyo aṭṭhaṅgiko maggo* in addition to right concentration:

> That one-pointedness of mind, *bhikkhus*, which is equipped (*parikkhāta*) with these seven factors is called noble right concentration along with its supports and its equipment.[105]

This notion of *ariyo sammā-samādhi sa-upaniso sa-parikkhāro* is referred to in a number of places in the Nikāyas[106] and is obviously of some significance in connection with the *ariyo aṭṭhaṅgiko maggo*. The *Mahācattārīsaka-sutta* constitutes its fullest treatment in the Nikāyas, and as such must be judged a *sutta* of considerable importance. In the Chinese versions of the Āgamas the equivalent to the *Mahācattārīsaka-sutta* apparently finds its place in the equivalent to the *magga-saṃyutta*.[107] The recurring theme of the *Mahācattārīsaka-sutta* is the priority of right view with regard to 'noble right concentration along with its supports and equipment': 'with regard to this, right view comes first' (*tatra sammā-diṭṭhi pubbaṃ-gamā*). This is the starting point of the *sutta*, and the exposition that follows falls into three sections.[108] Each opens with a statement of the priority of right view, and proceeds to explain just how this is so.

The first section explains that right view comes first because it knows wrong view as wrong view and right view as right view (*micchā-diṭṭhiṃ micchā-diṭṭhī ti pajānāti sammā-diṭṭhiṃ sammā-diṭṭhī ti pajānāti sassa hoti sammā-diṭṭhi*). In the same way right view knows wrong and right thought, wrong and right speech, wrong and right action, wrong and right livelihood. In each case the *sutta* states that there are two kinds of right view, thought, speech, action and livelihood. One kind is with *āsavas*, concerned with merit (*puñña-bhāgiya*) and resulting in acquisition (*upadhi-vepakka*). The second kind is *ariya*, without

---

[103] See S V 17-8.

[104] M III 71-8.

[105] M III 71: *yā kho bhikkhave imehi sattaṅgehi cittassa ekaggatā parikkhātā ayaṃ vuccati bhikkhave ariyo sammā-samādhi sa-upaniso iti pi sa-parikkhāro iti pi.*

[106] In addition see D II 217; S V 21; A IV 40.

[107] See C. Akanuma, op. cit., p. 75.

[108] M III 71-5, 75-6, 76-7.

āsavas, transcendent (*lokuttara*), a factor of the path (*maggaṅga*).[109] Each of the five parts of the first section concludes by stating that as the *bhikkhu* strives to abandon the item in question—view, thought, speech, action, or livelihood—as wrong and arouse it as right , his striving is right-striving. As he mindfully abandons what is wrong and attains and dwells in what is right, his mindfulness is right mindfulness. So 'these three *dhammas* flow around after (*anuparidhavanti*), revolve around (*anuparivattanti*) right view—namely right view, right striving and right mindfulness'.

The second section of the *sutta* explains the way in which right view comes first, with the following formula that sees the factors as consecutive:

> For one of right view, *bhikkhus*, right thought appears; for one of right thought, right speech appears; for one of right speech, right action appears; for one of right action, right livelihood appears; for one of right livelihood, right striving appears; for one of right striving, right mindfulness appears; for one of right mindfulness, right concentration appears; for one of right concentration right knowledge appears; for one of right knowledge, right freedom appears. Thus, *bhikkhus*, the learner on entering is possessed of eight factors, the *arahant* of ten factors.[110]

Finally the third section consists of another formula again in explanation of how *sammā-diṭṭhi* comes first:

> For one of right view, wrong view wastes away and those various bad unskilful *dhammas* that come into being conditioned by wrong view, they too waste away for him; the various skilful *dhammas* that have right view as their condition reach fulfilment by development.[111]

This is repeated nine more times substituting in turn for right and wrong view, right and wrong thought, speech, action, livelihood, striving, mindfulness, concentration, knowledge and freedom.

The *Mahācattārīsaka-sutta* quite clearly constitutes an exposition of how noble right concentration with its supports and equipment comes into being, and how right view leads the way in all spiritual practice. The basic notion would seem straightforward enough. To use the image of the journey, if one wants to go somewhere one must have an initial understanding of where one is and how one got there, along with where one wants to go and how to get there. This, in other terms, is an initial appreciation of the four truths. Specifically in the *Mahācattārīsaka-sutta*, where one is and also how one got there, is typified by wrong view, etc., where one wants to go and how to get there is typified by

---

109 Cf. how Dhs adds the terms *maggaṅga* and *magga-pariyāpanna* when defining the eight factors for *lokuttara-citta*.

110 M III 76: *sammā-diṭṭhissa bhikkhave sammā-saṃkappo pahoti; sammā-saṃkappassa sammā-vācā pahoti; sammā-vācassa sammā-kammanto pahoti; sammā-kammantassa sammā-ājīvo pahoti; sammā-ājīvassa sammā-vāyāmo pahoti; sammā-vāyāmassa sammā-sati pahoti; sammā-satissa sammā-samādhi pahoti; sammā-samādhissa sammā-ñāṇaṃ pahoti; sammā-ñāṇassa sammā-vimutti pahoti. iti kho bhikkhave aṭṭhaṅga-samannāgato sekho pāṭipado dasaṅga-samannāgato arahā hoti.* (I emend *sekho paṭipado* to *sekho pāṭipado* (cf. M I 354; III 300); *PED*, s.v. *sekha*, is misleading; Ce (1974) reads just *sekho*.)

111 M III 76: *sammā-diṭṭhissa bhikkhave micchā-diṭṭhi nijjiṇṇā hoti; ye ca micchā-diṭṭhi-paccayā aneke pāpakā akusalā dhammā sambhavanti te cassa nijjiṇṇā honti. sammā-diṭṭhi-paccayā ca aneke kusalā dhammā bhāvanā-pāripūriṃ gacchanti.*

right view, etc. Thus it is that right view must lead the way in knowing what wrong view, etc. and what right view, etc. are. But while right view has precedence because of its function of knowing and seeing what is wrong and what is right, in the actual task of abandoning what is wrong and causing what is right to arise, right view must be supported by right striving and right mindfulness. Thus the first section emphasizes that right view must in some sense lead the way because it is what 'sees', but three *dhammas*, namely right view, right striving and right mindfulness, continually interact with the other factors in order to promote them in their 'right' aspect.

Of great importance here is the fact that in this first section, the *sutta* distinguishes between two levels of right view, thought, speech action and livelihood,[112] the ordinary skilful variety concerned with merit, and the *ariya* factor of the transcendent path. This is taken up in the commentary which distinguishes here between right view that is concerned with ordinary *vipassanā* or 'insight' and right view that is concerned with the path—the *lokuttara-magga.*[113] What this indicates is two quite distinct stages in the coming into being of *ariya* right concentration along with its supports and equipment. First there is the turning away from wrong view, etc., and the turning towards right view, etc. that are of the ordinary skilful variety. Secondly there is the attainment of right view, etc. as noble, without *āsavas*, *lokuttara*, a factor of the path. It is precisely this second stage that must be understood as *ariyo sammā-samādhi sa-upaniso sa-parikkhāro*.

At this point the second section of the *Mahācattārīsaka-sutta* becomes relevant. Once again right view leads the way, but this is now the stage of the 'learner who has come to the way' (*sekho pāṭipado*)—the way that leads to the cessation of suffering, the *ariyo aṭṭhaṅgiko maggo*. Such a learner has brought the eight items to the stage of being factors of the *ariya-magga*, and endowed with these eight factors he begins to bring two further items into being, namely right knowledge and right freedom, such that, endowed with all ten factors in full, he becomes an *arahant*. This brings us to the final section of the *sutta* where once again right view is said to lead the way in the final and absolute wasting away of the ten items in their wrong aspects, and their coming to full development in their right aspects. This contrast between the eight factors of the learner and the ten factors of the one who has nothing to learn (*asekha*) or *arahant*, as already noted, occurs with some frequency in the Nikāyas.

The *Mahācattārīsaka-sutta* is an exposition of the processes involved in the passing from wrong view, etc. to right view, etc. that is ordinary and skilful, and from here to right view, etc. that is *ariya* and without *āsavas*; and from here to the full development of right view, etc. Throughout it is emphasized that right view leads the way. Thus right view comes first not just as the preliminary stage in spiritual practice, not just as the preparation or basis for

[112] Why the *sutta* stops with *sammā-ājīva* and does not continue with *sammā-vāyāma*, *-sati*, and *-samādhi* is unclear. These are dealt with within the body of the *sutta* as a whole, so perhaps one should ask why *sammā-diṭṭhi* is repeated here. The answer in this case would seem to be to do with the great emphasis on the priority of *sammā-diṭṭhi* in the *sutta*.

[113] Ps IV 131.

higher stages, rather it comes first at all stages of spiritual practice. The treatment of the factors as consecutive steps takes on the character not so much of a map showing the stages of spiritual practice, as of a working model illustrating the operation of spiritual practice at whatever stage. In the *Dhamma-saṅgaṇi* the items embraced by the factors of the path are understood to indicate the path the mind is following at any given time, the direction in which it is going. In the *Mahācattārīsaka-sutta* right view, closely followed by right striving and right mindfulness, interacts with the other factors of the path leading the way down the path that will eventually become the *ariyo aṭṭhaṅgiko maggo*. Just like the *Dhammasaṅgaṇi*, the *Mahācattārīsaka-sutta* sees in the eight factors not the successive stages of the spiritual path, but rather the process that is active at all stages of the path.

One more aspect of the *Mahācattārīsaka-sutta's* treatment of the factors of the path seems to me to be of particular interest. It serves both to bring out what I have already said and also adds something of a further dimension. I refer to the actual contrast between the eight or ten items in their wrong aspect, on the one hand, and in their right aspect, on the other hand. Exactly this contrast is made again and again within the *magga-saṃyutta* and in many other places in the Nikāyas.[114] Amongst the seven sets this kind of contrast is peculiar to the *ariyo aṭṭhaṅgiko maggo*, and must be reckoned as one of the most distinctive and characteristic aspects of its treatment in early Buddhist literature. In the *Mahācattārīsaka-sutta* this contrast is particularly striking and well developed. It is made throughout the *sutta* and also forms the real climax—it is what actually gives the *sutta* its title.

The 'great forty', the twenty items in the party of the unskilful (*akusala-pakkha*) and the twenty items in the party of the skilful (*kusala-pakkha*), are contained in the third section. Wrong view counts as the first item that contributes to what is unskilful; 'the various bad unskilful *dhammas* that come into being with wrong view as their condition' count as the second item. In the same way wrong thought, speech, action, livelihood, striving, mindfulness, concentration, knowledge and freedom each give two items and complete the twenty. The ten items beginning with right view are considered in a similar fashion: right view itself as the first item, 'the various skilful *dhammas* with right view as their condition' as the second. So the 'great forty' is counted.

The 'great forty' consists, then, of two sequences of items balancing each other: one is negative and unskilful, the other positive and skilful. The first is headed by wrong view and the second by right view; these lead the way into an unskilful and skilful cycle respectively. Significantly the opening *sutta* of the *magga-saṃyutta* gives exactly these two cycles in a formula, that reflects the second section of the *Mahācattārīsaka-sutta*:

> Ignorance comes first, *bhikkhus*, in the attaining of unskilful *dhammas*; after [come] lack of self-respect and disregard for consequence. For one given to ignorance, for one who is ignorant, *bhikkhus*, wrong view appears; for one of wrong view, wrong thought ... wrong speech ... wrong action ... wrong livelihood ... wrong striving ...

---

114 M I 42-5; S II 168-9; III 109; V 1-2, 12-4, 15-7, 17-20, 23; A II 220-5; V 211-49.

> wrong mindfulness ... wrong concentration appears. Knowledge comes first, *bhikkhus* in the attaining of skilful *dhammas*; after [come] self-respect and regard for consequence. For one given to knowledge, for one who has knowledge, *bhikkhus*, right view appears; for one of right view, right thought ... right speech ... right action ... right livelihood ... right striving ... right mindfulness ... right concentration appears.[115]

Looked at in this way, the whole treatment of the *micchā-diṭṭhi* sequence and the *sammā-diṭṭhi* sequence begins to resemble another set of two alternative cycles, one negative, one positive, frequently found in the Nikāyas. I refer, of course, to the *anuloma* and *paṭiloma* sequences of conditioned arising (*paṭicca-samuppāda*).[116] The great emphasis on the priority of *sammā-diṭṭhi* in leading the way in the positive cycle in the *Mahācattārīsaka-sutta*, is exactly an application of what might be called the first principle of *paṭicca-samuppāda*: that *avijjā* comes first in the sequence of conditions that result in the coming into being of this whole mass of *dukkha*, and that the cessation of *avijjā* comes first in the sequence of conditions that result in the cessation of this whole mass of *dukkha*.

The significance of this is, I think, that we might speak of the law of *paṭicca-samuppāda* in the Nikāyas, and also of the law of the eight-factored path. These are in a sense two aspects of essentially the same thing, namely *dhamma*. According to early Buddhist literature the law of *paṭicca-samuppāda* is not something that can be avoided, it is not something that there is any choice about; it is the law of the universe and endures whether or not a Tathāgata arises in the world.[117] Either the cycle of *paṭicca-samuppāda* will tend towards the accumulation of 'this mass of *dukkha*' or it will tend towards its cessation; it cannot be otherwise. The 'law of the eight-factored path' can be understood similarly. The eight factors embrace eight essential aspects of existence—eight aspects that cannot be avoided. As long as these eight aspects are *sammā* or 'right' they continue to interact 'properly' and move in a skilful direction towards the cessation of *dukkha*. When they are *micchā* or 'wrong' they interact wrongly and move away from the cessation of suffering. What ultimately issues from the skilful interaction or cycle is the *ariyo aṭṭhaṅgiko maggo* itself. All this highlights a tension that exists in Buddhist thought between descriptive *dhamma* (how things are, *paṭicca-samuppāda*) and prescriptive *dhamma* (how things ought to be, the *ariyo aṭṭhaṅgiko maggo*).

This view of the *ariyo aṭṭhaṅgiko maggo* might be summed up like this. There are various eight-factored paths, some *micchā*, some *sammā*. These 'paths' are there all the time, and whether we like it or not we inevitably follow

---

115 S V 1-2: *avijjā bhikkhave pubbaṃ-gamā akusalānaṃ dhammānaṃ samāpattiyā anudeva ahirikaṃ anottappaṃ. avijjā-gatassa bhikkhave aviddasuno micchā-diṭṭhi pahoti. micchā-diṭṭhissa micchā-saṃkappo ... micchā-vācā ... micchā-kammanto ... micchā-ājīvo ... micchā-vāyāmo ... micchā-sati ... micchā-samādhi pahoti. vijjā bhikkhave pubbaṃ-gamā kusalānaṃ dhammānaṃ samāpattiyā anudeva hirikaṃ ottappaṃ. vijjā-gatassa bhikkhave viddasuno sammā-diṭṭhi pahoti. sammā-diṭṭhissa sammā-saṃkappo ... sammā-vācā ... sammā-kammanto ... sammā-vāyāmo ... sammā-sati ... sammā-samādhi pahoti.* (Cf. A V 211-2.)

116 E.g. S II 1.

117 S II 25; cf. A I 286.

one variety or the other, sometimes *micchā*, sometimes *sammā*. The *ariyo aṭṭhaṅgiko maggo* then becomes a particular variety of eight-factored paths in general. It is the eight-factored path as it really should be, it is the eight-factored path as it truly is, while the eight-factored paths that exist for us ordinarily are either—when they are *micchā*—distortions of this reality, or—when they are *sammā*—partial or momentary reflections of it.

I should add here that I do not wish to deny that there may well be a logic by which the eight factors of the path can be understood as characterizing the progressive stages of a spiritual path. Indeed Frauwallner himself suggests a quite attractive correspondence between the *sāmañña-phala* account of the path and the eight factors: right view corresponds to the initial confidence (*saddhā*) in the awakening of the Tathāgata; right thought, right speech and right action to the practice of *sīla*; right livelihood to the way of life of the monk as described at the conclusion of the *sīlas*; right striving to his trying to avoid future unskilful *dhammas* and to arouse future skilful *dhammas*; right mindfulness to the preparations for meditation; right concentration to the various meditation attainments.[118] Yet it is surely significant that the Nikāyas themselves never attempt such a correspondence, although the Buddhist tradition can on occasion do something rather similar with the factors, as is shown by the following passage from Harivarman's **Satyasiddhi-śāstra*:

> The right view is when one having the wisdom born of listening believes that the five aggregates of elements are impermanent and suffering, etc. When the knowledge turns to be reflective it is called right thought. As a result of this thought one attempts to eradicate sins and cultivate merits; that is right endeavour. In due course he, being ordained in the order follows good conduct and adheres to right speech, right action and right livelihood. As a result of these restraints the foundations of mindfulness, trances and concentrations are received in order. And as a result of the latter again the yogin secures a true knowledge of things as they are. This is the order of eight constituents of the path.[119]

What I do suggest, however, is that this is not the primary way of understanding the *ariyo aṭṭhaṅgiko maggo* in the Nikāyas. I suggest, then, that the process formula in the case of the factors of the path is intended to show the continuing priority of right view at all stages of the spiritual path: how one speaks, acts and thinks at any time is dependent on one's vision of oneself and the world.[120]

At this point it is worth pursuing the question of the way in which right view is understood to develop a little further. Peter Masefield has argued that there is in the Nikāyas an unbridgeable gap between right view that is ordinary and right view that is transcendent, a factor of the path, noble and without *āsavas*.[121] He then goes on to consider how this second kind of right view (i.e the path-factor) is seen as being acquired in the Nikāyas. According to a

---

118 Frauwallner, *HIP*, pp. 147-8.

119 Satya Trsl 43. It is, perhaps, significant that Harivarman here changes the place of *samyak-vyāyāma*.

120 Cf. the account of the path-factors at Mp II 71-3; Vibh-a 115-6.

121 Masefield, op. cit., p. 43.

Majjhima and *Aṅguttara* saying there are two conditions for the arising of right view, namely 'the utterance of another' (*parato ghosa*) and 'appropriate bringing to mind' (*yoniso manasikāra*).[122] Masefield proceeds to ignore the question of *yoniso manasikāra* as a condition for the arising of right view, in the case of ordinary disciples (*sāvakas*) of the Buddha, and concentrates on *parato ghosa*.[123] This he takes as meaning the 'sound from the Beyond'.[124] This is then taken as support for his main thesis: the sound of the beyond is mediated to other disciples only by the Buddha and his immediate disciples—this is the only way of gaining noble right view, which is religious truth 'revealed' in sound.

Many of Masefield's ideas and suggestions are of great interest and not without their attraction. I should not wish to deny that *parato ghosa* might mean 'the roar or thunder from beyond'; what I would wish to deny is that this excludes the meaning 'the utterance of another'. For, from the Nikāyas' point of view, to hear the utterance of one who speaks *dhamma* is perhaps precisely to hear 'the sound from beyond'. In the course of bringing to life a neglected dimension of the Nikāya's outlook, Masefield fails, I think, to relate this to other dimensions.

The thinking that underlies the notion of *parato ghosa* and *yoniso manasikāra* as the 'conditions for the arising of right view'[125] finds expression in different terms elsewhere in the Nikāyas. In the *bojjhaṅga-saṃyutta* appropriate bringing to mind is said to be the internal condition for the development of the *bojjhaṅgas*, and having a good friend (*kalyāṇa-mittatā*) the external condition.[126] Again, in the *Saṃgīti-sutta* and *Vibhaṅga* we find the notion of three kinds of wisdom: wisdom produced by reflection (*cintā-mayā paññā*), wisdom produced by hearing (*suta-mayā paññā*) and wisdom produced by development (*bhāvanā-mayā paññā*).[127] The *Vibhaṅga* defines wisdom produced by reflection as openness to knowledge[128] not gained by hearing from another (*khantiṃ ... parato assutvā paṭilabhati*); wisdom produced by hearing as openness to knowledge gained by hearing from another (*khantiṃ ... parato sutvā paṭilabhati*); and wisdom produced by development as all wisdom of the one who has

---

[122] M I 294; A I 87; whether *ariya* right view or ordinary right-view is intended here is not actually specified; but the Ps II 346 takes it as both (*sammā-diṭṭhiyā uppādāyā ti vipassanā-sammā-diṭṭhiyā ca magga-sammā-diṭṭhiyā ca*).

[123] Masefield, op. cit., p. 50, but Ps II 346 is misrepresented here; while it does say that *yoniso manasikāra* is the means of acquiring right view for *pacceka-buddhas* and *sabbaññu-buddhas*, it does *not* say that *parato ghosa* is the means for *sāvakas*; what they need are *both* conditions: 'Therein for disciples, even for Dhammasenāpati [i.e. Sāriputta], the two conditions conduce to the gaining [of right view].' (*tattha sāvakesu Dhammasenāpatino dve paccayā laddhuṃ vattanti yeva.*)

[124] Masefield, op. cit., p. 52. In discussing the meaning of *parato ghosa* Masefield cites Sn 696, 698 (id., pp. 51) but ignores Sn 818 (*sutvā paresaṃ nigghosaṃ*) which surely must be translated as 'hearing the outcry of others'.

[125] A I 87 also states that *parato ghosa* and *ayoniso manasikāra* are conditions for the arising of *micchā-diṭṭhi*, a fact which Masefield acknowledges as awkward to his thesis (op. cit., p. 52).

[126] See below, p. 256.

[127] D III 219; Vibh 324, 325; they do not appear to be mentioned elsewhere in the canon; in later writings *suta-mayā paññā* is given first. The list is also known to Buddhist Sanskrit sources, e.g. Abhidh-k 334.

[128] On *khanti* in this sense see *BHSD*, s.v. *kṣānti*.

spiritual attainments (*sabbā pi samāpannassa paññā*).[129] These three kinds of wisdom and their connection with *parato ghosa* and *yoniso manasikāra* are fully explored in the *Peṭakopadesa* and *Nettippakaraṇa*; I give just one illustrative quotation:

> The Teacher or a fellow practitioner in the position of a teacher teaches someone *dhamma*. Having heard this *dhamma* he gains confidence. Therein, whatever is investigation, energy, consideration, examination, this is wisdom produced by hearing. Whatever is investigation, consideration, examination, contemplation in dependence on what is thus heard, this is wisdom produced by reflection. The knowledge that arises either at the stage of seeing or the stage of development for one engaged in bringing to mind by means of these two kinds of wisdom is wisdom produced by development. From the utterance of another there is wisdom produced by hearing; from appropriate bringing to mind undertaken individually there is wisdom produced by reflection; the knowledge that arises both as a result of the utterance of another and as a result of appropriate bringing to mind undertaken individually is wisdom produced by development.[130]

The point here is that 'right view', whether initiated by hearing another's utterance or by appropriate bringing to mind, develops by means of the interaction of these two.

8. The ariyo aṭṭhaṅgiko maggo and the notion of 'path'

The commentaries preserve the following explanation of the expression *ariyo aṭṭhaṅgiko maggo*:

> It is noble due to its remoteness from the defilements to be slain by the appropriate path, due to bringing about the state of a noble, and due to bringing about the acquisition of the noble fruit. It is eight-factored in that it has eight factors; like an army of four parts, like musical instruments of five kinds, there is only the sum of parts, there is not something separate from the parts. It is a *magga* in that it is traced (*maggīyati*) by those whose goal is *nibbāna*, or it traces (*maggati*) *nibbāna*, or killing defilements it goes along (*mārento gacchati*).[131]

The term *magga* or 'path' is used in the Abhidhamma, both canonical and commentarial, to refer to four specific spiritual attainments, namely stream-attainment, once-return, non-return, and *arahant*-ship. These four attainments constitute the four varieties of *lokuttara-magga*; they are the four 'ways' (*paṭipadā*) that lead specifically to the cessation of suffering. In the Abhidhamma literature this usage of the term *magga* might seem to acquire its

---

[129] Vibh 325 = Sv III 1002; for further definition see Vibh-a 410-2 = DAṬ III 272-4.

[130] Nett 8 : *yassa satthā vā dhammaṃ desayati aññataro vā garu-ṭṭhāniyo sabrahma-cārī, so taṃ dhammaṃ sutvā saddhaṃ paṭilabhati. tattha yā vīmaṃsā ussāhanā tulanā upaparikkhā ayaṃ suta-mayi paññā. tathā sutena nissayena yā vīmaṃsā tulanā upaparikkhā manasânupekkhanā ayaṃ cintā-mayi paññā. imāhi dvīhi paññāhi manasikāra-sampayuttassa yaṃ ñāṇaṃ uppajjati dassana-bhūmiyaṃ vā bhāvanā-bhūmiyaṃ vā ayaṃ bhāvanā-mayi paññā. parato ghosā suta-mayi paññā, paccatta-samuṭṭhita yoniso manasikārā cintā-mayi paññā, yaṃ parato ca ghosena paccatta-samuṭṭhitena ca yoniso manasikārena ñāṇaṃ uppajjati ayaṃ bhāvanā-mayi paññā.* (Cf. Peṭ 2, 186, 232-6; 252-3, 260; Nett 50, 60.)

[131] Vibh-a 114 : *ariyo ti taṃ taṃ magga-vajjhehi kilesehi ārakattā, ariya-bhāva-karattā, ariya-phala-paṭilābha-karattā ca ariyo. aṭṭha aṅgāni assā ti aṭṭhaṅgiko. svāyaṃ caturaṅgikā viya senā pañcaṅgikaṃ viya turiyaṃ aṅga-mattaṃ eva hoti aṅga-vinimmutto natthi. nibbānatthikehi maggīyati, nibbānaṃ vā maggati kilese vā mārento gacchatī ti maggo.* (Cf. Ud-a 305; Nidd-a I 67.)

ultimate contradictory form. The image of a path, it might be thought, ought to imply 'a path along with one travels from beginning to end'; yet in the Abhidhamma literature 'path' comes to describe an experience so specific that it is, at least in the fully developed systems, seen as lasting only a single moment (or at most fifteen thought moments, if we choose to follow the traditions of the Sarvāstivāda). But what I have tried to show above is that in the Nikāyas the *ariyo aṭṭhaṅgiko maggo* was always primarily conceived of as a way of practising or of going along; it is a path in the sense of how one goes, rather than where one goes. I mean by this that the image of the 'path' in the Nikāyas seems much more concerned with how one travels or one's means of conveyance than with the sequence of places through which one passes on the journey. This is particularly clear with the image of the *ariyo aṭṭhaṅgiko maggo* as a 'divine vehicle' (*brahma-yāna*). If one considers this image in the light of the *Mahācattārīsaka* treatment, the point seems to be that on the one hand there is a kind of consistency about how one travels at all stages of the journey, on the other hand a transformation occurs: one may start in a chariot and finish in a chariot, yet the chariot one sets out in is old, broken and in need of repair, the chariot one arrives in is suited to a god.

The eight factors are, then, thought of as eight items that are to be collectively brought to rightness. We start with the condition of the ordinary man (*puthujjana*) which is characterized by the continual fluctuation of the eight items (sometimes they are 'right', sometimes they are 'wrong'); we finish with the condition of the *arahant* which is characterized by the eight items being firmly and fully 'right'. The notions of stream-attainment, and so on, must always have served the purpose in Buddhist thought of defining possible stages in this process of the mind's turning away from wrong view, etc., beginning with the grosser manifestations and continuing until the subtlest forms are left behind. Once there are stages, there are points of transition between the stages; the precise nature of these points of transition is the domain of Abhidhamma, which defines them ever more closely and subtly. While the Abhidhamma literature does add new details, it does so within an existing framework.

The traditional image of finding an ancient path in the jungle provides a convenient point of reference for the summing up of the notion of the *ariyo aṭṭhaṅgiko maggo* in the Nikāyas, for the image seems to me to present what is in fact a rather exact model of the Nikāya conception of spiritual progress:

> As if, *bhikkhus*, a person wandering in the forest, in the jungle were to see an ancient path, an ancient road along which men of old had gone. And he would follow it, and as he followed it he would see an ancient city, an ancient seat of kings which men of old had inhabited, possessing parks, gardens, lotus-ponds, with high walls, a delightful place. And then that person would tell the king or his minister: 'You should surely know, sir, that while wandering in the forest, in the jungle I saw an ancient path ... an ancient city ... a delightful place. Claim that city, sir!' And then the king or the king's minister would claim that city. And after a time that city would become prosperous and wealthy, with many people, filled with people, achieving growth and prosperity. Just so, I saw an ancient path, the ancient road along which the fully awakened ones of old had gone ... namely the

> noble eight-factored path ... I followed it and following it I knew directly old age and death, the arising of old age and death, the cessation of old age and death, the way leading to the cessation of old age and death.[132]

Let us consider this from the point of view of the king informed of the existence of the path and the city in the jungle. He is clearly to be likened to one instructed by the Buddha concerning the *ariyo aṭṭhaṅgiko maggo* as the way leading to the cessation of suffering. Having been informed of the path and city, of its general whereabouts, the king must find the path in the jungle himself. Likewise the Buddha's disciple, the *bhikkhu*, following the instructions concerning the abandoning of wrong view and so on, and the development of right view and so on, sets out to find the *ariyo aṭṭhaṅgiko maggo*; thus he develops right view and so on that are ordinary and concerned with merit. Now, the king or his ministers who have set out into the jungle have accepted the existence of the path and city on trust; wandering in the jungle doubts may arise, but as soon as they come across the path and see the way before them leading to a city all those doubts will be dispersed. Similarly, as the *bhikkhu* develops ordinary right view and so on, he may doubt the existence of a path that leads to the cessation of suffering, but when in the course of that development he comes across right view and so on that is noble, when, that is, he comes across the *ariyo aṭṭhaṅgiko maggo* and sees that it truly does lead on to the cessation of suffering, how can he doubt it? This is surely the significance of the stream-attainer's being characterized as one who has complete trust (*avecca-ppasāda*) in the Buddha, Dhamma and Saṃgha, as one who has overcome doubt. One who has found the path and sees that it leads to the city, has only to follow that path and enter the city. Thus the *bhikkhu* who has gained the path develops the eight factors along with right knowledge and right freedom and finally destroys the *āsavas*.

In conclusion it is worth noting how Jaina sources give the path of spiritual progress a structure that shows quite definite parallels to this. The spiritual path is understood as consisting of fourteen successive stages called *guṇa-sthānas*. The fourth of these is known as *samyag-dṛṣṭi* which, according to P.S. Jaini, is understood as an initial flash or experience of insight (*darśana*).[133] He writes:

> Thus it is said that a soul which retains its samyak-darśana at the time of death will not fall into hells or the lower tiryañca destiny. Even more important, it will

---

132 S II 105-6: *seyyathâpi bhikkhave puriso araññe pavane caramāno passeyya purāṇaṃ maggaṃ purāṇañjasaṃ pubbakehi manussehi anuyātaṃ. so taṃ anugaccheyya taṃ anugacchanto passeyya purāṇaṃ nagaraṃ purāṇaṃ rāja-dhānim pubbakehi manussehi ajjhāvutthaṃ ārāma-sampannaṃ vana-sampannaṃ pokkharaṇī-sampannaṃ uddāpavantaṃ ramaṇīyaṃ. atha kho so bhikkhave puriso rañño vā rāja-mahāmattassa vā āroceyya. yagghe bhante jāneyyāsi. ahaṃ addasaṃ araññe pavane caramāno purāṇaṃ maggaṃ ... purāṇaṃ nagaraṃ ... ramaṇīyaṃ. taṃ bhante nagaraṃ māpehī ti. atha kho bhikkhave rājā vā rāja-mahāmatto vā taṃ nagaraṃ māpeyya. tad assa nagaraṃ aparena samayena iddhaṃ ceva phītaṃ ca bahujanaṃ ākiṇṇa-manussaṃ vuddhi-vepulla-ppattaṃ. evam eva khvāhaṃ bhikkhave addasaṃ purāṇaṃ maggaṃ purāṇañjasaṃ pubbakehi sammā-sambuddhehi anuyātaṃ ... ayaṃ eva ariyo aṭṭhaṅgiko maggo ... taṃ anugacchiṃ. taṃ anugacchanto jarā-maraṇaṃ abbhaññāsiṃ, jarā-maraṇa-samudayaṃ abbhaññāsiṃ, jarā-maraṇa-nirodhaṃ abbhaññāsiṃ, jarā-maraṇa-nirodha-gāminiṃ paṭipadaṃ abbhaññāsiṃ.*

133 P.S. Jaini, *The Jaina Path of Purification*, Berkeley, 1979, pp. 144-5.

> remain in bondage *no longer* than the amount of time required to take in and use up half of the available karmas in the universe ... [134]

Further the arising of *samyag-darśana* is associated with the arising of eight factors (*aṣṭâṅga*) which are subsequently cultivated and brought to perfection. These turn out to be rather different in nature from the eight path-factors in Buddhist literature, and the image of the path does not appear to be used.[135] Of note, however, is the inclusion of freedom from doubt (*niḥśaṅkita*) and freedom from delusive views (*amūḍha-dṛṣṭi*). From the point of view of general principle the fourth *guṇa-sthāna* bears considerable resemblance to stream-attainment, which abandons doubt, and the view of individuality, cuts off rebirth in a place of regress, and destines one for awakening. Of course, Jaini is following here exgetical literature removed by as much as 1,200 years from the time of Mahāvīra. But however one views the origins of these parallels—whether as deriving from a common earlier source or as the result of deliberate borrowing at some later date—their very existence tends to indicate a particular way of looking at the structure of spiritual development that modern expositions of the *ariyo aṭṭhaṅgiko maggo* have failed to make clear.

---

[134] Ibid.
[135] Id., pp. 151-6.

PART TWO

THE SEVEN SETS COLLECTIVELY

CHAPTER SEVEN

THE SEVEN SETS IN THE NIKĀYAS

1. Preliminary remarks: different usages distinguished

In this chapter I wish to discuss the treatment of the seven sets collectively in the earlier parts of the Pāli canon, and begin to come to some conclusion about just what the seven sets represent for this literature. The seven sets are listed together some seventy-four times in the *Vinaya-piṭaka* and the Nikāyas.[1] As I have noted above, it is not always easy to determine what counts as a parallel passage, and what as mere repetition—especially, in this case, in the *Saṃyutta-nikāya*. But it seems reasonable to suggest that these seventy-four times the sets are listed represent some twenty-seven distinct occasions upon which the seven sets are collectively cited.[2]

As I hope to make clear, these passages are of four basic types. The first type is distinguished by the fact that it presents the seven sets as '*dhammas* taught' by the Buddha. The second type presents the seven sets more specifically as representing the path or practice to be undertaken by the *bhikkhu*. In the third type of passage the seven sets form a part of more extended lists of items and appear to be treated rather more generally. Finally there is the *mahā-vagga* of the *Saṃyutta-nikāya*; although I have already referred to its treatment of the individual sets, it deserves also to be considered as a distinctive treatment of the seven sets collectively.

2. The appeal to the seven sets as dhammas taught by the Buddha

It seems appropriate to begin here with an important passage from the *Mahāparinibbāna-sutta* that is frequently cited as an instance in the Nikāyas where the seven sets occur as a definite group.[3] This passage is of additional interest as a starting point since it happens to afford a considerable amount of parallel material in Buddhist Sanskrit sources and in Chinese and Tibetan translations. First of all, however, it is worth placing the passage in question in its proper context in the Pāli version of the *Mahāparinibbāna-sutta*.

The *sutta* opens on Vulture Peak near Rājagaha with a discussion of those

---

[1] The only text of the *Khuddaka-nikāya* that turns out to be relevant is the *Udāna* which lists the seven sets once in a passage that has a parallel in both the *Vinaya-piṭaka* and *Aṅguttara-nikāya*; the *Niddesa* and *Paṭisambhidāmagga* I do not take as belonging to the earlier parts of the Pāli canon.

[2] Vin II 236-41 = A IV 197-204 = 204-8 = Ud 51-6 (4 'times'; 1 'occasion'). Vin III 93, 94, 95, 97 (4 'times'; 1 'occasion'). Vin IV 26, 27, 28 (3 'times'; 1 'occasion'). D II 120; III 102, 127 (3 'times'; 3 'occasions'). M II 11, 238, 245; III 81; 289, 296 (6 'times'; 6 'occasions'); S III 96, 153-4; IV 359-73 (34 'times'); V 49-50, *54 (3 times), *135-6, *138, *191, *240, *242, *246, *250, *252, *291, *308-9 (50 'times'; 11 'occasions'). A I 39-40, 295-7; IV 125-7; V 175 (4 'times'; 4 'occasions'). (An asterisk before a reference indicates that the occurrence is lost in the abbreviations of the text.)

[3] E.g. Warder, *IB*, p. 81.

conditions that will prevent the decline (*aparihāniya-dhamma*) of the Saṃgha. Whatever historical value one attaches to the details of person and place in this introductory section (and Bareau, for one, attaches very little),[4] it is clear that it carefully sets the mood for the rest of the *sutta*: our concern is the imminent death of the Buddha and the future of the Saṃgha and his teaching. According to the narrative the Buddha then journeys in stages from Rājagaha to Vesālī. Not far from Vesālī at Beluva the Buddha decides to spend the rainy season. At this point the Buddha falls ill, whereupon Ānanda questions the Buddha concerning any final instructions he might have for the Saṃgha before he dies. The Buddha responds with what is again a well known passage:

> But what, Ānanda, does the *bhikkhu-saṃgha* expect of me? *Dhamma* is taught by me, Ānanda, making no 'inside' and no 'outside'; in this connection, Ānanda, the Tathāgata does not have the closed fist of the teacher with regard to *dhammas*.[5]

After this the Buddha retires to the Cāpāla-cetiya. I have already discussed this incident at some length in connection with the *iddhi-pādas*; the culmination is the announcement of the Buddha's imminent death—after three months have passed. The Buddha then requests Ānanda to assemble the *bhikkhus* who live in the neighbourhood of Vesālī at the Kūṭāgāra-sālā where he addresses them with the passage concerning the seven sets:

> Then the Blessed One approached the meeting hall; having approached he sat down on the prepared seat. Seated he addressed the *bhikkhus*: 'So, *bhikkhus*, those *dhammas* that I have directly known and taught to you—having properly grasped them, you should practise them, develop them, make them great so that the spiritual life might continue and endure long; this will be for the good of the many, for the happiness of the many, for the sake of compassion for the world, for the benefit, good and happiness of devas and men. And what, *bhikkhus*, are the *dhammas* that I have known directly and taught to you ... ? Just these—the four establishings of mindfulness, the four right endeavours, the four bases of success, the five faculties, the five powers, the seven factors of awakening, the noble eight-factored path ... ' Then the Blessed One addressed the *bhikkhus* [further]: 'Now let me address you, *bhikkhus*, the nature of conditions is to decay; work with heedfulness, the *parinibbāna* of the Tathāgata will not be long ... '[6]

As is well known, the rest of the *Mahāparinibbāna-sutta* goes on to detail how the Buddha continues his journey; at Pāvā he has his last meal and falls ill for a second time and then moves on to Kusinārā where the *parinibbāna* takes place. The passage concerning the seven sets by no means constitutes the

---

[4] Bareau, *RBB* II 7-16.

[5] D II 100: *kiṃ panânanda bhikkhu-saṃgho mayi paccāsiṃsati. desito Ānanda mayā dhammo anantaraṃ abāhiraṃ karitvā, na tatthânanda tathāgatassa dhammesu ācariya-muṭṭhi.*

[6] D II 119-120: *atha kho bhagavā yena upaṭṭhāna-sālā ten'upasaṃkami, upasaṃkamitvā paññatte āsane nisīdi. nisajja kho bhagavā bhikkhū āmantesi. tasmāt iha bhikkhave ye vo mayā dhammā abhiññāya desitā te vo sādhukaṃ uggahetvā āsevitabbā bhāvetabbā bahulīkātabbā yathay-idaṃ brahma-cariyaṃ addhaniyaṃ assa cira-ṭṭhitikaṃ, tad assa bahu-jana-hitāya bahu-jana-sukhāya lokânukampāya atthāya hitāya sukhāya deva-manussānaṃ. katame ca te bhikkhave dhammā mayā abhiññāya desitā ... seyyathīdaṃ cattāro satipaṭṭhānā cattāro samma-ppadhānā cattāro iddhi-pādā pañcindriyāni pañca balāni satta bojjhaṅgā ariyo aṭṭhaṅgiko maggo ... atha kho bhagavā bhikkhū āmantesi. handa dāni bhikkhave āmantayāmi vo, vaya-dhammā saṃkhārā appamādena sampādetha, na ciraṃ tathāgatassa parinibbānaṃ bhavissati.*

Buddha's last discourse—the narrative states that the Buddha subsequently gave *dhamma* talks (*dhammiṃ kathaṃ karoti*) at various places and also gives some details of what was said on specific occasions. While this is so, the passage itself and the immediate context of the announcement of the imminent *parinibbāna* of the Buddha make it abundantly clear that this is intended as an important and essential summary of the Buddha's teaching. That this is so is underlined by a consideration of parallel sources.

The Pāli *Mahāparinibbāna-sutta* can be conveniently considered alongside the Mūlasarvāstivādin *Mahāparinirvāṇa-sūtra* which exists in Sanskrit as well as in Chinese and Tibetan translation.[7] Bareau's detailed analysis of the *parinirvāṇa* traditions also takes into account additional Chinese translations of further recensions of the same material.[8] All these recensions apparently include a version of the present incident, namely a summary of the Buddha's teaching based on the seven sets and given by the Buddha in the context of the announcement of his imminent *parinirvāṇa*.[9]

The Mūlasarvāstivādin version is worth setting out in full here, since it illustrates both a basic correspondence with the Pāli version as well as interesting variations in matters of detail:

> Then the Blessed One approached the meeting hall. Having approached he sat down on the prepared seat before the *bhikṣu-saṃgha*. Seated the Blessed One addressed the *bhikṣus*: 'Impermanent are conditions, *bhikṣus*, they are unstable, uncertain, their nature is to change. In so far as this is so, one should condition all conditions, one should desist (from them). So, *bhikṣus*, those *dharmas* which conduce to good and happiness in the world of the here and now, to good and happiness in the future—having grasped and mastered those [*dharmas*], *bhikṣus* should thus preserve them, give instruction in them, teach them, so that the spiritual life might endure long; this will be for the good of the many, for the happiness of the many, for the sake of compassion for the world, for the benefit, good and happiness of devas and men. And what are those *dharmas* ... ? Just these, the four establishings of mindfulness, the four right abandonings, the four bases of success, the five faculties, the five powers, the seven factors of awakening, the noble eight-factored path.'[10]

---

[7] See E. Waldschmidt *MPS*.

[8] The Dharmaguptaka *Dīrghâgama* (trsl. Buddhayaśas and Tchou Fo-nien, 412-3 CE) = A; *Buddhanirvāṇa-sūtra* (trsl. Po Fa-tsou, 290-306 CE) = B; *Parinirvāṇa-sūtra* (trsl. 317-402 CE) = C; *Mahāparinirvāṇa-sūtra* (trsl. Fa-hien, 417 CE) = D. See Bareau, *RBB* II 4.

[9] Bareau, *RBB* II 196: 'Cet épisode est raconté par les six MPNS. Dans cinq d'entre eux, il suit immédiatement celui dans lequel le Buddha annonce à Ānanda le rejet de ses compositions vitales et lui fait des reproches, alors que, dans le chinois A, il le précède immédiatement; mais, dans tous les cas, il vient aussitôt après les divers événements qui se sont déroulés près du sanctuaire de Cāpāla entre le Bienheureux et Ānanda demeurés seuls.'

[10] *MPS* (Waldschmidt) 222-4: *atha bhagavān yenopasthāna-śālā tenopasaṃkrāntaḥ. upasaṃkramya purastād bhikṣu-saṃghasya prajñapta evâsane nyasīdat. niṣadya bhagavān bhikṣūn āmantrayate sma. anityā bhikṣavaḥ sarva-saṃskārā adhruvā anāśvāsikā vipariṇāma-dharmaṇo yāvad alam eva bhikṣavaḥ sarva-saṃskārān saṃskārituṃ alaṃ virantum. tasmāt tarhi bhikṣavo ye te dharmā dṛṣṭa-dharma-hitāya saṃvartante dṛṣṭa-dharma-sukhāya samparāya-hitāya samparāya-sukhāya te bhikṣubhir udgṛhya paryavāpya tathā tathā dhārayitavyā grāhayitavyā vācayitavyā yathedaṃ brahmacaryaṃ cira-sthitikaṃ syāt tad bhaviṣyati bahu-jana-hitāya bahu-jana-sukhāya lokânukampāyârthāya hitāya sukhāya deva-manuṣyānām. katame te dharmā dṛṣṭa-dharma-hitāya saṃvartante ... tadyathā catvāri smṛty-upasthānāni catvāri samyak-prahāṇāni catvāri ṛddhi-pādāḥ pañcendriyāṇi*

The opening formula of this Mūlasarvāstivādin version seems to parallel in spirit what comes at the close of the Pāli passage; a more direct Pāli parallel to this opening formula—though still with interesting variation—is found in a different Nikāya context.[11] The formula used in the body of the Mūlasarvāstivādin version and applied more directly to the seven sets is also slightly different from the formula used in the Pāli version. Once again a direct Pāli parallel to this formula exists, though it appears to be very rare in the Nikāyas.[12] Bareau gives no information on the formulas used in the Chinese translations, but does comment that one Chinese translation details the seven sets. Two of the Chinese translations also apparently add to the list of the seven sets, between the *ṛddhi-pādas* and *indriyas*, the four *dhyānas*.[13] I shall return to the significance of this below. Finally one should note that the Mūlasarvāstivādin version of the *Mahāparinirvāṇa-sūtra* gives the seven sets in another context as well, namely the context of the Buddha's first illness and his remark concerning the closed fist of the teacher.[14]

Already, I think, we have good grounds for thinking that as far as the early Buddhist tradition is concerned, the seven sets should be seen as encapsulating the essential teaching and practice of Buddhism.[15] As far as the Pāli canon is concerned, however, there are a number of passages citing the seven sets that bear close comparison with this *Mahāparinibbāna-sutta* passage. Although these passages seem to have been largely overlooked, they do, I think, make the nature of the appeal to the seven sets rather clearer.

The *Pāsādika-sutta*[16] opens with the Buddha dwelling among the Sakkas immediately after the death of Nigaṇṭha Nāthaputta at Pāvā. The *sutta* then recounts how at Nigaṇṭha Nāthaputta's death the Nigaṇṭhas become split and start quarrelling with each other. Cunda Samaṇuddesa relates the matter to Ānanda who suggests that they put it before the Buddha. The Buddha responds with a discussion of the relationship between teacher (*satthar*),

---

pañca balāni sapta bodhy-aṅgāny āryâṣṭâṅgo mārgaḥ. (Cf. *Divyâvadāna* (ed. E.B. Cowell and R.A. Neil, Cambridge, 1886), pp. 207-8.)

[11] Cf. D II 198: *evaṃ aniccā kho Ānanda saṃkhārā evaṃ addhuvā … anassāsikā kho Ānanda saṃkhārā, yāvañ c'idaṃ Ānanda alaṃ eva sabba-saṃkhāresu nibbindituṃ alaṃ virajjituṃ alaṃ vimuccituṃ*.

[12] At A IV 281-9 (passim) we find *cattāro dhammā kula-putassa diṭṭha-dhamma-hitāya saṃvattanti diṭṭha-dhamma-sukhāya*, and *cattāro dhammā kula-putassa samparāya-hitāya saṃvattanti samparāya-sukhāya*. According to *PTC* (s.v. *diṭṭha-dhamma-sukhāya, -hitāya*) this is the only occurrence in the Pāli canon.

[13] Bareau, *RBB* II 202. Cf. Warder, *IB*, p. 77.

[14] There is a lacuna in the Sanskrit manuscript at this point: *mama khalv ānanda naivaṃ bhavati mamâsti bhikṣu-saṃghaḥ. ahaṃ bhikṣu-saṃghaṃ parihariṣyāmîti* [lacuna] *tadyathā catvāri smṛty-upasthānāni* … (*MPS* 197). Snellgrove (*BSOAS* 36 (1973), p. 401) translates the relevant portion from the Tibetan as follows: 'Ānanda, I do not have the idea that the order of monks is mine, that I must cleave to the order and lead it, so how should I have a last exhortation, even a slight one, with which to instruct the order? Whatever teachings I have had which were relevant to the order of monks, I have already taught them as the principles which must be practised, namely the four *smṛty-upasthānas* … As Buddha I do not have the closed-fistedness of a teacher who thinks he must conceal things as unsuitable for others.'

[15] Cf. Warder, *IB*, pp. 81-2.

[16] D III 117-41.

dhamma and pupils (*sāvaka*). He concludes[17] that although he is now old, *dhamma* is well proclaimed by him, an *arahant* and *sammāsambuddha*; among his pupils are *bhikkhus* and *bhikkhunīs* who are elders, middle-aged and novices, among his pupils are both *upāsakas* and *upāsikās*. He continues:

> A man speaking rightly who would say of something, 'The spiritual life is well proclaimed—accomplished and complete in every respect, without deficiency and without excess, well set forth, whole and complete', would say it of this [spiritual life, this *dhamma*][18]. So, Cunda, regarding those *dhammas* which I have known directly and taught to you, you should all meet and come together to chant meaning for meaning, word for word, and not to dispute so that the spiritual life might continue and endure long; this will be for the good of the many, for the happiness of the many, for the sake of compassion for the world, for the benefit, good and happiness of devas and men. And what, Cunda, are those *dhammas* ... ? Just these, the four establishings of mindfulness ... the noble eight-factored path.[19]

This passage marks what is more or less the halfway point in the *Pāsādika-sutta* and as such seems to act as a kind of pivot for the *sutta* as a whole. The *sutta* continues by detailing what are in effect a number of ways in which the tradition of the teacher and his pupils can be preserved. The emphasis is on avoiding dispute and reaching clear agreement: the *bhikkhus* should not quarrel, on the other hand they should not allow the tradition to be distorted.

The second passage I wish to consider here comes from the *Sāmagāma-sutta*.[20] In some ways this has the appearance of an alternative *Majjhima-nikāya* version of the *Dīgha-nikāya's Pāsādika-sutta*. Apart from the mention of the Buddha's specific place of residence among the Sakkas at Sāmagāma, the *Sāmagāma-sutta* opens in exactly the same manner as the *Pāsādika-sutta*: Nigaṇṭha Nāthaputta has just died and the Nigaṇṭhas become split and begin quarrelling; Cunda Samaṇuddesa and Ānanda put the matter before the Buddha.[21] This time, however, Ānanda concludes with a more specific point:

> This occurs to me, lord: let not a dispute arise in the Saṃgha after the passing of the Blessed One. Such a dispute would be to the detriment, unhappiness and

---

[17] D III 125-6.

[18] So Sv III 911.

[19] D III 127-8: *yaṃ kho taṃ Cunda sammā-vadamāno vadeyya: sabbâkāra-sampannaṃ sabbâkāra-paripūraṃ anūnaṃ anadhikaṃ svākkhātaṃ kevala-paripūraṃ brahma-cariyaṃ suppakāsitan ti idaṃ eva taṃ sammā-vadamāno vadeyya ... suppakāsitan ti. tasmāt iha Cunda ye vo mayā dhammā abhiññā desitā tattha sabbeh'eva saṃgamma samāgamma atthena atthaṃ vyañjanena vyañjanaṃ saṃgāyitabbaṃ no vivaditabbaṃ yathayidaṃ brahma-cariyaṃ addhaniyaṃ assa cira-ṭṭhitikaṃ ... katame ca te Cunda dhammā ... seyyathīdaṃ cattāro satipaṭṭhānā ... ariyo aṭṭhaṅgiko maggo ...*

[20] M II 243-51.

[21] Interestingly the *Saṃgīti-sutta* (D III 207) is said to have been delivered by Sāriputta also at the time of Nigaṇṭha Nāthaputta's death, when the Buddha was staying at Pāvā in the mango-grove of Cunda Kammāraputta (who prepared the Buddha's last meal). Bareau (*RBB* II 254-5) comments on the possible association of the name Cunda (both layman and *bhikkhu*) with the city of Pāvā in Buddhist tradition. As a great 'compendium' of *dhammas* the *Saṃgīti-sutta* would also seem to act as a point of reference in the settling of disputes; it too opens with the formula concerning the long duration of the spiritual life for the good of the many.

> disadvantage of the many; it would be to the detriment and suffering of devas and men.[22]

The Buddha responds:

> What do you think, Ānanda? Those *dhammas* which I have directly known and taught to you, namely the four establishings of mindfulness ... the noble eight factored path—regarding these *dhammas*, Ānanda, do you see any two monks who have opinions at variance with one another?[23]

Ānanda replies that he does not but suggests that after the Buddha's passing those who live taking him as their refuge (*paṭissayamāna*) might become involved in dispute about the proper way of life (*ajjhājīve*) and about the code of discipline (*adhipātimokkhe*),[24] and that this would be to the disadvantage of the many. The Buddha, however, replies that dispute about such matters is of little matter (*appa-mattaka*); it is dispute about the path (*magga*) and the way (*paṭipadā*) that is really to the disadvantage of the many. The Buddha then proceeds to detail six roots of dispute (*vivāda-mūla*) and how they are to be abandoned, four points that can constitute matters of formal controversy (*adhikaraṇa*), seven ways of settling such matters,[25] and six *dhammas* that make for affection and concord amongst fellow spiritual practitioners.

The last passage I wish to consider here is taken from the *Kinti-sutta*[26]—the *sutta* that immediately precedes the *Sāmagāma-sutta*. This *sutta* begins with a question put by the Buddha to the *bhikkhus*:

> What do you think of me, *bhikkhus*? That the *samaṇa* Gotama teaches *dhamma* for the sake of the robe? Or that the *samaṇa* Gotama teaches *dhamma* for the sake of alms ... or for the sake of lodgings ... or for the sake of different states of being?[27]

The *bhikkhus* reply that they do not think in this way, but rather that 'as one who is compassionate, desirous of good, the Blessed One teaches *dhamma* out of compassion' (*anukampako bhagavā hitesi anukampaṃ upādāya dhammaṃ deseti*). Immediately the Buddha responds:

> So, *bhikkhus*, there are those *dhammas* that I have directly known and taught to you, namely the four establishings of mindfulness ... the noble eight-factored path. You should all train yourselves therein united, in concord, not disputing. While

---

[22] M II 245: *tassa mayhaṃ bhante evaṃ hoti mā heva bhagavato accayena saṃghe vivādo uppajji. so vivādo bahu-janâhitāya bahu-janâsukhāya bahuno janassa anatthāya ahitāya dukkhāya deva-manussānan ti.*

[23] M II 245: *taṃ kiṃ maññasi Ānanda ye vo mayā dhammā abhiññā desitā seyyathīdaṃ cattāro satipaṭṭhānā ... ariyo aṭṭhaṅgiko maggo passasi no tvaṃ Ānanda imesu dhammesu dve pi bhikkhū nānā-vāde ti.*

[24] On these terms cf. *CPD*, s.vv. *ajjhājīve, adhipātimokkhe*: 'with regard to the rigours of the regimen' and 'regarding the code of discipline' respectively; *CPD* refers to Ps IV 38 for technical definitions.

[25] These seven *adhikaraṇa-samatha-dhammas* constitute the last seven rules of the *pātimokkha*; their equivalents are also found in the Mūlasarvāstivādin and Mahāsāṃghika *Prātimokṣa-sūtras*, see C. Prebish, *Monastic Discipline*, Pennsylvania, 1975, pp. 106-9.

[26] M II 238-43.

[27] M II 238: *kinti vo bhikkhave mayi hoti. cīvara-hetu samaṇo Gotamo dhammaṃ deseti piṇḍa-pāta-hetu vā ... senâsana-hetu vā ... iti bhavâbhava-hetu vā ...*

> you are training yourselves united, in concord, not disputing there might be two *bhikkhus* who hold opinions about *dhamma*[28] at variance with one another.[29]

The Buddha then goes on to discuss ways of dealing with possible areas of contention and friction: where there is disagreement about meaning and wording (both together and each separately); where a *bhikkhu* commits some offence (*āpatti*) or transgression (*vītikamma*); where argument and ill-feeling exist between two groups.

These four passages beginning with the *Mahāparinibbāna-sutta* all more or less concern themselves with the long term fortunes of the Saṃgha and the maintenance of the tradition established by the Buddha. The nature of the appeal to the seven sets in this particular context is worth considering carefully. In all four passages the seven sets are described as *dhammas* that the Buddha has gained direct knowledge (*abhiññā*) of and then taught to the *bhikkhus*. For their part, the *bhikkhus* should grasp these *dhammas* well (*sādhukaṃ uggahetvā*), practise them (*āsevitabba*), develop them (*bhāvetabba*), make them great (*bahulīkatabba*)—so the *Mahāparinibbāna-sutta*; they should come together and with regard to these *dhammas* (*tattha*) they should chant meaning for meaning and word for word (*atthena atthaṃ vyañjanena vyañjanaṃ saṃgāyitabbaṃ*) and not dispute—so the *Pāsādika-sutta*; they should train themselves in these *dhammas* united, in concord and without disputing—so the *Kinti-sutta*. The *Sāmagāma-sutta* opens with the question of dispute, but, says the Buddha, there is no dispute among the *bhikkhus* about the *dhammas* embraced by the seven sets; we are then told that disputes about the details of the way of life are of little importance; it is disputes about the path and way that matter. The implication seems clear: if the *bhikkhus* preserve the *dhammas* embraced by the seven sets in the above manner, then no disputes of importance will arise and the tradition will be preserved for the good and benefit of the many. The *Mahāniddesa*, apparently taking up this notion, states that agreement about *dhamma* (*dhamma-sāmaggi*) consists in the seven sets—collectively they find satisfaction, clarity, stillness, release (*te ekato pakkhandanti pasīdanti santiṭṭhanti vimuccanti*); there is no dispute or argument about these *dhammas* (*na tesaṃ dhammānaṃ vivādo vippavādo atthi*).[30]

The first thing that follows from this is, I think, that the appeal to the four establishings of mindfulness, and the rest, is not an appeal to *dhammas* as 'teachings' or 'doctrines'—at least not in the limited sense of a body of teachings or doctrines that can exist apart from the actual experience and practice of those teachings, apart from the actual path and way. The nature of the appeal to the seven sets is a matter of appeal to practice and experience rather than an appeal to theory and scripture. The appeal ultimately rests on the fact that the seven sets embrace *dhammas* that the *bhikkhu* can gain

---

28 On *abhi-dhamme* in this passage see *CPD*, s.v. *abhidhamma*, and Norman, *PL*, p. 97.

29 *tasmāt iha bhikkhave ye vo mayā dhammā abhiññā desitā seyyathīdaṃ cattāro satipaṭṭhānā … ariyo aṭṭhaṅgiko maggo, tattha sabbeh'eva samaggehi sammodamānehi avivadamānehi sikkhitabbaṃ. tesañ ca vo bhikkhave samaggānaṃ sammodamānānaṃ avivadamānānaṃ sikkhataṃ siyaṃsu dve bhikkhū abhi dhamme nānā-vādā.*

30 Nidd I 132.

personal direct knowledge of, they constitute *dhamma* that is 'to be known by the wise each one for himself' (*paccattaṃ veditabbo viññūhi*).[31]

It might be objected that in talking of 'chanting meaning for meaning and word for word' the *Pāsādika-sutta* especially implies precisely an appeal to scriptural authority. This raises the question of the proper understanding of the notion of *dhamma* in the Nikāyas, the question of the relationship between what the commentaries call *dhamma* as 'tradition' (*pariyatti*, *āgama*) and *dhamma* as practice and attainment (*paṭipatti*, *paṭivedha*, *adhigama*).[32] I shall return to this presently. However, it seems to me that the appeal to the seven sets is a classic instance showing that the authority of the former rests in its capacity to conduce to the latter. The yardstick is a practical test.

The question of difference of opinion over meaning (*attha*) and wording (*vyañjana*) is in fact dealt with in some detail in the *Kinti-sutta*. Difference of opinion over *vyañjana* is once more regarded as something of little consequence (*appa-mattaka*).[33] Difference of opinion over *attha* is a potentially more serious affair. The solution proffered here seems to be that the two sides in a dispute over *attha* should accept that some matters may be hard to grasp (*duggahīta*) others easy (*sugahīta*).[34] I take it that this implies that since differences of opinion over the *satipaṭṭhānas* and so on ultimately concern quite subtle matters of practical experience, *bhikkhus* should guard against attachment to particular interpretations of their theoretical formulation. Whether this is so or not, it seems to me that the appeal to the seven sets must be taken as in exactly the same spirit as the formula I quoted in connection with the *satipaṭṭhānas* and which occurs in the *Mahāparinibbāna-sutta* in the context of Ānanda's request for some final instruction from the Buddha:

> Therefore, Ānanda, you should dwell with yourselves as island, with yourselves as refuge, not with some other refuge; with *dhamma* as island, with *dhamma* as refuge, not with some other refuge.[35]

A passage that bears some resemblance to the four passages so far considered is found in the *Sampasādanīya-sutta*.[36] Here the seven sets are simply listed as skilful *dhammas* taught by the Buddha:

> Now, lord, this is unsurpassable: the way the Blessed One teachers *dhamma* with regard to skilful *dhammas*. Therein these are skilful *dhammas*, namely the four establishings of mindfulness ... the noble eight-factored path. Here, lord, a *bhikkhu* by the destruction of the *āsavas* himself knows directly in the here and now, realizes, attains and dwells in the freedom of mind, the freedom of wisdom that is without *āsavas*.[37]

---

[31] E.g. D II 93.

[32] On these terms see Carter, *Dhamma*, pp. 131-5.

[33] M II 240. An example of difference with regard to *vyañjana* is given at Ps IV 29 as *satipaṭṭhāno* (masculine) and *satipaṭṭhānaṃ* (neuter).

[34] M II 239-41.

[35] Cf. above, pp. 67, 230.

[36] D III 99-116.

[37] D III 102, *aparaṃ pana bhante etad ānuttariyaṃ yathā bhagavā dhammaṃ deseti kusalesu dhammesu. tatr'ime kusalā dhammā seyyathīdaṃ cattāro satipaṭṭhānā ... ariyo aṭṭhaṅgiko maggo.*

This, then, is the first of the sixteen *ānuttariyas* or 'unsurpassables' of the Buddha. The practical way in which the seven sets collectively constitute the highest realization of the Buddhist path is here explicit.

Returning to the usage of the seven sets as a reference point or yardstick in order to preserve and maintain the tradition, this invites comparison with the principle cited in connection with the four *mahâpadesas* or 'great authorities'.[38] According to this principle any statements or expressions (*pada-vyañjana*) that are claimed by a *bhikkhu* to have the status of *dhamma-vinaya* or the instruction of the teacher (*satthu sāsanaṃ*) are 'to be grasped well and brought into Sutta and compared with Vinaya; if being brought into Sutta they do in fact enter into Sutta, if being compared with Vinaya they do in fact bear comparison with Vinaya' (*tāni pada-vyañjanāni sādhukaṃ uggahetvā sutte otaretabbāni vinaye sandassetabbāni ... tāni ce sutte otariyamānāni vinaye sandassiyamānāni sutte c'eva otaranti vinaye ca sandissanti*), then one should conclude that the statements and expressions in question do represent the word of the Buddha. Étienne Lamotte has discussed the *mahâpadesas* at some length in two contexts. Commenting in the *Traité* on the question of the criterion of authenticity he says:

> Le point de vue orthodoxe, traditionaliste, est celui du pieux Aśoka dans l'édit de Bairat ... «Tout ce qu'a dit le bienheureux Buddha est bien dit» (*e kechi bhaṃte bhagavatā Budhena bhāsite sarve se subhāsite*). Par conséquent, diront les rédacteurs du canon, pour savoir si une doctrine ou un texte est parole du Buddha, il faudra le confronter avec les recueils d'écritures bouddhiques qui seuls font autorité.[39]

He goes on to paraphrase the passage concerning the *mahâpadesas* as follows:

> Quand un texte est proposé ... il faut voir si ce texte (*pada-vyañjanāni*) se trouve dans le Sūtra (*sutte otaranti*) et apparait dans le Vinaya (*vinaye sandissanti*).[40]

He concludes by suggesting that, with the development of Buddhist literature, it is increasingly the intrinsic merits of the text itself that determines its acceptance or otherwise as the authentic word of the Buddha:

> Finalement le critère d'autorité est complètement abandonné. Pour admettre un sūtra, on ne s'inquiète plus de savoir s'il a été prêché par le Buddha en un lieu donné à telle ou telle personne; on se demande seulement si les doctrines qu'il renferme sont, oui ou non, utiles et profitables. C'est le triomphe de la critique interne sur la critique externe, du subjectivisme sur l'objectivité. L'ancienne formule «Tout ce que le Buddha a dit est bien dit» est renversé et on proclame communément: «Tout ce qui est bien dit a été dit par le Buddha».[41]

Certainly Lamotte here regards this way of thinking as typical of a later text such as the **Mahāprajñāpāramitā-śāstra*, but rather curiously in a footnote on

---

idha bhante bhikkhu āsavānaṃ khayā anāsavaṃ ceto-vimuttiṃ paññā-vimuttiṃ diṭṭhe va dhamme sayaṃ abhiññā sacchikatvā upasampajja viharati. (Cf. also S III 94-9, cited above, p. 152-3.)

38 D II 123-6; A II 167-70.

39 Lamotte, *Traité*, I 80.

40 Id., p. 81.

41 Id., pp. 81-2.

the next page he quotes an *Aṅguttara* passage: *yaṃ kiñci subhāsitaṃ sabbaṃ taṃ bhagavato vacanaṃ*.[42]

In all this Lamotte appears to understand the *mahâpadesa* passage primarily in terms of an appeal to a commonly accepted corpus of literary texts. Elsewhere,[43] however, he prefers to to understand it precisely in the light of the fact that ancient Buddhism lacked an agreed and fixed canon of scriptures. This is surely nearer the truth:

> In order that a text proposed with reference to one of the four Great Authorities be guaranteed, it is not necessary for it to be literally reproduced in the Scriptures, it is enough that its general purport be in keeping with the spirit of the Sūtras, the Vinaya and the Buddhist doctrine in general.[44]

He goes on to cite the *Nettippakaraṇa* in support of this conclusion. More recently L.S. Cousins too has suggested that the particular terms of the *mahâpadesa* passage (*otaranti* and *sandissanti*) should be understood in the light of the traditions preserved by the *Peṭakopadesa* and *Nettippakaraṇa*.[45] According to these, categories such as the aggregates (*khandha*) spheres (*āyatana*), elements (*dhātu*), truths (*sacca*) and conditioned arising (*paṭicca-samuppāda*) are to be used to analyze the contents of a discourse and place it in its context in the teaching as a whole:

> What is envisaged for sutta is not then a set body of literaure, but rather a traditional pattern of teaching. Authenticity lies not in historical truth, although this is not doubted, but rather in whether something can accord with the essential structure of the *dhamma* as a whole. If it cannot, it should be rejected. If it can, then it is to be accepted as the utterance of the Buddha. We may compare from the later commentarial tradition: 'Whosoever ... might teach and proclaim the *dhamma*, all that is accounted as actually taught and proclaimed by the Teacher.'[46]

I think the usage of the seven sets collectively in the passages that have been under consideration begins to throw some light on what is happening here, and also shows why any notion of a gradual shift from a principally text based criterion of authenticity to one based on practical merit is misconceived. Our problem is the very notion of *dhamma* in Buddhist literature. In contexts where there is a question of the Buddhist tradition it is all too easy to render '*dhamma*' as 'teaching' or 'doctrine', yet this fails to convey a fundamental nuance of the notion of *dhamma*. There is in the appeal to the seven sets a kind of equivocation that is inherent in the notion of *dhamma* as at once truth itself—truth that is to be directly known and realized—and teachings about the

---

[42] A IV 164, quoted Lamotte, *Traité*, I 84 (n. 2).

[43] 'The Assessment of Textual Authenticity in Buddhism', *BSR* I (1983-4), pp. 4-15 (originally published as 'La critique d'authenticité dans le bouddhisme', *India Antiqua*, Leiden, 1947, pp. 213-22; although published three years after the appearance of *Traité* I, it seems likely that this represents Lamotte's more considered opinion; the *mahâpadesas* are discussed again briefly at *HBI*, pp. 180-1).

[44] Id., p. 13.

[45] Denwood and Piatigorsky, *BSAM*, pp. 2-3. The relevant passages are Peṭ 11, 98-101; Nett 21-2, 63-70, 107. Cf. Jaini, Abhidh-dī, introduction, p. 27 on Nett.

[46] Denwood and Piatigorsky, *BSAM*, p. 3.

truth—teachings that indicate how the truth is to be directly known and realized.

What, I think, needs to be distinguished here are two conceptual pairs. The first pair contrasts *dhamma* as tradition with *dhamma* as path; the second pair *dhamma* as the teaching of specifically the historical Buddha, the *samaṇa* Gotama, with *dhamma* as the teaching of all Buddhas and wise men. What is important is that there exists a certain parallelism between these two pairs: the first members of each pair are related, as are the second members of each pair. So, *dhamma* as tradition is represented basically by the *Tipiṭaka*; what the *Tipiṭaka* contains is the theory or teaching about *dhamma* as path, *dhamma* that is to be put into practice, directly known and realized. Now what is remembered in the *Tipiṭaka* is basically considered to be the teaching of one particular historical teacher, namely the *samaṇa* Gotama. But the teaching of the *samaṇa* Gotama is not regarded as his original invention or discovery, it is the teaching common to all Buddhas; *dhamma* is not just *samaṇa* Gotama's 'truth', it is the 'truth' of all Buddhas; it is a 'truth' that potentially all can come to know directly. In other words the first member of each of the conceptual pairs that I have distinguished is particular and historical in nature, the second member is universal and transcendent.

In the appeal to the seven sets as a reference point of truth, there is a sense in which the four elements that make up the two conceptual pairs revolve around the seven sets. The seven sets can be singled out as a constant point of reference because they encapsulate *dhamma* that is at once the tradition of the *samaṇa* Gotama and *dhamma* that is to be personally and individually directly known. If one asks why the appeal is not made to the aggregates, spheres, elements, truths or conditioned arising, then the answer must be, I think, that these items of the teaching are in some sense subordinate to the seven sets; knowledge of them only exists to the extent that the seven sets are directly known and realized, developed, made great; that is to say, they are not so much *dhamma* that is to be developed (*bhāvetabba*) and realized (*sacchikātabba*) as *dhamma* that is to be fully known (*pariññeyya*). I drew attention in an earlier chapter to reasons for thinking that the criterion of 'truth' in Buddhist thought was always more or less the usefulness or profitability of something; the question asked was: 'In what way does this conduce to the goal, the cessation of suffering?' And in the context of the appeal to the seven sets it seems that teachings about the *satipaṭṭhānas* and so on could only be considered as 'authentic' or 'true' in so far as they conduce to direct knowledge and realization of them.

As a footnote to this discussion I wish to draw attention to one more passage, which relates how the chief of the asuras, Pahārāda, visits the Buddha who asks him what wonderful and marvelous things (*acchariyā abbhutā dhammā*) *asuras* perceive in the great ocean and which cause them to delight in it. Pahārāda lists eight such things. The Buddha responds by listing eight corresponding wonderful and marvelous things that *bhikkhus* perceive in the *dhamma-vinaya* and which cause them to delight in it. The seventh in the list is of relevance here. Just as the ocean has many and various treasures (*bahu-*

ratana, aneka-ratana) such as pearls, jewels, lapis lazuli, shells, crystal, coral, rubies, silver, gold and emeralds, so too does the *dhamma-vinaya* have many and various treasures, namely the four establishings of mindfulness, the four right endeavours, the four bases of success, the five faculities, the five powers, the seven factors of awakening and the noble eight-factored path.[47] The way in which the seven sets are singled out here as the jewels or treasures of the Buddha's *dhamma-vinaya* seems to represent a poetic and imaginative echo of the appeal to the seven sets as *dhammas* directly known by the Buddha and subsequently taught to his pupils.

3. The seven sets as the path

I have already suggested that the appeal to the seven sets as a yardstick or reference point must ultimately be seen as an appeal to *dhamma* as practice and realization—that is, to *dhamma* as path. The association of the seven sets with the path is also already apparent in the characterization of each one of the seven sets in turn as the middle way between the ways of sensual indulgence and 'burning away'.[48]

A succinct and explicit characterization of the seven sets as path (*magga*) occurs in the ancient expositions or 'old commentary' to the fourth 'offence involving defeat' (*pārājika*) and eighth 'offence involving expiation' (*pācittiya*) in the *Vinaya-piṭaka*.[49] The fourth *pārājika* is said by the Buddha to consist in a *bhikkhu's* announcing an attainment beyond normal human capacity (*uttari-manussa-dhamma*), saying that he sees when in fact he does not. A detailed exposition of this then follows in which the term *uttari-manussa-dhamma* is defined as *jhāna*, liberation (*vimokkha*), concentration (*samādhi*), attainment (*samāpatti*), knowledge and vision (*ñāṇa-dassana*), development of the path (*magga-bhāvanā*), realization of the fruit (*phala-sacchikiriyā*), abandoning of defilements (*kilesa-pahāna*), the absence of the hindrances from the mind (*vinīvaraṇatā cittassa*), 'delight in empty-dwellings' (*suññâgāre abhirati*). The expression *magga-bhāvanā* is in turn explained as *cattāro satipaṭṭhānā cattāro samma-ppadhāna cattāro iddhi-pādā pañca indriyāni pañca balāni satta bojjhaṅgā ariyo aṭṭhaṅgiko maggo.*[50] It might be felt that this already simply reflects later Abhidhamma conceptions, since the date of this old commentary embed-

---

[47] The whole basic passage listing the two sets of eight *dhammas* occurs four times in the Pāli canon: A IV 197-204 (which I follow here) has the Buddha in conversation with Pahārāda; at A IV 204-8 the passage is introduced by an incident concerning the recital of the *pātimokkha* after which the Buddha alone simply lists the two sets of eight items; Ud 51-6 is identical with this latter version except that an *udāna* (= Th 447) is appended ; Vin II 236-40 again follows this second version except that certain words are transposed to the end of the passage. Frauwallner (*EVBBL*, pp. 147-8) argues that A IV 197-204 represents the earliest version.

[48] See above, p. 200; another passage I have already considered and which is also suggestive of the notion of the seven sets as the path is S III 94-9 (see, p. 293).

[49] Vin III 87-109 (fourth *pārājika*); IV 23-30 (eighth *pācittiya*).

[50] Vin III 93, 94, 95, 97. The exposition of the eighth *pācittiya* is similar to that of the fourth *pārājika*, the difference being that the claim to *uttari-manussa-dhamma* is not false, but is made to one who has not received *upasampadā*; for the seven sets as *magga-bhāvanā* see Vin IV 26, 27, 28.

ded in the text of the Pāli *Vinaya-piṭaka* is difficult to determine with any precision.[51]

Certainly, as I stated at the outset of this study, later treatises of different traditions provide treatments of the seven sets that identify them with the path (*magga/mārga*) in a variety of ways. At this point I should like to begin to look more closely at the possible Nikāya antecedents of this. A good place to start is a *sutta* I referred to above in connection with the noble eight-factored path, the *Mahāsaḷāyatanika-sutta.*[52] According to this *sutta* when the *bhikkhu* does not know and does not see according to what is (*ajānaṃ apassaṃ yathā-bhūtaṃ*) the six senses, the six kinds of sense object, their contact or interaction (*samphassa*) and the feeling that arises conditioned by their interaction (*samphassa-paccayā uppajjati vedayitaṃ*), then he is impassioned (*sārajjati*) with regard to these things; the five aggregates of grasping continue to perpetuate themselves (*āyatiṃ pañc'upādāna-kkhandhā upacayaṃ gacchanti*), and in the end he experiences suffering of both body and mind (*so kāya-dukkhaṃ pi ceto-dukkhaṃ pi paṭisaṃvedeti*). However, when the *bhikkhu* does know and see according to what is the six senses, the six kinds of sense-object, their interaction and the feeling that arises conditioned by their interaction, then he is not impassioned with regard to these things; the five aggregates of grasping diminish in the future (*āyatiṃ pañc'upādāna-kkhandhā apacayaṃ gacchanti*) and eventually he experiences happiness of both body and mind (*so kāya-sukhaṃ pi ceto-sukhaṃ pi paṭisaṃvedeti*).

> The view of one who exists accordingly is his right view[53]; the thought of one who exists accordingly is his right thought; the striving of one who exists accordingly is his right striving; the mindfulness of one who exists accordingly is his right mindfulness; the concentration of one who exists accordingly is his right concentration. His bodily actions, his actions of speech and his livelihood have been previously well purified. Thus for him the noble eight-factored path reaches full development.
>
> As he develops the noble eight-factored path thus, the four establishings of mindfulness also reach full development; the four right endeavours ... the four bases of success ... the five faculties ... the five powers ... the seven factors of awakening also reach full development. For him these two *dhammas*, calm and insight, occur yoked together.[54]

---

[51] K.R. Norman (*PL*, p. 19) suggests that its method of word analysis (*pada-bhājaniya*) perhaps indicates that it belongs to the same period as the *Niddesa*, that is more or less to the latest stratum of the canon. He goes on to comment (id., p. 21) that the Sanskrit text of the Mahāsāṃghika-Lokottaravādin *Bhikṣunī-vinaya* includes a word commentary that is not the same as the Pāli *pada-bhājaniya*.

[52] M III 287-90.

[53] Miss Horner translates: 'Whatever is the view of what really is, that is for him right view; whatever is aspiration for what really is, that is for him right aspiration ... ' (M Trsl III 337-8). But it seems more natural to take *yathā-bhūtassa* as balanced by *assa* (K.R. Norman, private communication), in which case *yathā-bhūtassa* refers back to the *bhikkhu* who knows and sees the senses, etc. in accordance with what is, and experiences bodily and mental happiness; this at least is how the commentary takes it: '*yathā-bhūtassa*: of the one who has become endowed with mental happiness associated with skilful consciousness' (*kusala-citta-sampayutta-ceto-sukha-samaṅgī-bhūtassa*), (Ps V 103). Some MSS read *tathā-bhūtassa*, as does Vibh-a 319 in quoting this passage.

[54] M III 289: *yā yathā-bhūtassa diṭṭhi sā'ssa hoti sammā-diṭṭhi yo yathā-bhūtassa saṃkappo svāssa hoti sammā-saṃkappo yo yathā-bhūtassa vāyāmo svāssa hoti sammā-vāyāmo yā yathā-bhūt-*

And so the exposition concludes that the *dhammas* that should be fully known (*pariññeyya*) by direct knowledge (*abhiññā*), namely the five aggregates of grasping, are fully known; the *dhammas* that should be abandoned by direct knowledge, namely ignorance and craving for existence (*avijjā ca bhava-taṇhā ca*), are abandoned; the *dhammas* that should be developed by higher knowledge, namely knowledge and freedom (*vijjā ca vimutti ca*), are realized. So when a *bhikkhu* brings to fulfilment the development of the noble eight-factored path, he at the same time brings to fulfilment the development of the four *satipaṭṭhānas* and so on. In other words, the final stage of the development of the noble eight-factored path represents the culmination of the development of all seven sets.

Already, it is not so hard to see how we get from here to the more specific and technical formulations of the *Visuddhimagga* (when it says that the seven sets are associated with the transcendent path and fruit moments) or the *Abhidharmakośa* (when it uses the seven sets to characterize the successive stages of the path). In fact, viewed in the light of the *Mahāsaḷāyatanika-sutta* the shift represented by the later formulations becomes really rather subtle. It is a question not so much of a radical recasting of the Nikāya thought-world as of gently placing a finger upon something that is rather intangible and elusive in the Nikāya formulations. The spirit of the later formulations is certainly not entirely inconsonant with the spirit of the Nikāya formulations. Nor is the *Mahāsaḷāyatanika* formula an isolated instance. The *mahā-vagga* of the *Saṃyutta-nikāya* makes quite a lot of a slightly different version of the same formula. This version is initially given in full in the *magga-saṃyutta* with an introductory simile:

> As, *bhikkhus*, in the sky various winds blow: east winds and west winds, north winds and south winds, winds of dust and winds free of dust, cool winds and warm winds, gentle winds and strong winds—just so, *bhikkhus*, when a *bhikkhu* develops and makes great the noble eight-factored path, the four establishings of mindfulness also reach full development; the four right endeavours ... the four bases of success ... the five faculties ... the five powers ... the seven factors of awakening also reach full development.[55]

The usage of this formula in the *mahā-vagga* is particularly interesting in that, apart from its occurrence in the *magga-saṃyutta*, it is also understood to

---

assa sati sā'ssa hoti sammā-sati yo yathā-bhūtassa samādhi svāssa hoti sammā-samādhi. pubbe va kho pan'assa kāya-kammaṃ vacī-kammaṃ ājīvo suparisuddho hoti. evaṃ assâyaṃ ariyo aṭṭhaṅgiko maggo bhāvanā-pāripūriṃ gacchati. tassa evaṃ imaṃ ariyaṃ aṭṭhaṅgikaṃ maggaṃ bhāvayato cattāro pi satipaṭṭhānā bhāvanā-pāripūriṃ gacchanti cattāro pi samma-ppadhānā bhāvanā-pāripūriṃ gacchanti cattāro pi iddhi-pādā bhāvanā-pāripūriṃ gacchanti pañca pi indriyāni bhāvanā-pāripūriṃ gacchanti pañca pi balāni bhāvanā-pāripūriṃ gacchanti satta pi bojjhaṅgā bhāvanā-pāripūriṃ gacchanti. tass'ime dve dhammā yuganandhā vattanti samatho ca vipassanā ca.

[55] S V 49: *seyyathâpi bhikkhave ākāse vividhā vātā vāyanti puratthimā pi vātā vāyanti pacchimā pi vātā vāyanti uttarā pi vātā vāyanti dakkhiṇā pi vātā vāyanti sarajā pi vātā vāyanti arajā pi vātā vāyanti sītā pi vātā vāyanti uṇhā pi vātā vāyanti parittā pi vātā vāyanti adhimattā pi vātā vāyanti. evaṃ eva kho bhikkhave bhikkhuno ariyaṃ aṭṭhaṅgikaṃ maggaṃ bhāvayato ariyaṃ aṭṭhaṅgikaṃ maggaṃ bahulīkaroto cattāro pi satipaṭṭhānā bhāvanā-pāripūriṃ gacchanti cattāro pi samma-ppadhānā cattāro pi iddhi-pādā pañca pi indriyāni pañca pi balāni satta pi bojjhaṅgā bhāvanā-pāripūriṃ gacchanti.*

occur in each of the relevant *saṃyuttas*: the *bojjhaṅga-*, *satipaṭṭhāna-*, *indriya-*, *samma-ppadhāna-*, *bala-* and *iddhi-pāda-saṃyuttas*; in addition it is also understood to occur in the *jhāna-saṃyutta*—a fact of special interest. However, in the case of each of these repetitions the occurrence of the formula is indicated only by a mnemonic verse and not given in full.[56] Presumably what is intended is not mere repetition but that the relevant categories should be substituted in the original formula for the noble eight-factored path. This is clearly the procedure that operates for the other formulaic treatments that are indicated by mnemonic verse in the *mahā-vagga*. Unless this is so it is difficult to see how the formula might be made relevant to the *jhāna-saṃyutta*. In this particular case the formula should read, I think:

> Just so, *bhikkhus*, when a *bhikkhu* develops and makes great the four *jhānas*, the four establishings of mindfulness also reach full development; the four right endeavours ... the noble eight-factored path also reaches full development.

This association of the four *jhānas* with the seven sets is in itself of some importance and significance since it seems to correlate with the same association found in two of the Chinese translations of the *Mahāparinirvāṇa-sūtra*.

The casting of each of the seven sets in turn in the role played by the noble eight-factored path in the initial version brings to the fore a dimension that is really only latent in the *Mahāsaḷāyatanika* version: the bringing to a state of full development of any one of the seven sets involves also the bringing to a state of full development of each of the other sets; one set cannot be fully developed without at the same time the other sets being fully developed. That is to say, any one of the seven sets is seen as embracing all seven. This kind of notion has already in part been adumbrated especially in chapters one and two where I drew attention to the way in which the Nikāyas on occasion fit the stages of the Buddhist path into the structure of either the four *satipaṭṭhānas* or the four *samma-ppadhānas*. Moreover, one has only to consider for a moment the items that constitute the seven sets and the way in which these are defined in the Nikāyas in order to realize the extent of the overlap and cross-referencing inherent in the basic Nikāya treatment of the sets.

Finally, the *Nettippakaraṇa*—a text in which the association of the expression *bodhi-pakkhiyā dhammā* has become more or less firmly associated with the seven sets—gives another slightly different version of the *Mahāsaḷāyatanika* formula:

> When the four establishings of mindfulness are being developed, the four right endeavours reach full development; when the four right endeavours ... the four bases of success ... the five faculties ... the five powers ... the seven factors of awakening are being developed, the noble eight-factored path reaches full development. What is the reason? All *dhammas* leading to awakening, contributing to awakening have one characteristic by reason of the characteristic of leading out.[57]

---

[56] The simile occurs in the *balakaraṇīya-vagga* of the *mahā-vagga* which is common to the *saṃyuttas* mentioned above; for the relevant mnemonic verses see S V 136, 138, 191, 240, 246, 250, 252, 291, 309.

[57] Nett 31, 83: *catusu satipaṭṭhānesu bhāviyamānesu cattāro samma-ppadhānā bhāvanā-pāripūriṃ gacchanti. catusu samma-ppadhānesu ... catusu iddhi-pādesu ... pañc'indriyesu ... pañca balesu ...*

The wording here brings out even more explicitly the relationship of reciprocity that exists between the seven sets, and brings us one step nearer, I think, to the more technical Abhidhamma formulations. This principle of reciprocity is summed up in the *Peṭakopadesa* as 'when one *dhamma* that contributes to awakening is spoken of, then all *dhammas* that lead to awakening are spoken of' (*ekamhi bodhi-pakkhiya-dhamme vutte sabbe bodha-gamaniyā dhammā vuttā*).[58]

Before turning to a number of other similes that illustrate the process of the development of the seven sets, I should briefly mention the treatment of the sets in the *Piṇḍapātapārisuddhi-sutta*.[59] This is perhaps the most developed account of the path incorporating the seven sets in the Nikāyas. In this *sutta* the Buddha gives an account of how a *bhikkhu* should proceed if he wishes to dwell 'by the dwelling of emptiness' (*suññatā-vihārena*). First he should reflect on (*paṭisañcikkhitabbaṃ*) his alms round and consider whether or not there was any compulsion (*chanda*), desire (*rāga*), hate (*dosa*), delusion (*moha*), repugnance (*paṭigha*) with regard to the objects of the five senses and the mind. If there was, then the effort should be made (*vāyamitabbaṃ*) for the abandoning (*pahānāya*) of unskilful *dhammas*; if there was not, then he should dwell in joy and gladness training day and night in skilful *dhammas* (*bhikkhunā ten'eva pīti-pāmujjena vihātabbaṃ ahorattânusikkhinā kusalesu dhammesu*).[60] Next the *bhikkhu* should reflect on the five kinds of sensual desire (*kāma-guṇa*): are they abandoned in him? If not he should make an effort for their abandoning; if they are, he again should train himself night and day in skilful *dhammas*. In precisely the same way the *bhikkhu* considers whether the five hindrances (*nīvaraṇa*) are abandoned; whether the five aggregates of grasping are fully known (*pariññāta*); whether in turn the four *satipaṭṭhānas*, four *samma-ppadhānas*, four *iddhi-pādas*, five *indriyas*, five *balas*, seven *bojjhaṅgas* and *ariyo aṭṭhaṅgiko maggo* are developed (*bhāvita*); whether calm and insight are developed; and whether knowledge and freedom are realized (*sacchikata*). In each case if the answer is no, then the appropriate effort is to be made; if the answer is yes, then the *bhikkhu* should dwell in joy and gladness, training himself in skilful *dhammas* night and day. The account finishes with a statement of the universal and timeless nature of this scheme of things: those *bhikkhus* who in the past purified their alms round, all did so having reflected and considered just so again and again; likewise with those who will do so in the future and who do so now.

---

satta bojjhaṅgesu bhāviyamānesu ariyo aṭṭhaṅgiko maggo bhāvanā-pāripūriṃ gacchati. kena karaṇena. sabbe hi bodhaṃ-gamā dhammā bodhi-pakkhiyā niyyānika-lakkhaṇena eka-lakkhaṇā. (Cf. Mil 358.)

[58] Peṭ 188.

[59] M III 293-7.

[60] Miss Horner takes *vihātabbaṃ* here as if from *vijahati*; apart from sense, *ten'eva tvaṃ Rāhula pīti-pāmujjena vihareyyāsi ahorattânusikkhī kusalesu dhammesu* (M I 417-9) would suggest this is mistaken.

Effectively this is a scheme of the whole Buddhist path set out in seven stages:

(i) attention to and reflection on the five senses and mind.
(ii) abandoning of the five *kāma-guṇas*
(iii) abandoning of the five *nīvaraṇas*
(iv) full knowledge of the five *upādāna-kkhandhas*
(v) development of the four *satipaṭṭhānas* ... *ariyo aṭṭhaṅgiko maggo*
(vi) development of *samatha* and *vipassanā*
(vii) realization of *vijjā* and *vimutti*

The seven sets are here used to characterize what appears to be specific and relatively advanced stages of the path. The abandoning of the *kāma-guṇas* and *nīvaraṇas* might be thought of as implying the development of ordinary concentration or *jhāna*; the full knowledge of the *upādāna-kkhandhas* as implying the development of wisdom that directly knows *nibbāna*. In that case the seven sets are here seen as essentially what the *bhikkhu* properly develops only during the final stages of the path. If this way of looking at the *Piṇḍapātapārisuddhi-sutta* is valid it in fact once more represents a rather good correspondence with the general principle expressed in the commentarial tradition, namely the association of the seven sets with the four transcendent paths and fruits beginning with stream-attainment.[61]

The passage I wish to turn to next is common to both the *Saṃyutta-* and *Aṅguttara-nikāyas*.[62] With its accompanying similes it makes the way in which the Nikāyas conceive of the seven sets as representing the path to awakening a little clearer:

> When a *bhikkhu* is not engaged in development, although the wish might arise thus, 'O that my mind might be freed from the *āsavas* as a result of not grasping', still his mind is not freed from the *āsavas* as a result of not grasping. Why is this? 'Because of the state of undevelopment' is what should be said. Because of the state of undevelopment of what? Because of the state of undevelopment of the four establishings of mindfulness ... the noble eight-factored path.[63]

This is then illustrated by a simile:

> Suppose, *bhikkhus*, there were eight or ten or twelve hen's eggs that were not

---

[61] The commentary (Ps V 105-6) in fact pitches the *sutta* at a rather more specific and absolute level, so that already at the abandoning of the *kāma-guṇas* there is the path of non-return (*anāgāmi-magga*); at the abandoning of the five *nīvaraṇas* there is *arahant*-ship. The development of the seven sets thus represents the final consummation of the path in the reaching of *arahant*-ship. The reason for the commentary's interpretation is probably to do with the fact that the exposition is addressed to Sāriputta and that the term *suññatā-vihāra* is taken to mean *suññatā-phala-samāpatti-vihāra*. In other words the *sutta* is understood to concern the highest perfection of spiritual faculties. However, I do not think that this necessarily invalidates my more general interpretation.

[62] See S III 153-5; A IV 125-7.

[63] S III 153 = A IV 125 (with minor variations): *bhāvanânuyogam ananuyuttassa bhikkhave bhikkhuno viharato kiñ câpi evaṃ icchā uppajjeyya aho vata me anupādāya āsavehi cittaṃ vimuccеyyā ti, atha khvassa neva anupādāya āsavehi cittaṃ vimuccati. taṃ kissa hetu. abhāvitattā ti'ssa vacaniyaṃ. kissa abhāvitattā. abhāvitattā catunnaṃ satipaṭṭhānānaṃ ... ariyassa aṭṭhaṅgikassa maggassa.*

properly sat upon, not properly warmed, not properly nurtured by the hen. Although the wish might arise for the hen, 'O that the chicks should pierce the eggshell with the points of their claws or with their beaks and break out safely', still those chicks would be unfit to break out ... [64]

The whole is now repeated in its positive form. Thus when a *bhikkhu* does engage in development, although the wish that his mind might be freed from the *āsavas* as a result of absence of grasping does not arise, still his mind is in fact freed from the *āsavas*. Why? Because of the state of development of the four *satipaṭṭhānas*, and so on. Similarly, if a hen tends to her eggs properly, even if there is no wish that the chicks should break out of their shells, still those chicks will be fit to break out.[65] This positive treatment is further filled out by the addition of two more similes:

> As, *bhikkhus*, a carpenter or carpenter's apprentice, when inspecting the handle of his knife, sees the marks of his fingers and the mark of his thumb, yet has no knowledge that so much of the handle has been worn away by him today, so much yesterday, so much previously; but when the last bit has been worn away, then he has knowledge. Just so, *bhikkhus*, a *bhikkhu* who dwells engaged in development has no knowledge that so much of the *āsavas* has been worn away by him today, so much yesterday, so much previously; but when the last bit has been worn away, then he has knowledge.[66]

> Suppose, *bhikkhus*, that there were an ocean going ship lashed with reed ropes that, having sailed the sea for six months, had been beached for the winter; the ropes affected by the wind and heat, drenched by the clouds of the rainy season would slacken with ease and become rotten. Just so, *bhikkhus*, for a *bhikkhu* who dwells engaged in development the fetters slacken and become rotten.[67]

These descriptions and similes bring out very clearly a number of important aspects of the Nikāya conception of the spiritual path. First the path is something that is gradual and cumulative; secondly and on the other hand this gradual and cumulative path comes to a quite specific and definite culmination or climax. These two aspects are both implicit in the succinct expression of the

---

[64] S III 154 = A IV 125-6: *seyyathâpi bhikkhave kukkuṭiyā aṇḍāni attha vā dasa vā dvādasa vā tān'assu kukkuṭiyā na sammā adhisayitāni na sammā pariseditāni na sammā paribhāvitāni. kiñ câpi tassa kukkuṭiyā evaṃ icchā uppajjeyya aho vata me kukkuṭapotakā pāda-nakha-sikhāya vā mukha-tuṇḍakena vā aṇḍa-kosaṃ padāletvā sotthinā abhinibbhijjeyyun ti, atha kho abhabbā va te kukkuṭa-potakā ... sotthinā abhinibbhijjituṃ.*

[65] The simile of the hen is also found at M I 104 and 357; a rather different application of the same image is also found at Vin III 3 = A IV 176.

[66] S III 154-5 = A IV 127: *seyyathâpi bhikkhave palagaṇḍassa vā palagaṇḍantevāsissa vā vāsi-jaṭe dissante aṅguli-padāni dissanti aṅguṭṭha-padaṃ, no ca khvassa evaṃ ñāṇaṃ hoti ettakaṃ vata me ajja vāsi-jaṭassa khīṇaṃ ettakaṃ hiyyo ettakaṃ pare ti. atha khvassa khīṇe khīṇante va ñāṇaṃ hoti. evaṃ eva kho bhikkhave bhāvanânuyogaṃ anuyuttassa bhikkhuno viharato kiñ câpi na evaṃ ñāṇaṃ hoti. ettakaṃ vata me ajja āsavānaṃ khīṇaṃ ettakaṃ hiyyo ettakaṃ pare ti. atha khvassa khīṇe khīṇante va ñāṇaṃ hoti.*

[67] S III 155 = A IV 127: *seyyathâpi bhikkhave samuddikāya nāvāya vetta-bandhana-baddhāya chammāsāni udake pariyādāya hemantike thale ukkhittāya vātātapa-paretāni bandhanāni, tāni pāvussakena meghena abhippavaṭṭhāni appa-kasiren'eva paṭippassambhanti pūtikāni bhavanti. evaṃ eva kho bhikkhave bhāvanânuyogaṃ anuyuttassa bhikkhuno viharato appa-kasiren'eva saṃyojanāni paṭippassambhanti pūtikāni bhavanti.* (This simile of the ship is repeated in the *balakaraṇīya-vagga* of the *mahā-vagga* of the *Saṃyutta-nikāya*, illustrating the development of each of the seven sets and four *jhānas* in turn; see S V 51.)

commentaries here: 'the path of *arahant*-ship acquired gradually' (*anupubbâdhigato arahatta-maggo*).[68] The notion that the process of awakening is at once something gradual and something sudden is thus suggested. But there is a further aspect to the conception of the path here—one that tends to draw these two somewhat divergent aspects back together. The path is thus here conceived of as essentially a natural process. Its final consummation is seen as simply the natural unfolding and consequence of the setting in motion and maintenance of the appropriate practice. The appropriate practice is engagement in the development of the seven sets. The mere self-conscious wish that the conclusion of the path be reached is inadequate to bring it about, while the development of the seven sets will have its natural result quite apart from any such wish. Furthermore, the process involved in the gradual progress towards awakening—that is the process of the development of the seven sets—is essentially the same as the process involved in the final consummation, in awakening itself—that is the full development of the seven sets. Any difference is one of order rather than kind. This is particularly evident in the image of the wearing away of the knife handle.

These are ideas that I have already suggested are involved to some extent in the Nikāyas' understanding of the noble eight-factored path. I also suggested in conclusion that the treatment of the noble eight-factored path in the Nikāyas involved a certain fusion of or deliberate ambiguity with regard to the notions of *dhamma* as prescriptive and descriptive. These are things that are evident once more in the notion of the path as a natural process of unfolding, and are worth pursuing a little further at this point.

4. The path as 'stream'

In an important section of his recent book *Selfless Persons* Steven Collins has considered several distinct patterns of imagery that are repeatedly exploited and played upon in Buddhist literature.[69] His treatment indicates, I think, how these patterns of imagery form an imaginative substrate to the more abstract and theoretical formulations of the Nikāyas that can to some extent be used to bring the latter to life. Certainly the relevant sections of Collins' book are of some interest since in the academic pursuit of Buddhism the imaginative thought world of the Nikāyas has received rather scant and often unimaginative treatment.[70]

Regarding the usage of vegetation imagery in connection with the processes involved in progress along the path, Collins has the following to say:

> We can, I think, gain empathy into the psychological attitude recommended here from one particularly ingenious application of the image. There are three 'urgent duties' [*accayikāni karaṇīyāni*] of a householding farmer. He must plough and

---

[68] Spk II 330 = Mp IV 62.

[69] S. Collins, *SP*, pp. 165-76 (house imagery); 218-24 (vegetation imagery); 247-61 (river imagery).

[70] Apart from Collins' work, one of the few recent attempts to take the imagery of the Nikāyas seriously albeit within the compass of a brief and general article is B.G. Gokhale, 'The Image-World of the *nikāyas*', *JAOS* 100 (1980), pp. 445-52.

> harrow his field quickly, he must plant the seed quickly, and he must be quick to water it. Although he has these three urgent duties to perform, he cannot hasten the growth of his crops by saying 'let the crops spring up today ... ear tomorrow ... ripen on the next day!' It is rather a natural process of seasonal change [*utu-pariṇāma*] which brings the crops to ripening. In the same way, although a monk has the three urgent duties of 'the higher training in morality, concentration and insight', he has no 'magic power or influence' [*iddhi vā anubhāvo vā*] to hasten their development. In a psychological perspective, this depiction of Buddhist training suggests the feeling of inculcating a natural process of personal growth, rather than the magical or 'occult' production of spiritual states. Seeds work slowly, beneath the ground, as the process of character development in Buddhist training is meant to work slowly, beneath the level of conscious perception.[71]

The passage cited here by Collins is clearly rather similar in intent to the passages I have just cited in connection with the seven sets, although the imagery is of a rather different nature. Later Collins turns his attention to the imagery of 'streams, rivers and water in general' and attempts to make a distinction between the 'positive' and 'negative' evaluation the themes and concepts illustrated by such imagery receive in Buddhist thought. Collins' treatment is not always, I think, entirely satisfactory.

He surely quite rightly points out that river imagery in the classical texts of the Pāli tradition is not brought into play with the specific aim of illustrating the paradoxes of difference and identity involved in the concept of change, as has sometimes been assumed.[72] However, according to Collins:

> The 'positive' uses of river and water imagery in the *Theravāda* tradition cannot be brought into a single piece with the conceptual analysis of *bhavaṅga* and the mind-in-saṃsāra. When images of water are applied to matters of individual psychology the idea is not that of a moving flowing current, but of a still, cool, deep and peaceful expanse, as in a lake or the ocean. In so far as the idea of *moving* [Collins' emphasis] water is used positively, it refers to the Buddhist religious life and Community in its entirety, and not to matters of individual psychology.[73]

By way of illustrating the negative usage of water imagery in the Nikāyas Collins states a little earlier that, 'The process of Dependent Origination, which keeps one within the temporal world of saṃsāra, is compared to the flow of rain water down hillsides, into streams, lakes and rivers and finally into the sea.'[74] On inspection this appears to be a rather loose statement on the part of Collins. The usage he here refers to is found in the *nidāna-saṃyutta* of the *Saṃyutta-nikāya*.[75] Yet the simile is used here not to illustrate the usual forwards (*anuloma*) and backwards (*paṭiloma*) sequence of twelve links (*nidāna*), but a distinctive 'negative' and then 'positive' sequence, illustrating quite explicitly not the process whereby one is kept within the temporal world of *saṃsāra* but how one is released from it. Thus from the condition of ignorance (*avijjā*) there are volitional activities (*saṃkhāra*); from these, consciousness

---

[71] Id., p. 222. The passage cited occurs at A I 239-40; cf. 229-33.
[72] Collins, *SP*, pp. 252-8.
[73] Id., p. 259.
[74] Id., p. 249.
[75] S II 32; cited by Collins, *SP*, p. 306, n. 11.

(*viññāṇa*); from this, mind and form (*nāma-rūpa*); from this, the six spheres of sense (*āyatana*); from these, contact (*phassa*); from this, feeling (*vedanā*); from this, craving (*taṇhā*); from this, grasping (*upādāna*); from this, becoming (*bhava*); from this, birth (*jāti*); from this old-age and death (*jarā-maraṇa*); from this, suffering (*dukkha*). At this point, instead of then describing how from the cessation of ignorance there is the cessation of volitional activities, and so on, the present *sutta* continues: from the condition of suffering there is confidence (*saddhā*); from this, gladness (*pāmojja*); from this, joy (*pīti*); from this, tranquillity (*passaddhi*); from this, happiness (*sukha*); from this, concentration (*samādhi*); from this, knowledge and vision (*ñāṇa-dassana*); from this, disenchantment (*nibbidā*); from this, dispassion (*virāga*); from this, freedom (*vimutti*); from this, knowledge with regard to the destruction of the *āsavas* (*āsava-kkhaye ñāṇaṃ*).[76] I take it that Collins would regard this as referring to matters of individual psychology, but I cannot see how the Nikāyas' evaluation of this might be accurately characterized as 'negative'.

The simile referred to by Collins here is worth quoting in full:

> Just as, *bhikkhus*, when the *deva* rains with huge raindrops upon a mountain top, the water running down with the slope fills-up the mountain crevices, clefts and gullies; when full, the mountain crevices, clefts and gullies fill up the pools; when full, the pools fill up the lakes; when full, the lakes fill up the streams; when full, the streams fill up the rivers; when full, the rivers fill up the great ocean, the sea.[77]

This simile is in fact found on at least five other occasions in the four Nikāyas.[78] On three occasions the simile is used unambiguously to illustrate either the development and coming to completion of the process of spiritual growth or the potential inherent in something for spiritual growth.[79] In each of two adjacent *suttas* the simile is twice repeated, on both occasions illustrating first a negative sequence, and secondly a positive sequence.[80] The two latter *suttas* begin with the notion of ignorance as 'specifically conditioned' (*idapaccayā avijjā*) and discuss the 'food' (*āhāra*) for ignorance. It is worth recalling in this connection the various discussions in the *bojjhaṅga-saṃyutta* of the 'foods' for the hindrances and the foods for the factors of awakening.

In the *mahā-vagga* of the *Saṃyutta-nikāya* we find other examples of the

---

[76] S II 29-32; I have already cited part of this sequence in connection with the *bojjhaṅgas*.

[77] *seyyathâpi bhikkhave uparipabbate thulla-phusitake deve vassante taṃ udakaṃ yathā ninnaṃ pavattamānaṃ pabbata-kandara-padara-sākhā paripūreti. pabbata-kandara-padara-sākhā paripūrā kusubbhe paripūrenti. kusubbhā paripūrā mahāsobbhe paripūrenti. mahāsobbhā paripūrā kunnadiyo paripūrenti. kunnadiyo paripūrā mahānadiyo paripūrenti. mahānadiyo paripūrā mahāsamuddaṃ sāgaraṃ paripūrenti.*

[78] See index of similes, *JPTS* (1906-07), p. 69, s.v. *udaka*.

[79] At S V 396 it illustrates the potential inherent in the three kinds of 'intelligent trust' (*avecca-ppasāda*) and conduct pleasing to the *ariyas*; at A I 243-4 the potential inherent in the assembly that is united (*samaggā parisā*); at A II 140 the potential inherent in hearing *dhamma* at the appropriate time (*kālena*), discussion of *dhamma* at the appropriate time, calm at the appropriate time and insight at the appropriate time.

[80] A V 113-6, 116-9: *asappurisa-saṃseva* > *asaddhamma-savana* > *assaddhiya* > *ayoniso-manasikāra* > *asatasampajañña* > *indriyâsaṃvara* > three *duccaritas* > five *nīvaraṇas* > *avijjā*; *sappurisa-saṃseva* > *saddhamma-savana* > *saddhā* > *yoniso-manasikāra* > *sati-sampajañña* > *indriya-saṃvara* > three *sucaritas* > four *satipaṭṭhānas* > seven *bojjhaṅgas* > *vijjā-vimutti*.

positive usage of moving water or river imagery. The following illustrates the practice of each of the seven sets and seems intended to draw attention to the gradual and cumulative process of their development—a development that as it progresses becomes inevitable:

> Just as, *bhikkhus*, the Gaṅgā river tends to the east, flows to the east, slides to the east, so, *bhikkhus*, the *bhikkhu* who develops and makes great the noble eight-factored path [... the seven factors of awakening ... the four establishings of mindfulness ... the five faculties ... the four right endeavours ... the five powers ... the four bases of success] tends to *nibbāna*, flows to *nibbāna*, slides to *nibbāna*.[81]

The application of this image is taken a little further when the Buddha asks the *bhikkhus* whether they think that a great crowd of people taking picks and baskets might be able to make the Gaṅgā river, tending, flowing and sliding to the east as it does, tend, flow and slide to the west. No, they respond. Similarly, continues the Buddha, it cannot be that kings, ministers, friends and relatives should make a *bhikkhu* who develops the noble eight-factored path, and the rest, turn to the lesser life by offering him goods. What is the reason?

> Certainly, *bhikkhus*, it cannot be that the mind that has long tended to seclusion, flowed to seclusion, slid to seclusion should turn to the lesser life.[82]

Once more this does not, I think, refer to 'the Buddhist religious life and Community in its entirety' as distinct from 'matters of individual psychology'. The point is simple enough, just as the arising of *dukkha* is conditioned (*paṭicca-samuppanna*), so too is the path leading to its cessation,[83] so too is the practice and development of the four *satipaṭṭhānas*, the four *samma-ppadhānas*, the four *iddhi-pādas*, the five *indriyas*, the five *balas*, the seven *bojjhaṅgas* and the *ariyo aṭṭhaṅgiko maggo*. In fact it is just this that, as far as the Nikāyas are concerned, makes the spiritual path possible. What the simile of the rain filling gullies, streams and rivers that eventually over flow into the sea brings out, is the way in which the Nikāyas conceive of *dhammas*—whether unskilful or skilful—as naturally tending to perpetuate their own kind so that they gather momentum, snow-ball, accumulate and build up to a final culmination. This is the way of things, this is what *dhammas* do, this is *dhamma*.

Collins argues that river imagery is used in Buddhist literature to characterize the flowing stream of desire and attachment by which the ordinary man gets swept along.[84] Collins is certainly quite right in this, but the imagery also involves an exact inverse corollary. Indeed, Collins hints at it when he notes

---

[81] S V 38: *seyyathâpi bhikkhave Gaṅgā nadī pācīna-ninnā pācīna-poṇā pācīna-pabbhārā. evaṃ eva kho bhikkhave bhikkhu ariyaṃ aṭṭhaṅgikaṃ maggaṃ bhāvento ariyaṃ aṭṭhaṅgikaṃ maggaṃ bahulīkaronto nibbāna-ninno nibbāna-poṇo nibbāna-pabbhāro.* (In the *Gaṅgā-peyyāla* (S V 38-40) this simile is applied to the *ariyo aṭṭhaṅgiko maggo* a total of twelve times; six variations are achieved by substituting different rivers for the Gaṅgā, and a further six by substituting 'ocean' (*samudda*) for 'east'. In the *mahā-vagga* the *Gaṅgā-peyyāla* should be repeated in full for all seven sets and the four *jhānas*.

[82] S V 53: *yañ hi taṃ bhikkhave cittaṃ dīgha-rattaṃ viveka-ninnaṃ viveka-poṇaṃ viveka-pabbhāraṃ taṃ vata hīnāyâvattissatī ti netaṃ ṭhānaṃ vijjati.* (Again this should be repeated in full for all seven sets and the four *jhānas*.)

[83] Cf. the application of *paṭicca-samuppāda* to *lokuttara-citta* at Vibh 172-3, 179-80, 186-7, 189.

[84] See especially Collins, *SP*, pp. 250-2; he cites in particular S IV 174-5 and 114.

that those who make progress along the Buddhist path are often said to go upstream (*uddhaṃ-sota*) or against the stream (*paṭisota-gāmin*) as opposed to with the stream (*anusota-gāmin*).[85] Yet he seems not to follow this up. The conclusion I think one should draw from the Nikāyas usage of this imagery is that there are in a sense two distinct 'streams': the stream or current that tends to desire and selfishness and that ordinary humanity is always in danger of getting caught up in, and the stream or counter current that tends to absence of desire and selflessness and which is most fully realized in the actions, speech and thought of the 'noble ones' (*ariya*).

Thus I think Collins is quite wrong to suggest that when the noble eight-factored path is called 'stream' (*sota*), it refers to 'the Buddhist religious life and community in its entirety, and not to matters of individual psychology'.[86] I have in some measure already tried to make clear how in the Nikāyas the association of 'stream-attainment' (*sotâpatti*) with the noble eight-factored path characterizes a specific stage in the development of the Buddhist path. I think the nature of this stage and just why it comes to be seen as a quite specific psychological event in the Abhidhamma literature is beginning to become clearer. What lies behind the imagery of 'stream-attainment' is perhaps something like this. As skilful and wholesome *dhammas* are nurtured and developed, the stream or current of unskilful and unwholesome *dhammas* is weakened and begins gradually to lose hold. If the process of development is maintained sooner or later a point is reached when the stream or current of skilful and wholesome *dhammas* must once and for all become the overpowering current of the mind; the 'stream' is attained and the mind now tends, flows and slides inexorably towards *nibbāna*.[87]

It seems to me that in his discussion of river imagery Collins is in danger of introducing a dichotomy between 'negative' and 'positive' evaluation precisely at the point where the thought-world of the Nikāyas in a sense equivocates. Collins is rather nearer the mark, I think, when he notes:

> In the end, the flowing stream of sense-desire must be 'cut' or 'crossed' completely; nevertheless, for the duration of the Path, a monk must perforce work with motivational and perceptual processes as they ordinarily are, that is to say based on desire. Accordingly for this specific context, the imagery can be used without the extreme condemnation it carries in the passages I have cited so far.[88]

Strictly the imagery of water in the passages I have been discussing must be characterized as neutral—if, that is, the characterization *dhamma* can be properly called 'neutral' in the Nikāyas. For the imagery here illustrates 'the way things are', but this 'way things are' is actually what allows there to be a cessation of suffering; the way things are is, it turns out, the way we want things to be.

What I have tried to show so far in this chapter is that underlying the

---

[85] Collins, *SP*, p. 250; he cites M I 168; S I 136; A II 5; Sn 319; A I 223; D II 237.

[86] Cf. Collins, *SP*, pp. 259-60.

[87] Peter Masefield, however, offers (op. cit., pp. 134-5) an intriguing interpretation of *sotâpanna* as 'one who attains the ear [of *dhamma*]'.

[88] Collins, *SP*, p. 251.

apparent simplicity of these Nikāya passages concerning the seven sets is a developed, sophisticated and subtle psychology that already adumbrates in important respects much of what is spelt out and made explicit in the early Abhidhamma literature.

5. *The Mahā-vagga of the Saṃyutta-nikāya*

Having looked at certain particular treatments of the seven sets collectively in the Nikāyas, it is worth now considering some of the features that stand out in the overall treatment of the seven sets in the *mahā-vagga* of the *Saṃyutta-nikāya*. The *mahā-vagga* contains separate chapters or collections (*saṃyutta*) of *suttas* devoted to each of the seven sets, as well as collections devoted to a number of other topics.

Apart from the material that is distinctive to and characteristic of each particular set of items, these collections of *suttas* also exhibit a certain number of common features in the form of various recurrent themes and set formulaic treatments. Indeed a considerable proportion of the *mahā-vagga* consists entirely of the repetition of stock formulas applied to each of the seven sets in turn. Although the usage of set formulas is certainly not confined to these sections, I am speaking principally of the *Gaṅgā-peyyāla*, the *appamāda-*, *bala-karaṇīya-*, *esana-* and *ogha-vaggas*, which apply the same formulaic treatments in the case of the *ariyo aṭṭhaṅgiko maggo*, *bojjhaṅgas*, *satipaṭṭhānas*, *indriyas*, *samma-ppadhānas*, *balas*, *iddhi-pādas* and in addition—as I have already noted—to the four *jhānas*. Indeed the *samma-ppadhāna-*, *bala-* and *jhāna-saṃyuttas* consist of nothing more than the repetition of these five formulaic treatments. Such repetition of formulaic treatments has the effect of making the presentation of the *mahā-vagga* as a literary text impracticable without extensive abbreviations. Certainly all manuscripts and printed editions would appear to exhibit such abbreviations, although their precise extent varies.[89] Even with abbreviations the PTS edition runs to 478 pages.

This means that in important respects we are not presented with a fixed literary text so much as a method or technique for dealing with certain themes according to set patterns. Such a technique while demonstrating how the parts should be related to the whole, also allows for a certain amount of freedom and improvisation; once the principles, themes and patterns are familiar, any portion of the material might be expanded or abbreviated as seemed fit. Thus in order to understand what the *mahā-vagga* as a whole has to offer on the matter of the seven sets what we must do is to attempt to bring out those particular themes and patterns that are considered appropriate to all seven sets.

---

[89] Cf. L. Feer's comments S V v-ix. The conventions of classical Indian music would seem to provide an interesting parallel: the performance of an individual *rāga* may well last in excess of an hour, but the same *rāga* performed for record may well last only fifteen minutes.

(i) The seven sets are to be developed and made great

Perhaps the most obvious feature of the *mahā-vagga* treatment—so obvious that one almost simply overlooks it—is the extent to which derivatives of *bhāveti* and *bahulīkaroti* are used in connection with the seven sets. As far as the noble eight-factored path, the awakening-factors, the establishings of mindfulness, the faculties, the right endeavours, the powers and the bases of success are concerned, what the *bhikkhu* must do above all is simply 'bring them into being' (*bhāveti*) and 'make them become great' (*bahulīkaroti*).[90] How this will bring to the *bhikkhu* all the fruits of the spiritual life is stated again and again on nearly every other page of the *mahā-vagga*.

Developed and made great the *ariyo aṭṭhaṅgiko maggo*, the seven *bojjhaṅgas*, the four *satipaṭṭhānas*, the four *iddhi-pādas* conduce to going from this shore to the farther shore (*apārā-pāraṃ-gamanāya saṃvattanti*);[91] for whomever these are initiated (*āraddha*), the noble path leading to the right destruction of *dukkha* is initiated (*āraddho tesaṃ ariyo maggo sammā-dukkha-kkhaya-gāmī*);[92] developed and made great the seven *bojjhaṅgas*, the four *satipaṭṭhānas*, the four *iddhi-pādas* are 'noble, leading out; for the one who practises them they lead out to the right destruction of *dukkha*' (*ariyā niyyānika niyyanti tak-karassa sammā-dukkha-kkhayāya*);[93] they conduce to complete turning away, dispassion, cessation, peace, direct knowledge, awakening, *nibbāna* (*ekanta-nibbidāya virāgāya nirodhāya upasamāya abhiññāya sambodhāya nibbānāya saṃvattanti*).[94]

The *ariyo aṭṭhaṅgiko maggo* is the path, the way to full knowledge of *dukkha*, to full knowledge of the three feelings, to the allaying of passion (*rāga-virāga*), to the abandoning of the fetters, (*saṃyojana-pahāna*), to abolishing of the tendencies (*anusaya-samugghāṭana*), to full knowledge of the journey (*addhāna-pariññā*), to the destruction of the *āsavas* (*āsava-kkhaya*), to realization of the fruit of knowledge and freedom (*vijjā-vimutti-phala-sacchikiriyā*), to knowledge and vision (*ñāṇa-dassana*), to *nibbāna* without grasping (*anupāda-parinibbāna*).[95] The *ariyo aṭṭhaṅgiko maggo* leads to the deathless (*amata-gāmin*), to the restraint and destruction of greed, hate and delusion (*rāga-, dosa-, moha-vinaya, -kkhaya*);[96] it leads to *nibbāna* (*nibbāna-gama*), goes to *nibbāna* (*nibbāna-parāyana*), has its conclusion in *nibbāna* (*nibbāna-pariyosāna*);[97] it is to be developed for the abandoning of the five classes of object of sensual desire.[98]

---

90 (a) *bhāveti, bahulīkaroti/bhāvita, bahulīkata*: S V 2, 5, 11-2, 14-5, 24-5, 30-8, 38-41, 41-51 (*ariyo aṭṭhaṅgiko maggo*); 63-4, 67-70, 73-5, 78-9, 82-7, 90, 93, 98-100, 129-34, 134-5, 137-8 (*bojjhaṅga*); 166-7, 172-4, 176-7, 190-1 (*satipaṭṭhāna*); 220-4, 232-3, 235-6, 239-42 (*indriya*); 224-6 (*samma-ppadhāna*); 249-52 (*bala*); 255-7, 267, 271, 273-5, 284-5, 290-1 (*iddhi-pāda*). (b) *bhāvetabba*: S V 21-2, 54-62 (*magga*); 136-7, 139-40 (*bojjhaṅga*); 178-9, 190-2 (*satipaṭṭhāna*); 240-1, 242-3 (*indriya*); 246-8 (*samma-ppadhāna*); 250-1, 252-3 (*bala*); 258, 291-3 (*iddhi-pāda*).

91 S V 24-5, 81, 180, 254.

92 S V 23-4, 82, 179-80, 254-5.

93 S V 82, 166, 255.

94 S V 82, 179, 255.

95 S V 6-7, 21-2, 27-9.

96 S V 8.

97 S V 11-2.

98 S V 22.

The seven *bojjhaṅgas* turn towards awakening (*bodha*), towards penetrative insight (*nibbedha*), towards growth (*vuddhi*) and not decay (*aparihāna*), towards the realization of the fruit of knowledge and freedom;[99] they constitute the path and the way that turns towards the destruction and cessation of craving (*taṇhā-kkhaya, taṇhā-nirodha*);[100] they constitute the path that crushes the army of Māra (*māra-sena-pamaddano maggo*).[101]

Developing and making great the seven sets, the *bhikkhu* abandons and destroys the *āsavas*;[102] he abandons the fetters;[103] he is in training (*sekha*) and he is trained (*asekha*); [104] he is a stream attainer, a once returner, a non-returner, or an *arahant*.[105]

Two thorough treatments are represented by the *esanā-* and *ogha-vaggas*, sections which as I indicated above are common to the treatment of all seven sets in the *mahā-vagga*. According to these, then, the seven sets are to be developed for the sake of direct knowledge (*abhiññā*), full knowledge (*pariññā*), complete destruction (*parikkhaya*) and abandoning of the three desires (*esanā*), the three modes (*vidha*) [of pride], the three *āsavas*, the three becomings (*bhava*), the three sufferings (*dukkhatā*), the three wastelands (*khila*), the three stains (*mala*), the three destructions (*nigha*), the three feelings (*vedanā*), the three cravings (*taṇhā*); the four floods (*ogha*), the four graspings (*upādāna*), the four ties (*gantha*), the seven tendencies (*anusaya*), the five kinds of object of sensual desire (*kāma-guṇa*), the five hindrances (*nīvaraṇa*), the five aggregates of grasping (*upādāna-kkhandha*), the five lower fetters (*orambhāgiyāni saṃyojanāni*), the five higher fetters (*uddhambhāgiyāni saṃyojanāni*).[106]

So the seven sets individually and collectively when developed and made great lead to the fruits of the spiritual life. But exposition of the theme of the seven sets as the path to awakening does not end here in the *mahā-vagga*; it is extended to the individual factors of the path, awakening factors, faculties and powers.[107] Thus in the *Gaṅgā-peyyāla, appamāda-, balakaraṇīya-, esanā-*, and *ogha-vaggas* of each of these four sets it is stated at some length how the *bhikkhu* develops in turn each of the individual path-factors, awakening-factors, faculties and powers dependent on seclusion (*viveka-nissita*), dependent on dispassion (*virāga-nissita*), dependent on cessation (*nirodha-nissita*), ripening in release (*vosagga-pariṇāmin*);[108] he develops each one in turn as that which concludes in the restraint of greed, hate and delusion (*rāga-, dosa-, moha-vinaya-pariyosāna*); he develops each one in turn as that which plunges into the

---

99 S V 72, 83; 87; 94; 93, 97, 126.
100 S V 86-7
101 S V 99.
102 S V 8, 28 (*magga*); 72 (*bojjhaṅga*); 190 (*satipaṭṭhāna*); 220-2, 236 (*indriya*); 256-7, 275-6, 284, 288-9 (*iddhi-pāda*).
103 S V 14 (*magga*); 88 (*bojjhaṅga*); 177-8 (*satipaṭṭhāna*); 236 (*indriya*).
104 S V 14 (*magga*); 174-5 (*satipaṭṭhāna*); 229-30 (*indriya*).
105 S V 25-6 (*magga*); 174-5, 188 (*satipaṭṭhāna*); 200-1, 236-7 (*indriya*).
106 S V 54-62; 136-7; 139-40; 191-2; 240-3; 246-8; 250-3; 291-3.
107 The *satipaṭṭhānas, samma-ppadhānas* and *iddhi-pādas* are excluded since as aspects of what is essentially a unity it appears to be considered inappropriate or unnecessary to itemize them in quite the same way as the *maggaṅgas, bojjhaṅgas, indriyas* and *balas*.
108 On the *viveka-nissita* formula see above, Chapter 5.6.

deathless (*amatogadha*), goes to the deathless (*amata-parāyana*), concludes in the deathless (*amata-pariyosāna*); he develops each one in turn as that which tends, flows and slides to *nibbāna* (*nibbāna-ninna, -poṇa, -pabbhāra*).[109] All this is entirely consistent with the tendency to see the seven sets as representing a description of the path, as corresponding to the fourth of the four noble truths—the reality of the way leading to the cessation of suffering.

(ii) Prior and supporting conditions

Another theme that recurs in the treatment of the seven sets throughout the *mahā-vagga* is that of prior and supporting conditions that are conducive to the development of the seven sets and form a suitable basis for their development. The two items most consistently singled out in this connection are 'conduct' (*sīla*) and 'heedfulness' (*appamāda*).

As I have already indicated, a chapter on heedfulness—the *appamāda-vagga*—is common to all seven sets. This chapter consists of ten different similes illustrating how 'whatever skilful *dhammas* there are, they all are rooted in heedfulness and come together in heedfulness; heedfulness is reckoned the chief of these *dhammas*' (*ye keci kusalā dhammā sabbe te appamāda-mūlakā appamāda-samosaraṇā, appamado tesaṃ dhammānaṃ aggaṃ akkhāyati*); and so 'the *bhikkhu* who is heedful can be expected to develop and make great' (*appamattass'etaṃ bhikkhuno pāṭikaṅkhaṃ ... bhāvessati bahulīkarissati*) the noble eight-factored path, the awakening-factors, the establishings of mindfulness, the faculties, the right endeavours, the powers, the bases of success.[110] Similarly the *balakaraṇīya-vagga*, also common to all seven sets, opens with three similes illustrating how 'the *bhikkhu* depending on conduct, established in conduct develops and makes great the noble eight-factored path' (*bhikkhu sīlaṃ nissāya sīle patiṭṭhāya ariyaṃ aṭṭhaṅgikaṃ maggaṃ bhāveti bahulīkaroti*).[111]

The way in which conduct and heedfulness are fundamental to the development of the seven sets is also emphasized within the distinctive portions of the

[109] In extending the application of *amatogadha*, etc. and *nibbāna-ninna*, etc. to the individual *bojjhaṅgas*, *indriyas* and *balas* I depart from the PTS edition of the text as edited by Leon Feer. Feer seems to regard the repetitions in the *mahā-vagga* as rather excessive (cf. S V iii) and, lest they should get out of hand, restricts the *amatogadha* and *nibbāna-ninna* formulas to the initial exposition of the *Gaṅgā-peyyāla, appamāda-, balakaraṇīya-, esanā-* and *ogha-vaggas* in the context of the *magga-saṃyutta* (see S V 38-62). In the context of the *bojjhaṅga-, indriya-* and *bala-saṃyuttas* Feer confines the exposition of these sections to the *viveka-nissita* and *rāga-vinaya-pariyosāna* formulas. Clearly this is all that is *explicit* in some manuscripts, but equally clearly other manuscripts understand all four formulas to be relevant here. Thus with regard to the *Gaṅgā-peyyāla*, etc., some Burmese manuscripts state *yad api magga-saṃyuttaṃ vitthāretabbaṃ tad api bojjhaṅga-saṃyuttaṃ vitthāretabbaṃ* (S V 140; cf. 243 n. 4, 251 n. 3); certain Ceylonese manuscripts apparently include the other formulas in the *peyyālas* (see S V 243 n. 1, 251 n. 2). The commentary gives no reason why all four formulas should not be relevant in each case; on the contrary it seems to imply that at least in the case of the *bojjhaṅga-saṃyutta* they are all relevant: *Gaṅgā-peyyālâdayo magga-saṃyutte vutta-nayena veditabbā* (Spk III 176). The *amatogadha* formula is in fact applied directly to the individual *indriyas* in the body of the *indriya-saṃyutta* (see S V 220), while the *nibbāna-ninna* formula is used of each set as a *whole* in the *Gaṅgā-peyyāla* treatment; there would thus appear to be no technical reason for excluding them.

[110] S V 41-5; (135, 138, 191, 240, 242, 246, 250, 252, 291).

[111] S V 45-54 (passim); (135, 138, 191, 240, 242, 245, 250, 252, 291).

saṃyuttas devoted to the individual sets. In 'the repetitions of the sun' (*suriyassa peyyālo*), peculiar to the *magga-saṃyutta*,[112] the accomplishment of conduct and heedfulness (*sīla-*, *appamāda-sampadā*) are two of seven items that are the prelude and signal of the arising of the noble eight-factored path (*ariyassa aṭṭhaṅgikassa maggassa uppādāya etaṃ pubbaṃ-gamaṃ etaṃ pubba-nimittaṃ*), exactly as the dawn is the prelude and signal of the rising sun (*suriyassa udayato etaṃ pubbaṃ-gamaṃ etaṃ pubba-nimittaṃ yad idaṃ aruṇ-aggaṃ*).[113] The other five items here are having good friends (*kalyāṇa-mittatā*), accomplishment (*sampadā*) of the wish to act (*chanda*), of self (*attā*), of view (*diṭṭhi*), of proper bringing to mind (*yoniso manasikāra*). In the 'one *dhamma* repetitions' (*eka-dhamma-peyyāla*), again peculiar to the *magga-saṃyutta*, the same seven items are singled out as individual *dhammas* particularly useful for the arising of the noble eight-factored path (*eka-dhammo bahu-pakāro ariyassa aṭṭhaṅgikassa maggassa uppādāya*),[114] and as affording the means by which the noble eight-factored path once arisen reaches full development: 'I see no other single *dhamma*, *bhikkhus*, by means of which the noble eight-factored path not yet arisen arises, or the noble eight-factored path once arisen reaches full development.' (*nâhaṃ bhikkhave aññaṃ eka-dhammaṃ pi samanupassāmi yena anuppanno vā ariyo aṭṭhaṅgiko maggo uppajjati, uppanno vā ariyo aṭṭhaṅgiko maggo bhāvanā-pāripūriṃ gacchati*).[115] That the *bojjhaṅgas* and *satipaṭṭhānas* must be developed dependent on *sīla* is also further emphasized on a number of other occasions,[116] as is also the importance of *appamāda* for the development of the *bojjhaṅgas* and *indriyas*.[117]

Thus of the seven items mentioned in the 'repetition of the sun' and 'one *dhamma* repetitions' of the *magga-saṃyutta* it is *sīla* and *appamāda* that are the most generally emphasized as prior and supporting conditions for the development of the seven sets. However, 'having good friends' (*kalyāṇa-mittatā*) and 'proper bringing to mind' (*yoniso manasikāra*) receive some additional attention in both the *magga-* and *bojjhaṅga-saṃyuttas*. In the former 'having good friends' is termed 'the entire spiritual life' (*sakalaṃ brahma-cariyaṃ*);[118] in the latter the relationship between the dawn and the rising sun is now likened to the relationship between having good friends and the arising of the awakening-factors, and to the relationship between proper bringing to mind and the arising of the awakening-factors.[119] Proper bringing to mind is further explained as the internal factor or condition (*ajjhattikaṃ aṅgaṃ*) and having good friends as the external factor or condition (*bāhiraṃ aṅgaṃ*) for the arising of the awakening factors.[120]

---

[112] But cf. above, p. 165, n. 102.
[113] S V 29-32.
[114] S V 32-5.
[115] S V 35-8.
[116] S V 63-4, 78, 143-4, 165-6, 171-2, 187-8.
[117] S V 91, 232.
[118] S V 2-4.
[119] S V 78-9, 101; *kalyāṇa-mittatā* and *yoniso-manasikāra* are also associated with the *bojjhaṅgas* at A I 14-5.
[120] S V 101-2. See also comments on *parato ghosa* above, pp. 221-3.

I do not intend to discuss these items further individually.[121] What I have said in other contexts should be sufficient to make it clear that what these various passages with their similes seem intended to show is how the maintenance and continuance of certain conditions, disciplines and tendencies of the mind will gradually give rise to and support the development of those spiritual faculties encompassed by the seven sets. Thus the seven sets are presented here as representing something psychologically and spiritually more specific and definite that arises and develops naturally out of the generality of the proper supporting conditions. In terms appropriate to the imaginative thought world of the Nikāyas, it is as if the continuing support of the right conditions in the shape of *sīla*, *appamāda*, proper bringing to mind, good friends and so on is the continuing rain of the *deva* on the mountain top that initiates the trickle that eventually will become the Gaṅgā flowing majestically towards the ocean. The literary form of much of the *mahā-vagga* here seems to echo the sense. The abundant repetitions, not just with the recurrence of the themes but in the actual structure of sections such as the *appamāda-* and *balakaraṇīya-vaggas*, have their own cumulative effect.

(iii) Some further similes

I have already commented on a number of similes both in the *mahā-vagga* and elsewhere that illustrate the gradual and inevitable nature of the development of the seven sets—a development that is seen as reaching a decisive and definite culmination. Apart from the Gaṅgā similes, the ship simile and the simile of the various winds in the sky, the *mahā-vagga* contains a number of other important similes illustrating the development of each of the seven sets in turn. For the most part these similes occur in the *balakaraṇīya-vagga*, common to all of the sets.

A tree that leans, tends and inclines to the east (*pācīna-ninna*, *-poṇa*, *-pabbhāra*) will, when cut at the root, fall to the east; in the same way a *bhikkhu* developing and making great the noble eight-factored path and the rest leans, tends and inclines to *nibbāna*.[122] Just as a pot that is upset spills out its water and cannot be refilled with it (*kumbho nikkujjo vamateva udakaṃ no paccāvamati*), so a *bhikkhu* who develops and makes great the noble eight-factored path and the rest spills out bad unskilful *dhammas* and cannot be refilled with them.[123] Just as a stem of wheat or grass that is appropriately directed (*sammā-paṇihita*) can pierce the skin and draw blood (*lohitaṃ uppādessati*) when the hand or foot is placed on it, so the *bhikkhu* by appropriately directed development of the path can pierce ignorance, draw knowledge and realize *nibbāna* (*bhikkhu sammā-paṇihitāya magga-bhāvanāya avijjaṃ chijjati vijjaṃ*

---

[121] On *kalyāṇa-mittatā* see S. Collins, '*Kalyāṇamitta* and *Kalyāṇamittatā*', *JPTS* (1986), pp. 51-72; on *appamāda* cf. comments in chapter one (pp. 43-4); on *atta-sampadā* cf. the instruction to the *bhikkhus* to dwell *atta-dīpa* and *atta-saraṇa*, explained in terms of the *satipaṭṭhāna* formula (see above, p. 67); on *chanda* cf. comments above (pp. 90-1, 114-5).

[122] S V 47-8.

[123] S V 48; cf. A V 337 and different application of *kumbha* simile to just the *ariyo aṭṭhaṅgiko maggo* at S V 20.

uppādessati nibbānaṃ sacchikarissati); in this connection he develops the noble eight-factored path and the rest.[124] Just as in the last month of the hot season when the dust and dirt rise up, a great cloud out of season suddenly causes it to disappear and settle (*gimhānaṃ pacchime māse uggataṃ rajo-jallaṃ taṃ enaṃ mahā akāla-megho ṭhānaso antaradhāpeti vūpasameti*), so a *bhikkhu* developing and making great the noble eight-factored path and the rest suddenly causes bad unskilful *dhammas* that continually arise (*uppannuppanne*) to disappear and settle.[125] Just as a great cloud that has arisen is dispersed, made to disappear and settle by a great wind (*uppannaṃ mahā-meghaṃ taṃ enaṃ mahā-vāto antarāy'eva antaradhāpeti vūpasameti*), so a *bhikkhu* developing and making great the noble eight-factored path and the rest disperses the bad unskilful *dhammas* that continually arise, he makes them disappear and settle.[126]

(iv) The seven sets as normative

A final theme of the *mahā-vagga* is that which presents the seven sets as 'normative': the seven sets illustrate the nature and law of things, and are at once central and peculiar to the teaching of a Buddha. There are two formulaic cycles illustrating this theme; one may be termed the 'past-future-present' formula, the other the 'not-apart-from-the-training-of-a-Sugata' formula. One of the passages in the first cycle is a variation of a passage I referred to above in chapter one:

> All those Blessed Ones who in the past were *arahants*, fully awakened ones, abandoning the five hindrances, defilements of the mind that weaken wisdom, their minds well established in the four establishings of mindfulness, developed in accordance with what is the seven factors of awakening and awakened to the unsurpassable full awakening. All those Blessed Ones who in the future will be *arahants*, fully awakened ones ... will awaken to the unsurpassable full awakening. And the Blessed One, an *arahant*, a fully awakened one now ... awakens to the unsurpassable full awakening.[127]

Similarly all those *samaṇas* and *brāhmaṇas* who abandoned the three forms of pride in the past, who will abandon them in the future, and who abandon them in the present—all have done so, will do so and do so now as a result of developing and making great the seven factors of awakening (*sattannaṃ bojjhaṅgānaṃ bhāvitattā bahulīkatattā*).[128] All those *samaṇas* and *brāhmaṇas*

---

[124] S V 49; cf. S V 10.

[125] S V 50.

[126] S V 50-1.

[127] S V 160-1 (= D II 81-3; III 99-101): *ye pi te bhante ahesuṃ atītaṃ addhānaṃ arahanto sammāsambuddhā sabbe te bhagavanto pañca nīvaraṇe pahāya cetaso upakkilese paññāya dubbalī-karaṇe catusu satipaṭṭhānesu supatiṭṭhita-cittā satta bojjhaṅge yathā-bhūtaṃ bhāvetvā anuttaraṃ sammā-sambodhiṃ abhisambujjhiṃsu. ye pi te bhante bhāvissanti anāgataṃ addhānaṃ ... abhisam-bujjhissanti. bhagavā pi bhante etarahi arahaṃ sammāsambuddho ... abhisambuddho.* (Cf. above, p. 58.)

[128] S V 98. Cf. S V 86: 'I see no single *dhamma, bhikkhus*, other than the seven awakening-factors such that when developed and made great it turns towards the abandoning of those *dhammas* connected with the fetters.' (*nâhaṃ bhikkhave aññaṃ eka-dhammaṃ pi samanupassāmi yo evaṃ bhāvito bahulīkato saṃyojanīyānaṃ dhammānaṃ pahānāya saṃvattati, yathayidaṃ bhikkhave satta bojjhaṅgā.*)

who achieved partial or full meditational power (*iddhi-padesa, samattaṃ iddhiṃ*) in the past, or will achieve it in the future, or achieve it in the present—all have done so, will do so, and do so now as a result of developing and making great the four bases of success.[129] All those *bhikkhus* who by the destruction of the *āsavas*, have in the here and now directly known, realized, attained and dwelt in the freedom of mind, the freedom of wisdom that is without *āsavas* in the past, or will dwell in it in the future, dwell in it now—all have done so, will do so, and do so now as a result of developing and making great the four bases of success.[130]

The form of the second formulaic cycle is as follows:

> When these eight *dhammas* are as yet unarisen as [*dhammas* that are] developed and made great, they do not arise apart from the appearance of a Tathāgata, an *arahant*, a fully awakened one. Which are the eight? They are right view, right thought, right speech, right action, right livelihood, right effort, right mindfulness, right concentration.[131]

A number of variations are achieved by making certain changes: they do not arise outside the training of a Sugata (*nâññatra sugata-vinaya*); or the eight *dhammas* are considered as purified, cleansed, without blemish, defilements gone (*parisuddhā pariyodātā anaṅgaṇā vigatupakkilesā*).[132] In the *bojjhaṅga-* and *indriya-saṃyuttas* the same formula is applied to the awakening-factors and faculties.[133]

Thus the treatment of the seven sets by way of these two formulas—the 'past-future-present' formula and the 'not-apart-from' formula—is not systematic or comprehensive; that is to say, not all of the seven sets are treated by way of each formula: the *ariyo aṭṭhaṅgiko maggo* is not treated by way of the 'past-present-future' formula, and the *satipaṭṭhānas* and *iddhi-pādas* not by way of the 'not-apart-from' formula; while the *samma-ppadhānas* and *balas* do not feature at all.

Whether we should attempt to see some method in this, or whether it is better viewed as largely a matter of chance might be made clearer by a detailed study of the Chinese Āgamas. My own suspicion is that the latter is nearer the mark. Thus the *Mahāparinibbāna-sutta* passage which states that the four classes of *samaṇa* are only found in that *dhamma-vinaya* where the *ariyo aṭṭhaṅgiko maggo* is found is rather close in intent to the 'past-future-present' formula.[134] While the fact that the *samma-ppadhānas* and *balas* do not feature here is largely consistent with the fact that, of the seven sets, these two clearly receive rather less individual attention in the Nikāyas than the others. The

---

129 S V 255-6; cf. 273-5; 269-71; 288 (of Moggallāna); 289 (of the Tathāgata).

130 S V 256-7.

131 S V 14: *atth'ime bhikkhave dhammā bhāvitā bahulīkatā anuppannā uppajjanti naññatra tathāgatassa pātubhāvā arahato sammāsambuddhassa. katame attha. seyyathīdaṃ sammā-diṭṭhi ... sammā-samādhi.*

132 S V 14-5.

133 S V 77, 235.

134 See above, p. 204.

Peṭakopadesa in fact uses a variation on the 'past-present-future' formula in the context of the thirty-seven *bodhi-pakkhiyā dhammā*:

> The four establishings of mindfulness ... the noble eight-factored path—these are the thirty-seven *bodhi-pakkhiyā dhammā*. Those *dhammas* which conduce to *nibbāna* for past, future and present blessed Buddhas, Paccekabuddhas and disciples, they are the path.[135]

At this point I can perhaps make one or two further comments on the notion of *dhamma* and its relationship to the seven sets in the Nikāyas. What I want to say follows on from what was said at the conclusion of the section of this chapter dealing with the seven sets as *dhammas* taught by the Buddha. What the passages just considered suggest then is that if the *samaṇa*, the *brāhmaṇa* or the *bhikkhu* practises in a certain way, that is to say, develops and makes great the seven sets, then the natural consequence of this will be the cessation of suffering, will be awakening. This is the truth that the Nikāyas claim to expound, this is *dhamma*. Put like this, *dhamma* is for the Nikāyas not so much an absolute statement of truth as an observation of cause and effect; on the basis of this observation the seven sets are suggested as a prescription if the desired effect happens to be the cessation of suffering; the teachings about the seven sets are not so much a final statement about the way things are as useful to the one who desires to arrive at the cessation of suffering.

But this is not strictly the end of the story for the Nikāyas. The development of the seven sets has in the past, will in the future and does in the present bring about the cessation of suffering—it always was so, it always will be so, and it is so now. Inherent in this kind of thinking is the notion that in some sense the universal and fundamental nature of things has been tapped. Thus if the path to awakening is set out in terms of the seven sets, it does in some sense actually represent a description of the way things are—the way things have been, and always will be.

So, we are told, anyone who has come to the cessation of suffering must have come by this path, the path that is encompassed in the development of the seven sets. Or, turning this around, any path that ends in the cessation of suffering must essentially be this path. This kind of thinking is of some importance to our understanding of the seven sets in the Nikāyas. This is precisely why the Nikāyas can describe the seven sets as collectively and individually reaching the end of the path to awakening, why the seven sets are bound up together, why the full development of any one of the sets brings to fulfilment all seven. The seven sets are essentially just different ways of looking at or describing the same thing, namely what is seen as the one reality of the truth of the path leading to the cessation of suffering. But the teachings about the seven sets are not necessarily the absolute or final description of that truth or of the path; as I have already suggested, for the Nikāyas such teachings can

---

[135] Peṭ 114: *cattāro satipaṭṭhānā yāva ariyo aṭṭhaṅgiko maggo, evaṃ ete sattatiṃsa bodhi-pakkhikā dhammā. ye dhammā atītānāgata-paccuppannānaṃ buddhānaṃ bhagavantānaṃ pacceka-buddhānaṃ sāvakānañ ca nibbānāya saṃvattanti, so maggo.* (Cf. Asaṅga's *Śrāvakabhūmi*, quoted Wayman, *JIP* 6 (1978), p. 418.)

only be 'true' in so far as they are effective, since it is what is effective, what works, what brings about the cessation of suffering that constitutes the path, that constitutes what is true, what is *dhamma*.

Finally, we are told this path is not found outside the training of a Sugata or apart from the appearance of a Tathāgata. This does begin to look rather more like an absolute and exclusive claim on the part of the Nikāyas, and possibly should be taken as such. Yet in one sense it is merely the consequence of the internal consistency of the Nikāya thought-world, of the particular function of certain concepts. For to say that there is no path apart from the teaching of a Buddha is merely the corollary of the notion that the one—anyone—who discovers and teaches the way to the cessation of suffering should be called 'buddha', for this is what Buddhas do. Yet the teaching of Buddhas is not something at variance with the teaching of other wise men:

> I do not quarrel with the world, *bhikkhus*, but the world quarrels with me. One who speaks *dhamma* does not quarrel with anyone in the world. Of that to which the wise men of the world do not assent, I too say that it is not so. Of that to which the wise men of the world assent, I too say that it is so.[136]

6. The powers of the one who has destroyed the āsavas

This discussion of the way in which the seven sets are used in the Nikāyas to describe the course and final consummation of the path to awakening is conveniently brought to a conclusion by turning briefly to the notion of the particular powers that belong to the one who has come to the end of the path, namely the powers that belong to the one who has destroyed the *āsavas* (*khīṇâsava-bala*). The Nikāyas give these powers as seven, eight or ten in number. The full ten are as follows:

> Here, sir, for a *bhikkhu* for whom the *āsavas* are destroyed [i] all conditions are well seen by means of right wisdom as they are, as impermanent ... this is a power of the *bhikkhu* for whom the *āsavas* are destroyed, and depending on it he recognizes the destruction of the *āsavas*: 'The *āsavas* are destroyed for me.' [ii] ... sensual desires are well seen by means of right wisdom as they are, as like a fire pit ... this is a power ... 'The *āsavas* are destroyed for me.' [iii] ... his mind leans towards, tends towards, inclines towards, is intent upon seclusion, it delights in absence of desire, it is completely removed from those *dhammas* that form a basis for the *āsavas* ... this is a power ... 'The *āsavas* are destroyed for me.' [iv] ... the four establishings of mindfulness are developed, well developed ... this is a power ... 'The *āsavas* are destroyed for me.' [v] ... the four right endeavours ... [vi] ... the four bases of success ... [vii] ... the five faculties ... [viii] ... the five powers ... [ix] ... the seven factors of awakening ... [x] ... the noble eight-factored path is developed, well developed ... this is a power ... 'The *āsavas* are destroyed for me.'[137]

---

136 S III 138: *nâhaṃ bhikkhave lokena vivadāmi loko ca mayā vivadati. na bhikkhave dhamma-vādī kenaci lokasmiṃ vivadati. yaṃ bhikkhave natthi sammataṃ loke paṇḍitānaṃ ahaṃ pi taṃ natthī ti vadāmi. yaṃ bhikkhave atthi sammataṃ loke paṇḍitānaṃ ahaṃ pi taṃ atthī ti vadāmi.*

137 For the ten *khīṇâsava-balas* see A V 175, Paṭis II 173-4: *idhâvuso khīṇâsavassa bhikkhuno aniccato sabbe saṃkhārā yathā-bhūtaṃ samma-ppaññāya sudiṭṭhā honti, yaṃ p'āvuso khīṇâsavassa bhikkuno ... honti, idaṃ pi khīṇâsavassa bhikkhuno balaṃ hoti yaṃ balaṃ āgamma khīṇâsavo*

Rather interestingly when the list of the seven *khīṇâsava-balas* is given, it does not simply consist of the seven sets (iv-x) as might have been guessed. What is omitted are the references to the *samma-ppadhānas*, the *iddhi-pādas* and the *balas*.[138] The list of eight *khīṇâsava-balas* restores the *iddhi-pādas*, but once again omits the *samma-ppadhānas* and *balas*.[139] Why this variation, and what principles govern the omissions?

It seems that the *khīṇâsava-balas* should be seen as an attempt to define the special capacities of a *khīṇâsava* or *arahant* in much the same way as the ten *tathāgata-balas* define the special capacities of a Buddha. Thus the fluctuation between seven, eight and ten *khīṇâsava-balas* might be seen as concerned with the definition of the minimum number of special powers, the basic capacities common to all *arahant*s. Certainly the early history of Buddhist thought would seem to bear witness to such concerns.[140] The theoretical problem is, then, that although all individuals looked upon as *arahants* need not be expected to exhibit precisely the same capacities, by definition they must still exhibit some common traits.

So why may the *samma-ppadhānas* be omitted from the list of *khīṇâsava-balas*? It seems that in some sense 'endeavour' or 'strength' is simply not seen as crucial for the *arahant* in quite the same way as it is for one who is actively developing the path. That this is so would seem to follow from the way in which the four *samma-ppadhānas* appear to be understood as *viriya*, especially in its capacity of maintaining what has been achieved and checking any falling back. This would also appear to tie in with the Abhidhamma tradition that omits *samma-ppadhāna* from the reckoning at the time of the occurrence of the transcendent fruition (*lokuttara-phala*) consciousness.

Above I discussed how the *iddhi-pādas* are especially associated with the acquiring of facility in a variety of meditation attainments. In particular this facility is considered to result in a number of different meditation powers. It is clear from the later tradition that the full development and mastery of such powers was regarded not as an absolute prerequisite of the destruction of the *āsavas* (although certainly useful to that end) but rather as the particular domain of the master and adept of *jhāna*. Presumably, then, whether or not the *iddhi-pādas* are counted among the special powers of the one who has destroyed the *āsavas* is indicative in some measure of the distinction made in later writings between the practitioner who follows the vehicle of calm (*samatha-*

---

bhikkhu āsavānaṃ khayaṃ paṭijānāti khīṇā me āsavā ti … aṅgāra-kāsûpamā kāmā yathā-bhūtaṃ samma-ppaññāya sudiṭṭhā honti … balaṃ hoti … khīṇā me āsavā ti … viveka-ninnaṃ cittaṃ hoti viveka-poṇaṃ viveka-pabbhāraṃ vivekaṭṭhaṃ nekkhammâbhirataṃ vyantibhūtaṃ sabbaso āsava-ṭṭhāniyehi dhammehi … balaṃ hoti … khīṇā me āsavā ti … cattāro satipaṭṭhānā bhāvitā honti subhāvitā … balaṃ hoti … khīṇā me āsavā ti … cattāro samma-ppadhāna … cattāro iddhi-pādā … pañca indriyāni … pañca balāni … satta bojjhaṅgā … ariyo aṭṭhaṅgiko maggo bhāvito hoti subhāvito … balaṃ hoti … khīṇā me āsavā ti.

[138] D III 283-4.

[139] A IV 223-5.

[140] Cf. K. Werner, 'Bodhi and Arahattaphala: from Early Buddhism to Early Mahāyāna', Denwood and Piatigorsky, *BSAM*, pp. 167-81.

yāna) and the practitioner who follows the vehicle of pure insight (*vipassanā-yāna*).[141] The reason why the *balas* can be omitted from the reckoning when talking of the *khīṇâsava-balas* is perhaps simply because to say of the *indriyas* that they are 'developed, well developed' is to say precisely that they are *balas*.

---

[141] Cf. L.S. Cousins, 'Samatha-yāna and Vipassanā-yāna' in Dhammapala, *BSHS*, pp.56-68.

CHAPTER EIGHT

THE SEVEN SETS EXPANDED

1. In the four Nikāyas

So far I have confined myself to Nikāya passages that deal more or less exclusively with the seven sets. Of course the treatments in the *Mahāsaḷāyatanika-* and *Piṇḍapātapārisuddhi-suttas* do bring in other items, principally calm (*samatha*) and insight (*vipassanā*), but it remains fair to say that the seven sets still function here as a more or less self-contained group. However, at this point in my study I need to look at a number of Nikāya passages that expand the seven sets by bringing various items into rather more direct association with them.

The first passage I wish to consider in this context is the *asaṃkhata-saṃyutta*.[1] The *asaṃkhata-saṃyutta* consists of variations on the following basic form:

> I shall teach you, *bhikkhus*, the unconditioned and the path leading to the unconditioned. Hear it. And what, *bhikkhus*, is the unconditioned? That which is the destruction of passion, the destruction of hatred, the destruction of delusion—this is called the unconditioned. And what is the path leading to the unconditioned? Mindfulness concerned with body—this is called the path leading to the unconditioned. Thus, *bhikkhus*, the unconditioned and the path leading to the unconditioned is taught by me to you. That which should be done by a teacher desiring the welfare of his pupils, out of compassion, depending on compassion has been done by me for you. There are roots of trees, there are empty places; meditate, *bhikkhus*, do not be heedless, do not be regretful later. This is my instruction to you.[2]

Into this framework, in place of 'mindfulness concerned with body' (*kāya-gatā sati*) as an explanation of 'the path leading to the unconditioned' (*asaṃkhata-gāmi maggo*), ten different items are then substituted giving ten more rehearsals of this basic *sutta* form. The ten items are:

(i) calm and insight (*samatho vipassanā cā*)
(ii) concentration with initial and sustained thought (*savitakko savicāro samādhi*), concentration without initial thought yet with sustained thought (*avitakka-vicāra-matto samādhi*), concentration without initial and sustained thought (*avitakko avicāro samādhi*)

---

[1] S IV 359-73.

[2] S IV 359: *asaṃkhatañ ca vo bhikkhave desissāmi asaṃkhata-gāmiñ ca maggaṃ, taṃ suṇātha. katamañ ca bhikkhave asaṃkhataṃ. yo bhikkhave rāga-kkhayo dosa-kkhayo moha-kkhayo idaṃ vuccati bhikkhave asaṃkhataṃ. katamo ca bhikkhave asaṃkhata-gāmi maggo. kāya-gatā sati, ayaṃ vuccati bhikkhave asaṃkhata-gāmi maggo. iti kho bhikkhave desitaṃ vo mayā asaṃkhataṃ desito asaṃkhata-gāmi maggo. yaṃ bhikkhave satthārā karaṇīyaṃ sāvakānaṃ hitesinā anukampena anukampaṃ upādāya kataṃ vo taṃ mayā. etāni bhikkhave rukkha-mūlāni etāni suññâgārāni jhāyatha mā pamādattha mā pacchā-vippaṭisārino ahuvattha. ayaṃ kho vo amhākaṃ anusāsanī ti.*

TABLE 6. THE 7 SETS EXPANDED IN THE NIKĀYAS

Asaṃkhata-saṃyutta	Mahāsakuludāyi-sutta	Ānâpānasati-sutta	Aṅguttara: eka-nipāta
1 kāya-gatā sati		arahants	
2 samatha-vipassanā		opapātikas	
3 samādhis		sakad-āgāmins	4 jhānas
3 samādhis		anāgāmins	4 ceto-vimuttis (mettā, etc.)
4 satipaṭṭhānas	4 satipaṭṭhānas	4 satipaṭṭhānas	4 satipaṭṭhānas
4 samma-ppadhānas	4 samma-ppadhānas	4 samma-ppadhānas	4 samma-ppadhānas
4 iddhi-pādas	4 iddhi-pādas	4 iddhi-pādas	4 iddhi-pādas
5 indriyas	5 indriyas	5 indriyas	5 indriyas
5 balas	5 balas	5 balas	5 balas
7 bojjhaṅgas	7 bojjhaṅgas	7 bojjhaṅgas	7 bojjhaṅgas
ariyo aṭṭhaṅgiko maggo	ariyo aṭṭhaṅgiko maggo	ariyo aṭṭhaṅgiko maggo	ariyo aṭṭhaṅgiko maggo
	8 vimokkhas	mettā-bhāvanā	8 abhibhâyatanas
	8 abhibhâyatanas	karuṇā-bhāvanā	8 vimokkhas
	10 kasiṇâyatanas	muditā-bhāvanā	10 kasiṇâyatanas
	4 jhānas	upekkhā-bhāvanā	20 saññās
	sāmañña-phala (final 8)	asubha-bhāvanā	10 indriyas-balas × 4 jhānas
		anicca-saññā-bhāvanā	10 indriyas-balas × 4 ceto-vimuttis
		ānâpāna-sati-bhāvanā	5 indriyas
			5 balas

(iii) empty concentration (*suññato samādhi*), signless concntration (*animitto samādhi*), wishless concentration (*appaṇihito samādhi*)
(iv) the four establishings of mindfulness
(v) the four right endeavours
(vi) the four bases of success
(vii) the five faculties
(viii) the five powers
(ix) the seven factors of awakening
(x) the noble eight-factored path

The *asaṃkhata-saṃyutta* then continues by breaking down these ten groups into their constituent parts so that each of these parts is itself said to be equivalent to the path leading to the unconditioned. This procedure gives a further forty-five rehearsals of the basic *sutta* form. Of course, as far as the seven sets are concerned the implications of such a procedure are familiar enough: the totality of each of the sets is a complete path; each item of each of the sets is also a complete path—these are ideas that have already been met with in the course of this study. Once again what is brought out is the essential unity of the seven sets and the path—how each of the sets and each of the items that make up each of the sets are in some sense equivalent. What of the items brought into association with the seven sets? The expansion of the seven sets here would seem to follow a principle of numerical progression: first we have a single item (*kāya-gatā sati*), followed by one pair and two sets of three, and finally the seven sets in numerical order beginning with the four establishings of mindfulness. This gives a total of forty-six items. As was seen in chapter one, *kāya-gatā sati* is merely another way of looking at the first establishing of mindfulness; so in the *asaṃkhata-saṃyutta* the seven sets are effectively once more brought into association with *samatha* and *vipassanā* (as in the *Mahāsaḷāyatanika-* and *Piṇḍapātapārisuddhi-suttas*), and also six varieties of *samādhi*.

Three other Nikāya passages take the extension of the seven sets rather further than this; the connection between the seven sets as a self-contained yardstick of Buddhist teaching or as a description of the Buddhist path that is at once concise and complete seems to become more tenuous. The seven sets are apparently just examples, along with other examples, of what the Buddha and his followers teach and practise.

According to the *Mahāsakuludāyi-sutta*[3] there are five reasons why the pupils of the Buddha esteem, revere, think highly of, honour and rely on him (*pañca dhammā yehi mama sāvakā sakkaronti garukaronti mānenti pūjenti sakkatvā garukatvā upanissāya viharanti*).[4] The fifth of these reasons is that the Buddha explains to his pupils various paths or ways:

> Moreover, Udāyi, explained by me to my pupils is the way entering upon which my pupils develop the four establishings of mindfulness ... the four right endeavours ... the four bases of success ... the five faculties ... the five powers ... the seven factors of awakening ... the noble eight-factored path ... the eight liberations ... the eight

[3] M II 1-22.
[4] M II 9.

spheres of mastery ... the ten *kasiṇâyatanas* ... the four *jhānas* ... the way entering upon which my pupils know thus: 'This body of mine has form, consists of the four great elements, is born of mother and father, is sustained by cooked rice and gruel; its nature is to be impermanent, to run down, to wear away, to break up, to perish, and this consciousness of mine is tied to it, bound to it.' ... [They] create from this body another body, having form, mind-made, with all limbs, not lacking in any faculty ... [They] enjoy various kinds of power ... [They,] by means of the divine ear-element, purified, surpassing the human, hear sounds, both divine and human, far and near ... [They,] embracing with the mind the minds of other beings, of other persons, know [them] ... [They] recall various former existences ... [They,] by means of the divine eye, purified, surpassing the human see beings arising and falling—inferior or refined, fair or ugly, well-born or ill-born, they know beings as faring according to their actions ... [They,] by the destruction of the *āsavas*, in the here and now directly know for themselves, realize, attain and dwell in the freedom of mind, the freedom of wisdom that is without *āsavas*.[5]

In the first instance the list of seven sets seems here to be once more extended according to a principle of numerical progression: two sets of eight—the *vimokkhas* and *abhibhāyatanas*—are added, and one set of ten—the *kasiṇâyatanas*. The *vimokkhas* and *abhibhāyatanas* are two sets of categories not specifically discussed at great length in the later literature. This at least in part appears to be because they are considered to overlap with matters dealt with in detail under the more general headings of *jhāna* and formless attainment. Thus, as far as the *Dhammasaṅgaṇi* is concerned, the *abhibhāyatanas* seem to be concerned with mastery and facility in certain aspects of *jhāna* practice.[6] The *vimokkhas* would appear to embrace *jhāna* of both the form and formless spheres.[7] The ten *kasiṇas*, however, are rather more central to the exposition of *jhāna* in such works as the *Visuddhimagga* and *Vimuttimagga* than are the *vimokkhas* and *abhibhāyatanas*.[8] Having reached ten *kasiṇâyatanas* by way of

---

5 M II 11-22: *puna ca paraṃ Udāyi akkhātā mayā sāvakānaṃ paṭipadā yathā paṭipannā me sāvakā cattāro satipaṭṭhāne bhāventi ... cattāro samma-ppadhāne ... cattāro iddhi-pāde ... pañc-indriyāni ... pañca balāni ... satta bojjhaṅge ... ariyaṃ aṭṭhaṅgikaṃ maggaṃ ... aṭṭha vimokkhe ... aṭṭha abhibhāyatanāni ... dasa kasiṇâyatanāni ... cattāri jhānāni ... paṭipadā yathā paṭipanno me sāvakā evaṃ pajānanti: ayaṃ kho me kāyo rūpī catum-mahā-bhūtiko mātā-pettika-sambhavo odana-kummāsūpacayo aniccucchādana-parimaddana-bhedana-viddhaṃsana-dhammo idañ ca pana me vi-ññāṇaṃ ettha sitaṃ ettha paṭibaddhaṃ ... imamhā kāya aññaṃ kāyaṃ abhinimminanti rūpiṃ mano-mayaṃ sabbaṅga-paccaṅgiṃ abhinindriyaṃ ... aneka-vihitaṃ iddhi-vidhaṃ paccanubhonti ... dibbāya sota-dhātuyā visuddhāya atikkanta-mānusikāya ubho sadde suṇanti dibbe ca mānuse ca ye dūre santike ca ... para-sattānaṃ para-puggalānaṃ cetasā ceto paricca pajānanti ... aneka-vihitaṃ pubbe-nivāsaṃ anussaranti ... dibbena cakkhunā visuddhena atikkanta-mānusakena satte passanti cavamāne upajjamāne hīne paṇīte suvaṇṇe dubbaṇṇe sugate duggate yathā-kammûpage satte pajān-anti ... āsavānaṃ khayā anāsavaṃ ceto-vimuttiṃ paññā-vimuttiṃ diṭṭhe va dhamme sayaṃ abhiññā sacchikatvā upasampajja viharanti.* (The text details in full each of the items mentioned.)

6 See Dhs 42-52 where the eight *abhibhāyatanas* (with slight variations from the Nikāya formulation) are treated as an aspect of *jhāna* that is *rūpâvacara*; cf. As 187-90.

7 The fourth, fifth, sixth and seventh *vimokkhas* straightforwardly correspond to the four formless attainments respectively; the eighth *vimokkha* is *saññā-vedayita-nirodha*; the formulation of the second *vimokkha* (*ajjhattaṃ arūpa-saññī bahiddhā rūpāni passati*) suggests that it is a shorthand for all eight *abhibhāyatanas* which consist of variations on the theme *ajjhattaṃ arūpa-saññī eko bahiddhā rūpāni passati*. For a more detailed exposition of the *vimokkhas* see Paṭis II 38-40.

8 Dhs 31-42 gives only eight *kasiṇas*; Vism has ten but with *āloka* for *viññāṇa*; the *Vimuttimagga* has all eleven.

numerical progression, the *Mahāsakuludāyi-sutta* abandons this principle and gives next the four *jhānas*. The eight individual items that follow after the *jhānas* correspond to the eight items that follow the *jhānas* in the *sāmañña-phala* schema. In effect it seems that we have two lists: one list consists of the seven sets along with the eight *vimokkhas*, eight *abhibhāyatanas* and ten *kasiṇâyatanas*; the other of the *sāmañña-phala* schema beginning with the four *jhānas*.

To move on to the second passage, near the beginning of the *Ānâpānasati-sutta* the Buddha is described as surveying the *bhikkhu-saṃgha* and commenting:

> There are, *bhikkhus*, *bhikhus* in this *bhikkhu-saṃgha* who are *arahants* who have destroyed the *āsavas* ... who by the destruction of the five lower fetters are ones who will arise spontaneously [in the pure abodes] ... who by the destruction of three fetters and the weakening of greed, hatred and delusion are once returners ... who by the destruction of three fetters are stream attainers ... who dwell engaged in the development of the four establishings of mindfulness ... the four right endeavours ... the four bases of success ... the five faculties ... the five powers ... the seven factors of awakening ... the noble eight-factored path ... loving kindness ... compassion ... sympathetic joy ... equipoise ... ugliness ... the notion of impermanence ... mindfulness of breathing in and out.[9]

This list is a little different in character from the preceding. We begin with the four basic types of noble person. Presumably what follows are the practices and meditations that the one aspiring to the state of the noble person must develop: these are the seven sets; the four meditations often collectively referred to as the 'immeasurables' (*appamaññā*)[10] or 'divine abidings' (*brahma-vihāra*);[11] the meditation on ugliness; the notion of impermanence; mindfulness of breathing in and out. The items added to the list of seven sets here agree in large measure with additional items singled out for association with the *bojjhaṅgas* in both the *Saṃyutta-nikāya* and also the commentaries.[12] This is especially so if we can take *anicca-saññā* as implying something similar to the development of insight or what the commentaries call '*jhāna* as a basis for insight' (*vipassanā-pādaka-jjhāna*). This agreement should possibly be seen as connected with the fact that the account of the path associated with *ānâpāna-sati* in this *sutta* and also elsewhere, culminates specifically in the complete development of the seven *bojjhaṅgas*.

The third and final expansion of the seven sets[13] in the four primary

---

9 M III 80-2: *santi bhikkhave bhikkhū imasmiṃ bhikkhu-saṃghe arahanto khīṇâsavā ... pañcannaṃ orambhāgiyānaṃ saṃyojanānaṃ parikkhayā opapātikā ... tiṇṇaṃ saṃyojanānaṃ parikkhayā rāga-dosa-mohānaṃ tanuttā sakad-āgāmino ... tiṇṇaṃ saṃyojanānaṃ sotâpannā ... catunnaṃ satipaṭṭhānānaṃ bhāvanânuyogaṃ anuyuttā viharanti ... catunnaṃ samma-ppadhānānaṃ ... catunnaṃ iddhi-pādānaṃ ... pañcannaṃ indriyānaṃ ... pañcannaṃ balānaṃ ... sattanaṃ bojjhaṅg-ānaṃ ... ariyassa aṭṭhaṅgikassa maggassa ... mettā-bhāvanânuyogaṃ ... karuṇā-bhāvanânuyogaṃ ... muditā-bhāvanânuyogaṃ ... upekkhā-bhāvanânuyogaṃ ... asubha-bhāvanânuyogaṃ ... anicca-saññā-bhāvanânuyogaṃ ... ānâpāna-sati-bhāvanânuyogaṃ anuyuttā viharanti.*

10 E.g. D III 223

11 E.g. D II 196.

12 See above, pp. 179-80.

13 A I 38-43.

Nikāyas is the most exhaustive; it is to be found in the *eka-nipāta* of the *Aṅguttara-nikāya* and is based on the following formula:

> If a *bhikkhu* develops the first *jhāna* for even a mere finger snap then, *bhikkhus*, he is called a *bhikkhu* who dwells as one whose meditation is not in vain; practising the instruction of his teacher, following his advice, he does not eat the country's almsfood for nothing.[14]

A further one hundred and ninety repetitions of this basic formula follow, each one substituting a different single item where the initial statement has 'develops the first *jhāna*'. The full one hundred and ninety-one variations are achieved by substituting the following items: the development of the four *jhānas* (1-4); the development of the four *ceto-vimuttis* of loving kindness, compassion, sympathetic joy and equipoise (5-8); the four parts of the basic *satipaṭṭhāna* formula (9-12); the four parts of the *samma-ppadhāna* formula (13-16); the development of the four *iddhi-pādas* (17-20); the development of the five *indriyas* (21-25); the development of the five *balas* (26-30); the development of the seven *bojjhaṅgas* (31-7); the development of the eight path-factors (38-45); the eight items elsewhere termed *abhibhāyatana* (46-53); the eight items elsewhere termed *vimokkha* (53-61); the development of ten *kasiṇas* (62-71); the development of twenty 'notions' or 'ideas' (*saññā*) (72-91);[15] the development of ten varieties of recollection (*anussati*) and mindfulness (*sati*) (92-101).[16] The remaining ninety items are achieved by combining each of the five *indriyas* and five *balas* with each of the four *jhānas* and four *ceto-vimuttis* beginning with loving kindness (102-181);[17] finally, for good measure, we have the recapitulation of the development of the five *indriyas* and five *balas* singly (182-191).

It would be hard to detect any clear system or pattern in these three extended lists. Certainly they seem to be casting their nets wider in order to give a more representative impression of the range and depth of early Buddhist yogic or meditation practice. Yet it remains true to say that none of them appears to make any real attempt to be exhaustive and comprehensive. Moreover, the lists are hardly uniform in character, they seem to represent collections of rather miscellaneous items. While in one or other of the lists all

---

[14] A I 38: *accharā-saṃghāta-mattaṃ pi ce bhikkhave bhikkhu paṭhamaṃ jhānaṃ bhāveti ayaṃ vuccati bhikkhave bhikkhu aritta-jjhāno viharati satthu sāsana-karo ovāda-paṭikaro amoghaṃ raṭṭha-piṇḍaṃ bhuñjati.*

[15] The twenty *saññās* are: *asubha-, maraṇa-, āhāre paṭikkūla-, sabba-loke anabhirata-, anicca-, anicce dukkha-, dukkhe anatta-, pahāna-, virāga, nirodha-, anicca-, anatta-, maraṇa-, āhāre paṭikkūla-, sabbe-loke anabhirata-, atthika-, puḷavaka-, vinīlaka-, vicchiddaka-, uddhumātaka-saññā.* The list is rather odd in that a number of items occur twice in a rather haphazard way. It seems to be based on a list of ten *saññās* (A V 105) and the list of five kinds of corpses (e.g. S V 129-31). D III 251 gives a list of six *nibbedha-bhāgiya-saññās* (*anicca-, anicce dukkha-, dukkhe anatta-, pahāna-, virāga-, nirodha-*), and D III 253 a list of seven *saññās* (*anicca-, anatta-, asubha-, ādīnava-, pahāna-, virāga-, nirodha-*).

[16] These are: *buddhânussati, dhammânussati, saṃghânussati, sīlanussati, cāgânussati, devatânussati, ānâpāna-sati, maraṇa-sati, kāya-gatā sati, upasamânussati.* These ten are the same as in the later literature (e.g. Vism VII-VIII).

[17] The *bhikkhu* thus develops *saddhindriya* accompanied by the first *jhāna* (*paṭhama-jjhāna-sahagataṃ saddhindriyaṃ bhāveti*), then *viriyindriya* accompanied by the first *jhāna*, and so on through the remaining *indriyas* and *balas*. The sequence of ten is then repeated with the other *jhānas* and four *ceto-vimuttis*.

forty *kamma-ṭṭhānas* or thirty-eight *ārammaṇas* current in the later literature are found, it does not seem to me that these Nikāya exercises in extending the seven sets can be viewed as mere lists of meditation subjects in the manner of the lists of forty *kamma-ṭṭhānas* and thirty-eight *ārammaṇas*.

So are these extended Nikāya lists perhaps best viewed as accidental chance compositions—the result of the idle whims of the *bhāṇakas* whose work underlies the Pāli canon? It would be difficult to answer such a question definitely without a detailed comparison of the Pāli sources with the Chinese Āgamas. However, two points can perhaps be made at this stage. First, the sequence of seven sets appears to be firm and fixed enough to withstand any insertion into the actual body of the list. Thus where the number of items in an additional set makes this possible (i.e. in the case of the four *jhānas*, four *brahma-vihāras*, eight *vimokkhas* and eight *abhibhāyatanas*), they cluster around the sequence of seven sets rather than being incorporated into it. Secondly, it would seem to be fair to characterize the common element in all the additional items associated with the seven sets as *jhāna* or *samādhi*. In effect what we have are the four *jhānas* themselves along with various *jhāna* type meditations and practices that are the vehicle for the development of *jhāna*.

2. In the rest of Buddhist literature

Before attempting to draw any conclusions from the material so far considered in this chapter it is worth briefly surveying the rest of Buddhist literature for comparable extended lists that appear to be based on or incorporate the seven sets.

Beginning with the *Khuddaka-nikāya* of the Pāli canon, two recurrent lists in the *Paṭisambhidāmagga* stand out in particular; I call these list A and list B.[18] It is list B that occurs the most frequently in the *Paṭisambhidāmagga*, and is the characteristic feature of the treatment of the seven sets in this text.[19] I shall describe that treatment more fully and generally in chapter ten. Here it is simply worth noting that these two lists appear to be largely peculiar and distinctive to the *Paṭisambhidāmagga*. There appears to be no precedent for the combination of just these items in the earlier literature, nor any obvious corresspondence with lists found in the later literature. Again we are left with something of a problem. Either we view them as rather arbitrary in nature, or we accept that underlying them is a careful plan and particular logic which must, however, remain largely inaccessible to us apart from guesswork and speculation. In the context of a work as intricate as the *Paṭisambhidāmagga* their very peculiarity suggests that the latter is in fact the case. In spite of the difficulties one or two comments are in order. I leave aside the question of the order of the seven sets here and the repetition of the *indriyas*, *balas*, *bojjhaṅgas* and *maggaṅgas* which are considered first item by item and then set by set; this

---

[18] These two lists are set out in Table 7, p. 271.

[19] For list A see Paṭis I 16-8; II 120. For list B (i) see Paṭis I 21-2, 180-2; II 29, 124-5, 160-2. For list B (ii) see Paṭis I 73-6; II 84-5, 90-1, 142-6, 216-7.

TABLE 7. THE 7 SETS EXPANDED IN THE PAṬISAMBHIDĀMAGGA

	A	B (i)	B (ii)
1-5	indriyas (5)	indriyas (5)	maggaṅgas (8)
6-10	balas (5)	balas (5)	bojjhaṅgas (7)
11-17	bojjhaṅgas (7)	bojjhaṅgas (7)	balas (5)
18-25	maggaṅgas (8)	maggaṅgas (8)	indriyas (5)
26	indriya	indriya	indriya
27	bala	bala	bala
28	bojjhaṅga	bojjhaṅga	bojjhaṅga
29	magga	magga	magga
30	satipaṭṭhāna	satipaṭṭhāna	satipaṭṭhāna
31	samma-ppadhāna	samma-ppadhāna	samma-ppadhāna
32	iddhi-pāda	iddhi-pāda	iddhi-pāda
33	sacca	sacca	sacca
34	payoga	samatha	samatha
35	phala	vipassanā	vipassanā
36	vitakka	samatha-vipassanā	samatha-vipassanā
37	vicāra	yuganandha	yuganandha
38	pīti	sīla-visuddhi	sīla-visuddhi
39	sukha	citta-visuddhi	citta-visuddhi
40	citta	diṭṭhi-visuddhi	diṭṭhi-visuddhi
41	āvajjana	vimokkha	vimokkha
42	vijānana	vijjā	vijjā
43	pajānana	vimutti	vimutti
44	sañjānana	khaye ñāṇaṃ	khaye ñāṇaṃ
45	ekodi	anuppāde ñāṇaṃ	anuppāde ñāṇaṃ
46		chanda	
47		manasikāra	
48		phassa	
49		vedanā	
50		samādhi	
51		sati	
52		paññā	
53		vimutti	
54		amatogadhaṃ nibbānaṃ	

latter feature does in fact have some parallels with the treatment of the sets in the *Vibhaṅga*.[20]

In list A *jhāna* is once more to the fore, this time under the guise of the *jhāna* factors, namely *vitakka*, *vicāra*, *pīti* and *sukha*; *citta* apparently stands in for *cittass'ekaggatā*. These five terms are followed by 'adverting' (*āvajjana*)[21] and then by 'discriminating' (*vijānana*), 'knowing' (*pajānana*) and 'conceiving' or 'noting' (*sañjānana*). This in fact does in part tie in with discussions found elsewhere in Pāli literature. For instance two sections of the *Mahāvedalla-sutta* are devoted to a discussion of the close relationship between *paññā* and *viññāṇa*, and *vedanā*, *saññā* and *viññāṇa* respectively.[22] Buddhaghosa too in the course of his account of the nature of *paññā* devotes some space to the question of its relationship to *saññā* and *viññāṇa*.[23] Buddhaghosa's account implies that although *pajānana* is 'knowing' in a different mode from *sañjānana* and *vijānana*, it nevertheless builds on the basis of these.[24] It looks, then, as if the sequence *āvajjana*, *sañjānana*, *pajānana*, *vijānana* might be viewed as adding up to insight (*vipassanā*). In other words, what the latter half of list A does is breakdown *samatha* and *vipassanā* into its constituent parts: the *jhāna*-factors and various modes of 'knowing' respectively. What we then have in list A are the seven sets culminating in 'truth' (*sacca*), which suggests 'vision of the four truths'; this is followed by 'application' (*payoga*) and 'result' or 'fruit' (*phala*) considered by way of *samatha* and *vipassanā* which together add up to a unification (*ekodi*) of mind. This way of understanding list A seems to be confirmed by list B (i and ii). The four truths here are explicitly followed by the coupling of *samatha* and *vipassanā*; this leads on to purification of conduct, mind and view; knowledge and freedom; and the destruction of the *āsavas*—all in some sense representing the culmination of the development of the seven sets. The list now begins to bear some resemblance to the *Mahāsaḷāyatanika-sutta's* account of the path.

The *Theragāthā* contains a sequence of ten verses with a recurring refrain that has some of the characteristics of an expanded list of the seven sets:

> One should know the goal as one's own, one should inspect the teaching for what is fitting to the one who has entered into the state of the *samaṇa*.
>
> A good friend here, undertaking of the training in full, attentiveness to teachers—this is fitting for the *samaṇa*.
>
> Respect for the Buddhas, homage to the Dhamma as it is, and esteem for the Saṃgha—this is fitting for the *samaṇa*.
>
> A purified and blameless livelihood along with good conduct and associations; stilling of the mind—this is fitting for the *samaṇa*.

---

[20] See below, Chapter 10.4.

[21] A term of some significance in the commentarial accounts of the consciousness process.

[22] M I 292-3.

[23] Vism XIV 3-5.

[24] I am thinking particularly of his simile here: *saññā* is like a child who 'knows' a particular object as round and figured, *viññāṇa* is like a villager who 'knows' the object as a coin; *paññā* is like a money changer who 'knows' the value of the coin, whether it is genuine or not, etc.

> Right conduct, restraint and a pleasing way of acting; application with regard to higher consciousness—this is fitting for the *samaṇa*.
>
> Forest lodgings, remote, with little noise are to be resorted to by the sage—this is fitting for the *samaṇa*.
>
> Virtue and great learning, discrimination of *dhammas* as they are, understanding of the truths—this is fitting for the *samaṇa*.
>
> Thinking, 'This is impermanent', he should develop the notion of not-self and the notion of ugliness; absence of delight in the world—this is fitting for the *samaṇa*.
>
> And he should develop the awakening factors, the bases of success, the faculties and powers, the noble eight-factored path—this is fitting for the *samaṇa*.
>
> The sage should abandon craving, he should split the *āsavas* and their roots, he should dwell freed—this is fitting for the *samaṇa*.[25]

Certain features are immediately familiar from the extended lists already considered and from the treatment of the seven sets elsewhere in the four Nikāyas: the good friend; the emphasis on good conduct; the stilling of the mind; the development of the ideas of impermanence, not-self and ugliness; the destruction of the *āsavas*. Such irregularities and peculiarities as there are—for example the omission of the *satipaṭṭhānas* and *samma-ppadhānas*—are presumably to be explained by reference to the fact that we are dealing with verse.

Moving on to the para-canonical literature,[26] a passage in the *Nettippakaraṇa* gives as opposed to the sixty-two kinds of view (as expounded in the *Brahmajāla-sutta*)[27] 'forty-three *bodhi-pakkhiyā dhammā*, eight *vimokkhas* and ten *kasiṇ-âyatanas*'.[28] Apparently we are expected to know what the forty-three *bodhi-pakkhiyā dhammā* in question are. The context gives no obvious clues, but Dhammapāla's commentary tells us that they consist of the seven sets together with six kinds of *saññā*, namely the notions or ideas of impermanence, suffering, not-self, abandoning, dispassion and cessation.[29] In the *Dīgha-nikāya* these are appropriately enough called 'six ideas concerned with penetrative wisdom (*nibbedha-bhāgiya*)'.[30] It is difficult to see how we might do better than this. Dhammapāla continues: 'Having in this way indicated the opposite by

---

[25] Th 587-96; *vijāneyya sakaṃ atthaṃ avalokeyyātha pāvacanaṃ/ yañ c'ettha assa paṭirūpaṃ sāmaññaṃ ajjhupagatassa// mittaṃ idha kalyāṇam. sikkhā-vipulaṃ samādānaṃ/ sussūsā ca garūnaṃ etaṃ samaṇassa paṭirūpaṃ// buddhesu sāgaravatā dhamme apaciti yathā-bhūtaṃ/ saṃghe ca citti-kāro etaṃ samaṇassa paṭirūpaṃ// ācāra-gocare yutto ājīvo sodhito agārayho/ cittassa saṇṭhapanaṃ etaṃ samaṇassa paṭirūpaṃ// cārittaṃ atha vārittaṃ iriyā-pathiyaṃ pasādaniyaṃ/ adhicitte ca ayogo etaṃ samaṇassa paṭirūpaṃ// āraññakāni senâsanāni pantāni appa-saddāni/ bhajitabbāni muninā etaṃ samaṇassa paṭirūpaṃ// sīlañ ca bahu-saccañ ca dhammānaṃ pavicayo yathā-bhūtaṃ/ saccānaṃ abhisamayo etaṃ samaṇassa paṭirūpaṃ// bhāveyya aniccan ti anatta-saññaṃ asubha-saññañ ca/ lokamhi ca anabhiratiṃ etaṃ samaṇassa paṭirūpaṃ// bhāveyya ca bojjhaṅge iddhi-pādāni indriya-balāni/ aṭṭhaṅga-maggaṃ ariyaṃ etaṃ samaṇassa paṭirūpaṃ// taṇhaṃ pajaheyya munī samūlake āsave padāleyya/ vihareyya vimutto etaṃ samaṇassa paṭirūpaṃ//*

[26] Two sequences from the *Niddesa* can be viewed as extended lists based on the seven sets, but I have chosen to deal with them in another context, see below, pp. 279, 292-3.

[27] D I 1-46.

[28] Nett 112.

[29] Nett-a 237: *tecattalīsaṃ bodhi-pakkhiyā dhammā ti anicca-saññā dukkha-saññā anatta-saññā pahāna-saññā virāga-saññā nirodha-saññā cattāro satipaṭṭhānā ... ariyo aṭṭhaṅgiko maggo ti.*

[30] D III 251.

way of *vipassanā*, in order to indicate it by way of *samatha* he mentions the eight *vimokkhas* and ten *kasiṇâyatanas*.'[31] This suggests that Dhammapāla understood this extended list as indicating how the seven sets fulfil both *samatha* and *vipassanā*.

The *Milindapañha* also provides several examples of extended lists based on or incorporating the seven sets:

> Morality, your majesty, has the characteristic of being the foundation for all skilful *dhammas*: morality is the foundation for the faculties, powers, awakening factors, path, establishings of mindfulness, right endeavours, bases of success, *jhāna*, liberations, concentration, and [other] attainments.[32]
>
> Moreover, your majesty, the sun moves satisfying the mass of people; just so the world along with its *devas* is to be satisfied by the yogin, by the practitioner of yoga, by conduct, morality, merit, observance, practice; by *jhāna*, liberations, concentration, attainments, faculties, powers, awakening-factors, establishings of mindfulness, right endeavours, bases of success ... Moreover, your majesty, the sun reveals what is good and bad; just so by the yogin, by the practitioner of yoga the faculties, powers, awakening-factors, establishings of mindfulness, right endeavours, bases of success, ordinary and transcendent *dhammas* are to be revealed.[33]

One extremely extended and miscellaneous list describes how in the *dhamma*-city of the Blessed One there dwell the following sorts of people: those versed in Suttanta (*suttantika*), Vinaya (*venayika*) and Abhidhamma (*ābhidhammika*); those who give talks on *dhamma* (*dhamma-kathika*); chanters (*bhāṇaka*) of the *Jātaka*, the *Dīgha*, the *Majjhima*, the *Saṃyutta*, the *Aṅguttara*, the *Khuddaka*; those who have accomplished (*sampanna*) morality (*sīla*), concentration (*samādhi*) and wisdom; those devoted to the development of the awakening-factors (*bojjhaṅga-bhāvanā-rata*), practitioners of insight (*vipassaka*), those intent on the highest good (*sad-attham anuyuttā*); those who dwell in the forest (*āraññaka*), at the roots of trees (*rukkha-mūlika*), in the open (*abbhokāsika*), on heaps of grass (*palāla-puñjaka*), in the cemetery (*sosānika*), always sitting (*nesajjika*); those entering the way (*paṭipannaka*), those established in the fruit (*phalaṭṭha*), those in training (*sekha*), those endowed with the fruit (*phala-samaṅgin*); stream-attainers, once-returners, never-returners, *arahants*; those who have three knowledges (*tevijja*), those who have six direct knowledges (*chal-abhiñña*), those with power (*iddhimant*), those who have reached the perfection of wisdom (*paññāya pāramiṃ gatā*); those skilled (*kusala*) in the establishings of mindfulness, the right endeavours, the bases of success, the faculties, the powers, the awakening-factors, the excellent path, the *jhānas*, *vimokkhas*, and

---

[31] Nett-a 237: *evaṃ vipassanā-vasena paṭipakkhaṃ dassetvā samatha-vasena dassetuṃ aṭṭha-vimokkha dasa ca kasiṇâyatanānī ti vuttaṃ*.

[32] Mil 33: *patiṭṭhāna-lakkhaṇam mahā-rāja sīlaṃ sabbesaṃ kusalānaṃ dhammānaṃ: indriya-bala-bojjhaṅga-magga-satipaṭṭhāna-samma-ppadhāna-iddhi-pāda-jhāna-vimokkha-samādhi-samāpattīnaṃ sīlaṃ patiṭṭhā*.

[33] Mil 389-90: *puna ca paraṃ mahā-rāja suriyo mahā-jana-kāyaṃ santāpento carati, evaṃ eva kho mahā-rāja yoginā yogâvacarena ācāra-sīla-guṇa-vatta-paṭipattiyā jhāna-vimokkha-samādhi. samāpatti-indriya-bala-bojjhaṅga-satipaṭṭhāna-samma-ppadhāna-iddhi-pādehi sa-devako loko santāpayitabbo ... puna ca paraṃ mahā-rāja suriyo kalyāṇa-pāpake dasseti, evaṃ eva kho mahā-rāja yoginā yogâvacarena indriya-bala-bojjhaṅga-satipaṭṭhāna-samma-ppadhāna-iddhi-pāda-lokiya-lokuttara-dhammā dassetabbā*. (The omission of the *magga* from these two sequences is curious.)

peaceful and happy form and formless attainments—crowded and teeming with these *arahants*, the *dhamma*-city was like a grove of reeds.[34] Once more in these *Milindapañha* passages it is the *jhānas* and *jhāna*-type meditations and attainments that are most closely associated with the sequence of the seven sets.[35]

Looking further afield in Buddhist literature, the following is an example of an extended list based on the seven sets from the Mahāyāna *prajñāpāramitā* literature:

> Subhūti said: 'Which are the *dharmas* that are skilful or contribute to awakening? Which *dharmas* are Pratyeka-buddha-*dharmas*, Bodhisattva-*dharmas* and also Buddha-*dharmas*—[*dharmas*] that are comprised and reach a conclusion in the perfection of wisdom?' The Blessed One said: 'Just these: the four establishings of mindfulness, the four right abandonings, the four bases of success, the five faculties, the five powers, the seven awakening-factors, the noble eight-factored path, the four noble truths, the gateways to liberation—the empty, the signless, the wishless—the four *dhyānas*, the four immeasurables, the four formless attainments, the six direct knowledges, the perfections of giving, morality, patience, strength, concentration and wisdom ... '[36]

No doubt further examples from Mahāyāna *sūtras* and the *prajñāpāramitā* literature might be searched out[37] but from the point of view of present concerns this one example suffices to show that in this type of literature too, familiar additional sets are at times juxatposed with the sequence of seven sets. It is worth noting that even here the list of seven sets is self contained and once more resists any insertion directly into its sequence. All the additional sets have already been seen appended to the list of the seven sets in the Nikāyas apart, that is, from the four truths and six perfections.[38] The addition of the six perfections is of course to be expected in a *prajñāpāramitā* text. The addition of

---

34 Mil 341-2.

35 The changed order of the sets in these passages corresponds to the order of the sets in the *Paṭisambhidāmagga* lists.

36 *Śatasāhasrikāprajñāpāramitā* (ed. P. Ghosa, Calcutta, 1902), p. 1636: *Subhūtir āha/ katame bhagavān kuśala-dharmmā bodhi-pakṣāḥ vā ke dharmmaś ca pratyeka-buddha-dharmmaś ca bodhisattva-dharmmaś ca buddha-dharmmaś ca ye prajñā-pāramitāyāṃ saṃgrahaṃ samavasaraṇaṃ gacchanti/ bhagavān āha/ tad yathā catvāri smṛty-upasthānāni/ catvāri samyak-prahāṇāni/ catvāra ṛddhi-pādāḥ/ pañcendriyāṇi/ pañca-balāni/ satta-bodhy-aṅgāni/ āryyâṣṭâṅgo mārgaḥ/ catvāryy āryya-satyāni/ śūnyatânimittâpraṇihita-vimokṣa-mukhāni/ catvāri dhyānāni/ catvāryy apramāṇāni/ catusra ārūpya-samāpattayaḥ/ ṣaḍ-abhijñāḥ/ dāna-pāramitā/ śīla-pāramitā/ kṣānti-pāramitā/ vīrya-pāramitā/ samādhi-pāramitā/ prajñā-pāramitā* ... (Cf. pp. 274-5 where thirty-seven *bodhi-pakṣā dharmmāḥ* are mentioned in the context of various other items: four *dhyānas*, four *apramāṇas*, four *ārūpya-samāpatti*, six *abhijñās*, ten *tathāgata-balas*. These passages, along with other passages relevant to the *bodhi-pākṣikā dharmāḥ* from the same work, are cited but not quoted by Dayal, op. cit., p. 82.)

37 E.g. *Śatasāhasrikā*, pp. 1427-39; *Pañcaviṃśatisāhasrikā* (E. Conze, *The Large Sūtra on Perfect Wisdom*, Part I, London, 1961, pp. 140- 3); *Daśasāhasrikā* (S. Konow, 'The Two First Chapters of the Daśasāhasrikā Prajñāpāramitā', *Avhandlinger utgitt av Det Norske Videnskaps-Akademi i Oslo*, II. Hist.-Filos. Klasse 1941, No. I, pp. 1-117). G. Roth also cites some interesting extended lists in some 1st/2nd century CE works dealing with the significance of the various parts of a stupa ('The Symbolism of the Buddhist Stūpa' in A.L. Dallapiccola (ed.), *The Stūpa: Its Religious, Historical and Architectural Significance*, Wiesbaden, 1980, pp. 183-209).

38 For the three gateways to liberation cf. the second set of three *samādhis* in the *asaṃkhata-saṃyutta*; I take the four *ārūpya-samāpattis* as comprised in the eight *vimokkhas*, and the six *abhijñās* as comprised in the *sāmañña-phala* schema.

the four truths is in general terms hardly surprising, but more specifically the immediate juxtaposition of the seven sets and the four truths would seem to correspond to the stage by stage account of the path in Sarvāstivādin manuals.[39] However, as I shall consider presently, it is not wihout a certain precedent in the *mahā-vagga* of the *Saṃyutta-nikāya*. But before turning to this, it is worth noting that Bareau records as a thesis of the Vibhajyavāda (according to the *Vibhāṣā*) that there are forty-one *bodhi-pākṣikā dharmāḥ*—the thirty-seven along with the four truths.[40]

Alongside all these examples of extended lists based around the seven sets should be placed the actual headings that form the basis for the *mahā-vagga* of the *Saṃyutta-nikāya*, as well as what we know of the headings used in the corresponding portions of other recensions of the *saṃyukta* material. Thus I have set out [41] the twelve divisions of the Pāli *mahā-vagga* alongside the twenty-one divisions that Anesaki has identified in what he calls the *magga-vagga* of the Chinese *Saṃyuktâgama* translations.[42] These lists are of a rather different make-up from the lists so far considered. The reasons that lie behind the changed order in the Pāli must remain obscure, as must those behind the omission of the *iddhi-pādas* from the Chinese. The Chinese list seems to include rather a large number of miscellaneous additional items. Anesaki's analysis indicates, however, that the items towards the end of the list—especially those from fifteen onwards—have rather little space devoted to them.[43] It should also be borne in mind that Anesaki's list is something of a reconstruction—an attempt to bring order to what are apparently rather disordered texts showing no clear divisions.[44] Thus it is not entirely clear how far we should regard Anesaki's analysis as final.

I shall return to the *saṃyutta/saṃyukta* lists presently. First, I wish to turn briefly to the *mātikās/mātṛkās* that provide the subject headings for four

---

[39] See below, pp. 335-6, 337-9.

[40] Bareau, *SBPV*, p. 174; however, he refers to La Vallée Poussin's Abhidh-k Trsl IV 281 where it is noted that the Vibhajyavādins have a list of forty-one [*bodhipākṣikas*] adding the four *ārya-vaṃśas*; Lamotte notes the same at *Traité*, III 1121. Interestingly, Vasubandhu includes the four *ārya-vaṃśas* at the beginning of his account of the path before the practice of *aśubha-bhāvanā* and *ānâpāna-smṛti* (Abhidh-k 336 ff.).

[41] See Table 8, p. 277.

[42] See Anesaki, op. cit., pp. 68-76. Anesaki sees eight major divisions underlying the Chinese *Saṃyuktâgama* material: (i) *Khandha-vagga*, (ii) *Saḷāyatana-vagga*, (iii) *Nidāna-vagga*, (iv) *Sāvaka-vagga*, (v) *Magga-vagga*, (vi) *Puggala-vagga*, (vii) *Sagāthā-vagga*, (viii) *Tathāgata-vagga*, (he uses Pāli-forms). As far as can be ascertained various recensions of the *Saṃyukta* material seem to have been agreed in devoting major divisions to the *skandhas*, *āyatanas*, *pratītya-samutpāda* and *mārga* (i.e. a major division devoted more or less to the seven sets), but the detailed constitution of these major divisions is largely unknown, except in the case of the Chinese *Saṃyuktâgamas*; see Anesaki, op.cit., pp. 68- 70; J. Bronkhorst, 'Dharma and Abhidharma', *BSOAS* 48 (1985), p. 317.

[43] Anesaki, op. cit., p. 73. Note that the treatment of the six *āyatanas* in this context appears to be secondary in that they also form the basis of a major division of the Chinese *Saṃyuktâgamas*; see id., p. 71.

[44] Id., p. 70: 'When we come to the two extant versions of the Saṃyukta in Chinese ... the classifications are in utter confusion.' Cf. E. Mayeda, 'Japanese Studies on the Schools of the Chinese Āgamas' in H. Bechert (ed.), *Zur Schulzugehörigkeit von Werken der Hīnayāna Literatur*, Göttingen, 1985, pp. 94-103; Mayeda comments on the difficulties of the reconstruction of the arrangement of the fifty vol. *Saṃyuktâgama* (probably Sarvāstivādin); a sixteen vol. and one vol. *Saṃyuktâgama* trsl appear incomplete.

TABLE 8. SAṂYUTTA/SAṂYUKTA TABLES OF CONTENTS: MAHĀ-VAGGA/MĀRGA-VARGA

Saṃyutta-nikāya	Saṃyuktâgama*
magga (8)	smṛty-upasthāna
bojjhaṅga (7)	indriya
satipaṭṭhāna (4)	bala
indriya (5, etc.)	bodhy-aṅga
samma-ppadhāna (4)	mārga
bala (5)	ānâpāna
iddhi-pāda (4)	śaikṣa
Anuruddha	avetya-prasāda/srota-āpatti
jhāna (4)	deva
ānâpāna	tad-rūpa
sotâpatti	samyak-prahāṇa
sacca (4)	dhyāna
	traividyā
	asaṃskṛta
	samudra
	ṣaḍ-āyatana
	bīja
	loka
	śāstṛ
	Rāhula
	bhikṣu

* See Anesaki, op.cit., pp. 72-3. (I have sanskritized the forms given by Anesaki.)

TABLE 9. THE MĀTIKĀ/MĀTṚKĀ OF THE VIBHAṄGA, ETC.

Vibhaṅga	**Dhātukathā**	**Dharmaskandha***	**Arthaviniścaya-sūtra**
khandha (5)	khandha (5)	śikṣā-pada (5)	skandha (5)
āyatana (12)	āyatana (12)	srota-āpatty-aṅga (4)	upādāna-skandha (5)
dhātu (18)	dhātu (18)	avetya-prasāda (4)	dhātu (18)
sacca (4)	sacca (4)	śramaṇya-phala (4)	āyatana (12)
indriya (22)	indriya (22)	abhijñā-pratipad (4)	pratītya-samutpāda (12)
paccayâkāra (12)	paṭicca-samuppāda (12)	ārya-vaṃsa (4)	ārya-satya (4)
satipaṭṭhāna (4)	satipaṭṭhāna (4)	samyak-prahāṇa (4)	indriya (22)
samma-ppadhāna (4)	samma-ppadhāna (4)	ṛddhi-pāda (4)	dhyāna (4)
iddhi-pāda (4)	iddhi-pāda (4)	smṛty-upasthāna (4)	ārūpya-samāpatti (4)
bojjhaṅga (7)	jhāna (4)	ārya-satya (4)	brahma-vihāra (4)
maggaṅga (8)	appamañña (4)	dhyāna (4)	pratipad (4)
jhāna (4 + 4)	indriya (5)	apramāṇā (4)	samādhi-bhāvanā (4)
appamañña (4)	bala (5)	ārūpya-dhātu (4)	smṛty-upasthāna (4)
sikkhā-pada (5)	bojjhaṅga (7)	bhāvanā-samādhi (4)	samyak-prahāṇa (4)
paṭisambhidā (4)	magga (8)	bodhy-aṅga (7)	ṛddhi-pāda (4)
ñāṇa	phassa	kṣudraka-vastu	indriya (5)
khuddaka-vatthu	vedanā	indriya (22)	bala (5)
dhamma-hadaya	sañña	āyatana (12)	bodhy-aṅga (7)
	cetanā	skandha (5)	mārga (5)
	citta	dhātu (6/18/62)	ānâpāna-smṛti (16)
	adhimokkha	pratītya-samutpāda (12)	srota-āpatty-aṅga (4)
	manasikāra		tathāgata-bala (10)
			vaiśāradya (4)
			pratisaṃvid (4)
			āveṇika-dharma (18)
			mahāpuruṣa-lakṣaṇa (32)
			anuvyañjana (80)

* See J. Takakusu, *JPTS*, 1905, pp. 111-5; E. Frauwallner, *WZKS* 8 (1964), pp. 73-4.

works: the *Vibhaṅga*, the *Dhātukathā*, the *Dharmaskandha* and the *Arthaviniś-caya-sūtra*.[45] I take the latter two texts as representative of the literature of the wider Buddhist tradition. These tables of topics are again of a rather different nature from the lists so far considered. They are not collations that focus primarily on the sphere of what is actually to be practised and developed. They attempt to embrace the whole of Buddhist teaching in a rather more explicit and straightforward way. What are apparently considered the most important headings covering the full range and expanse of early Buddhist teaching are singled out in order to give summaries of the teaching in all its various aspects. While some topics are peculiar to one or other of the lists, or are subsumed under a different heading in different lists, it is not hard to identify a common core.[46] This common core in fact corresponds quite closely with the topics that receive special attention in the *Saṃyutta-nikāya* and *Saṃyuktâgama*. These *mātikās/mātṛkās* also invite comparison with Nikāya works such as the *Saṃgīti-* and *Dasuttara-suttas*, and also the *Kumāra-pañha* and *Mahā-pañha*, which are all in their different ways attempts to give accounts of the teaching in all its aspects.[47] From the point of view of present concerns it is enough to consider the role of the seven sets when brought into such a context. A number of features are immediately noticeable in these *mātikās/mātṛkās*. There is a tendency to treat the five *indriyas* not in the context of the seven sets but as subsumed in the full list of twenty-two *indriyas*, which are then grouped with the *khandhas*, *āyatanas*, *dhātus*, *paṭicca-samuppāda* and *saccas*;[48] the *balas* have no separate existence apart from the *indriyas* in the *Vibhaṅga* and *Dharma-skandha*. The *Arthaviniścaya-sūtra* is the only one of the four to maintain the sequence of all seven sets; the other three texts tamper with it in various ways. In contrast to the Nikāyas, there is a tendency for these *mātikās/mātṛkās* to insert additional sets of four directly into the sequence of the seven sets.

3. Conclusions

What are the implications of all these different extended lists for our under-

[45] See Table 9, p. 278.

[46] Cf. A.K. Warder, 'The Mātikā', introductory essay to *Mohavicchedanī*, London, 1961, pp. xix-xxvii. A slightly different and shorter version of the same list occurs repeatedly in the *Niddesa* which talks of being skilled (*kusala*) in *khandha, āyatana, dhātu, paṭicca-samuppāda, satipaṭṭhāna, samma-ppadhāna, iddhi-pāda, indriya, bala, bojjhaṅga, magga, phala, nibbāna* (see Nidd I 69, 71-2, 1-5, 171; Nidd II (Ne 1959) 41, 120; cf. Nidd I 45, 340-1; Nidd II (Ne 1959) 133, 142, 200. 203, 225, 229).

[47] The *Kumāra-pañha* (Khp 2), the *Mahā-pañha* (A V 48-54) and a variation on the latter (A V 54-9) each give ten items corresponding to the numbers from one to ten. The seven sets feature sporadically; the *Kumāra-pañha* gives the seven *bojjhaṅgas* and *ariyo aṭṭhaṅgiko maggo* for the numbers seven and eight, but the four *ariya-saccas* and five *upādāna-kkhandhas* for four and five; the variation on the *Mahā-pañha* gives the four *satipaṭṭhānas* and five *indriyas*. Rather similarly, various of the seven sets feature in the numerical system of the *Dasuttara-sutta*: the four *satipaṭṭhānas*, the seven *bojjhaṅgas* and *ariyo aṭṭhaṅgiko maggo* as four, seven and eight *dhammas* respectively to be developed (*bhāvetabba*); the five *indriyas* as five *dhammas* concerned with distinction (*visesa-bhāgiya*), though one Chinese translation treats them as 'to be developed'; see J.W. de Jong, 'The Daśottarasūtra' in his *Buddhist Studies*, Berkeley, 1979, pp. 252-73. The less selective method of the *Saṃgīti-sutta* means that all seven sets feature.

[48] I have commented on what I believe to be the significance of this in Chapter 4.5.

standing of the role of the seven sets in early Buddhist literature? Before attempting to answer this question one should perhaps remind oneself that the list of the seven sets both in its own right and under the guise of the thirty-seven *bodhi-pakkhiya-dhammas/bodhi-pākṣika-dharmas* continues to remain an important and distinct list of items in probably all varieties of post-canonical Buddhist literature—it continues to crop up in Abhidharma, Mahāyāna and even in tantric texts.[49] The fact that this is so means that the extended lists based around the seven sets cannot be viewed as the end result of some simple process that involved the gradual accretion of further sets until finally the list of seven sets was superseded and ceased to be of importance as a distinct list. This simply does not happen. Nor, I think, can we view the existence of extended lists as an indication that the sequence of the seven sets was not yet established as a separate and distinct list. It seems to me that the passages I have considered in chapter seven are quite sufficient to show that the sequence of seven sets was already firmly established as a distinct and separate list in the period of the four primary Nikāyas. As far as the whole of the Pāli canon is concerned, it should also be noted here that the *Vibhaṅga* gives the seven sets the appellation *saddhamma*.[50] So if the *Peṭakopadesa* talks of thirty-seven *bodhi-pakkhikā dhammā*,[51] but the *Nettippakaraṇa* of forty-three *bodhi-pakkhiyā dhammā*, it is not out of any uncertainty about the seven sets as a distinct and separate list.

The fact that the seven sets remain important as a distinct list in the later tradition despite the existence of extended lists both in the Nikāyas and later literature must indicate that the list of seven sets acquired a certain authority rather early in the history of Buddhist thought. Possibly this authority can be adequately explained merely by reference to the ancientness of the list, yet I think we ought to go a little further than this. For in fact the very existence of the extended lists alongside the fixed list of seven sets already in the Nikāya period suggests that in appreciating the authority of the seven sets we have not simply to do with their ancientness. If this is the sole source of authority, why is the sequence of seven sets not always respected, why are further sets added? It seems reasonable to suggest that it is in order to bring out something of the nature of the seven sets as conceived and worked out already in the Nikāyas. Thus, in the Nikāya lists especially, what we consistently have are the seven sets along with a variety of meditation subjects. What is being indicated, I think, are the particular contexts in which the seven sets are developed. In other words, the seven sets remain a distinct set of items not simply because they came down as a bare and distinct list from ancient times and therefore had to be fitted in somehow, but because rather early on—well before the end of the period of the four primary Nikāyas—they began to be understood and elaborated together in a quite specific way as a description of the unfolding of

[49] For an indication of the extent of the importance of the seven sets/thirty-seven *bodhi-pākṣika-dharmas* in a wide range of Buddhist literature see the 'Note on the seven sets/thirty-seven *bodhi-pākṣika-dharmas* in non-Pāli sources' below, pp. 357-8.

[50] Vibh 372.

[51] Peṭ 114, 138.

the Buddhist path from beginning to end. The particular quality of the description of the Buddhist path in terms of the seven sets is something I shall return to at the conclusion of this study, but it has, I think, to do with the rather elaborate system of 'cross-referencing' inherent in the seven sets, the way in which they inter-relate with each other and also draw together various Nikāya themes. The kind of thinking that underlies this is, I think, fundamental to Buddhist thought and psychology of meditation. Thus the description of the path in terms of the seven sets is important in that it is suggestive of a certain depth and subtlety along with a certain simplicity and conciseness.

In a recent article[52] Johannes Bronkhorst has suggested that we can view the expansion of the seven sets as the result of attempts to complete the list with meditational states.[53] According to Bronkhorst, first the four *dhyānas* were added—he cites the Chinese translations of the *Mahāparinirvāṇa-sūtra* and some further *Dīrghâgama* and *Madhyamâgama* passages.[54] Next were added the four *apramāṇas* (he cites the *mātikā* of the *Dhātukathā*) and finally the four *ārūpyas* or 'formless attainments', giving a list of ten sets: the four *smṛty-upasthānas*, four *samyak-prahāṇas*, four *ṛddhi-pādas*, four *dhyānas*, four *apramāṇas*, four *ārūpyas*, five *indriyas*, five *balas*, seven *bodhy-aṅgas*, *āryâṣṭâṅga-mārga*.[55] In fact Bronkhorst can find no example of just this sequence of ten sets anywhere in Buddhist literature, but suggests that it must have been the source of the appropriate portion of *Saṃgīti-sūtra's* section of 'fours', and cites four different versions of the *sūtra* to this effect; of this portion of the *Saṃgīti-sūtra's* section of fours he says that it is 'difficult to doubt that this enumeration was taken from an earlier list' of ten sets, and gives the list of ten as above.[56] Yet this seems certainly dubious, and amounts, I think, to a rather unconvincing and indeed unhelpful line of speculation that tends to distract attention from the way in which the seven sets are actually handled and understood in the early literature. Not the least of its problems is that it totally ignores the various other extended lists that I have been considering in this chapter. The lists that Bronkhorst cites, on the other hand, are somewhat hypothetical in nature. The only hard evidence for the expansion to nine sets is the occurrence of this sequence within the body of the *mātikā* of the *Dhātukathā*. But this *mātikā* contains rather more than just these nine sets and, as I have suggested, its nature is such that it is not clear that it is entirely valid to extract the sequence of nine sets in the way Bronkhorst does. The evidence for the list of ten sets is even more tentative—the sequence of these ten sets does not appear to occur even within the body of some longer list. The whole procedure begins to look dubious. The point is that we have no grounds for believing that lists of *just* these sets—either nine or ten—*ever* played a part in the exposition of Buddhist thought.

Of the three expanded lists considered by Bronkhorst we are thus left with

---

52 'Dharma and Abhidharma', *BSOAS* 48 (1985), pp. 305-20.

53 Id., p. 306.

54 Ibid., n. 8.

55 Id., p. 307.

56 Ibid.

the expanded list of eight sets—the seven together with the four *dhyānas*—as the only one that is certainly witnessed in the literature. As I have already indicated, this fact is of some interest since the occurrence of this list of eight sets in the Chinese Āgamas seems to find close harmonies in the Pāli Nikāyas. The association of the four *jhānas*—and only the four *jhānas*—with the seven sets is quite explicit in the application of common treatments in the *mahā-vagga* of the *Saṃyutta-nikāya*; that is to say, on the basis of the *mahā-vagga* one would have to single out eight sets and not seven. Again I have argued that *jhāna* or at least a state of meditation close to *jhāna* is consistently implicit in much of the Nikāya treatment of the seven sets individually. Similarly in what I have considered as the Nikāya treatment of the seven sets as 'path' or 'practice', and in the various extended lists, *samatha*, *samādhi* and the *jhānas* are certainly recurrent themes: in the *Mahā-saḷāyatanika-sutta* we have the coupling of *samatha* and *vipassanā*, in the *Piṇḍapātapārisuddhi-sutta*, the abandoning of the five *nīvaraṇas* and *samatha* and *vipassanā*; in the *asaṃkhata-saṃyutta*, *samatha* and *vipassanā* along with *savitakko savicāro samādhi, avitakko vicāra-matto samādhi* and *avitakko avicāro samādhi*—merely a different way of looking at the *jhānas*; in the *Mahāsakuludāyi-sutta*, the four *jhānas* and *abhibhāyatanas*; in the *eka-nipāta* treatment the four *jhānas* along with the *brahma-vihāras* receive special emphasis—this in a section entitled *jhāna-vagga*.

What lies behind all this is not the mechanical accumulation of lists of meditation states. It is rather a feeling that in one sense and in certain contexts the list of the seven sets is not quite specific, is not quite enough. As I said above, what is lacking is an indication of the context in which the seven sets are to be developed. So we are told that the seven sets are developed in association with the practice of *jhāna*, in association with the practice of the *brahma-vihāras*, in association with *ānâpāna-sati* or with some other meditation subject or practice. This means, I think, that the treatment of the seven sets as a definite list of thirty-seven *bodhi-pakkhiya-dhammas* in the later literature must be seen as related rather more closely to their treatment in the early literature than might have been supposed. Unless this is so it is difficult to see why the later literature should have felt the need to develop the notion of thirty-seven *bodhi-pakkhiya-dhammas*, given that other more extended lists were available.

I have already pointed out some of the ways in which the Nikāya handling of the seven sets begins to approach and imply something of the more explicit statements concerning the seven sets as the thirty-seven *bodhi-pakkhiya-dhammas* in the later literature. Before passing on to look at the Abhidhamma treatment more closely it is worth just considering once more the nature of the topics brought into association with the seven sets in the *mahā-vagga* of the *Saṃyutta-nikāya*. The *Anuruddha-saṃyutta* seems to be attracted by association with the *satipaṭṭhānas*, which are mentioned in every *sutta*. I have already discussed the *jhāna-saṃyutta*. Next is the *ānâpāna-saṃyutta*; *ānâpāna-sati* is an aspect of the first *satipaṭṭhāna* (*kāye kāyânupassanā*) and is treated as such in the *(Mahā-)Satipaṭṭhāna-sutta*; the treatment in the *ānâpāna-saṃyutta* follows in general that found in the *Ānâpānasati-sutta*, which gives special emphasis to all four *satipaṭṭhānas* and the *bojjhaṅgas*. The *Ānâpānasati-sutta* opens, as I have already pointed out, with an extended list based around the seven sets. This list culminates in *ānâpāna-sati*. The commentary states here that the reason why *ānâpāna-sati* is the only one of the items in the list to be explained in full is because of the large number of *bhikkhus* who take it as their *kamma-ṭṭhāna*.[57] The practice of *ānâpāna-sati* seems to have something of a special status within the tradition as the practice of the Buddha on the night of his awakening.[58] It does not seem unreasonable to suggest that, in the case of the *mahā-vagga*, *ānâpāna-sati* is where it is because it is regarded as the normative vehicle on the basis of which the seven sets are 'to be developed and to be made great'. Finally there are the *sotâpatti-* and *sacca-saṃyuttas*. Their appearance just here shows a clear correspondence with the notion, explicit both in the *Visuddhimagga* and *Abhidharmakośa*, that stream attainment and definite knowledge of the four truths coincide with the culmination of the development of the seven sets. Of course the actual structure and ordering of the Nikāyas is likely to be rather later than the contents itself. Yet, with the proviso that Anesaki's list is somewhat tentative, it is worth noting that much the same sets seem to cluster most closely around the seven sets in the Chinese *Saṃyuktâgama* translations.

---

[57] Ps IV 139: *yasmā pan'ettha ānâpāna-kamma-ṭṭhāna-vasena abhiniviṭṭhā bahū bhikkhū, tasmā sesa-kamma-ṭṭhānāni saṃkhepena kathetvā ānâpāna-kamma-ṭṭhānaṃ viṭṭhārena kathento ānâpāna-sati bhikkhave ti ādiṃ āha.*

[58] E.g. Ps II 291; cf. Paravahera Vajirañāṇa Mahāthera, *Buddhist Meditation in Theory and Practice*, Kuala Lumpur, 1962, p. 227.

CHAPTER NINE

DHAMMAS THAT CONTRIBUTE TO AWAKENING

1. The expression bodhi-pakkhiyā dhammā in the canon

I have already noted that 'thirty-seven *bodhi-pakkhiyā dhammā*' becomes a standard way of referring to the seven sets in post-canonical Buddhist literature, and that while the expression occurs in a number of passages in the Pāli canon, it is not found in any context where the seven sets appear as a definite group, nor is the number of *bodhi-pakkhiyā dhammā* anywhere specified as thirty-seven.[1] So what exactly is understood by the expression in these canonical passages? What are its implications and connotations? Is the expression understood to define a particular set of items—a set of items other than the seven sets?

What does the expression *bodhi-pakkhiyā dhammā* mean? The Pāli textual tradition bears witness to a number of variations in the form of both parts of the adjectival compound *bodhi-pakkhiya.* As far as the meaning of the term in the Nikāyas is concerned these variations would appear to be of little consequence. Yet the term *bodhi-pakkhiya* has in the course of the history of modern Buddhist scholarship been the occasion for a number of academic footnotes and asides concerning these variations and other matters. Since the term is one that is central to the present study it is perhaps as well to consider all this rather carefully.

The term *bodhi-pakkhiya* occurs in some eighteen different contexts within the Pāli canon.[2] However, in these various contexts we find forms not only ending in *-pakkhiya* but also in *-pakkhika.* It is clear that alternation between the *-pakkhiya* and *-pakkhika* forms as we now have it is often the result of the predelictions of manuscript copyists. In the absence of critical editions[3] of the texts it is virtually impossible to determine any consistent preference for one form or the other among the different works of the canon. The sometimes rather limited variant readings indicated in PTS editions suggest that in many, if not in most, instances some manuscripts of a given text read *bodhi-pakkhiya* and others *bodhi-pakkhika.*[4] On the other hand where no variants are recorded[5]—if this does in fact reflect the state of the manuscripts—*bodhi-pakkhika* appears the more regular form. The *aṭṭhakathās* show that in one case at least

[1] But Lamotte notes (*Traité*, III 1120) that the *Ekottarikâgama* ('texte tardif et farci d'interpolations mahāyānistes') does qualify the seven sets as thirty-seven *bodhi-pākṣikas.*

[2] Vin III 23; D III 97; S V 227, 231, 237-9; A III 70-1, 300-1; IV 351-2; Paṭis I 18; II 115, 122; Ap 28, 314; It 75, 96; Th 900; Vibh 244, 249-50.

[3] Cf. O. von Hinüber, 'On the Tradition of Pāli Texts in India, Ceylon and Burma' in *Buddhism in Ceylon and Studies on Religious Syncretism in Buddhist Countries*, ed. H. Bechert, Göttingen, 1978, pp. 48-58.

[4] It appears that in general Burmese MSS prefer *-pakkhiya*, Ceylonese and Thai *-pakkhika* (cf. C.A.F. Rhys Davids' comments at Vibh xiv); but the rule is not absolute, cf. below, p. 286, n. 13.

[5] Vin III 23; D III 97; A III 70-1, 300-1; IV 351-2; Ap 28, 214; Paṭis I 18; II 115, 122, Vibh 244.

the variation between *bodhi-pakkhiya* and *bodhi-pakkhika* is ancient.[6] In other cases the PTS edition of the text reads *bodhi-pakkhika* with no variants recorded, yet all manuscripts of the commentary apparently read *bodhi-pakkhiya* without further comment.[7] The Pāli manuscript tradition preserves, then, forms in both *-pakkhiya* and *-pakkhika*, and one must surmise that these were already largely interchangeable in ancient times. Probably they should be regarded as simply reflecting the preferences of particular Middle Indo-Aryan dialects for either the ending *-iya* or *-ika*.

Buddhist Sanskrit sources similarly evidence a variety of forms: *bodhi-pakṣā dharmāḥ*, *bodhi-pakṣikā dharmāḥ*, *bodhi-pakṣyā dharmāḥ* and *bodhi-pākṣikā dharmāḥ*.[8] Now *-pakṣa*[9] might represent a sanskritization of Middle Indo-Aryan *-pakkha*; both *-pakṣika* and *-pākṣika* might represent sanskritizations of Middle Indo-Aryan *-pakkhika*, while *-pakṣya* might represent, a sanskritization of *-pakkhiya* and indeed *-pakkha*. Classical Sanskrit literature records the following adjectival formations derived from the substantive *pakṣa* ('wing' or 'side'): *pakṣin*, *pakṣya*, *pakṣīya* and *pākṣika*.[10]

What we appear to have then in *-pakkhiya* and *-pakkhika* is an adjectival formation in either *-iya* or *-ika*, derived from the substantive *pakṣa*, possibly with *vṛddhi*; compounded with *bodhi-* it would mean 'siding with' or 'taking the part of awakening'. The evidence of Buddhist Sanskrit literature also suggests a Middle Indo-Aryan form **bodhi-pakkhā dhammā* deriving from an Old Indo-Aryan *-pakṣa* or *-pakṣya*.[11] Since *-pakṣya* may not be recorded in the sense of 'siding with' until rather later in the history of Sanskrit literature',[12] the former is perhaps to be preferred; the whole expression would then mean something like '*dhammas* whose side/party is (that of) awakening', '*dhammas* that take the side of awakening', or even '*dhammas* that are the wings of awakening'. I shall return to the question of the meaning of *pakṣa/pakkha* at the beginning of section three of this chapter. In conclusion, it seems doubtful that one might meaningfully talk of the 'original' or 'correct' form of the expression. The texts (Pāli and Buddhist Sanskrit) indicate an absence of concern about the exact form, and it is difficult to see at what point in the history of the language and literature it would have been otherwise.

Two variations in the first member of the compound *bodhi-pakkhiya* are

---

6 Commenting on *bodhi-pakkhiyānaṃ dhammānaṃ* at It 75, Dhammapāla draws attention to the alternative reading: *bodhi-pakkhikānan ti pi pāṭho* (It-a II 73-4).

7 E.g. Mp III 259 to A III 70; Mp III 351 to A III 300.

8 Q.v. *BHSD*; different forms sometimes appear in the same text.

9 Edgerton regards *bodhi-pakṣa* as 'rare, and possibly only a phonetic variant of the commoner -pakṣya' (*BHSD*, s.v. *bodhi-pakṣa*), but it may not be as rare as he suggests; it seems to be the regular form in the *prajñāpāramitā* texts (not cited by Edgerton here) and cf. Abhidh-k 382 n.9.

10 Q.v., BR, MW; *pakṣiya* is recorded in the *Harivaṃśa* in the sense of 'siding with'; Pāṇini also gives the expression *pūrva-pakṣīya* (q.v., MW), 'situated on the front side', but there appears to be no corresponding **bodhi-pakṣīyā dharmāḥ* in Buddhist Sanskrit texts. Turner cites Pkt *pakkhia* under Skt *pākṣika*.

11 Cf. the adjectival usage of *kusala-pakkha* at M III 77: *iti kho bhikkhave vīsati kusala-pakkhā vīsati akusala-pakkhā*.

12 See BR and MW, s.v. *pakṣya*.

also found. First there is the alternation between *bodhi-* and *bodha-*,[13] and secondly the addition on one occasion in the four primary Nikāyas of the prefix *sam-*, giving *sambodha-pakkhika*.[14] The alternation between the *-i* and *-a* stem forms has no obvious significance in early Buddhist literature.[15] As for *sambodha*, I commented in the course of my discussion of the *bojjhaṅgas* that in a late canonical work such as the *Paṭisambhidāmagga* (where we have such sequences as *bujjhanti*, *anubujjhanti*, *paṭibujjhanti*, *sambujjhanti* and indeed *bodhi-pakkhiyaṭṭhena*, *anubodhi-pakkhiyaṭṭhena*, *paṭibodhi-pakkhiyaṭṭhena*, *sambodhi-pakkhiyaṭṭhena*) it is not unreasonable to see the addition of the various prefixes as imparting a specific meaning.[16] However, it is equally clear that in the Nikāyas *sambojjhaṅga* and *bojjhaṅga* are regularly equivalents. In the context of the four primary Nikāyas there seem to be no good grounds for thinking that *sambodha-pakkhikā dhammā* are conceived of as anything different from *bodha-pakkhikā dhammā*.[17]

These, then, are the basic facts concerning the occurrence of the term *bodhi-pakkhiya* in the Pāli canon. However, commenting on *bodhi-pakṣika-dharma* in a note to his translation of the *Mahāvastu*, J.J. Jones wrote as follows:

> *Pakṣika* is the Pāli *pakkhika* or *pakkhiya* ... The term *pakṣika* has been taken as a derivative of *pakṣa*, and has accordingly been rendered either 'being on the side of' or 'forming the wings of' ... This interpretation seems to be borne out by the fact that in BSk. the forms *bodhipakṣa* and *-pakṣya* are more frequent than *-pakṣika*. At

---

[13] For *bodha-* see S V 227, 231, 237-9. It is not at all clear what is the 'correct' reading in many instances. D III 97 has *bodhi-pakkhiya* as does Sv III 872 and Sv (Be 1902) III 48, but Sv (Ce 1925) II 632 has *bodha-pakkhiya*; DAṬ III 63 has *bodha-pakkhiya* but records as variants *bodhi-pakkhiya* (Be Chaṭṭhasaṃgāyanā, one Sinhalese MS), *bodhi-pakkhika* (two Sinhalese MSS). At S V 227, 231, 237-9 Feer is not consistent about which form he prefers, but the variant readings he notes show that the Burmese prefer *bodhi-pakkhiya* and the Sinhalese *bodha-pakkhika*. Mp IV 162 (to A IV 251) has *sambodha-pakkhika* and *sambodhassa*, but records Be (1924) as reading *sambodhi-pakkhiya* and *sambodhissa*. Vibh-a 346 reads *bodhi-pakkhiya*, following Be (1902), but gives two Sinhalese MSS as reading *bodha-*; but Sinhalese MSS do on occasion have *bodhi-pakkhiya* (cf. variant given at Vibh 250). For the *-a* stem cf. *sambodha-gāmino* (Sn p. 140), though Sn also has *sambodhi* (Sn 478, 503, 693, 696).

[14] A IV 352; variant *sambodhi-*.

[15] *PED*, *BHSD*, s.vv. *bodha*, *bodhi*. Edgerton comments that the usage of *bodha* in Buddhist, non-Buddhist and Jaina Sanskrit is much the same, whereas *bodhi* is very rare in non-Buddhist and non-Jaina texts. It is clear from the stock commentarial exegesis of *bojjhaṅga* (see above, Chapter 5.9) that whether *bodhi* is glossed as *ñāṇa* or *ariya-puggala* hinges on whether the commentators take *bodhi-* as *bodhi* or *bodhin*, and not on whether they read *bodhi-* or *bodha-* , as Ñāṇamoli implies at Paṭis Trsl 316 n. 2; likewise *bodha-* might be taken in two ways, as 'awakening' itself or as an adjective descriptive of the one who is awakening, i.e. 'the awakening [man]'.

[16] See above, p. 184-5.

[17] It is not clear to me why Hare says (A Trsl IV 231 n. 1) of *sambodha-pakkhikā dhammā* 'the context clearly shows that it is not the same as *bodhipakkhiyā dhammā*'; possibly it is because he understands the latter to refer straightforwardly to the seven sets. Citing the commentary he ignores the extent to which the explanation of *sambodha-pakkhika* here corresponds with that of *bodhi-pakkhiya* elsewhere (see Chapter 9.3); clearly the commentarial tradition takes them as basically equivalent. *PED*, s.v. *sambodha* does give 'the insight belonging to the three higher stages of the path' but without stating its authority; Mp IV 162 states that *sambodha* at A IV 352 has to do with all four paths (*catu-magga-saṃkhātassa sambodhassa*), while Sp I 229 takes *bodhi* to refer only to the path of *arahant*-ship. Thus it is clear that the commentaries interpreted these terms in the Nikāyas as they saw fit according to particular contexts.

> the same time, as the word *pakkhika* does definitely occur in the older Pāli texts, it cannot be regarded as certain that the term as well as the complete formula originated among the Sanskritists or quasi-Sanskritists as Har Dayal maintains ... There is every possibility that the Pāli *pakkhika* is more original, and the etymology of this, viz. from *pakkha*, Sk. suffix *-prakhya*, 'like', 'resembling' would seem to suit its application in this formula better than the derivation from *pakṣa*, 'wing' or 'side'. For then *bodhipakṣikadharma* would mean a '*bodhi*-like quality or condition.' On this supposition all the BSk. forms are due to a wrong Sanskritization of the Pāli *pakkha, pakkhika.*[18]

I shall turn to Har Dayal's comments presently, but what of Jones' suggestion that *bodhi-pakkhiyā dhammā* might be an erroneous formation for an expression that originally signified '*bodhi*-like *dhammas*'?

As I have suggested, there are possibly grounds for preferring the reading *-pakkhika*, but it is difficult to see why and even how Jones derived this from *-prakhya*—the dictionaries record no such forms as **prakhyika* or **prākhyika*. On the other hand, Pāli *pakkhika* does represent a quite regular Middle Indo-Aryan equivalent to the perfectly correct Sanskrit *pākṣika*. Jones appears to be quite alone in relating *pakkhika* to *prakhya.*[19] The suggestion that we have to do with an expression meaning '*bodhi*-like *dhammas*' might be better founded on the assumption that *bodhi-pakkha* and not *bodhi-pakkhika* represents the 'correct' form; *pakkha* might very well represent Sanskrit *prakhya*. Yet the usage of Pāli *pakkha* in the sense of Sanskrit *prakhya* is not reliably attested,[20] while the postulated *bodhi-pakkhā dhammā*, as I have already pointed out, still makes good sense in terms of Sanskrit *-pakṣa*: '*dhammas* that take the side of awakening'.

The existence of various adjectival formations derived from a common substantive and having little difference in meaning is, of course, quite normal in both Sanskrit and Middle Indo-Aryan. Expressing a rather similar notion to Sanskrit *pakṣin, pakṣīya, pakṣya* and *pākṣika* are a number of derivatives from *bhāga*: *bhāgika, bhāgin, bhāgya.*[21] These all mean, more or less, 'having a share in'. Similarly in Pāli we find *bhāgin* and *bhāgiya.*[22] These adjectival derivatives from *bhāga* prove particularly relevant to the question of the meaning of *bodhi-pakkhiya* in the Pāli canon, since *-pakkhiya/-pakkhika* is often found juxtaposed with *-bhāgiya* in a way that suggests they should be taken as alternative ways of expressing a similar idea:

> *ye keci bhikkhave dhammā kusalā kusala-bhāgiyā kusala-pakkhikā sabbe te appamāda-mūlakā.*[23]

A further indication of this overlap in meaning and usage is the way in which *-pakkhiya/-pakkhika* and *bhāgiya* are on occasion apparently glossed by the

---

18 Mvu Trsl II 272 n.1.

19 Cf. Childers, *PED*, *PTC*, s.v. *pakkhika*.

20 *PED* (s.v. *pakkha*, 2) does take *pakkha* in *mātu-pakkha* and *pitu-pakkha* at Mil 75 as equivalent to *prakhya*, though the Skt expressions *mātṛ-pakṣa* and *pitṛ-pakṣa* (q.v., MW) suggest that it is mistaken in doing so; *PED* cites no further examples.

21 Q.v., MW.

22 Q.v. *PED*.

23 S V 91; misprinted as *kusalâkusala-bhāgiya*; cf. A I 11.

same phrase. Thus to describe something as *nibbedha-bhāgiya* indicates that it 'turns towards' or 'conduces to' (*saṃvattati*) penetrative wisdom;[24] similarly something that is *bodha-pakkhika* is said to 'turn towards' or 'conduce to' awakening.[25] At this point it is worth comparing the expression *bodhi-pakkhiyā dhammā* to an expression found in a prose section of the *Suttanipāta*: 'skilful *dhammas* which are noble, lead out, lead to awakening' (*kusalā dhammā ariya niyyānikā sambodha-gāmino*).[26] In conclusion, to treat *-pakkhika* or *-pakkhiya* in the expression *bodhi-pakkhiya* or *bodhi-pakkhikā dhammā* as anything other than a derivative of *pakṣa* seems perverse; the basic meaning of the expression must be taken as '*dhammas* that side with or take the part of awakening'.

What of Dayal's comments referred to in the above quotation from Jones? In his study of the bodhisattva according to the Sanskrit sources Dayal states:

> The Pāli word *bodhi-pakkhiya* is probably derived from the Sanskrit form, which was the earlier of the two, as this word does not occur often in the *Nikāyas* or *Milindapañho* ... The term emphatically refers to *bodhi* and not to the *nirvāṇa* of the Pāli scriptures. Both the term and the complete formula seem to have orginated among the Sanskritists or quasi-Sanskritists, who were the forerunners of the Mahāyāna. The Pāli rendering points to *pakṣya* as the correct Sanskrit form ... [27]

What has already been said should make it clear why I regard Dayal's comments concerning the correct form to be misconceived. The more surprising claim is that the Pāli usage of the term *bodhi-pakkhiya* is a borrowing from 'Sanskritists or quasi-Sanskritists'. The bases of this claim, namely that the term is found only infrequently in the Nikāyas and *Milindapañha* and that the reference to *bodhi* is suggestive of the Mahāyāna, are certainly dubious. Dayal refers to Buddhist Sanskrit works such as the *Mahāvastu*, *Mahāvyutpatti*, the *Lalitavistara*, the *Saddharmapuṇḍarīka* and the *Daśabhūmika-sūtra*. Yet we have no reason for thinking that these works are older than Pāli works such as the *Peṭakopadesa*, and *Milindapañha* which mention 'thirty-seven *bodhi-pakkhiyā dhammā*' explicitly. Furthermore the term *bodhi-pākṣika* (and variants) hardly occurs with greater frequency in the Buddhist Sanskrit works mentioned than *bodhi-pakkhiya* does in paracanonical Pāli literature; and although rare in the canon it is not *that* rare. Finally, it is true that the term *bodhi* is taken up in certain concepts associated with the development of the Mahāyāna, but the usage of derivatives from the root *budh* is hardly to be regarded as an exclusive feature of the Mahāyāna. As I stated at the outset of this study, it is clear that the expression *bodhi-pakkhiyā dhammā/bodhi-pākṣikā dharmāḥ* should be regarded as part of the common heritage of ancient Buddhism.

---

[24] S V 87.

[25] S V 237. Cf. also the juxtaposition of *vighāta-pakkhiya* (variant: *-pakkhika*) and *anibbāna-saṃvattanika* at S V 97; M I 115; As 382.

[26] Sn p. 140.

[27] Dayal, op. cit., p. 81. Rather curiously he seems to regard *pakṣa* meaning 'wing' and *pakṣa* meaning 'side' as two distinct homonyms: 'It seems probable that the form *pakṣya* is not related to the word *pakṣa*, which means "wing". That simile would not be very appropriate as no bird has thirty-seven wings.' He goes on to say that *pakṣya* 'is derived from the substantive *pakṣa*, which means "a side, party, faction".'

2. Usage and application of the expression

Six of the canonical passages that speak of *bodhi-pakkhiyā dhammā* employ the expression 'to dwell engaged in the development of *bodhi-pakkhiyā dhammā*' (*bodhi-pakkhiyānaṃ dhammānaṃ bhāvanânuyogaṃ anuyutto viharati*).[28] First there is a *Vinaya* passage (Vin) that constitutes part of the preamble to the final formulation of the first of the four *pārājika* rules of training, the transgression of which involves the *bhikkhu* in 'defeat'. The particular rule in question is the one prohibiting sexual intercourse. A number of *bhikkhus* from Vesālī are represented as eating, drinking and bathing as much as they like; without proper reflection, without first renouncing the training and declaring their weakness they indulge in sexual intercourse. Some time later they think better of their back sliding and request that Ānanda should put the matter before the Buddha in the following terms:

> Even now, Ānanda, if we might obtain the 'going-forth' in the presence of the Blessed One, if we might obtain ordination—even now as practitioners of insight into skilful *dhammas* we would dwell engaged in the development of *bodhi-pakkhikā dhammā* during the first and last parts of the night.[29]

Two *Aṅguttara-nikāya* passages (A.1 and A.2) make use of a slightly fuller version of essentially the same formula:

> Therefore, *bhikkhus*, I say that you should train thus: we shall be guarded as to the doors of the [sense-] faculties; knowing the right amount in food, engaged in wakefulness, as practitioners of insight into skilful *dhammas* we shall dwell engaged in the development of *bodhi-pakkhikā dhammā* during the first and last parts of the night.[30]

In each of these *Aṅguttara* passages the formula occurs both in a negative version (regarding the consequences when *bhikkhus* are not guarded as to the doors of the sense-faculties, and so on) and a positive version as quoted. In the first passage the Buddha addresses a *bhikkhu* who complains: 'My body becomes drugged, directions are not clear to me, *dhammas* are not apparent to me, weariness and lethargy invade my mind and remain [there], I practise the spiritual life without enthusiasm, and I have doubt about *dhammas*.'[31] Taking heed of the Buddha's instructions, the *bhikkhu* subsequently attains *arahant*-ship. In the second passage the Buddha admonishes a group of *bhikkhus*, recently gone-forth, for their laziness, asking them whether they have seen or heard of a *samaṇa* or *brāhmaṇa* who is unguarded as to the doors of the

---

[28] Vin III 23; A III 70-1, 300-1; It 75, 96; Vibh 244.

[29] Vin III 23: *idāni ce pi mayaṃ bhante Ānanda labheyyāma bhagavato santike pabbajjaṃ labheyyāma upasampadaṃ idāni pi mayaṃ vipassakā kusalānaṃ dhammānaṃ pubba-rattâpara-rattaṃ bodhi-pakkhikānaṃ dhammānaṃ bhāvanânuyogaṃ anuyuttā vihareyyāma.*

[30] A III 70-1, 300-1: *tasmā ti ha vo bhikkhave evaṃ sikkhitabbaṃ: indriyesu gutta-dvārā bhavissāma bhojane mattaññavo jāgariyaṃ anuyuttā vipassakā ... bhāvanânuyogaṃ anuyuttā viharissāma.*

[31] A III 69: *etarahi me bhante madhuraka-jāto c'eva kāyo, disā ca me na pakkhāyanti. dhammā ca maṃ na ppaṭibhanti, thīna-middhañ ca me cittaṃ pariyādāya tiṭṭhati, anabhirato ca brahma-cariyaṃ carāmi, atthi ca me dhammesu vicikicchā ti.* The formula is thus initially directed to one individual and as quoted needs adjustment for the singular; however, the instructions are generalized for all *bhikkhus* at the close of the *sutta*.

sense-faculties, and so forth, but has nevertheless attained the liberation of mind and wisdom that is without *āsavas*. They have not, and neither has the Buddha.

Turning to the *Itivuttaka*, we find two passages (It.1 and It.2) that employ the expression 'dwelling engaged in the development of *bodhi-pakkhiyā dhammā*' as the second part of a threefold series. The first of these concerns the three occasions on which a *deva*-cry issues forth among the *devas*:

> [i] At that time, *bhikkhus*, when an *ariya-sāvaka* shaves off his hair and beard, puts on orange robes and intends to go forth from the home into homelessness, a *deva*-cry issues forth among the *devas*: 'This *ariya-sāvaka* intends to do battle with Māra.' [ii] At that time when an *ariya-sāvaka* dwells engaged in the development of the seven *bodhi-pakkhiyā dhammā*, a *deva*-cry issues forth ... : 'This *ariya-sāvaka* does battle with Māra.' [iii] At that time when an *ariya-sāvaka* by the destruction of the *āsavas* directly knows for himself in the here and now, realizes, attains and dwells in the liberation of mind, the liberation of wisdom that is without *āsavas*, a *deva*-cry issues forth ... : 'This *ariya-sāvaka* is victorious in the battle; victorious he enters into the front-line of the battle.'[32]

In the second passage the Buddha explains how 'in this *dhamma-vinaya* the *bhikkhu* who has lovely virtue, lovely *dhamma* and lovely wisdom is called one who is whole, accomplished, the best of men':[33]

> [i] How does a *bhikkhu* have lovely virtue? Here, *bhikkhus*, a *bhikkhu* has virtue and dwells restrained by the restraint of the *pātimokkha*; endowed with good conduct and good associates, seeing danger in the slightest of faults, he undertakes and trains in the rules of training. [ii] How does a *bhikkhu* have lovely *dhamma*? Here, *bhikkhus*, a *bhikkhu* dwells engaged in the development of the seven *bodhi-pakkhiyā dhammā*. [iii] How does a *bhikkhu* have lovely wisdom? Here, *bhikkhus*, a *bhikkhu* by the destruction of the *āsavas* ... dwells in the liberation of mind, the liberation of wisdom that is without *āsavas*.[34]

Finally the following forms the opening passage of the 'analysis according to Suttanta' of the chapter on *jhāna* in the *Vibhaṅga*:

> Here a *bhikkhu* dwells restrained by the restraint of the *pātimokkha*; endowed with good conduct and good associates, seeing danger in the slightest of faults, he undertakes and trains in the rules of training; guarded as to the doors of the [sense-] faculties, knowing the right amount in food, engaged in wakefulness during

---

[32] It 75: *yasmiṃ bhikkhave samaye ariya-sāvako kesa-massuṃ ohāretvā kāsāyāni vatthāni acchādetvā agārasmā anagāriyaṃ pabbajjāya ceteti tasmiṃ samaye devesu deva-saddo niccharati: eso ariya-sāvako mārena saddhiṃ saṃgāmāya cetetī ti. yasmiṃ samaye ariya-sāvako sattannaṃ bodhi-pakkhiyānaṃ dhammānaṃ bhāvanânuyogaṃ anuyutto viharati tasmiṃ samaye ... : eso ariya-sāvako mārena saddhiṃ saṃgāmetī ti. yasmiṃ samaye ariya-sāvako āsavānaṃ khayā anāsavaṃ ceto-vimuttiṃ paññā-vimuttiṃ diṭṭhe va dhamme sayaṃ abhiññā sacchikatvā upasampajja viharati tasmiṃ samaye ... : eso ariya-sāvako vijita-saṃgāmo taṃ eva saṃgāma-sīsaṃ abhivijiya ajjhāvasatī ti.*

[33] It 96: *kalyāṇa-sīlo bhikkhave kalyāṇa-dhammo kalyāṇa-pañño imasmiṃ dhamma-vinaye kevalī vusitavā uttama-puriso ti vuccati.*

[34] Ibid.: *kathañ ca bhikkhave bhikkhu kalyāṇa-sīlo. idha bhikkhave bhikkhu sīlavā hoti pātimokkha-saṃvara-saṃvuto viharati ācāra-gocara-sampanno aṇumattesu vajjesu bhaya-dassāvī samādāya sikkhati sikkhā-padesu ... idha bhikkhave bhikkhu sattannaṃ bodhi-pakkhiyānaṃ dhammānaṃ bhāvanânuyogaṃ anuyutto viharati ... idha bhikkhave bhikkhu āsavānaṃ khayā anāsavaṃ ceto-vimuttiṃ paññā-vimuttiṃ ... viharati.*

the first and last parts of the night, he is continually and wisely engaged in the development of *bodhi-pakkhikā dhammā*.[35]

This *Vibhaṅga* passage (Vibh) goes on to detail how the *bhikkhu* acts with clear comprehension in everything he does, how he retires to a suitable place, sits crosslegged, abandons the five hindrances and attains the four *jhānas* and four formless attainments.

What are we to make of these passages? I shall for the moment ignore the question of the 'seven' in the *Itivuttaka* passages. The way in which the six passages embrace various common elements is abundantly clear. Moreover these various elements that make up the passages also represent stock phrases and formulas that are scattered throughout the canon. If we exclude the phrase *vipassakā kusalānaṃ dhammānaṃ* and the actual expression concerning the *bodhi-pakkhiyā dhammā*, none of the various elements is unique to these passages. This suggests that one might collate the six passages in order to produce a synoptic version:

(a) He shaves off his hair and beard, puts on orange robes and goes forth from the home into homelessness.

[It.1]

(b) He (has virtue and) dwells restrained by the restraint of the *pātimokkha*; endowed with good conduct and good associates, seeing danger in the slightest of faults, he undertakes and trains in the rules of training.

[It.2, Vibh]

(c) Guarded as to the doors of the [sense-] faculties, knowing the right amount in food, engaged in wakefulness (during the first and last parts of the night),

[A.1, A.2, Vibh]

(d) as a practitioner of insight into skilful *dhammas*,

[Vin, A.1, A.2]

(e) (he dwells) (continually and wisely) engaged in the development of *bodhi-pakkhikā dhammā* (during the first and last parts of the night).

[Vin, A.1, A.2, It.1, It.2, Vibh]

(f) By the destruction of the *āsavas* he directly knows for himself in the here and now, realizes, attains and dwells in the liberation of mind, the liberation of wisdom that is without *āsavas*.[36]

[(A.1), A.2, It.1, It.2]

---

[35] Vibh 244: *idha bhikkhu pātimokkha-saṃvara-saṃvuto ... sikkhā-padesu ... indriyesu gutta-dvāro bhojane mattaññū pubba-rattâpara-rattaṃ jāgariyânuyogaṃ anuyutto sātaccaṃ nepakkaṃ bodhi-pakkhikānaṃ dhammānaṃ bhāvanânuyogaṃ anuyutto.*

[36] *kesa-massuṃ ohāretvā kāsāyāni vatthāni acchādetvā agārasmā anagāriyaṃ pabbajati. (sīlavā hoti) pātimokkha-saṃvara-saṃvuto viharati ācāra-gocara-sampanno aṇumattesu vajjesu bhaya-dassāvī samādāya sikkhati sikkhā-padesu. indriyesu gutta-dvāro bhojane mattaññū (pubba-rattâpara-rattaṃ) jāgariyaṃ anuyutto vipassako kusalānaṃ dhammānaṃ (sātaccaṃ nepakkaṃ) (pubba-rattâpara-rattaṃ) (sattannaṃ) bodhi-pakkhiyānaṃ dhammānaṃ bhāvanânuyogaṃ anuyutto (viharati) āsavānaṃ khayā anāsavaṃ ceto-vimuttiṃ paññā-vimuttiṃ diṭṭhe va dhamme sayaṃ abhiññā sacchi-*

What the above synoptic version of the whole formula does is to bring *bodhi-pakkhiyānaṃ dhammānaṃ bhāvanā* into perspective within what amounts to a summary of the whole Buddhist path; development of *bodhi-pakkhiyā dhammā* is apparently conceived of as a specific stage or practice within the general schema of the Buddhist path.[37] This is perhaps also reflected in the following verses from the *Theragāthā*:

> But he is one who is mindful, desiring little, content, untroubled; he delights in seclusion, [stays] secluded; his strength is always firm.
>
> For him *dhammas* are skilful, siding with awakening; and he is one without *āsavas*—thus it is spoken by the great seer.[38]

However, Lamotte has commented with reference to some of the passages I have just been considering:

> Dans les Nikāya et les Āgama, l'expression *bodhipākṣika dharma* est plutôt rare et de contenu encore mal défini. L'Aṅguttara, III p. 70, 300 (cf. Vibhaṅga, p. 244) range parmi eux: la garde des sens (*indriyesu guttadvāratā*), la sobriété (*bhojane mattaññutā*) et la vigilence (*jāgariy'ānuyoga*).[39]

Certainly it is not possible on the basis of these passages alone to be very specific about just how *bodhi-pakkhiyā dhammā* are conceived of, but surely it is a misreading of the passages in question to suggest that there *indriyesu gutta-dvāratā*, *bhojane mattaññutā* and *jāgariyânuyoga* are all considered *bodhi-pakkhiyā dhammā*.

The six passages so far considered prompt comparison with a rather interesting sequence that occurs several times in the *Mahāniddesa*, defining the content of the expression 'skilful *dhammas*'. According to the *Niddesa* skilful *dhammas* consist of or in the following: the right-way (*sammā-paṭipadā*), the way forward (*anuloma-paṭipadā*), the way leading forward (*apaccanīka-paṭipadā*), the way following on (*anvattha-paṭipadā*), the way of *dhamma* (*dhammânudhamma-paṭipadā*); the fulfilment of virtues (*sīlesu pāripūrikāritā*), guarding the doors of the sense-faculties (*indriyesu gutta-dvāratā*), knowing the right

---

katvā upasampajja viharati. (For the various elements cf.: [a] D I 63, 115, 136, 250; II 29, 42, 241, 249; III 60, 76; M I 163, 179, 240, 267, 343-4, 451; II 55, 66, 75, 89, 101, 166, 211; III 33; S II 219-20; A I 107; II 207-8; III 217, 226, 386, 399; IV 118; V 205; [b] D I 63; III 78; M I 33, 355; III 2, 11, 134; S V 187; A I 63-4, 244; II 14, 22, 39; III 113, 135, 138, 151, 262, IV 189, 352, 357; V 23, 71-2, 131, 198, 338; [c] D I 63; M I 32, 273-4, 354, 470-1; III 6, 134-5; S II 218-9; IV 103, 175; A I 113; II 39; III 199; IV 166; [f] D I 156; II 92; III 281; M I 35, 71, 74, 210, 284, 289, 357, 482, 490; II 22; III 12, 99, 103, 275; S II 214, 217, 222; V 203, 220, 257, 266, 268, 275, 305, 346, 358, 376, 406; A I 107, 123-4, 220, 232-4, 236, 246, 256, 273, 291; II 6, 23, 36, 87, 146, 214, 238; III 19, 83, 114, 119, 131, 134-5, 142, 262, 281-2, 300-1; IV 13, 83, 119, 140-1, 145-6, 314-5, 400; V 10-5, 36, 38, 69, 200-1, 340. See *PTC* under various head words.)

[37] *CPD* (s.v. *ācāra-gocara-sampanna*) comments of the formula marked (b) in the synoptic table: 'The formula (also occurring with slight variations) often is a unit in an enumeration of several *aṅga*, *dhamma* characterizing a *vinayadhara*, an *ariyasāvaka*, etc., or constituting necessary qualifications or a degree in spiritual development.' In principle this might equally apply to (a), (c), (d), (e) and (f).

[38] Th 899-900: *sato ca hoti appiccho santuṭṭho avighātavā| paviveka-rato vitto niccaṃ āraddha-vīriyo|| tassa dhammā ime honti kusalā bodhi-pakkhikā| anāsavo ca so hoti iti vuttaṃ mahesinā||*

[39] *Traité*, III 1120.

amount in food (*bhojane mattaññutā*), engaging in wakefulness (*jāgariyânu-yoga*), mindfulness and clear comprehension (*sati-sampajañña*); engaging in the development of the four establishings of mindfulness, the four right endeavours, the four bases of success, the five faculties, the seven awakening-factors, the noble eight-factored path.[40]

It seems to me rather too much of a coincidence that here the *Niddesa* inserts the seven sets just at the point where in the other passages we have '(as a practitioner of insight into skilful *dhammas*) he dwells engaged in the development of *bodhi-pakkhiyā dhammā* (during the first and last parts of the night)'. At the very least this must indicate that by the time of the *Niddesa* the seven sets had come to represent for the tradition what *bodhi-pakkhiyā dhammā* represents for the earlier tradition. Possibly we can go further and suggest that the *Niddesa* implies here a conscious and deliberate identification of the seven sets with the expression *bodhi-pakkhiyā dhammā*. If so it probably constitutes the earliest such identification we have.

Returning to the four primary Nikāyas, an *Aṅguttara* passage would seem to confirm that the development of *bodhi-pakkhiyā dhammā* is conceived of as something rather specific that pertains to the higher stages of the path. This occurs in the *navaka-nipāta*. The Buddha explains how wanderers from other schools should be answered if they ask about the conditions or supports (*upanisā*) for the development of *sambodha-pakkhikā dhammā*:

> Here, sirs, a *bhikkhu* is one who has good friends, good companions, good associates. This is the first support for the development of *sambodha-pakkhikā dhammā*. Furthermore a bhikkhu has virtue and dwells restrained by the restraint of the *pātimokkha*; endowed with good conduct and good associates, seeing danger in the slightest of faults, he undertakes and trains in the rules of training. This is the second support ... Furthermore a *bhikkhu* easily, readily, without difficulty finds just that kind of talk which concerns application and leads to the opening of the heart, namely talk of wanting little, contentment, seclusion, detachment, initiating strength, virtue, concentration, wisdom, freedom, knowledge and vision and freedom. This is the third support ... Furthermore a *bhikkhu* dwells having initiated strength for the abandoning of unskilful *dhammas* and the arousing of skilful *dhammas*; he is firm, steadfast and resolute with regard to skilful *dhammas*. This is the fourth support ... Furthermore a *bhikkhu* has wisdom; he is endowed with the wisdom that attains to the rise and fall [of things], that is noble, penetrating, and attains to the right destruction of suffering. This is the fifth support for the development of *sambodha-pakkhikā dhammā*.[41]

---

[40] Nidd I 13-4, 361-2, 468-9; the same basic sequence occurs with some additions or omissions (the first five items) at Nidd I 54-5, 143-4, 219, 332, 361-2, 365, 468-9, 480, 502.

[41] A IV 351-2: *idhâvuso bhikkhu kalyāṇa-mitto hoti kalyāṇa-sahāyo kalyāṇa-sampavaṅko. sambodha-pakkhikānaṃ dhammānaṃ āvuso ayaṃ paṭhamā upanisā bhāvanāya. puna ca paraṃ āvuso bhikkhu sīlavā hoti ... sikkhati sikkhā-padesu ... ayaṃ dutiyā upanisā ... puna ca paraṃ āvuso bhikkhu yâyam kathā abhisallekhikā ceto-vivaraṇa-sappāyā seyyathīdaṃ appiccha-kathā santuṭṭhi-kathā paviveka-kathā asaṃsagga-kathā viriyârambha-kathā sīla-kathā samādhi-kathā paññā-kathā vimutti-kathā vimutti-ñāṇa-dassana-kathā evarūpiyā kathāya nikāma-lābhī hoti akiccha-lābhī akasira-lābhī ... ayaṃ tatiyā upanisā ... puna ca paraṃ āvuso bhikkhu āraddha-viriyo viharati akusalānaṃ dhammānaṃ pahānāya kusalānaṃ dhammānaṃ upasampadāya thāmavā daḷha-parakkamo anikkhitta-dhuro kusalesu dhammesu ... ayaṃ catutthā upanisā ... puna ca paraṃ āvuso bhikkhu paññavā hoti udayattha-gāminiyā paññāya samannāgato ariyāya nibbedhikāya sammā-dukkha-kkhaya-gāminiyā ... ayaṃ pañcamī upanisā bhāvanāya.*

The Buddha goes on to review these five conditions as follows:

> Of the *bhikkhu*, *bhikkhus*, who is one who has good friends, good companions, good associates, this is to be expected (*pāṭikaṅkhaṃ*): he will have virtue ... he will undertake and train in the rules of training. Of the *bhikkhu* who is one who has good friends ... this is to be expected: he will easily, readily and without difficulty find just that kind of talk which concerns application ... talk about knowledge and vision and freedom. Of the *bhikkhu* who is one who has good friends ... this is to be expected: he will dwell ... firm, steadfast and resolute with regard to skilful *dhammas*. Of the *bhikkhu* who is one who has good friends ... this is to be expected: he will have wisdom ... that attains to the right destruction of suffering.[42]

These five supports for the development of *sambodha-pakkhikā dhammā* are thus interconnected and bound up together. In so far as all this makes clear what the conditions for the development of the *sambodha-pakkhikā dhammā* are, it also makes clear what the *sambodha-pakkhikā dhammā* themselves are not: they are clearly seen as something different from the *generality* of conditions and practices that constitute the Buddhist path; on the other hand they emerge directly out of those conditions. The passage continues:

> By the *bhikkhu* who establishes [himself] in these five *dhammas*, four further *dhammas* are to be developed: [the meditation on] ugliness is to be developed in order to abandon passion; loving kindness is to be developed in order to abandon ill will; mindfulness of breathing in and out is to be developed in order to cut off [discursive] thought; the idea of impermanence is to be developed in order to abolish the conceit, 'I am'. For the *bhikkhu* who has the idea of impermanence, the idea of not-self is present; one who has the idea of not-self gains the abolition of the conceit, 'I am', [gains] *nibbāna* in the here and now.[43]

Since these four further *dhammas* are the *dhammas* that arise on the basis of the supports for the *sambodha-pakkhikā dhammā*, it seems fair to assume that the passage intends us to understand that these four further *dhammas* are in fact the *sambodha-pakkhikā dhammā* themselves. At anyrate, if they are not indeed identical with them, it seems that at least they should be seen as in some sense embracing *sambodha-pakkhikā dhammā*.[44]

At this point I need to return to the fact that the number of *bodhi-pakkhiyā dhammā* is specified as seven in the *Itivuttaka*. One other Nikāya passage also talks of seven *bodhi-pakkhiyā dhammā*:

> A *khattiya*, Vāseṭṭha, restrained in body, speech and mind, as a consequence of developing the seven *bodhi-pakkhiyā dhammā* attains full *nibbāna* in the here and now. A *brāhmaṇa* too ... A *vessa* too ... A *sudda* too ... A *samaṇa* too, restrained

---

[42] A IV 352-3.

[43] A IV 353: *tena ca pana bhikkhave bhikkhunā imesu pañcasu dhammesu patiṭṭhāya cattāro dhammā uttariṃ bhāvetabbā: asubhā bhāvetabbā rāgassa pahānāya; mettā bhāvetabbā vyāpādassa pahānāya; ānâpāna-sati bhāvetabbā vitakkûpacchedāya; anicca-saññā bhāvetabbā asmi-māna-samugghātāya. anicca-saññino bhikkhave bhikkhuno anatta-saññā saṇṭhāti. anatta-saññi asmi-māna-samugghātaṃ pāpuṇāti diṭṭhe va dhamme nibbānan ti.*

[44] The same nine *dhammas* are detailed at Ud 35-7 without any mention of *bodhi-pakkhiya-dhamma*; here the first five *dhammas* are specifically termed 'five *dhammas* that lead to the ripening of unripe freedom of mind' (*aparipakkāya ceto-vimuttiyā pañca dhammā paripākāya saṃvattanti*).

in body, speech and mind, as a consequence of developing the seven *bodhi-pakkhiyā dhammā* attains full *nibbāna* in the here and now.[45]

So what are the seven *dhammas* referred to in these passages as *bodhi-pakkhiya*? The old commentary of the 'word-analysis' (*pada-bhājaniya*) type that forms an important part of the text of *Vibhaṅga* has this to say with regard to the *Vibhaṅga* passage quoted above (which does not specify the number seven):

> Therein, which are [the] *bodhi-pakkhikā dhammā*? The seven factors of awakening—the mindfulness factor of awakening ... the equipoise factor of awakening.[46]

In the light of this it seems reasonable to assume that talk of seven *bodhi-pakkhiyā dhammā* in other contexts should also be taken as a reference to the seven *bojjhaṅgas*.[47] But can we simply conclude that *bodhi-pakkhiyā dhammā* was originally always merely an alternative expression for the seven *bojjhaṅgas*? I think not.

Obviously, as I have taken it, the *Aṅguttara* passage concerning the supports for the development of *sambodha-pakkhikā dhammā* is a complicating factor. The usage of the expression *bodhi-pakkhiyā dhammā* in the *indriya-saṃyutta* further complicates matters:

> Just so, *bhikkhus*, of whatever *bodhi-pakkhiyā dhammā* there are, the faculty of wisdom is reckoned the pinnacle, that is for awakening. And which, *bhikkhus*, are [the] *bodhi-pakkhiyā dhammā*? The faculty of confidence is a *bodhi-pakkhiyo dhammo*; it turns towards awakening. The faculty of strength ... The faculty of mindfulness ... The faculty of concentration ... The faculty of wisdom is a *bodhi-pakkhiyo dhammo*; it turns towards awakening.[48]

---

[45] D III 97: *khattiyo pi Vāseṭṭha kāyena saṃvuto vācāya saṃvuto manasā saṃvuto sattannaṃ bodhi-pakkhiyānaṃ dhammānaṃ bhāvanaṃ anvāya diṭṭhe va dhamme parinibbāyati. brāhmaṇo pi ... vesso pi ... suddo pi ... samaṇo pi ...* (Of the three versions of the *Aggañña-sutta* that come down in Chinese translation, the *Dīrghâgama* version talks of 'seven thoughts of awakening' at this point, while the *Madhyamâgama* version talks of the 'seven components of awakening'. Neither of the Chinese expressions involved is apparently usual for either *bodhi-pākṣika-dharma* or *bodhy-aṅga*. The third version uses a different formula at this point: 'With his mind well established in the four establishings of mindfulness he develops the seven factors of awakening.' (Cf. above, pp. 58-9.) See K. Meisig, *Das Sūtra von den vier Ständen*, pp.162-3.)

[46] Vibh 249-50: *tattha katame bodhi-pakkhikā dhammā. satta bojjhaṅgā: sati-sambojjhaṅgo ... upekkhā-sambojjhaṅgo.*

[47] We can add to this the fact that at Paṭis II 115, 122 *bodhi-pakkhiya* is used in explanation of *bojjhaṅga*, while the term *bojjhaṅga* is also on occasion explained in terms similar to those used in explanation of *bodhi-pakkhiya*: 'they turn towards *bodha*, *bhikkhus*, therefore they are called *bojjhaṅgas*' (*bodhāya saṃvattantī ti kho bhikkhū tasmā bojjhaṅgā ti vuccanti*) (S V 72; cf. Paṭis II 115). The commentaries get around the problem of 'seven' rather neatly. According to both Buddhaghosa and Dhammapāla there are seven *bodhi-pakkhiyā dhammā* because there are seven sets (Sv III 872: *sattannaṃ bodhi-pakkhiyānan ti cattāro satipaṭṭhānā ti ādi koṭṭhāsa-vasena sattannaṃ. paṭipātiyā pana satta-tiṃsāya bodhi-pakkhiyānaṃ dhammānaṃ*. It-a 73-4: *sattannan ti koṭṭhāsato sattannaṃ pabhedato pana te satta-tiṃsa honti ... evaṃ pabhedato satta-tiṃsa-vidhā pi satipaṭṭhānâdi koṭṭhāsato satt'eva hontī ti vuttaṃ sattannan ti*). While it may seem a little unlikely that this expresses the intention of the *Dīgha* or *Itivuttaka*, taking the seven sets as 'seven *dhammas*' is not entirely without precedent in the Nikāyas in that they are treated in the *sattaka-nipāta* of the *Aṅguttara-nikāya*, see A IV 125-7 and above, pp. 245-6.

[48] S V 227, 231, 237-9: *evaṃ eva kho bhikkhave ye keci bodha-pakkhiyā dhammā paññindriyaṃ tesaṃ aggaṃ akkhāyati yad idaṃ bodhāya. katame ca bhikkhave bodha-pakkhiyā dhammā. saddh-indriyaṃ bhikkhave bodha-pakkhiyo dhammo taṃ bodhāya saṃvattati. viriyindriyaṃ ... satindriyaṃ ... samādhindriyaṃ ... paññindriyaṃ ...* I have now discussed all canonical passages known to me

It is perhaps important to note that this passage occurs six times in the *indriya-saṃyutta* illustrated on each occasion by a different simile. In other words, it is not an isolated passage, but is in fact made rather a lot of. In the context of the *mahā-vagga* it is also perhaps significant that this treatment is restricted to the *indriyas*. Clearly its application to the *satipaṭṭhānas*, *samma-ppadhānas* and *iddhi-pādas* would not work. The reason for its omission in the case of the *balas* is probably best explained by the fact that they are considered entirely by way of the common formulaic treatments. Its omission from the treatment of the *ariyo aṭṭhaṅgiko maggo* is interesting; the nature of the treatment of the *ariyo aṭṭhaṅgiko maggo* in the Nikāyas is such that to single out *sammā-diṭṭhi* as the 'pinnacle' of the eight factors might just be seen as inappropriate. However, when it comes to the *bojjhaṅgas*, it is not so clear that the same applies to *dhamma-vicaya-sambojjhaṅga*.[49]

At first glance the application of the expression *bodhi-pakkhiyā dhammā* to the five *indriyas* would seem to contradict what I have been arguing, namely that we must understand the expression *bodhi-pakkhiyā dhammā* as indicating something quite specific in the Nikāyas. I suggested in chapter four that the five *indriyas* can be thought of as representing for the Nikāyas the five spiritual faculties considered by way of their most general capacities, yet here they are being identified with *bodhi-pakkhiyā dhammā*. However, I also drew attention in chapter four to a certain tension in the way the *indriyas* are handled in the *indriya-saṃyutta*; this tension manifests as a moot point of Abhidharma among certain schools, some among them suggesting that strictly speaking it is only confidence, strength, mindfulness, concentration and wisdom that are transcendent that can be termed *indriyas*.

It is perhaps not so hard to trace the line of thinking involved here. If the five *indriyas* are the spiritual faculties considered by way of their most general capacity, then corresponding to that general capacity is the capacity perfected, the capacity of each *indriya*, when uncluttered by defilements, to function as it really should. It is only when they function as they ideally should that their true nature as *indriyas* is properly manifest. The *indriyas* are at once the five basic and the five essential spiritual faculties; they are the five 'cardinal virtues', to use Conze's expression. Hence they are singled out as *bodhi-pakkhiyā dhammā* in the *indriya-saṃyutta*.

However, the problem of the precise import of *bodhi-pakkhiyā dhammā* in the canon remains. We must accept that *bodhi-pakkhiyā dhammā* is used in the

---

that employ the term *bodhi-pakkhiya*, apart from two verses in the *Apadāna* which appear to add little in the present context: 'Whoever in the world have followings and are called teachers, they teach to their gatherings *dhamma* that is handed down from one to another. But you, great hero, do not teach *dhamma* to creatures in this manner; having awakened to the truths, [you teach *dhamma* that] solely sides with awakening.' (Ap 28: *ye keci gaṇino loke satthāro ti pavuccare/ paraṃ-parā-gataṃ dhammaṃ deseti parisāya te// na h'eva tvaṃ mahā-vīra dhammaṃ desesi pāṇinaṃ/ samaṃ saccāni bujjhitvā kevalaṃ bodhi-pakkhikaṃ//*); 'In walking up and down or in endeavour; in strength that sides with awakening—having summoned up knowledge with regard to these, I dwell as I wish.' (Ap 314: *caṅkame vā padhāne vā viriye bodha-pakkhike// tesu ñāṇaṃ upānetvā viharāmi yad-icchakaṃ//*)

[49] Mil does indeed single out *dhamma-vicaya-sambojjhaṅga*; see above, p. 185.

canon not simply in the sense of the seven *bojjhaṅgas* or the five *indriyas* or the four 'further' *dhammas* given in the *navaka-nipāta* of the *Aṅguttara*. These are all attempts to give particular content to an expression that was originally used apart from a particular content. This is not the same thing as saying that *bodhi-pakkhiyā dhammā* was originally used as a rather vague and indeterminate expression. What it means is that the specific implications of the expression *bodhi-pakkhiyā dhammā* were not immediately connected with the specific implications of other expressions and concepts. In other words, it took time for various elements to be fully integrated.

Why are the seven *bojjhaṅgas* and five *indriyas* originally proffered in answer to the question: 'Which are [the] *bodhi-pakkhiyā dhammā*?' How one should approach this question suggests itself if one considers the nature of *bodhi-pakkhiyā dhammā* alongside that of *kusala-pakkhiyā dhammā* or, more simply, *kusala-dhammas*. What we need to ask is in what sense *bodhi-pakkhiyā dhammā—dhammas* that side with or take the part of awakening—are different from *kusala-pakkhiyā dhammā—dhammas* that side with or take the part of the skilful. Certainly *bodhi-pakkhiyā dhammā* and indeed the seven sets are also *kusala-dhammas*. But can everything that might be termed a *kusala-dhamma* equally be termed a *bodhi-pakkhiyo dhammo*. All the indications are, I think, that it cannot. A *bodhi-pakkhiyo dhammo* is rather a special variety of *kusala-dhamma*. We must surmise that a *bodhi-pakkhiyo dhammo*, a *dhamma* that sides with awakening, is a *dhamma* that sides more or less directly with awakening; in comparison with the generality of *kusala-dhammas*, a *bodhi-pakkhiyo dhammo* is a *kusala-dhamma* that is rather more immediately and closely bound up with and involved in *bodhi*. So the nature of *bodhi-pakkhiyā dhammā* hinges on the way *bodhi* itself is understood.

The nature and treatment of the seven *bojjhaṅgas* that I outlined in chapter five make it clear how *bodhi* is basically thought of as a particular variety of *jhāna*. The general understanding of the exegetical tradition is of some relevance at this point. With regard to the *bojjhaṅgas* it provides two basic perspectives on *bodhi*: it is either the assemblage of seven *dhammas* or, more specifically, it is the special knowledge inherent in that assemblage; in particular the special knowledge is represented by the one *bojjhaṅga*, *dhamma-vicaya*. If we reconsider the canonical *bodhi-pakkhiyā dhammā* passages rather similar themes are apparent. In the *Vibhaṅga* the development of *bodhi-pakkhiyā dhammā* is considered as an aspect of the practice of *jhāna*. Buddhaghosa's comment is worth noting here:

> Engaged in the development of *bodhi-pakkhiyā dhammā*: this is an indication that his practice shares in penetrative wisdom.[50]

The fifth of the five supports for the development of *sambodha-pakkhikā dhammā* is wisdom that attains to the rise and fall [of things] (*udayattha-gāminī*) and is penetrating (*nibbedhika*). The four 'further' *dhammas* in the *Aṅguttara*

---

[50] Vibh-a 324: *bodhi-pakkhiyānaṃ dhammānaṃ bhāvanânuyogaṃ anuyutto ti idaṃ assa paṭipattiyā nibbedha-bhāgiyatta-paridīpanaṃ.*

correspond to the greater part of the items directly associated with the *bojjhaṅgas* in the *Saṃyutta-nikāya* and according to the tradition preserved in the commentaries.[51] Of the five *indriyas* it is the faculty of wisdom that is singled out as the pinnacle of all *bodhi-pakkhiyā dhammā*.

So *bodhi* is a special variety of *jhāna*. What is special about it is the fact that it embraces a particular kind of knowledge. In discussing *bodhi-pakkhiyā dhammā* we are concerned with the particular *dhammas* that are directly involved in the cultivation of that special kind of *jhāna*. Obviously this is why the seven *bojjhaṅgas* are early on directly associated with the expression *bodhi-pakkhiyā dhammā*. Yet, also fairly clearly, there is a sense in which the perspective of the seven *bojjhaṅgas* is felt to be not quite broad enough in this respect. The *dhammas* that are directly and immediately involved in the meditation experience that is awakening are felt to be rather more far reaching than just these seven *dhammas*. The seven *bojjhaṅgas* are, after all, cultivated in a particular context. This is, in fact, precisely the significance of much of the Nikāya treatment of the seven sets: the seven *bojjhaṅgas* must be seen as existing in a reciprocal relationship with the other sets.

It begins to emerge how the notion of the thirty-seven *bodhi-pakkhiyā dhammā* constitutes one of various strands of thinking in the Nikāyas. The nature of this fusion, and just why the seven sets are brought together under the rubric 'thirty-seven *bodhi-pakkhiyā dhammā*' is something I shall return to at the conclusion of this study.

3. The commentarial exegesis

At this point it might prove helpful to consider how the explanation of the bare expression *bodhi-pakkhiyā dhammā* is taken up in the later literature. As far as the actual meaning of the expression is concerned, the paracanonical *Peṭakopadesa* and *Nettippakaraṇa* do not add substantially to its understanding. Yet these two texts do serve to underline the general Suttanta interpretation that is suggested by the canonical usage. Accordingly expressions such as 'those *dhammas* ... that conduce to *nibbāna*' and '*dhammas* that lead to awakening' are found as glosses for or in the context of discussion of *bodhi-pakkhiyā dhammā*.[52]

Before turning to the commentarial tradition proper it is worth registering the range of meanings and usages recorded for *pakṣa* in Sanskrit literature. The primary meaning of the word would seem to be 'wing';[53] it can then mean the 'flank' or 'side' of anything, and subsequently comes to denote 'a side, party, faction; multitude, number, troop, set, class of beings; partisan, adherent, follower'.[54] The usage of *pakṣa* as a collective noun denoting a group or set consisting of a number of members, and then as a way of referring to one of

---

[51] See above, pp. 179-80.

[52] Peṭ 114 (*ye dhammā ... nibbānāya saṃvattanti*); 188 (*bodha-gamaniyā dhammā*); Nett 31 (*bodhaṃ-gamā dhammā*).

[53] Cf. Mayrhofer, s.v. *pakṣa*.

[54] MW s.v. *pakṣa*. The other most important meaning of *pakṣa* is the half of a lunar month.

the members of such a set underlies, I think, what the commentaries have to say about *bodhi-pakkhiyā dhammā*. Once more we have the notion of 'awakening' as at once a single *dhamma* and the sum of an assemblage or collective of *dhammas* operating together.

The commentarial tradition preserves a number of fairly succinct analyses of the term *bodhi-pakkhiya* some of which are worth quoting in full. In the *Visuddhimagga* Buddhaghosa states:

> These thirty-seven *dhammas* [i.e. the *satipaṭṭhānas*, etc.] are called *bodhi-pakkhiyas* due to their being in the party of the noble path which has the name 'awakening' in the sense of waking up. 'Due to their being in the party', i.e. due to their being established in the condition of aiding.[55]

The *Mahā-ṭīkā* comments:

> Alternatively, awakening in the sense of waking up is the arising of the path consciousness. *Bodhi-pakkhiyas* are items in the party [of *bodhi*] due to their suitability to the waking-up-activity of this [consciousness].[56]

Presumably the point of the *Mahā-ṭīkā's* comment here is to give a slightly broader perspective. Buddhaghosa here identifies *bodha* with the noble path; that is to say, I think, the eight factors that constitute the path. *Bodhi-pakkhiyas* are then seen as those items whose relationship to the eight factors of the path is one of 'aiding', 'helping', 'supporting' or 'contributing'. The *Mahā-ṭīkā* gives an alternative view whereby *bodha* is seen as the 'arising of the path consciousness' (*magga-cittuppāda*), that is to say the whole complex of *citta* and *cetasika*, of mind and associated mental factors, that makes up the path consciousness. *Bodhi-pakkhiyas* are then seen as those items that are adapted to the particular function of this *citta*, namely awakening. The *Mahā-ṭīkā* includes in this all mental *dhammas* present at that time.

Turning to the *aṭṭhakathās*, we find the following:

> 'Of *bodhi-pakkhikā* [*dhammā*]': of items in the party of awakening; 'they are aids to the path-knowledge of *arahant*-ship' is the meaning.[57]
>
> 'Of *sambodha-pakkhikā* [*dhammā*]': of items in the party of awakening, [here] a designation for the four paths; 'they are aids' is the meaning.[58]
>
> 'Of *bodhi-pakkhiyā dhammā*': of *dhammas* that are items in the party of path-knowledge, [here] designated awakening to the four truths.[59]

The foregoing come to us by way of Buddhaghosa; Dhammapāla in the *Itivuttakaṭṭhakathā* comments:

---

[55] Vism XXII 33: *ime satta-tiṃsa dhammā bujjhanaṭṭhena bodho ti laddha-nāmassa ariya-maggassa pakkhe bhavattā bodhi-pakkhiyā nāma. pakkhe bhavattā ti upakāra-bhāve ṭhitattā.* (Cf. Paṭis-a II 482; III 618.)

[56] Vism-mhṭ (Ne) III 1606: *bujjhanaṭṭhena vā bodho magga-cittuppādo. tassa bujjhana-kiriyāya anuguṇa-bhāvato pakkhe bhavā ti bodhi-pakkhiyā.*

[57] Sp I 229: *bodhi-pakkhikānan ti bodhissa pakkhe bhavānaṃ arahatta-magga-ñāṇassa upakārakānan ti attho.*

[58] Mp IV 162: *sambodha-pakkhikānan ti catu-magga-saṃkhātassa sambodhassa pakkhe bhavānaṃ upakārakānan ti attho.*

[59] Vibh-a 346-7: *bodhi-pakkhiyānaṃ dhammānan ti catu-sacca-bodhi-saṃkhātassa magga-ñāṇassa pakkhe bhavānaṃ dhammānaṃ.*

> 'Of *bodhi-pakkhiya* [*dhamma*]': of items in the party of the noble person or just of path-knowledge which [here] have the name 'awakening' in the sense of waking up; of *bodhi-pakkhiyas*, 'of those things that belong to the set of *bodhi'* is the meaning ... 'they possess the party of *bodhi* or they are appointed to the party of *bodhi'* is the meaning.[60]

Finally, the *aṭṭhakathā* to the *Paṭisambhidāmagga* has this to say:

> 'In the sense of *bodhi-pakkhiya*': due to being in the party of the *yogin* who has the name 'awakening' in the sense of waking up. This is an indication of their aiding the *yogin*.[61]

As with the analysis of the *bojjhaṅgas*, we have a number of different perspectives on what constitutes *bodhi*; it is 'knowledge' (of the four truths), it is the 'path', it is the 'path-consciousness', it is the 'noble person'; and *bodhi-pakkhiyā dhammā* are what 'aid', 'assist' or 'support' this knowledge, this path, this path consciousness, this noble person; they cause it to succeed or prosper (*upakāraka*).[62]

The use of the term *upakāraka* in this context is not without significance, in that it possesses certain technical Abhidhamma connotations. In the Pāli commentaries the term is used especially to define and illustrate the way in which one *dhamma* can be a condition (*paccaya*) for the arising of another. The following definition is given by way of introduction to the twenty-four *paccayas* of the Theravādin Abhidhamma:

> Now as to characteristic, a *paccaya* has the characteristic of an *upakāraka*, for when one *dhamma* is an *upakāraka* either for the maintenance or for the arising [of another *dhamma*], then the one is said to be a *paccaya* for the other.[63]

The Burmese monk, U Nārada, has explained *upakāraka* as follows:

> This means that when a state is present, the other states that are connected with it will (1) arise if they have not arisen, (2) continue to exist if they have already arisen, or (3) gradually develop while in existence. The ultimate states of reality cannot make efforts on their own or plan to do so. But if one of them is present the accomplishments of the connected states are brought about.[64]

The introduction of the notion of the twenty-four *paccayas* is of some importance. If *bodhi-pakkhiyā dhammā* are *paccayas* for *bodhi*, then in what way are they *paccayas*? Which of the twenty-four *paccayas* are relevant to the relationship that exists between *bodhi-pakkhiyā dhammā* and *bodhi*? A complete answer to this question would probably have the effect of expanding the

---

[60] It-a 73-4: *bodhi-pakkhiyānan ti bujjhanaṭṭhena bodhī ti laddha-namassa ariya-puggalassa magga-ñāṇass'eva vā pakkhe bhavānaṃ; bodhi-pakkhiyānaṃ bodhi-koṭṭhāsiyānan ti attho ... bodhi-pakkha-vantānaṃ bodhi-pakkhe vā niyuttānan ti attho.*

[61] Paṭis-a III 600: *bodhi-pakkhiyaṭṭhenā ti bujjhanaṭṭhena bodho ti laddha-nāmassa yogissa pakkhe bhavattā. ayaṃ etesaṃ yogino upakāratta-niddeso.* (Cf. I 100; at II 482 and III 618 we also have a parallel to Vism XXII 33, but reading just *ariyassa* where Vism has *ariya-maggassa*.)

[62] Cf. MW s.v. *upa-kṛ*.

[63] Vism XVII 68 = Tikap-a 11-2: *lakkhaṇato-pana upakāra(ka)-lakkhaṇo paccayo. yo hi dhammo ṭhitiyā vā uppattiyā vā upakārako hoti so tassa paccayo ti vuccati.* (Cf. Abhidh-av 58; Moh 322.)

[64] Paṭṭh Trsl I xii.

present study to the infinite proportions that the *Paṭṭhāna* itself is said to possess. But a general point can be made here. The list of twenty-four *paccayas* can be considered by way of two basic aspects. The first concerns those *paccayas* that illustrate the various relationships that exist simultaneously between *dhammas* that arise together in a given assemblage or complex at a given moment in time. The second concerns those *paccayas* that focus on the relationships that exist between *dhammas* over a period of time; that is to say, the way in which a *dhamma* that arises at one time can be related to a *dhamma* that arises at another time.[65] The foregoing suggests two ways of considering *bodhi-pakkhiyā dhammā* in the Abhidhamma. First, *bodhi-pakkhiyā dhammā* arise in one moment along with *bodhi*; they assist and contribute to the event called 'awakening'—however, precisely, that is thought of. Secondly, they are prior conditions that make for the arising of *bodhi* at some point in the future. What needs to be borne in mind in turning to a consideration of the seven sets in the Abhidhamma, is how remote these conditions can be from the actual event of 'awakening' and still be meaningfully called *bodhi-pakkhiyā dhammā*. What is the accepted Abhidhamma usage?

Before turning to the Abhidhamma treatment of the seven sets, it is worth noting some definitions of *bodhi-pākṣikā dharmāḥ* from the northern tradition. Lamotte quotes the following *Vibhāṣā* definition:

> Pourquoi sont-ils nommés *bodhipākṣika*? Les deux savoirs du saint, le savoir de la destruction des impuretés (*āśravakṣayajñāna*) et le savoir que celles-ci ne renaîtront plus (*anutpādajñāna*) recoivent le nom de Bodhi parce qu'ils comportent l'intelligence complète des quatre verités. Si un dharma est favorable à cette intelligence complète il reçoit le nom de *bodhipākṣika*.[66]

Vasubandhu gives the following:

> [*Bodhi* is] knowledge of destruction and knowledge of non-rising. By division of persons three *bodhis* arise: *śrāvaka-bodhi*, *pratyeka-bodhi* and unsurpassable *samyak-sambodhi* ... **Due to their being adapted to this [i.e. *bodhi*] there are thirty-seven in its party**—because of being adapted to *bodhi*, thirty-seven [*dharmas*] belonging to the party of *bodhi* arise.[67]

Finally the author of the *Abhidharmadīpa* states:

> Moreover this *bodhi*, which consists of knowledge of destruction and of non-arising, divides into three by means of the division of persons. The three *bodhis* are those of

[65] The first aspect is illustrated especially by the *paccayas* of conascence (*sahajāta*), reciprocity (*aññam-añña*), association (*sampayutta*), presence (*atthi*), non-departure (*avigata*); the second aspect by precedence (*anantara*), immediate precedence (*samanantara*), strong remote support (*upanissaya*), prior nascence (*pure-jāta*), posterior nascence (*paccha-jāta*), repetition (*āsevana*), dissociation (*vippayutta*), absence (*natthi*), departure (*vigata*). A number of the twenty-four *paccayas* cover both these two aspects either because of subvarieties or particular circumstances that mean that a given relationship can exist both between conascent (*sahajāta*) *dhammas* and *dhammas* that arise at different moments (*nāna-kkhaṇika*). Cf. F. Lottermoser, 'The Doctrine of Relationship (*Paṭṭhāna*)', unpublished MA thesis, University of Mandalay, 1969/70.

[66] Lamotte, *Traité*, III 1119.

[67] Abhidh-k 383: *kṣaya-jñānam anutpāda-jñanaṃ ca. pudgala-bhedena tisro bodhaya utpadyante, śrāvaka-bodhiḥ pratyeka-bodhir anuttarā samyaksambodhir iti* ... ***tadanulomyataḥ saptatriṃśat tu tat-pakṣyāḥ*** *bodher anulomatvād bodhi-pakṣyāḥ saptatriṃṣad utpadyante.*

a Buddha, *pratyeka-buddha* and *śrāvaka* [respectively] ... The *dharmas* that incline towards these three kinds of *bodhi* are namely the thirty-seven, beginning with the *smṛty-upasthānas*.[68]

The rather more restricted definition of *bodhi* in northern sources has already been noted. The usage of such terms as *anuloma* ('adapted to') and *anukūla* ('inclining to') where in the Pāli commentaries we seem to have *upakāraka* is of some interest, for it appears to parallel something we find in the *Vimuttimagga*. In the *Vimuttimagga* account of the final stages of the path (as in the *Visuddhimagga* account) knowledge of the path of stream attainment is immediately preceded by 'adaptive knowledge' (*anuloma-ñāṇa*) and 'knowledge of the state of lineage' (*gotra-bhū-ñāṇa*).[69] It is at the stage of *anuloma-ñāṇa* that the thirty-seven *bodhi-pakkhiyā dhammā* begin to come into their own:

> Q. What is adaptive knowledge? The knowledge which conforms to the four foundations of mindfulness ... and the factors of the Noble Eightfold Path.[70]

All this suggests that we should not be misled by English translations such as 'helping', 'aiding', 'favourable to', 'conducive to' and so on, into thinking that the relationship between *bodhi-pakkhiyā dhammā* and *bodhi* is one of rather vaguely and generally assisting in the bringing about of awakening. On the contrary, they appear to be thought of as rather closely and definitely related to *bodhi*. In conclusion '*dhammas* that contribute to awakening' would seem to be a generally applicable translation of the expression, which is neither too imprecise nor too technical.

---

[68] Abhidh-dī 357-8: *sā punar eṣā bodhiḥ kṣayânutpāda-jñāna-rūpā satī pudgala-bhedena tridhā bhidyate. tisro bodhayaḥ buddha-pratyeka-buddha-śrāvaka-bodhayaḥ ... tasyāḥ punas tri-prakārāyā bodher anukūla-dharmāḥ smṛty-upasthānâdayaḥ sapta-triṃśan nāmataḥ.*

[69] It is not quite clear from the text whether or not Vimutt here sees these as momentary in the way Vism does; cf. below, p. 334.

[70] Vimutt Trsl 301. Cf. below, pp. 334-5.

CHAPTER TEN

THE SEVEN SETS IN THE ABHIDHAMMA

1. The Visuddhimagga: the classic developed account

In the previous chapter I discussed the meaning of the term *bodhi-pakkhiya* both in the Nikāyas and the later literature without too much regard for the specific association of the term with the seven sets in the paracanonical and postcanonical literature. What I wish to do now is to consider directly the treatment of the seven sets collectively in the Pāli Abhidhamma, both canonical and commentarial. Rather than beginning with the canonical Abhidhamma, the most convenient course to follow is to begin with Buddhaghosa's standard account of the thirty-seven *bodhi-pakkhiyā dhammā* in chapter twenty-two of the *Visuddhimagga*.[1] This can then serve as a point of reference when dealing with the canonical Abhidhamma texts. I have already had occasion to refer to what this section of the *Visuddhimagga* has to say about the seven sets individually; now the picture needs to be completed by an account of what it has to say about the seven collectively.

The relevant section is introduced under the heading *bodhi-pakkhiyānaṃ paripuṇṇa-bhāvo*—'the fulfilment of the things that contribute to awakening'. This heading itself is suggestive. We are concerned here with the arising of the four kinds of path knowledge. These four knowledges are thus seen as representing the fulfilment of the various conditions that contribute to awakening. Having discussed each of the sets in turn, Buddhaghosa then says:

> In the prior stage [i.e. the stage prior to the arising of the transcendent path] when ordinary insight occurs, these thirty-seven *dhammas* are found in a series of consciousnesses in the following way. For one apprehending the body in the fourteen ways [described in the *Satipaṭṭhāna-sutta*], there is the *satipaṭṭhāna* of watching body; for one apprehending feeling in the nine ways, there is the *satipaṭṭhāna* of watching feeling; for one apprehending mind in the sixteen ways, there is the *satipaṭṭhāna* of watching mind; for one apprehending *dhammas* in the five ways, there is the *satipaṭṭhāna* of watching *dhammas*. For one who sees that there has arisen in another unskilfulness that is previously unarisen in himself, and thinks: 'It has arisen in one practising thus, I will not practise thus, and it will not arise in me'—for such a one at the time of striving thus for the non-arising [of unskilful *dhammas*], there is the first *samma-ppadhāna*; for one who sees unskilfulness pertaining to his own behaviour, at the time of striving for [its] abandoning, there is the second; for one striving to arouse in himself previously unarisen *jhāna* or insight, there is the third; for one arousing again and again what has thus arisen so that it does not decay, there is the fourth *samma-ppadhāna*. At the time of

[1] It seems reasonable to regard Vism XXII 33-43 as the standard commentarial account; it is presumably what is referred to as the full discussion of the *bodhi-pakkhiyas* at Ps III 255 (*ayaṃ ettha saṃkhepo vitthārato panâyaṃ bodha-pakkhiya-kathā Visuddhimagge vuttā*); cf. Sv II 564 (*etesaṃ pana bodhi-pakkhiya-dhammānaṃ vinicchayo sabbâkārena Visuddhimagge ñāṇa-dassana-visuddhi-niddese vutto*). Mahānāma also follows it, apart from a number of minor variations, at Paṭis-a III 618-20.

arousing skilfulness having made *chanda* chief, there is *chandiddhi-pāda*, [and similarly for *viriyiddhi-pāda*, *cittiddhi-pāda* and *vīmaṃsiddhi-pāda*]. At the time of refraining from wrong speech, there is right speech, [and similarly for wrong-action and wrong-livelihood]. But at the time of the arising of the four knowledges [i.e. the four path-knowledges] [these thirty-seven *dhammas*] are found in a single consciousness. At the moment of fruition, leaving aside the four *samma-ppadhānas*, the remaining thirty-three are found.[2]

When they are found in a single consciousness in this way, just the one mindfulness which has *nibbāna* as its object is called 'four *satipaṭṭhānas*' by virtue of its accomplishing the function of abandoning the notions of beauty, etc. with regard to body, etc. And just the one strength is called 'four *samma-ppadhānas*' by virtue of its accomplishing the function of non-arising of things not arisen, and so on. As for the remaining [items] there is no decrease or increase.[3]

Buddhaghosa continues with a mnemonic verse:

> Nine in one way, one in two ways, and in four and five ways; and in eight ways, and in nine ways—thus they are in six ways.[4]

The explanation of this verse can be conveniently set out as follows:

(i) **nine in one way**
chanda — iddhi-pāda
citta — iddhi-pāda
pīti — bojjhaṅga
passaddhi — bojjhaṅga
upekkhā — bojjhaṅga
saṃkappa — maggaṅga
vācā — maggaṅga
kammanta — maggaṅga
ājīva — maggaṅga

(ii) **one in two ways**
saddhā — bala, indriya

---

[2] Vism XXII 39: *iti ime satta-tiṃsa bodhi-pakkhiyā dhammā pubba-bhāge lokiya-vipassanāya vattamānāya cuddasa-vidhena kāyaṃ pariganhato ca kāyânupassanā-satipaṭṭhānaṃ nava-vidhena vedanaṃ pariganhato ca vedanânupassanā-satipaṭṭhānaṃ soḷasa-vidhena cittaṃ pariganhato ca cittânupassanā-satipaṭṭhānaṃ, pañca-vidhena dhamme pariganhato ca dhammânupassanā-satipaṭṭhānaṃ; imasmiṃ atta-bhāve anuppanna-pubbaṃ parassa uppannaṃ akusalaṃ disvā, yathā paṭipannass' etaṃ uppannaṃ, na tathā paṭipajjissāmi, evaṃ me etaṃ n'uppajjissatī ti tassa anuppādāya vāyamana-kāle paṭhamaṃ samma-ppadhānaṃ, attano samudācāra-ppattaṃ akusalaṃ disvā tassa pahānāya vāyamana-kāle dutiyaṃ, imasmiṃ atta-bhāve anuppanna-pubbaṃ jhānaṃ vā vipassanaṃ vā uppādetuṃ vāyamantassa tatiyaṃ, uppannaṃ yathā na parihāyati evaṃ punap-punaṃ uppādentassa catutthaṃ samma-ppadhānaṃ; chandaṃ dhuraṃ katvā kusaluppādana-kāle chandiddhi-pādo, micchā-vācāya viramaṇa-kāle sammā-vācā ti evaṃ nānā-cittesu labbhanti; imesaṃ pana catunnaṃ ñāṇānaṃ uppatti-kāle eka-citte labbhanti phala-kkhaṇe ṭhapetvā cattāro samma-ppadhāne avasesā te-ttiṃsa labbhanti.* (In the above the remaining *iddhi-pādas* and *viratis* are to be supplied according to Vism-mhṭ (Ne) III 1610.)

[3] Vism XXII 40: *evaṃ eka-citte labbhamānesu c'etesu ekā vā nibbānârammaṇā sati kāyâdīsu subha-saññâdi-pahāna-kicca-sādhana-vasena cattāro satipaṭṭhānā ti vuccati; ekaṃ eva ca viriyaṃ anuppannānaṃ anuppādâdi-kicca-sādhana-vasena cattāro samma-ppadhānā ti vuccati. sesesu pana hāpana-vaddhanaṃ natthi.*

[4] Vism XXII 41: *nava eka-vidhā eko dvedhâtha catu-pañcadhā| aṭṭhadhā navadhā c'eva iti chadhā bhavanti te||*

(iii) **one in four ways**
samādhi — *indriya, bala, bojjhaṅga, maggaṅga*

(iv) **one in five ways**
paññā — *iddhi-pāda* (*vīmaṃsā*), *indriya, bala, bojjhaṅga* (*dhamma-vicaya*), *maggaṅga* (*sammā-diṭṭhi*)

(v) **one in eight ways**
sati — *satipaṭṭhāna* (× 4), *indriya, bala, bojjhaṅga, maggaṅga*

(vi) **one in nine ways**
viriya — *samma-ppadhāna* (× 4), *iddhi-pāda, indriya, bala, bojjhaṅga, maggaṅga*

Buddhaghosa concludes with some further verses:

> Without division there are just fourteen items that contribute to awakening; by way of sets they are sevenfold, by way of division they are thirty-seven.
>
> Because of performing an individual function and because of similarity in occurrence, they are all produced in the production of the noble path.[5]

With the exception of the identification of *vīmaṃsā* with *paññā*,[6] the basic correspondences involved here are all explicit in the four Nikāyas. The Sarvāstivādin based northern texts arrive at a slightly different breakdown of the thirty-seven *dharmas*, but this is due to other considerations.[7]

A number of questions arise from Buddhaghosa's account: (i) What precisely is the nature of the different consciousnesses that give rise to the thirty-seven *bodhi-pakkhiyā dhammā* in the stage prior to the arising of the transcendent path? In what kind of ordinary *lokiya* consciousness exactly are *bodhi-pakkhiyā dhammā* present? (ii) What precisely is the significance of the fact that only the first three sets and the three kinds of refraining are detailed with regard to *bodhi-pakkhiyā dhammā* that are *lokiya*? (iii) Why are the four *samma-ppadhānas* excluded from the fruit moment? (iv) A point is made of the fact that the one *sati* and the one *viriya* are termed 'four *satipaṭṭhānas*' and 'four *samma-ppadhānas*' respectively at the *lokuttara* path moment, but how precisely are we to understand the occurrence of all four *iddhi-pādas* in a single consciousness?

For the moment I shall restrict my comments to matters that relate to questions (ii) and (iv). If one considers for a moment the point that at the moment of the *lokuttara* path it is the one *sati* and the one *viriya* that is regarded as the fulfilment of all four *satipaṭṭhānas* and all four *samma-ppadhānas*, together with the fact that Buddhaghosa details only the first three sets and the three path factors of right speech, action and livelihood, then what is going on is clear enough. As I have discussed above, according to the

---

[5] Vism XXII 43: *cuddas'eva asambhinnā hont'ete bodhi-pakkhiyā/ koṭṭhāsato satta-vidhā satta-tiṃsa pabhedato// sakicca-nipphādanato sarūpena ca vuttito/ sabbe va ariya-maggassa sambhave sambhavanti te//*

[6] This is made in the *Vibhaṅga*.

[7] See below, p. 3387.

commentaries (apparently following the *Dhammasaṅgaṇi*) the only times that all three kinds of refraining (*virati*) occur in a single moment of consciousness is at the time of the occurrence of the four transcendent path and fruit types of consciousness. In a sense the presence of all three of these factors is precisely what defines the *citta* as transcendent. Ordinarily, at a given time, the mind refrains from only one of wrong speech, wrong action, wrong livelihood. In a rather similar way, then, mindfulness found in a single moment of *lokiya* consciousness is regarded as mindfulness concerned with the body, or with feeling, or with mind, or with *dhammas*—but it cannot be concerned with all four at once. What Buddhaghosa seems to be saying here is that as the practitioner develops *vipassanā* any given arising of *sati* takes only one object at a time. This object will be classifiable as *rūpa-kkhandha* (first *satipaṭṭhāna*), *vedanā-kkhandha* (second *satipaṭṭhāna*), *viññāṇa-kkhandha* (third *satipaṭṭhāna*), or *saññā-kkhandha* or *saṃkhāra-kkhandha* (fourth *satipaṭṭhāna*).[8] However, when the mind is transcendent, when its object is *nibbāna*, it cannot be understood by way of just one of the *satipaṭṭhānas*, for *nibbāna* is not *rūpa*, not *vedanā*, not *viññāṇa*, not *saññā*, not *saṃkhāras*. But this is to be viewed, not as the absence of the *satipaṭṭhānas*, but as the occurrence of all four *satipaṭṭhānas* together. The implications of this are rather interesting. Making the same point the other way round, we can say that in the fulfilment of the *satipaṭṭhānas*, the object of the mind ceases to be body, feeling, mind, ideas and formations but becomes *nibbāna*. This is particularly important for the understanding of the fourth *satipaṭṭhāna*, namely watching *dhammas* or *dhamma* (*dhammânupassanā*). In a sense the practice of all the *satipaṭṭhānas* involves the watching of *dhammas*—*rūpas*, *vedanās*, *cittas* are no less *dhammas* than are *saññās* and *saṃkhāras*, than are *nīvaraṇas* and *bojjhaṅgas*. However, it is only when they are truly seen as *dhammas*, rising and falling, that there is *dhammânupassanā*; at that stage the point seems to be that practitioner sees not *dhammas* so much as *dhamma* itself, which, it seems, amounts to seeing *nibbāna*. This fits with the Nikāya notion that all four *satipaṭṭhānas* are fulfilled in *ānâpāna-sati*: what begins as *ānâpāna-sati* or *kāyânupassanā* gradually transforms itself into *dhammânupassanā*. To sum up, in ordinary *citta* the four *satipaṭṭhānas* are mutually exclusive, and the fact that *sati* only fulfils the role of one *satipaṭṭhāna* is what defines *citta* as ordinary.[9]

Buddhaghosa's comments suggest that in the same way the four modes of *samma-ppadhāna* are also viewed as mutually exclusive in the case of a single moment of *lokiya* consciousness. Similarly, since only one of *chanda*, *viriya*, *citta* and *vīmaṃsā* can operate as *adhipati* at any given time, the four *iddhipādas* too are viewed as mutually exclusive in a single moment of *lokiya* consciousness. What this means is that what in general distinguishes ordinary *lokiya* consciousness from *lokuttara* as far as *bodhi-pakkhiyā dhammā* are

[8] This applies generally to the practice of *vipassanā*; in the case of *samatha*, at the time of the occurrence of *rūpâvacara-jjhāna* and the first and third formless attainments the object of the mind is considered to be *paññatti* or 'concept'; in the case of the second and fourth formless attainments it is the *citta* of the previous formless attainment.

[9] Cf. Chapter 10.4.

concerned, is the fact that at any given time only a maximum of twenty-six may be found.[10] Transcendent *citta* is thus the kind of consciousness that completes or fulfils the conditions that contribute to awakening: all thirty-seven are found.[11]

All this makes all the more curious Buddhaghosa's failure to comment on what is involved in the notion of all four *iddhi-pādas* being present in a single moment of transcendent consciousness. With such questions in mind, I wish now to turn to the seven sets in the canonical Abhidhamma works.

2. *The Paṭisambhidāmagga*

The *Paṭisambhidāmagga* clearly belongs to a rather late stratum of the Pāli canon.[12] It has been suggested[13] that its rightful home is the *Abhidhamma-piṭaka* and not the *Khuddaka-nikāya* of the *Sutta-piṭaka*. Of course this depends on what we understand to be the necessary features of an 'abhidhamma' text. It would be difficult to relate the *Paṭisambhidāmagga* directly to the unified system of thought that seems to underlie the *Dhammasaṅgaṇi*, *Vibhaṅga*, *Dhātukathā* and *Paṭṭhāna*, neither does it seem that its method could be rightly characterized as 'without regard for exposition' (*nippariyāyena*). But to view Abhidhamma in its early phase as exclusively concerned with such a system of thought is perhaps to be too much influenced by the method of the later manuals such as the *Abhidhammatthasaṃgaha*. The *Paṭisambhidāmagga* is perhaps indicative of an early Abhidhamma technique of providing extended improvisations on Suttanta themes. These themes are woven into a pattern so intricate that it becomes impossible to unravel, at least formally. One of the threads woven into the pattern by the *Paṭisambhidāmagga* is spun of the seven sets. In what follows I shall make some attempt to trace its course.

The seven sets are immediately in evidence among the titles of the thirty 'talks' (*kathā*) that make up the *Paṭisambhidāmagga*, only the *samma-ppadhānas* are without their own 'talk'. Yet there seems to be no discernable system to the way in which the seven sets are treated. They are not treated in a block, and their order is without precedent. In fact, the way they are picked out seems almost deliberately haphazard, and there appears to be no common method to their treatment in their respective *kathās*; on the contrary, the 'talks' seem intentionally designed to treat their subject matter in different and not entirely expected ways. The *indriya-kathā* (IV) concerns itself exclusively with the five spiritual *indriyas* (there is no mention of the other seventeen) but does bring in all seven sets at the close. The *magga-kathā* (IX) discusses the four paths and eight path-factors; again all seven sets are brought in. The *bojjhaṅga-kathā*

---

10 One *satipaṭṭhāna*, one *samma-ppadhāna*, one *iddhi-pāda*, five *indriyas*, five *balas*, seven *bojjhaṅgas*, six *maggaṅgas*.

11 Following the principle that *lokuttara-citta* corresponds to a level of concentration equal to *rūpâvacara-jjhāna*, thirty-seven is a maximum that can be reduced by two: *pīti* and *sammā-saṃkappa* (= *vitakka*) are absent above the levels of the third and first *jhānas* respectively (cf. below, p. 331, n. 102).

12 Cf. Norman, *PL*, p. 87; A.K. Warder's introduction to Ñāṇamoli, Paṭis Trsl xxxiii-iv.

13 Paṭis II iv; Paṭis Trsl xxxiii; cf. Frauwallner, *WZKS* 16 (1972), pp. 124-32.

(XIII) concerns the *bojjhaṅgas* again bringing in all seven sets. The *bala-kathā* (XIX) begins with an account of the five *balas* but then immediately moves on simply to define the individual items in a list of sixty-eight *balas*. The *iddhi-kathā* (XXII) discusses ten kinds of *iddhi* and includes an account of the *iddhi-pādas*. Finally, the *satipaṭṭhāna-kathā* gives a fairly straightforward but in certain respects distinctive account of the *satipaṭṭhānas*.

While from this it might seem that the seven sets receive a somewhat incomplete and uneven treatment, when the *Paṭisambhidāmagga* is taken as a whole it is clear that the seven sets are in fact rather central to its system. In all, the sequence of seven sets features in twelve of the thirty *kathās*, and in some repeatedly.[14] Of the references to the seven sets that constitute isolated and self-contained statements or treatments[15] two can be singled out. First, there is the general Abhidhamma type direct association of the seven sets with the four transcendent paths and fruits:

> Which *dhammas* are transcendent? The four establishings of mindfulness, the four right endeavours, the four bases of success, the five faculties, the five powers, the seven awakening-factors, the noble eight-factored path, the four noble paths, the four fruits of *samaṇa*-ship and *nibbāna*—these *dhammas* are transcendent.[16]

Secondly, in the 'talk on the fine extract to be drunk' (*maṇḍapeyya-kathā*) it is the seven sets along with the four noble truths that are singled out as the 'fine extract' or 'distilled essence' of the teaching (*desanā*).[17] This shows clearly that the seven sets were taken by the *Paṭisambhidāmagga* as the central core of the Buddha's teaching.

Apart from these isolated passages the *Paṭisambhidāmagga's* treatment of the seven sets revolves around an extended list that I have already referred to. What I found convenient to treat as two lists (A and B) in chapter eight,[18] in fact in certain contexts form parts of one extended composite list. This full list (hereafter C) would appear to occur seven times in the whole of the *Paṭisambhidāmagga*.[19] I calculate that list C contains a total of 382/386 items.[20] The list is of such a nature that certain items are continually recalled or returned to in various ways. Associated with each of the items in the list is an *attha*; that is, a 'meaning', 'aim', 'purpose', 'objective' or even 'effect'.[21] The initial exposition

---

[14] The twelve are the *ñāṇa-kathā* (I), *ānâpāna-kathā* (III), *indriya-kathā* (IV), *vimokkha-kathā* (V), *magga-kathā* (IX), *maṇḍapeyya-kathā* (X), *bojjhaṅga-kathā* (XIII), *dhammacakka-kathā* (XVII), *lokuttara-kathā* (XVIII), *mahā-paññā* (XXI), *abhisamaya-kathā* (XXIII).

[15] I.e. Paṭis II 56, 86, 166, 190-3, 198-200.

[16] Paṭis II 166: *katame dhammā lokuttarā. cattāro satipaṭṭhānā ... ariyo aṭṭhaṅgiko maggo cattāro ariya-maggā cattāri ca sāmañña-phalāni nibbānañ ca ime dhammā lokuttarā.*

[17] Paṭis II 86; the *ariyo aṭṭhaṅgiko maggo* is the 'distilled essence' of the spiritual life (*brahma-cariya*) itself (cf. the conclusions of Chapter 6).

[18] See pp. 270-2.

[19] Paṭis I 15-22, 23, 27, 34, 35; II 118-25. This adds up to 6 times in the *ñāṇa-kathā* (5 times lost in *peyyālas*; cf. Paṭis Trsl) and once in the *bojjhaṅga-kathā*.

[20] forty-four miscellaneous items; forty-five items of list A; ten miscellaneous; fifteen based on *citta*; forty-two based on *ekatta*; twenty miscellaneous; forty based on *chanda, viriya, citta, vīmaṃsā*; sixteen/twenty based on four truths; fifty-four miscellaneous, fifty-four items of list B.

[21] Cf. A.K. Warder's discussion, Paṭis Trsl x-xi. Paṭis seems to deliberately play on the usage of *attha*; its general meaning in Paṭis seems to amount to 'nature'.

TABLE 10. THE PAṬISAMBHIDĀMAGGA AṬṬHAS FOR THE SEVEN SETS

saddhindriya	commitment (*adhimokkha*)
viriyindriya	taking on (*paggaha*)
satindriya	standing near (*upaṭṭhāna*)
samādhindriya	non-distraction (*avikkhepa*)
paññindriya	seeing (*dassana*)
saddhā-bala	that which is unshakeable by distrust (*assaddhiye akampiyaṃ*)
viriya-bala	that which is unshakeable by laziness (*kosajja*)
sati-bala	that which is unshakeable by heedlessness (*pamāda*)
samādhi-bala	that which is unshakeable by agitation (*uddhacca*)
paññā-bala	that which is unshakeable by ignorance (*avijjā*)
sati-sambojjhaṅga	standing near
dhamma-vicaya-sambojjhaṅga	discrimination (*pavicaya*)
viriya-sambojjhaṅga	taking on
pīti-sambojjhaṅga	suffusing (*pharaṇa*)
passaddhi-sambojjhaṅga	peace (*upasama*)
samādhi-sambojjhaṅga	non-distraction
upekkhā-sambojjhaṅga	judgement (*paṭisaṃkhāna*)
sammā-diṭṭhi	seeing
sammā-saṃkappa	setting [one's thought] on [something] (*abhiniropana*)
sammā-vācā	embracing (*pariggaha*)
sammā-kammanta	undertaking (*samuṭṭhāna*)
sammā-ājīva	cleansing (*vodana*)
sammā-vāyāma	taking on
sammā-sati	standing near
sammā-samādhi	non-distraction
indriya	overlordship (*adhipateyya*)
bala	that which is unshakeable
bojjhaṅga	leading out (*niyyāna*)
magga	cause (*hetu*)
satipaṭṭhāna	standing near
samma-ppadhāna	endeavouring (*padhāna*)
iddhi-pāda	succeeding (*ijjhana*)

N.B. For the last seven items cf. As 237: *niyyānaṭṭhena* is given for *magga* (though *hetvaṭṭhena* is added at As 154) and *bujjhanaṭṭhena* for the *bojjhaṅgas*.

of the list in the *ñāṇa-kathā* states that the *aṭṭha* of each item is 'to be directly known' (*abhiññeyya*). As the list unfolds it becomes apparent how the *aṭṭha* of certain items is to be directly known in terms of other items in the list.[22] The items directly associated with the seven sets, which I have in places already referred to, are set out in full at the end of this section. The next exposition states that the *aṭṭhas* are to be fully known (*pariññeyya*); next seeing the *aṭṭhas* one abandons (*passanto pajahati*); seeing the *aṭṭhas* one develops (*passanto bhāveti*); seeing the *aṭṭhas* one realizes (*passanto sacchikaroti*). In the seventh and final exposition in the *bojjhaṅga-kathā*, the *bojjhaṅgas* are what awake to (*bujjhanti*) the various *aṭṭhas*. Rather more regularly in the *Paṭisambhidāmagga* the concluding portion of list C is focused upon; this consists of the fifty-four items of list B (i and ii).[23] In the *ñāṇa-kathā* we are told that at the moment of each of the four paths and four fruits each of the fifty-four items is 'then come forth' by means of its particular *aṭṭha* (e.g. *sotâpatti-magga-kkhaṇe dassanaṭṭh-ena sammā-diṭṭhi tadā samudāgatā*). In the *ānâpāna-kathā* as a *bhikkhu* knows one-pointedness of mind by way of each of the sixteen stages (*vatthu*) of mindfulness of breathing, he 'applies' or 'connects' each of the fifty-four items by means of its *aṭṭha* (e.g. *adhimokkhaṭṭhena saddhindriyaṃ samodhāneti*).[24] In the *magga-kathā* the form is rather different. Right view is not to be known, or whatever, 'by means of its aim of seeing' or 'in the sense of seeing', rather the path of seeing is right view (*dassana-maggo sammā-diṭṭhi*), the path of setting [one's thought] on [something] is right thought (*abhiropana-maggo sammā-saṃkappo*), and so on for the rest of the individual path-factors, awakening-factors, powers and faculties. However, in the sense of overlordship the faculties are the path (*adhipateyyaṭṭhena indriyaṃ maggo*), *nibbāna* that plunges into the deathless is the path in the sense of conclusion (*amatogadhaṃ nibbānam pariyosānaṭṭhena maggo*).[25] The same pattern is followed in the *maṇḍpeyya-kathā*: the distilled essence of seeing is right view (*dassana-maṇḍo sammā-diṭṭhi*), in the sense of overlordship the faculties are the distilled essence (*adhipateyyaṭṭhena indriyaṃ maṇḍo*), *nibbāna* that plunges into the deathless is the distilled essence in the sense of conclusion (*amatogadhaṃ nibbānaṃ pariy-osanaṭṭhena maṇḍo*).[26]

In certain contexts the individual *indriyas*, *balas*, *bojjhaṅgas* and *maggaṅgas*

---

[22] E.g. *avikkhepaṭṭho abhiññeyyo* (Paṭis I 15.23); *samādhindriyassa avikkhepaṭṭho abhiññeyyo* (Paṭis I 16.16-7); *avikkhepaṭṭhena samādhindriyaṃ abhiññeyyaṃ* (Paṭis I 21.6-7); *niyyānaṭṭho abhiññeyyo* (Paṭis I 16.2); *bojjhaṅgānaṃ niyyānaṭṭho abhiññeyyo* (Paṭis I 17.5-6); *cittassa niyyān-aṭṭho abhiññeyyo* (Paṭis I 17.31-2).

[23] Paṭis I 73-6 (× 8), 180-94 (× 16); II 29, 84-5, 90-1, 142-3 (× 2), 145-6 (× 2), 160-5 (× 6), 216-7 (× 9). This adds up to a total of 48 times.

[24] Cf. correction to PTS text at Paṭis Trsl 207 n. 21. The same formula is used in the *indriya-kathā*; again cf. correction to PTS text at Paṭis Trsl 235 n. 9-10.

[25] Cf. Paṭis II 143, 146 where the same formula is used for two of the rehearsals of list B in the *virāga-kathā*.

[26] Cf. The *virāga-kathā*: 'the dispassion of seeing is right view' (*dassana-virāgo sammā-diṭṭhi*), etc., 'the freedom (*vimutti*) of seeing is right view', etc.; the *dhammacakka-kathā*: 'the faculty of trust is *dhamma*, he sets that *dhamma* in motion' (*saddhindriyaṃ dhammo, taṃ dhammaṃ pavatteti*), etc.; the *abhisamaya-kathā*: 'the convergence of seeing is right view', etc. ('convergence' is Ñāṇamoli's translation of *abhisamaya*).

are itemized and the other sets left out of the reckoning,[27] presumably because they cannot be individualized in quite this way. One treatment is of particular interest in that it attempts to bring out the unity of the various items embraced by these four sets:

> What is the development of the one taste? For one who develops the faculty of trust in the sense of commitment, four faculties have one taste by virtue of the faculty of trust. This is the development of the faculties in the sense of one taste. For one who develops the faculty of strength ... For one who develops right concentration in the sense of non-distraction, seven path-factors have one taste by virtue of right-concentration. This is the development of the path-factors in the sense of one taste. This is the development of the one taste.[28]

The *Paṭisambhidāmagga* is a frustrating text to use if one is trying to cull specific facts and pieces of information from its pages. This is well illustrated by the *bojjhaṅga-kathā*, which begins by simply listing the seven *bojjhaṅgas*. It then asks in what sense they are *bojjhaṅgas* (*kenaṭṭhena bojjhaṅga*). Nearly the whole of the *kathā* is devoted to answering this question. I have counted that there are in fact 609 answers—that is, 609 senses in which the *bojjhaṅgas* are *bojjhaṅgas*. The initial twenty-seven centre around words and notions derived from the root *budh*, but the next 200 range rather wider. These are followed by answers based on the 382 items of the full list C. In short, the *Paṭisambhidāmagga* appears to relate the *bojjhaṅgas* to everything it can think of.

In order to begin to make sense of its method, it appears that one needs to ask not so much what it says but what it does. It is clear that in the *Paṭisambhidāmagga* the full list C, and especially its final portion (= list B) is intended to focus on the path to awakening in general, and the nature of the awakening experience in particular—list B is consistently related to the transcendent stages. One thing that seems to follow from the *Paṭisambhidāmagga's* method is that the awakening experience must be understood as an experience of many different dimensions and many different aspects. It is an experience of many facets and subtleties. It is an experience of great richness and, above all, of great depth. It is sometimes suggested that one of the universals of mystical literature is the claim that the highest mystical experience is ineffable, beyond language. The effect of the *Paṭisambhidāmagga's* treatment is not entirely dissimilar. So much is said about the awakening experience, that what is said defies simple description. In this respect its technique has something in common with some of the *prajñāpāramitā* texts.

At the same time as suggesting the richness and depth of the awakening experience the *Paṭisambhidāmagga* also suggests something of its simplicity. All the different dimensions are woven into a coherent whole. All the different aspects simply follow from the fullness and completeness of what is yet one

---

[27] Paṭis I 28-30, 88-91; II 86-8, 88-90, 132-9, 219-24.

[28] Paṭis I 28-30: *katamā eka-rasa-bhāvanā. adhimokkhaṭṭhena saddhindriyaṃ bhāvayato saddhindriyassa vasena cattāri indriyāni eka-rasā hontī ti indriyānaṃ eka-rasaṭṭhena bhāvanā. paggahaṭṭhena viriyindriyaṃ bhāvayato ... avikkhepaṭṭhena sammā-samādhiṃ bhāvayato sammā-samādhissa vasena satta maggaṅga eka-rasā hontī ti maggaṅgānaṃ eka-rasaṭṭhena bhāvanā. ayaṃ eka-rasa-bhāvanā.*

simple moment of 'awakening'. The *Paṭisambhidāmagga* is thus a classic *ekâbhisamaya* text.[29] The awakening experience is simple, unitary, self-contained and complete in itself. Even so the constitution of the extended lists in the *Paṭisambhidāmagga* shows how the awakening experience is related to the whole of the teaching, to the whole of the path from beginning to end. The *Paṭisambhidāmagga* thus develops a way of thinking that I have already suggested is inherent in the understanding of the noble eight-factored path in the four Nikāyas and later finds expression in Buddhaghosa's treatment of the moment of the transcendent path as the fulfilment of that which contributes to awakening (*bodhipakkhiya-paripuṇṇa-bhāva*).

3. The seven sets in the Dhammasaṅgaṇi

The portion of the *Dhammasaṅgaṇi* that is relevant here is 'the section on the arising of consciousness' (*cittuppāda-kaṇḍa*).[30] This takes the form of an analysis of different varieties of consciousness (*citta*) according to the divisions of the first triplet (*tika*) of the Abhidhamma *mātikā*: *dhammas* that are skilful (*kusala*); *dhammas* that are unskilful (*akusala*); *dhammas* that are undetermined (*avyākata*). The *Dhammasaṅgaṇi's* analysis in this respect falls into fourteen basic parts:

kusala

(1) *kāmâvacara-kusala* [Dhs 9-30]
(2) *rūpâvacara-kusala* [Dhs 31-55]
(3) *arūpâvacara-kusala* [Dhs 55-6]
(4) × *adhipati* [Dhs 56-60]
(5) *lokuttara* [Dhs 60-75]

akusala

(6) *kāmâvacara-akusala* [Dhs 75-87]

avyākata

(7) *kāmâvacara-kusala-vipāka* [Dhs 87-97]
(8) *rūpâvacara-kusala-vipāka* [Dhs 97]
(9) *arūpâvacara-kusala-vipāka* [Dhs 97-9]
(10) *lokuttara-vipāka* [Dhs 99-117]
(11) *kāmâvacara-akusala-vipāka* [Dhs 117-20]
(12) *kāmâvacara-kiriya* [Dhs 120-3]
(13) *rūpâvacara-kiriya* [Dhs 123]
(14) *arūpâvacara-kiriya* [Dhs 123-4]

Each of these fourteen basic parts of the *cittuppāda-kaṇḍa* details a number of different kinds of *citta* distinguished according to various principles. Each kind of *citta* that is distinguished is treated in the text by way of what the commentary calls three 'great sections' (*mahā-vāra*):[31] the section that deter-

---

[29] Cf. A.K. Warder's comments, Paṭis Trsl xxv.
[30] Dhs 9-124.
[31] As 55.

mines *dhammas* (*dhamma-vavatthāna*); the section of groups (*saṃgaha*) or sets (*koṭṭhāsa*), and the section on emptiness (*suññata*). In the text of the *Dhammasaṅgaṇi* these three great sections are indicated and fully elaborated only in the case of the first kind of skilful *citta* belonging to the sphere of sense-desire (*kāmâvacara*).[32] I have already commented on the role of the *saṃgaha-* or *koṭṭhāsa-vāra* in the course of my discussion of the *ariyo aṭṭhaṅgiko maggo*.[33] Essentially the *suññata-vāra* would seem to involve a review of the *koṭṭhāsa-vāra* from the perspective of 'emptiness'; from the point of view of content it adds nothing new, though from the point of view of the spirituality of the *Dhammasaṅgaṇi* it is not without some significance. What I wish to do here is to consider a little more closely for each kind of *citta* the extent to which the seven sets feature or do not feature, both in the initial determination of *dhammas* and also among the groupings and sets brought out in the *koṭṭhāsa-* and *suññata-vāras*.

The *dhamma-vavatthāna-vāra* for the first kind of *citta* distinguished begins by simply listing fifty-six *dhammas* as being present when there arises *kāmâvacara-kusala-citta* that is accompanied by pleasant feeling (*somanassa-sahagata*) and associated with knowledge (*ñāṇa-sampayutta*). There then follows a 'word -analysis' (*pada-bhājaniya*) which defines each of the fifty-six *dhammas* in turn. It becomes clear in the process of this analysis that a number of the fifty-six *dhammas* represent different aspects of what are essentially equivalents. The fifty-six fall fairly clearly into the following groups:[34]

(i) *phassa, vedanā, saññā, cetanā, citta*
(ii) *vitakka, vicāra, pīti, sukha, cittass'ekaggatā*
(iii) *saddhindriya, viriyindriya, satindriya, samādhindriya, paññindriya, manindriya, somanassindriya, jīvitindriya*
(iv) *sammā-diṭṭhi, sammā-saṃkappa, sammā-vāyāma, sammā-sati, sammā-samādhi*
(v) *saddhā-bala, viriya-bala, sati-bala, samādhi-bala, paññā-bala, hiri-bala, ottappa-bala*
(vi) *alobha, adosa, amoha*
(vii) *anabhijjhā, avyāpāda, sammā-diṭṭhi*
(viii) *hiri, ottappa*
(ix) *kāya-citta-passaddhi; kāya-citta-lahutā; kāya-citta-mudutā; kāya-citta-kammaññutā; kāya-citta-pāguññatā; kāya-citta-ujukatā*
(x) *sati, sampajañña*
(xi) *samatha, vipassanā*
(xii) *paggaha, avikkhepa*

---

32 Dhs 9-26. The name *dhamma-vavatthāna-vāra* does not occur in the text (though where the commentary understands it to close is indicated by the words *pada-bhājaniyaṃ niṭṭhitaṃ* at Dhs 17); the names *koṭṭhāsa-* and *suññata-vāra* do occur (Dhs 25, 26 respectively). The actual indication of these sections in the text may not be original, but the use of the commentarial terminology is convenient when discussing the method of Dhs.

33 See pp. 212-4.

34 Identified in the commentary; for a full discussion see Nyanaponika, *AS*, pp. 31-93.

Groups (ii)-(vi) are immediately suggestive of groups frequently found elsewhere in the canonical literature. We have all five *jhāna*-factors, eight (of the twenty-two) faculties, five of the eight path-factors, seven powers and three motivations (*hetu*).[35] The other groups are also suggestive of various Nikāya contexts—pairs such as *sati* and *sampajañña* and *samatha* and *vipassanā* especially have become familiar in the course of this study. I shall return to the way the *Dhammasaṅgaṇi* defines these fifty-six items when I come to *lokuttara-citta*. For the moment I simply make the general observation that the correspondences inherent in the *Dhammasaṅgaṇi* definitions reduce fifty-six items to thirty.

Essentially the *koṭṭhāsa-vāra* and *suññata-vāra* bring out the groups I have already identified, but with rather more besides. The initial exposition of the *koṭṭhāsa-vāra* for the first kind of *citta* reads as follows:

> At that time there are four *khandhas*, two *āyatanas*, two *dhātus*, three *āhāras*, eight *indriyas*; there is a five-factored *jhāna*, a five-factored *magga*; there are seven *balas*, three *hetus*; there is one *phassa*, one *vedanā*, one *sañña*, one *cetanā*, one *citta*, one *vedanā-kkhandha*, one *saññā-kkhandha*, one *saṃkhāra-kkhandha*, one *viññāṇa-kkhandha*; one *manāyatana*, one *manindriya*, one *mano-viññāṇa-dhātu*, one *dhammâyatana*, one *dhamma-dhātu*.[36]

The constitution of these various elements is then spelt out in some detail. It is worth noting the general resemblance the structure of the *koṭṭhāsa-vāra* bears to the *mātikās/mātṛkās* of the *Vibhaṅga*, *Dhātukathā* and *Dharmaskandha*. As far as the seven sets are concerned it is clear that the *indriyas*, *balas* and path factors are fundamental to the *Dhammasaṅgaṇi's* treatment of all eight kinds of skilful consciousness belonging to the sense sphere.

It is important to understand how the various groups or sets brought out in the *koṭṭhāsa-* and *suññata-vāras* are directly related to the correspondences that the preceding 'world analysis' makes between various of the fifty-six items. Thus the 'word analysis' of *vitakka*, sees it as at once a *jhāna*-factor (*vitakka*) and a path-factor (*sammā-saṃkappa*); *cittass'ekaggatā* is seen as at once a *jhāna*-factor (*cittass'ekaggatā*), a faculty (*samādhindriya*), a power (*samādhi-bala*) and a path-factor (*sammā-samādhi*), and so on. This multiplicity of aspect which the fifty-six items possess is thus reiterated in the *koṭṭhāsa-* and *suññata-vāras*.

A consideration of the *Dhammasaṅgaṇi's* treatment of the remaining varieties of skilful consciousness—of the form-sphere (*rūpâvacara*), of the formless sphere (*arūpâvacara*), and transcendent (*lokuttara*)—and also of the various kinds of unskilful consciousness (which always belongs to the sense sphere) reveals a similar state of affairs. With one interesting exception—the unskilful consciousness associated with doubt (*vicikicchā-sampayutta*) which I shall come back to—the relevant *indriyas*, *balas* and path-factors are brought

---

[35] Group (vii) is in a sense incomplete; we have here the last three of the ten *kusala-kamma-pathas* (e.g. D I 139); cf. Nyanaponika, *AS*, p. 80.

[36] Dhs 17. Why the *koṭṭhāsa-* and *suññata-vāras* should invert the order of the *jhāna* factors and *indriyas* as given in the *dhamma-vavatthāna-vāra*, I do not know.

out.[37] However, when we come to certain kinds of undetermined (*avyākata*) consciousness, the position is rather different. Although the abbreviations in the text make it rather difficult in places to determine precisely what is going on, a number of points are quite clear.[38]

The eight varieties of skilful resultant consciousness (*kusala-vipāka-citta*) that in the later literature number among those types of *citta* termed 'without motivation' (*ahetuka*)[39] are each in the relevant *dhamma-vavatthāna-vāras* said to possess 'one pointedness of mind' (*cittass'ekaggatā*). In the case of *kāmâvacara-kusala-citta* this was further explained in the subsequent 'word analysis' by reference to, amongst other things, *samādhindriya*, *samādhi-bala* and *sammā-samādhi*.[40] In the case of these eight varieties of *kusala-vipāka-citta*, however, the subsequent 'word analysis' does not refer to *samādhindriya*, *samādhi-bala* and *sammā-samādhi*.[41] Moreover the relevant *koṭṭhāsa-vāra* treatment states in this connection not that there are four *indriyas*, but that there are just three (*manindriya*, *jīvitindriya* and one of *sukhindriya*, *somanassindriya* and *upekkh-indriya*), while no mention at all is made of *balas*, *jhānaṅgas* or *maggaṅgas*.[42] In other words, although 'one-pointedness of mind' is a component of these eight kinds of *kusala-vipāka-citta*, the *Dhammasaṅgaṇi* makes a point of not treating it as an *indriya*, *bala*, *jhānaṅga* or *maggaṅga*. One needs also to take account here of the fact that the *kusala-vipāka-mano-dhātu* (often referred to in the commentaries by way of its function of *sampaṭicchana* or 'receiving')[43] and the two *kusala-vipāka-mano-viññāṇa-dhātus* (often referred to in the commentaries by way of their function of *santīraṇa* or 'investigating')[44] are said, in the initial determination of *dhammas*, to possess both *vitakka* and *vicāra*—items missing from the five-sense consciousnesses. The second of the *mano-viññāṇa-dhātus* also has *somanassindriya* (in place of *upekkhindriya* in the first and in the *mano-dhātu*) and hence *pīti*. But none of these four items is treated as a path-factor or *jhāna*-factor in these varieties of *citta*.[45]

---

[37] The treatment of *arūpâvacara* consciousness is so abbreviated in the text that one cannot actually see that this is so, but it seems safe to assume that it is to be elaborated following the pattern of the fourth/fifth *jhāna* of the *rūpâvacara*.

[38] Nyanaponika has drawn attention to some of these ('Gradations of Intensity among Parallel Factors', *AS*, pp. 95-9), but he has overlooked the commentarial material.

[39] The eight are the five consciousnesses related to each of the five senses (Dhs 87-90), the mind-element (Dhs 91-2), and the two mind-consciousness-elements (Dhs 92-6).

[40] See Dhs 10 (S. 11).

[41] The PTS text is misleading and inaccurate in this respect. Dhs 88 (§ 438), 90 (§ 450), 92 (§ 464), 94 (§ 479), 95 (§ 493) all read: *yā tasmiṃ samaye cittassa ṭhiti ... pe ... ayaṃ tasmiṃ samaye cittass'ekaggatā hoti*. In addition Dhs 92 (§ 464) and 94 (§ 479) refer the *pe* back to Dhs 10 (§ 11), but this is surely mistaken since the definition of *cittass'ekaggatā* here includes *samādhindriya*, *samādhi-bala* and *sammā-samādhi*, all of which are omitted from the initial determination of *dhammas* at Dhs 91 (§ 455) and 92-3 (§ 469). At Dhs 88 (§ 438) Buddhaghosa apparently read just *yā tasmiṃ samaye cittassa ṭhiti ayaṃ tasmiṃ samaye cittass'ekaggatā* (see As 262: *cittassa ṭhitī ti ekaṃ eva padaṃ vuttaṃ*). This corrected reading is to be preferred in the other four instances listed above; cf. C.A.F. Rhys Davids, Dhs Trsl 115 (n. 1), 119 (n.1), 121 (§§ 463-7), 123 (§ 470-82), 124-5 (§§ 485-96).

[42] Dhs 90 (§ 453), 92 (§ 467), 94 (§ 482), 96 (§ 496).

[43] As 263.

[44] As 264.

[45] See Dhs 92.

Similar considerations apply to the *Dhammasaṅgaṇi's* treatment of the seven types of *akusala-vipāka-citta*, and to the three *kiriya* types of *citta* without motivation—the *mano-dhātu*, or 'mind-element' that performs the function of adverting to the doors of the five senses,[46] and the two *mano-viññāṇa-dhātus*, namely what the commentary understand as the 'laughter-producing' (*hāsayamāna*) *citta* of the *arahant*,[47] and the *citta* that adverts to the mind-door.[48] However, in the case of the two latter types there is a complication that I discussed in connection with the *indriyas* and *balas* in chapter four (p. 143), namely that *cittass' ekaggatā* is counted as *samādhindriya* though not apparently as a *bala*, *jhānaṅga* or *maggaṅga*. Finally, returning to *akusala-citta*, in the type that is associated with doubt (*vicikicchā-sampayutta*),[49] *cittass' ekaggatā*, although present, is not counted an *indriya*, *bala* or *maggaṅga*; it is, however counted a *jhānaṅga*, while other relevant items are also counted *indriyas*, *balas* and *maggaṅgas* in this kind of *citta*.[50] This clearly has something to do with the opposing natures of 'one-pointedness of mind' and *vicikicchā*, which is seen in the commentaries as a basic wavering (*kampana*, *calayati*)[51] of the mind. So although *cittass' ekaggatā* is weak, this kind of *citta* is not seen as completely devoid of *jhāna*- and path-factors in the way the *ahetuka* types of *citta* are.

What is the significance of all this? One can do little better here than refer to a number of comments made in the *Atthasālinī*. With regard to the omission of *samādhindriya* and other terms from the account of *cittass' ekaggatā* in the twice-five sense-consciousnesses, the *Atthasālinī* has the following to say:

> For this too[52] is a weak *citta*, and only the degree of stability [necessary] for occurrence is found here—it is unable to obtain the state of increased and strong stability. In the *saṃgaha-vāra* the *jhāna*- and path-factors are not brought out. Why? For *jhāna* follows in the wake of *vitakka*, and a path in the wake of motivations; by nature *jhāna*-factors are not found in *citta* without *vitakka*, and path-factors in *citta* without motivation, therefore neither are brought out here.[53]

A little later on, with regard to the *kusala-vipāka-mano-dhātu*, which does contain *vitakka*, the *Atthasālinī* comments:

> Since this *citta* is neither skilful nor unskilful, neither *sammā-saṃkappa* nor *micchā-saṃkappa* are stated. In the *saṃgaha-vāra*, although the *jhāna*-factor is found [in this

---

[46] Dhs 120 (§§ 566–7); cf. As 294.

[47] Dhs 120–2 (§§ 568–73); cf. As 294.

[48] Dhs 122 (§§ 574–5); cf. As 295.

[49] Dhs 85-6 (§§ 422–6).

[50] See Dhs 85 (§ 424); once more delete *pe*; cf. As 259 and p. 315, n. 41, above. Dhs 86 (§ 425) tells us that at that time there are four *indriyas* (*viriyindriya*, *manindriya*, *upekkhindriya*, *jīvitindriya*); there is four-factored *jhāna* (*vitakka*, *vicāra*, *upekkhā*, *cittass' ekaggatā*); there is a two-factored path (*micchā-saṃkappa*, *micchā-vāyāma*); and there are three *balas* (*viriya-bala*, *ahirika-bala*, *anottappa-bala*).

[51] As 259.

[52] The other *citta* that is weak is the *vicikicchā-sampayutta* variety just mentioned.

[53] As 262: *idam pi hi dubbala-cittaṃ pavatti-ṭṭhiti-mattam ev' ettha labbhati; saṇṭhiti-avaṭṭhiti-bhāvaṃ pāpuṇituṃ na sakkoti. saṃgaha-vāre jhānaṅga-maggaṅgāni na uddhaṭāni. kasmā. vitakka-pacchimakaṃ hi jhānaṃ nāma hetu-pacchimako maggo nāma, pakatiyā avitakka-citte jhānaṅgaṃ na labbhati ahetuka-citte ca maggaṅgan ti tasmā idha ubhayaṃ pi na uddhaṭaṃ.* (On *saṇṭhiti* and *avaṭṭhiti*, see As 143–4.)

> *citta*], because of following the pattern of the five-sense consciousnesses, it is not brought out; but path-factors are not even found, so they are not brought out.[54]

Thus two reasons are given for the fact that *jhāna*-factors are not brought out. In the first place, *jhāna*-factors are seen to exist dependent, in some sense, upon *vitakka*.[55] That is to say, it is only by virtue of application of the mind to its object with sufficient force and conviction that *cittass' ekaggatā* can warrant the epithet *jhānaṅga*. Presumably, then, even in the second, third, fourth and fifth *jhānas* (of the fivefold system) where there is no *vitakka*, the remaining *jhānaṅgas* are such by virtue of their 'following in the wake' of the *vitakka* that contributed to the arising of the first *jhāna*. In the second place, it seems that direct association with the twice-five sense-consciousnesses is what tends to weaken would-be *jhāna*-factors. In other words, what the *Atthasālinī* seems to be suggesting is that *jhāna*-factors are those forces of the mind that need to be developed if the mind is to be able to free itself from the distractions of the five senses; their development allows the mind to pass unhindered from the sphere of sense-desire (*kāmâvacara*) to the sphere of form (*rūpâvacara*). The nearer the mind comes to *rūpâvacara* consciousness, the more the *jhāna*-factors come into their own, the more fully they are *jhāna*-factors.

As for the path-factors, that their presence depends in some sense on the 'motivations',[56] and that they are stated only in skilful and unskilful *citta* would seem to be equivalent points. If one is to think in terms of the three motivations of skilful *citta* (i.e. *amoha*, *alobha* and *adosa*) and the three motivations of unskilful *citta* (i.e. *moha*, *lobha* and *dosa*), then *citta* that is *avyākata* is excluded on both accounts.

As far as the *Dhammasaṅgaṇi* itself is concerned, all this amounts, I think, to a principle that can be stated quite generally and simply. It is only with regard to consciousness that has a certain force, strength or power that one should speak of *balas*, *jhānaṅgas* and *maggaṅgas*. This kind of *citta* is characteristically skilful or unskilful; that is to say, it is the kind of consciousness that constitutes a *kamma*, or fulfils the active function of 'running' (*javana*)—according to the commentarial theory of the consciousness process (*citta-vīthi*).[57] Consciousness, on the other hand, that operates more automatically and is bound up with the twice-five sense-consciousnesses is considered to be relative-

---

[54] As 264 : *yasmā pan' etaṃ cittaṃ neva kusalaṃ nâkusalaṃ tasmā sammā-saṃkappo ti vā micchā-saṃkappo ti vā na vuttaṃ. saṃgaha-vāre labbhamānaṃ pi jhānaṅgaṃ pañca-viññāṇa-sote patitvā gatan ti na uddhaṭaṃ; maggaṅgaṃ pana na* labbhati evā ti na uddhaṭam*. (*For the reading *pi na* or *pana na* as against just *pana* in the PTS edition, see As Trsl 351 (n. 1) and variant given at As 508 (revised edition, 1979); the *na* is supported by *maggaṅgāni alābhato yeva* at As 264.24.) The logic behind the usage of *labbhati* and *uddhaṭa* here seems to be as follows: *maggaṅgas* are said to be 'not found', because although *vitakka* and *cittass' ekaggatā* are stated in the initial determination of *dhammas*, *sammā-saṃkappa* and *sammā-samādhi* are not, and therefore they are 'not brought out' in the *saṃgaha-vāra*; but because *vitakka*, *vicāra* and *cittass' ekaggatā* are stated in the initial determination of dhammas, *jhāna*-factors are said to be 'found', but they are still not 'brought-out' in the *saṃgaha-vāra*. Cf. Dhs-mṭ (Be) 126.

[55] Cf. Abhidh-av 31: *sabhāvenâvitakkesu jhānaṅgāni na uddhare.*

[56] Cf. Abhidh-av 31: *sabbâhetuka-cittesu maggaṅgāni na c' uddhare.*

[57] See L. S. Cousins, 'The Paṭṭhāna and the Development of the Theravādin Abhidhamma', *JPTS* 9 (1981), pp. 22–46.

ly weak; there are no *balas*, *jhānaṅgas* or *maggaṅgas*, and even *indriyas* can be said to be present in only a very limited sense.

As far as they can be ascertained from an abbreviated text, the details of the *Dhammasaṅgaṇi's* handling of the *indriyas*, *balas*, *jhānaṅgas* and *maggaṅgas* for the remaining types of *citta* are set out below.[58] For this I have adopted the classic commentarial schema of eighty-nine *cittas*, but follow the order of the *Dhammasaṅgaṇi* arrangement.[59] I include in this table the *adhipatis* (as an indication of the extent of the relevance of the *iddhi-pādas*) and the *bojjhāṅgas*. A few comments are in order.[60]

Although it cannot be definitely determined from the text of the *Dhammasaṅgaṇi*, the *Atthasālinī* seems to be of the view that the seventeen *vipāka-cittas* (42-58) should all be taken as having *indriyas*, *balas* and *jhānaṅgas*;[61] possibly we should exclude the *maggaṅgas* on the principle that they are only properly relevant to actively skilful and unskilful *citta*. The same considerations apply to the seventeen *kiriya-cittas* of the *arahant* (73-89).[62] Buddhadatta's *Abhidhammâvatāra* provides some assistance in determining the commentarial position on these matters,[63] but also raises the problem of later divergence from the traditions of the *Dhammasaṅgaṇi*. Buddhadatta brings out *jhāna*-factors in all but the twice-five sense-consciousnesses, and this is clearly at odds with the text of the *Dhammasaṅgaṇi* as we have it. For in the *Dhammasaṅgaṇi* the treatment of the remaining eight types of *ahetuka-citta* is not different from that of the twice-five sense-consciousnesses in this respect; the relevant *koṭṭhāsa-vāras* plainly omit the *jhāna*-factors (although *cittass'ekaggatā* and some variety of *vedanā* are given as present).[64]

I should reiterate here something that I mentioned in chapter six. The treatment of the *maggaṅgas* with regard to the eight varieties of *lokuttara-citta* (18-21, 59-62)—the four paths and the four fruits (*lokuttara-vipāka*)—is rather special on two accounts. Not only are *sammā-diṭṭhi*, *-saṃkappa*, *-vācā*, *-kammanta*, *-ājīva*, *-vāyāma*, *-sati* and *-samādhi* stated in the initial determination of *dhammas* present, [65] and brought out as an eight-factored path in the *koṭṭhāsa-vāra*,[66] but in addition the detailed definition of terms, the *pada-bhājaniya*,

---

[58] See Table 11, p. 319.

[59] The schema of eighty-nine *cittas* can be seen as a convenient simplification of the Dhs method. The Dhs, by the use of the four *adhipatis* and four *paṭipadās*, etc., multiplies the varieties of some kinds of *citta*, and is perhaps rather less rigid and more fluid.

[60] The Dhs here seems to provide the key to the understanding of *indriya-paccaya*, *jhāna-paccaya*, *magga-paccaya* and *adhipati-paccaya* in the *Paṭṭhāna*, i.e. we should only speak of these *paccayas* in the cases where the Dhs indicates the presence of *indriyas*, *jhānaṅgas*, *maggaṅgas* and *adhipatis*. Note how, in the list of twenty-four *paccayas*, the sequence *āhāra-paccaya*, *indriya-paccaya*, *jhāna-paccaya*, *magga-paccaya* corresponds directly to the order of the relevant items in the *koṭṭhāsa-vāra* of the Dhs.

[61] Cf. As 266 (*sesaṃ sabbaṃ aṭṭhasu kusalesu vutta-sadisaṃ eva*), 289 (*sesaṃ kusale vutta-nayen' eva veditabbaṃ*).

[62] Cf. As 295-6

[63] Abhidh-av 30-1. A resolution of his summary is set out in Appendix II.

[64] See Dhs 88 (§ 441); 92 (§ 467), 94 (§ 482), 96 (§ 496), 118 (§ 560), 119 (§§ 562, 564), 121 (§ 572), 122 (§ 574).

[65] See Dhs 60.

[66] See Dhs 68.

TABLE 11. THE PRESENCE OF INDRIYAS, ETC. IN DIFFERENT CLASSES OF CONSCIOUSNESS ACCORDING TO THE DHAMMASAṄGAṆI, ATTHASĀLINĪ AND ABHIDHAMMÂVATĀRA

	citta	indriya	jhānaṅga	maggaṅga	bala	bojjhaṅga	adhipati
1-8	kāmâvacara-kusala (8)	×	×	×	×		×
9-13	rūpâvacara-kusala (5)	×	×	×	×		×
14-17	arūpâvacara-kusala (4)	×	×	×	×		×
18-21	lokuttara(-kusala) (4)	×	×	× ×	×	×	×
22-33	akusala (12)[1]	×	×	×	×		
34-38	kusala-vipāka (5)	[×]					
39	kusala-vipāka-mano-dhātu	[×]	A				
40-41	kusala-vipāka-mano-viññāṇa-dhātu (2)	[×]	A				
42-49	mahā-vipāka (8)	×	×	?A	×		
50-54	rūpâvacara-vipāka (5)	×	×	?A			
55-58	arūpâvacara-vipāka (4)	×	×	?A			
59-62	lokuttara-vipāka (4)	×	×	× ×	×	×	×
63-67	akusala-vipāka (5)	[×]					
68	akusala-vipāka-mano-dhātu	[×]	A				
69	akusala-vipāka-mano-viññāṇa-dhātu (2)	[×]	A				
70	kiriya-mano-dhātu	[×]	A				
71-72	kiriya-mano-viññāṇa-dhātu (2)	×	A		A[2]		
73-80	kāmâvacara-kiriya (8)	×	×	?A	×		?
81-85	rūpâvacara-kiriya (5)	×	×	?A	×		?
86-89	arūpâvacara-kiriya (4)	×	×	?A	×		

KEY

× 'brought out'

[×] while certain items of the 22 are 'brought out' as *indriyas*, items usually classed as or equivalent to the five spiritual indriyas are not

× × all 8 *maggaṅgas* are 'brought out' in *lokuttara-citta*

? Dhs and As are not explicit

A the position of Abhidh-av (where apparently at odds with Dhs and As or where they are not explicit)

1 *cittass'ekaggatā* is not 'brought out' as *indriya*, *bala* or *maggaṅga* in *vicikicchā-sampayutta-citta*

2 the treatment of the *balas* in these *cittas* is problematic

comments of each of these eight items and their equivalents that they are 'factors of the path' and that they are 'included in the path' (*magga-pariyāpanna*).[67] This added emphasis on the path is because, it seems, the presence of all eight path-factors, which defines *lokuttara-citta*, brings to completion and fulfilment the *ariyo aṭṭhaṅgiko maggo*. Another distinctive feature of the *Dhammasaṅgaṇi's* treatment of the eight *lokuttara* varieties of *citta* is that, where appropriate, *dhamma-vicaya-sambojjhaṅga, sati-, viriya-, pīti-, passaddhi-* and *samādhi-sambojjhaṅga* are brought out.[68] This is confined to the detailed definition of terms or *pada-bhājaniya*,[69] and is not a feature of the *koṭṭhāsa-vāra*.

I referred to the relationship between the *iddhi-pādas* and *adhipati* in chapter three. The *Dhammasaṅgaṇi* confines its treatment of the *adhipatis* to actively skilful and unskilful *citta* (1-33), and also to the four *lokuttara-vipāka* (59-62).[70] According to the *Atthasālinī*, *kāmâvacara-citta* may or may not have an *adhipati* depending on particular circumstances; *rūpâvacara* and *arūpâvacara* always has an *adhipati*.[71] Once more this appears to have something to do with the dynamics and power of different types of consciousness; it fits well with the notion of the *iddhi-pādas* as tied up with the potential for growth inherent in different types of consciousness, which are then seen as the bases for further development.

Finally we need to note that the *Dhammasaṅgaṇi* makes it explicit that the breakthrough to stream-attainment, and so on takes place in a state of mind equivalent in some sense to that of *rūpâvacara-jjhāna*. In other words, it makes explicit a point already noted, namely that 'awakening' is itself conceived of as a kind of *jhāna*. The *Dhammasaṅgaṇi* introduces the various types of *lokuttara* consciousness by the following formula:

> At that time when one develops transcendent *jhāna*, which leads out and brings about dispersal, for the sake of abandoning wrong views and for achieving the first stage, [and when] secluded from sensual desires ... one attains and dwells in the first *jhāna* ... at that time there is ... [72]

Three parts of this formula are then varied. 'For the sake of abandoning wrong views and for achieving the first stage' is replaced first by 'for the weakening of passion for the objects of sensual desire and illwill, and for achieving the second path' (*kāma-rāga-vyāpādānaṃ patānu-bhāvāya dutiyāya bhummiyā pattiyā*), then by 'for the sake of abandoning passion for the objects of sensual desire and illwill without remainder, and for achieving the third stage' (*kāma-rāga-vyāpādānaṃ anavasesa-ppahānāya tatiyāya bhummiyā pattiyā*), and finally by 'for the sake of abandoning without remainder passion for the world of

[67] See Dhs 61-8, 75, 117; As 292.
[68] On the omission of *upekkhā-sambojjhaṅga* see above, p. 157, n. 69.
[69] See Dhs 61-8, 75, 117; As 292.
[70] Could we also include the seventeen *kiriya* (73-89)?
[71] See As 213. Of *vipāka-citta*, why the *lokuttara* alone has *adhipatis* is discussed at As 291. Cf. Abhidh-av 11: *honti sâdhipatin'eva lokuttara-phalāni tu| vipāke'dhipati natthi ṭhapetvā||*
[72] Dhs 60: *yasmiṃ samaye lokuttaraṃ jhānaṃ bhāveti niyyānikaṃ apacaya-gāmiṃ diṭṭhi-gatānaṃ pahānāya paṭhamāya bhummiyā pattiyā vivicc'eva kāmehi ... pe ... paṭhamaṃ jhānaṃ upasampajja viharati ... tasmiṃ samaye hoti ...*

forms and the formless, conceit, agitation and ignorance (*rūpa-rāga-arūpa-rāga-māna-uddhacca-avijjā*) and for achieving the fourth stage';[73] we thus have the paths of stream-attainment, once-return, non-return and *arahant*-ship. Next, for 'first *jhāna*' any of the remaining four *jhānas* of the fivefold system may be substituted.[74]

However, from the point of view of present concerns, the most important variable in the formula is the following: in place of 'transcendent *jhāna*' we can have 'transcendent *magga*', 'transcendent *satipaṭṭhāna*', 'transcendent *samma-ppadhāna*', 'transcendent *iddhi-pāda*', 'transcendent *indriya*', 'transcendent *bala*', 'transcendent *bojjhaṅga*', 'transcendent *sacca*', 'transcendent *samatha*', 'transcendent *dhamma*', 'transcendent *khandha*', 'transcendent *āyatana*', 'transcendent *dhātu*', 'transcendent *āhāra*', 'transcendent *phassa*', 'transcendent *vedanā*', 'transcendent *saññā*', 'trasncendent *cetanā*', 'transcendent *citta*'.[75] These twenty 'great methods' (*mahā-naya*) apply equally to *lokuttara-vipāka* consciousness. This list can perhaps be compared to list B in the *Paṭisambhidāmagga*; both lists seem intended as a way of reviewing the transcendent mind from all possible aspects. The way in which the 'path' comes first of the seven sets perhaps reflects the perspective of the *Mahāsaḷāyatanika-sutta* where the 'path' is seen as the fulfilment of the seven sets.

So, nothing is said in the *Dhammasaṅgaṇi* about the *satipaṭṭhānas* and *samma-ppadhānas* apart from *lokuttara-citta*. In so far as the *iddhi-pādas* are identifiable with the *adhipatis*, they occur in skilful and unskilful *citta*, but are especially characteristic of *rūpâvacara* and *arūpâvacara* consciousness according to the *Atthasālinī*, a fact that is suggestive of their particular association with meditational power. *Indriyas* appear to be the most universally applicable category, while *balas* and *maggaṅgas* are restricted to skilful and unskilful conscious, though matters are complicated as far as *balas* are concerned by the 'laughter producing' *citta* of the *arahant*. The *bojjhaṅgas* are restricted to *lokuttara* consciousness, while the *maggaṅgas* also receive special emphasis in this context. All seven sets are considered as characteristic of *lokuttara-citta*.

4. The seven sets in the Vibhaṅga

When we turn to the second book of the *Abhidhamma-piṭaka*, the *Vibhaṅga*, the seven sets are dealt with directly and not obliquely as in the *Dhammasaṅgaṇi*. The *Vibhaṅga*, then, gives an account of all seven sets except that, as I have already pointed out, the five spiritual *indriyas* are dealt with in the context of the full list of twenty-two *indriyas*, and the five *balas* do not feature at all as distinct items; presumably this is because the *Vibhaṅga's* particular method of analysis would fail to distinguish them from the five spiritual *indriyas*.

In the *Vibhaṅga*, each of the five chapters devoted to the *satipaṭṭhānas*, *samma-ppadhānas*, *iddhi-pādas*, *bojjhaṅgas* and *magga* respectively has three

---

[73] See Dhs 74-5.
[74] See Dhs 70-2.
[75] See Dhs 73, 107-8; cf. As 237-8.

sections: an analysis according to Suttanta (*suttanta-bhājaniya*), an analysis according to Abhidhamma (*abhidhamma-bhājaniya*), and a section of question and answer (*pañhâpucchaka*). I have already, in the course of the analysis of the sets individually, referred to the appropriate *suttanta-bhājaniya* sections, so now I wish to look more closely at the general principles of the *abhidhamma-bhājaniya* treatment of the sets. The *pañhâpucchaka* sections, to which I shall also refer, extend the Abhidhamma analysis by putting each of the sets through the matrix of the Abhidhamma triplets and couplets set out at the beginning of the *Dhammasaṅgaṇi*. Thus it is asked how many of the twenty-two *indriyas*, and so on, are skilful, how many unskilful and how many undetermined, and so on for the rest of the twenty-two triplets and 100 couplets.[76]

The *abhidhamma-bhājaniya* for the *indriya-vibhaṅga* is quite straightforward.[77] It consists simply of twenty-two registers of terms defining each of the *indriyas*. The registers given for the five spiritual *indriyas* agree exactly with those given for the corresponding terms in the word analysis for the first kind of *citta* treated in the *Dhammasaṅgaṇi*. Thus *saddhindriya* is related to *saddhā-bala*; *viriyindriya* to *viriya-bala* and *sammā-vāyāma*; *satindriya* to *sati-bala* and *sammā-sati*; *samādhindriya* to *samādhi-bala* and *sammā-samādhi*; *paññindriya* to *paññā-bala*, *dhamma-vicaya* and *sammā-diṭṭhi*. However, there is no use of the actual terms *bojjhaṅga* and *maggaṅga*. Examination of the *pañhâpucchaka* shows that the five spiritual *indriyas* are not here understood in their exclusively *lokuttara* aspect or even in their skilful aspect; as in the *Dhammasaṅgaṇi*, they are seen as *indriyas* in their general aspect, whether skilful, unskilful or undetermined.[78]

In the *abhidhamma-bhājaniya* for the *satipaṭṭhānas*,[79] however, the four activities of dwelling watching body, feeling, mind and *dhamma* are treated exclusively as aspects of *lokuttara* consciousness. The basic formula for *lokuttara-jjhāna* is borrowed directly from the *Dhammasaṅgaṇi*,[80] and the four phrases *kāye kāyânupassī*, *vedanāsu vedanânupassī*, *citte cittânupassī*, *dhammesu dhammânupassī* are inserted one at a time in four consecutive rehearsals of the formula. At the conclusion of each rehearsal we are told that 'whatever at this time is *sati*, *anussati* ... *sammā-sati*, *sati-sambojjhaṅga*, *maggaṅga*, *magga-pariyāpanna*, this is called *satipaṭṭhāna* and remaining *dhammas* are associated (*sampayutta*) with *satipaṭṭhāna*.' This, then, is the full register for *lokuttara* mindfulness as given in the *Dhammasaṅgaṇi*.[81] Next we have a fifth rehearsal (omitted in the PTS text) of the basic *lokuttara-jjhāna* formula in answer to the bare question, 'Therein what is *satipaṭṭhāna*?' This is called the bare (*suddhika*)

---

[76] See Table 12, pp. 328-9.

[77] Vibh 122-4.

[78] At Vibh 125 we are told that six *indriyas* may be skilful, unskilful and undetermined; the arithmetic of this only works if *viriyindriya* and *samādhindriya* are counted among these six; the way in which the *indriyas* are treated generally can also be determined by reference to a number of other triplets in the *pañhâpucchaka* for the *indriyas*; see table.

[79] Vibh 202-5.

[80] See Dhs 60 (§ 277); abbreviated at Vibh 203.

[81] E.g. Dhs 62 (§ 290).

satipaṭṭhāna method in the commentary.[82] The formula concludes with the same summary statement as the previous rehearsals. This completes the treatment of *satipaṭṭhāna* for skilful *lokuttara* consciousness. The *Vibhaṅga* then relates *satipaṭṭhāna* to the basic *Dhammasaṅgaṇi* formula for *lokuttara-vipāka* types of *jhāna*[83] according to the same pattern of five rehearsals (this time the 'bare' *satipaṭṭhāna* method is included in the PTS text).

These basic rehearsals relate only to the first *jhāna* and to the first path and fruit—those of stream-attainment. Though the text of the *Vibhaṅga* gives no definite indications, the commentary takes it that the basic rehearsals of the formula should be expanded in full according to the method of the *Dhamma-saṅgaṇi*; that is to say, by way of the fourfold and fivefold system of *jhāna* and so forth. Taking into account all possible variables, the commentary states that the ten basic methods expand to 80,000.

The fifth rehearsals—the two 'bare' *satipaṭṭhāna* methods of skilful *lokuttara* and *lokuttara-vipāka* respectively—are of some interest. The precise wording here is in doubt. Certainly we need to insert a paragraph into the PTS *Vibhaṅga* text for the skilful *lokuttara* type:[84]

> *tattha katamaṃ satipaṭṭhānaṃ. idha bhikkhu yasmiṃ samaye lokuttaraṃ jhānaṃ bhāveti niyyānikaṃ apacaya-gāmiṃ diṭṭhi-gatānaṃ pahānāya paṭhamāya bhūmiyā pattiyā, vivicc'eva kāmehi. pe. paṭhamaṃ jhānaṃ upasampajja viharati dukkha-paṭi-padaṃ dandhâbhiññaṃ (dhammesu dhammânupassī) yā tasmiṃ samaye sati anussati. pe. sammā-sati sati-sambojjhaṅgo maggaṅgaṃ magga-pariyāpannaṃ, idaṃ vuccati satipaṭṭhānaṃ.*[85]

Our problem is the inclusion or otherwise of the phrase *dhammesu dhammânu-passī*. Printed oriental editions seem to be fairly consistent in including the phrase for the skilful *lokuttara* bare *satipaṭṭhāna* method, and rather less so in including it for the *lokuttara-vipāka*. The *Mūla-ṭīkā*, while not perhaps finally deciding the issue, does offer some clues:

> In the *abhidhamma-bhājaniya*, [first] with [the words] 'And how does he dwell watching body with regard to body? Here at the time when a *bhikkhu* ... [and] direct knowledge slow; he watches body with regard to body—whatever at that time is *sati* ... ' and so forth, the persons are determined and the [different] *satipaṭṭhānas* distinguished by way of approach [i.e. *kāya, vedanā, citta, dhamma*]. Next, with [the words] 'Therein what is *satipaṭṭhāna?* Here at the time when a *bhikkhu* ... direct knowledge slow ... whatever at that time is *sati* ... ' and so forth, by not citing the persons and not making any distinction of approach, the bare *satipaṭṭhāna* method is stated by way of one *sati* accomplishing four functions. This is the distinction between the two methods here.[86]

---

[82] See Vibh-a 287.

[83] See Dhs 99 (§ 505).

[84] After Vibh 203.38; U Thiṭṭila, Vibh Trsl 264-5, includes this passage, as do printed oriental editions.

[85] For the *vipāka* at Vibh 205.15-28 we have: *tattha katamaṃ satipaṭṭhānaṃ ... tass'eva lokuttarassa kusalassa jhānassa katattā bhāvitattā vipākaṃ vivicc'eva kāmehi. pe. paṭhamaṃ jhānaṃ upasampajja viharati dukkha-paṭipadaṃ dandhâbhiññaṃ suññataṃ dhammesu dhammânupassī, yā tasmiṃ samaye ...*

[86] *Mūla-ṭīkā* Be (1960), to Vibh-a 287: *abhidhamma-bhājaniye 'kathañ ca kāye kāyânupassī viharati? idha bhikkhu yasmiṃ samaye// pa// dandhâbhiññaṃ kāye kāyânupassī// yā tasmiṃ samaye satī' ti ādinā āgamana-vasena visesitāni satipaṭṭhānāni puggale ṭhapetvā desetvā puna 'tattha*

The *pa* in the text of the *Mūla-ṭīkā* surely shows that the text of the *Vibhaṅga* that the author of the *Mūla-ṭīkā* had before him had something between *dandhâbhiññaṃ* and *yā tasmiṃ samaye sati* in the bare *satipaṭṭhāna* formula. Since a number of manuscripts and printed editions have *dhammesu dhammânupassī* precisely at this point, it seems reasonable to view it as an authentic part of the text. It is difficult to see why the *vipāka* should be different from the *kusala* in this respect—the *aṭṭhakathā* and *ṭīkā* fail to make any comment. It would seem that the *Mūla-ṭīkā's* point about the different *satipaṭṭhānas* being distinguished or not, and the persons being cited or not refers to the difference in the form of the initial questions: *kathañ ca kāye kāyânupassī viharati*, etc., and *tattha katamaṃ satipaṭṭhānaṃ*. The point about the one mindfulness fulfilling four functions in *lokuttara* consciousness refers back to the *Visuddhimagga's* account. If we are correct in reading *dhammesu dhammânupassī* in the bare *satipaṭṭhāna* method, then we seem to have an expression of the notion that at the level of *lokuttara* consciousness all four *satipaṭṭhānas* collectively resolve into *dhammesu dhammânupassanā* (cf. section one of this chapter).

Rather interestingly this would appear to have rather close parallels with the understanding of the four *smṛty-upasthānas* in the *Abhidharmakośa*. Vasubandhu states[87] that the first three *smṛty-upasthānas* have individual objects (*amiśrâlambana, asambhinnâlambana*) that fall into the categories of *kāya*, *vedanā* or *citta*. However, *dharma-smṛty-upasthāna* can be of two varieties: that which has an individual object—a *dharma* that does not fall into the categories of *kāya*, *vedanā* or *citta*; and that which has a unified object (*samastâlambana*). This more advanced stage of *dharma-smṛty-upasthāna* unifies the watching of *kāya*, *vedanā*, *citta* and other *dharmas*, and gives rise to the kind of *dharma-smṛty-upasthāna* that constitutes the four *nirvedha-bhāgīyas*, i.e. the stages of the path that are concerned with actively developing the penetrative wisdom that leads directly to the *lokottara* path.[88] This seems to be making a very similar point to the one made in the Pāli sources, and in the *Vibhaṅga* in particular. For the *Abhidharmakośa*, in the higher stages of the path, one *smṛty-upasthāna* fulfils the functions of all four *smṛty-upasthānas*; this one *smṛty-upasthāna* is to be considered a variety of *dharma-smṛty-upasthāna*. The main difference vis à vis the Pāli sources is that this kind of *smṛty-upasthāna* is not strictly confined to transcendent (*lokuttara/lokottara*) consciousness. Probably this difference should be seen simply as a point of strict Abhidharma, and should, I think, be related to the Theravādin notion that the *lokuttara* path-consciousness endures for but a single moment, as opposed to the fifteen moments of the Sarvāstivādin system. The *ekâbhisamaya* outlook of the Theravādins is bound to emphasize the special quality of the moment that finally and at once fulfils all that was previously only partially fulfilled. What

---

katamaṃ satipaṭṭhānaṃ? idha bhikkhu yasmiṃ samaye// pa// dandhâbhiññaṃ// pa// yā tasmiṃ samaye satī' ti ādinā puggalaṃ anāmasitvā āgamana- [reading with *Anuṭīkā*] *visesānañ ca akatvā catu-kicca-sādhakeka-sati-vasena suddhika-satipaṭṭhāna-nayo vutto ti ayaṃ ettha naya-dvaye viseso//*

[87] Abhidh-k 343.

[88] See Abhidh-k 343-4.

both systems seem to understand is that the final stages of the path involve a fundamental transformation of awareness whereby the practitioner sees not so much isolated *dhammas/dharmas* as *dhamma/dharma* itself. This transformation is sealed by the transcendent path, but presumably in the Theravāda, as in the Sarvāstivāda, the higher stages of 'ordinary insight', i.e. the stages that would be thought of as concerned with the development of the *lokiya-bodhi-pakkhiya-dhammas* (see section six of this chapter), would also be seen as already actively participating in this transformation. In other words, the four *nirvedha-bhāgīyas* correspond rather closely to the stages of the *lokiya-bodhi-pakkhiya-dhammas.*

So the treatment of the *satipaṭṭhānas* in the *abhidhamma-bhājaniya* brings us back to their treatment in the *Satipaṭṭhāna-sutta.* For the distinguishing of the four individual *satipaṭṭhānas* at the level of *lokuttara* consciousness suggests that each *satipaṭṭhāna* in some sense can be developed up to the stage of *lokuttara* consciousness. At the same time the bare *satipaṭṭhāna* method suggests that in the actual arising of *lokuttara* consciousness all four *satipaṭṭhānas* are fulfilled.

Turning now to the *abhidhamma-bhājaniya* for the *samma-ppadhānas,*[89] we find that they are treated here similarly to the *satipaṭṭhānas.* First each of the four parts of the *samma-ppadhāna* formula is combined with the basic skilful *lokuttara-jjhāna* formula from the *Dhammasaṅgaṇi,* giving us four successive rehearsals. Finally, we once more have a fifth rehearsal—a 'bare' *samma-ppadhāna* method. Presumably this once more relates to the *Visuddhimagga* point that in the path-consciousness, one *viriya* fulfils the function of all four *samma-ppadhānas.* One should note here that there appears to be no suggestion in the text that it is the fourth *samma-ppadhāna* that should be seen as fulfilling the functions of all four. A basic contrast with the *satipaṭṭhāna* treatment is the fact that the *samma-ppadhānas* are not combined with *lokuttara-vipāka* consciousness: there are no *samma-ppadhānas* in the fruition *citta.* Indeed the answer to the very first question in the *pañhâpucchaka* confirms the point: the *samma-ppadhānas* are just skilful. This is taken up in the *bodhi-pakkhiya-kathā* of the *Visuddhimagga,* as already noted. The *Vibhaṅga* commentary here states simply that 'in the *vipāka* there is no function to be performed by the *samma-ppadhānas*'.[90]

The *abhidhamma-bhājaniya* treatment of the *iddhi-pādas*[91] does not quite follow the pattern of the *satipaṭṭhāna* and *samma-ppadhāna* treatments. To begin with the *iddhi-pādas* are taken in two quite distinct ways. The first method treats them by way of their standard Suttanta formula: 'the *iddhi-pāda* that is furnished both with concentration gained by means of *chanda* ... *viriya* ... *citta* ... *vīmaṃsā,* and with forces of endeavour'. Each of the four parts is in turn related to the *Dhammasaṅgaṇi lokuttara-jjhāna* formula as in the cases of the *satipaṭṭhānas* and *samma-ppadhānas.* There follows a brief 'word-commentary' virtually identical to the one found in the *suttanta-bhājaniya.* The *iddhi* is

---

89 Vibh 211-4.
90 Vibh-a 302: *vipāke pana samma-ppadhānehi kattabba-kiccaṃ n'atthī ti vipāka-vāro na gahito ti.*
91 Vibh 220-4.

once more defined as the 'success', 'growth', 'attainment' and so on, of all *dhammas* present. The basis of this 'success'—the *iddhi-pāda*—is the totality of skilful *dhammas* that have arisen at that time.[92]

This first way of taking the *iddhi-pādas* is followed by what the commentaries call the *uttara-cūḷa-bhājaniya*[93] in which the four *iddhi-pādas* are defined succinctly as *chandiddhi-pāda, viriyiddhi-pāda, cittiddhi-pāda* and *vīmaṃsiddhi-pāda*. Once more these four are in turn related to the *lokuttara-jjhāna* formula from the *Dhammasaṅgaṇi*. No 'word-commentary' follows, but each rehearsal continues with a statement that shows that it is *chanda* itself—or *viriya, citta,* or *vīmaṃsā*—that is being taken as the 'basis of success';[94] remaining *dhammas* are associated with *chandiddhi-pāda*, and so on.

So there is no 'bare' method for the *iddhi-pādas*. There are just two ways of taking each of the four *iddhi-pādas*. According to the first, the totality of skilful *dhammas* is seen as the *iddhi-pāda*, according to the second just *chanda, viriya, citta* or *vīmaṃsā*.[95] What is also remarkable is that there is no treatment of the *iddhi-pādas* with regard to *lokuttara-vipāka* consciousness. Again this omission is confirmed by the answer to the first question in the *pañhâpucchaka*: all four *iddhi-pādas* are just skilful.[96] This treatment raises two problems. In the *Visuddhimagga* account of the *bodhi-pakkhiya-dhammas* Buddhaghosa appears to take it that four *iddhi-pādas* can be said to be present in some sense at the time of the arising of both the *lokuttara* path-consciousness and the *lokuttara* fruit-consciousness. But in what sense? Secondly, why are the *iddhi-pādas* excluded from *vipāka-citta* in the *Vibhaṅga* but not in the *Visuddhimagga*?

The answer to these problems should possibly be seen as connected with the two ways of looking at the *iddhi-pādas* in the *abhidhamma-bhājaniya*. The very fact that there are two alternative ways of taking the *iddhi-pādas* here, suggests that even according to Abhidhamma analysis the way of handling the *iddhi-pādas* cannot be as strict and as final as it can be with other categories. To the extent that the *iddhi-pādas* are to be related to the notion of *adhipati*, it appears that only one *iddhi-pāda* could function at any time. However, this strict way of taking the *iddhi-pādas* would appear to be confined to the *uttara-cūḷa-bhājaniya* and *pañhâpucchaka*. If it is the totality of skilful *dhammas* that constitutes the *iddhi-pādas* at the time of *lokuttara* consciousness then there is perhaps a sense in which all four *iddhi-pādas* can be said to be present at once, or can be said to be fulfilled at once. The relationship of the *iddhi-pādas* to the four *adhipatis* would seem to suggest that they should be regarded as present in

---

[92] Vibh 221-3 (passim): *iddhi-pādo ti tathā-bhūtassa phasso vedanā. pe. paggaho avikkhepo.* (Cf. discussion of *suttanta-bhājaniya* above, Chapter 3.3.)

[93] Vibh 223-4; see Vibh-a 308.

[94] E.g. Vibh 216: *yo tasmiṃ samaye chando chandīkatā kattu-kamyatā kusalo dhamma-cchando, ayaṃ vuccati chandiddhi-pādo.*

[95] Cf. Moh 160-1.

[96] See Vibh 224. It is clear that the *pañhâpucchaka*, despite being introduced by the full Suttanta *iddhi-pāda* formula, considers the *iddhi-pādas* from the point of view of the narrower *uttara-cūḷa-bhājaniya* definition; this comes out in the section on the couplets: e.g. *vīmaṃsiddhi-pādo hetu, tayo iddhi-pādā na hetu* and *tayo iddhi-pādā bāhirā, cittiddhi-pādo ajjhattiko* (see Vibh 225).

lokuttara-vipāka consciousness—as I have noted, the *Atthasālinī* and *Abhidhammâvatāra* make a point of the fact that *lokuttara-vipāka* is the only variety of *vipāka-citta* to possess *adhipatis*. Yet the equation of the *adhipatis* and *iddhi-pādas* is not something absolute.

The *Mahā-ṭīkā* to the *Visuddhimagga* comments that when it is said that, excepting the four *samma-ppadhānas*, the remaining thirty-three *bodhi-pakkhiya-dhammas* are found in the fruition consciousness, this is 'by way of exposition' (*pariyāyato*).[97] This comment is presumably made with regard to the fact that strictly the seven sets encompass fourteen *dhammas* and not thirty-seven, and that *viriya* is, of course, still a constituent of the fruit, although not reckoned as 'four *samma-ppadhānas*'. This suggests that the whole question of counting the thirty-seven *dhammas* in *lokuttara* consciousness is ultimately a matter of 'exposition'; the fact that the way of construing the *iddhi-pādas* is not entirely fixed would seem to make this doubly so.

The exclusion of the *iddhi-pādas* from the *lokuttara-vipāka* is in many ways quite consistent with the way they are understood in the literature. The *phala* is essentially a passive kind of consciousness; it is not seen as something actively involved in the dynamics of spiritual growth. It is noticeable that the commentarial discussion of various kinds of *iddhi* and *iddhi-pāda* leaves the *phala* entirely out of the reckoning.[98] Thus the path of non-return may be viewed as the basis for the *iddhi* of the path of *arahant*-ship, but it does not seem that the fruit of non-return should be viewed as such a basis.

Next in the *Vibhaṅga* comes the analysis of the seven *bojjhaṅgas*. In the *abhidhamma-bhājaniya*[99] first of all the seven *bojjhaṅgas* are related collectively to the *lokuttara-magga*, and then individually. Thus we are told that at the time of developing *lokuttara-jjhāna* at the level of the first *jhāna* there are seven *bojjhaṅgas* (which are defined in the text), and remaining *dhammas* are associated with these *bojjhaṅgas*. Following this, the seven *bojjhaṅgas* are related individually to the *lokuttara-jjhāna* formula. The first of these subsequent rehearsals concludes, then, with a statement that whatever is *sati* at that time, that is *sati-sambojjhaṅga*, and remaining *dhammas* are associated with *sati-sambojjhaṅga*. Each of the other six *bojjhaṅgas* is treated similarly. There are thus eight basic rehearsals of the *lokuttara-jjhāna* formula: one for the seven *bojjhaṅgas* collectively, and one for each of the *bojjhaṅgas* individually. Again the commentary suggests that each of these is to be expanded following the pattern of the *Dhammasaṅgaṇi*. The seven *bojjhaṅgas* are then related to *lokuttara-vipaka* consciousness in precisely the same way, with eight rehearsals of the basic formula.

We have here the notion that the *bojjhaṅgas* form a collective function, along with the notion that the whole, that is to say *lokuttara* consciousness, exists in some sense only by virtue of its relationship to each individual *bojjhaṅga*. It is also worth drawing attention to the way in which the treatment

[97] Vism-mhṭ (Ne 1972) III 1620.
[98] Vibh-a 307.
[99] Vibh 229-32.

TABLE 12. THE VIBHAṄGA'S ANALYSIS OF THE SETS BY THE TWENTY-TWO TRIPLETS OF THE ABHIDHAMMA-MĀTIKĀ

TRIPLETS 1–11

		1			2			3			4			5			6			7			8			9			10			11		
		a	b	c	a	b	c	a	b	c	a	b	c	a	b	c	a	b	c	a	b	c	a	b	c	a	b	c	a	b	c	a	b	c
INDRIYA	cakkhu			×	□	□	□			×	×				×				×	□	□	□			×			×			×			×
	sota			×	□	□	□			×	×				×				×	□	□	□			×			×			×			×
	ghāna			×	□	□	□			×	×				×				×	□	□	□			×			×			×			×
	jivhā			×	□	□	□			×	×				×				×	□	□	□			×			×			×			×
	kāya			×	□	□	□			×	×				×				×	□	□	□			×			×			×			×
	mano	×	×	×	×	×	×	×	×	×	×	×	×	×	×	×	×	×	×	⊠	⊠	⊠	×	×	×	×	×	×	×	×	×	×	×	×
	itthi			×	□	□	□			×	×				×				×	□	□	□			×			×			×			×
	purisa			×	□	□	□			×	×				×				×	□	□	□			×			×			×			×
	jīvita	×	×	×	⊠	⊠	⊠	×	×	×	×	×	×	×	×	×	×	×	×	⊠	⊠	⊠	×	×	×	×	×	×	×	×	×	×	×	×
	sukha			×	□	□	□	×			×				×				×	□	□	□			×			×			×			×
	dukkha			×	□	□	□	×			×				×				×	□	□	□			×			×			×			×
	somanassa	×	×	×	□	□	□	×	×	×	×	×	×	×	×	×	×	×	×	⊠			×	×	×	×	×	×	×	×	×	×	×	×
	domanassa		×		□	□	□		×			×		×			×			□	□	□	×	×		×	×		×					×
	upekkhā	×	×	×	□	□	□	×	×	×	×	×	×	×	×	×	×		×	□	□	□	×	×	×	×	×	×	×	×	×	×	×	×
	saddhā	×		×	×		×	×	×	×	×	×	×		×	×	×	×	×	×	×	×			×			×	×	×	×	×	×	×
	viriya	×	×	×	×	×	×	×	×	×	×	×	×	×	×	×	×	×	×	⊠	⊠	⊠	×	×	×	×	×	×	×	×	×	×	×	×
	sati	×		×	×		×	×	×	×	×	×	×		×	×	×	×	×	×	×	×			×			×	×	×	×	×	×	×
	samādhi	×	×	×	×	×	×	×	×	×	×	×	×	×	×	×	×	×	×	⊠	⊠	⊠	×	×	×	×	×	×	×	×	×	×	×	×
	paññā	×		×	×		×	×	×	×	×	×	×		×	×	×	×	×	×	×	×			×			×	×	×	×	×	×	×
	anaññātaññasāmīti	×			×		×		×				×			×	×	×	×	×	×	×			×			×		×		×		
	aññā	×		×	×		×	×	×				×			×	×	×	×	×	×	×			×			×		×	×	×		
	aññatāvin			×	×		×						×			×	×	×	×	×	×	×			×			×			×		×	
	satipaṭṭhāna	×		×	×		×	×	×				×			×	×	×	×	×	×	×			×			×		×	×	×	×	
	samma-ppadhāna	×			×		×		×				×			×	×	×	×	×	×	×			×			×		×	×	×		
	iddhi-pāda	×			×		×		×				×			×	×	×	×	×	×	×			×			×		×	×	×		

TRIPLETS 12–22

		12			13			14			15			16			17			18			19			20			21			22		
		a	b	c	a	b	c	a	b	c	a	b	c	a	b	c	a	b	c	a	b	c	a	b	c	a	b	c	a	b	c	a	b	c
INDRIYA	cakkhu	×			–	–	–		×				×	–	–	–	×	□	×	×	×	×	–	–	–	×	×	×	–	–	–		×	
	sota	×			–	–	–		×				×	–	–	–	×	□	×	×	×	×	–	–	–	×	×	×	–	–	–		×	
	ghāna	×			–	–	–		×				×	–	–	–	×	□	×	×	×	×	–	–	–	×	×	×	–	–	–		×	
	jivhā	×			–	–	–		×				×	–	–	–	×	□	×	×	×	×	–	–	–	×	×	×	–	–	–		×	
	kāya	×			–	–	–		×				×	–	–	–	×	□	×	×	×	×	–	–	–	×	×	×	–	–	–		×	
	mano	×	×	×	⊠	⊠	⊠	×	×	×	×	×	×	⊠	⊠	⊠	×	×	×	×	×	×	⊠	⊠	⊠	×	×	×	⊠	⊠	⊠			×
	itthi	×			–	–	–		×				×	–	–	–	×	□	×	×	×	×	–	–	–	×	×	×	–	–	–			×
	purisa	×			–	–	–		×				×	–	–	–	×	□	×	×	×	×	–	–	–	×	×	×	–	–	–			×
	jīvita	×	×	×	⊠	⊠	⊠	×	×	×	×	×	×	×	×	×	×	×	×	×	×	×	⊠	⊠	⊠	×	×	×	⊠	⊠	⊠			×
	sukha	×			×				×				×	□	□	□	×	□	×	×	×	×			×	×	×	×	×	×	×			×
	dukkha	×			×				×				×	□	□	□	×	□	×	×	×	×			×	×	×	×	×	×	×			×
	somanassa	×	×	×	⊠	⊠	⊠	×	×	×	×	×	×	⊠	⊠	⊠	×	×	×	×	×	×	⊠	⊠	⊠	×	×	×	×	×	×			×
	domanassa	×			⊠	⊠		×			×		×	□	□	□	×	×	□	×	×	×	⊠	⊠	⊠	×	×	×	×	×	×			×
	upekkhā	×	×	×	⊠	⊠	⊠	×	×	×	×	×	×	⊠	⊠	⊠	×	×	×	×	×	×	⊠	⊠	⊠	×	×	×	⊠	⊠	⊠			×
	saddhā	×	×	×	⊠	⊠	⊠		×	×		×	×	⊠	⊠	⊠	×	×	×	×	×	×	⊠	⊠	⊠	×	×	×	⊠	⊠	⊠			×
	viriya	×	×	×	⊠	⊠	⊠	×	×	×	×	×	×	⊠	⊠	⊠	×	×	×	×	×	×	⊠	⊠	⊠	×	×	×	⊠	⊠	⊠			×
	sati	×	×	×	⊠	⊠	⊠		×	×		×	×	⊠	⊠	⊠	×	×	×	×	×	×	⊠	⊠	⊠	×	×	×	⊠	⊠	⊠			×
	samādhi	×	×	×	⊠	⊠	⊠	×	×	×	×	×	×	⊠	⊠	⊠	×	×	×	×	×	×	⊠	⊠	⊠	×	×	×	⊠	⊠	⊠			×
	paññā	×	×	×	⊠	⊠	⊠		×	×		×	×	⊠	⊠	⊠	×	×	×	×	×	×	⊠	⊠	⊠	×	×	×	⊠	⊠	⊠			×
	anaññātaññasāmīti			×			×			×		×			×	⊠	×	×	□	×	×	×	□	□	□	×	×	×		×				×
	aññā			×			×			×		×	×		⊠	⊠	×	×	×	×	×	×	□	□	□	×	×	×		×				×
	aññatāvin			×			×			×			×	□	□	□	×	□	×	×	×	×	□	□	□	×	×	×		×				×
	satipaṭṭhāna			×			×			×		×	×		⊠	⊠	×	×	×	×	×	×	□	□	□	×	×	×		×				×
	samma-ppadhāna			×			×			×		×	×		×	⊠	×	×	□	×	×	×	□	□	□	×	×	×		×				×
	iddhi-pāda			×			×			×		×	×		×		×	×	□	×	×	×	□	□	□	×	×	×		×				×

BOJJHAṄGA	sati	× ×	× ×	× ×	×	×	× × ×	× × ×	×	×	× ×	× ×	×	×	×	× ×	⊠⊠	× × ×	× × ×	□□□	× × ×	×	×
	dhamma-vicaya	× ×	× ×	× ×	×	×	× × ×	× × ×	×	×	× ×	× ×	×	×	×	× ×	⊠⊠	× × ×	× × ×	□□□	× × ×	×	×
	viriya	× ×	× ×	× ×	×	×	× × ×	× × ×	×	×	× ×	× ×	×	×	×	× ×	⊠⊠	× × ×	× × ×	□□□	× × ×	×	×
	pīti	× ×	×	× ×	×	×	× × ×	×	×	×	× ×	× ×	×	×	×	× ×	⊠⊠	× × ×	× × ×	□□□	× × ×	×	×
	passaddhi	× ×	× ×	× ×	×	×	× × ×	× × ×	×	×	× ×	× ×	×	×	×	× ×	⊠⊠	× × ×	× × ×	□□□	× × ×	×	×
	samādhi	× ×	× ×	× ×	×	×	× × ×	× × ×	×	×	× ×	× ×	×	×	×	× ×	⊠⊠	× × ×	× × ×	□□□	× × ×	×	×
	upekkhā	× ×	× ×	× ×	×	×	× × ×	× × ×	×	×	× ×	× ×	×	×	×	× ×	⊠⊠	× × ×	× × ×	□□□	× × ×	×	×
MAGGAṄGA	sammā-diṭṭhi	× ×	× ×	× ×	×	×	× × ×	× × ×	×	×	× ×	× ×	×	×	×	× ×	⊠⊠	× × ×	× × ×	□□□	× × ×	×	×
	sammā-saṃkappa	× ×	×	× ×	×	×	× × ×	×	×	×	× ×	× ×	×	×	×	× ×	⊠⊠	× × ×	× × ×	□□□	× × ×	×	×
	sammā-vācā	× ×	× ×	× ×	×	×	× × ×	× × ×	×	×	× ×	× ×	×	×	×	× ×	⊠⊠	× × ×	× × ×	□□□	× × ×	×	×
	sammā-kammanta	× ×	× ×	× ×	×	×	× × ×	× × ×	×	×	× ×	× ×	×	×	×	× ×	⊠⊠	× × ×	× × ×	□□□	× × ×	×	×
	sammā-ājīva	× ×	× ×	× ×	×	×	× × ×	× × ×	×	×	× ×	× ×	×	×	×	× ×	⊠⊠	× × ×	× × ×	□□□	× × ×	×	×
	sammā-vāyāma	× ×	× ×	× ×	×	×	× × ×	× × ×	×	×	× ×	× ×	×	×	×	× ×	⊠⊠	× × ×	× × ×	□□□	× × ×	×	×
	sammā-sati	× ×	× ×	× ×	×	×	× × ×	× × ×	×	×	× ×	× ×	×	×	×	× ×	⊠⊠	× × ×	× × ×	□□□	× × ×	×	×
	sammā-samādhi	× ×	× ×	× ×	×	×	× × ×	× × ×	×	×	× ×	× ×	×	×	×	× ×	⊠⊠	× × ×	× × ×	□□□	× × ×	×	×

KEY

The 22 triplets are set out in Table 13 (p. 330)

× falls or may fall into triplet category a/b/c

□ should not or may should not be said to fall into triplet-category a/b/c

– is without object (triplets 13, 16, 19, 21)

E.g. The full analysis of the 22 *indriyas* by triplet 16 reads as follows: 'Seven *indriyas* are without object; four *indriyas* should not be said to have the path as object, to be connected with the motivations of the path, to have the path as overlord; *anaññātaññassāmītindriya* does not have the path as object, is connected with the motivations of the path, may have the path as overlord, or may should not be said to have the path as overlord; *aññindriya* does not have the path as object, may be connected with the motivations of the path, may have the path as overlord, may should not be said to be connected with the motivations of the path, or to have the path as overlord; nine *indriyas* may have the path as object, may be connected with the motivations of the path, may have the path as overlord, may should not be said to have the path as object, to be connected with the motivations of the path, or to have the path as overlord.' [Vibh 127]

TABLE 13. THE 22 TRIPLETS OF THE ABHIDHAMMA-MĀTIKĀ

(Dhs 1-2; for the Pāli text see page 360)

1 [a] skilful *dhammas*; [b] unskilful *dhammas*; [c] undetermined *dhammas*.

2 [a] *dhammas* accompanied by pleasant feeling; [b] *dhammas* accompanied by unpleasant feeling; [c] *dhammas* accompanied by not-unpleasant-not-pleasant feeling.

3 [a] *dhammas* that are results; [b] *dhammas* that have results; [c] *dhammas* that neither are results nor have results.

4 [a] *dhammas* that have been grasped and can be subject to grasping; [b] *dhammas* that have not been grasped but can be subject to grasping; [c] *dhammas* that have not been grasped and cannot be subject to grasping.

5 [a] *dhammas* that are defiled and connected with defilement; [b] *dhammas* that are undefiled and connected with defilements; [c] *dhammas* that are undefiled and not connected with defilement.

6 [a] *dhammas* with initial and sustained thinking; [b] *dhammas* without initial thinking but still with sustained thinking; [c] *dhammas* without initial and sustained thinking.

7 [a] *dhammas* associated with joy; [b] *dhammas* associated with happiness; [c] *dhammas* associated with equipoise.

8 [a] *dhammas* to be abandoned by seeing; [b] *dhammas* to be abandoned by development; [c] *dhammas* to be abandoned neither by seeing nor by development.

9 [a] *dhammas* connected with motivations to be abandoned by seeing; [b] *dhammas* connected with motivations to be abandoned by development; [c] *dhammas* connected with motivations to be abandoned neither by seeing nor by development.

10 [a] *dhammas* which lead to accumulation; *dhammas* which lead to dispersal; *dhammas* which lead neither to accumulation nor to dispersal.

11 [a] *dhammas* concerned with training; [b] *dhammas* that are beyond training; [c] *dhammas* that are neither concerned with training nor beyond training.

12 [a] small *dhammas*; [b] *dhammas* that have become great; [c] immeasurable *dhammas*.

13 [a] *dhammas* that have a small object; [b] *dhammas* that have an object that has become great; [c] *dhammas* that have an immeasurable object.

14 [a] deficient *dhammas*; [b] middle *dhammas*; [c] refined *dhammas*.

15 [a] *dhammas* destined to wrongness; [b] *dhammas* destined to accomplishment; [c] *dhammas* without fixed destiny.

16 [a] *dhammas* that have the path as object; [b] *dhammas* that are connected with the motivations of the path; [c] *dhammas* that have the path as overlord.

17 [a] *dhammas* that have arisen; [b] *dhammas* that have not arisen; [c] *dhammas* that will arise.

18 [a] past *dhammas*; [b] future dhammas; [c] present *dhammas*.

19 [a] *dhammas* that have a past object; [b] *dhammas* that have a future object; [c] *dhammas* that have a present object.

20 [a] *dhammas* that are within; [b] *dhammas* that are without; [c] *dhammas* that are within and without.

21 [a] *dhammas* that have an object within; [b] *dhammas* that have an object without; [c] *dhammas* that have an object within and without.

22 [a] *dhammas* that can be indicated and offer resistance; [b] *dhammas* that cannot be indicated but offer resistance; [c] *dhammas* that cannot be indicated and do not offer resistance.

of the *bojjhaṅgas* contrasts with that of the *indriyas*. The *pañhâpucchaka* for the *indriyas* makes it clear that *viriya*, for example, as an element of skilful or unskilful *citta* of any kind is to be reckoned *viriyindriya*. However from the *pañhâpucchaka* for the *bojjhaṅgas*, it is apparent that it is only as a constituent of *lokuttara* consciousness that *viriya* is to be reckoned *viriya-sambojjhaṅga*. The same principle operates in the case of the remaining *bojjhaṅgas*.

So finally there is the *magga-vibhaṅga*. In principle the *abhidhamma-bhājaniya* for the *magga*[100] follows the method adopted for the *bojjhaṅgas*; the path factors are related to *lokuttara-jjhāna*, both skilful and resultant, collectively and then individually. In the case of the path factors, however, we have the complication of the eight-factored path and—omitting *sammā-vācā*, *sammā-kammanta* and *sammā-ājīva* from the reckoning—the five-factored path.

Both the eight-factored and the five-factored paths are each collectively related to the *lokuttara-jjhāna* formula with concluding statements following the usual form: 'this is called the eight-factored path; remaining *dhammas* are associated with the eight-factored path' and 'this is called the five-factored path; remaining *dhammas* are associated with the five-factored path'.[101] However, it is only the five factors that are individually related to the *lokuttara-jjhāna* formula, with concluding statements following the form: 'this is called right view; remaining *dhammas* are associated with right view'. I have already referred to the ancient Abhidharma discussions concerning the eight- and five-factored path. The Pāli commentaries wholeheartedly reject the notion of a five-factored *lokuttara* path. Does the *Vibhaṅga* here preserve a tradition at odds with the received commentarial thinking on the matter? It is just possible, but if it were truly the case one would expect the eight-factored and five-factored paths to be given equal weight as alternatives; that is to say, one would expect both to be related to *lokuttara-jjhāna* collectively and individually. One might also expect there to be mention of a seven-factored and even four-factored path.[102] The fact that there is not suggests that it is the special function of the five factors that is being highlighted rather than alternative paths. This, at any rate, is how the commentary takes it:

> So what is the point of including this 'five-factored path'? In order to indicate the extra function. For when one abandons wrong speech and fulfils right speech, then there is no right action and right livelihood. Just these five active factors abandon wrong speech, while right speech fulfils itself by way of refraining ... The five-factored path is included in order to indicate the extra function of these five active factors.[103]

---

[100] Vibh 236-41.

[101] See Vibh 237-8.

[102] *Sammā-saṃkappa* (= *vitakka*) is absent in the second, third, fourth and fifth *jhānas* of the fivefold system. The possibility of there being a *lokuttara* path with only seven *maggaṅgas* is recognized at As 226, 228; similarly there may only be six *bojjhaṅgas* present (*pīti-sambojjhaṅga* is absent after the third *jhāna* in the fivefold system). The possibility of these variations is inherent in the *Vibhaṅga* in the *pañhâpucchaka* sections; cf. triplets two and seven.

[103] Vibh-a 320: *atha pañcaṅgiko maggo ti idaṃ kiṃ atthaṃ gahitan ti. atireka-kicca-dassanatthaṃ. yasmiṃ hi samaye micchā-vācaṃ pajahati, sammā-vācaṃ pūreti, tasmiṃ samaye sammā-kammanta-sammā-ājīvā natthi. imāni pañca kārāpakaṅgān'eva micchā-vācaṃ pajahanti sammā-vācā*

The commentary spells this out for right action and livelihood as well. So, in other words, the five path-factors are universally active in the development of right speech, and the rest, but the latter are only active in the refraining from wrong speech, wrong action and wrong livelihood respectively.

As with the *bojjhaṅgas*, the *pañhâpucchaka* makes it quite clear that the path factors are here treated exclusively as constituents of *lokuttara* consciousness. The *Vibhaṅga* is not here concerned with the path-factors in their more general aspect. That this is so is also apparent from the fact that the definitions of the individual path-factors in the *abhidhamma-bhājaniya* include the terms *magg-aṅga* and *magga-pariyāpanna*.

What are the general conclusions to be drawn from this treatment? In the first place the *Vibhaṅga* gives a strict Abhidhamma account of the *indriyas*, *satipaṭṭhānas*, *samma-ppadhānas*, *iddhi-pādas*, *bojjhaṅgas* and *maggaṅgas*. According to this account strictly one only talks of the five last mentioned categories with reference to *lokuttara* consciousness. For it seems that it is only at this time that they come into their own. This is what they are geared to; this is their ultimate point of reference. Apart from *lokuttara* consciousness, strictly one should talk only of *indriyas*. It seems, then, that when the *satipaṭṭhānas* and so on are spoken of in the context of ordinary skilful *citta*, it is only in so far as that *citta* approximates to or is geared towards the development of *lokuttara* consciousness. It should be noted that the *jhānas* are treated quite differently from the seven sets in the *Vibhaṅga*; they are not confined to *lokuttara* consciousness (which is, however, included) but are treated by way of ordinary *rūpâvacara* skilful and resultant *citta*.

5. The thirty-seven bodhi-pakkhiyā dhammā: ordinary and transcendent

As noted above, in the *Visuddhimagga* a distinction is made between the thirty-seven *bodhi-pakkhiyā dhammā* as *lokiya* or 'ordinary' and *lokuttara* or 'transcendent'. In fact the commentaries repeatedly draw attention to this distinction:[104] when *samatha* and *vipassanā* are being actively developed during 'the prior stage' (*pubba-bhāga*, i.e. the stage prior to the arising of the *lokuttara* path) we can speak of the *bodhi-pakkhiyā dhammā* as *lokiya*; when the *lokuttara* path and fruit arise the *bodhi-pakkhiyā dhammā* are themselves *lokuttara*. What does this strictly mean? In what kinds of consciousness does the commentarial tradition understand 'ordinary' *bodhi-pakkhiyā dhammā* to be present? What exactly is the extent of the 'prior stage' and what precisely is to be reckoned as *samatha* and *vipassanā*?

These questions are worth considering initially in relationship to the varieties of *citta* distinguished in the *Dhammasaṅgaṇi*. Which of these might be said to possess 'ordinary' *bodhi-pakkhiyā dhammā*? Clearly we can exclude all unskilful and all *vipāka* consciousness on the grounds that the development of *samatha* and *vipassanā* must involve active skilful consciousness. Of the eight

---

pana sayaṃ virati-vasena pūrati ... imaṃ etesaṃ pañcannaṃ kārāpakaṅgānaṃ kiccâtirekakataṃ dassetuṃ pañcaṅgiko maggo ti gahitaṃ.

[104] Cf. Sp II 494; Sv II 564; III 883-4; Ps III 243-4; IV 28-9; Mp II 49-51, 70, 73; It-a 73-4.

kāmâvacara skilful *cittas*, the four dissociated from knowledge (*ñāṇa-vippayutta*) can also be excluded on the grounds that there is no *vipassanā* apart from knowledge. This leaves the four *kāmâvacara* skilful *cittas* associated with knowledge,[105] and the various kinds of *rūpâvacara* and *arūpâvacara* skilful *citta*. Are we to conclude that whenever any of these varieties of *citta* occurs, the relevant fourteen *dhammas* are to be termed 'ordinary' *bodhi-pakkhiyā dhammā*? After all, the *Dhammasaṅgaṇi* does bring out the pair *samatha* and *vipassanā* in these varieties of consciousness.[106] It seems clear that in principle these are the varieties of *citta* to be associated with 'ordinary' *bodhi-pakkhiyā dhammā*, but there is perhaps a little more to the commentarial understanding of the matter than this. The question can be taken a little further by pursuing the notion of the *pubba-bhāga* or 'prior stage'.

In general, the term *pubba-bhāga* appears to be a straightforward relative term—the 'prior stage' it signifies depends on its precise point of reference. However, its usage seems to indicate that what it refers to is most characteristically whatever is *immediately* prior to something else; that is to say, a *pubba-bhāga* is the initial stage of some particular further stage.[107] The usage of the term *pubba-bhāga* in connection with the exposition of the *iddhi-pādas* brings this out most clearly.[108] An *iddhi-pāda* is to be understood as a *pubba-bhāga* for an *iddhi*. It is said that the meaning of this is to be explained with reference to either access concentration (cf. *samatha*) or insight. Accordingly if the point of reference is the first *jhāna*, then the *pubba-bhāga* is the 'preparation' (*parikamma*) for the first *jhāna*; if the point of reference is the path of stream-attainment, then the *pubba-bhāga* is the insight for the path of stream-attainment (*sotâpatti-maggassa vipassanā*).

The association of *pubba-bhāga* with *parikamma* is of some significance. In the description of the consciousness process that *immediately* precedes full absorption (*appanā*) of form-sphere *jhāna*, formless-sphere attainments and the *lokuttara* path and fruit types of consciousness, *parikamma* appears as a technical term.[109] This consciousness process focuses on the actual transition from the ordinary sense-sphere consciousness to form-sphere, formless-sphere or *lokuttara* consciousness. The moment of transition is understood to be preceded by three or four moments of ordinary *kāmâvacara* skilful *citta* associated with knowledge.[110] These four moments of consciousness may be termed 'preparation' (*parikamma*), 'access' (*upacāra*), 'conformity' (*anuloma*) and 'state of lineage' (*gotra-bhū*) respectively.[111] By an alternative method the initial three (*parikamma*, *upacāra* and *anuloma*) may be *collectively* termed *parikamma* or *upacāra* or *anuloma*. It seems that it is with reference to this that

---

105 See Dhs 9-29; the four *ñāṇa-sampayutta* are the first, second, fifth and sixth types of *citta* distinguished.

106 Cf. Dhs 9.

107 As 378 characterizes the *pubba-bhāga* and *apara-bhāga* of sleep as *thīna-middha*.

108 See above, p. 88.

109 See Vism IV 74-5, XIV 121, XXI 129-30.

110 Abhidh-s IV 7; see (JPTS (1884), p. 18).

111 When there are only three initial moments of *citta*, it is the *parikamma* moment that is taken as missing.

the *parikamma* for the first *jhāna* is taken as an *iddhi-pāda* or *pubba-bhāga*. Quite consistently, the term *pubba-bhāga* is elsewhere identified with *upacāra* concentration.[112] The significance of this is that the notion of 'access-concentration' involves not only a momentary consciousness that is passed through on the way to full absorption, but also a more definite and enduring stage; *upacāra* is a level of concentration to be cultivated in its own right.[113] It seems that the *pubba-bhāga* with regard to the arising of the *lokuttara* path might be taken in a similar way; that is to say it might be taken to indicate either a momentary stage passed through immediately prior to the arising of *lokuttara* consciousness, or a more enduring stage that nevertheless corresponds in level more or less to the momentary stage. In other words, if one's point of reference is the *lokuttara* path-knowledge, then the *pubba-bhāga* is *samatha* and *vipassanā* that either immediately precedes its arising, or approximates and is close to it in character. In this connection it is worth quoting a commentarial gloss:

> 'He does not take up the sign': he does not know that, having reached conformity and the state of lineage, the meditation subject has been established by him; he is unable to take up the sign in his mind. In this *sutta* the *satipaṭṭhānas* connected with insight of the prior stage only are spoken of.[114]

This outlook is perhaps to be related to a brief comment in a later Abhidhamma work, the *Paramatthavinicchaya*, to the effect that the *bodhi-pakkhiyā dhammā* are seen at the stage of watching the rise and fall of things (*udaya-bbaya-dassana*).[115] According to Buddhaghosa and the author of the *Paramatthavinicchaya*, watching rise and fall (*udaya-bbayânupassanā*) is characteristic of both the fifth *visuddhi* (knowledge and vision of path and not-path) and the sixth *visuddhi* (knowledge and vision of the way).[116] The knowledge connected with watching rise and fall at the stage of the fifth *visuddhi* is initially disabled by the ten defilements (*upakkilesa*) of insight. Having overcome the ten defilements, the practitioner completes the fifth *visuddhi* and enters the stage of the sixth *visuddhi* which begins once more with the watching of rise and fall, and culminates in the momentary 'knowledge of conformity' (*anuloma-ñāṇa*) that signals the arising of the *lokuttara* path. According to Buddhadatta the last of the nine knowledges that add up to the sixth *visuddhi* is called 'conformity' because it conforms both to the previous eight knowledges and to the *bodhi-pakkhiya-dhammas*.[117] So *anuloma-ñāṇa* is what links the domain of the advanced stages of insight to the domain of the *bodhi-pakkhiya-dhammas*

---

112 Vism III 6: 'And that which is one-pointedness in the prior-stage of the absorption concentrations—this is access concentration.' (*yā ca appanā-samadhīnaṃ pubba-bhāge ekaggatā ayaṃ upacāra-samādhi.*)

113 Cf. Vism III 6, 106, IV 32-3.

114 Spk III 150 (to S V 150, quoted above, p. 52): *nimittaṃ na uggaṇhātī ti imaṃ me kamma-ṭṭhānaṃ anulomaṃ vā gotrabhuṃ vā ahacca ṭhitan ti na jānāti. attano cittassa nimittaṃ gahituṃ na sakkoti. imasmiṃ sutte pubba-bhāga-vipassanā satipaṭṭhānā va kathitā.*

115 See *Paramatthavinicchaya* v. 996, *JPTS* 10 (1985), p. 210.

116 See Vism 93-104, XX 2-9; *Paramatthavinicchaya*, *JPTS* 10 (1985), pp. 210-11.

117 Abhidh-av 124: *purimānaṃ pan'aṭṭhannaṃ ñāṇānaṃ anulomato| bodhi-pakkhiya-dhammānaṃ uddhañ ca anulomato|| ten'eva taṃ hi saccânuloma-ñāṇaṃ pavuccati|* (Cf. Vimutt Trsl 301, quoted above, p. 302).

proper, namely the *lokuttara* paths and fruits. To then view the advanced stages of insight as the particular domain of the *lokiya* or ordinary *bodhi-pakkhiya-dhammas* requires only a small shift in one's perspective.

It seems possible, then, to form a fairly clear idea of the particular domain of the ordinary *bodhi-pakkhiyā dhammā* as understood in the commentaries. But one should note here that the notion of *pubba-bhāga* is sometimes extended to the notion of *sabba-pubba-bhāga* or 'the prior stage of all'.[118] Thus the *Vibhaṅga* commentary states that the discussion of the *samma-ppadhānas* is twofold, *lokiya* and *lokuttara*; the *lokiya* discussion refers to the *sabba-pubba-bhāga*.[119] This might suggest that at whatever stage in a *bhikkhu's* practice skilful *viriya* arises, it can be appropriately termed *samma-ppadhāna*. But this principle would not seem to apply equally to all seven sets. Even when the application of the *bojjhaṅgas* is extended beyond the confines of *lokuttara* paths and fruit, and beyond the confines of strong insight, the usage of the term is still fairly tight: the *kasiṇa-jjhānas* that are a basis for insight and the *jhānas* of breathing in and out, ugliness and the *brahma-vihāras*.[120] If one recalls the treatment of the *Dhammasaṅgaṇi*, all this is perhaps indicative of a certain hierarchy underlying the conception of the seven sets, that is to say one might speak of *samma-ppadhāna*, *indriyas* and *balas* in rather more contexts than one might speak of *bojjhaṅgas*. This is certainly rather suggestive when considered alongside the Sarvāstivādin conception of the seven sets as spanning the various stages of the path to awakening.

6. *The thirty-seven bodhi-pākṣikā dharmāḥ according to the Sarvāstivāda*

In this section I do not intend to attempt a systematic and comprehensive account of the thirty-seven *bodhi-pākṣikā dharmāḥ* according to Sarvāstivādin Abhidharma sources; such an undertaking would extend this study indefinitely. Rather I wish to draw attention to the basic features and principles of the treatment of the thirty-seven *dharmas* in Sarvāstivādin Abhidharma texts—and also other texts that bear a kinship relationship to the Sarvāstivādin Abhidharma system. This will help to throw the Theravādin Abhidhamma treatment into relief. My basic sources for this section are the **Abhidharmahṛdaya* (or

---

118 At Mp I 70 the *sabba-pubba-bhāga* of *mettā* is clearly distinguished from both 'access' and 'absorption'; it is 'the mere suffusion of friendliness towards beings' (*mettāya sabba-pubba-bhāgo nama neva appanā na upacāro sattānaṃ hita-pharaṇa-mattaṃ evā ti*). The same passage continues: 'But here it should be understood that he practises just by the mere occurrence of a suffusion of friendliness which is the prior stage of *mettā*.' (*idha pana mettā-pubba-bhāgena hita-pharaṇa-pavattana-matten'eva āsevatī ti veditabbaṃ.*) I do not think that the equation of *mettāya pubba-bhāgo* and *mettāya sabba-pubba-bhāgo* in this particular context can be taken to mean, as Aronson suggests (*LCSJE*, p. 224), that the two expressions are used as simple equivalents in all contexts; Aronson's conclusion that *mettāya pubba-bhāgo* is always necessarily something different from 'access', therefore appears to me unsound. (Cf. Aronson, *LCSJE*, pp. 112-8, 160-4, 223-4.)

119 Vibh-a 291: *ayaṃ hi samma-ppadhāna-kathā nāma duvidhā lokiyā lokuttarā ca. tattha lokiyā sabba-pubba-bhāge hoti.*

120 See above, p. 180.

-sāra) of Dharmaśrī,[121] the **Abhidharmâmṛtarasa* of Ghoṣaka,[122] the **Satya siddhi-śāstra* (or *Tattva-*) of Harivarman,[123] the *Abhidharmakośa-bhāṣya* of Vasubandhu, the *Abhidharmadīpa*, whose author is unknown, and the *Abhidharmasamuccaya* of Asaṅga.[124] The precise dating of these texts is, as always, problematic, but the first three of the aforementioned works seem certainly to pre-date the *Abhidharmakośa* (4th-5th centuries CE), while the *Abhidharmadīpa* certainly assumes the *Kośa*.[125]

Like the Pāli sources, these Buddhist Sanskrit sources identify the *bodhipākṣikā dharmāḥ* with the *mārga* or 'path'. As we have seen, strictly the Pāli Abhidhamma sources tend to identify the seven sets or thirty-seven *bodhipakkhiyā dhammā* with the actual arising of the *lokuttara* path, i.e. the culmination of the path, though a more general identification of the seven sets with the path seems to be assumed in the Suttanta formulations. Buddhist Sanskrit sources, too, tend to see the relationship of the thirty-seven *dharmas* to the path in broad terms.[126]

So the Sarvāstivādin Abhidharma understands the thirty-seven *bodhi-pākṣikā dharmāḥ* to be one possible way of characterizing the path to awakening. However, the Sarvāstivādin Abhidharma does, of course, preserve its own account of the consecutive stages of the path to awakening—the counterpart to the account of the seven *visuddhis* in the *Visuddhimagga*. The basic features of this Sarvāstivādin account of the stages of the path have been well documented by others,[127] and since the treatment of the *bodhi-pākṣikā dharmāḥ* is to some extent geared to this gradual account, it is as well to set it out in brief here.

The complete path to awakening is usually conceived of as made up of five paths: 'the path of equipment' (*sambhāra-mārga*), 'the path of application' (*prayoga-mārga*), 'the path of vision' (*darśana-mārga*), 'the path of development' (*bhāvanā-mārga*), and 'the path of the adept' (*aśaikṣa-mārga*).[128] The *sambhāra-mārga* consists of the various practices that are considered the necessary preliminaries to the cultivation of the path proper; it culminates in the practice of *aśubha-bhāvanā* and *ānâpāna-smṛti*.[129] The practice of *aśubha-bhāvanā* and *ānâpāna-smṛti* results in *śamatha* or *samādhi*, and it is at this point

---

[121] *The Essence of Metaphysics*, translated and annotated by C. Willemen, Bruxelles, 1975; *Le Coeur de la Loi Suprême*, traduit et annoté par I. Armelin, Paris, 1978. (References are to the former).

[122] *La Saveur de l'Immortel: La version chinoise de l'Amṛtarasa de Ghoṣaka (T. 1553)*, traduite et annotée par J. Van Den Broek, Louvain, 1977.

[123] *Satyasiddhiśāstra of Harivarman*, Vol. II, English Translation, N. Aiyaswami Sastri, Baroda, 1978 (English translation from Skt text reconstructed on the basis of the Chinese).

[124] *Le Compendium de la Super-doctrine (philosophie) (Abhidharmasamuccaya) d'Asaṅga*, traduit et annoté par W. Rahula, Paris, 1971.

[125] For additional references to non-Pāli sources see below, pp. 357-8.

[126] By means of the seven sets one attains *nirvāṇa* (Amṛta Trsl 201); the truth of the path consists of the thirty-seven *bodhi-pākṣikā dharmāḥ* (Satya Trsl 41); the path is called *bodhi-pākṣika* (Abhidh-k 382; Abhidh-dī 356).

[127] La Vallée Poussin, Abhidh-k Trsl IV iv-xi; Lamotte, *HBI*, pp. 678-85; Conze, BTI, pp. 175-7; H.V. Guenther, *PPA*, pp. 215-32.

[128] Also called the *viśeṣa-* or *niṣṭhā-mārga*.

[129] Abhidh-k 337 (VI 8-9).

that the practitioner begins to develop the four *smṛty-upasthānas* proper.[130] Borne of the practice of the fourth *smṛty-upasthāna*[131] (which here, as noted, subsumes the other three) are the four stages of penetrative wisdom (*nirvedha-bhāgīya*) that constitute the *prayoga-mārga*: 'sparks' (*uṣma-gata*), 'summits' (*mūrdhan*), 'acceptance' (*kṣānti*) and the state that constitutes the peak of ordinary experience, the *laukikâgra-dharma*. This last is momentary and signals the immediate arising of the transcendent *darśana-mārga*. In the *Abhidharma-kośa-bhāṣya* Vasubandhu's account of the four *nirvedha-bhāgīyas* sees them as an extension of the practice of the fourth *smṛty-upasthāna*.[132] The *nirvedha-bhāgīyas* are developed only in the preliminary to full *dhyāna* (i.e. the *anāgamya*; cf. the Theravādin notion of *upacāra*) or in the *dhyānas* themselves (including the *dhyānântara* or 'in between *dhyāna*' without *vitarka* but still with *vicāra*); they are not developed in the four formless attainments.[133] The momentary stage of *laukikâgra-dharma* is still considered to be 'with *āsravas*' (*sâsrava*). The *darśana-mārga* consists of fifteen moments of consciousness that are said to be 'without *āsravas*' (*anāsrava*).[134] There follows a sixteenth moment which completes the vision of the four truths in sixteen aspects. This sixteenth moment constitutes the beginning of the *bhāvanā-mārga*.[135] The fifteen moments are equivalent to path-attainment and the sixteenth moment to fruit attainment.[136] Like the *nirvedha-bhāgīyas*, these sixteen consciousnesses occur only at the levels of the *anāgamya*, *dhyānântara*, and four *dhyānas*.[137] The culmination of the *bhāvanā-mārga* is the 'diamond like concentration' (*vajropama-samādhi*) of the path of *arhant*ship that issues in *bodhi* itself: knowledge with regard to non-arising (*anutpāda-jñāna*) and knowledge with regard to destruction (*kṣaya-jñāna*).[138] The fruit of *arhant*-ship is equivalent to the *aśaikṣa-mārga*.

This summary account of the Sarvāstivādin path will suffice for present purposes. Alongside it I wish to consider the thirty-seven *bodhi-pākṣikā dharmāḥ* by way of three topics:[139] (i) the consideration of the thirty-seven *dharmas* as ten *dravyas* or 'elements'; (ii) the distribution of the seven sets over the five paths of equipment, application, vision, development and the adept; (iii) the distribution of the thirty-seven *dharmas* through the various levels of existence, beginning with the realm of sense-desire (*kāma-dhātu*).

---

130 Abhidh-k 341 (VI 14a): *niṣpanna-śamathaḥ kuryāt smṛty-upasthāna-bhāvanām.*

131 Abhidh-k 343 (bh to VI 17a): *tasmād dharma-smṛty-upasthānād evam abhyastāt krameṇoṣma-gataṃ nāma kuśala-mūlam utpadyate.*

132 Abhidh-k 345 (bh to VI 19c): *ta eta uṣma-gatâdayaḥ smṛty-upasthāna-svabhāvatvāt prajñâtmakā ucyante.*

133 Abhidh-k 346 (VI 20 c-d).

134 Abhidh-k 345 (bh to VI 19c), 350 (bh to VI 26a).

135 Abhidh-k 353 (bh to VI 28c-d).

136 Abhidh-k 353-4 (VI 29-31). The nature of the path and fruit attainment (whether of stream-attainment, once-return or non-return) is determined by previous practice in the course of the *laukika-bhāvanā-mārga*.

137 Abhidh-k 352 (bh to VI 27d): *yad bhūmiko'gra-dharmas tad bhūmikāny etāni ṣoḍaśa cittāni; te punaḥ ṣaḍ-bhūmikā ity uktaṃ prāk.*

138 See Abhidh-k 364-5 (VI 44-5). I have commented on the restricted usage of the term *bodhi* in Sarvāstivādin Abhidharma above.

139 Cf. Lamotte, *Traité*, III 1132-3.

The dravyas

Just as in the Theravādin system the various correspondences inherent in the Nikāya definitions of the seven sets are resolved to give a list of fourteen *dhammas*, so in the Sarvāstivādin system, except that the Sarvāstivādins generally arrive at only ten *dravyas*.[140] The discrepancy is to be explained by reference to the four *ṛddhi-pādas* and the three path-factors *samyag-vāk*, *samyak-karmânta* and *samyag-ājīva*. Thus the *ṛddhi-pādas* are reduced to just one item, namely *samādhi*, and the three path-factors to one item, namely *śīla*. That this should be so is not entirely surprising. As we have seen, the method of taking the *iddhi-pādas* is somewhat undecided or fluid in Theravādin Abhidhamma texts. The *Abhidharmakośa-bhāṣya* also notes that certain teachers (the Vaibhāṣikas according to the *Vyākhyā* of Yaśomitra) took the *ṛddhi-pādas* as four items (*chanda*, *citta*, *vīrya*, *mīmāṃsā*) and thus added *chanda* and *citta* to their list of *dravyas*.[141] Opinion also seems to have varied on whether to take the three path-factors as one, two or three items.[142] Thus the author of the *Abhidharmadīpa* distinguishes *samyag-vāk* and *samyak-karmânta* but not *samyag-ājīva*, giving a list of eleven *dravyas*;[143] while the *Abhidharmakośa* refers to a Vaibhāṣika list of eleven *dravyas* whereby *samyag-vāk* and *samyak-karmânta* are taken as one item, *samyag-ājīva* as a separate item.[144] Lamotte notes that the *Vibhāṣā*, in addition to ten and eleven *dravyas*, allows twelve;[145] he does not elaborate, but such a total might be arrived at by either taking the *ṛddhi-pādas* as three and the *śīlâṅgas* as one, or the *ṛddhi-pādas* as one and the *śīlâṅgas* as three.

The distribution of the seven sets

Both the *Abhidharmakośa* and *Abhidharmadīpa* give the following account of the way in which the seven sets can be allocated to the various stages of the path:[146]

ādi-karmika	—	*smṛty-upasthāna*
uṣma-gata	—	*samyak-prahāṇa*
mūrdhan	—	*ṛddhi-pāda*
kṣānti	—	*indriya*
laukikâgra-dharmas	—	*bala*

---

140 Abhidh-h Trsl 139; Amṛta Trsl 208-9; Abhidh-k 383-4 (VI 67-9).

141 Abhidh-k 384 (bh to VI 69c-d): *ye tv āhuḥ samādhir evarddhiḥ pādaś chandâdaya iti, teṣāṃ dravyatas trayodaśa bodhi-pakṣyāḥ prāpnuvanti chanda-cittayor ādhikyāt*. (They get thirteen because they also count two *śīlâṅgas*; see below.)

142 Cf. the *Atthasālinī* discussion of these three path-factors; see above, p. 196.

143 Abhidh-dī 358: *dravyatas tv ekadaśa: śraddhâdīni pañca balāni prīti-praśrabdhy-upekṣā-samyaksaṃkalpa-vāk-karmântaś ca ṣaḍ iti*.

144 Abhidh-k 383-4 (bh to VI 19a-b): *vaibhāṣikānām ekadaśa kāya-vāk-karmaṇor asambhinnatvāt śīlâṅgāni dve dravye iti*.

145 *Traité*, III 1132.

146 Abhidh-k 384-5 (bh to VI 70); Abhidh-dī 362.

darśana-mārga	—	*mārgâṅga*
bhāvanā-mārga	—	*bodhy-aṅga*

Of note here is the inverting of the *bodhy-aṅgas* and *mārgâṅgas*, though it is pointed out that some teachers follow the order of Sūtra and thus identify the *bodhy-aṅgas* with the *darśana-mārga* and the *mārgâṅgas* with the *bhāvanā-mārga*.

In the *Jewel Ornament of Liberation*, sGam.po.pa preserves a slightly different tradition for which I have been unable to find an Indian source that gives full details, though the *Madhyântavibhāga-bhāṣya* all but does so:[147]

	(smaller)	—	*smṛty-upasthāna*
sambhāra-mārga	(mediocre)	—	*samyak-prahāṇa*
	(greater)	—	*ṛddhi-pāda*
prayoga-mārga	*uṣma-gata* *mūrdhan*	—	*indriya*
	kṣānti *laukikâgra*	—	*bala*
darśana-mārga		—	*bodhy-aṅga*
bhāvanā-mārga		—	*mārgâṅga*

The **Abhidharmahṛdaya* makes use of a different terminology but again seems to want to view the seven sets as developed successively:[148]

upasthāna	—	*smṛty-upasthāna*
vyāyāma	—	*samyak-prahāṇa*
cittaikâgratā	—	*ṛddhi-pāda*
indriya (mṛdu)	—	*indriya*
indriya (tīkṣṇa)	—	*bala*
darśana-mārga	—	*bodhy-aṅga*
bhāvanā-mārga	—	*mārgâṅga*

A similar progressive view of the seven sets seems inherent in the following from the *Abhidharmasamuccaya*, again involving rather different terminology:[149]

---

147 *Jewel Ornament of Liberation*, translated by H.V. Guenther, London, 1959, pp. 112-4, 232-4. The *Madhyântavibhāga-bhāṣya* (IV 8-10) identifies the first two of the *nirvedha-bhāgīyas* with the *indriyas*, and the second two with the *balas;* it identifies the *bodhy-aṅgas* with the *darśana-mārga* and the *mārgâṅgas* with the *bhāvanā-mārga* (see S. Anacker, *Seven Works of Vasubandhu*, Delhi, 1984, pp. 249-5, 448) but is silent on the question of the *sambhāra-mārga*.

148 Abhidh-h Trsl 140. Abhidh-h Trsl (II) 194 gives the term *sthiti* for *upasthāna*; this might indicate 'abode' or 'resting place', echoing the various Nikāya treatments of the *satipaṭṭhānas* as the *gocara* of the *bhikkhus*. The association of *samyak-prahāṇa* with *vyāyāma* ('striving'), *ṛddhi-pāda* with *cittaikâgratā* ('one-pointedness') and *indriya* and *bala* with weak and sharp faculties follows the usual pattern.

149 Abhidh-sam Trsl 116-7. The seven paths might be translated as the path of examining things, the path of striving, the path of preparation for concentration, the path of application to comprehension, the path that adheres to comprehension, the path of comprehension, the path that leads out to purification.

vastu-parīkṣā-mārga	—	*smṛty-upasthāna*
vyāvasāyika-mārga	—	*samyak-prahāṇa*
samādhi-parikara-mārga	—	*ṛddhi-pāda*
abhisamaya-prayogika-mārga	—	*indriya*
abhisamaya-śliṣṭa-mārga	—	*bala*
abhisamaya-mārga	—	*bodhy-aṅga*
viśuddhi-nairyāṇika-mārga	—	*mārgâṅga*

The occurrence of the 37 bodhi-pākṣikas in the different levels[150]

This is most conveniently set out in tabular form. The Sarvāstivādin treatment of the *bodhi-pākṣikā dharmāḥ* in this respect in fact shows broad agreement with the *Dhammasaṅgaṇi*: the seven *bodhy-aṅgas* and eight *mārgâṅgas* are generally excluded from the *kāma-dhātu*. This relates to the fact that the *mārgâṅgas* and *bodhy-aṅgas* are said to be *anāsrava* because of their association with *lokottara* comprehension of the four truths, which cannot be achieved by consciousness of the *kāma-dhātu* type. In other words, these two categories are only relevant to *lokottara* consciousness. In the *Dhammasaṅgaṇi*, although *maggaṅgas* are brought out in *kāmâvacara-citta*, they are brought out fully and completely only in the *lokuttara*. Interestingly, though, the Sarvāstivādin texts bear witness to a certain amount of discussion concerning the proper way to handle the *mārgâṅgas*. The *Amṛtarasa* states that of the seven sets the seven *bodhy-aṅgas* are always without *āsravas*; the remaining six sets may be either with or without *āsravas*.[151] However, it goes on to note that some teachers are of the view that both the *bodhy-aṅgas* and the *mārgâṅgas* are only without *āsravas*. Again, in keeping with the view that it is just the *bodhy-aṅgas* that are only without *āsravas*, the *Abhidharmadīpa* excludes the *bodhy-aṅgas* alone from the *kāma-dhātu*. The *Abhidharmakośa*, however, sides with those who are of the opinion that both the *bodhy-aṅgas* and *mārgâṅgas* are only without *āsravas*, while the rest may be either with or without.[152] The principal divergence from the Theravādin system in all this would seem to be that *lokottara* comprehension (*abhisamaya*) of the four truths can take place in the *anāgamya* and first three *ārūpya-samāpattis* in addition to the *dhyānântara* and four *dhyānas*, which correspond to the five *jhānas* of the Theravādins. But the *ārūpyas* that are *anāsrava* are restricted to the *lokottara-bhāvanā-mārga*; the *darśana-mārga* is never of the *ārūpya* level.[153]

What are the general conclusions to be drawn from this treatment of the

---

150 Abhidh-h Trsl 140-1; Amṛta Trsl 209; Abhidh-dī 365; Abhidh-k 385-6 (VI 71-3). See Table 14, p. 341.

151 Despite the fact that Amṛta excludes both the *bodhy-aṅgas* and *mārgâṅgas* from the *kāma-dhātu*.

152 Abhidh-k 385 (VI 71).

153 E.g. see Abhidh-k 365 (bh to VI 44d) (on three *ārūpyas* as *vajropama-samādhi*), 368 (bh to VI 48 c-d). Cf. L. Schmithausen 'On some aspects of descriptions or theories of "liberating insight" and "enlightenment" in early Buddhism' in *Studien zum Jainismus und Buddhismus (Gedenkschrift für Ludwig Alsdorf)*, ed. K. Bruhn and A. Wezler, Wiesbaden, 1980, pp. 240-4.

TABLE 14. THE OCCURRENCE OF THE BODHI-PĀKṢIKAS IN DIFFERENT LEVELS

		Present	Absent
kāma-dhātu	Abhidh-h	22	*7 bodhy-aṅgas*, 8 *mārgâṅgas*
	Amṛta	22	*7 bodhy-aṅgas*, 8 *mārgâṅgas*
	Abhidh-k	22	*7 bodhy-aṅgas*, 8 *mārgâṅgas*
	Abhidh-dī	30	*7 bodhy-aṅgas*
anāgāmya	all	36	*prīti*
dhyāna (1)	all	37	
dhyānântara	all	35	*prīti*, *saṃkalpa*
dhyāna (2)	all	36	*saṃkalpa*
dhyāna (3-4)	all	35	*prīti*, *saṃkalpa*
ārūpya (1-3)	Abhidh-h	31	*prīti*, *saṃkalpa*, 3 *śīlâṅgas*,[1] *kāya-smṛty-upasthāna*[2]
	Amṛta	32	*prīti*, *saṃkalpa*, 3 *śīlâṅgas*
	Abhidh-k	32	*prīti*, *saṃkalpa*, 3 *śīlâṅgas*
	Adhidh-dī	32	*prīti*, *saṃkalpa*, 3 *śīlâṅgas*
bhavâgra	Abhidh-h	21	*7 bodhy-aṅgas*, 8 *mārgâṅgas*, *kāya-smṛty-upasthāna*
	Amṛta	22	*7 bodhy-aṅgas*, 8 *mārgâṅgas*
	Abhidh-k	22	*7 bodhy-aṅgas*, 8 *mārgâṅgas*
	Abhidh-dī	25	*7 bodhy-aṅgas*, 3 *śīlâṅgas*, *prīti*, *saṃkalpa*[3]

NOTES

1 The 3 *śīlâṅgas* are absent from the first 3 *ārūpyas* because they are *avijñapti-rūpa*.
2 Yaśomitra takes up the question of why Abhidh-k does not exclude *kāya-smṛty-upasthāna* from the *ārūpyas* (Abhidh-k-vy 605).
3 Abhidh-dī appears to count *prīti-sambodhy-aṅga* twice in this calculation (365: *bhavâgre pi śīlâṅga-traya-prīti-saṃkalpa-bodhy-aṅga-varjitaḥ pañca-viṃśatiḥ*).

thirty-seven *bodhi-pākṣikā dharmāḥ*? In the first place it is clear that the distribution of the seven sets over the successive stages of the path to awakening is not something fixed or final; it is offered as a way of looking at the *bodhi-pākṣikā dharmāḥ* rather than the final word on their nature. Thus although the *Abhidharmakośa* associates the *smṛty-upasthānas* with the *ādi-karmika* or one beginning meditation, it also gives an account of the *nirvedha-bhāgīyas* solely in terms of *smṛty-upasthāna*. The *Amṛtarasa* similarly notes that the four *smṛty-upasthānas* are included in the attainments of all the different levels.[154] Again, the fact that it is said that all seven sets may be without *āsravas* can only mean that in some sense all thirty-seven *bodhi-pākṣikā dharmāḥ* are understood to be present in *lokottara* consciousness. In other words, although from one point of view the *smṛty-upasthānas* and *samyak-prahāṇas* can be looked at as characteristic of the earlier stages of the path, what is practised at one stage is not left behind but is rather carried over into the next stage. The perspective of the Sarvāstivādin Abhidharma is not then so different from that of Theravādin Abhidhamma when it sees the attainment of the transcendent path as involving the fulfilment, and hence 'presence', of thirty-seven *bodhi-pakkhiyas* all at once.

---

[154] Amṛta Trsl 201.

CONCLUSION

Alex Wayman has criticized A.K. Warder for taking the seven sets/thirty-seven *bodhi-pakkhiyā dhammā* as representing the 'basic doctrines of Buddhism as originally propounded by the Buddha':[1]

> If he is going to intelligently insist that these constitute the Buddha's original doctrine, he should admit—which he does not—that the only teaching of the Buddha amounted to the details of the Buddhist path as followed by the monks, and so there were no characteristic doctrines of Buddhism as contrasted with monkish practice, no instructions to the laymen of how they could lead a Buddhist life without going into a monastery, and so on.[2]

It seems to me that Wayman is both right and wrong here. He is right to criticize Warder's particular presentation of the seven sets as the Buddha's basic teaching, but wrong in thinking that, as the essence of the teaching or the *saddhamma* itself, they necessarily reduce the Buddha's teaching to 'monkish practice'. Wayman is rather happier when Warder indicates that the Buddha's 'doctrine has to do with causation':

> This is just one of the many correct statements in this book that are not integrated into a total image of early Buddhism, because the author insists on the thirty-seven *bodhi-pakṣyadharmas* for the chief role.[3]

The more telling criticism here is that of failure to present an integrated picture of early Buddhism. What I hope the present study has shown at least is that the Nikāya and Abhidhamma understanding of the seven sets does in fact fully integrate them with Buddhist teaching as a whole. The presentation of the seven sets in early Buddhist thought is in fact adapted rather precisely to early Buddhist ideas of causation (*paṭiccasamuppāda*).

Before I go on to make some concluding remarks about the thirty-seven *bodhipakkhiyā dhammā*, I should like to reiterate something that I said in my introduction. This study is essentially an attempt to explore the logic and coherence of early Buddhist meditation theory; it does not expressly try to search out inconsistencies and contradictions in order to lay bare the various strata of historical development and retrieve the early, essential and original message of the Buddha. In fact, I have come to rather few, if any, definite conclusions about the historical development of the notion of the *bodhi-pakkhiyā dhammā*. While I trust I have been sufficiently mindful of historical considerations, what I have tried to show is that, if allowed, the outlook of the earlier (i.e. Nikāya) and later (i.e. Abhidhamma and commentaries) tradition has a certain coherence and consistency. At any rate it is possible to read them in this way, and to read them in this way makes at least as good sense as do the conclusions arrived at by homing in on certain apparent inconsistencies and

---

1 Warder, *IB*, p. 82.
2 *JIP* 6 (1978), pp. 418–9.
3 *JIP* 6 (1978), p. 419.

contradictions. This study contains ample evidence, I think, to suggest that before we come to any conclusions about the chronological stratification of the Nikāyas we need to pay much more careful attention to the nature of the processes that govern the creation and spread of oral literatures; before we throw away the Abhidhamma and the commentaries, we need to be very sure that we have understood what it is they are saying, and how it is they are actually interpreting the texts.

Jhāna

At this point I wish to trace not so much the evolution of the Nikāya and Abhidhamma understanding of the seven sets and *bodhi-pakkhiyā dhammā* as its logic. A 'path to awakening' must in some sense be conceived of as a process of change and development. One starts somewhere and finishes somewhere else. In the beginning there is ignorance (*avijjā*), at the end there is 'awakening'. But what exactly is 'awakening'? True, it seems ultimately in the Abhidhamma to be conceived of as a species of knowledge, but the experience of this knowledge has definite and far reaching consequences. Awakening is not the mere transformation of *avijjā* into *vijjā*; it is the transformation of wrong view, wrong thought, wrong speech, wrong action, wrong livelihood, wrong striving, wrong mindfulness and wrong concentration into right view, right thought, right speech, right action, right livelihood, right striving, right mindfulness and right concentration. It is thus an inner transformation of thought, word and deed; in short a transformation of the 'person' (chapter five, section nine). The teaching of the path to awakening is concerned with how this transformation occurs. I should like here to try to summarise the understanding of the Buddhist path that I think emerges from this study.

The path to awakening is then about a process of transformation—it is about how to effect that transformation. The transformation in question is the transformation of the 'unawakened' mind of the ordinary man into the 'awakened' mind of the *arahant*. The texts' presupposition is that such a transformation is possible—there is a way in which the unawakened mind can be woken up. The theory and practice of the path to awakening involves coming 'to know' the relationship between the unawakened mind and the awakened mind: in what ways is it similar, in what ways is it different? The outlook of the body of texts considered above is that the ordinary unawakened mind is not to be understood as uniform in character. In fact the ordinary mind is very complex and very subtle; it is of many different kinds; it has many different and contradictory tendencies. Some of these kinds of mind and some of these tendencies are more useful than others in trying to wake up the mind. Some kinds of ordinary mind actively perpetuate the sleep of the defilements, while some kinds of ordinary mind actually approximate rather closely to the waking mind itself. In other words, some states of mind, some tendencies are to be cultivated, others are to be curbed. The task, then, is to maximise these *kusala* or 'skilful' tendencies, to use the technical terminology of the texts. How does one go about this? The problem is that in ordinary everyday states of mind, while these skilful tendencies may often arise, they are always in danger of being crowded out. The texts immediate solution is that we must attempt to still the mind—we must practise calm (*samatha*) and concentration (*samādhi*). According to the texts, in calm, still states of mind the natural 'skilful' tendencies of the mind tend to come into their own—they naturally grow and strengthen, and the mind becomes clearer. Indeed the mind is by nature shining and bright—defilements are what are alien to it.[4] So, in the technical terminlogy of the texts, one must cultivate the *jhānas*. The texts appear to understand that when the mind is stilled in the *jhānas* some very powerful skilful forces or tendencies become available to the mind—these powerful skilful forces are none other than the 'ordinary' *bodhi-pakkhiyā dhammā*. One might say that in the course of cultivating *jhāna* the mind has generated—or exposed—these very powerful skilful forces. The forces are not essentially peculiar to these states of mind, indeed the same tendencies of confidence, strength, mindfulness, concentration, wisdom, etc. are present at other times, but in *jhāna* they are fully activated. The mind that has settled in *jhāna* is thus rather close to 'waking up'—with a little nudge from 'the good friend' (*kalyāṇa-mitta*) it might actually start out of its sleep; if it attends to things in an appropriate way (*yoniso manasikāra*) an even deeper transformation than *jhāna* may take place.

Traditionally Buddhist meditation theory talks of two things in this context: *samatha* and *vipassanā* or *samādhi* and *paññā*. *Samatha/samādhi* is the bare and pure stilling of the mind—which is what is seen as making the powerful forces available to the mind in the first place. *Vipassanā/paññā* is the wielding of those forces to a particular end—as the *Milindapañha* puts it, the various other factors of awakening allow the sword of wisdom to perform its task.

Samatha and *vipassanā* and *samādhi* and *paññā* are, of course, in a sense artificial abstractions. According to Abhidhamma theory, in practice, when the mind is stilled in *jhāna* there is always some element of *paññā* involved—in fact a being whose natural mind (*bhavaṅga-citta*) is devoid of wisdom is said to be unable to cultivate the *jhānas*.[5] Again, when the mind is developing wisdom there must be present some degree of concentration. So in talking of *samatha* and *vipassanā* we are really talking about different focuses: do we focus on *samatha* or do we focus on *vipassanā*? As far as we know the ancient Buddhist schools were unanimous that, in order that the mind should 'wake up', it needs to develop both *samatha* and *vipassanā*. Wisdom may be what actually cuts the 'fetters' but it cannot perform this function without some degree of concentration. The ancient (and modern) debate concerning *samatha* and *vipassanā* centres not on whether *samatha* or *samādhi* are essential for awakening, but on the question of what degree of *samatha* or *samādhi* is required. The Theravādin Abhidhamma traditions, beginning with the *Dhammasaṅgaṇi* and followed by Buddhaghosa, are clear that one needs full *jhāna* or 'absorption'—at least at the actual moment of awakening, if not before. As we saw in chapter ten, the

---

[4] A I 10.

[5] Abhidh-s 19.

Vaibhāṣika traditions differ in that they appear to allow an 'access' type of concentration as sufficient.

The whole question of *samatha* and *vipassanā* has caused a certain amount of discussion in modern accounts of traditional Buddhist meditation theory. Because Buddhist theory allows that the *jhānas* can be developed apart from the actual 'world transcending' wisdom that wakes the mind up, a conclusion is drawn that the *jhānas* are somehow not really 'Buddhist'—Buddhism borrowed them from what went before and added the distinctively 'Buddhist' *vipassanā* meditation. Thus, from the point of view of true 'Buddhist' meditation, the *jhānas* are something of a diversion. In recent years this line has perhaps been most clearly taken by W.L. King in his book *Theravāda Meditation: the Buddhist transformation of yoga.*

There are a number of problems. In the first place Buddhist theoretical abstractions are confused with the question of historical development. As we saw in chapter six, the theory of the Buddhist path works (sometimes) with the hierarchy of *sīla/samādhi/paññā*. I shall attempt to sum up what I see as the implications of this hierarchy. In the first place what it conveys is the idea that it is possible to have basically 'skilful' conduct without having actually developed states of concentration or the *jhānas*. However, the keeping of *sīla*, the practice of good conduct, will naturally tend to bring about calm and peace such that if good conduct is firmly established, when one tries to develop states of concentration, progress is likely to be easier than otherwise. The corrolary of this is that if one tries to develop states of concentration without the basis of good conduct, one is likely to find that one will need to attend to conduct before states of concentration can succeed and be firmly established. In short, real good conduct without meditation attainments is possible, but real meditation attainment without good conduct is not. Again, it is possible to have good conduct and to have meditation attainments without having developed the wisdom that penetrates to the four truths; but one cannot have that wisdom without in some measure having established good conduct and some level of concentration. Of course, I think the theory is meant to allow that someone who seemingly has rather 'bad' conduct might, apparently out of the blue, have an experience of deep 'world-transcending' penetrative insight, but such an experience if 'true' would, according to the principles of the hierarchy under discussion, have to involve also both a transformation of *sīla*, and a degree of *samādhi* equivalent to *jhāna*. The basic principle holds good: *sīla* can stand without *samādhi* and *paññā*, but *samādhi* and *paññā* cannot stand without *sīla*; *sīla* and *samādhi* can stand without *paññā*, but *paññā* cannot stand without *sīla* and *samādhi*.

In modern scholarly writings this piece of Buddhist theorizing tends to be confused with historical development: the *jhānas* are not truly 'Buddhist', they are borrowed from a pre-existing 'yogic' tradition. What is original 'Buddhist' teaching is *vipassanā*. But what does this really mean? What precisely do we mean by 'Buddhist' here? If we mean invented and taught by the historical Buddha, then we have to acknowledge that we really have no idea what the Buddha borrowed from the pre-existing nascent 'yogic' tradition of India and what the Buddha added as 'new'; all we can safely say, as I pointed out in my introduction, is that it is clear that he inherited something. While I would not want to go along with everything Bronkhorst says in his book on 'the two traditions of meditation' in ancient India, he does highlight a basic fact: we do not have any clear evidence of the *jhāna* meditations prior to their appearance in early Buddhist texts—the *jhānas* surface first in Buddhist writings.

W.L. King's *Theravāda Meditation* is one of the fullest descriptions of traditional Theravādin meditation theory to be published in recent years. This book certainly provides what is a generally useful and comprehensive account, but in the light of the present study it also certainly perpetuates certain misunderstandings.

For King the *jhānas* and formless attainments, from the perspective of strict Theravādin 'orthodoxy', are to be characterized as 'alien' and 'non-Buddhist'—they are derived from 'Brahmanical-yogic spirituality' (p. viii). *Vipassanā*, on the other hand, is the 'Buddhist heart of the Theravāda meditational discipline' (p. 82). Many problems are raised by this view of Theravādin Buddhist meditation. One is the simple lumping together of the *jhānas* and formless attainments. Indeed King aknowledges this as a problem (pp. 14-16) but concludes that 'the series [of *jhānas* and formless attainments] is continuous in quality and method through all eight stages' and is of the view that '"jhanic" as a characterizing adjective applies equally well to the four jhānas *and* to the four immaterial states' (p. 41). But this simple compounding of the *jhānas* and the formless attainments is full of problems. As King himself aknowledges, in the story of Gotama's abandoning of the practice of severe austerities the *jhānas* are seemingly presented as the alternative to—almost the rejection of—the earlier 'yogic' teaching, which seems to encompass both the practice of severe austerities and the practice of the formless attainments taught to Gotama by Āḷāra Kālāma and Uddaka Rāmaputta. Can we afford to simply pass over this presentation of the *jhānas* in the face of other evidence that also suggests that the *jhāna* meditations were central to early Buddhist meditation theory? Again, to oppose 'Buddhist' and 'Brahmanical-yogic' spirituality in the way King does in the context of the fourth or third century BCE is surely historically inadequate. The evidence of Buddhist, Jaina and Brahmanical texts suggests that there were numerous groups practising and experimenting with, loosely speaking, 'yogic' techniques and formulating various theories and ideas about them; furthermore the relationship of the Brahmanical tradition to the emerging 'yogic' tradition is hardly clear cut. No doubt everybody was borrowing ideas and practices from everybody else.

The present study suggests that we must see the *jhāna* meditations as at the heart of early Buddhist meditation theory, and, at least as far as the Theravāda tradition goes, they continue to occupy a central place in the meditation theory of the Abhidhamma and commentaries. There can be no doubt that for the Nikāyas, the Abhidhamma and the commentaries the *jhānas* represent central, mainstream (i.e. 'Buddhist') meditation; more or less everything is continually being related back to the *jhānas*. As we have seen, as far as the seven sets are concerned, this is particularly clear with the treatment of the four establishings of mindfulness, the four bases of success and the seven factors of awakening. When the list of the seven sets is expanded in the Nikāyas and other classes of Buddhist literature it is the four *jhānas*/*dhyānas* and other meditation practices leading to *jhāna*/*dhyāna* that are immediately and most often brought in. This indicates the 'context' in which the seven sets were understood to be developed. Thus in the Abhidhamma and commentaries too the seven sets are collectively associated with *lokuttara-jjhāna* (cf. the *Dhammasaṅgaṇi*), and individually (i.e. as *lokiya-bodhi-pakkhiya-dhammas*) with especially the advanced stages of *samatha* and *vipassanā*. The stage of the *lokiya-bodhi-pakkhiya-dhammas* seems to correspond in some measure to the stages of the *nirvedha-bhāgīyas* in the Sarvāstivādin account of the path; the latter are especially associated with the *smṛty-upasthāna*, *samyak-prahāṇa*, *ṛddhi-pādas*, *indriyas* and *balas* in the *Abhidharmakośa*.

Furthermore, according to the texts studied here, the awakening experience itself was essentially understood as a species of *jhāna*—that is, it is a meditation experience that shares the characteristic features of *jhāna*, yet it is a special *jhāna*, a *jhāna* in which *paññā* plays a special role, and a *jhāna* that establishes the eight factors of the noble path in the subsequent deeds, words and thoughts of the person attaining it. This conclusion is based in the first place on the terminology associated with the factors of awakening, but is reinforced by the whole thrust of our study of the thirty-seven *bodhi-pakkhiyā dhammā*. The question of the origin of the *jhāna* meditations is a separate issue, and something that is probably unanswerable. To ask whether they are 'Buddhist' or 'non-Buddhist' seems to me essentially misconceived. All we know is that they first become explicit in and are a central feature of early Buddhist texts.

The Nikāyas seem consistently to conceive of a turning point or point of cross-over in the process of the path to awakening. This crucial point is encountered in several guises. Most generally it might be characterized as the point of cross-over from the state of the ordinary man (*puthujjana*) to that of the 'noble person' (*ariya-puggala*). Spiritually and psychologically this turning point is the point at which the pull of awakening, becomes overwhelming. Although there is not full or final awakening, the gravitation towards awakening is now the most significant force at work in the mind (chapter seven, section four). The lower limit of this turning point is stream-attainment and is marked by the establishing of the eight factors of the 'noble path' beginning with right view. Hitherto these factors were unstable (chapter six, section seven).

This breakthrough to the noble eight-factored path is not, it seems, always presented in the Nikāyas as a formal 'meditation' experience. Classically it might take the form, perhaps, of a sudden and radical change of heart—a sudden seeing prompted by the gradual discourse of the Buddha, for example. There are in the Nikāyas also notions such as those of the *saddhânusārin* and *dhammânusārin* which are rather close to the notion of stream-attainer and indeed at times hard to distinguish from it. Generally, however, they seem to stand slightly lower in the scale of persons. This has the effect of defining the 'turning point' as something specific that nevertheless covers a certain range of types of experience. This somewhat looser Nikāya conception of the path of stream-attainment seems to find a counterpart in the commentarial notion of the 'lesser stream-attainer' (chapter four). The general notion of stream-attainment appears sometimes to be used in the Nikāyas to characterize the stage of spiritual development of the ideal layfollower or householder.[6] The stream-attainer is one who has abandoned doubt, the view of individuality, and holding on to precept and vow; he has trust or faith based in understanding in the Buddha, Dhamma and Saṃgha. Moreover, while he need not be a celibate, his conduct is pleasing to the 'noble ones' and he has abandoned the grosser kinds of unwholesome behaviour that can lead to rebirth in the places of regress; his behaviour thus conforms to the five precepts.

The Nikāyas may not always present the turning point in spiritual development as a formal 'meditation' experience (or even as issuing from immediately prior spiritual practice), but what clearly interests the texts, what they continually return to, is the precise nature of the mind at the turning point. What kind of mind is it that produces such a fundamental and far-reaching change of heart? What is so special about it? What is different about it? How is it related to other types of mind? What are the factors that contribute to it? A concern with such questions is quite apparent from the description contained in the gradual discourse, and much of the early Abhidhamma is in one way or another an exploration of such matters. The state of mind that the gradual discourse focuses upon is described as well (*kalla*), open (*mudu*), free of hindrances (*vinīvaraṇa*), joyful (*udagga*), at peace (*pasanna*). The terminology used here clearly also relates to the kind of mind that is brought about by the practice of *jhāna*. Here, then, is the explicit path of meditation. And what the path of meditation issues in is a particular kind of *jhāna* termed *bodhi* and characterized by the seven *bojjhaṅgas* (chapter five). In the Nikāyas the path of meditation is neatly summed up as abandoning the five hindrances, establishing the mind in the four establishings of mindfulness and developing the seven awakening-factors; this path finds one of its fullest elaborations in the *Ānâpāna-sati-sutta* (chapter one). What is significant about the path of meditation, however, is that it only succeeds in a specific context and under certain conditions—conditions such as having a 'good friend', continual application and heedfulness (*appamāda*), the basis of *sīla*; the hindrances must be starved of food and the awakening-factors nourished (chapter five). The factors that make for the particular mental state of peace and balance that allows the mind to awake are varied and subtle.

In all this, I arrive, via a completely different route, at conclusions that have something in common with the findings of J. Bronkhorst (*The Two Traditions of Meditation in Ancient India*) and T. Vetter (*The Ideas and Meditative Practices of Early Buddhism*). Both these scholars argue that that the *jhānas* represent mainstream early Buddhist meditation; unlike Vetter, who argues that the *jhāna* meditation path early on gave way to the meditation based on

---

[6] See especially the *sotâpatti-saṃyutta* (S V 343-413); many of these *suttas* are addressed to layfollowers and relate the 'factors of stream-attainment' to lay-practice.

'discriminating insight', I maintain that the *jhānas* continue to be of paramount importance for the Abhidhamma and the commentaries. What I suggest is that a book such as King's relies far too heavily on Buddhaghosa's *Visuddhimagga* sytematisation of the path under the headings of 'conduct', 'consciousness' and 'understanding'. This separating out of the three categories is certainly a useful device for a presentation of the Buddhist path, but the structure of the *Visuddhimagga* can make it appear that much of the account of the development of *samatha* given under the heading 'purification of consciousness' (*citta-visuddhi*) has rather little bearing on the remaining five 'purifications', which are therefore to be understood more or less exclusively in terms of wisdom and insight. The result of following Buddhaghosa too closely can be a rather distorted and misleading account of Theravādin meditation theory. My point here is not that Buddhaghosa gets it wrong, but that in failing to have an adequate grasp of the theory of meditation presented in the Nikāyas and Abhidhamma, modern scholars misunderstand Buddhaghosa. The treatment of the seven sets in the Nikāyas and Abhidhamma, on the other hand, seems to make clear and emphasize the ancient conception of the path as the yoking together of calm and insight (cf. the *Ānâpānasati-sutta*). The mind is stilled and brought to a state of happiness and balance; awakening arises directly in this soil. Thus in emphasizing the interdependence and reciprocity of the various elements that contribute to the path, the teaching of the seven sets presents us with a rather more integrated view of the path to awakening.

Abhidhamma

To recapitulate somewhat, to follow the path to awakening is to undergo a process of transformation. Such processes have a beginning, middle and an end. Specifically the Buddhist path to awakening conerns the 'ordinary' unawakened mind (beginning) coming to a critical point where 'waking up' is in some sense understood to be near (middle) such that it is only a matter of time until the occurrence of final perfect awakening (end). The question is: what mental forces, what mental qualities effect this waking process? what helps it along, what hinders it? From one point of view, Buddhist texts are full of different descriptions of this one process. (One might also venture to suggest that it is the critical 'middle' stage that is the particular focus of many texts.) If we find the process at all interesting we might, like the early *ābhidhammikas*, feel we want to focus in on particular parts and get a closer look so that we can see exactly what is going on. That is, we can attempt to distinguish the stages within a stage, the processes that make up the process. Now what the early *ābhidhammikas* tell us they saw when they did precisely this is more of the same. The more one focuses in on a process and tries to observe the processes operating within a process, the more one comes to see that all small scale processes are essentially reflections of large scale processes. This, it seems, is the kind of thinking that underlies the view of *paṭicca-samuppāda* (which is found in the early Abhidhamma) as extending over a period of time or as being decsriptive of a single arising of consciousness.[7] The processes that operate in the microcosm are the same as the processes that operate in the macrocosm—*dhammas* are only Dhamma. In fact there is only one process—wherever one looks and however closely one looks there is only Dhamma. The process that binds one to *saṃsāra* is in the end precisely the process that liberates one. It does not seem unreasonable to extend this way of thinking to the seven sets. The handle of the carpenter's knife is worn away bit by bit each day by the repeated process of wearing away until suddenly, all at once, it is completely worn away and the process of wearing away is complete. Just so the seven sets are developed little by little until suddenly, all at once, they are fully developed and the path to awakening is complete (chapter seven, sections three and four).

What I am trying to suggest, then, is that in taking the traditional lists and exploring their application, the early *ābhidhammikas* were not contributing to the ossification of Buddhist teaching, but were rather developing something that was at the heart of early Buddhism. The concerns of the early Abhidhamma were precisely the same concerns as those of the Nikāyas. The concerns of the early Abhidhamma are practical rather than purely theoretical or scholastic; they arise directly out of the concerns of the Nikāyas themselves: what is going on in the mind when one tries to train it and wake it up? Thus the Abhidhamma enterprise continues a way of conceptualizing and exploring the processes of meditation and spiritual development that is clearly evidenced from the beginnings of Buddhism. In this respect, as I suggested earlier, I take a line quite opposite to that taken by Peter Masefield in his recent book, *Divine Revelation in Pāli Buddhism*, in which he presents a rather extreme form of the argument that the *ābhidhammika* monks had completey lost touch with the spirit (or rather 'sound') of the earlier tradition.

Path

Perhaps the most general point about the nature of the path to awakening as understood in the Nikāyas and Abhidhamma is that the end is essentially the means. If awakening results in right view, etc., then the way to awakening is equally right view, etc. (chapter six). I pointed out in chapter one that the Nikāyas seem to suggest that by developing just one of the thirty-seven

---

[7] See Vibh 135-192. Cf. Vibh-a 199-200: 'Thus, as one who lays out the great earth and spreads out the sky, the Teacher, whose knowledge is unobstructed in respect of all *dhammas*, shows in the *suttanta-bhājaniya* the mode of conditions without knot or tangle by way of different [moments of] *citta*. And now, since the mode of conditions is not only [relevant] to different [moments of] *citta* but also to a single *citta*, therefore in order to show the mode of conditions for a single *citta*-moment in its different aspects by way of the *abhidhamma-bhājaniya*, he sets out the *mātikā* accordingly with the [words] beginning: *avijjā-paccayā saṃkhāro*.'(*evaṃ mahāpaṭhaviṃ pattharanto viya ākāsaṃ vittharayanto viya ca sabba-dhammesu appaṭihata-ñāṇo satthā suttanta-bhājaniye nigganṭhiṃ nijjaṭaṃ paccayâkāraṃ nānā-citta-vasena dassetvā, idāni yasmā na kevalaṃ ayaṃ paccayâkāro nānā-cittesu yeva hoti eka-citte pi hoti yeva, tasmā abhidhamma-bhājaniya-vasena eka-citta-kkhaṇikaṃ paccayâkāraṃ nāna-ppakārato dassetuṃ avijjā-paccayā saṃkhāro ti ādinā nayena mātikaṃ tāva ṭhapesi*.) Vibh 135-8 does not give the standard later description which extends the twelve links over three lives (cf. Vism XVII 273-98); it is couched in rather more general terms. Cf. Abhidh-k 132-3 which distinguishes (amongst other types) *pratītya-samutpāda* that is momentary (*kṣaṇika*) and extended (*prakārṣika*).

dhammas (any aspect of the four *satipaṭṭhānas*) to its full one comes to the conclusion of the path to awakening. Or, the full development of the first *satipaṭṭhāna* actually involves the development of all four *satipaṭṭhānas*, and the conclusion of the path is again reached. Similarly in chapter two the four *samma-ppadhānas* were found on occasion to be interpreted so as to embrace the whole path. Again in chapter three the notion of *iddhi-pāda* (especially in the commentarial analysis) was interpreted on a number of different scales involving in some cases the conclusion of the path. In chapter four it was found that it is through development of the *indriyas* that one is an *arahant*, etc. I need not go on. If one of the seven sets—or even just one of the thirty-seven *dhammas*—is sufficient for awakening, then what purpose is served by the other sets, and by the other thirty-six *dhammas*?[8] The answer seems to be to show that the path and awakening itself is at once simple and multi-dimensional. This is most clearly seen in some of the treatments common to all seven sets. The bringing to fulfilment of any one of the seven sets cannot be accomplished without bringing to fulfilment all seven sets. For, as the *Nettippakaraṇa* puts it, all *dhammas* that lead to awakening and contribute to awakening have but one characteristic, the characteristic of 'leading out'. In other words, there exists between the thirty-seven *dhammas* a relationship of reciprocity and radical interdependence.

Finally, in the Abhidhamma/Abhidharma traditions we find two perspectives: one that sees the seven sets as indicative of the gradual progress of the path, and one that sees them as characterizing its final culmination. In chapter ten I suggested that these two perspectives should not be considered peculiar to the Sarvāstivāda and Theravāda respectively, and thus mutually exclusive. Rather they amount to a difference of emphasis in each tradition. After all, once again we have only an application of the principle of momentary and extended *paṭicca-samuppāda/pratītya-samutpāda*. For the Pāli commentaries, inspired perhaps by the *ekâbhisamaya* traditions found in a text such as the *Paṭisambhidāmagga*, what above all distinguishes the transcendent mind from the ordinary mind is that the latter only ever partially fulfils the conditions that contribute to awakening, the transcendent mind in a moment fulfils them completely. One might sum up the two Abhidhamma/Abhidharma perspectives as follows. From the perspective of the beginning of the path the unknown way stretches out ahead; yet from the perspective of its conclusion it is apparent that all the factors that contributed to it at once find their fulfilment. So while the perspective of the whole path is never lost in the teaching of the seven sets, its point of focus, its orientation is always the consummation of the path. As we have seen, the expression 'development of *bodhi-pakkhiyā dhammā*' was

---

[8] Cf. *Traité*, III 1143-4: Question.—Les quatre fixations de l'attention (*smṛty-upasthāna*) étant suffisantes pour obtenir le chemin (*mārga*), pourquoi parler de trente-sept auxiliaires? ... Réponse.—Bien que les quatre fixations-de-l'attention soient suffisantes pour obtenir le chemin, il faut aussi prêcher les quatre efforts corrects (*samyak-pradhāna*) et les autres dharma auxiliaires. Pourquoi? Chez les êtres, les pensées (*citta*) sont multiples (*nānāvidha*) et dissemblables (*viṣama*); leurs entraves (*saṃyojana*) aussi sont multiples, et les choses qu'ils aiment ou dont il se détachent sont multiples.

originally used in the Nikāyas as generally descriptive of the higher stages of the path. The expression *bodhi-pakkhiyā dhammā* focuses on *bodhi* in much the same way as *bojjhaṅga* does, but is less specific. The actual notion of the 'thirty-seven *bodhi-pakkhiyā dhammā*' derives, I think, from the association of the term *bodhi-pakkhiya* with the *bojjhaṅgas* on the one hand, and the association of the *bojjhaṅgas* with the ancient sequence of seven sets on the other. This imparts something of the specific perspective of the *bojjhaṅgas* to the whole, to all thirty-seven *dhammas*, while retaining the broader perspective of sets such as the *satipaṭṭhānas* and noble eight-factored path.

So what is the place of the seven sets in Buddhist thought? For the *Vibhaṅga* they are simply the *saddhamma*. For the *Paṭisambhidāmagga* they are, together with the four truths, the essence of the teaching. The Nikāyas, for their part, state that *bhikkhus* should preserve the establishings of mindfulness, the right endeavours, the bases of success, the faculties, powers, awakening-factors and noble eight-factored path so that the spiritual life endures, out of compassion for the world, for the good and happiness of the many. But we are not to confuse the preservation of the *dhamma* as teaching with the preservation of *dhamma* as knowledge and experience. What seems to underlie the Nikāyas outlook here is the understanding that all those who have in the past, will in the future and also now come to the end of the path to awakening do so by the development of the seven sets. Teachings about the seven sets are only *saddhamma* in so far as they conduce to the realization of *dhamma*; teachings that conduce to the realization of *dhamma* are teachings about the seven sets.

I have suggested that *lokiya-bodhi-pakkhiya-dhammas* are seen as primarily relevant to the more advanced stages of *samatha* and *vipassanā*. But I do not think this means that talk of *bodhi-pakkhiya-dhammas* should be absolutely excluded from all other contexts. According to the *Dhammasaṅgaṇi*, *samatha* and *vipassanā* may be seen as general characteristics of skilful *kāmâvacara* consciousness.[9] This means that acts of giving (*dāna*), and conduct in conformity with the precepts (*sīla*) may, like certain meditation states, be associated with a mind that reflects the nature of the awakening mind. This has some bearing on the kind of distinction that Spiro and others have tried to make between the 'kammatic' or 'merit making' Buddhism of the majority of the Buddhist populace, and the 'nibbānic' or 'release producing' Buddhism of an orthodox meditating elite.[10] From the perspective of the path to awakening understood in terms of the Nikāya and Abhidhamma teaching of the seven sets such a distinction is artificial and misconceived. Many of the classic merit-making activities might be brought into the scheme of the path to awakening by way of the faculty of confidence or faith, or, more significantly perhaps, by way of the establishings of mindfulness, for the standard list of *anussatis* or 'recollections' (which the *Niddesa* directly relates to the practice of the four *satipaṭṭhānas*)[11] includes the recollection of the Buddha, Dhamma and Saṃgha,

---

9 The four *ñāṇa-sampayutta-cittas*; Dhs 9-27, 28-9.

10 M.E. Spiro, *Buddhism and Society: A Great Tradition and its Burmese Vicissitudes*, London, 1970, e.g. pp. 11-3.

11 E.g. Nidd I 10.

which are standard popular lay meditations in all Buddhist countries. Thus one of the things the early Abhidhamma seems concerned to show is that the kind of mind in which 'awakening' arises is not necessarily or always so far removed from the kinds of mind that might 'ordinarily' be experienced. And why should this not be so? To develop just one of the *dhammas* that contribute to awakening is to develop them all. The beginning of the path is in a sense already its end, the end is in a sense not different from its beginning. In the words of T.S. Eliot:

> *In my beginning is my end …*
> *In my end is my beginning.*

APPENDIX

I SUMMARY OF TEXTUAL REFERENCES

A. PASSAGES IN THE PĀLI CANONICAL AND PARACANONICAL SOURCES DEALING WITH THE SEVEN SETS INDIVIDUALLY

(4) *satipaṭṭhāna*/basic formula
D II 83, 94-5, 100, 216, 290-314: III 58-77, 101, 141, 221, 276, 283.
M I 55-63, 83, 221, 224, 301, 339-40; III 82-8, 135-6, 252.
S III 93; IV 211; IV 73-4, 141-92, 196, 294-306, 329-40.
A II 218, 256; III 12, 81ff, 155, 386, 450; IV 223-5, 300-1, 457-8, V 56, 114-8, 175, 194-5, 350, 352.
Th 100, 166, 352, 765, 1090.
Nidd I 9-10, 21, 241-4, 347, 399, 475.
Paṭis I 177-96; II 13-21, 152-5, 164-5, 232-5.
Ap 26, 44, 518.
Vibh 105, 193-207, 236.
Kv 63, 155-9.
Peṭ 4, 71, 90, 95, 98, 121, 138, 185, 201, 247, 249, 257.
Nett 7, 94, 123.
Mil 178, 332, 368, 375, 388, 399, 402, 407, 407, 418.

(4) *samma-ppadhāna*/basic formula
D II 312; III 221.
M I 301; II 26-8, 129; III 251.
S V 9, 196, 198, 244-8, 268-9.
A I 153; II 15, 74, 256; III 12; IV 462-3;
Dhs 234
Vibh 105, 208-15, 216, 235.
Peṭ 71, 98, 128, 183, 185.
Nett 18, 123.
Mil 371.

(4) *iddhi-pāda*
D II 103, 115-8, 213; III 77, 221.
M I 103.
S I 116, 132; V 254-93.
A II 256; III 81-2; IV 225, 309, 463.
Ud 62.
Th 595; Thī 233.
Paṭis I 19, 111-5; II 205.
Ap 44, 443, 518.
Vibh 216-26.
Peṭ 247.
Nett 15-6.
Mil 140, 400.

(3/4/5, etc.) *indriya*
Vin I 294.
D III 239, 278, 284.
M I 19-20, 164, 479.
S V 193-204, 219-43.
A I 42-4, 118-9; II 141, 149-52; III 277-8, 281-2; IV 225, 264-6; V 56.
Th 352, 437, 595, 672, 1114; Thī 170-1.
Nidd I 115, 233. Paṭis II 1-34.
Dhs passim.
Vibh 122-34.
Kv 589-92.
Yam *see* indriya-yamaka

Paṭṭh passim.
Peṭ 37, 41, 89, 71-2, 79, 88, 97-8, 128-9, 171, 179, 183, 185-6.
Nett 7, 19, 28, 100-1.
Mil 33ff, 43.

(2/4/5/7) *bala*
Vin I 294.
D III 213, 229, 253.
S V 249-53.
A II 141; III 10-2, 245, 277-8, 281-2, IV 3-4.
Th 352, 437, 595, 672, 1114; 170-1.
Nidd I 14,151.
Paṭis II 166-76.
Peṭ 37, 79, 179, 189.
Nett 100-1.

(7) *bojjhaṅga*
Vin I 294.
D III 79, 83; 303-4; III 101, 106, 226, 251, 282, 284.
M I 11, 61-2; III 85-8, 275.
S I 54; V 24, 63-140, 161, 312, 331-40.
A I 14, 53; II 16, 237; III 386, 390; IV 23, 148, 225; V 58, 114-8, 194-5, 211, 233, 253.
Khp 2.
Dhp 89.
Th 161-2, 352, 437, 595, 672, 725, 1114; Thī 21, 45, 170-1.
Paṭis II 115-29.
Dhs 61-8, 232.
Vibh 199-201, 227-34, 249.
Peṭ 10, 12, 56, 103, 122, 141, 167-8, 189, 248.
Nett 82-3, 94.
Mil 83, 336, 340, 356.

***ariyo aṭṭhaṅgiko maggo/sammā-diṭṭhi*, etc.**
Vin I 10.
D I 157, 165; II 151, 251, 311; III 284, 286.
M I 15-6, 42-3, 48-55, 118, 221-4, 299-301, 446, 508; II 82; III 231, 251, 289.
S I 88; II 42, 57, 106ff, 168-9; III 59ff; 86, 109, 158-9; IV 133; 175, 220-3, 233,252-62.
A I 177, 180, 217, 297; II 34, 220-5; III 242, 411-6; IV 190, 225, 348; V 58, 211-49, 349, 352.
It 18.
Khp 2.
Vv 19.
Pv 61.
Th 35; 349, 421, 980, 1115; Thī 171-2, 215, 222.
Paṭis II 82-5.
Ap 6, 314.
Cp 103. Dhs passim.
Vibh 104-6, 235-43.
Kv 431-3, 99-601.
Peṭ 10, 54, 55, 124-6, 130, 132, 165, 191, 238.
Nett 51-2.
Mil 218.

B. PASSAGES LISTING THE SEVEN SETS (CANONICAL AND PARACANONICAL)

Vin II 240; III 93, 94, 95, 97; IV 26, 27, 28.
D II 120; III 102, 127.
M II 11, 238, 245; III 81, 289, 296.
S III 96, 153-4; IV 360-8; V 49-50.
A I 39-40, 295-7; IV 125-7, 203, 208; V 175.
Ud 51-6.
Nidd I 13-4, 45, 54-5, 69, 71-2, 85, 87, 105, 132, 138, 143, 144, 171, 212, 219, 221, 234, 322, 324, 332, 338, 340-1, 343, 361-2, 365, 398, 455-6, 468-9, 480, 481, 502.
Nidd II passim.

Paṭis I 16-7, 21-2, 23, 27, 34, 35, 73-6, 180-2; II 29, 56, 86, 90-1, 120, 124-5, 142-3, 145-6, 173-4.
Dhs 73, 107, 116.
Vibh 372.
Dhātuk passim.
Kv 74-6, 85-9, 169-71, 182-4, 190-2, 221, 232-6, 245-6, 270, 271-3, 308, 470, 480, 507, 514, 515, 516, 524, 526, 604, 608.
Peṭ 114-5.
Nett 31,83.
Mil 33, 37, 330, 342-3, 358.

C. DHAMMAS THAT CONTRIBUTE TO AWAKENING

bodhi-/bodha-/sambodhi-/sambodha-/-pakkhiyā/-pakkhikā (dhammā)
Viṇ III 23.
D III 97.
S V 227, 237-9.
A III 70-1, 300-1; IV 351.
It 75, 96.
Th 900.
Paṭis I 18; II 115, 122.
Vibh 244, 249-50.
Ap 28, 314.
Peṭ 114, 138, 188, 212.
Nett 31, 83, 112.
Mil 237, 300.

D. PRINCIPAL COMMENTARIAL PASSAGES

satipaṭṭhāna
Sv III 741-806; Ps I 225-302; Paṭis-a III 695-7; Vibh-a 214-88; Moh 153-7.

samma-ppadhāna
Ps III 243-54; Spk III 164-5; Vibh-a 289-301; Moh 157-9.

iddhi-pāda
Sv II 641-3; DAṬ 262-9; Ps II 69; Spk III 255-7; Vibh-a 303-9; Vism XII 50-3; Moh 159-61.

indriya
Vibh-a 125-9; Moh 139-4.

bojjhaṅga
Ps I 85; Spk III 138-9; Paṭis-a III 600; As 217; Vibh-a 310-8; Moh 161-4.

magga
Paṭis-a I 162-96; Vibh-a 114-22, 319-22; Moh 164-6.

The seven sets
Mp II 49-73; Ud-a 303-6; Nidd-a I 66-7; Paṭis-a I 95-7; III 618-20.
Vism XXII 32-42.

E. A NOTE ON THE 7 SETS/BODHIPĀKṢIKA-DHARMAS IN NON-PĀLI SOURCES

1 **Sūtra**—For citations of the seven sets in the Chinese Āgamas see Lamotte, *Traité* III 1120; J. Bronkhorst, *BSOAS* 48 (1985), pp. 305-6. *Arthaviniścaya-sūtra* and commentary (Artha 28-42, 172-7, 208-33); *Avadānaśataka* (ed. J.S. Speyer, St. Petersburgh, 1906-09, I 122, 136, 340; II 171); *Karuṇāpuṇḍarīka-sūtra* (see Dayal, op. cit., p. 80); *Kāśyapaparivarta* (ed. A.v. Staël-Holstein, Shanghai, 1926, p. 75); *Gaṇḍvyūha* (ed. D.T. Suzuki and H. Idzumi, Kyoto, 1934-36, 2nd ed. 1949, p. 495); *Daśabhūmika-sūtra* (ed. J. Rahder, Louvain, 1926, pp. 42, 57); *Divyâvadāna* (pp. 207-8, 350, 616); *Dharmasaṃgraha* (pp. 9-11); *Śatasāhasrikā Prajñāpāramitā* (pp. 56-7, 133, 162, 274, 1410, 1427-39, 1473, 1636); *Pañcaviṃśati-sāhasrikā Prajñāpāramitā* (E. Conze, *The Large Sūtra on Perfect Wisdom*, Part I, London, 1961, pp. 140-3); *Aṣṭadaśasāhasrikā Prajñāpāramitā* (ed. E. Conze, Rome, 1962, pp. 16-7, 216-8); *Daśasāhasrikā Prajñāpāramitā* (S. Konow, *Avhandlinger utgitt av Det Norske Videnskaps-Akademi i Oslo*, 1941, II Historisk-Filofisk Klasse, pp. 96-7); *Mahāvastu* (II 394-5); *Mahāvyutpatti* (pp. 16-7); *Laṅkāvatāra-sūtra* (ed. B. Nanjio, Kyoto, 1923, p. 213); *Lalitavistara* (ed. S. Lefmann, Halle, 1902, pp. 9, 424); *Saddharmapuṇḍarīka* (p. 458);

Samādhirāja-sūtra (see Dayal, op. cit., p. 80); *Vimalakīrtinirdeśa* (É. Lamotte, *L'Enseignement de Vimalakīrti*, Louvain, 1962, (pp. 117, 139, 201-2, 216, 378); *Saṃdhinirmocana-sūtra* (ed. É. Lamotte, Louvain, 1935, pp. 82-3, 205).

2 **Śāstra**—**Abhidharmahṛdaya* (Abhidh-h Trsl 137-41); **Abhidharmâmṛtarasa* (Amṛta Trsl 201-9); *Abhidharmakośa-bhāṣya* (Abhidh-k 382-6); *Abhidharmadīpa* (Abhidh-dī 356-65); *Abhidharma-samuccaya* (Abhidh-sam Trsl 117-24); *Bodhisattvabhūmi* (ed. Wogihara, Tokyo, 1930-36, pp. 227, 236, 259); *Madhyântavibhāga-bhāṣya* (Anacker, op.cit., pp. 246-51, 446-9); **Mahāprajñāpāramitā-śāstra* (Lamotte, *Traité*, III 1138-1207); *Mahāyānasūtrâlaṃkāra* chapter XVIII (ed. S. Bagchi, Darbhanga, Bihar, 1970, pp. 128-53; Trsl S. Lévi, Paris, 1911, pp. 225-65); *Bhāvanākrama* of Kamalaśīla (José Van Den Broeck, *La Progression dans la méditation*, Bruxelles, 1977, pp. 47-8); **Satyasiddhiśāstra* (Satya Trsl 41-4, 448-9); *Saundarananda* of Aśvaghoṣa (ed. E.H. Johnston, London, 1928, XVII 24); *Śikṣāsamuccaya* (ed. C. Bendall, St. Petersburgh, 1897-1902, pp. 12,52, 283); *Śrāvakabhūmi* (A. Wayman, 'Analysis of the Śrāvakabhūmi Manuscript', *University of California Publications in Classical Philology*, XVII (1961), Berkeley, pp. 75-6, 97-102).

See also Dayal (op.cit., pp. 80-2), *BHSD* (s.vv. *bodhipakṣa, bodhipakṣya, bodhipākṣika*), Lamotte (*Traité*, III 1120-1). Some other relevant works are *Caityavibhāga-vinayodbhāva-sūtra* and *Stūpalakṣaṇakārikā-vivecana* (see G. Roth, 'The Symbolism of the Buddhist Stūpa' in *The Stūpa: Its Religious, Historical and Architectural Significance*, ed. A.L. Dallapiccola, Wiesbaden, 1980, pp. 183-209); *Cakrasaṃvara-tantra* (see Warder, *IB*, p. 498); *Jewel Ornament of Liberation* of sGam. po.pa (Trsl H.V. Guenther, London, 1959, pp. 112-4, 232-4).

The foregoing is not intended to be exhaustive or comprehensive by any means, but it is illustrative of the importance of the thirty-seven *bodhipākṣika-dharmas*/seven sets in a wide range of Buddhist literature.

II RESOLUTION OF BUDDHADATTA'S SUMMARY OF THE PRESENCE OF INDRIYAS, ETC. IN THE CLASSES OF CITTA (Abhidh-av 30-1)

Buddhadatta here adopts the schema of 121 *cittas*, multiplying the eight *lokuttara-cittas* by the fivefold *jhāna* system.

INDRIYA

16 cittas have 3 indriyas

16 cittas: 2 × 5 viññāṇa, 2 mano-dhātu (kusala-, akusala-vipāka), 3 mano-viññāṇa-dhātu (2 kusala-, 1 akusala-vipāka), 1 kiriya-mano-dhātu
3 indriyas: 1 'feeling' indriya, jīvitindriya, manindriya

1 citta has 4 indriyas

1 citta: 1 akusala (vicikicchā-sampayutta)
4 indriyas: upekkhā, jīvitindriya, viriya, manindriya

13 cittas have 5 indriyas

13 cittas: 11 akusala, 2 kiriya-mano-viññāṇa-dhātu
5 indriyas: 1 'feeling' indriya, jīvitindriya, viriya, samādhi, manindriya

12 cittas have 7 indriyas

12 cittas: 12 kamavacara (ñāṇa-vippayutta)
7 indriyas: 1 'feeling' indriya, jīvitindriya, saddhā, viriya, sati, samādhi, manindriya

39 cittas have 8 indriyas

39 cittas: 12 kāmâvacara (ñāṇa-sampayutta), 15 rūpâvacara, 12 arūpâvacara
8 indriyas: 1 'feeling' indriya, jīvitindriya, saddhā, viriya, sati, samādhi, paññā, manindriya

40 cittas have 9 indriyas

40 cittas: 40 lokuttara
9 indriyas: 1 'feeling' indriya, jīvitindriya, saddhā, viriya, sati, samādhi, paññā, 1 lokuttara 'knowledge' indriya, manindriya

JHĀNAṄGA

29 cittas have 5 jhāna-factors

29 cittas: 12 kāmâvacara (somanassa-sahagata), 4 akusala (somanassa-sahagata), 3 rūpâvacara (1st jhāna), 8 lokuttara (1st jhāna), 1 kusala-vipāka-mano-viññāṇa-dhātu (somanassa-sahagata), 1 kiriya-mano-viññāṇa-dhātu (somanassa-sahagata)

37 cittas have 4 jhāna-factors

11 cittas: 3 rūpâvacara (2nd jhāna), 8 lokuttara (2nd jhāna)
4 factors: vicāra, pīti, sukha, cittass'ekaggatā
26 cittas: 12 kāmâvacara (upekkhā-sahagata), 8 akusala (upekkhā-sahagata), 2 mano-dhātu (kusala-, akusala-vipāka), 2 mano-viññāṇa-dhātu (kusala-, akusala-vipāka, upekkhā-sahagata), 1 kiriya-mano-dhātu, 1 kiriya-mano-viññāṇa-dhātu (upekkhā-sahagata)
4 factors: vitakka, vicāra, upekkhā, cittass'ekaggatā

11 cittas have 3 jhāna-factors

11 cittas: 3 rūpâvacara (3rd jhāna), 8 lokuttara (3rd jhāna)
3 factors: pīti, sukha, cittass'ekaggatā

34 cittas have 2 jhāna-factors

34 cittas: 6 rūpâvacara (4th, 5th jhāna), 12 arūpâvacara, 16 lokuttara (4th, 5th jhāna)
2 factors: upekkhā, cittass'ekaggatā

10 cittas have no jhāna-factors

2 × 5 viññāṇa

MAGGAṄGA

18 cittas have no path-factors

18 ahetuka

1 citta has 2 path-factors

1 citta: 1 vicikicchā-sampayutta
2 factors: micchā-saṃkappa, micchā-vāyāma

7 cittas have 3 path-factors

7 cittas: 7 akusala (4 diṭṭhi-gata-vippayutta, 2 paṭigha-sampayutta, 1 uddhacca-sampayutta)
3 factors: micchā-saṃkappa, micchā-vāyāma, micchā-samādhi

40 cittas have 4 path-factors

4 cittas: 4 akusala (diṭṭhi-gata-sampayutta)
4 factors: micchā-diṭṭhi, micchā-saṃkappa, micchā-vāyāma, micchā-samādhi
12 cittas: 12 kāmâvacara (ñāṇa-vippayutta) **4 factors:** sammā-saṃkappa, sammā-vāyāma, sammā-sati, sammā-samādhi
24 cittas: 12 rūpâvacara (2nd-5th jhāna), 12 arūpâvacara
4 factors: sammā-diṭṭhi, sammā-vāyāma, sammā-sati, sammā-samādhi

15 cittas have 5 path-factors

15 cittas: 12 kāmâvacara (ñāṇa-sampayutta), 3 rūpâvacara (1st jhāna)
5 factors: sammā-diṭṭhi, sammā-saṃkappa, sammā-vāyāma, sammā-sati, sammā-samādhi

32 cittas have 7 path-factors

32 cittas: 32 lokuttara (2nd-5th jhāna)
7 factors: sammā-diṭṭhi, sammā-vaca, sammā-kammanta, sammā-ājīva, sammā-vāyāma, sammā-sati, sammā-samādhi

8 cittas have 8 path-factors

8 cittas: 8 lokuttara (1st jhāna)

BALA

2 cittas have 2 balas

2 cittas: 2 kiriya-mano-viññāṇa-dhātu
2 balas: viriya, samādhi

1 citta has 3 balas

1 citta: 1 vicikicchā-sampayutta
3 balas: viriya, ahirika, anottappa

11 cittas have 4 balas

11 cittas: 11 akusala
4 balas: viriya, samādhi, ahirika, anottappa

12 cittas have 6 balas

12 cittas: 12 kāmâvacara (ñāṇa-vippayutta)
6 balas: saddhā, viriya, sati, samādhi, hiri, ottappa

79 cittas have 7 balas

79 cittas: 12 kāmâvacara (ñāṇa-sampayutta), 15 rūpâvacara, 12 arūpâvacara, 40 lokuttara
7 balas: saddhā, viriya, sati, samādhi, paññā, hiri, ottappa

16 cittas have no balas

Remaining ahetuka

III THE 22 TRIPLETS OF THE ABHIDHAMMA MĀTIKĀ

[1] kusalā dhammā, akusalā dhammā, avyākatā dhammā; [2] sukhāya vedanāya sampayuttā dhammā, dukkhāya vedanāya sampayuttā dhammā, adukkha-m-asukhāya vedanāya sampayuttā dhammā; [3] vipākā dhammā, vipāka-dhamma-dhammā, neva-vipāka-na-vipāka-dhamma-dhammā; [4] upādiṇṇupādāniyā dhammā, anupādiṇṇupādāniyā dhammā, anupādiṇṇa-anupādāniyā dhammā; [5] saṃkiliṭṭha-saṃkilesikā dhammā, asaṃkiliṭṭha-saṃkilesikā dhammā, asaṃkiliṭṭha-asaṃkilesikā dhammā; [6] savitakka-savicārā dhammā, savitakka-vicāra-mattā dhammā, avitakka-avicārā dhammā; [7] pīti-sahagatā dhammā, sukha-sahagatā dhammā, upekkhā-sahagatā dhammā; [8] dassanena pahātabbā dhammā, bhāvanāya pahātabbā dhammā, neva dassanena na bhāvanāya pahātabbā dhammā; [9] dassanena pahātabba-hetukā dhammā, bhāvanāya pahātabba-hetukā dhammā, neva dassanena na bhāvanāya pahātabba-hetukā dhammā; [10] ācaya-gāmino dhammā, apacaya-gāmino dhammā, nevâcaya-gāmino na apacaya-gāmino dhammā; [11] sekkhā dhammā, asekkhā dhammā, neva sekkhā nâsekkhā dhammā; [12] parittā dhammā, mahaggatā dhammā, appamāṇā dhammā; [13] parittârammaṇā dhammā, mahaggatârammaṇā dhammā, appamāṇârammaṇā dhammā; [14] hīnā dhammā, majjhimā dhammā, paṇītā dhammā; [15] micchatta-niyatā dhammā, sammatta-niyatā dhammā, aniyatā dhammā; [16] maggârammaṇā dhammā, magga-hetukā dhammā, maggâdhipatino dhammā; [17] uppannā dhammā, anuppannā dhammā, uppādino dhammā; [18] atītā dhammā, anāgatā dhammā, paccuppannā dhammā; [19] atītârammaṇā dhammā, anāgatârammaṇā dhammā, paccuppannârammaṇā dhammā; [20] ajjhattā dhammā, bahiddhā dhammā, ajjhatta-bahiddhā dhammā; [21] ajjhattârammaṇā dhammā, bahiddhârammaṇā dhammā, ajjhatta-bahiddhârammaṇā dhammā; [22] sanidassana-sappaṭighā dhammā; anidassana-sappaṭighā dhammā; anidassana-appaṭighā dhammā.

GLOSSARY OF PĀLI AND SANSKRIT TERMS

This is a glossary of selected Pāli terms; where they differ, relevant Sanskrit forms are given in brackets after the Pāli.

akusala (akuśala)	unskilful, unwholesome
aṅga	limb, part, factor
aṭṭha-kathā	commentary
adhipati	overlord
anāgamya	non-attainment (as stage of meditation; cf. *upacāra* and *samantaka*)
anāgāmin	one who does not return
anupassanā (anupaśyanā)	watching, contemplation
anussati (anusmṛti)	recollection, mindfulness
appamāda (apramāda)	heedfulness, alertness, lack of carelessness
abhidhamma (abhidharma)	further dhamma, third section of the Buddhist canon and system of thought expounded on its basis
abhibhāyatana	(class of) meditation attainment
arahant (arhant)	one who has completed the path
ariya (ārya)	noble
arūpâvacara	belonging to the sphere of the formless
asubha (aśubha)	ugliness
asura	one of the jealous gods
āgama	section of the Buddhist canon (cf. *nikāya*)
ānâpāna	breathing in and out
ānuttariya	unsurpassable
ābhidhammika	one versed in Abhidhamma
āyatana	sphere (of the senses)
ārammaṇa	object of consciousness, subject of meditation
āsava (āsrava)	(defiling) influx
iddhi (ṛddhi)	(meditational) success or power
iddhi-pāda (ṛddhi-pāda)	basis of success
indriya	(controlling) faculty
upacāra	access (as stage of meditation; cf. *anāgamya* and *samantaka*)
upasampadā	higher ordination
upadāna-kkhandha	aggregate of grasping
upekkhā (upekṣā)	equipoise
ekaggatā (ekâgratā)	one-pointedness (of mind)
ekâyana	one-going
kamma-ṭṭhāna	subject of meditation
kammanta (karmânta)	action
karuṇā	compassion
kalyāṇa-mitta	the good friend
kāma	sensual desire, object of sensual desire
kāma-guṇa	(five) classes of object of sensual desire
kāmâvacara	belonging to the sphere of sense-desire
kāya	body
kusala (kuśala)	unskilful, unwholesome
khandha (skandha)	aggregate

cakka-vattin (cakra-vartin)	wheel-turning king, universal monarch
citta	mind, (class of) consciousness
cetasika (caitta)	concomitant of consciousness
ceto-khila	barrenness of mind
chanda	desire to act, purpose
jhāna (dhyāna)	state of absorption in meditation
jhānaṅga	limb or factor of *jhāna*
ñāṇa (jñāna)	knowledge
ṭīkā	subcommentary
taṇhā (tṛṣṇā)	thirst, craving
tika	triplet
dassana (darśana)	seeing
diṭṭhi (dṛṣṭi)	(wrong) view
duka	couplet
deva(tā)	god
dhamma (dharma)	law, teaching, ultimate constituent of reality
dhamma-vicaya (dharma-pravicaya)	discernment of *dhamma*
dhātu	element
nikāya	section of the canon (cf. āgama)
nipāta	numerical section of the of the *Aṅguttara-nikāya*
nimitta	sign, mental image (as object of meditation)
niraya	hell
nīvaraṇa	hindrance
nekkhamma	desirelessness
paccaya (pratyaya)	condition
paccupaṭṭhāna	manifestation
paññā (prajñā)	wisdom
paṭicca-samuppāda (pratītya-samutpāda)	dependent arising
pada-ṭṭhāna	footing, basis
pada-bhājaniya	word analysis
padhāna (pradhāna)	endeavour
pabbajjā	going forth
pahāna (prahāṇa)	abandoning
passaddhi (praśrabdhi)	tranquillity
pātimokkha (prātimokṣa)	the rule of the Saṃgha
pārājika	offence involving 'defeat'
pīti (prīti)	joy
pubba-bhāga	prior or initial stage
puthujjana	ordinary man
phala	fruit, result, stage of attainment (cf. *magga*)
phassa (sparśa)	contact
bala	power
bojjhaṅga (bodhy-aṅga)	factor of awakening
bodhi	awakening
bodhi-pakkhiya (bodhi-pākṣika)	contributing to awakening
brahma-vihāra	divine dwelling (as a meditation attainment)
bhāvanā	development
bhikkhu (bhikṣu)	monk

bhikkhunī (bhikṣunī)	nun
magga (mārga)	path, stage of attainment (cf. *phala*)
maggaṅga (mārgâṅga)	limb or factor of the path
mātikā (mātṛkā)	scheme of categories or topics
micchā (mithyā)	wrong
muditā	sympathetic joy
mettā (maitrī)	loving kindness
yoga	(spiritual) work
yogâvacara	practitioner of *yoga*
rasa	taste, property, function
rūpa	form, materiality
rūpâvacara	belonging to the sphere of form
lakkhaṇa (lakṣaṇa)	characteristic (mark)
loka	world
lokiya (laukika)	belonging to the world, ordinary
lokuttara (lokottara)	(world) transcendent
vagga (varga)	chapter, section
vara	portion, section
vāyāma (vyāyāma)	effort
vicāra	sustained thought
vicikicchā (vicikitsā)	doubt
viññāṇa (vijñāna)	consciousness
vitakka (vitarka)	initial thought
vipassanā (vipaśyanā)	insight
vibhaṅga	analysis
vimokkha (vimokṣa)	liberation
viriya (vīrya)	strength, vigour
visuddhi	purification
vīmaṃsā (mīmāṃsā)	investigation
vedanā	feeling
saṃkappa (saṃkalpa)	thought
saṃkhāra (saṃskāra)	(volitional) force
saṃgha	community of Buddhist monks and nuns
sakadāgāmin (sakṛdāgāmin)	one who returns once
sacca (satya)	truth, reality
saññā (saṃjñā)	recognition
sati (smṛti)	mindfulness
satipaṭṭhāna (smṛty-upasthāna)	establishing of mindfulness
saddhā (śraddhā)	confidence, faith
samatha (śamatha)	calm
samantaka	neighbouring (as stage of meditation; cf. *anāgamya* and *upacāra*)
samādhi	concentration
sammā (samyak)	right, perfect
samma-ppadhāna (samyak-pradhāna)	right endeavour
sīla (śīla)	morality, ethical conduct
sukha	happiness
sotâpanna (srotâpanna)	one who has attained the 'stream'
hetu	cause, motivation

ABBREVIATIONS

Except in the case of dictionaries and other works of reference abbreviated titles of secondary sources are not listed; for these see under the author's name and appropriate work in BIBLIOGRAPHY (C).

A. PĀLI AND SANSKRIT TEXTS

For full citation of editions used see BIBLIOGRAPHY (A). In the footnotes -a or -ṭ after an abbreviated title indicates *aṭṭha-kathā* or *ṭīkā* respectively; Trsl indicates a translation from Pāli, Sanskrit, Chinese or Tibetan into a modern European language, for which see BIBLIOGRAPHY (B).

A	Aṅguttara-nikāya
Ap	Apadāna
Abhidh-av	Abhidhammavatara
Abhidh-k	Abhidharmakośa(bhāṣya)
Abhidh-k-vy	Abhidharmakośavyākhyā
Abhidh-dī	Abhidharmadīpa
Abhidh-s	Abhidhammatthasaṃgaha
Abhidh-sam	Abhidharmasamuccaya
Abhidh-h	*Abhidharmahṛdaya
Amṛta	*Abhidharmâmṛtarasa
Artha(-n)	Arthaviniścayasūtra(-nibandhana)
As	Atthasālinī (= Dhs-a)
It	Itivuttaka
Ud	Udāna
Kv	Kathāvatthu
Khp	Khuddakapāṭha
Ch-Up	Chāndogya-upaniṣad
J	Jātaka
Tikap	Tikapaṭṭhāna
Th	Theragāthā
Thī	Therīgāthā
D	Dīgha-nikāya
DAṬ	Dīghanikāyaṭṭhakathā-ṭīkā
Dukap	Dukapaṭṭhāna
Dhātuk	Dhātukathā
Dhp	Dhammapada
Dhs	Dhammasaṅgaṇi
Nidd I	Mahāniddesa
Nidd-a I	Mahaniddesaṭṭhakathā (= Saddhammapajjotikā)
Nidd II	Cullaniddesa
Nett	Nettippakaraṇa
Paṭis	Paṭisambhidāmagga
Paṭis-a	Paṭisambhidāmaggaṭṭhakathā (= Saddhammappakāsinī)
Paṭṭh	Paṭṭhāna
Pugg	Puggalapaññatti
Peṭ	Peṭakopadesa
Ps	Papañcasūdanī (= M-a)
Bṛh-Up	Bṛhadāraṇyaka-upaniṣad
M	Majjhima-nikāya
Mil	Milindapañha
Mp	Manorathapūraṇī (= A-a)
MPS	Mahāparinirvāṇasūtra
MBh	Mahābhārata
Mhv	Mahāvaṃsa
YS	Yoga-sūtras

Vin	Vinayapiṭaka
Vibh	Vibhaṅga
Vibh-a	Vibhaṅgaṭṭhakathā (= Sammohavinodanī)
Vimutt	Vimuttimagga
Vism	Visuddhimagga
Vism-mhṭ	Visuddhimagga-mahāṭīkā
S	Saṃyutta-nikāya
Satya	*Satyasiddhi-śāstra
Sadd	Saddanīti
Sn	Sutta-nipāta
Sp	Samantapāsādikā (= Vin-a)
Spk	Sāratthappakāsinī (= S-a)
Sv	Sumaṅgalavilāsinī (= D-a)

B. JOURNALS

AO	*Acta Orientalia*, Copenhagen
BEFEO	*Bulletin de l'École Française d'Extrême Orient*, Paris
BSOAS	*Bulletin of the School of Oriental and African Studies*, London
BSR	*Buddhist Studies Review*, London
HR	*History of Religions*, Chicago
IHQ	*Indian Historical Quarterly*, Calcutta
IIJ	*Indo-Iranian Journal*, Dordrecht
IT	*Indologica Taurinensia*, Turin
JA	*Journal Asiatique*, Paris
JAOS	*Journal of the American Oriental Society*, New Haven
JAS	*Journal of Asian Studies*, Berkeley
JIABS	*Journal of the International Association of Buddhist Studies*, Madison
JIP	*Journal of Indian Philosophy*, Dordrecht
JPTS	*Journal of the Pāli Text Society*, London
JRAS	*Journal of the Royal Asiatic*, Society, London
PBR	*Pāli Buddhist Review*, London
RS	*Religious Studies*, Cambridge
TASJ	*Transactions of the Asiatic Society of Japan*
UCR	*University of Ceylon Review*, Colombo
WZKS	*Wiener Zeitschrift für die Kunde Süd- und Ostasiens*, Vienna

C. DICTIONARIES AND OTHER STANDARD WORKS OF REFERENCE

BHSD	*Buddhist Hybrid Sanskrit Dictionary*, F. Edgerton, Yale, 1953
BR	O. Böhtlingk and R. Roth, *Sanskrit Wörterbuch*, St. Petersburgh, 1852-75
Childers	R. Childers, *A Dictionary of the Pāli Language*, London, 1875
CPD	*A Critical Pāli Dictionary*, Copenhagen, 1924-
DPPN	*Dictionary of Pāli Proper Names*, 2 vols, G.P. Malalasekera, London, 1937-38
ERE	*Encyclopaedia of Religion and Ethics*, ed. J. Hastings, Edinburgh, 1908-26
Mayrhofer	M. Mayrhofer, *A Concise Etymological Sanskrit Dictionary*, Heidelberg, 1956-80
MW	Sir Monier Monier-Williams, *A Sanskrit-English Dictionary*, Oxford, 1899
PED	*Pāli-English Dictionary*, T.W. Rhys Davids and W. Stede, PTS, London, 1921-25
PTC	*Pāli Tipiṭakaṃ Concordance*, PTS, London, 1955-
Turner	R.L. Turner, *A Comparative Dictionary of the Indo-Aryan Languages*, London, 1966; Indexes, 1969

D. GENERAL

Common abbreviations listed in dictionaries (e.g. *Collins English Dictionary*, London and Glasgow, 1979) are not listed here.

Be	Edition in Burmese characters
Ce	Edition in Sinhalese characters
Ne	Edition in Nāgarī characters
Pkt	Prakrit

PTS	Pāli Text Society
Skt	Sanskrit
Tib	Tibetan
Trsl	Translation/Translated

BIBLIOGRAPHY

A. PĀLI AND SANSKRIT TEXTS

Aṅguttara-nikāya I-V, ed. R. Morris, E. Hardy, PTS, London, 1885-1900. (A)
Atthasālinī, ed. E. Muller (1897), revised ed. PTS, London, 1979. (As)
Apadāna I-II, ed. M.E. Lilley, PTS, London, 1925-27. (Ap)
Abhidhammatthasaṃgaha, ed. T.W. Rhys Davids, JPTS, 1884, pp. 1-48. (Abhidh-s)
Abhidhammâvatara, Buddhadatta's Manuals I, ed. A.P. Buddhadatta, PTS, London, 1915. (Abhidh-av)
Abhidharmakośabhāṣya, ed. P. Pradhan, Patna, 1967. (Abhidh-k)
Abhidharmadīpa, ed. P.S. Jaini, Patna, 1977. (Abhidh-dī)
Arthaviniścaya-sūtra, ed. with its commentary (*nibandhana*) N.H. Samtani, Patna, 1971. (Artha, Artha-n)
Avadānaśataka I-II, ed. J.S. Speyer, St. Petersburgh, 1906-09.
Aṣṭadaśasāhasrikāprajñāpāramitā, ed. (with trsl) E. Conze, Rome, 1962.
Itivuttaka, ed. E. Windisch, PTS, London, 1890. (It)
Itivuttakaṭṭhakathā I-II, ed. M.M. Bose, PTS, London, 1934-36. (It-a)
Udāna, ed. P. Steinthal, PTS, London, 1885. (Ud)
Udānaṭṭhakathā, ed. F.L. Woodward, PTS, London, 1926. (Ud-a)
Upaniṣads, The Principal, ed. (with trsl) S. Radhakrishnan, London, 1953.
Kathāvatthu I-II, ed. A.C. Taylor, PTS, London, 1894-97. (Kv)
Kathāvatthu-aṭṭhakathā, ed. N.A. Jayawickrama, PTS, London, 1979. (Kv-a)
Khuddakapāṭha, ed. (with *aṭṭhakathā*) H. Smith, London, 1915. (Khp, Khp-a)
Cullaniddesa, ed. Bhikkhu Jagdish Kashyap (et al.), Nava Nālanda Mahāvihāra, 1959. (Nidd II Ne)
Jātaka I-VI, ed. V. Fausboll, London, 1877-96. (J)
Tikapaṭṭhāna I-III, ed. (with commentary) C.A.F. Rhys Davids, PTS, London 1921-23. (Tikap, Tikap-a)
Theragāthā and *Therīgāthā*, ed. H. Oldenberg, R. Pischel, 2nd ed., PTS, London, 1966. (Th, Thī)
'Daśasāhasrikā Prajñāpāramitā, The two first chapters of the,' (restoration of the Skt Text from the Tib), S. Konow, *Avhandlinger utgitt av Det Norske Videnskaps-Akademi i Oslo*, 1941, Historisk-Filosofisk Klasse, pp. 1-117.
Divyâvadāna, ed. E.B. Cowell and R.A. Neil, Cambridge, 1886.
Dīgha-nikāya I-III, ed. T.W. Rhys Davids, J.E. Carpenter, W. Stede, PTS, London, 1890-1911. (D)
——, ed. Balangoda Ananda Maitreya Nayaka Thera, Buddha Jayanti Tripiṭaka Series, Vol. VII, Colombo, 1962. (D Ce)
Dīghanikāyaṭṭhakathā-ṭīkā (= *Līnatthappakāsinī/Sumaṅgalavilāsinī-purāṇaṭīkā*) I-III, ed. L. de Silva, PTS, London, 1970. (DAṬ)
Dukapaṭṭhāna, ed. C.A.F. Rhys Davids, London, 1906.
Dhammapada: Dhammapadaṭṭhakathā, ed. H.C. Norman, PTS, London, 1906-14. (Dhp)
Dhammasaṅgaṇi, ed. E. Muller, PTS, London, 1885. (Dhs)
Dharmasaṃgraha, ed. K. Kasawara, F. Max Muller, H. Wenzel, Oxford, 1885; reprinted Amsterdam, 1972.
Dharmaskandha, Fragmente des, ed. S. Dietz, Göttingen, 1984
Dhātukathā, ed. E.R. Gooneratne (1892), revised, PTS, London, 1963. (Dhātuk)
Nettippakaraṇa, ed. E. Hardy, PTS, London, 1902. (Nett, Nett-a)
Nettippakaraṇaṭṭhakathā, ed. Widurupola Piyatissa Thera. (Simon Hewavitarne Bequest, Vol. IX), Colombo, 1921. (Nett-a Ce)
Paṭisambhidāmagga I-II, ed. A.C. Taylor, PTS, London, 1905-07. (Paṭis)
Papañcasūdanī I-V, ed. J.H. Woods, D. Kośambi, I.B. Horner, PTS, London, 1922-38. (Ps)
Paramatthavinicchaya, ed. A.P. Buddhadatta, JPTS 10 (1985), pp. 154-226.
Puggalapaññatti, ed. R. Morris, PTS, London, 1883. (Pugg)
Peṭakopadesa, ed. A. Barua, PTS, London, 1949. (Peṭ)
Majjhima-nikāya I-III, ed. V. Trenckner, R. Chalmers, PTS, London, 1888-1902. (M)
——, ed. Labugama Lankananda Thera, Buddha Jayanti Tripiṭaka Series, Vol. XII, Colombo, 1974. (M Ce)

Madhyântavibhāga(bhāṣya), S. Anacker, *Seven Works of Vasubandhu*, Delhi, 1984, pp. 191-286, 424-63. (Text and translation.)
Manorathapūraṇī I-V, ed. M. Walleser, H. Kopp, PTS, London, 1924-57. (Mp)
Manorathapūraṇī-ṭīkā, Chaṭṭhasaṃgāyanā ed., Rangoon, 1961. (Mp-ṭ Be)
Mahāniddesa I-II, ed. L. de La Vallée Poussin, E.J. Thomas, PTS, London, 1916-17. (Nidd I)
Mahāparinirvāṇasūtra, ed. E. Waldschmidt, Berlin, 1950; (Text in Sanskrit und Tibetisch, verglichen mit dem Pāli nebst einer Übersetzung der chinesischen Entsprechung im Vinaya der Mūlasarvāstivādins). (MPS)
Mahābhārata, ed. V.S. Sukthankar et al., Poona, 1931-. (MBh)
Mahāvaṃsa, ed. W. Geiger, PTS, London, 1908. (Mhv)
Mahāvastu Avadāna I-II, ed. R. Basak, Calcutta, 1963-68.
Mahāvyutpatti, ed. I.P. Minaev, N.D. Mironov, St. Petersburgh, 1911.
Milindapañha, ed. V. Trenckner, PTS, London, 1880. (Mil)
Milinda-ṭīkā, ed. P.S. Jaini, PTS, London, 1961. (Mil-ṭ)
Mūla-ṭīkā (Be), Chaṭṭhasaṃgāyanā ed., Rangoon, 1960.
Yamaka I-II, ed. C.A.F. Rhys Davids, PTS, London, 1911-13. (Yam)
Yoga-sūtras, ed. M.N. Dvivedi, Madras, 1930. (YS)
Vinayapiṭaka I-V, ed. H. Oldenberg, London, 1879-83. (Vin)
Vibhaṅga, ed. C.A.F. Rhys Davids, PTS, London, 1904. (Vibh)
Visuddhimagga, ed. H.C. Warren, revised D. Kosambi, Harvard, 1950. (Vism)
Visuddhimagga-mahāṭīkā: Visuddhimaggo with Paramatthamañjusāṭīkā I-III, ed. Rewatadhamma, Varanasi, 1972. (Vism-mhṭ Ne)
Śatasāhasrikāprajñāpāramitā, ed. P. Ghosa, Calcutta, 1902.
Saṃyutta-nikāya I-V, ed. L. Feer, PTS, London, 1884-98. (S)
Saddanīti I-V, ed. H. Smith, Lund, 1928-66. (Sadd)
Saddhammapajjotikā I-III, ed. A.P. Buddhadatta, PTS, London, 1931-40. (Nidd-a I)
Saddhammappakāsinī I-III, ed. C.V. Joshi, PTS, London, 1933-47. (Paṭis-a)
Saddharmapuṇḍarīka, ed. H. Kern, B. Nanjio, St. Petersburgh, 1912.
Samantapāsādikā I-VII, ed. J. Takakusu, M. Nagai, PTS, London, 1924-47. (Sp)
Sammohavinodanī, ed. A.P. Buddhadatta, PTS, London, 1923. (Vibh-a)
Sāratthappakāsinī I-II, ed. F.L. Woodward, PTS, London, 1921-37. (Spk)
Suttanipāta, ed. D. Andersen, H. Smith, PTS, London, 2nd ed. 1968. (Sn)
Sumaṅgalavilāsinī I-III, ed. T.W. Rhys Davids, J.E. Carpenter, W. Stede, PTS, London, 1886-1932. (Sv)
——, ed. Saya U Pye, Pyi Gyi Mundyne Piṭaka Press, Rangoon, 1902. (Sv Be)
——, ed. Boruggamuwe Siri Revata Thero, Simon Hewavitarne Bequest, Vol. 19, Colombo, 1925. (Sv Ce)
Saundarananda, ed. (with trsl) E.H. Johnston, London, 1928.
Sphuṭârtha-Abhidharmakośavyākhyā, ed. V. Wogihara, Tokyo, 1932-36. (Abhidh-k-vy)

B. TRANSLATIONS INTO MODERN EUROPEAN LANGUAGES FROM PALI, SANSKRIT, CHINESE AND TIBETAN

Anacker, S., *Seven Works of Vasubandhu*, Delhi, 1984.
Armelin, I., *Le Coeur de la loi suprême*, Paris, 1978. (Abhidh-h Trsl II)
Aung, S.Z., Rhys Davids, C.A.F., *Points of Controversy*, PTS, London, 1915. (Kv Trsl)
Conze, E., *The Large Sūtra on Perfect Wisdom*, Part I, London, 1961. (= *Pañcaviṃśatisāhasrikā-prajñāpāramitā* Trsl)
Cowell, E.B. et al., *The Jātaka* I-VI, London, 1895-1907. (J Trsl)
Ehara, Rev. N.R.M., Soma Thera and Kheminda Thera, *The Path of Freedom by the Arahat Upatissa*, 1st ed. Colombo, 1961, reprinted Buddhist Publication Society, Kandy, 1977. (Vimutt Trsl)
Feer, L., *Avadānaśataka: Cent légendes bouddhiques*, Paris, 1891.
Guenther, H.V., *sGam.po.pa's Jewel Ornament of Liberation*, London, 1959.
Horner, I.B., *The Book of Discipline* I-VI, London, 1938-60. (Vin Trsl)
——, *Middle Length Sayings* I-III, PTS, London, 1954-59. (M Trsl)
——, *Milinda's Questions* I-II, London, 1963-64. (Mil Trsl)
Jones, J.J., *The Mahāvastu* I-III, London, 1949-56.
Lamotte, É., *Saṃdhinirmocana-sūtra*, Louvain, 1935. (Tibetan text, French translation.)
——, *L'Enseignement de Vimalakīrti*, Louvain, 1962.
[Lamotte, Traité] = **Mahāprajñāpāramitā-śāstra* Trsl; see BIBLIOGRAPHY (C).

La Vallée Poussin, L. de, *L'Abhidharmakośa de Vasubandhu*, 6 vols, Paris, 1923-31. (Abhidh-k Trsl)
Law, B.C., *A Designation of Human Types*, PTS, London, 1922. (Pugg Trsl)
——, *The Debates Commentary*, PTS, London, 1940. (Kv-a Trsl)
Bhikkhu Ñāṇamoli, *The Path of Purification*, Colombo, 1956. (Vism Trsl)
——, *The Guide*, PTS, London, 1962. (Nett Trsl)
——, *Piṭaka Disclosure*, PTS, London, 1964. (Peṭ Trsl)
——, *The Path of Discrimination*, PTS, London, 1982. (Paṭis Trsl)
U Nārada, *Discourse on Elements*, PTS, London, 1962. (Dhātuk Trsl)
——, *Conditional Relations* I-II, PTS, London, 1969-81. (Paṭṭh Trsl)
Norman, K.R., *Elders' Verses* I-II, PTS, London, 1969-71. (Th and Thī Trsl)
——, *The Group of Discourses*, PTS, London, 1984. (Sn Trsl)
Rahula, W., *Le Compendium de la Super-doctrine (philosophie) (Abhidharmasamuccaya) d'Asaṅga*, Paris, 1971. (Abhid-sam Trsl)
Rhys Davids, T.W. and C.A.F., *Dialogues of the Buddha* I-III, London, 1899-1921. (D Trsl)
Rhys Davids, C.A.F., *Buddhist Psychological Ethics*, 3rd ed., PTS, London, 1974. (Dhs Trsl)
Rhys Davids, C.A.F. and Woodward, F.L., *Minor Anthologies* I-II, London, 1931-35. (Dhp, Khp, Ud and It Trsl)
——, *The Book of Kindred Sayings* I-V, PTS, London, 1917-30. (S Trsl)
Sastri, A., *Satyasiddhiśāstra of Harivarman*, Vol. II, English Translation, Baroda, 1978. (Satya Trsl)
U Thiṭṭila, *The Book of Analysis*, PTS, London, 1969. (Vibh Trsl)
Pe Maung Tin, *The Expositor* I-II, PTS, London, 1920-22. (As Trsl)
Van Den Broeck, J., *La Saveur de l'immortel: La version chinoise de l'Amṛtarasa de Ghoṣaka (T. 1553)*, Louvain, 1977. (Amṛta Trsl)
——, *La Progression dans la meditation (Bhāvanākrama de Kamalaśīla)*, Brussels, 1977.
Willemen, C., *The Essence of Metaphysics*, Brussels, 1975. (Abhidh-h Trsl I)
Woodward, F.L. and Hare, E.M., *The Book of Gradual Sayings* I-V, PTS, London, 1923-26. (A Trsl)

C. SECONDARY SOURCES

Adikaram, E.W., *The Early History of Buddhism in Ceylon*, Migoda, Ceylon, 1946.
Akanuma, C., *The Comparative Catalogue of Chinese Āgamas and Pāli Nikāyas*, Nakoya, Japan, 1929.
Anesaki, M., 'The Four Buddhist Āgamas in Chinese (A concordance of their parts and of the corresponding counterparts in the Pāli Nikāyas)', *TASJ* 35 (1908), pp. 1-149.
Armelin, I., *Le Roi détenteur de la roue solaire en révolution, cakravartin, selon le brahmanisme et selon le bouddhisme*, Paris, 1975.
Aronson, H.B., 'Love, Compassion, Sympathetic Joy and Equanimity', Ph.D. thesis, University of Winsconsin, 1975. (*LCSJE*)
——, 'Equanimity (Upekkhā) in Theravādin Buddhism' in Narain, *SPB*, pp. 1-18.
Bareau, A., *Les Sectes bouddhiques du Petit Véhicule*, Saigon, 1955. (*SBPV*)
——, *Recherches sur la biographie du Buddha dans les Sūtrapiṭaka et les Vinayapiṭaka anciens*, 3 vols, Paris, 1963, 1970, 1971. (*RBB*)
Barua, B.M., 'Faith in Buddhism' in *Buddhistic Studies*, ed. B.C. Law, Calcutta, 1931, pp. 329-49.
Basham, A.L., *The Wonder that was India*, London, 1967.
——, *History and Doctrines of the Ājīvikas*, London, 1951.
Bechert, H., 'The Date of the Buddha Reconsidered', *IT* 10 (1982), pp. 29-36.
——, 'A Remark on the Problems of the Date of Mahāvīra', *IT* 11 (1983), pp. 287-90.
——, 'Remarks on the Date of the Historical Buddha', *Buddhist Studies (Bukkyō Kenkyū)* 17 (1988), pp. 97-117.
Bechert, H. (ed.)., *Buddhism in Ceylon and Studies on Religious Syncretism in Buddhist Countries*, Göttingen, 1978. (*BCSRS*)
——, *The Language of the Earliest Buddhist Tradition*, Göttingen, 1980. (*LEBT*)
Bloch, J., *Les Inscriptions d'Aśoka*, Paris, 1955.
Bhikkhu Bodhi, 'Transcendental Dependent Arising', *The Wheel Publication* 277/278, Kandy, 1980.
Braithwaite, R.B., 'An Empiricist's View of the Nature of Religious Belief' in *Christian Ethics and Contemporary Philosophy*, ed. I.T. Ramsey, London, 1966, pp. 53-73.
Bronkhorst, J., 'Dharma and Abhidharma', *BSOAS* 48 (1985), pp. 305-20.

——, *The Two Traditions of Meditation in Ancient India*, Stuttgart, 1986.
Brough, J., 'Thus Have I Heard ...', *BSOAS* 13 (1950), pp. 416–26.
——, *The Gāndhārī Dharmapada*, London, 1962.
Bucknell, R., 'The Buddhist Path to Liberation: An Analysis of the Listing of Stages', *JIABS* 7 (1984), pp. 7-40.
Carter, J.R., *Dhamma: Western Academic Approaches and Sinhalese Buddhist Interpretations: A Study of a Religious Concept*, Tokyo, 1978.
Chang, G.C.C., *The Buddhist Teaching of Totality: The Philosophy of Hwa Yen Buddhism*, London, 1972.
Charlesworth, M.J., *Philosophy of Religion: The Historic Approaches*, London, 1972.
Chau, T.M., *The Chinese Madhyama Āgama and the Pāli Majjhima Nikāya: A Comparative Study*, Saigon, 1964.
Ch'en, K.K.S., *Buddhism in China: A Historical Survey*, Princeton, 1964 .
Collins, S., *Selfless Persons: Imagery and Thought in Theravāda Buddhism*, Cambridge, 1982. (*SP*)
——, 'Self and Non-self in Early Buddhism', *Numen* 28 (1982), pp. 250–61.
——, 'Buddhism in Recent British Philosophy and Theology', *RS* 21 (1985), pp. 475-93.
——, 'Kalyāṇamitta and Kalyāṇamittatā', *JPTS* (1986), pp. 51-72.
Cone, M. and Gombrich, R.F., *The Perfect Generosity of Prince Vessantara: A Buddhist Epic*, Oxford, 1977.
Conze, E., *Buddhist Thought in India*, London, 1962. (*BTI*)
——, *Thirty Years of Buddhist Studies*, Oxford, 1967.
——, 'Contradictions in Buddhist Thought', *Mélanges Lamotte*, pp. 41-52.
Cousins, L.S., 'Buddhist *Jhāna*: Its nature and attainment according to the Pāli sources', *Religion* 3 (1973), pp. 115-31.
——, 'The Paṭṭhāna and the Development of the Theravādin Abhidhamma', *JPTS* (1981), pp. 22-46.
——, 'Pāli Oral Literature' in Denwood and Piatigorsky, *BSAM*, pp. 1-11.
——, 'Samatha-yāna and Vipassanā-yāna' in Dhammapala, *BSHS*, pp. 56-68.
Dasgupta, S., *Yoga as Philosophy and Religion*, London, 1924.
Dayal, H., *The Bodhisattva Doctrine in Buddhist Sanskrit Literature*, London, 1932.
Denwood, P., and Piatigorsky, A. (ed.), *Buddhist Studies: Ancient and Modern*, London, 1983. (*BSAM*)
Dhammapala, G. et al. (ed.), *Buddhist Studies in Honour of Hammalava Saddhatissa*, Nugegoda, 1984, (*BSHS*)
Doore, G., 'The "Radically Empiricist" Interpretation of Early Buddhist Nirvāṇa', *RS* 15 (1979), pp. 65-70.
Dutt, N., 'Place of Faith in Buddhism', *IHQ* 14 (1940), pp. 639-49.
Edgerton, F., 'Did the Buddha Have a System of Metaphysics?', *JAOS* 79 (1959), pp. 81-5.
Eliade, M., *Yoga: Immortality and Freedom*, 2nd ed., Princeton, 1969.
Ergardt, J.T., *Faith and Knowledge in Early Buddhism*, Leiden, 1977.
Evans-Pritchard, E.E., *Essays in Social Anthropology*, London, 1962.
Faddegon, B., 'The Catalogue of Sciences in the Chāndogya-Upaniṣad', *AO* 4 (1926), pp. 42-54.
Frauwallner, E., *The Earliest Vinaya and the Beginnings of Buddhist Literature*, Rome, 1956. (*EVBBL*)
——, 'Abhidharma Studien: II Die kanonischen Abhidharma-Werke', *WZKS* 8 (1964), pp. 59-99.
——, 'Abhidharma Studien: III Der Abhisamayavādaḥ; IV Der Abhidharma der anderen Schulen', *WZKS* 15 (1971), pp. 69-121; *WZKS* 16 (1972), pp. 95-152.
——, *History of Indian Philosophy* I, Delhi, 1973; originally published as *Geschichte der indischen Philosophie*, Salzburg, 1953. (*HIP*)
——, *Studies in Abhidharma Literature and the Origins of Buddhist Philosophical Systems*, Albany, 1995.
French, H.W., 'The Concept of *iddhi* in Early Buddhist Thought', *PBR* 2 (1977), pp. 42-54.
Geiger, W., *Pāli Literature and Language*, Calcutta, 1943; originally published as *Pāli Literatur und Sprache*, Strassburg, 1916.
Gethin, R., 'The Five Aggregates in the Nikāyas and Early Abhidhamma', unpublished dissertation submitted in part fulfilment of the requirements for the degree of MA in Buddhist Studies, University of Manchester, 1982.
——, 'The Five *khandhas*: Their Treatment in the Nikāyas and Early Abhidhamma', *JIP* 14 (1986), pp. 35-53.
Gokhale, B.G., 'The Image-world of the *Nikāyas*', *JAOS* 100 (1980), pp. 445-52.
Gombrich, R.F., *Precept and Practice*, Oxford, 1971.
——, 'Notes on the Brahminical Background to Buddhist Ethics' in Dhammapala, *BSHS*, pp. 91–102.

——, 'Recovering the Buddha's Message', *The Buddhist Forum*, Volume I, *Seminar Papers 1987-88*, ed. T. Skorupski, London, 1990, pp. 5-20.
Gomez, L.O., 'The Bodhisattva as Wonder Worker' in *Prajñāpāramitā and Related Systems*, Studies in honor of Edward Conze, ed. L. Lancaster, Berkeley, 1977, pp. 221-61.
Gonda, J., *Vedic Literature*, Wiesbaden, 1975.
Grant, R.M., A *Historical Introduction to the New Testament*, London, 1963.
Gudmunsen, C., *Wittgenstein and Buddhism*, London, 1977.
Guenther, H.V., *Philosophy and Psychology in the Abhidharma*, 3rd ed., Berkeley, 1976.
Hara, M., 'Note on Two Sanskrit Religious Terms *bhakti* and *śraddhā*', *IIJ* 7 (1964), pp. 123-45.
——, 'Review of H. Köhler, *Śrad-dhā in der vedischen und altbuddhistischen Literatur*', *IIJ* 19 (1977), pp. 105-8.
——, '*Śraddhāviśeṣa*', *IT* 7 (1979), pp. 262-73.
Harvey, P., 'The Concept of the Person in Pāli Buddhist Literature', unpublished Ph.D. thesis, University of Lancaster, 1981/82.
Hick, J., *Faith and Knowledge*, New York, 1957.
Hinüber, O. von, 'On the Tradition of Pāli Texts in India, Ceylon and Burma' in Bechert, *BCSRS*, pp. 48-58.
Hirakawa, A., 'The Meaning of "Dharma" and "Abhidharma"', *Mélanges Lamotte*, pp. 159-75.
Hirakawa, A. (et al.), *Index to the Abhidharmakośabhāṣya (P. Pradhan Edition)*, Tokyo, 1973.
Holt, J.C., *Discipline: The Canonical Buddhism of the Vinayapiṭaka*, Delhi, 1981.
Hurvitz, L., 'Fa-sheng's Observations on the Four Stations of Mindfulness' in *Mahāyāna Buddhist Meditation: Theory and Practice*, ed. M. Kiyota, Honolulu, 1978, pp. 207-48.
Jacob, G.A., *A Concordance of the Principal Upaniṣads and Bhagavadgītā*, Bombay, 1891; reprinted Delhi, 1971.
Jaini, P.S., 'On the Theory of Two Vasubandhus', *BSOAS* 21 (1958), pp. 48-53.
——, 'The Buddha's Prolongation of Life', *BSOAS* 21 (1958), pp. 546-52.
——, 'The Sautrāntika Theory of *bīja*', *BSOAS* 22 (1959), pp. 236-49.
——, *The Jaina Path of Purification*, Berkeley, 1979.
Jayasuriya, W.F., *The Psychology and Philosophy of Buddhism*, Kuala Lumpur, 1963.
Jayatilleke, K.N., *Early Buddhist Theory of Knowledge*, London, 1963.
Jong, J.W. de, *Buddhist Studies*, ed. G. Schopen, Berkeley, 1979.
Karunadasa, Y., *The Buddhist Analysis of Matter*, Colombo, 1967.
Katz, S.T. (ed.), *Mysticism and Philosophical Analysis*, London, 1978.
Keith, A.B., *Buddhist Philosophy in India and Ceylon*, Oxford, 1923.
Kern, H., *Manual of Indian Buddhism*, Strassburg, 1896.
Kheminda Thera, *Path, Fruit and Nibbāna*, Colombo, 1965.
King, W.L., *Theravāda Meditation: The Buddhist Transformation of Yoga*, Pennsylvania, 1980.
Köhler, H., *Śrad-dhā in der vedischen und altbuddhistischen Literatur*, Wiesbaden, 1973.
Lamotte, É., *Histoire du bouddhisme indien*, Louvain, 1958. (*HBI*)
——, *Le Traité de la grande vertu de sagesse de Nāgārjuna* I-III, Louvain, 1944-70. (*Traité*)
——, 'The Assessment of Textual Authenticity in Buddhism', *BSR* 1 (1983/84), pp. 4-15.
——, 'The Assessment of Textual Interpretation in Buddhism', *BSR* 2 (1985), pp. 4-24.
——, 'Problems Concerning the Minor Canonical Texts' in Dhammapala, *BSHS*, pp. 148-58.
[Lamotte, É.,] *Indianisme et Bouddhisme (Mélanges offerts à Mgr Étienne Lamotte)*, Louvain, 1980. (*Mélanges Lamotte*)
La Vallée Poussin, L. de, 'Faith and Reason in Buddhism', *Transactions of the Third International Congress for the History of Religions* (Oxford, 1908) II 32-43.
Law, B.C., *History of Pāli Literature*, 2 vols , London, 1933.
Ledi Sayadaw, 'The Requisites of Enlightenment (Bodhipakkhiya-Dīpanī)', *The Wheel Publication* 171/174, Kandy, 1971.
Lesser, A.H., 'Eastern and Western empiricism and the "No-self" theory', RS 15 (1979), pp. 55-64.
Lévi, S., and Chavannes, E., 'Les Seize arhat protecteurs de la loi', *JA*, 11me série, 8 (1916), pp. 5-50, 189-304.
Lin Li Kouang, *L'Aide mémoire de la vraie Loi (Saddharma-Smṛtyupasthāna-sūtra)*, Paris, 1949.
Lord, A.B., *The Singer of Tales*, Harvard, 1960.
Lottermoser, F., 'The Doctrine of Relationship (Paṭṭhāna)', unpublished MA thesis, University of Mandalay, 1969/70.
——, *Quoted Verse Passages in the Works of Buddhaghosa: Contributions towards the study of the lost sīhalaṭṭhakathā literature*, doctoral dissertation, Göttingen, 1982.
Ludowyk-Gyomroi, E., 'Note on the Interpretation of "*Pasīdati*"', *UCR* 1 (1) (1943), pp. 74-82.
——, 'The Valuation of Saddhā in Early Buddhist Texts', UCR 5 (2) (1947), pp. 32-49.

Mahasi Sayadaw, *The Progress of Insight*, Kandy, 1965.
Malalasekera, G.P., et al. (ed.), *Encyclopaedia of Buddhism*, Colombo, 1961.
Masefield, P., *Divine Revelation in Pāli Buddhism*, Colombo/London, 1986.
Matilal, B.K., 'Ignorance or Misconception? - A Note on Avidyā in Buddhism' in *Buddhist Studies in Honour of Walpola Rahula*, ed. S. Balasooriya et al., London, 1980.
Mayeda, E., 'Japanese Studies on the Schools of the Chinese Āgamas' in *Zur Schulzugehörigkeit von Werken der Hīnayāna-Literatur*, ed. H. Bechert, Göttingen, 1985, pp. 94-103.
Meisig, K., *Das Śrāmaṇyaphala-sūtra: Synoptische Übersetzung und Glossar der chinesischen Fassungen verglichen mit dem Sanskrit und Pāli*, Wiesbaden, 1987.
——, *Das Sūtra von den vier Ständen: Das Aggañña-sutta im Licht seiner chinesischen Parallelen*, Wiesbaden, 1988.
Mizuno, K., *Primitive Buddhism*, Yamaguchi-ken, 1969.
Monier-Williams, Sir Monier, *Buddhism, in its connexion with Brahmanism and Hinduism, and its contrast with Christianity*, London, 1889.
Moore, P., 'Buddhism, Christianity and the Study of Religion' in Denwood and Piatgorsky, *BSAM*, pp. 74-91.
Sodō Mori, 'The Vitaṇḍavādins (Sophists) as Seen in the Pāli Aṭṭhakathās' in *Essays on Pāli and Buddhist Civilization*, Society for the study of Pāli and Buddhist Civilization, Tokyo, 1982, pp. 171-88.
——, 'Aṭṭhakathācariyas and Aṭṭhakathikas', *Journal of Indian and Buddhist Studies* 31 (1983), pp. 977-83.
——, *A Study of the Pāli Commentaries*, Tokyo, 1984.
Nakamura, H., *Indian Buddhism: A Survey with Bibliographical Notes*, Tokyo, 1980.
——, 'Common Elements in Early Jain and Buddhist Literature', *IT* 11 (1983), pp. 303-30.
Nagao, G.M., 'Tranquil Flow of Mind: An Interpretation of Upekṣā', *Mélanges Lamotte*, pp. 245-58.
Ñāṇamoli Thera, *Mindfulness of Breathing*, 4th ed., Kandy, 1981.
Narain, A.K. (ed.), *Studies in Pāli and Buddhism*, Delhi, 1979. (*SPB*)
Nattier, J.J. and Prebish, C.S., 'Mahāsāṃghika Origins: The Beginnings of Buddhist Sectarianism', *HR* 16 (1976/77), pp. 237-72.
Norman, K.R., 'Pāli and the Language of the Heretics', *AO* 37 (1976), pp. 117-26.
——, 'The Dialects in which the Buddha Preached' in Bechert, *LEBT*, pp. 61-77.
——, 'The Four Noble Truths: A Problem of Pāli Syntax' in *Indological and Buddhist Studies* (Volume in Honour of J.W. de Jong on his sixtieth Birthday), ed. L.A. Hercus et al., Canberra, 1982, pp. 377-91.
——, *Pāli Literature*, Wiesbaden, 1983. (*PL*)
——, 'The Role of Pāli in Early Sinhalese Buddhism' in Bechert, *BCSRS*, pp. 28-47.
——, 'On translating from Pāli', *One Vehicle*, Singapore, 1984, pp. 77-87.
——, 'The Value of the Pāli Tradition', *Buddha Jayanti Annual*, Calcutta, 1984, pp. 1-9.
Nyanaponika Thera, *Abhidhamma Studies*, 3rd ed., Kandy, 1976.
Nyanaponika Thera, *The Heart of Buddhist Meditation*, London, 1962.
Nyanatiloka, *Guide Through the Abhidhamma-piṭaka*, 3rd ed., Kandy, 1971.
Oldenberg, H., *Buddha: His Life, His Doctrine, His Order*, Delhi, 1971. (First published London, 1882.)
Pande, G.C., *Studies in the Origins of Buddhism*, Allahabad, 1957.
Piatigorsky, A., *The Buddhist Philosophy of Thought*, London, 1984.
Pina, C., 'Notes on Meditational States in Buddhism', *East and West* (Rome) 27 (1977), pp. 335-44.
Potter, K.H., 'Does Indian Epistemology Concern Justified True Belief?', *JIP* 12 (1984), pp. 307-27.
Prebish, C.S., 'A Review of Scholarship on the Buddhist Councils', *JAS* 33 (1974), pp. 239-54.
——, *Monastic Discipline: the Sanskrit Prātimokṣa Sūtras of the Mahāsāṃghikas and Mūlasarvāstivādins*, Pennsylvania, 1975.
Przyluski, J. and Lamotte, E., 'Bouddhisme et Upaniṣad', *BEFEO* (1932), pp. 141-69.
Rahula, W., *History of Buddhism in Ceylon*, 2nd ed., Colombo, 1966.
——, *What the Buddha Taught*, 2nd ed., London, 1967.
Renou, L. and Filliozat, J., *L'Inde Classique* III, Hanoi, 1953.
Rhys Davids, C.A.F., 'Index of Similes', *JPTS* (1906-07), pp. 52-151; 'Addenda', *JPTS* (1908), pp. 180-8.
——, 'The Abhidhamma-piṭaka and Commentaries', *JRAS*, 1923, pp. 243-50.
——, 'The Two Ends and the Middle Way: A Suggested Reconstruction', *JRAS*, 1932, pp. 114-24.

——, 'Curious Omissions in Pāli Canonical Lists', *JRAS* (1935), pp. 721-4.
Roth, G., 'The Symbolism of the Buddhist Stūpa' in *The Stūpa: Its Religious, Historical and Architectural Significance*, ed. A.L. Dallapiccola, Wiesbaden, 1980, pp. 183-99.
Ruegg, D.S., *La Théorie du Tathāgatagarbha et du Gotra*, Paris, 1969.
——, 'Pāli *gotta/gotra* and the term *gotrabhū* in Pāli and Buddhist Sanskrit' in *Buddhist Studies in Honour of I.B. Horner*, ed. L.S. Cousins et al., Dordrecht, 1974, pp. 199-210.
Saddhatissa, H., *Buddhist Ethics*, London, 1970.
——, *The Buddha's Way*, London, 1971.
Schayer, S., 'Precanonical Buddhism', *Archi Orientalni* (Prague) 7 (1935), pp. 121-32.
Schmithausen, L., 'Die vier Konzentrationen der Aufmerksamkeit', *Zeitschrift für Missionwissenschaft und Religionwissenschaft*, 60 (1976), pp. 241-66.
——, 'On some aspects of descriptions or theories of "liberating insight" and "enlightenment" in early Buddhism', *Studien zum Jainismus und Buddhismus (Gedenkschrift für Ludwig Alsdorf)*, Herausgegeben von K. Bruhn und A. Wezler, Wiesbaden, 1981, pp. 199-250.
——, 'The *Darśanamārga* Section of the *Abhidharmasamuccaya*', *Contributions on Tibetan and Buddhist Religion and Philosophy*, ed. E. Steinkellner and H. Tauscher, Vienna, 1983, pp. 259-74.
Sharpe, E.J., *Comparative Religion: A History*, London, 1975.
——, *Understanding Religion*, London, 1983.
Smart, N., *The Religious Experience of Mankind*, London and Glasgow, 1971.
——, *Secular Education and the Logic of Religion*, London, 1968.
Snellgrove, D.L., 'Śākyamuni's Final Nirvāṇa', *BSOAS* 36 (1973), pp. 399-411.
——, *Indo-Tibetan Buddhism: Indian Buddhists and their Tibetan Successors*, Boston, 1987.
Soma Thera, *The Way of Mindfulness*, 5th ed., Kandy, 1981.
Southwold, M., *Buddhism in Life: The anthropological study of religion and the Sinhalese practice of Buddhism*, Manchester, 1983.
Spiro, M.E., *Buddhism and Society*, London, 1971.
Staal, F., *Exploring Mysticism*, Harmondsworth, 1975.
Stace, W.T., *Mysticism and Philosophy*, London, 1960.
Stcherbatsky, T., *The Central Conception of Buddhism and the Meaning of the Word 'dharma'*, London, 1923.
Streng, F.J., 'The Buddhist Doctrine of Two Truths as Religious Philosophy', *JIP* 1 (1971), pp. 262-71.
Strong, J.S., 'The Legend of the Lion-Roarer: A Study of the Buddhist Arahat Pindola Bhāradvāja', *Numen* 26 (1979), pp. 50-88.
Takakusu, J., 'On the Abhidharma Literature of the Sarvāstivādins', *JPTS* (1905), pp. 65-146.
Thapar, R., *Aśoka and the Decline of the Mauryas*, Oxford, 1961.
Thomas, E.J., *The History of Buddhist Thought*, 2nd ed., London, 1951.
Vajirañāṇa, *Buddhist Meditation in Theory and Practice*, 2nd ed., Kuala Lumpur, 1975.
Vermes, G., *Jesus the Jew*, London, 1973.
Vetter, T., *The Ideas and Meditative Practices of Early Buddhism*, Leiden, 1988.
Vogel, C., *The Teachings of the Six Heretics*, Wiesbaden, 1970.
Warder, A.K., 'On the Relationships between Early Buddhism and Other Contemporary Systems', *BSOAS* 18 (1956), pp. 43-63.
——, 'The Concept of a Concept', *JIP* 1 (1971), pp. 181-96.
——, 'Dharmas as Data', *JIP* 1 (1971), pp. 272-95.
——, 'Is Nāgārjuna a Mahāyānist?' in *The Problem of Two Truths in Buddhism and Vedānta*, ed. M. Sprung, Dordrecht, 1973, pp. 78-88.
——, *Indian Buddhism*, 2nd ed., Delhi, 1980. (*IB*)
Wayman, A., 'Regarding the translations of the Buddhist terms *saññā/saṃjñā, viññāṇa/vijñāna*' in *Malalasekera Commemoration Volume*, ed. O. H. de A. Wijesekera, Colombo, 1976, pp. 325-35.
——, 'Analysis of the Śrāvakabhūmi Manuscript', *University of California Publications in Classical Philology*, 17, Berkeley, 1961.
——, 'Indian Buddhism', *JIP* 6 (1978), pp. 415-27.
Werner, K., *Yoga and Indian Philosophy*, Delhi, 1977.
——, 'Bodhi and Arahattaphala: from early Buddhism to early Mahāyāna' in Denwood and Piatigorsky, *BSAM*, pp. 167-81.
Whaling, F. (ed.), *Contemporary Approaches to the Study of Religion* (Vol. I The Humanities), Berlin, 1984. (*CASR*)

Whitney, W.D., *The Roots, Verb-forms and Primary Derivatives of the Sanskrit Language*, Leipzig, 1885.

Winternitz, M., *History of Indian Literature* II, Calcutta, 1933. (English translation; orginally published as *Geschichte der indischen Literatur*, Leipzig, 1909-20.)

Woods, R. (ed.), *Understanding Mysticism*, London, 1981.

INDEX

Italicized numbers indicate that the reference is to be found in the footnotes on that page.

Lightning Source UK Ltd.
Milton Keynes UK
10 February 2010

149840UK00001B/86/A

9 781851 682850